Food Preparation

FOR THE PROFESSIONAL

Food Preparation

FOR THE PROFESSIONAL

THIRD EDITION

DAVID A. MIZER

MARY PORTER

BETH SONNIER

KAREN EICH DRUMMOND

JOHN WILEY & SONS, INC.

New York / Chichester / Weinheim / Brisbane / Singapore / Toronto

This book is printed on acid-free paper. ♾

Library of Congress Cataloging-in-Publication Data:
Food preparation for the professional / David A. Mizer . . . [et al.].—
—3rd ed.
p. cm.
ISBN 0-471-25187-9 (cloth : alk. paper)
1. Quantity cookery. 2. Food service. I. Mizer, David A.
TX820.F63 1999
641.5′7—dc21 99-31227

Printed in the United States of America.

10 9 8 7 6 5 4 3 2 1

Preface

This third edition of *Food Preparation for the Professional* comes straight out of today's foodservice kitchens. Its focus is on *doing*—what to do, how to do it, and why. It is designed to train undergraduate hotel and restaurant students in the principles, techniques, and skills needed to prepare food for production. These skills are necessary for people who will likely manage some aspect of food production during their career.

The text centers its teaching around the actual preparation of different kinds of foods. Not only does it give specific instructions for basic dishes; it also explains clearly, in everyday terms, what is going on in the pot or the oven or the mixing bowl as raw foods are turned into finished menu items. Thus, the student can absorb the principles of cooking in terms of real food products and actual cooking processes. Step-by-step instructions and illustrations explain techniques essential to the dish being prepared. The student's learning experiences, repeated and reinforced as the chapters unfold, build into a real-world body of knowledge and understanding.

Although the book's point of view is the cook's point of view and its scope is deliberately limited to the cook's sphere, it teaches principles of good management from the bottom up—quality in raw and finished products, good planning and production techniques, sanitation, service to the customer, and the faithful carrying out of management policies. There is also a wealth of detailed information on foods and cooking that every manager should know.

WHAT'S NEW

In addition to new recipes and illustrations, the text has been updated, nutritional information has been added, and current cooking trends are explored. The book has been reorganized, so that now there are 17 chapters instead of 18, and much of the text has been updated.

Chapter 1, "The Kitchen," has been reorganized to allow for a full explanation of staff structure before the reader moves on to examples of typical kitchens. The kitchen profiles have been updated to include current terminology and organizational structure where appropriate.

Whereas the organization of Chapter 2, "Sanitation and Safety," has remained the same, much of the content in this vital area has been revised and updated. Tables provide the latest information on bacteria, viruses, and parasites that are of concern to foodservice professionals. A section also has been added on the Hazard Analysis Critical Control Point (HACCP) system.

In Chapter 3, "Prepreparation," a section titled "Planning Your Own Production" was moved here from the end of the book.

In Chapter 4, "Cooking, Equipment, and Measurement," the authors have discussed cooking methods separate from cooking equipment in order to make the material easier for students to understand. Newer types of equipment, such as combination ovens and induction burners, are discussed and illustrated, and there is a much more complete section on pots, pans, hand tools, and small equipment. The topic of measurement has also been switched to this chapter from Chapter 5.

Chapter 5, "Menus, Nutrition, and Recipes," now includes the topic of menus (which originally was found in the back of the book) and a short section on nutrition and nutrients in foods. The chapter concludes with a discussion of standardized recipes and converting recipes.

Chapter 6, "Building Flavor, Body, and Texture," has been updated so as to provide information and recipes on vegetable stocks and vegetable purees. The section on seasonings, flavorings, and flavor builders has been greatly expanded to include more charts and drawings of herbs and spices.

Chapter 7, "Soups," has minor revisions, such as a change of name from potage to naturally thickened or purée soups.

In Chapter 8, "Sauces," the classical sauces are more clearly explained. The category of yellow sauces has been broadened and renamed butter sauces in this edition. The butter sauces include everything from simple melted butter to hollandaise. This chapter now includes sections on purée sauces, salsa and relish, and pan gravy.

New sections on legumes and grains in Chapter 9, "Vegetables, Grains, and Pasta," give much information on cooking and using these recent additions on menus. The pasta section now includes photographs and a recipe to make pasta.

Chapters 10 ("Meat Cookery"), 11 ("Poultry Cookery"), and 12 ("Fish and Shellfish Cookery") appear in a revised order. As appropriate, cooking methods have been updated, along with doneness temperatures. The chapter on fish and shellfish now contains more charts that give information on fin fish, as well as a separate section on shellfish that goes into detail about six popular forms of shellfish.

In Chapter 13, "Breakfast, Beverages, and Dairy Products," recipes are now included for the egg dishes described in the text, such as fried, scrambled, and boiled eggs. The section on coffee and tea has been greatly expanded, to better reflect current beverage choices. More information on cheeses is given using a chart format.

The section on hors d'oeuvres that originally appeared in Chapter 14 ("Pantry Production") has been moved to its own chapter. Hors d'oeuvres are covered in more detail in Chapter 15 ("Hors d'Oeuvres and Food Presentation"), and recipes have been added. Food presentation has been moved from the end of the book into this chapter, as a way to summarize the topic before the final two chapters on baking—Chapter 16, "The Bakeshop," and Chapter 17, "Desserts." Several recipes have been added to these final two chapters.

OBJECTIVES AND PHILOSOPHY

As with the second edition, our aim is to provide the student with the following essential information.

1. *A thorough grasp of basic cooking principles and techniques.* We want the student to gain a real understanding of cooking. The industry needs people who know how a recipe works and why. By reducing cooking to its simplest terms—basic recipes, basic ratios or proportions, basic cooking techniques and principles—we can show how ingredients in a given dish function to produce that dish. Then it becomes easy to understand not only that dish

but also others made in the same way. Cooking becomes not a bewildering succession of individual recipes but a fascinating series of elaborations on a few simple themes.

2. *A vocabulary of cooking, processing, and menu terms, with precise definitions and pronunciations.* We want to equip the student with the tools for quick communication and easy understanding, which are often missing in the interchange between supervisors and workers in foodservice kitchens. Well-defined terms, correctly used, will smooth both communication and relationships.
3. *A working knowledge of the foods, equipment, and methods of preparation in common use in today's kitchens.* We want students not only to be familiar with this basic core of information but also to know how to put foods, equipment, and methods to use; how to work with them; and how to choose between them. It is useless to know *what* if you do not also know *how, when, where,* and *why.*
4. *A feeling for the real world of food preparation and for the practical application of classroom learning.* We want students to absorb information as it relates to the working world rather than to see it merely as rules and facts coming from a printed page. We use realistic problems and settings, and we give detailed information on how to deal with a sauce that is too thick or too thin, how a broiler cook sets up for cooking steaks to order, and so on. We talk about many kinds of operations and responses to different conditions (e.g., different styles of cooking and service, different clienteles, and different menus and cuisines).
5. *Knowledge of quality standards and a sense of pride and pleasure in producing good food efficiently and in presenting it attractively.* We want students to know what excellence is and to set their sights high, even though they won't achieve perfection on the first or even on the tenth try. Although time, costs, and other on-the-job realities often require compromises, the goal is always quality—the best quality that circumstances will allow. Inferior food has no potential for sale or profit. So we teach students tastes, textures, eye appeal, and mise en place, along with such practical matters as batch cooking, portion control, and converting recipes. Along the way we hope to convey some of the fascination of food and cooking and the challenge of creating good things to eat.

PEDAGOGICAL AIDS

In addition to the chapter objectives, summaries, vocabulary or key terms, and review questions, the book includes many important features.

Recipes—Prototypes of the most important kinds of dishes provide the basis for text discussion. Additional mini-recipes show how the pattern of a basic dish can be applied and reapplied to provide endless menu versatility.

Illustrations—More than 300 illustrations provide what words alone cannot convey: techniques, equipment, sequence of steps, specific foods, food cuts, plate layouts, temperatures, proportions, and so on. Always functional, the illustrations are an integral part of the text, amplifying and reinforcing its teachings.

How-to-do-it—Often text-and-picture combinations show how to do many things, such as how to cut with a french knife, use a pastry bag, shuck an oyster, truss a bird, flip eggs, and many other tasks.

Tables and charts—Designed specifically for this text, the tables and charts in the book present valuable reference information in an easy-to-use format.

Key terms—Key terms are highlighted in boldface type. They are precisely defined and phonetically pronounced at their first appearance. Key concepts are fully discussed for greater understanding.

Glossary—The Glossary at the back of the book gathers all the text terms together for ready reference and adds others that the student is likely to encounter in reading or on the job.

Instructor's Manual—We offer an *Instructor's Manual* (ISBN 0-471-37676-0) with this book, which outlines points of emphasis for teaching each chapter. It also suggests exercises and activities to further the student's gradual progression toward insight, understanding, and mastery of techniques and skills. The *Instructor's Manual* also supplies test questions and answers for each chapter as well as Transparency Masters covering content and key figures.

Contents

Chapter 6

BUILDING FLAVOR, BODY, AND TEXTURE / 157

Chapter 7

SOUPS / 193

Chapter 8

SAUCES / 219

Chapter 9

VEGETABLES, GRAINS, AND PASTA / 245

Chapter 10

MEAT COOKERY / 287

Chapter 11

POULTRY COOKERY / 313

Chapter 12

FISH AND SHELLFISH COOKERY / 333

Chapter 13

BREAKFAST, BEVERAGES, AND DAIRY PRODUCTS / 367

Chapter 14

PANTRY PRODUCTION / 401

Chapter 15

HORS D'OEUVRES AND FOOD PRESENTATION / 429

Chapter 17

DESSERTS / 481

Chapter 1

THE KITCHEN

"*There's a romance to it*—and maybe something a little bit crazy. . . . " This is the owner-manager of a restaurant talking about the foodservice industry. His face, his voice, the sparkle in his eyes tell you that he is a man who loves what he is doing, that all the unpredictables and problems and demands on his time ("unreal, sometimes!") are worth it—maybe even part of the romance. "It's a whole new world every day," he says, with a mixture of frustration and relish. "And of course there's a profit to be made."

"There is a fascination about hospital foodservice—at least for me," says a dietitian who is tops in her profession. "I get involved in other aspects of dietetics—teaching, research—but I'm always being drawn back to hospital kitchens in some way—designing them, placing students, getting involved in day-to-day operations."

"It's the creativity you have," says a sous-chef in a large hotel, "taking some plain thing like a chicken or a piece of sole or beef and preparing an elegant meal, and the satisfaction you get when somebody tells you, 'Hey, that was delicious!' I've always been fascinated with it. I started when I was 14."

"Foodservice is an industry where people can really make a difference." The woman speaking manages an employee foodservice unit serving a thousand meals a day. "I can make a difference, the cook can, the cashier can—we make the difference in whether this restaurant is good or bad. I think that's why I like it, why other people like it. We have an effect on what we're doing, and we can see it happen."

Whatever the lure of foodservice as a career, whatever your own special career goals, it is important to understand cooking and to learn basic food preparation techniques. Even if you are headed for a management career and never expect to cook professionally, a knowledge of cooking will be very important to you. You can't write a job description for a cook, or hire one intelligently, unless you understand the skills needed and how to judge them. You need to know how a product should look and taste when it comes from a new cook you have just hired, and what to do about it if it isn't right. You should be able to fill in for the cook in an emergency. (One manager in such a situation discovered she didn't even know how to turn on the gas ovens.) You ought to have done some cooking yourself in order to plan a day's production, so that you know how long things take and what you are asking of your employees. ("When they give me the story they don't have enough time," says the in-plant feeding manager, " 'Okay,' I say, 'I can do it in half the time—watch me!' And they know that I can.")

"Dietitians need training in cooking as well as in food science, in the presentation of food and the taste of it," the hospital dietitian says. "We get engrossed in the scientific aspects—the sodium in a piece of meat or potassium in milk. We need the cooking knowledge as well as the science."

If your goal is culinary skill, if you aspire to master all the arts of cooking, a good understanding of basic principles will help you on your way. It will enable you to make more sense of each of the many jobs you will have as you acquire the experience necessary for true mastery. You will know what to look for as you observe skilled cooks, and you can ask intelligent questions to get the most out of your education on the job.

After completing this chapter, you should be able to:

- Discuss the basic features of kitchen organization in today's foodservice establishments.
- Compare and contrast kitchens in different types of facilities.
- Describe the duties and responsibilities usually associated with typical kitchen positions.
- Trace the development of quantity cooking methods, equipment, traditions, and cuisines from early times to the present.

CHARACTERISTIC FEATURES OF FOODSERVICE KITCHENS

There are many different types of foodservice establishments. Most common are the commercial restaurants. Other examples include healthcare foodservices, employee foodservices, school and college foodservices, in-flight foodservice, banquet catering, and the large hotel with restaurants as well as room service. There are also many foodservices that do not fit into any of these categories.

Although there are many types of kitchens and every kitchen is different in some way, the tasks performed in these kitchens are similar. The differences arise from the menus, the kinds of meals served, the numbers served, and the production and service goals. But kitchens are all doing the same thing—preparing food for service—so all are alike in certain basic ways.

Consider the following:

- The kitchen is divided into **stations,** or preparation areas, according to the types of food prepared.
- There is equipment appropriate to the menu and to the number of meals to be served.
- There is a staff structure or hierarchy with clearly defined lines of **authority** and **responsibility.** Authority can be defined as the right and power to make the necessary decisions and take the necessary actions to get the job done. Responsibility refers to the obligation an individual has to carry out certain duties and activities. Each job in the kitchen requires a certain set of skills.

Let us look more closely at some of these features of foodservice kitchens.

KITCHEN STATIONS

Most kitchens, even small ones, have at least two stations, one for hot food and one for cold. Large operations may have more, the number and type depending on the menu and the volume of production. There are no formulas governing the number of stations or the way they are divided. It depends on what is most appropriate and efficient for each operation.

Each station typically has its own equipment, some of its own storage areas, its own **station head** or supervisor, and its own staff. In effect, each station is a little production department that is semi-independent within the larger kitchen structure.

EQUIPMENT

Each station of the kitchen has the equipment it needs to process, cook, and hold the menu items assigned to it in the volume needed. Again, there is no formula for what equipment is found at any given station. It depends not only on the menu and the volume of production but also on whether the kitchen makes everything from scratch or buys preprepared foods. A kitchen buying processed potatoes, for example, would have no need for an electric potato peeler.

At times, the same piece of equipment may be shared by more than one station. A slicer may be used by cooks responsible for cooking and slicing meats, as well as cooks slicing tomatoes for salads.

STAFF STRUCTURE

Each kitchen staff is organized in terms of who has responsibility for what and who reports to whom. Many kitchens have the structure of relationships plotted out in a formal **organization chart** such as those in Figures 1.2 to 1.7. Using the organization chart, you can see the different levels of management, with authority and responsibility handed down from the top, level by level. There may be as many variations in staff structure as there are kitchens. But there is always structure, and the lines of responsibility and authority must be clearly understood on all sides if the kitchen is to function properly.

Georges Auguste Escoffier (1846–1935), the most famous chef of his day, is credited with developing the kitchen **brigade system** (**brigade de cuisine**—bree-gahd de kwee-zeen) in which each position has a station and specific responsibilities. His system was begun in order to streamline how work was done in the hotel kitchens, such as the Savoy of London, which he managed.

The **chef de cuisine,** also called the **executive chef,** is at the top of the brigade. The executive chef is responsible for all kitchen operations, for the quality of the menu and the products served, for hiring and managing the kitchen staff, for controlling costs and meeting budgets, and for coordinating with departments not directly involved in food production. Duties may also include food purchasing, menu costing, and scheduling of employees. In a small kitchen, the executive chef is often called a working chef because he or she spends part of the time managing but most of the time actually working at production tasks. Whether in a small or large kitchen, this is a position requiring extensive training and experience, both as a cook and as a manager.

The executive chef is typically one level above the **sous-chef.** *Sous-chef* is French for under-chef, and it is pronounced soo-shef. This person fills in for the chef and directly supervises that menu items are appropriately prepared, portioned, and presented. The sous-chef assists the station chefs, also called section cooks. Larger operations often have an executive sous-chef along with several other sous-chefs.

Below the executive chef and the sous-chef in the kitchen hierarchy are the **station heads or chefs**—the **chefs de partie** (shefs de par-tee) as they are called in classical terminology. Each is in charge of a particular area of production. In the classical kitchen team, you might have the following station heads:

- **Sauté station chef** (*saucier*—so-see-ay), responsible for all sautéed items and for sauces.

This position is often considered the most demanding. The saucier may also be the sous-chef, especially in smaller establishments.

- **Fish station chef** (*poissonnier*—pwa-sawn-yay), responsible for all fish dishes. This position may be combined with the sauté station chef.
- **Roast station chef** (*rôtisseur*—ro-tee-sur), responsible for roasted and braised meats and meat dishes.
- **Grill station chef** (*grillardin*—gree-yar-dan), responsible for grilled and broiled meats, seafood, and poultry. This position may be combined with the roast station chef.
- **Fry station chef** (*friturier*—free-tour-yay), responsible for all fried foods. This position may be combined with the roast station chef.
- **Vegetable station chef** (*légumier*—lay-gum-yay), responsible for preparation of vegetables and starches.
- **Soup station chef** (*potager*—poh-ta-zhay), responsible for the preparation of soups and stocks.
- The **vegetable and soup station** chef positions are often combined into one, called the *entremetier*—on-tra-met-yay.
- **Pantry chef** (*garde manger*—gardmon-zhay), responsible for the preparation of all cold foods, such as salads and cold appetizers,
- **Pastry chef** (*pâtissier*—pa-tees-yay), responsible for the preparation of all baked items, including desserts, breads, and pastries.
- **Relief cook** (*tournant*—toor-non), also called swing cook or rounds cook, a cook with all-round skills and constantly changing duties who relieves any of the other positions.

These positions are defined in a classical sense. In the real world, they are combined, altered, and adapted to fit the specific goals of the operation.

A station head, such as the pantry chef, may have additional staff consisting of **station cooks,** also called **line cooks,** and helpers with varying degrees of skill. Station cooks are responsible for preparing certain menu items. In smaller kitchens, the staff for many stations may be simply the station chef. Each station head must be fully skilled in the preparation of every dish made by the station. Station heads must also have administrative skills. Each must be able to plan and carry out production schedules for the station, supervise the workers, and train each worker in the skills required.

The term cook can be confusing. A **cook** is any person responsible for the preparation of food. This title has broad application; it may refer to persons who are accomplished and well paid, or to those who simply make sandwiches, or to anyone in between.

An **apprentice** is an individual who is receiving formal training for a career in foodservice. Apprentices rotate among kitchen stations and may be assigned according to their level of skill.

A **helper** is a person in training or one lacking the skills necessary to merit the title of cook. This is an entry-level job at the first rung of the kitchen ladder.

Figure 1.1 describes nutrition professionals found in healthcare foodservices.

Given the variety of kitchens and kinds of operations today, there is no way to attach specific duties or rank to a title, job, or station. Each operation has its own staff structure, and every well-organized kitchen has a written description of each job and the duties and skills it requires. Table 1.1 will give you some idea of the vast spread of opportunities available in the industry. Experience and education are requirements for

Figure 1-1 NUTRITION PROFESSIONALS IN HEALTHCARE FOODSERVICE

In the United States, the largest and most visible group of professionals in the nutrition field are the over 50,000 **registered dietitians (RDs).** Registered dietitians have specialized education in human anatomy and physiology, medical nutrition therapy, foods and food science, the behavioral sciences, and foodservice management. Registered dietitians must complete at least a bachelor's degree, an internship or equivalent experience, and a qualifying examination. Continuing education is required to maintain RD status. Most registered dietitians are members of the **American Dietetic Association (ADA).**

Registered dietitians work in a variety of settings. For example, you will find them in hospitals, nursing homes, retirement communities, wellness centers, or business and industry. According to a 1995 ADA membership survey, almost 50 percent of dietitians work in clinical dietetics, and about 25 percent work in foodservice administration. Clinical dietitians provide nutrition services such as nutrition counseling. Administrative dietitians work in the foodservice itself. They may be in charge of food production, cafeteria service, patient service, or even catering in a large department. Many administrative dietitians work their way up the ranks to become the director of food and nutrition services.

A **dietetic technician** is a professional who works as a member of a foodservice or health team under the supervision of a dietitian in a healthcare setting. By completing a two-year associate degree program approved by the American Dietetic Association and passing a credentialing exam, dietetic technicians can become registered. Registered dietetic technicians are permitted to use the initials DTR to signify that they have passed the exam and are professionally competent.

positions of skill, but seldom does a given job require a specific level of either one.

At this point, let us look at some real kitchens in different kinds of foodservice establishments. You will see how they are similar and how and why they differ.

SOME TYPICAL KITCHENS

A QUICK-SERVICE RESTAURANT

Let us begin our tour with the most familiar kind of operation—a **quick-service restaurant.** We're visiting an actual facility at the lunch hour. Busy and crowded as it is, we are greeted cordially at the counter, and our order is taken and delivered in minutes. Call it quick service, or fast food, both are good names for it.

The kitchen in this facility is a shiny display of tile and stainless steel projecting an image of sanitation in silver. Grills, deep-fat fryers, microwave ovens, and toasters are the only pieces of cooking equipment. A whole crew of workers moves in synchronized fashion to cook, assemble, and serve the orders, each person carrying out one small step of the task. Behind them all is the manager, keeping everyone supplied, shifting people about as needed, solving problems as they arise. The result is speed, high volume, and happy customers.

Table 1-1 KITCHEN POSITIONS: REQUIREMENTS AND OPPORTUNITIES

	Four-Year Degree Required	*Four-Year Degree Helpful*	*Two-Year Degree Required*	*Two-Year Degree Helpful*	*Years Experience to Full Position*	*Opportunities in*						
						Quick-Service	*Hotel Kitchen*	*Small Restaurant*	*Large Restaurant*	*In-Flight Foodservice*	*Cruise Ship*	*School, Hospital*
Executive chef		X		X	5–10	⊗[a]	X		X	X	X	X
Working chef		X		X	5–10		X	X	X	X	X	X
Sous-chef		X		X	3–5		X	X	X	X	X	X
Sauce cook				X	2–5		X	X	X	X	X	X
Chef garde manger				X	2–5		X		X	X	X	
Pastry cook				X	2–5		X	X	X	X	X	X
Fish cook				X	2–5	X	X	X	X	X	X	X
Fry cook				X	1–3	X	X	X	X	X	X	X
Production manager		X		X	5–10	X	X	X	X	X	X	X
Sanitarian	X				E[b]	⊗[a]	X			X	X	X
Dietitian	X				E					⊗[a]		X
Dietetic technician			X		E							X
Pantry cook				X	1–3	X	X	X	X	X	X	X

[a]⊗ indicates corporate headquarters only.
[b]E = Entry-level positions.

How do they do it? The secret is simple. Everything is premeasured, precut, preportioned, preprocessed, electronically controlled, and precisely timed. Custom equipment does the cooking. It is practically person-proof, requiring only that things be put in it or on it and taken out or off again in response to electronic signals. Substituting precision for creative cooking, the system turns out the standardized products its customers love.

A quick-service operation, whether it is burgers or chicken or pizza or sandwiches or fish or whatever, is food preparation reduced to its simplest terms. It typically has a limited menu requiring a minimum of cooking equipment and cooking skills. Precut and preportioned raw products reduce labor to a minimum. Production is divided into a series of small tasks anyone can be trained to do.

A quick-service operation is typically one unit of a chain, all alike in menu, equipment, operation, product, quality, and image. The parent corporation provides the design and layout of the facility, writes the menu, sets the standards, and often trains both managers and crew. In company-owned stores, managers report to corporate management; in others, the units are franchises that are independently owned. The manager of a franchise store may also be the owner of the unit.

Staff structure in each unit is simple: a unit manager, an assistant manager, and a crew reporting directly to management (Figure 1.2). All are thoroughly trained in every procedure of cooking and service and are interchangeable on the job. Thus, during rush periods, any crew member can shift from one task to another without missing a beat. After the rush, the crew will drop to a handful, doubling up on duties and taking care of cleanup as well.

Figure 1-2 ORGANIZATION CHART FOR A QUICK-SERVICE UNIT

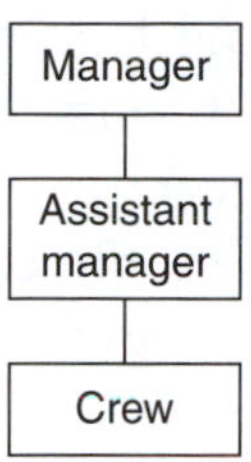

A HOTEL FOODSERVICE

Now, let us move to the other extreme in size and complexity and visit the kitchens of a large hotel in a big city. This hotel (also an actual operation) has a huge main kitchen that prepares all the food for a high-volume banquet service. Satellite kitchens serving various restaurant areas supplement the main kitchen production.

The minute you step into the main kitchen you are in a special world. Big as it is, it is crowded with people and food and movement and clatter. Sizes and quantities boggle the mind of the uninitiated visitor: 2500 servings of broccoli . . . steaks by the hundreds . . . a 20-gallon pot of soup . . . 40 liters of mayonnaise, one day's supply. The sights, scents, and sizzle of steaks, soups, and sauces seduce the senses and quicken the appetite. How can there be so many thin people among all these cooks?

A bank of ranges, ovens, fryers, grills, and broilers identifies the area, or station, where the hot foods are prepared—roasts, braised meats, steaks, chops, grilled chicken, fish, eggs, sauces. In any full-service kitchen, this is the backbone of the operation, its main production station. It has its own station chef and its own team of station cooks and helpers as well as its own special equipment and storage areas. The sauté chef is the station chef in this hotel. In other hotel kitchens, the head of this station may have a different specialty and a different title.

On either side of the range area are two more large production areas, the soup and vegetable station and the cold-food station. They, too, are separate departments, each with its own equipment, storage areas, station head, and staff. In this kitchen, the cold-food station is called the garde manger department. It produces all the cold food except pastries and ices—the salads and salad dressings, fruits for breakfast and dessert, cold meats and cheeses, canapés and cold hors d'oeuvres, buffet platters, decorated molds, ice carvings, display foods. The head of this department, the chef garde manger, uses the classical title for this culinary specialty. It represents a high level of skill in preparing elaborate cold foods and food displays. In a smaller operation offering simpler foods, this area might be called the salad station or the pantry.

Room service has a station to itself—a complete kitchen-within-a-kitchen laid out for the use of one cook. Another station belongs to the hotel butcher—something of a rarity these days. He breaks down or cuts up large pieces of meat into the special cuts required by the hotel menu. He also bones chickens, skins and fillets fish, opens oysters, watches over live lobsters, and turns meat scraps into cocktail meatballs. But he is one of the last of his kind. Pretrimmed and preportioned meats are rapidly making the hotel butcher obsolete.

Another unusual department of this kitchen is the pastry or bakeshop (most hotels and restaurants buy their baked goods readymade). The holding areas for this station are like scenes from a dream: a five-tiered and pillared wedding cake decked with the most delicate flowers and intricate scrollwork . . . a huge bar-mitzvah cake with the young man's name and tomorrow's date iced in thin tall lettering as distinctive as an artist's signature . . . cakes in various stages: ready for layering, ready for icing, ready for decorating, ready to be topped with ice cream and meringue for baked Alaska.

In the satellite kitchen of the hotel's expensive dinner restaurant is a set of production stations of a different kind. Here, each menu dish is prepared to the diner's order just before it is served. This is known as **à la carte cookery.**

Each station has its own chef, highly skilled, highly specialized—a sauté chef, a soup and vegetable chef, a garde manger chef. In a single evening, some of them cook for as many as 500 diners, one or a few portions at a time. The action is fast, the tension is high, the timing is critical. Perfect coordination with serving personnel is absolutely essential to get each dish to the diner at its peak of quality—worthy of its price tag. To the onlooker, it seems impossible, but they do it every night.

All the food production for the hotel's banquet service, restaurants, and employee cafeteria is the responsibility of one person, the executive chef. This is entirely a management role, complete with a private office, a secretary, and a handsome salary. But this chef came up through the kitchens and knows every station firsthand. Such intimate knowledge of food and cooking pays off every day in a hundred ways. Where so many different things are going on, where every day is different (maybe 500 meals on a really slow day and 5000 in one day a week later), where needs change from hour to hour, and the unpredictable happens frequently, only someone who knows cooking, cooks, and kitchens inside out is capable of running the show.

The executive chef reports to the **food and beverage director,** who has final responsibility

Figure 1-3 ORGANIZATION CHART FOR A HOTEL FOOD AND BEVERAGE DEPARTMENT

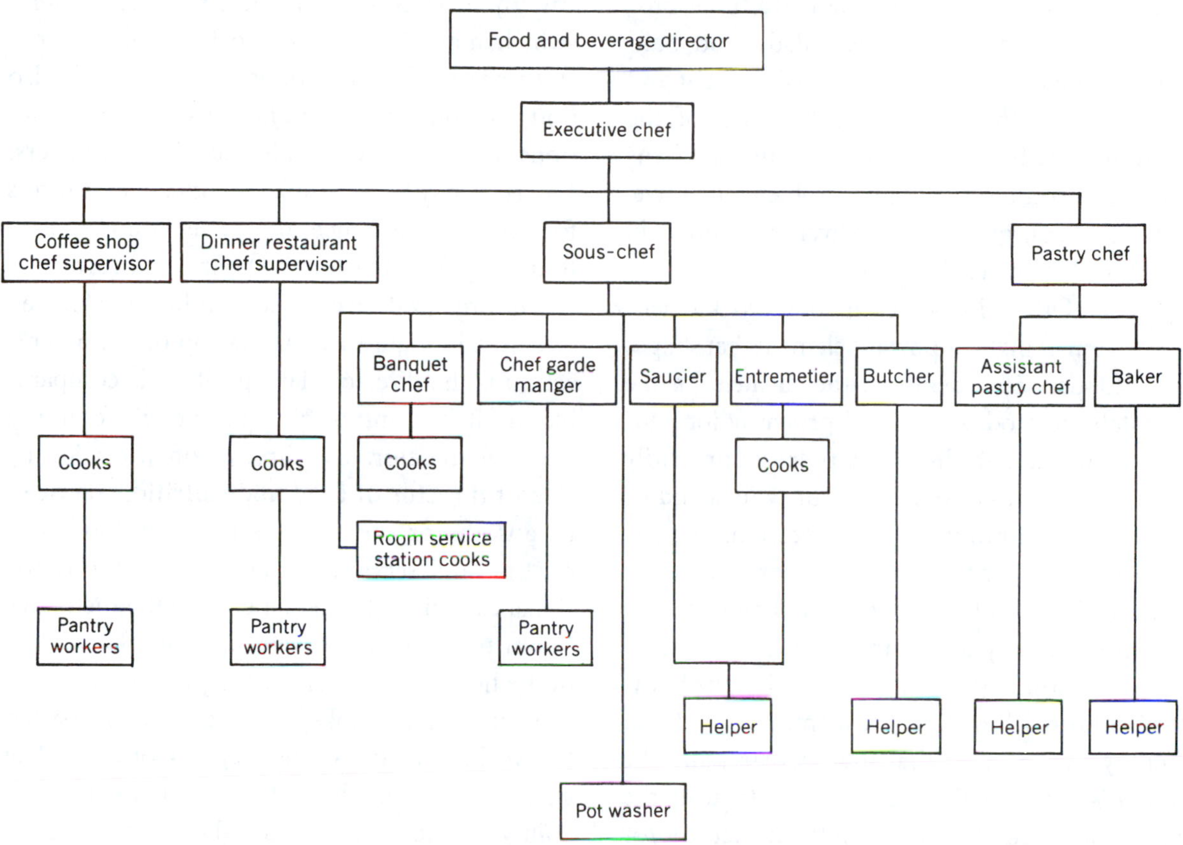

not only for the food side of this foodservice operation but for the service side and the beverage side as well.

An organization chart for this kitchen is given in Figure 1.3. Below the executive chef is the sous-chef, the pastry chef, the dinner restaurant chef, and the coffee shop chef. Below the sous-chef are the banquet chef, the station heads, and the butcher. Though it represents a specific kitchen, it is fairly typical of a hotel doing this volume of business. Station divisions may vary from one hotel to another; titles may vary; but the organizational structure is similar. Smaller hotel kitchen staffs may be simpler versions of the same pattern.

A HOSPITAL KITCHEN

Let us now visit a different type of large, complex operation—a hospital kitchen serving about 3000 meals a day. Not only does this kitchen look and feel clean, but clues to the importance of sanitation are everywhere. An entire room is devoted to hosing down and sanitizing the carts on which dirty trays have been stacked. The aides who dish out the food wear plastic gloves.

This kitchen is in many ways a simpler version of the hotel kitchen. There are three production stations—hot foods, salads, and baking—each having its own special equipment and storage areas and its own staff. Much of the equipment is like the hotel's. The two kitchens even have some of the same problems to solve: Both, for example, must deliver hot and cold foods to distant serving places.

Most of the differences in the two kitchens come from a single important element that shapes every foodservice operation: the clientele. In the hospital, the food is prepared primarily for people who are ill. In the hotel, it is prepared primarily for out-of-town visitors with money to spend or for people celebrating a special occasion. The difference means very different kinds of menus.

In the hospital kitchen, nutrition and medical nutrition therapy are primary concerns. **Nutrition** is the study of how food nourishes the body. **Medical nutrition therapy,** formerly called diet therapy, is a process that involves assessing the patient's nutritional status and then treating the patient as needed with a modified diet and/or counseling. Meals are carefully planned to provide a balanced diet. In addition, there are several versions of the patient menu to fit special needs—a liquid diet, a low-fat diet, a low-sodium diet, and so on. Since the right food is part of making the patient well, the kitchen works closely with the medical staff. Standardized recipes are scrupulously followed. Doctors' orders are carried out to the letter.

Since patients in a hospital eat all their meals there day after day, the menu changes daily. Contrast this with the hotel menu, where the offerings are the same every day. The hospital cook's assignments will change daily; the hotel cook will generally make the same things every day.

In addition to providing meals for patients, hospital foodservices prepare meals for hospital employees who frequent the employee cafeteria (which may also be open to hospital visitors). Within many hospital foodservices, you will also find someone in charge of catering special functions, such as a luncheon for hospital volunteers. Catering may be as simple as coffee and muffins for an early-bird meeting, or as complex as a four-course dinner for the board of directors.

The organization chart for this hospital kitchen is shown in Figure 1.4. At the top of the organization is the director. This position is comparable in kitchen authority to the hotel's food and beverage director. The director often carries the title of **director of food and nutrition services,** because he or she oversees not only food production and service, but also directs the nutritional care given to the patients by the dietitians.

On the production level, it is similar to that of the hotel kitchen. There is a production manager, and skilled cooks head the stations, assisted by workers with varying degrees of skill. The skills required of the station heads include the ability to follow a standardized recipe to produce a quality product and the capacity to supervise the workers on the station.

One senses calm and order in this kitchen. Perhaps it comes from the high degree of organization. Perhaps it is due to the nature of the operation—after all, demand is steady and predictable for the most part, and most problems are foreseeable. Perhaps it reflects the administrative skills of its top people. Perhaps it is all these things.

A MIDSCALE RESTAURANT

Next, let us look at a **midscale,** also called **midpriced, restaurant.** This is a broad term applying to restaurants that offer food at moderate prices with service that is not as fast as found in a quick-

Figure 1-4 ORGANIZATION CHART FOR A HOSPITAL FOOD AND NUTRITION DEPARTMENT

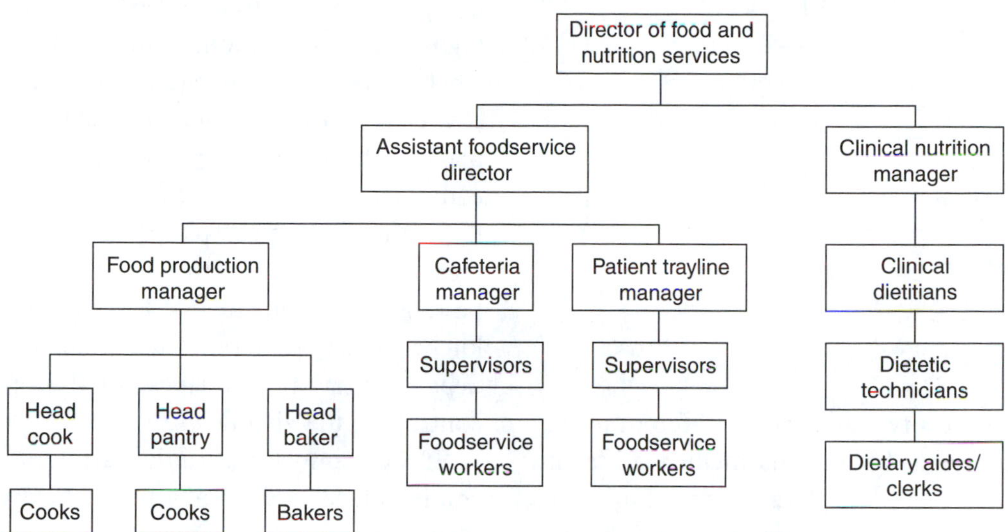

service restaurant. A midscale restaurant might be a family restaurant, a cafeteria, a Mexican restaurant, or a steakhouse. It usually has table service and an atmosphere that goes with the type of food.

The small midscale restaurant we have chosen (another real place) features extra-good food at modest prices in an atmosphere a local columnist described as "casual class." It has 130 seats and serves an average of 250 meals a day.

The kitchen would fit into one corner of one station of the big hotel or hospital kitchen. Its equipment is a mixture of old reliable and shiny new. It has two stations, cold and hot, and two cooks, one in charge of each station. A third staff member works as a prep person under the hot-food cook during prepreparation time and doubles as dish and pot washer during the service period. On weekends, a part-time cook backs up both cooks during the serving period.

We have timed our visit for the dinner hour. In spite of the small staff, the tiny kitchen seems full of people. What with a dishwasher and pot sink fitted in along one wall, and waiters coming in and going out, there are few square inches of space unused. But the layout has been well planned, the traffic patterns carefully calculated. The kitchen works.

Everything is ready that can be prepared ahead. A steam table holds hot foods ready for service. The few items cooked to order are done quickly with a minimum of motion. Though the pace is fast, things move smoothly. These cooks are skilled, with several years of experience and training behind them. They have to be experts to keep up with the orders.

In this small operation, there is no separate production supervisor. The kitchen staff reports directly to the restaurant manager. The manager knows cooks and cooking firsthand, though she plays no part in the kitchen operations other than to schedule the day's production. She also does the purchasing, plans the menu specials, and supervises the service personnel. Figure 1.5 shows the organization of this operation.

Figure 1-5 ORGANIZATION CHART FOR A MIDSCALE RESTAURANT

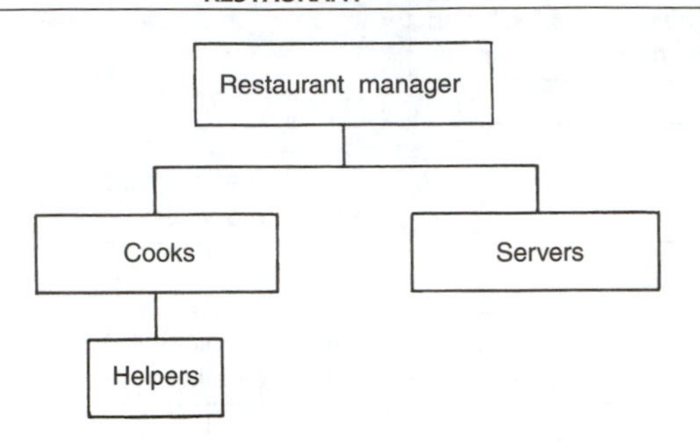

Every specialty restaurant is different in staff and equipment, because its menu is different. Its volume makes a difference, too. But its organization will not vary greatly from the pattern of this small restaurant, though there may be more cooks, more helpers, and more stations.

IN-FLIGHT FOODSERVICE KITCHEN

The in-flight foodservice kitchen we have chosen to visit works right around the clock seven days a week, preparing some 25,000 meals a day for an airline that averages 150 flights a day. It is one of a chain of 28 kitchens at airports across the country, serving some 50 airlines in all.

Each outgoing plane must have on board the correct number and types of meals for all the passengers, packed in special holding or cooking equipment that fits into each aircraft galley (there are different types). Every plane must depart on time. It has a departure slot in the air traffic control pattern and a landing slot in another city at a specific time. For the kitchen, this turns each day into a series of 150 inflexible deadlines.

The huge stainless steel and tile kitchen contains two food production areas—hot food and cold food—each with production and storage equipment similar to what we have seen in other high-volume operations. But, in this kitchen, when people talk about equipment, they are usually referring to the equipment that travels on the planes—the holding and heating and cooking equipment they must custom-load for each flight, the small square plates they must pack the meals in, and the trays they must set up for each passenger. Equipment is the focal point of this kitchen, and the equipment and sanitation (E&S) department is the heartbeat of the operation, controlling the vital flow.

E&S personnel unload the carts from the incoming planes, wash and sanitize the dishes and carts, and put everything in readiness to be packed and sent out again, usually within hours. It is up to this department to see that the equipment that must go out has come in and that there is enough of the right kind of everything to service each scheduled flight. The food department packs the equipment with its products. The ramp and dispatch department transports and installs the equipment on the outbound planes and brings back the used equipment to repeat the cycle.

The cold-food production area seems full of people—almost more people than food. Each worker performs one small step—washing lettuce, hulling strawberries, slicing roast beef, breaking parsley into sprigs of a specified size. For assembly, a moving belt carries the dishes for a menu item past assemblers, each of whom places one ingredient in its specified position on the dish. The moving belt is the caterer's version of plating, which is usually done in other kitchens by the cook. At the end of the line, each dish is checked, wrapped, loaded into a waiting cart, and rolled off to a cooler to await departure.

The hot-food area is much smaller, since only the entrées for the first-class passengers are made from scratch. They are prepared in 100-portion batches, assembled and chill-packed in individual portions, and held in refrigerators until use. Entrées for coach passengers are bought frozen, prepared by vendors to airline specifications.

Two to three hours before flight time, the exact number and kinds of meals for each plane are moved from the refrigerator to the ramp area. Here, another moving belt is activated, carrying the trays that will be served to the passengers. Assemblers position each tray mat, napkin, cup, salad, dressing, dessert, roll, butter—everything but the hot entrée, which will be added to the tray when it is served. These trays are then packed in dry ice and loaded into the equipment that fits into the plane's galley.

The hot entrées are also packed into equipment that fits the plane for which they are headed. If that equipment can heat or cook, the food is packed cold; otherwise, it is heated, packed hot, and kept hot until service two to five hours later. Both hot and cold equipment are then loaded onto the waiting truck that will service that particular flight.

Delivery to the plane completes the caterer's service goal. The caterer serves the airline rather than the individual customer. In fact, each airline it serves plans its own menus, develops its own recipes, and sets the quality standards and the budget. The caterer simply meets the airline's specifications.

Figure 1.6 shows how this huge foodservice operation is organized. The food manager is comparable to an executive chef or production manager. The ramp and dispatch manager and the equipment and sanitation manager have comparable responsibility in their own spheres. The sanitation side of the E&S is as important as the equipment

Figure 1-6 ORGANIZATION CHART FOR AN IN-FLIGHT FOODSERVICE OPERATION

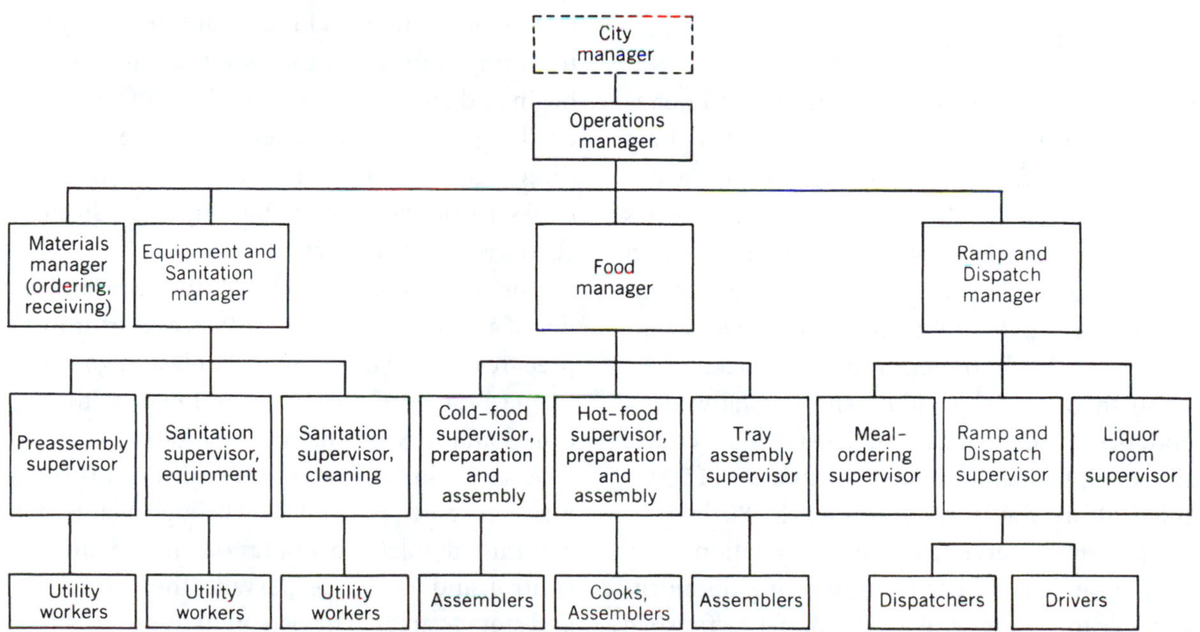

responsibility because of the many problems of handling and holding such large amounts of food safely under potentially hazardous conditions. The operations manager at the top of the chart would correspond to the food and beverage director. The food production supervisors are comparable to a sous-chef in a hotel kitchen, but unless there is an emergency they seldom do any food preparation.

Part of the challenge of everyone's job is the need to adjust to the unexpected. A situation can change dramatically minutes before flight time if a canceled flight from another airline adds an extra 200 passengers. The weather in airports 3000 miles away can play havoc with schedules, force changes in the type of plane, and turn the best laid plans into a game of musical chairs.

Overall, this is an intricate, complex, sophisticated operation. Everything is systematized and prescribed to the last detail and the airline calls the tune. Yet systems alone cannot do the job, and the caterer must remain flexible and sensitive if the operation is to meet the service goal.

A CRUISE SHIP KITCHEN

Cruise lines are noted for the quality, and quantity, of their food. The cruise ship we are visiting makes its way from one warm-weather port to another on cruises of three to seven days. It carries 1000 passengers. Food—really good food—is part of its tourist package and a major feature of its entertainment and shipboard activities. Deck luncheons, midnight buffets, morning snacks, afternoon snacks, teas, parading and singing waiters, and, of course, breakfast, lunch, and a six-course dinner all happen every day. Of its crew of 500, a full 200 are foodservice personnel—80 in production, 80 in service, and 40 in sanitation.

The kitchen is busy from morning till morning: Cleanup after the 1 A.M. buffet is finished only a few hours before breakfast prep begins. At noon and at dinnertime, the kitchen is a wall-to-wall buzz of activity as 1000 people are served in two sittings with a choice of six or seven entrées prepared to order. It is like serving two banquets back to back twice a day, but with the guests selecting the food.

A tour through the kitchen reveals the same banks of ovens, banks of ranges, steam tables, and full array of equipment found in many other kitchens. Since all baking is done aboard ship (no readymade bread or pastries), there is a full complement of baking ovens. A separate kitchen prepares three meals a day for the crew and serves as a training kitchen.

Most of the staff structure is similar to that of many land-based operations. The position of food manager is like that of a food and beverage director without the beverage responsibility. The assistant managers relieve the executive chef and sous-chef of responsibilities they would have in other kitchens. They are responsible for the smooth flow of production from storage areas to kitchen and from kitchen to dining room, and they see that all activities begin and end as they should. Perhaps the most challenging of their duties is the role of **expediter**—getting the à la carte entrées from the cooks to the servers at the height of the luncheon and dinner service.

The station cooks are all fully trained. The luxury of an ample labor force offers opportunity to prepare classical dishes found only at high prices in the best hotels, or to experiment with new dishes and new production techniques.

A sanitation officer ranks high on this organization chart (Figure 1.7). Through a large staff committed solely to sanitation, this manager's control and influence pervade the production and storage areas. The person in this job also has

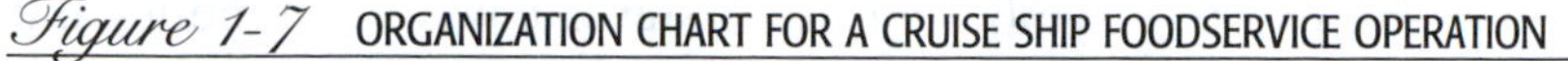

Figure 1-7 ORGANIZATION CHART FOR A CRUISE SHIP FOODSERVICE OPERATION

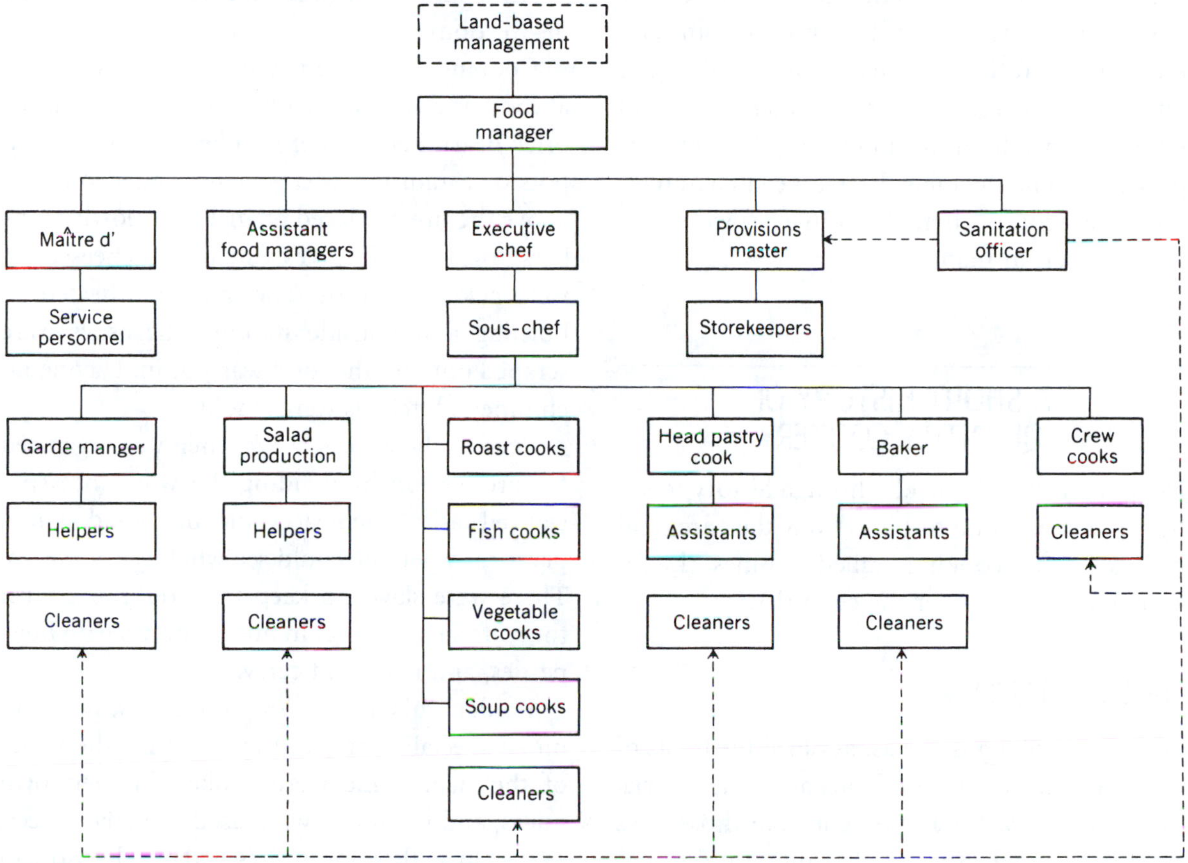

charge of chlorinating the drinking water, since there is no reliable source.

Everybody works 12 hours a day or more, seven days a week, except when the ship is in port. The work is difficult and the hours are long, but the ship's vacation atmosphere is stimulating, and when the passengers are off the ship sightseeing and shopping there are chances to take a few free hours and explore ports in foreign lands.

WHY KITCHENS DIFFER

Once you have examined several kitchens, you can begin to see that the menu and the service goal are the two most important factors dictating the physical organization, the equipment, the staff, and the structure of the organization chart. In the cruise ship kitchen, for example, you have special stations for plating in order to feed large numbers of people simultaneously. In the in-flight kitchen, on the other hand, you have a transportation department because the meals must be transported to aircraft for service at a later time. Hotel and hospital kitchens are also concerned with delivering foods at different times and places.

The **food production manager** is the person responsible for all levels of food handling, production, and often service of food. The exact amount of control depends on the size of the operation. This is the key position in any kitchen operation. Other typical titles are kitchen manager, foodservices manager, food manager, production supervisor, kitchen supervisor, to name a few. In a large kitchen having an executive chef, the sous-chef would be the production manager.

A SHORT HISTORY OF QUANTITY COOKERY

Now, let us travel quickly through history to see how kitchens came to be the way they are, and how styles of cooking, called cuisines (kwee-zeens), developed over the centuries.

THE EARLY EMPIRES

Quantity cooking is at least as old as the feasts of the kings and emperors of ancient Egypt, Assyria, Persia, and Israel. Banquet guests in those days often numbered a thousand or more, and sometimes whole herds of cattle were slaughtered for a single feast. Large households consumed food in quantity every day.

When the Romans built their empire, they helped themselves to the foods, the cooks, and the culinary splendors of the peoples they vanquished. The emperor Julius Caesar set a new record for quantity foodservice when he celebrated one of his military triumphs with a feast for 260,000 people that lasted for several days.

The Roman cook was typically a male slave brought from conquered Greece, where cooking skills and cuisine were highly developed. Cooks were in great demand in Rome, and cooking was considered an art. A good cook became a status symbol for his master. He was given money and presents and often became rich enough to buy his freedom.

Cooking in the Roman kitchen was done with a wood or charcoal fire built on a raised stone or brick hearth. Foods were cooked over the fire in pots or cauldrons. Meats were roasted on spits above the fire or placed on grills on glowing embers. Breads and cakes, including cheesecake, were baked in ovens. The oven was heated by burning a fire inside it; then the ashes were scraped out and the food was put in. Having no chimneys, kitchens were smoky.

Even in those days, the kitchen was organized for production by dividing the work into specialized tasks. The head cook supervised from a platform where he could see what was going on. There were slaves to keep the fires going, turn the spits, crush things in huge mortars with huge pestles, and fetch and carry.

Roman cuisine was long on meats, fish, and birds, specially bred and fattened for the tables of the rich. Some were cooked in their own juices, and the juices were used to make sauces, as we do with some dishes today. The Roman menu included most of the foods we use today in the way of vegetables, fruits, dairy products, grains, and spices, but olive oil was used for cooking and honey for sweetening. Though they searched the known world for rare and unusual foods, the Romans' cuisine was not delicate and refined but highly spiced and heavy.

MEDIEVAL EUROPE

After the barbarians overran the Roman Empire, the well-organized Roman kitchen and the elaborate Roman cuisine all but disappeared. Life in most of Europe was reduced to mere survival. People lived clustered in and about the noble's manor or the monastery and ate what was provided by the nobles or the monks. Quantity cooking, far from dying out, was more important than ever.

The food was cooked outdoors or over fires built in the middle of a great hall with a hole in the roof. Many a manor hall was dining room, living room, and bedroom for everyone. The food was boiled in cauldrons or roasted on hand-turned spits. It was served on slabs of hard bread, called *trenchers,* and eaten with the fingers. Kitchen workers were serfs, the medieval equivalent of slaves, so the labor supply was plentiful.

Food supplies were scanty—whatever could be grown in the fields with primitive plows, raised in the barnyard, or caught in the streams and forests. All in all, the early Middle Ages did not offer the cook much chance for fame and fortune.

After several hundred years, times began to improve. Trade revived, new techniques of farming were developed, kings and nobles and monasteries grew richer. The later Middle Ages were a time of pomp and pageantry, and the great halls of the manor houses and castles were scenes of lavish feasting. In fact, eating and drinking were the chief forms of entertainment. Often, there would be music and dancing between courses. It was the day of the juggler, the jester, and the wandering minstrel.

Kitchens by this time were separate rooms or separate buildings. They had fireplaces with chimneys, ovens for baking, and high vaulted ceilings for carrying away the smoke. But the spit and the cauldron at the open fire were still the means of food production, and the knife and the mortar and pestle were the primary processing tools. A cauldron for quantity production is illustrated in Figure 1.8.

The cook now had more and better raw materials to work with. Spices from the Far East were available, along with raisins, currants, almonds, and sugar from the Near East. The cook

Figure 1-8 COOKING WITH AN OPEN FIRE

A kettle of fish or a pot of stew for a large household required strength as well as cooking skill. (From Bartolomeo Scappi, *Dell arte dell cucinare* [*On the Arts of Cooking*], 1643. Courtesy Rare Books and Manuscripts Division, The New York Public Library, Astor, Lenox, and Tilden Foundations.)

still struggled, however, with problems of taste and texture. The salty taste of winter meats was moderated by soaking and boiling, by stewing meat with bland starchy foods or with honey or wine, or by masking the taste with spices or sauces. Tough meats—and most were tough—were minced or pounded. Fresh meats, poultry, and game were spit-roasted and brought whole to the serving table, where they were carved into small pieces (forks had not yet made their appearance) and tasted for poison before being served to the king or noble.

Chefs in royal households were now persons of importance, respected and well paid. The most famous chef of the period, head chef to King Charles VI of France, was, in fact, made a knight. His coat of arms, still to be seen on his tombstone, bears three cooking pots and six roses. Taillevent, as he called himself, wrote one of the earliest cookbooks, called *Le Viandier* (*The Meat Cook*). In it, he describes many new cooking techniques and dishes of his day, such as sauces thickened with bread crumbs and various kinds of stews.

NEW FOODS AND A NEW CUISINE

The sixteenth century brought new foods from across the seas following the voyages of Columbus and other explorers—turkey, potatoes, corn, red and green peppers, tomatoes, coffee, and chocolate. It also brought Italian cuisine to France when two 14-year-olds were married—Catherine de' Medici of Florence and the heir to the French throne, the future Henry II. Catherine brought with her to Paris a complete staff of Italian cooks. In Italy, some of the old Roman ways with food had survived, and a cuisine of considerable elegance had developed, enriched with foods and cooking techniques from other parts of the Mediterranean world.

Now, the French court learned to eat veal, artichokes, truffles, melons, macaroons, quenelles, ice cream, and frangipane tarts. They also adopted the more elegant Italian manners. Catherine even introduced the table fork, although she herself ate with her fingers. It took another century for the fork to catch on in France and England.

French cooks were quick to learn the new cuisine, and over the next several generations they built upon this foundation to develop the classical French cuisine we still enjoy today. The heavy, highly spiced medieval fare gave way to lighter foods more delicate in taste and texture. Vegetables and fruits and even flowers were added to the diet.

Fine food and fine cooking became favorite pastimes of the French nobility. Not only did they dine well, they learned to cook. Louis XV, who ruled France for much of the eighteenth century, was both an avid eater and an amateur cook, and he demanded the same of those around him. It became important to be a good cook, and especially to invent a new dish, if you wanted to succeed at the French court. So arose the multiplication of sauces and garnitures—the basic dish served with a certain sauce or a certain garnish or a certain set of vegetables. Many a garniture or sauce, however, was invented not by the person it was named for but by the chef.

It was the heyday of French chefs. They were honored and well paid. Their fame spread throughout Europe. Nobles from other countries sent their chefs to France for training or imported French chefs to head their kitchens.

But the chef's work was not easy. A dinner might require the preparation of a hundred or more different dishes. It is true that the kitchen had improved. Pots and pans were better. There were charcoal braziers—small burners containing live coals—and by the eighteenth century there were stoves with 12 or 20 grates. This equipment made it possible to sauté and to season and to manipulate the food in the pan, which could not be done near the roaring fires of the Middle Ages. But the cook still lacked clean and steady heat sources and power-driven equipment. Fortunately, for the chef and for French cuisine, there still were plenty of helpers for the menial tasks.

This grand era of French cookery ended in 1793 with the stroke of the guillotine by which Louis XVI lost his head. The French nobility fled to other countries or lost their fortunes or their heads as the French Revolution turned society upside down. Many fine chefs, finding themselves without jobs, opened their own eating places in Paris. So began the restaurant industry. Within 20 years there were some 500 restaurants in Paris.

CARÊME

During the period of upheaval, a young nobody named Marie-Antoine Carême worked his way into kitchens that served some of the surviving aristocrats. By working under one great chef and then another, he mastered all branches of cooking—pastry, sauces, cold foods, hot foods. He quickly became the most sought-after chef in Europe. Among his employers were the czar of Russia, the future king of England, and the French foreign minister Talleyrand. It is said that Talleyrand's dinner table was responsible for settling the peace of Europe after the Napoleonic Wars.

But Carême was also busy writing books, often working all day in the kitchen, then staying up most of the night to study and write. He considered it his life's work to pass on to the world his intimate knowledge of every phase of the chef's art and of classical cuisine. A passage from one of his books conveys a strong impression of his intensity and dedication, as well as a vivid picture of Talleyrand's kitchen:

Imagine yourself in a large kitchen such as that of the Foreign Minister at the moment of a great dinner. There one sees twenty chefs at their urgent occupations, coming, going, moving with speed in this cauldron of heat. Look at the great mass of live charcoal, a cubic meter for the cooking of the entrées, and another mass on the ovens for the cooking of the soups, the sauces, the ragouts, the frying and the bains-marie.

Add to that a heap of burning wood in front of which four spits are turning, one of which bears a sirloin weighing from 45 to 60 lb., another a piece of veal weighing 35 to 45 lb., the other two for fowl and game.

In this furnace everyone moves with tremendous speed; not a sound is heard; only the chef has the right to make himself heard, and at the sound of his voice, everyone obeys. Finally, to put the lid on our sufferings, for about half an hour the doors and windows are closed so that the air does not cool the dishes as they are being dished up. And in this way we pass the best days of our lives.

But honour commands. We must obey even though physical strength fails. But it is the burning charcoal which kills us!*

---

*Reprinted from *Larousse Gastronomique* by Prosper Montagne. Copyright 1961 by Crown Publishers, Inc. Used by permission of Crown Publishers, Inc.

Carême's kitchen in England (Figure 1.9) was much better. It had everything an extravagant prince could buy—spits turned ingeniously by fans powered by the heat of the fire itself, a wall-length bank of ovens and ranges, a mortar and pestle standing waist-high and two feet across, shelves upon shelves of gleaming copper utensils. Windows at the top of the high ceiling helped to cope with the heat and fumes.

Figure 1-9 CAREME'S KITCHEN

Here is the kitchen in which Carême produced elaborate dinner parties for the prince regent of England. Notice the spits for roasting on the right, the rows of copper cookware along the rear wall, the high ceiling with windows at the top for carrying off the smoke and heat and fumes from the charcoal. Below the hood on the left wall are ranges. Under the clock, a cook is using a waist-high mortar and pestle for grinding or puréeing. On the center table are silver serving dishes ready for the prince's table. The chef directs his brigade of assistants, cook's knife tucked in his belt. (Aquatint by John Nash, 1821, from his *Views of the Royal Pavilion at Brighton,* 1826. Photo courtesy Royal Pavilion, Art Gallery and Museums, Brighton.)

CLASSICAL CUISINE

The classical cuisine detailed in Carême's books was made up of hundreds of different dishes, each defined right down to the shape of the potato and the arrangement on the plate. In contrast to the heavy, spicy fare of medieval times, classical cuisine was light and delicate. The goals of the cook were to build flavor with the flavors of the foods themselves; to create, smooth, rich textures; to achieve an effect of luxury and elegance as pleasing to the eye as to the palate.

To distill the essence of the flavor of a meat might require days of cooking. The refinement of a sauce's texture might require several cooks for the straining and puréeing. The number of dishes served at a meal (a Carême menu for 40 guests lists 144 separate dishes) might require a very large kitchen staff.

It was a cuisine difficult to produce unless there was plenty of money for staffing the kitchen and buying foods that were often scarce and expensive. The chefs who opened restaurants in Paris after the Revolution had a hard time of it. They either modified their menus or went out of business. There were still plenty of rich people, however, especially among the new and powerful middle class. Eating was still the pleasure of the rich, and French cuisine continued to flourish and to develop still further. New dishes were invented reflecting the times—prepared à la financière and à la bourgeoise. The common touch became popular, too, in dishes à la meunière, à la bonne femme, à la paysanne (in the style of the miller, the housewife, the peasant). What we call classical cuisine today is this French cuisine of the nineteenth century, which, in turn, is an expanded, refined, and codified version of classical eighteenth-century cuisine.

Now, cooks got their training by working in the kitchens of successful restaurants and in the big hotels being built to cater to the rich. The skilled French chef who made it to the top was more in demand than ever.

ESCOFFIER

Georges Auguste Escoffier was the most famous chef of his day. He is also the master chef best known to our generation. Escoffier was a superb and imaginative cook. But more important to his profession, he radically changed the methods of foodservice and kitchen organization during his years of managing the kitchens of the Savoy and Carlton hotels in turn-of-the-century London.

Escoffier fathered the modern menu by serving a carefully planned sequence of courses. He constructed it as though it were a symphony of contrasting movements; the soup, he said, should be like an overture suggesting the theme. This system of planning and serving the food replaced the old system of serving 20 to 40 different dishes at once, elaborately arranged on the table to overwhelm the diners. The dishes would grow cold before they could be eaten, and diners had to eat only what they could reach. Escoffier's system of courses—one or two dishes per course, served to each person—ensured that diners received their food quickly at its proper temperature and its peak of quality, a primary goal of any foodservice today.

Escoffier also reorganized the work of the different kitchen stations, eliminating duplication and improving efficiency. He had the same purpose in mind—to speed the food to the waiting customer. More than anyone else, he pointed the developing restaurant industry toward success by catering to the customer's needs and desires.

THE CONTEMPORARY KITCHEN AND CUISINE

In one respect, Escoffier was very old fashioned. He refused to cook with gas or electricity, though both were available by the 1890s. He felt that only coal and charcoal could produce perfection of flavor in roasting and grilling. Spit-roasting gave way to oven-roasting only in the twentieth century.

The last hundred years have seen more change in kitchens and cooking than all the thousands of years preceding. Among the most revolutionary changes are the use of gas and electricity for cooking, cooling, and freezing; thermostatic controls for cooking and cooling; power-driven machines to perform the endless tasks of the apprentice and the slave; the discovery of bacteria and ways to cope with them; improvements in raw materials through agriculture, stock breeding, food processing, and refrigerated transportation; and the development of convenience and organic foods. Not the least important is the invention of the automobile, which has strung foodservice facilities along every highway in America and made it easy and pleasant to travel miles for a single meal.

Today's cuisine is changing, too. The variety of foods available in restaurants (and supermarkets, too) is staggering. Many categories of foods have exploded in size: pasta, grains, seafood, breads, fresh fruits, and vegetables. In many restaurants, the emphasis is on fresh: fresh fruits, locally grown vegetables, just-caught fish, bread baked fresh daily. More customers also want organic foods and vegetarian meals, and, indeed, more organic foods and vegetarian meals are being sold than ever before. (**Organic foods** have been grown without nearly any synthetic insecticides, fungicides, herbicides, and fertilizers).

We have also added dishes from all over the world, as well as American regions, to our menus. Besides the ever-popular Italian, Chinese, and Mexican cuisines, other cuisines such as Thai and Jamaican are growing in popularity. Chefs also blend ingredients, flavors, and techniques from various ethnic cuisines to develop new dishes, a practice termed **fusion cooking.**

Trends outside the world of foodservice can have much influence on what we eat and what our customers want. Two particularly important trends include an increased need for convenient meals for families because both parents are likely to be working and an increased concern about the relationship between what we eat and our health. A survey by *Restaurants & Institutions* in 1997 showed that more than half of all Americans choose what and where to eat for dinner between 5 P.M. and 8 P.M. This trend has helped increase restaurant sales. Every year, more and more Americans see the importance of good nutrition, especially as it relates to health. Nutrition is no longer considered a fad. The growing interest in nutrition has resulted in more choices for health-conscious customers at many restaurants.

SUMMING UP

The kitchen of every foodservice establishment is different—uniquely adapted to its own needs. These needs are determined by the nature and purpose of the operation, its menu, the volume of production, the clientele, the type of service, and such other factors as special dietary and sanitation requirements.

Yet all foodservice kitchens have certain things in common. They are typically divided into production stations. Each station prepares certain kinds of food and each has its own production area, equipment, storage, and staff. All kitchens have a staff structure—a network or ladder of relationships by which authority and responsibility are assigned. All kitchens have specific job categories, and each job requires a certain set of skills.

Job titles and the skills and experience required vary widely from one operation to another. Opportunities exist everywhere, and now is the time for you to begin looking at kitchens in action with a critical eye toward planning your own training and experience and setting your career goals.

The contemporary foodservice kitchen is so well equipped and so many convenience products are available that we sometimes hear it said that the cook's job is not to cook but to produce food. The fact is that good cooking is still essential to producing good food, and good food is the basis of every successful operation, whether it is a gourmet restaurant or a hospital, a school cafeteria or a cruise ship.

There is no reason why food produced on a large scale should not be good food—very good food. And there is no reason why intelligent cooking should cost more than mindless production. Many foodservices today are proving the point.

Whether your own goal is kitchen stardom or a management career, understanding good cooking from the inside out is essential to your success.

The Cook's Vocabulary

à la carte cookery
American Dietetic Association (ADA)
apprentice
authority
brigade system, brigade de cuisine
cook
dietetic technician
director of food and nutrition services
executive chef, chef de cuisine
expediter
fish station chef
food and beverage director
food production manager
fry station chef
fusion cooking
grill station chef
helper
medical nutrition therapy
midscale (midpriced) restaurant
nutrition
organic food
organization chart
pantry chef
pastry chef
quick-service restaurant
registered dietitian (RD)
relief cook, swing cook, rounds cook
responsibility
roast station chef
sauté station chef
soup station chef
sous-chef
station
station cook, line cook
station head, station chef, chef de partie
vegetable and soup station chef
vegetable station chef

Review Questions

Answer each question in complete sentences. Read each question carefully and make sure you answer all parts of the question. Organize your answer into more than one paragraph when appropriate.

1. How do you account for the differences between a hotel kitchen and a hospital kitchen? How do you account for the differences between a quick-service and a midscale restaurant?
2. Explain how the menu of an operation will affect its kitchen organization, equipment, and staff. Give examples.
3. After learning something about job opportunities and requirements, which jobs look most interesting to you? Why?
4. Compare a modern foodservice kitchen with one of Roman times, the Middle Ages, or the time of Carême in terms of the food prepared, the equipment, and the labor force. What is simpler today than it was in those days, and what problems does a modern operation have that were unknown in that earlier era?

Chapter 2

SANITATION AND SAFETY

First things first. Before you become absorbed in foods and cooking, let us focus on the kitchen as a work environment and open your eyes to its hazards. If you know how to practice sanitation and safety, the kitchen can be a safe, clean, tidy, and healthful place to work. But if you are negligent, you may bring suffering to victims of foodborne illness, cause accidents to yourself or your coworkers, or even bring disaster to the establishment where you work.

Foodborne illness is the sickness that results from eating foods contaminated with harmful bacteria and other microorganisms. Although you may not see, smell, or taste these "bugs," they may be present on the foods when they are purchased or get into the food during preparation, cooking, serving, or storage. Common symptoms of foodborne illness include diarrhea, abdominal cramps, fever, headache, and vomiting. These symptoms may come on as early as a half hour after eating contaminated food or may not develop for several weeks. They usually last only a day or two, and many people attribute it to the "flu." For most healthy people, foodborne illnesses are neither long lasting nor life threatening. However, the consequences can be severe and may require hospitalization and even lead to death in children, the elderly, and those with weakened immune systems.

Fortunately, foodborne illness is preventable with good sanitation procedures and practices. **Sanitation** means taking measures to keep food free of anything that might cause disease. Numerous health organizations—local, state, and federal—check the health standards and practices of food establishments. But the fact that these agencies exist and enforce regulations is not the real reason for paying special attention to sanitation and safety. For the true professional, it is a matter of personal pride and integrity as well as legal and economic good sense. When you consider how many people's lives may be affected by the way you practice sanitation day in and day out, your own professional standards are going to be the same as the goals of the health agencies.

In a single chapter, we can give you only a bare-bones discussion on sanitation and safety, but it should be enough to open your eyes and launch you safely as a cook.

After completing this chapter, you should be able to:

- List the three major categories of foodborne hazards.
- Explain how to keep bacteria, viruses and parasites from causing foodborne illness.
- Explain how to keep bacteria out of the

kitchen and how to prevent their spread from one food to another.

- Understand the role of temperature in preventing foodborne illness and the importance of keeping foods at safe temperatures during preparation, cooking, holding, and storage.
- Clean and sanitize equipment, utensils, and work surfaces properly.
- Avoid food spoilage and chemical and physical hazards.
- Discuss the seven steps in the Hazard Analysis Critical Control Point system.
- Work safely, avoiding burns, fires, cuts, back injuries and strains, and falls.

HAZARDS THAT CAUSE FOODBORNE ILLNESS

Foodborne hazards refer to biological, chemical, or physical hazards that can be carried by food, or multiply in food, and cause foodborne illness. Most foodborne illness is caused by **biological** (or living) **hazards,** which include bacteria, viruses, and parasites. **Chemical hazards** include poisonous substances unintentionally added to foods, such as pesticides or cleaning chemicals. **Physical hazards** include foreign objects, such as glass fragments or slivers of metal, that can get into food and cause harm.

Table 2-1 VIRUSES

Name	*Hepatitis A*	*Norwalk Virus*	*Rotavirus*
Disease	Hepatitis A	Norwalk gastroenteritis	Rotavirus gastroenteritis
Foods	Raw and lightly cooked oysters and clams, ready-to-eat foods such as salads, vegetables, luncheon meats, and sandwiches.	Raw and lightly cooked shellfish, ready-to-eat foods.	Ready-to-eat foods
Transmission	Transmitted by eating foods contaminated with hepatitis A. Foods (such as oysters) are contaminated due to polluted water or food is contaminated by worker with infectious hepatitis and poor personal hygiene.	Same as hepatitis.	Transmitted commonly in daycare centers and homes. Contaminated hands spread the virus to food.
Prevention	Good personal hygiene. Thoroughly cook shellfish. Don't let sick employees handle food.	Same as hepatitis.	Good personal hygiene. Don't let sick employees handle food.
Incubation	15–50 days	18–48 hours	1–3 days
Duration	1–2 weeks	1–2 days	4–8 days
Symptoms	Fever, abdominal pain, nausea, vomiting, fatigue, can be followed by jaundice and liver infection.	Nausea, vomiting, abdominal pain, diarrhea.	Diarrhea, vomiting, fever (especially in infants and children).

Table 2-2 PARASITES

Name	*Giardia lamblia*	*Trichinella spiralis*
Disease	Giardiasis	Trichinosis
Foods	Fresh vegetables	Pork and pork products
Transmission	Giardia is found in the feces of domestic pets, infected persons, and wild animals, and in defective water systems. It is transmitted to food via contaminated water or infected food handlers.	Parasite is found in some pork and wild-game animals.
Prevention	Good personal hygiene.	Cook pork to 145°F (63°C) and wild game to 165°F (74°C).
Incubation	1 week	2–5 days
Duration	Up to 1 month	Up to 1 year or more
Symptoms	Diarrhea	Nausea, vomiting, diarrhea, abdominal pain, muscle pain, fever.

Bacteria are tiny, single-cell organisms seen only with a microscope. They single-handedly cause more cases of foodborne illness than any other hazard. Bacteria are everywhere we look—in the air, in water, on our skin, and in our bodies. Some bacteria are beneficial. If it were not for bacteria, we would not have foods such as yogurt, buttermilk, sour cream, wine, aged meats, or cheeses. It is not the beneficial bacteria we fight but the disease-causing bacteria. Disease-causing bacteria are responsible for most foodborne illness. We can tolerate a small amount of them, but large numbers can make us quite sick. We give bacteria in foods the opportunity to grow to large numbers when we give them a temperature between 40 and 140°F (4–60°C), about 3 to 4 hours in this temperature zone, and a food that usually contains protein, such as meat, eggs, milk, or beans.

Viruses cause a number of different diseases, from the common cold to hepatitis A. Like bacteria, viruses are so small (in fact, they are much smaller than bacteria) that you can only see them with the help of a microscope. But this is where their similarities end. Viruses do not reproduce or multiply in foods, nor do they need a protein-containing food to survive. Viruses simply use foods to "hitchhike" a ride to their next victim. You only need to eat a food contaminated with a few viruses in order to get sick. Foodborne illness caused by viruses is most often due to poor personal hygiene (especially handwashing) or water contaminated with viruses. Viruses of most importance to foodservice are discussed in Table 2.1.

Parasites are also small, sometimes microscopic, organisms that must live on or inside another organism to survive. Parasites are known to occur in pork and some fish (see Table 2.2)—and they are generally not a problem when these foods are thoroughly cooked.

BACTERIA

There are many ways in which bacteria get into food. Bacteria may already be present in some foods, such as poultry, eggs, or ground beef. Also, equipment that has not been properly cleaned may harbor bacteria. Foodservice employees can

Figure 2-1 FOOD SAFETY THERMOMETER SHOWING EFFECT OF TEMPERATURE ON BACTERIAL GROWTH

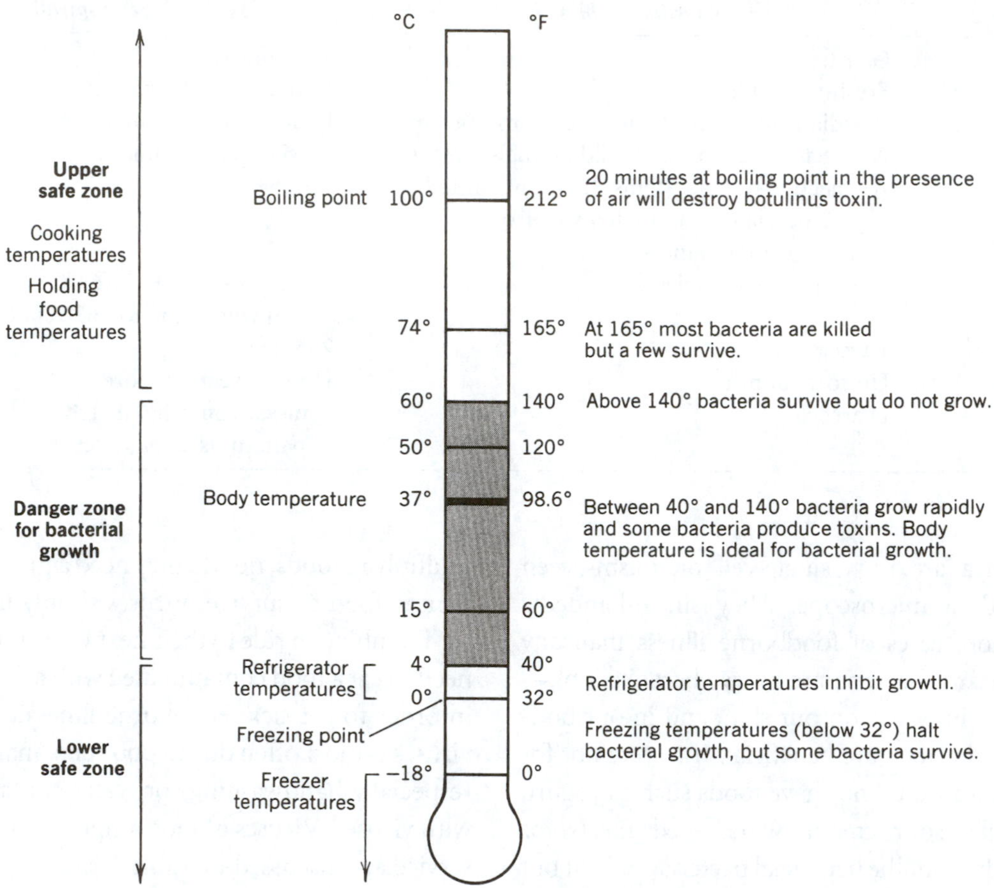

introduce bacteria into food by poor personal hygiene (especially dirty hands or improperly bandaged cuts, burns, and boils) or poor food-handling techniques.

Once bacteria are in food, they need food, moisture, and above all warmth in order to multiply. The key temperatures for bacterial growth range from 40 to 140°F (4–60°C). This is known as the bacterial growth range or the **temperature danger zone.** Below 40°F (4°C), such as in refrigerated storage, there is little or no growth. From 60 to 120°F (16–49°C), most bacteria reproduce well. Above 140°F (60°C), bacteria may survive but do not multiply. Above 165°F (74°C), most bacteria are killed. Figure 2.1 tells the temperature story graphically. Also, keep in mind that bacteria only need between 3 and 4 hours in the temperature danger zone to grow to sufficient numbers to cause foodborne illness.

Foods that can support the rapid growth of disease-causing bacteria are called **potentially hazardous foods.** Potentially hazardous foods usually contain protein. Protein is found in meat, poultry, seafood, eggs, milk and dairy products, and cooked rice, beans, and potatoes. Potentially hazardous foods also must contain some water. For example, dry rice or beans could not support bacterial growth. However, once cooked, bacteria can grow in them. In recent years, new foods have been added to the potentially hazardous list: cut melons, garlic in oil mixtures, and raw alfalfa sprouts.

Once bacteria have grown to sufficient numbers, they can cause foodborne illness in one of three different ways. Some bacteria create poisonous substances, or toxins, in foods that make people sick when eaten. The foodborne illness caused by eating foods containing toxins is called an **intoxication.** Unfortunately, cooking foods does not disable the toxins. Some bacteria produce toxins once they have entered the body (specifically, the intestines). This type of disease called a **toxin-mediated infection.** Other harmful bacteria attack the body directly. The foodborne illness caused by eating food that contains harmful bacteria is called a **bacterial infection.**

Table 2.3 lists bacteria that are of concern to anyone involved in food preparation or service. Fifty years ago we were dealing with only a lim-

Table 2-3 BACTERIA

Bacteria	*Bacillus cereus*	*Clostridium perfringens*
Disease	Gastroenteritis	*Perfringens* food poisoning
Type of illness	Intoxication or toxin-mediated infection	Toxin-mediated infection
Foods involved	Rice, potatoes, pasta, flour, cornstarch, spices, dry mixes, soybeans, tofu (vomiting disease); meats, milk, vegetables, fish (diarrhea disease).	Cooked meat, poultry, gravy, beans.
Transmission	Most often due to improperly held and cooled foods.	Most often due to foods that have been improperly cooked, cooled, and/or reheated.
Prevention	Hold hot foods above the danger zone. Cool foods rapidly to below 40°F (4°C). Reheat leftovers to 165°F (74°C). Don't reheat foods more than once.	Foods must be cooked to appropriate temperatures. Cool foods rapidly to below 40°F (4°C). Reheat leftovers to 165°F (74°C).
Incubation period	30 minutes–6 hours (vomiting type) 8–16 hours (diarrhea type)	8–14 hours
Duration of illness	6–24 hours (vomiting) 12–14 hours (diarrhea)	About 24 hours or less
Symptoms	Vomiting type: vomiting, nausea, abdominal cramps Diarrhea type: diarrhea, abdominal cramps, nausea.	Abdominal pain, cramps, diarrhea.
Bacteria	*Clostridium botulinum*	*Campylobacter jejuni*
Disease	Botulism	Campylobacteriosis
Type of illness	Intoxication	Infection
Foods involved	Low-acid canned or vacuum-processed foods that have been improperly processed. Grilled onions, garlic-in-oil products. Bulky cooked foods such as stews, meat/poultry/potatoes.	Meat or poultry, raw milk, contaminated water.

(*Continued*)

Table 2-3 (Continued)

Transmission	Improperly processed low-acid canned or vacuum-processed foods that are not boiled for more than 20 minutes Improperly held or cooled bulky foods.	Undercooked meat/poultry and raw milk may contain sufficient numbers of these bacteria.
Prevention	Don't use home-canned foods. Examine cans for dents, swelling, rust. Examine vacuum-packed foods carefully and refrigerate. Refrigerate garlic-in-oil. Cook foods thoroughly. Cook onions, etc. on grill to order. Cool foods properly.	Cook meats and poultry thoroughly. Avoid cross-contamination, especially by thoroughly washing hands, cutting boards, and knives. Don't use unpasteurized raw milk.
Incubation period	4–36 hours	2–5 days
Duration of illness	Several days to a year	1–7 days
	Headache, dizziness, double vision, fatigue, difficulty swallowing and breathing.	Fever, headache, muscle pain, diarrhea, stomach pain, nausea, vomiting, also can cause meningitis and urinary tract infection.
Bacteria	*Escherichia coli* 0157:H7	*Listeria monocytogenes*
Disease	Hemorrhagic colitis	Listeriosis
Type of illness	Infection or toxin-mediated infection	Infection
Foods involved	Hamburgers and other meats, unpasteurized milk and apple cider, some fresh fruits and vegetables.	Unpasteurized milk, dairy products, raw vegetables, meat, poultry, hot dogs, cold cuts.
Transmission	Undercooked meats and unpasteurized milk/apple cider, and some contaminated fruits/vegetables contain this bacterium.	Undercooked hot dogs and other meats/poultry, cold cuts, dairy products, and raw vegetables may contain bacteria. Unlike other bacteria, *Listeria* grow in the refrigerator.
Prevention	Cook beef and venison thoroughly. Avoid cross-contamination. Serve only pasteurized milk and pasteurized apple juice/cider. Wash fruits and vegetables thoroughly before eating.	Thoroughly cook meat/poultry. Timely use and rotation of luncheon meats.
Incubation period	1–2 days (can be up to 5 days)	1 day–3 weeks
Duration of illness	Usually 8 days, but can be much longer	Varies
Symptoms	Severe abdominal pain, nausea, vomiting, fever, bloody diarrhea, kidney failure, death.	Healthy adults: mild fever, muscle aches, headache, nausea, vomiting, diarrhea. Elderly, pregnant women, newborns, and those with weakened immune systems: septicemia, pharyngitis, meningitis, death.
Bacteria	*Salmonella*	*Shigella*
Disease	Salmonellosis	Shigellosis

Table 2-3 (Continued)

Type of illness	Infection	Toxin-mediated infection
Foods involved	Poultry, meat, shell eggs, milk, dairy.	Ready-to-eat salads (chicken, tuna, shrimp, potato), milk, dairy, poultry, raw vegetables, contaminated water or food.
Transmission	Salmonella are found sometimes in the foods noted. Some employees have the bacterium in their intestines and can transmit it via poor personal hygiene.	Shigella are commonly found in the intestines and feces of humans. They are usually transmitted through poor personal hygiene or contaminated water.
Prevention	Cook foods thoroughly. Hold hot foods above 140°F (60°C). Cool foods rapidly. Avoid cross-contamination, especially by thorough washing of hands, cutting boards, and knives. Stress good personal hygiene.	Same as Salmonella. Use sanitary water source.
Incubation period	8–48 hours	1–7 days
Duration of illness	4–7 days	3–5 days
Symptoms	Nausea, vomiting, fever, headache, abdominal cramps, diarrhea.	Diarrhea, fever, abdominal cramps, fatigue, dehydration.
Bacteria	*Staphylococcus aureus*	*Streptococcus pyogenes*
Disease	Staphylococcal food poisoning	Depends on symptoms
Type of illness	Intoxication	Infection
Foods involved	Ham, luncheon meats, other meats, ready-to-eat meat, vegetable and egg salads, dairy products, custards, cream-filled bakery items.	Salads (egg, potato, and lobster), eggs, custard, rice pudding, meat, sandwiches.
Transmission	Staphylococcus is commonly found on human skin, hair, and in nose, throat, cuts, boils, pimples. It is transmitted to food due to poor personal hygiene and the contaminated food is not held properly.	Streptococcus is found in the throat and on human skin. Food handlers with sore throats or skin infections usually contaminate foods due to poor personal hygiene.
Prevention	Don't allow food handlers with cuts, infections, or respiratory infection to work with food. Enforce good personal hygiene. Cook and cool foods properly. Keep ready-to-eat foods out of the danger zone.	Don't allow food handlers with sore throats or skin infections to work with food. Thoroughly cook foods and rapidly chill cooked foods.
Incubation period	1–7 hours	1–3 days
Duration of illness	1–2 days	Varies
Symptoms	Nausea, vomiting, abdominal pain, chills, sweating, occasionally diarrhea, dehydration.	Fever, tonsillitis, occasionally scarlet fever or rheumatic fever.

ited number of bacteria. Today, the list is much more extensive. Bacteria not previously recognized as important causes of foodborne illness—such as *Escherichia coli* 0157:H7—became more widespread. *E. coli* 0157:H7, which has caused deaths in children eating undercooked hamburgers in quick-service restaurants, was not well known outside of scientific circles until 1993. Listeria have caused death in at-risk populations such as the very young, very old, or those with weakened immune systems. Consider for a moment that the U.S. Centers for Disease Control and Prevention reports that about 1850 people become seriously ill from Listeria bacteria. Of these, 425 die.

Several bacteria will now be discussed in more detail. ***Staphylococcus aureus*** (staff-uh-luh-cock′-us or′-ee-us), generally referred to as staph, is the most common of all the toxin-producing bacteria. Staph bacteria produce their toxin in many foods—especially dairy products, foods containing eggs, sauces, and moist high-protein foods such as ham and other meats. They produce their toxins at temperatures characteristic of the preparation and holding of foods. It is very important to realize that these toxins are not killed by subsequent cooking or storage: Neither high temperatures nor low temperatures destroy them. The only way to fight these toxins is prevention.

Staph bacteria enter the kitchen most often on people. They are commonly found in the throat, nose, and hair and on the hands and skin, especially in infected areas such as cuts, boils, burns, pimples, and abrasions. People who have such infections should not be handling food at all. But even such precautions cannot eliminate staph bacteria: A cough or sneeze even from a healthy person may send staph bacteria toward food being prepared. Good personal hygiene is a must to stop staph from getting into foods.

A second type of toxin-producing bacteria is ***Clostridium botulinum*** (klos-trid′-ee-um botch-a-lee′-num). These bacteria produce the toxin causing **botulism** (botch′-a-lism), a deadly poisoning that can be fatal after a single bite. *C. botulinum* bacteria typically produce their toxin in low-acid foods in the absence of air—typically in canned or vacuum-packaged foods that have been improperly processsed. Commercial food processors are under strict regulations to subject canned foods to very high temperatures for long periods of time, and for the most part commercially canned foods are free of this dread toxin.

But errors do occur. You should always examine cans for dents, swelling, and rust or corrosion. Never use contents that look foamy, smell bad, or otherwise seem spoiled. (Don't even think about tasting these foods because you can die from a single taste of food contaminated with *C. botulinum*!) Be alert to announcements recalling certain lot numbers of canned goods. Keep foods out of the temperature danger zone and store vacuum-packed foods below 40°F (4°C). Botulism toxins can be destroyed by boiling for 20 minutes, so make sure foods are thoroughly cooked.

The problems *C. botulinum* cause are not limited to improperly processed canned and vacuum-packed goods. As thick, bulky foods are cooked, the heat drives away oxygen from the interior of the food. When not handled properly, these foods can create ideal conditions for the growth of these bacteria. For example, a cook may keep a pile of chopped onions or garlic in oil on the grill during meal service or leave baked potatoes out to cool. Both these foods could cause botulism. To prevent this, cook onions, garlic, or any other food in small batches or on request. Baked potatoes, or any leftover food for that purpose, should be cooled rapidly. If you buy commercially prepared garlic-in-oil products, keep them refrigerated.

Many kinds of bacteria attack the body directly, such as salmonella. **Salmonella** (sal-mun-ell′a) is probably the most common family of bacteria: There are more than 400 kinds, including typhoid. They are present in the intestines of all forms of animal life. They are spread by contact—to eggshells in hens, for example, and to almost anything in the kitchen that touches them. These bacteria can multiply in any environment containing moisture, oxygen, and favorable temperatures. It is almost impossible to keep them out of the kitchen. Your chief concern is to keep the numbers down.

Clostridium perfringens (klos-trid′-ee-um per-frin′-junz) bacteria, though far less common than salmonella, are especially dangerous in that they do not need oxygen to reproduce, only moisture and warmth, and they are found in most foods. Once in the body, *C. perfringens* makes a toxin that causes diarrhea and abdominal pain. It is most often due to foods (such as meat, poultry, gravy, and beans) that have been improperly cooked, cooled, and/or reheated. Like most cases of foodborne illness, it is preventable.

Campylobacter jejuni (camp-e-lo-back-ter ja-jun-e) is not a new bacterium, but is receiving more attention since it was identified as the most frequently isolated bacterium from persons with diarrhea. Campylobacter bacteria can exist in the human intestinal tract without causing any symptoms or illness. However, if people consume live bacteria in raw milk, contaminated water, or undercooked meat or poultry, they may acquire a campylobacter infection called **campylobacteriosis.** Symptoms usually occur within 2 to 10 days of eating the contaminated food and include fever, headache, and muscle pain, followed by diarrhea, stomach pain, and nausea. Complications can include urinary tract infections and meningitis.

Since you as a cook cannot tell whether bacteria and/or toxins are present in foods, your only course of action is to take every precaution you can. There are four basics of good sanitation that keep bacteria from reaching harmful levels:

- Limiting their entry
- Stopping their spread
- Preventing their growth
- Killing them

Before we start this discussion, we need to clearly understand the difference between clean and sanitary. A surface is considered to be **clean** when it is free of visible food or soiling. A clean surface is not necessarily sanitary. **Sanitary** means that it is free of harmful numbers of disease-causing microorganisms. To sanitize a plate, for example, you can expose it to very high heat or a chemical sanitizer. The following discussion will further enlighten you about sanitation basics.

KEEPING BACTERIA OUT

Bacteria enter the kitchen in a number of ways: with people, foods, flies, roaches, rats, and mice. Controlling all these sources of entry is an important way of keeping undesirable bacteria out of food preparation areas.

PEOPLE AS CARRIERS

People who handle food are a great threat to good sanitation. The places people go, the things they do, and the sanitation and personal hygiene habits they practice make it easy for them to harbor and transport bacteria. **Personal hygiene** refers to those actions we take to promote our health and cleanliness, such as eating right and taking a daily shower. Personal hygiene is important because the Centers for Disease Control has determined that it is involved in 59 percent of bacteria and 92 percent of viral foodborne illness.

Even when you are in perfect health, you have bacteria on your skin and in your mouth, nose, throat, and all parts of your body. Everyone does. Cleanliness of person and how to maintain that cleanliness are getting more and more attention from health agencies, and what it means to be clean becomes a necessary part of learning to be a cook.

First things first again: When you start working, you should never wear the same clothes in a food preparation area that you wear outside. Most operations today provide clean, sanitary uniforms or clothing for working in food preparation areas. If you are not provided with uniforms, it is your responsibility to have clean uniforms that you change at your workplace to limit the transportation of bacteria from outside.

Second, you should put a clean person into a clean uniform. You should wash regularly, especially those parts of you that harbor bacteria readily—your hair, hands, fingernails, and so on. You must wash your hands after you:

- Smoke
- Eat
- Use the restroom
- Touch money
- Touch raw foods
- Touch your face, hair, or skin
- Cough, sneeze, or blow your nose
- Comb your hair
- Handle anything dirty
- Take a break (and also before)

Today's public health regulations require numerous hand sinks in kitchens, placed so that they are available to each station. It can be assumed with some accuracy that an accessible hand sink will be used more often than one that is difficult to get to, but it is up to you to use it. Hand-sanitizing lotions do not replace handwashing.

Third, covering certain parts of your body is a must. Hair, no matter how long or short, should be covered to keep hairs from getting into food or onto food preparation surfaces. You normally lose at least 25 strands of hair daily. Long hair should be put up and netted to keep it restrained. Your hands should be covered with sanitary gloves whenever you handle foods ready to be served or foods that will not be heated to 140°F (60°C) or higher. Remember, however, that gloves can transmit bacteria as easily as hands can. Your gloves should be as clean as your hands should be. Never touch the food contact surfaces of plates, cups, glasses, or flatware with either your hands or your gloves.

Fourth, if you have any open cuts or burns, or if you are sick (especially with a sore throat or intestinal illness), you must tell your supervisor immediately. Unless open cuts can be completely covered with a waterproof bandage, you will not be able to work. If you are sick, you should not be handling food.

Table 2.4 summarizes positive personal hygiene practices.

FOODS AS CARRIERS

Foods are the second carrier of bacteria from outside. All foods and their containers entering the kitchen can bring bacteria with them. Yet, too often, the task of handling incoming foods is given little attention, and many bacteria enter and multiply before anyone is aware of the danger.

Table 2-4 POSITIVE PERSONAL HYGIENE PRACTICES

- Take a daily shower or bath and use deodorant. Showering helps wash away harmful germs and keeps you smelling good, too!
- Wash your hair as needed because oily, dirty hair is attractive to germs, and dandruff can flake into food.
- Brush your teeth often. Brushing reduces the number of germs in your mouth.
- Clip fingernails short. Long fingernails provide hiding places for dirt and germs.
- Do not use nail polish as it may chip into the food.
- Wear a clean and pressed uniform and apron because soiled clothing harbors germs that may be transferred to food.
- Wash your hands often to prevent contaminating foods.
- Do not use your apron as a hand towel because the apron will become contaminated and possibly transfer germs to food.
- Wear a hair restraint or covering because you lose over 25 strands of hair daily.
- Avoid excessive makeup, cologne, and jewelry as they may get into the food. Also, jewelry is a place where germs grow and jewelry is hard to keep clean.
- Cover all coughs and sneezes as germs are sent far and wide. Wash your hands after coughing and sneezing.
- Don't touch your face or other parts of your body while handling food because germs on your skin can then be introduced into food.
- Taste food properly. Don't use your fingers or a spoon that is reused. Use a plastic spoon or the two-spoon method; that is, use one spoon to dip into the food and the other to eat from.
- If feeling sick, even with a minor cold, speak to your supervisor immediately so you do not contaminate the food.
- Cover all cuts, burns, and boils with a bandage and plastic glove, and report them to your supervisor immediately.

You cannot keep all bacteria out, but there are several ways to keep their numbers down. Buy all products from reputable suppliers. Be sure frozen foods are received frozen from refrigerated vehicles and show no signs of thawing. Use your thermometer to make sure frozen foods are at 0°F (−18°C) or less, and refrigerated foods are at 41°F (5°C) or less. Carefully inspect all foods you receive to be sure they are not spoiled or contaminated. Check freshness dating. Look on the products for stamps of inspection and wholesomeness. Examine canned products for dents, swelling, missing labels, and dirt or rust. Reject any items that present problems.

Store all foods properly and quickly. Once in use, if you have any doubt about the quality, freshness, or safety of any item, don't use it. Don't even taste it. An old foodservice maxim goes like this: "If in doubt, throw it out."

PESTS AS CARRIERS

Roaches, rodents, and flies are the third common source of bacteria from outside. They are all notorious carriers and must be controlled and exterminated regularly. This is a job for professionals. Pesticides are poisons and are not to be handled by food handlers. These poisons could find their way into the food.

There are a number of things you can do to help prevent the harboring of pests. Cover all refuse containers. Keep all paper containers in which foods are received out of the kitchen. Cover all foods whenever production allows, and always cover them in storage. Keep your work area clean and free from anything that would attract pests.

The ways pests get into kitchens are beyond imagining. No one simple rule will keep them out; it takes constant awareness in key areas. Think clean, work clean, and clean!

STOPPING BACTERIAL SPREAD

Bacteria do not move on their own but are moved from one food to another. The transfer of bacteria in this way is called **cross-contamination.** It is most often the food handler—you—who transmits bacteria from one food to another via the dirty knife, towel, counter, sink, dish, cutting board, or your own two hands. It is particularly dangerous because you are probably unaware of it.

To a large degree, you can control this transfer of bacteria; it is one of the most important things you can do to maintain a sanitary kitchen. The first thing is to become aware of how it happens.

PRODUCT TO PRODUCT

All foods carry bacteria, just as all people do. But some are more likely than others to bring bacteria into the kitchen and to transmit them to other foods. Raw poultry, fish, meats, and eggs are the most likely carriers. Along with milk products, they are also the most susceptible to contamination from other foods as well as to bacteria brought in by people. Any food product can pass along bacteria to these more susceptible foods, or to any other food, via work surfaces, utensils, and hands.

To prevent product-to-product contamination, everything must be kept scrupulously clean. After you prepare one product on a work surface, you must clean and sanitize that surface before you prepare another product on it. Even when it is another batch of the same product, if there is a gap of more than 15 or 20 minutes between preparations, you must clean and sanitize that surface. And, as pointed out earlier, you must wash your hands whenever you are shifting from one preparation to another.

Once a piece of equipment, either large or small, has been used, it must be considered contaminated. Knives, tongs, serving utensils, even portion scales must not be overlooked. Can openers are a common offender: The cutting blade accumulates food, grows bacteria, and passes them on to the food in the next can. Contamination by large equipment—slicers, meat grinders, mixers, and cooking equipment—is just as likely to happen. The meat slicer is a frequent offender; it should be taken apart and cleaned hourly when used over a period of time. The same rule applies to everything, regardless of size: Clean and sanitize it between uses to prevent cross-contamination.

SPLASHING AND DRIPPING

Cross-contamination can also occur through splashing and dripping. Splashing can happen between stations, sending bacteria from one to another. Splashing can also happen when you wash your hands. Today's kitchens have splash guards on preparation tables and hand sinks to prevent this kind of cross-contamination. Splashing is also a cleaning hazard, especially in mopping and scrubbing: Dirty water may splash onto a clean surface or equipment or even onto food.

Dripping may occur when moisture from above, such as condensation from cooking, drops onto food products or preparation surfaces below. These overhead surfaces are often neglected in cleaning and can harbor bacteria, which drip with the condensation into food being prepared.

The most serious dripping hazard is one raw product dripping on another raw or cooked product. Raw meats, poultry, and fish are products that may drip. In storage, they should be placed on the lower refrigerator shelves so that they do not drip on any other food product. This is especially true of fish that have been iced to keep them fresh.

IMPROPER STORAGE

Improper storage is an open invitation to cross-contamination. To avoid it, store raw and cooked foods separately. Divide them into three categories:

- Raw, processed or unprocessed
- Processed ready to serve
- Cooked on premises

Though this sounds simple, it isn't always easy to tell which processed products are raw and which are cooked because foods come into the kitchen in so many different forms.

"Raw processed" includes bacon, breaded shrimp, frozen vegetables, and frozen dough—any products that have had some processing but must be cooked to be edible. "Processed ready to serve" includes such items as frozen cooked shrimp, smoked fish and meat products, franks, cold cuts, and cheeses. Any processed product that does not need further processing to be edible falls into this category.

"Cooked-on-premises" foods are such items as roasts and cooked dishes that are being held for later use. These foods should be stored separately from the other two categories. This does not mean that they cannot be stored in the same refrigerator or freezer. It means that they must be stored in separate sections, on racks or shelves that are clearly marked to indicate what is to be stored there.

There are other important storage rules for avoiding the spread of bacteria:

- Cover all foods. Label and date them.
- Store foods in properly sanitized containers.
- Store all products off the floor.
- Do not store decorative items (fat sculptures, ice carvings, flowers) with items to be consumed.

To avoid cross-contamination, proper storage is every bit as important as proper cleaning and handling.

When you carry foods from storage to preparation areas, do not bring them in the unsanitary boxes and bags in which they arrived. Transfer them to sanitary containers such as clean plastic carrying boxes or kitchen utensils such as pans or bowls. If you must use the original containers—egg cartons, for example—never put them on food preparation surfaces. This is especially important when you are preparing foods that will be served without being cooked.

PREVENTING BACTERIAL GROWTH

Preventing bacterial growth is primarily a matter of temperature. It requires knowing safe and unsafe temperatures; controlling cooking, holding, and storage temperatures; and limiting the time foods are exposed to unsafe temperatures.

Controlling temperature is possibly the most important way to serve safe food. Bacteria can multiply with fantastic speed by dividing—each into two, then those two into two each, and so on, until you have thousands in a matter of hours. A single organism, dividing every 20 minutes under ideal growth conditions, will produce more than 4000 bacteria in 4 hours and billions in 10 to 12 hours. The susceptible foods you have met before—milk and milk products, eggs, meats, poultry, seafood—are the foods most likely to provide favorable conditions for rapid multiplication.

We know that the secret to preventing multiplication is to keep hot foods hot (at or above 140°F/60°C) and cold foods cold (at or below 40°F/4°C). It is when foods are not in either of these temperature zones that we must give them the greatest attention. Foods must never be allowed to stand at room temperature. Body temperature, 98.6°F (37°C), is the ideal growth temperature for bacteria, and many areas in a kitchen are at or near body temperature.

Here are some simple hints for keeping foods from remaining in the danger zone longer than absolutely necessary:

- Prepare small batches of food as needed.
- Anything at room temperature more than 15 to 20 minutes cannot be considered in process and should be returned to heat or refrigeration.
- Cool foods as quickly as possible. The Centers for Disease Control has found that improper cooling of hot foods is the number one cause of foodborne illness. Small amounts may be refrigerated immediately using broad shallow pans (only 4 inches high) with the food no more than 3 inches for soups and 2 inches for thicker foods. Large amounts may be cooled by surrounding the container with ice or cold running water, stirring the food every few minutes. (This technique is illustrated in Figure 6.4.) Stir often and refrigerate when cool. Cooked foods must be cooled to 40°F (4°C) within 4 hours.
- Heat refrigerated foods to be served hot as quickly as possible, bringing them to a safe internal temperature (see Table 2.5). Never put food from the refrigerator into the steam table or other holding equipment without first cooking it.
- Measure food temperatures with a thermometer accurate to plus or minus 2°F (1°C). Measure food temperatures in several places, including the thickest part of the food. Clean and sanitize your thermometer before and after each use. See Figure 2.2 for types of thermometers.
- Regularly measure the temperatures of food being held, both hot and cold. Record in a log.
- Thaw frozen foods in the refrigerator. Do not let them sit thawing at room temperature; the outside will move into the danger zone while the inside is still thawing. You can also thaw foods under running drinkable water at a temperature of 70°F (21°C) or lower. The product should be completely covered with run-

Table 2-5 MINIMUM SAFE COOKING TEMPERATURES

Beef and pork roasts: 145°F (63°C) for 3 minutes
Ground beef: 155°F (69°C) for 15 seconds
Poultry, stuffed meats: 165°F (74°C) for 15 seconds
Eggs, beef, and pork (other than roasts), fish: 145°F (63°C) for 15 seconds
Previously cooked foods: 165°F (74°C)

SOURCE: 1999 Food Code.

Figure 2-2 TYPES AND USES OF THERMOMETERS

TYPES OF THERMOMETERS	SPEED	PLACEMENT	USAGE CONSIDERATIONS
LIQUID-FILLED 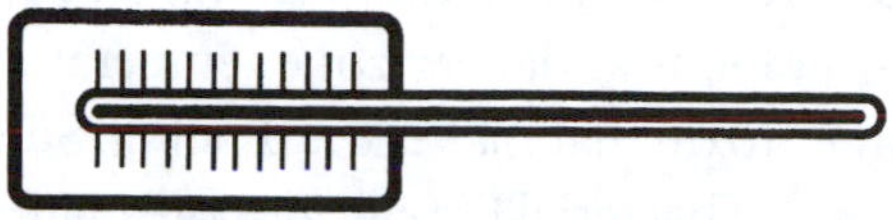	1 to 2 minutes	At least 2 inches deep in the thickest part of the food	• Used in roasts, casseroles, and soups • Can be placed in a food while it is cooking • Cannot measure thin foods • Calibration cannot be adjusted • Possible breakage while in food • Heat conduction of metal shield can cause false high reading
BIMETAL (oven-safe) 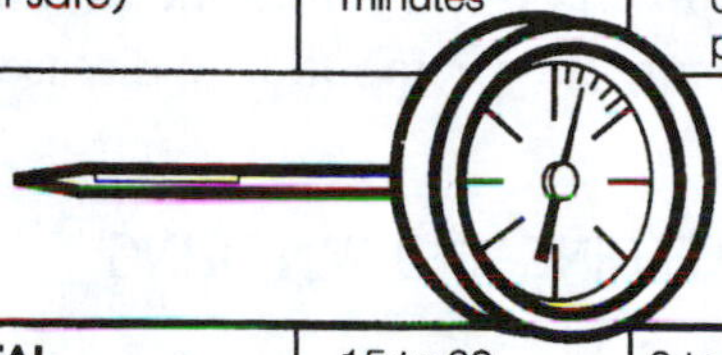	1 to 2 minutes	2 to 2 1/2 inches deep in the thickest part of the food.	• Can be used in roasts casseroles, and soups • Can be placed in a food while it is cooking • Not appropriate for thin foods • Heat conduction of metal stem can cause false high reading
BIMETAL (instant-read) 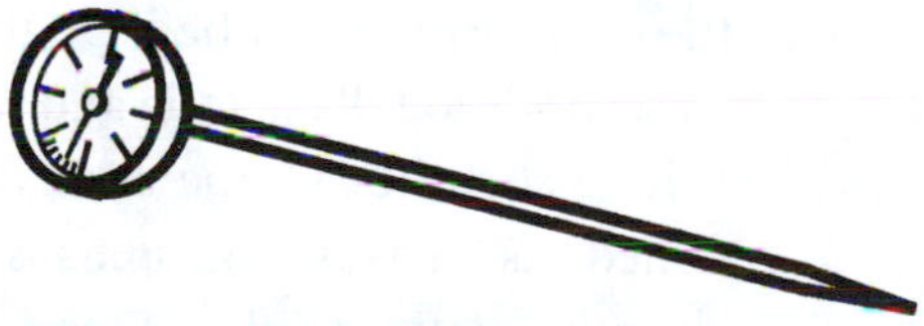	15 to 20 seconds	2 to 2 1/2 inches deep in the thickest part of the food	• Can be used in roasts, casseroles, and soups • Use to check the internal temperature of a food at the end of cooking time • Can be calibrated • Cannot measure thin foods unless inserted sideways • Cannot be used in an oven while food is cooking • Temperature is averaged along 2-3" of probe • Readily available in stores
THERMISTOR (digital) 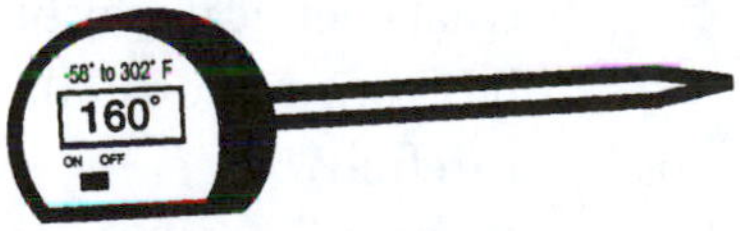	10 seconds	At least 1/2 inch deep in a food	• Gives faster reading • Can measure temperature in thin foods • Digital face easy to read • Cannot be used in an oven while food is cooking • Available in "kitchen" stores
THERMOCOUPLE (digital) 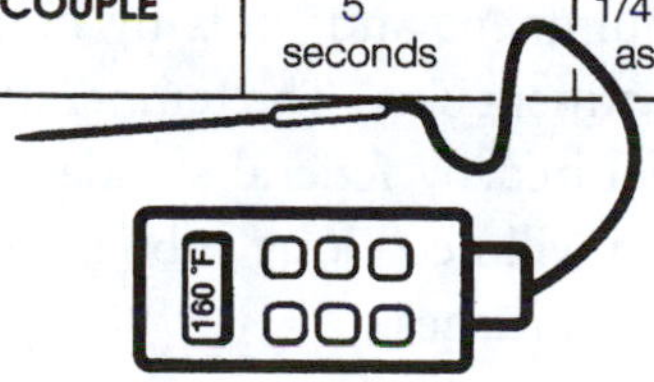	5 seconds	1/4 deep, or deeper, as needed	• Fastest • Can quickly measure even the thinnest foods • Digital face easy to read • Can be calibrated • More costly, may be difficult for consumers to find in stores

ning water for a period of time that does not allow thawed portions to be in the danger zone for more than 3 hours.

- Check interior temperatures of hot foods frequently to see that they are above 140°F (60°C). Check the food itself, not the holding unit.
- Check refrigerator temperatures frequently to see that they are well below 40°F (4°C)—comfortably in the lower safe zone. (Figure 4.27a shows a typical refrigerator thermometer.) Make sure refrigerator and freezer thermometers are in the warmest area. Space products so that cold air can circulate.
- Open refrigerator doors as little as possible to avoid a rise in temperature.

In short, avoid the hazardous temperature zone with all foods, especially susceptible foods such as eggs, raw poultry, raw meats (especially pork), cooked meats and poultry, milk, and combinations containing any of these products, such as stocks, sauces, puddings, and creams.

KILLING BACTERIA AND OTHER DISEASE-CAUSING ORGANISMS

KILLING BY COOKING

Ordinary cooking of foods destroys many disease-causing organisms. Others can survive low-temperature cooking (low oven temperatures or low-temperature frying). It is important to realize that it is not the temperature of the oven or the fry pan but the internal temperature of the food that must reach lethal levels.

Lethal temperatures vary widely depending on the kind of food, the kind of bacterium, and the length of time the food remains at a given temperature. It takes 3 to 10 minutes to destroy salmonella bacteria in a whole egg at 138°F (59°C) but less than a minute at 150°F (66°C). Most bacteria and other disease-producing organisms cannot survive a temperature of 165°F (74°C).

On the other hand, though a temperature of 165°F (74°C) will kill staph bacteria, it will not destroy toxin they may have already produced in foods at danger zone temperatures, and it is the toxin that makes the diner ill. Some special forms of bacterial life called spores can also outlive high temperatures and grow into active disease-causing organisms later on. (*C. perfringens* is one example.) So it is a mistake to think of cooking as a cure-all for foodborne disease.

CLEANING AND SANITIZING

Bacteria surviving on equipment and utensils can be killed by high temperatures or chemical solutions. The temperature of the final rinse water in the dishwasher must be kept at 180°F (82°C) for 10 seconds to kill bacteria and sanitize the dishes. Where such hot temperatures cannot be maintained, as in washing utensils by hand and in cleaning counters, floors, and large equipment, a chlorine or iodine solution is used in the final rinse to kill bacteria. State and local laws specify what chemical may be used in what quantity, and it is your responsibility to follow these guidelines carefully.

Here is a general procedure used for washing equipment and tools by hand in a three-compartment sink. The temperatures given are those required by federal standards. To follow them, you will need long rubber gloves and long-handled brushes.

- On the drainboard, scrape and prerinse with a spray in order to keep the wash water as clean as possible.

- In the first sink, wash with detergent in 140 to 150°F (60–66°C) water, removing all food particles and traces of grease. If necessary for utensils with baked-on foods, soak in detergent and scrape and prerinse again.
- In the second sink, rinse in clean warm water at 150 to 160°F (66–71°C). Change the water frequently or use a sink with an overflow drain and keep the water running.
- In the last sink, sanitize, using either an approved chemical disinfectant at the proper concentration or water at 180°F (82°C) for 10 seconds.
- Drain and allow to air dry. Wiping with a towel might recontaminate sanitized surfaces.

The same steps are followed using a dish or pot machine, except that the machine does the washing and rinsing and sanitizes with 180°F (82°C) water instead of a chemical solution.

The three steps of washing, rinsing, and sanitizing also apply to cleaning work surfaces and stationary equipment. Use clean cloths, sponges, and brushes that have been held in a chemical disinfectant and are used only for this purpose. Always unplug machinery with cutting blades before disassembling. Never place knives, sharp-edged tools, or cutting blades in a soapy sink: Immediately wash, rinse, and sanitize them and allow to air dry.

Clean and sanitize cutting boards, processing machines, can openers, and scales after each use. Clean and sanitize regularly and frequently everything that has contact with foods—refrigerators, mobile carts, worktables, deep fryers, steamers, ranges, ovens.

In addition to cleaning equipment, it is also very important to thoroughly wash fresh fruits and vegetables. This will be discussed in the next chapter.

OTHER FOODBORNE TROUBLEMAKERS

FOOD SPOILAGE

Food spoilage refers to any change in food that causes undesirable flavors, textures, or appearance. It is caused by the action of bacteria, yeasts, and molds on food. The spoiled food, if eaten, may cause illness. Spoilage can be prevented by storing foods at or below 40°F (4°C) and using them promptly, or storing them for longer periods at 0°F (−18°C) or below. Freezing slows down chemical change and inhibits bacterial growth, but it does not kill all bacteria.

Never use food that shows signs of spoilage—off color, off flavor, off odor, off feel (slimy or mushy). Don't use any food that has simply been kept too long, either: Spoilage does not often signal its presence. When in doubt, throw it out.

CHEMICAL HAZARDS

Chemical hazards fall into two categories: naturally occurring and synthetic (Table 2.6). Most cases of foodborne chemical poisoning are due to naturally occurring toxins in seafood and mushrooms. Three naturally occurring chemical hazards occur in seafood: ciguatoxin, scombrotoxin, and shellfish toxins. The symptoms each of these causes make it imperative that you buy seafood from reputable vendors and store and handle it correctly. Shellfish, in particular, should be purchased from sources approved by the Food and Drug Administration and the health departments of states located along the coast where the shellfish is harvested. Fresh seafood should be held at temperatures between 32 and 39°F (0–4°C).

Commercially raised mushrooms are generally safe to eat. The safety problem with mushrooms

Table 2-6 CHEMICALS IN FOODS

Naturally Occurring Chemicals	*Synthetic Chemicals*
Ciguatoxin	Cleaning products
Scombrotoxin	Pesticides
Shellfish toxins	Metals
Mycotoxins	Food additives

involves the gathering of wild mushrooms. Unfortunately, telling an edible from a poisonous mushroom can sometimes be impossible; you can't smell or taste a mushroom's toxins.

Mycotoxins are toxins produced by molds growing on food. Many mycotoxins are not destroyed by heat. Common foods containing mycotoxins include peanuts, pecans, Brazil nuts, walnuts, corn, and milk. These foods may contain mycotoxins called aflatoxin, which can cause cancer when consumed over a long period of time. The U.S. Food and Drug Administration and the U.S. Department of Agriculture monitor the levels of aflatoxin in peanut butter, milk, and other products. In addition, it is always wise to buy food from a reputable supplier; keep nuts dry and protected from humidity; and throw out milk, nuts, and corn if there is a question of spoilage or mold.

Synthetic chemicals may be brought into the kitchen in the form of cleaning compounds: Chlorine, iodine, cyanide, acids, and caustics are common poisons in cleaning supplies. Pesticides are also used in kitchens to exterminate insects and control rodents. These poisons can kill not only pests but also people.

Keep all these products away from food and food preparation surfaces and equipment. Store them in clearly labeled containers in a separate storage area away from food supplies. Never put any such products into an empty food or drink container; keep them in their original containers where they will not be mistaken for another product.

Another source of pesticide poisoning is the chemicals sprayed on fruits and vegetables. These are reduced by thoroughly washing all produce before use.

Metal residues in foods usually come from defective cooking utensils. A number of poisonous metals are used in making pots and pans—zinc, used in galvanizing buckets; cadmium, a common plating used in gray enamelware and in refrigerator shelves; lead, used in soldering tin cans and in glazing pottery; copper, used in pots, pans, bowls, and molds. High-acid foods such as fruits, fruit juices, and tomatoes can interact with such metals and cause poisoning.

If you find such utensils in your kitchen, check to be sure that galvanized utensils are not chipped, that copper does not have direct contact with food, and that all plated surfaces are not scratched or damaged. Today, most commercial cookware has eliminated these hazards, except for copperware. Copper cookware and molds are usually lined with tin to prevent metal poisoning. But tin is a soft metal and melts at a fairly low temperature. It can be scratched by scouring, and it can be ruined by leaving an empty pan on a burner, which may cause the pan to buckle and the lining to separate from the copper. Anything that exposes the copper is a food hazard, because copper interacts chemically with the moisture in the air, with acid, with salt, and with nearly everything else.

It is, however, safe to beat egg whites in a polished copper bowl, a technique important to the professional baker. The time it takes is not long enough to allow any interaction between egg and metal.

Food additives are substances added to food, intentionally or unintentionally. Additives perform a variety of useful functions in foods that are often taken for granted. Food additives must be tested for safety before being approved by the U.S. Food and Drug Administration for use. Two additives are of concern to a small number of persons sensitive to them: monosodium glutamate (MSG) and sulfites.

PHYSICAL HAZARDS

Foreign substances in food can sometimes cause trouble—not disease but injury. A can opener with a dull blade can produce metal shavings that may drop into the can's contents. The remedy is to throw out the contaminated food and replace the blade of the opener, and then assign someone to replace the blade on a regular basis.

Glasses can be broken by scooping up ice cubes in them; the pieces may not be found and may turn up in someone's glass of iced tea or Bloody Mary. The preventive is to use an ice scoop—always. Ingested glass or bits of metal can cause serious injury.

THE HAZARD ANALYSIS CRITICAL CONTROL POINT SYSTEM

The **Hazard Analysis Critical Control Point (HACCP)** system is a prevention-based food safety system. The seven steps in the HACCP process are designed to prevent the occurrence of foodborne illness. Using these steps, chefs and cooks use menus and recipes to identify the preparation steps when certain foods could be mishandled. Control procedures are then established to prevent mishandling, and these procedures are monitored. When control procedures are not properly followed, corrective action is taken.

The steps of the HACCP system are as follows (Loken, 1995):

1. Review your menu to identify potentially hazardous foods.
2. Observe those foods throughout your preparation, holding, and serving to identify critical control points. A **critical control point** is any point, step, or procedure in which a food safety hazard can be prevented, eliminated, or reduced.
3. Establish control procedures and critical limits. **Critical limits** are the criteria that must be met for each control procedure. A critical limit is frequently stated as a temperature range, such as at or below 40°F, or a time limit.
4. Establish monitoring procedures to adjust the process and maintain control. Typical monitoring procedures, such as temperature readings or visual observations, must be recorded.
5. Establish corrective actions to be taken when monitoring indicates that there is a deviation from an established critical limit. For example, this may involve disposing of the food.
6. Establish effective record-keeping procedures of the HACCP system.
7. Establish procedures to verify that the HACCP plan or system is working, such as regular review of records.

Figure 2.3 shows how the steps in the HACCP process have been used to identify potential hazards, critical control points, critical limits, monitoring procedures, and corrective actions for one menu item.

Figure 2-3 HACCP CHART FOR SEAFOOD SALAD

SEAFOOD SALAD

Flow Chart	Potential Hazards	CCP	Critical Limits	Monitoring Procedures	Corrective Action
Cooked Seafood / Dressing / Other Ingredients					
Receiving	Rapid bacterial growth; contamination; foreign objects	CCP	Chilled items below 40°F; frozen items with no signs of thawing; no spoilage, contamination or foreign objects	Visual inspection; Measure/record temperature	Reject thawed frozen items, chilled items above 40°F, and items with spoilage, contamination, or foreign objects
Prechill Ingredients (40°F)	Rapid bacterial growth	CCP	Chill in shallow pans to below 40°F	Measure/record cooler air temperature every 4 hours	Adjust thermostat
Mix Ingredients	Contamination		Minimize hand contact; use clean utensils	Observe employee and handling practices	Modify Standard Operating Procedures (SOPs) and production practices
Put in Dish or Storage Container	Contamination		Use clean dish or container	Observe employee and handling practices	Modify Standard Operating Procedures (SOPs) and production practices
Store in Cooler 40°F	Rapid bacterial growth	CCP	Product below 40°F	Measure/record cooler air temperature every 4 hours	Adjust temperature; stir
Replenish	Contamination		Avoid hand contact	Observe employee and handling practices	Modify Standard Operating Procedures (SOPs) and production practices
Display in Case (40°F)	Rapid bacterial growth	CCP	Product below 40°F	Measure/record temperature every 2 hours	Adjust thermostat; stir

▭ = **Critical Control Point**

Reprinted from *The HACCP Food Safety Manual,* Joan Loken, Copyright © 1995 by Joan Loken. Reprinted by permission of John Wiley & Sons, Inc.

KITCHEN SAFETY

The kitchen abounds in potential safety hazards: sharp knives sitting in the bottom of a sink full of soapy water, hot stoves and boiling water, steamers under pressure, wet floors. You can keep them "potential" if you recognize them and take appropriate precautions. The well-run kitchen has its own safety rules. When the rules are ignored or taken lightly, injuries, medical bills, lost work time, and possibly lost business result.

One of the most important safety precautions you can take is to know your cooking equipment and use it with respect. Every piece of equipment you use in cooking has an operator's manual furnished by the manufacturer. Study this manual. Learn how to operate the equipment correctly, what its safety hazards are, how to deal with them, how to clean and maintain the equipment, and how to turn off the power supply (which should always be done before cleaning). In particular, learn how to work with steam and gas. Electrical equipment has its dangers, too: sharp blades, moving pieces, the possibility of getting shocked if you get careless and touch the equipment with wet hands, for example, or fail to get a damaged cord fixed. Always ask for help with any unfamiliar equipment before you use it.

The most frequent kitchen accidents fall into four main categories: burns, cuts, strains, and falls.

BURNS AND FIRES

In the kitchen, you are surrounded by hot things—hot range tops and grills, hot fat in the fryer, hot pans, hot foods, steam under pressure. Not only are things hot, they are large scale—whole kettles of fat, multigallon pots of stew—so spills, if they occur, can be catastrophic. Some things are superhot: hot fat can be twice as hot as boiling water; broilers can heat up to 1200°F (650°C).

We could give you a long list of don'ts, but if your eyes are open to the dangers you won't need someone else's rules. You will work with caution and common sense. You will handle hot pans with dry towels or potholders (a wet towel will give you a steam burn). You will keep pan handles out of aisles so that no one can bump into them and upend the hot contents. You will remove covers from pots by tipping them away from you to send the steam in the other direction. You will not try to carry a heavy pot of hot food across a room alone. You will put foods slowly into the fryer as you step back, and make sure the basket is not overfilled. You will let equipment cool before cleaning it. You will work with appropriate clothing and shoes that protect you from burns. You will work with an awareness of those around you so that you don't create hazards for others. To ensure that customers do not get burned, you will warn them of hot plates and make sure lids of takeout containers are on tight.

In case of fire, make sure you know what to do. Know the precautions, equipment, and routines of your facility. Learn where the fire extinguishers are kept and how to operate them. In addition, you should know these things about fires:

- There are three common types of fires: **Class A,** an ordinary fire, such as burning wood, paper, or cloth; **Class B,** a grease or oil fire; **Class C,** an electrical fire.
- All types need oxygen to burn. If you can smother a fire, cutting off the oxygen supply, you can put it out—a lid on a kettle of burning fat, a blanket wrapped around burning clothing, carbon dioxide or foam on an electrical fire.
- Water will work only on an ordinary fire. It will make a grease or electrical fire worse.

Fire prevention is the best treatment. Work carefully. Keep equipment grease free, including hoods and vents. Don't turn your back on hot fat. Don't smoke in the kitchen. Make sure trash goes where it belongs (in the trash pail, of course). And report any frayed electrical cords, damaged plugs and outlets, and improperly operating pilot lights and gas smells. If a fire does start, call the fire department unless you can put it out immediately.

CUTS

Possibly the worst type of kitchen accident comes from careless handling of power-driven mixing and cutting machines. To classify such injuries as cuts is really the height of understatement.

As with cooking equipment, before you ever use a machine, study the operator's manual and attend a demonstration on its use. Learn how to operate the machine correctly, how to clean and maintain it, what its safety hazards are, and how to deal with them. In addition, follow these general precautions:

- Never touch food in a machine, even with a utensil, when the machine is in motion. If you must scrape, remove, or rearrange something, turn the machine off before you do it.
- Set the safety switch or pull the plug before cleaning a machine, changing an attachment, or handling a cutting part.
- Do not use equipment when wearing loose sleeves, ties, or dangling jewelery that may accidentally be pulled into a machine.

Cuts from hand tools seem minor in comparison to machine accidents, but they can be painful and incapacitating. They seldom occur when the tool is being used correctly for its appointed task. The trouble comes when you misuse a tool for another purpose, such as prying off a bottle cap with a knife point, or when your mind is on something else. Or you use a glass to get ice out of an ice machine—the glass may crack or break, and you won't be able to tell which is glass and which is ice.

Knives have their own set of rules. Don't gesture or turn around suddenly with a knife in your hand. If you must carry a knife across the room, point it down and carry it slightly behind you. Don't put it in your hip pocket; you could sit on it; and don't put it in the bottom of a sink full of water. To wash and dry a knife, wipe both sides at once with the sharp edge away from your hand and the towel.

STRAINS AND BACK INJURIES

Quantity food preparation can require a lot of lifting and carrying of heavy things. There are

Figure 2-4 LIFTING AND CARRYING

a. To lift a load from the floor, squat with one foot flat on the floor and lift with your leg muscles. Keep your knees bent and your back rounded. To set it down, slowly resume the original position.

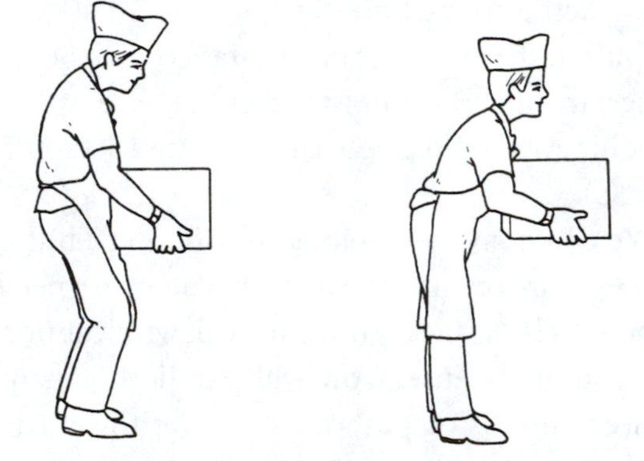

b. To carry a heavy load, keep your knees bent and your back rounded, with your load at waist level or below.

c. You can safely carry a heavy load on your back. You will automatically round your lower back to balance the load.

The wrong ways of lifting and carrying will make you arch your lower back and your neck. This pushes vertebrae together, pressing on disks and nerves.

ways of lifting and carrying that minimize the chance of strained muscles and back injuries.

Figure 2.4 shows right and wrong ways to lift and carry. The secret is to use your leg and stomach muscles instead of your back muscles. Keep your back rounded, so that your vertebrae do not pinch the cushioning disks between them or the nerves that run through them. Such injuries can be serious and do permanent damage. You can also strain muscles if you do not lift correctly.

To avoid carrying heavy things long distances, use a dolly or a cart or ask someone to help you.

FALLS

Falls are among the most common of kitchen accidents. They often happen because workers are unaware of the hazards. Most falls come from spills of food or grease. The simplest precaution is to wipe up a spill as soon as it happens and wipe it up clean. Another precaution is to use "Wet Floor" signs. Also, watch your step in any working area, since workers are not always aware of spills they have created. A fall can be compounded if the person falling is carrying something hot; then burns can be added to injuries. To prevent falls, you can also keep aisles and stairs clear, walk (don't run), use ladders properly, and wear shoes with skid-resistant soles and low heels.

You can see that cleanliness is as important to safety as it is to sanitation. If you keep your work area clean and use your tools and equipment properly, you can cook in safety and confidence. But be wary of overconfidence. If you begin to get the feeling that you'll never get hurt and you start to relax your caution, that's just when it will happen to you! Work seriously and professionally. Clowning and fooling around are invitations to accidents.

SUMMING UP

The practice of sanitation is just as important to the foodservice operation as the production of quality food. The hazards of foodborne disease are everywhere all the time.

The major enemy is the ever-present bacteria. Some types of bacteria produce toxins in food, notably staph, which is common, and *C. botulinum,* which is rare but deadly. Others attack the body directly. Of these, salmonella is common, and *C. perfringens* is noteworthy for surviving cooking.

Bacteria can multiply with unbelievable speed. We can never get rid of them entirely, but we can keep their numbers at safe levels in several ways. We can keep them from entering the kitchen along with people, foods, and pests. We can prevent their spread from one food to another by sanitary work habits, proper storage, and constant cleaning of tools, work surfaces, and hands. We can stop them from multiplying by keeping foods out of the danger zone temperatures of 40 to 140°F (4–60°C). We can kill them by cooking foods and sanitizing equipment touched by foods. We must think clean, work clean, and clean; we must make sanitation a habit.

Other hazards to which foods are susceptible are spoilage, contamination by chemicals from pesticides and cleaning supplies, metal residues from certain kinds of cooking utensils, and foreign substances such as broken glass or metal shavings.

The kitchen is full of safety hazards. Common accidents are burns, cuts, strains, back injuries, and falls. The best way to prevent them is to work with awareness, caution, and common sense. Handle all tools and equipment properly. Handle your body properly when lifting and carrying. Avoid spills and clean them up immediately if they happen. Know how to prevent fires and how to put them out. Think safety as you think sanitation and never take it for granted.

The Cook's Vocabulary

bacteria
bacterial infection
botulism
campylobacteriosis
clean
critical control point
critical limit
cross-contamination
foodborne hazards: biological, chemical, physical
foodborne illness
food additive
food spoilage
Hazard Analysis Critical Control Point (HACCP)
intoxication
mycotoxin
parasite
personal hygiene
potentially hazardous food
sanitary
sanitation
temperature danger zone
toxin-mediated infection
types of fires: Class A, B, C
virus

Review Questions

Answer each question in complete sentences. Read each question carefully and make sure you answer all parts of the question. Organize your answer into more than one paragraph when appropriate.

1. Of the many sanitation practices discussed in this chapter, which do you consider most important and why?
2. Of the four strategies for keeping bacteria at safe levels, which do you think is most important? From your own experience, which is the most commonly ignored?
3. What role does personal hygiene play in foodservice? How, specifically, can it affect sanitation?
4. In your opinion, what is the most serious kitchen safety hazard? How will you avoid it at work?
5. Cite instances you have seen in which cross-contamination could or did occur. How could they have been avoided?
6. List five tips for knife safety.
7. Discuss three other foodborne troublemakers besides bacteria.
8. Which muscles do you use if you are lifting correctly? If you are lifting incorrectly?

Chapter 3

PREPREPARATION

Go into the Yacht Club kitchen any midafternoon in summer. It hums with noise and action. Pans and trays clatter on counters; knives rap out staccato rhythms on cutting boards. A cook's mallet thumps veal down to scaloppine thinness. Water gushes from taps as vegetables are scrubbed. A rush of steam hisses from the cabinet steamer. Five prime ribs are sizzling gently in the convection oven. Pans sputter to themselves on the range. The mixer motor is purring hoarsely. The exhaust fans are droning. "Hot stuff coming through!" shouts a cook. "Somebody's burning the butter!" yells another.

All the cooks are intently busy. There is a formidable sense of bustle and hustle. Yet serving time is several hours away, and except for soup, prime rib, baked potatoes, and rice, every menu item will be finished in the few minutes before it is served. So what is everyone doing?

The blanket term for all this activity is prepreparation. In the hours before serving time, not only the cooks but a number of other persons from the executive chef to the kitchen helpers and potwashers are engaged in countless tasks that add up to precooking readiness.

As the serving hour draws near, a great crescendo of noise and activity crests and then suddenly subsides. Everything comes into sync. Quiet descends, and the cooks wait, relaxed and confident, for the first orders of the evening.

At such a moment, the old-school continental chef used to sit down to his glass of Pernod to savor the interlude of readiness that formed the threshold of triumphs to follow. Today, it is a coffee break, or a split between shifts, or time out for the employee meal. In continuous-service operations, there is no such moment; prepreparation and preparation go on simultaneously all the time.

In this chapter, we will look at some of the many tasks and techniques of prepreparation. This is an area neglected by most books on cookery, and yet it can make or break a dish, or a meal, or a restaurant.

After completing this chapter, you should be able to:

- Understand the importance of prepreparation and the meaning and importance of mise en place.
- Clean fresh produce properly.
- Use and care for knives and cutting machines correctly, and choose the appropriate tool or machine for the task.
- Identify standard food cuts.
- Define basic processing techniques.
- Hold and store foods properly for sanitation and product quality.
- Organize a production task or station efficiently.

THE MEANING OF PREPREPARATION

The tasks involved in turning raw products into menu dishes are separated into two groups: those that can be done ahead and those that are completed at or just before serving time. The terms used to describe this division of tasks are **prepreparation** (often shortened in kitchen jargon to preprep) and final preparation, or **finish cooking.**

If you were to make a casserole of chicken tetrazzini, for example, you would cook the spaghetti and the chicken ahead of time. You would dice the chicken, sauté the mushrooms, make the sauce, and grate the cheese ahead of time. Then you would assemble the dish in the casserole and refrigerate it. All this is prepreparation. The only steps left for final preparation are heating the dish and glazing it.

In food production, everything you can do ahead is done ahead—prepared. This is partly because there is a great deal that cannot be done ahead, partly because it is more efficient to spread the tasks throughout the time available, and partly because some things must be done before other things can be done in making many products. One of the most important aspects of food preparation is efficient organizing of prepreparation tasks.

There is a term used with pride throughout the profession—**mise en place** (meez on plass). Freely translated from the French, it means "everything in its proper place." A simpler English version is "a good setup." It means that the precooking procedures have been carried out with understanding and good organization, and everything is ready to go. As you pursue your career in the foodservice industry, you will be evaluated on your mise en place more than you can probably conceive at this point.

In this chapter, you will meet many other terms that are new to you, and you will meet everyday words with new meanings. How do you fold egg whites, for example? What about dice—is that something you roll at coffee break? Like every other trade or profession, food preparation has its own vocabulary.

There are several reasons for learning the specialized meanings of terms—learning them so thoroughly that they become part of your everyday vocabulary. They enable you to communicate with those around you and to understand what is going on. They help you to follow what you read, whether it is a recipe, a textbook, or a cookery dictionary. The right term is an excellent tool for finding information, both from people and from books. Many terms are interesting for their own sake. Much of the language of the kitchen goes back to classical times and earlier, and it carries pleasant overtones of banquets served to royalty and the culinary triumphs of such great chefs as Carême and Escoffier.

But there are problems. Some people use terms incorrectly. Some products are called by different names in different parts of the country. Some terms have different meanings in different operations. Some terms even the experts do not agree on. Many terms have changed in meaning over the years.

We need definitions to work with. "Define your terms," said Socrates, setting forth the first requirement for any fruitful discussion. We will go on defining terms throughout this book.

The definitions we will give you are as precise and yet as broadly applicable as we can make them. If they do not always agree exactly with those you find elsewhere, or with your own experience, perhaps they will intrigue you into working out better definitions of your own. Meantime, master ours as we explore prepreparation in more detail.

CLEANING

In many kitchens, the workday starts with the cleaning of the produce to be used that day. Kitchen slang for this phase of food preparation is **rough prep** or **prepping.** Some kitchens buy their produce already cleaned. But seldom is every cleaning need solved by purchasing, so it is important for you to know all the proper techniques.

The term cleaning, as applied to vegetables and other food products, can have multiple meanings. Most fruits and vegetables arrive at your door in anything but a clean condition. Some products are dirtier than others by virtue of the way they grow. Root vegetables such as carrots and beets have a lot of surface dirt. Lettuce, leeks, and other vegetables that grow in the earth or close to it may have a great deal of dirt in the leaves of the plant.

Cleaning such foods properly means washing them thoroughly, and "thoroughly" means getting them as clean and dirt free as possible. Cleanliness is of vital importance for a number of reasons. Insecticides, sprays, powders, and dirt are certainly not things that can be banished with sauces and seasonings. A gritty salad or vegetable is quite unpleasant and may be a health hazard.

Different vegetables are cleaned in different ways. The way a vegetable is cleaned is determined by its type and texture:

- Hard vegetables such as potatoes and carrots with skins should be scrubbed with a vegetable brush under cold running water. If they are to be peeled, they need not be scrubbed, but they should still be washed. You don't want to pass along dirt, sprays, or contamination to cut surfaces as you peel.
- Soft or fragile vegetables—such as tomatoes, asparagus, okra, and corn—and most fruits should be washed thoroughly in cold running water but not scrubbed.
- Leafy vegetables should be broken apart and washed thoroughly under cold running water to remove dirt from inside.

For large volume, it is sometimes necessary to clean vegetables by submerging them in water. This is not totally wrong, but using cold running water is certainly more desirable. Washing vegetables by submerging them means that you are washing the second item in the dirty water from the first.

When the submersion method is used, the vegetables are placed on large draining racks, which are then submerged in a sinkful of water. Leaf vegetables are plunged up and down to force water between the leaves. A raised screen placed on the bottom of the sink allows the dirt to settle. The water is changed frequently. After washing, the racks are removed from the sink and the produce is allowed to drain before storage.

Cold water is used for washing because it keeps vegetables crisp. Warm water wilts them. Both vegetables and fruits should be washed as close to use time as possible. They are then at their cleanest when used. In addition, some raw products begin to deteriorate after washing—mushrooms and berries, for example. Cleaned fresh fruits and vegetables are stored in the cooler, covered, until use.

Many items have portions that are discarded as part of the cleaning. With lettuce and cabbage, for example, the discolored outer leaves are discarded, along with the core. Tough parts, such as spinach stems and the bottoms of fresh asparagus and fresh broccoli stalks, are cut away; so are blemishes. Many fruits and vegetables are peeled; this can vary with the dish for which they are intended.

CUTTING

CUTTING TERMINOLOGY

Here are the basic cutting terms defined. You will meet others shortly.

- **Cut** To divide into pieces or to shape using a knife
- **Chop** To cut into pieces of no specified shape
- **Mince** To chop very fine
- **Dice** To cut into small uniform cubes
- **Slice** To cut into uniform slices, usually across the grain

Cutting, of course, is the general term that includes all the others. Chopping and mincing involve the same action but refer to different sizes of products—an important distinction. Dicing and slicing create specific kinds of cuts. Notice the word "uniform" in both definitions.

You may also meet some French cutting terms—concasser, émincer. **Concasser** (kon-kass-ay) is similar to chop; it means to cut rough-shaped but even-sized pieces. **Émincer** (ay-man-say) means to mince; it also means to slice thinly or cut into thin uniform strips.

Cutting is probably the most basic skill a cook must have—the ability to handle a knife quickly and efficiently to cut the exact size and shape of product needed. Although cutting machines often save time and labor, no machine can cut with the versatility and judgment of a good cook with a good knife. "He (or she) is a good hand with a knife" is high praise in the industry and an entry into almost any kitchen.

Figure 3-1 STATION SETUP FOR CUTTING

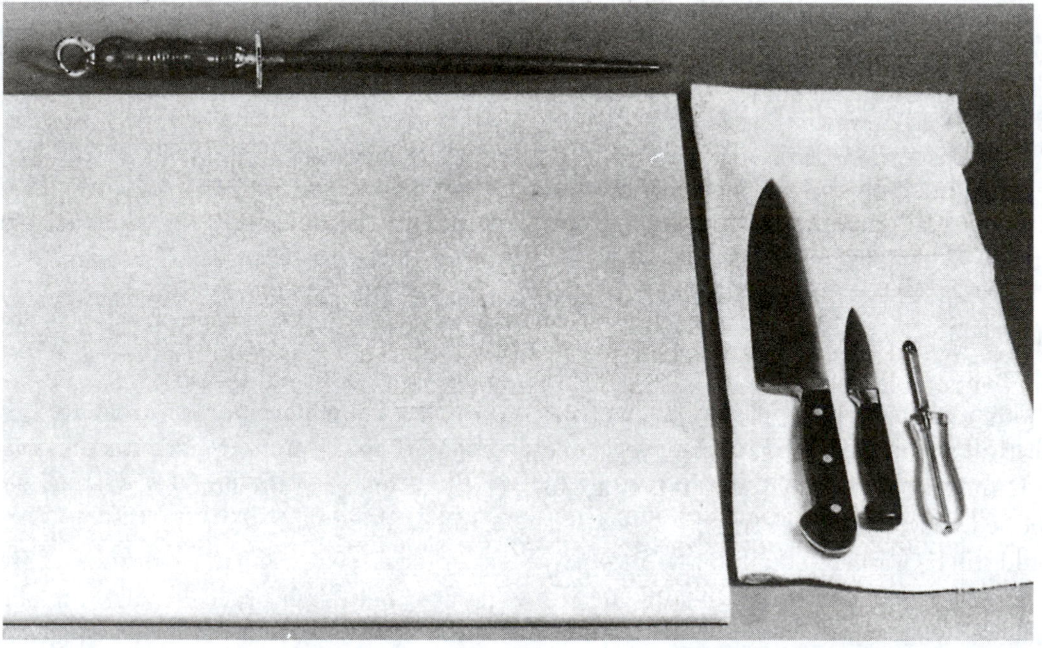

This heavy plastic cutting board is flanked on the right with the cook's most used cutting tools—the French knife, the paring knife, and the peeler—placed on a clean towel. Above the board is the steel. Left-handed cooks will reverse the arrangement. The board rests on a damp cloth so that it will not slip. (Photo by Patricia Roberts.)

THE KNIFE

The knife in question is the **French knife**—a fairly thick, rigid, wide-bladed knife with a distinctive triangular profile. It is illustrated in Figure 3.1, which shows a typical station setup for cutting. This knife is designed for heavy-duty cutting and chopping. Its sturdy blade is strong enough to withstand the constant beating it takes against the cutting board. The blade extends well below the knife handle, allowing the fingers to come all the way around under the handle without hitting the board (see Figure 3.2).

If you could have only one knife, it would probably be this one. The French knife is the cook's right hand. Most professional cooks have their own French knives and perhaps other hand tools as well. You can do your best work with a knife whose length, weight, balance, and handle grip suit you—a knife that feels good in your hand. It should be made of high-quality stainless steel that contains a high percentage of carbon steel, which helps the knife retain its sharpness. The **tang**—the extension of the blade into the handle—should run the entire handle length.

USING THE KNIFE

The French knife is used for many things, such as cutting, mincing, and puréeing. There are machines for doing such tasks. Then why use the knife? You will use it in the following situations:

- Whenever precise, uniform cuts are called for, such as cubes or slices, and you do not have a machine that makes these cuts. (The chopper chops; it does not and cannot make crisp, even cuts.)
- Whenever the knife takes less time than the machine. Cleaning a machine is time-consuming, and unless you must cut a large quantity, it is not worthwhile to use the machine.
- Whenever cutting foods whose texture would be spoiled by machine cutting, such as parsley or onions, which become crushed and juicy in a machine.

For a comfortable position while working, first stand at arm's length from the work surface with your heels together at a 45° angle. Then take a short step forward—with your left foot if you are right handed and your right foot if left-handed. Your body is now automatically placed at a 45° angle to the cutting board (Figure 3.3).

Figure 3-2 HOW TO HOLD A FRENCH KNIFE

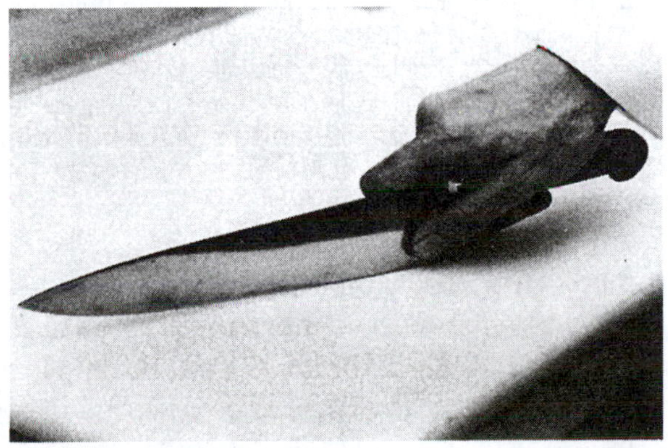

(Photo by Patricia Roberts.)

Figure 3-3 HOW TO POSITION YOURSELF FOR CUTTING

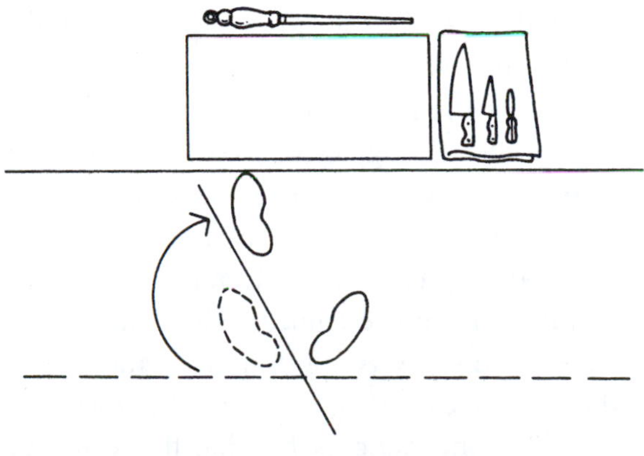

The diagonal line shows the angle of your body as you work.

Figure 3-4 HOW TO CUT WITH A FRENCH KNIFE

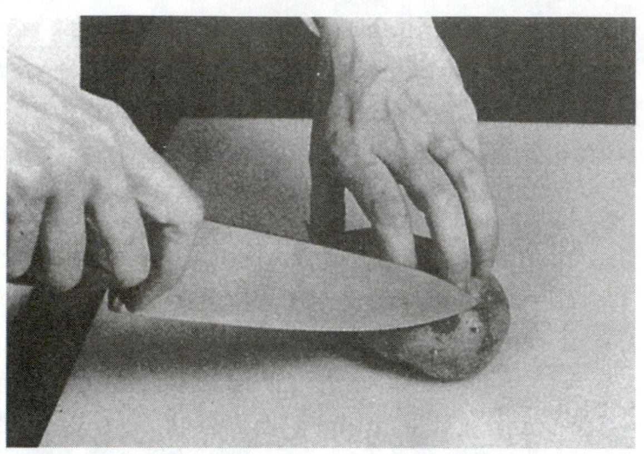

a. Place your other hand on top of the food you are going to cut, with your fingers curled. Your hand is relaxed. It holds the food lightly. Cut a thin piece off one side of a round food to make a flat place for it to rest on.

With the food resting on the flat place you have cut, place the knife tip on the food with its blade against your knuckles. Your knuckles should guide the blade, telling it where to cut. You can sight along them to see that they are in position to produce the thickness of slice you want.

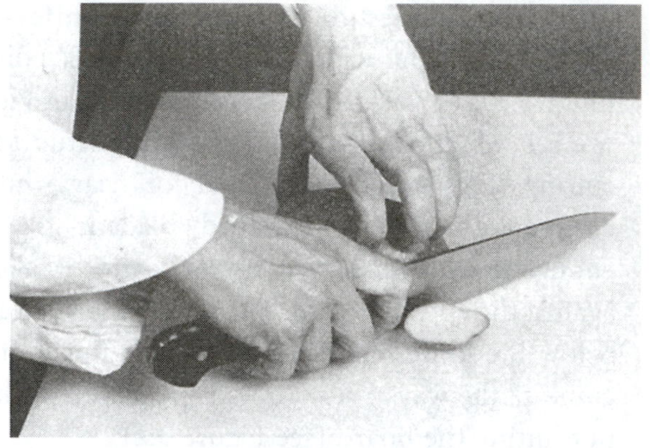

b. Cut through the food with a forward and downward stroke. The knife does the work.

Now, move your hand into position to guide the next cut. Bring the knife back to its starting position and repeat the stroke. The forward part of the blade does the cutting.

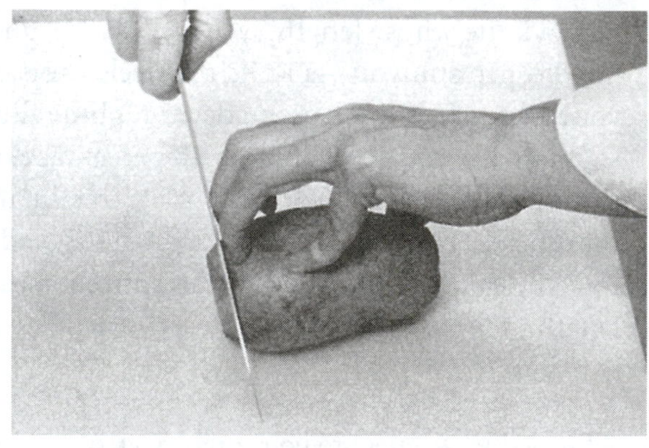

c. The knuckles guide the knife. Keep your hands relaxed, your knuckles in the guiding position. You can either move the action backward slice by slice or push the food under the knife with your guiding hand. In cutting thin foods, keep the tip of the knife on the cutting board and let it glide back and forth as you cut. (Photos by Patricia Roberts.)

This position allows you a natural movement with your shoulder, arm, and hand in line with each other. It will reduce fatigue, especially when you are working for long periods of time.

To learn how to cut with a French knife, first watch a demonstration and then try it yourself under supervision. Begin by holding the knife correctly. Figure 3.2 shows you how. Hold the base of the blade with your thumb and forefinger. Relax the remaining fingers loosely around the handle. This gives you good control. Many beginners hold the knife far back on the handle and push down with a forefinger along the top of the blade. The right grip takes far less effort and gives far more control. The knife is in balance. A simple wrist motion makes the weight of the knife itself do a good bit of the work.

While one hand is holding the knife, your other hand (called the **guiding hand**) holds the food lightly, just enough so the item doesn't slip (Figure 3.4). When held with your fingertips curled under, the knuckles of your guiding hand guide the knife into position. Now study carefully the photos and instructions in Figure 3.4. Then try them out yourself. Work very slowly until you have established a comfortable rhythm. Be sure the food is positioned for the knife, not the other way around.

Next, concentrate on making even cuts—pieces all the same thickness. Keep your knife straight. Do not try to get up speed until you have mastered the motions and the evenness. It takes weeks and months of concentrated practice for real proficiency.

Using the French knife to mince foods takes a slightly different technique. Figure 3.5 shows you how it is done. Minced parsley is often referred to in recipes as "chopped parsley."

A few foods don't lend themselves to straightforward cutting techniques. The onion is a special case because it is layered and the layers will separate. If you work with the layers rather than against them, you can cut the onion quickly and uniformly. Figure 3.6 shows you how. Minced shallots and garlic are also cut this way rather than using the mincing technique in Figure 3.5.

Puréeing is still another knife technique. To **purée** (pew-ray) is to mash a food to a fine pulp. It is usually done by forcing it through a sieve or putting it into a blender, but a small amount can be done with the blade of the French knife. Figure 3.7 shows you the technique.

SHARPENING THE KNIFE

Two tools will keep your knives sharp and true: the **stone** (short for **whetstone**) and the **steel.** The stone is for sharpening the knife initially; the steel is for removing any burrs from the knife edge (called **trueing the edge**). The steel is used to maintain the edge, in other words, keep it sharp as you use the knife, and it should therefore accompany your knife at all times. If you use the steel frequently as you work, you will seldom have to use the stone.

Figure 3.8 shows how to use the steel. Watch a demonstration before you try this yourself; then try it under supervision.

Figure 3-5 HOW TO MINCE

a. Cut the food coarsely, using the technique described in Figure 3-4. Then, with your cutting hand in its usual position, hold the knife tip in one place on the board with your other hand.

b. Rock the knife up and down in short strokes while moving the handle end in an arc that crosses the pile of food. Repeat, moving the arc backward and forward over the food until it reaches the desired fineness. After a number of passes across the food, you can scrape the pieces into a pile and go at it from a slightly different direction. (Photos by Patricia Roberts.)

Figure 3-6 HOW TO DICE ONIONS

a. Cut an onion in half lengthwise.

b. Place one half down on the cutting board and make an even series of lengthwise cuts as shown, leaving the segments attached at one end.

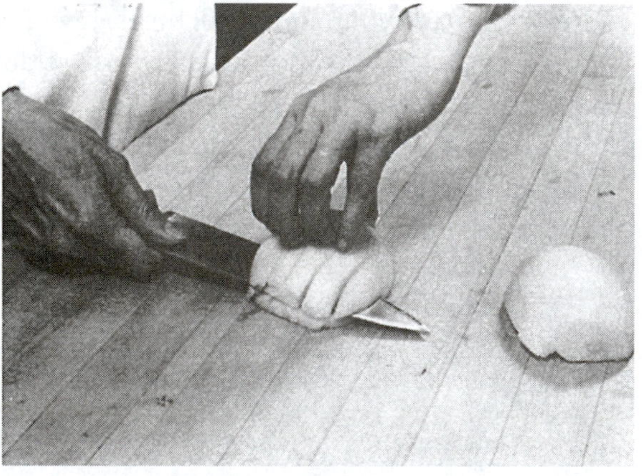

c. Holding the segments together, make a similar series of cuts parallel to the board, at right angles to the first series. Your hand is above the knife, well out of its way.

d. Now, make a series of cross cuts, and you have diced your onion. (Photos by Patricia Roberts.)

To sharpen a dull knife, you must start with the whetstone. Figure 3.9 shows how this is done. Watch a demonstration before you try it. Place the tip of your knife blade on one end of the flat stone. Hold the blade at a 20° angle to the stone. Move your knife slowly across the stone in a slow, even stroke from blade tip to base. Make the same number of strokes for each side of the blade and sharpen in one direction only. When your knife is sharp, finish with several strokes on the steel. Then wipe the blade to remove any steel dust. You will not need the whetstone again if you use your steel often enough.

If you have a good-quality electric knife sharpener, it can do a commendable job. However, a poor-quality one will not do an even job, and it

Figure 3-7 HOW TO PURÉE WITH A KNIFE

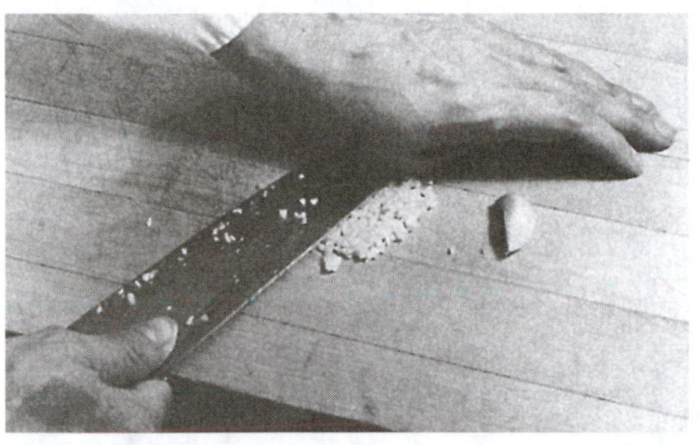

After mincing a food as shown in Figure 3.5 or 3.6, place the flat of the knife blade over it at a 20° angle, sharp edge flat on the cutting board. With your other hand, press down on the blade while you draw the flat of the blade hard across the food—in this case, garlic. Repeat until you have the fineness of purée desired. (Photo by Patricia Roberts.)

Figure 3-8 HOW TO USE THE STEEL

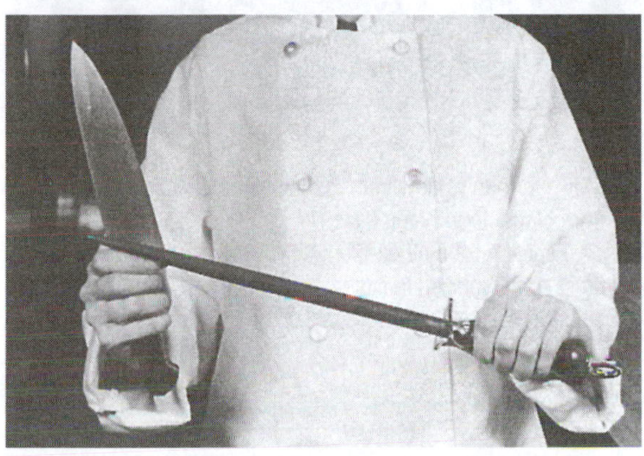

a. Hold the knife handle in your cutting hand. Hold your steel in front of you in your other hand. Place the base of your knife blade just below the tip of the steel, with the sharp edge of the blade resting on the steel at an angle of 15 or 20°.

b. Maintaining this angle, use a wrist motion to bring the blade across the length of the steel in one long stroke that ends with the tip of the knife near the base of the steel.

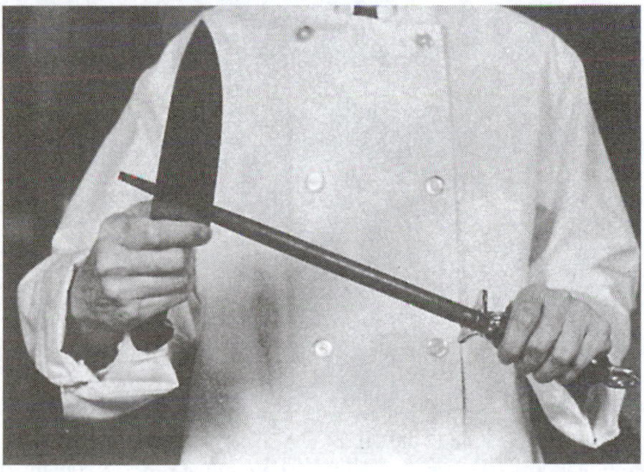

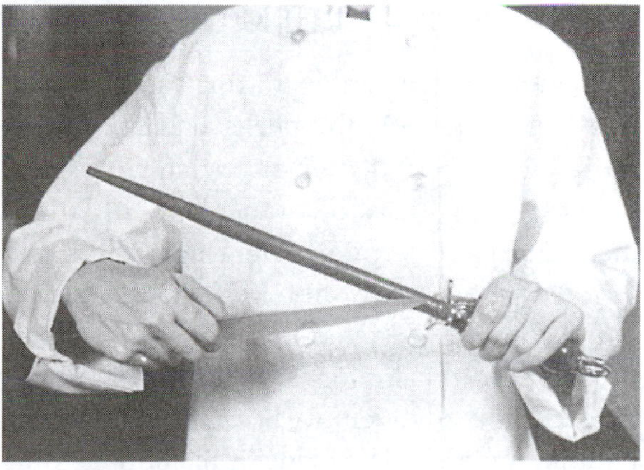

c. and ***d.*** Repeat this stroke with the other side of the sharp edge on the other side of the steel. Use this pair of strokes 10 or 12 times, always alternating sides of the blade edge. (Photos by Patricia Roberts.)

Figure 3-9 HOW TO USE THE STONE

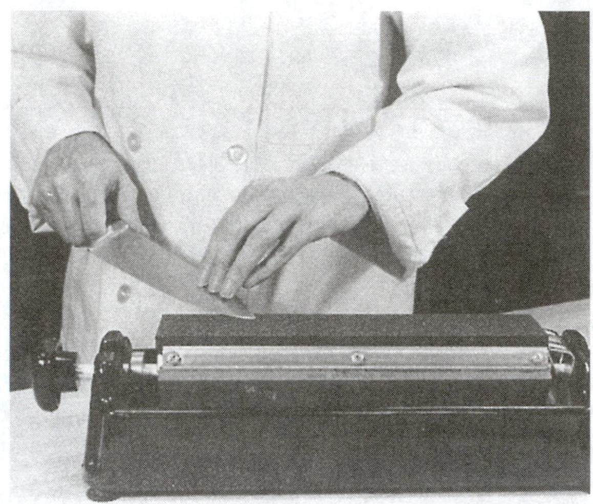

a. Place the tip of your knife blade on one end of the flat stone. Use the fingers of your other hand to apply a light, even pressure.

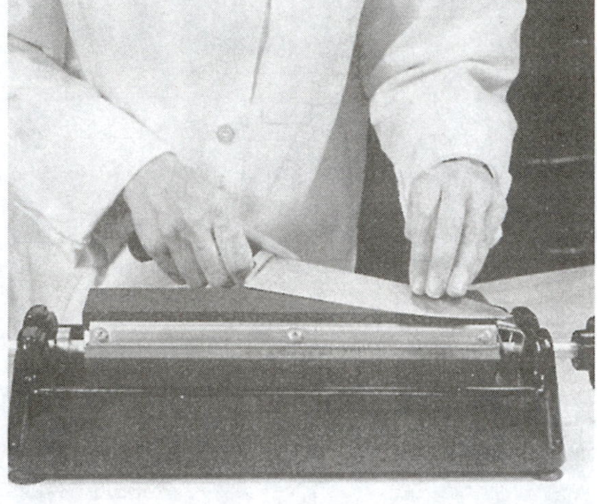

b. Move your knife slowly across the stone in a slow, even stroke from blade tip to blade base.

Repeat for the other side. Repeat the pair of strokes several times, until your knife is sharp. You can test it on your thumbnail. (Photos by Patricia Roberts.)

wears away the blade. Do not oversharpen your knife. It does not need to do the work of a razor. But don't be afraid to use a sharp knife. It is much safer than a dull one because it will do a good job and is less likely to slip out of position.

OTHER KNIVES AND CUTTING TOOLS

Two more indispensable cutting tools are pictured in Figure 3.1: the **peeler** and the **paring knife.** Figure 3.10 demonstrates how to use the peeler. Figure 3.11 shows other types of knives, including a utility knife, boning knife, slicer, and serrated slicer. A **utility knife** is a narrow, pointed knife used mostly in fruit and vegetable preparation and also for carving chicken. A **boning knife** is used to remove bones from raw meat, poultry, and fish. The blade of the boning knife may be either stiff or flexible. The stiff blade is

Figure 3-10

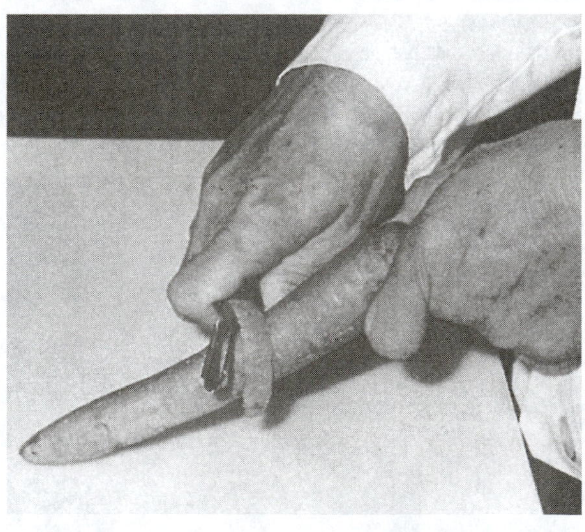

Holding the peeler and the product as shown, push the peeler away from you in a sweeping stroke the length of the product. (Photo by James C. Goering.)

better for boning meat and poultry; the flexible blade is better for lighter work such as filleting fish. **Slicers** do just the job their name implies: slicing. But they are not used to slice vegetables. Instead, a slicer is used to slice cooked meats, and a serrated slicer (it looks like it has teeth) is used to slice breads, cakes, and other items that you don't want to crush during the slicing process.

Figure 3.12 illustrates still other specialized hand tools for cutting. If there is a special cutting task of any sort, there is bound to be a special cutting tool to do it (see, for example, the **router** in Figure 3.14c).

Figure 3.13 shows the paring knife in action. It is used here for cutting the oval shape called **tourné** used in some classical dishes. The paring

Figure 3-11 OTHER KNIFE TYPES

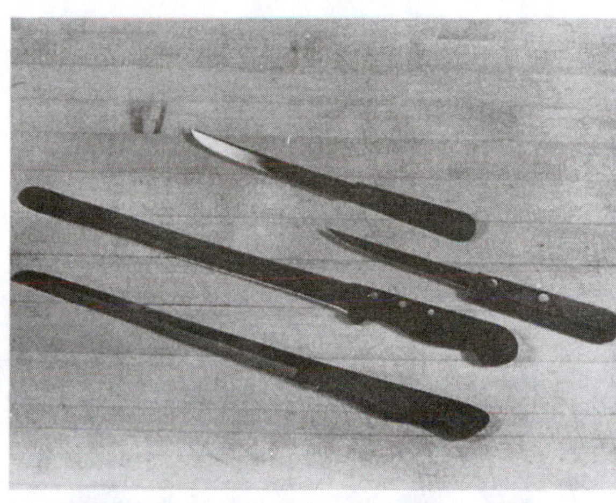

Top to bottom: utility, flexible boning, slicer, serrated. (Photo by Patricia Roberts.)

Figure 3-12 SOME SPECIALIZED CUTTING TOOLS

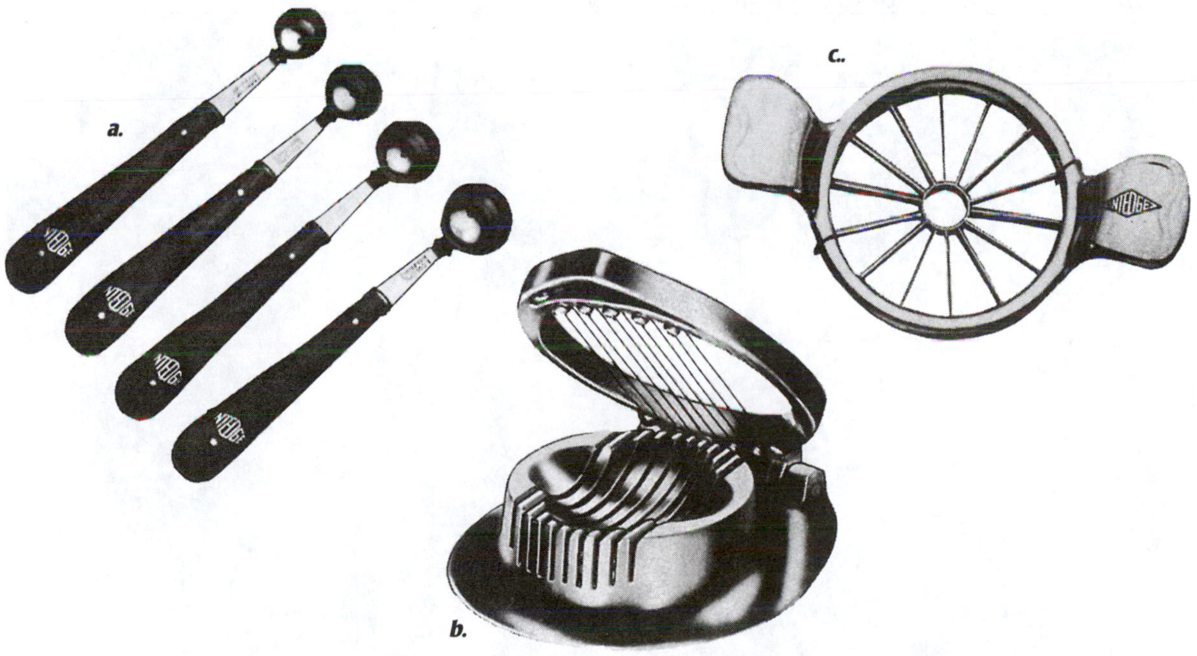

a. Ball cutters. (Photo courtesy Intedge Industries, Inc.) ***b.*** Egg slicer. (Photo courtesy Bloomfield Industries.) ***c.*** Apple corer/cutter. (Photo courtesy Intedge Industries, Inc.)

Figure 3-13 SHAPING WITH A PARING KNIFE

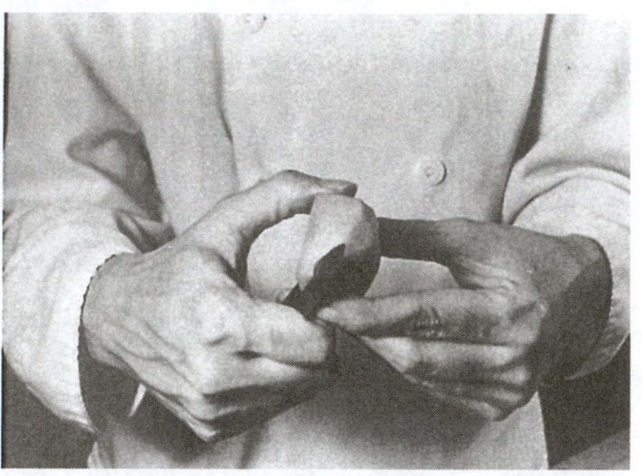

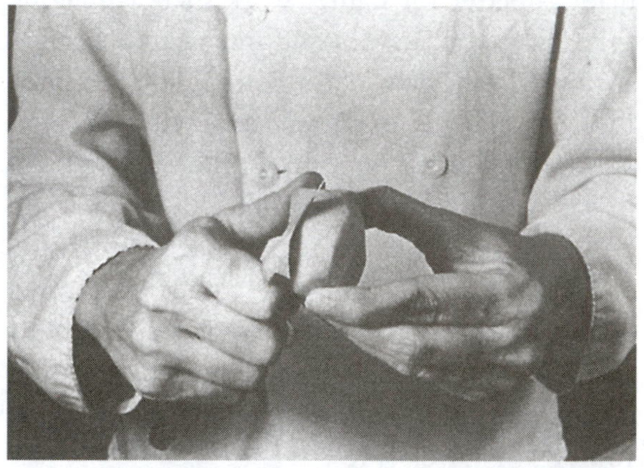

a. Curl your four fingers around the knife handle and part of the blade with the sharp edge toward you. You want your firm grip on the knife to be as close to the action as possible. Brace your thumb on the product. Hold the product firmly in your other hand.

b. Pull the knife slowly toward you. Make sure the blade bites firmly into the food. The thumb of your cutting hand steadies everything. (Photos by Patricia Roberts.)

Figure 3-14 USING THE PARING KNIFE TO MAKE GARNISHES

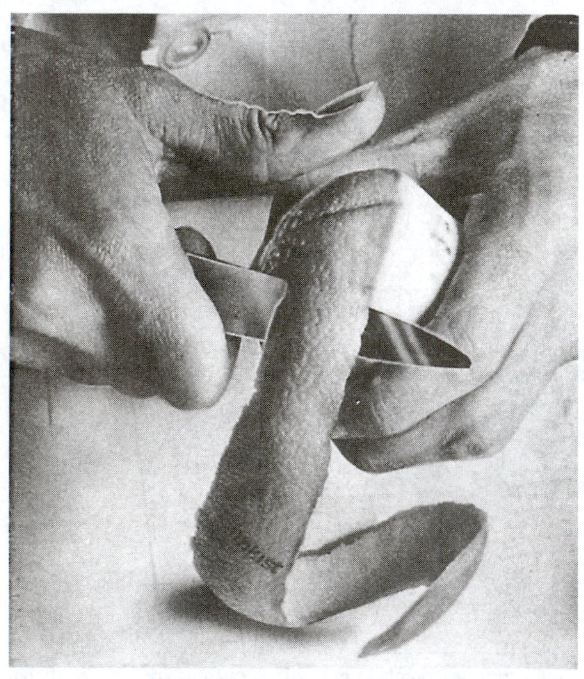

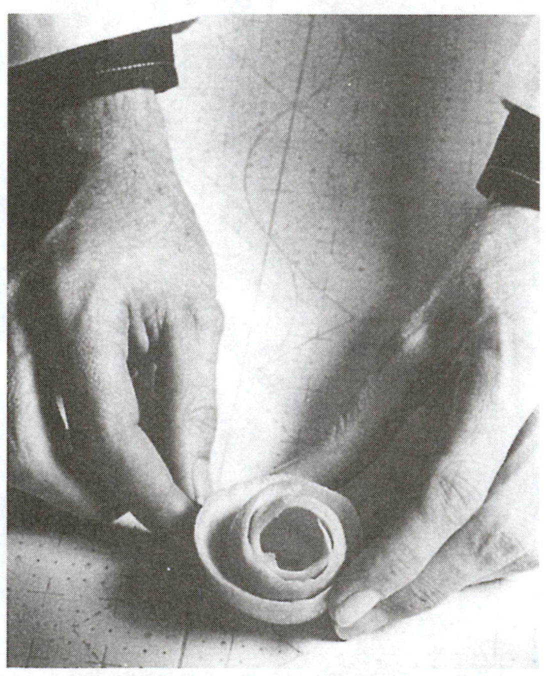

a. The rhythmic turning of the two hands in opposite directions yields a single long strip of orange peel.

b. The orange peel is rolled into a rose, skewed with a toothpick.

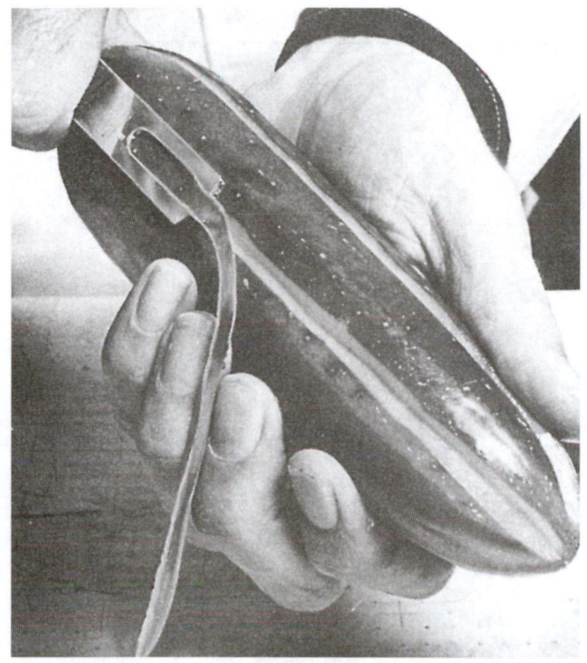

c. The cucumber is scored with a router. . . .

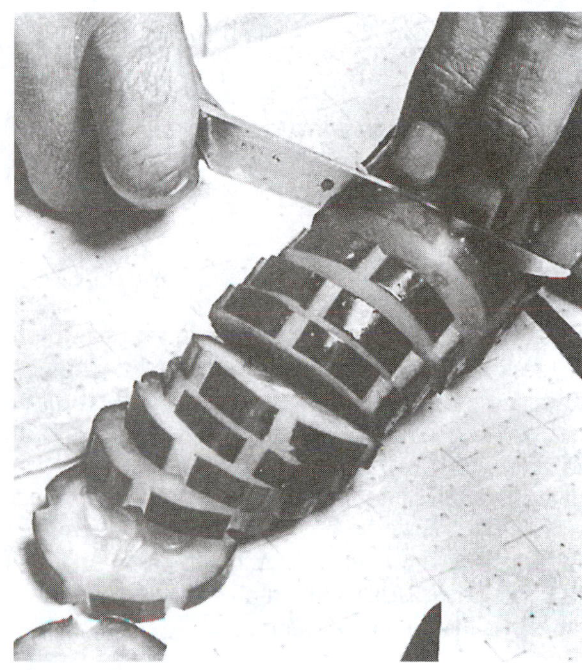

d. . . . then sliced . . .

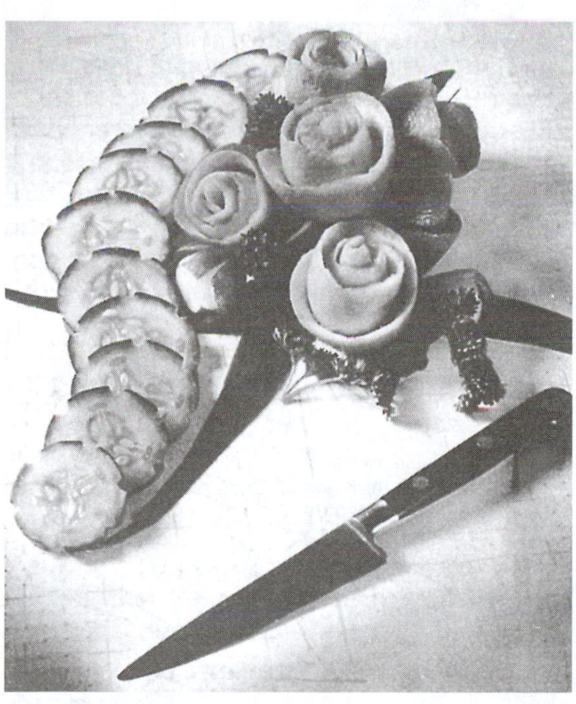

e. . . . and becomes part of a bouquet. (Photos courtesy *Dallas Times Herald*/Jay Dickman.)

Figure 3-15 COMMONLY USED FOOD CUTS

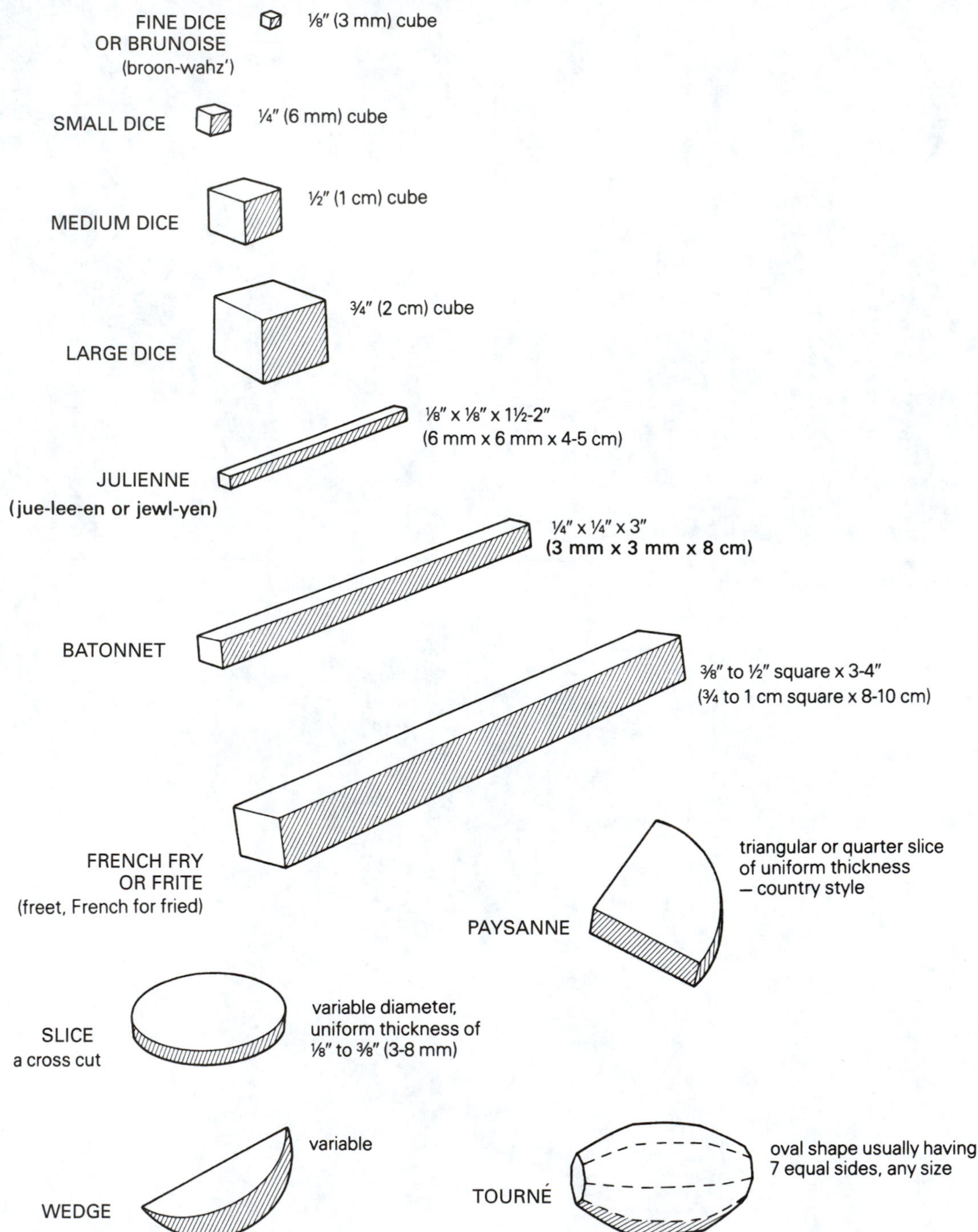

knife is also used for any cutting task requiring a short, sharp knife, such as making fancy garnishes (Figure 3.14). You can also use the paring knife as you do the French knife for cutting on the board.

Treat knives with tender loving care. Do not put them in the dishwasher and never put them in the bottom of a sink full of water. Always use a cutting board and clean the cutting board and knife after each use. Their surfaces can become unnoticed cross-contaminators, especially if used for cutting poultry, fish, or meat.

PRECISION CUTTING

The importance of careful cutting of vegetables cannot be overstated. For any one vegetable, pieces of the same size cook at the same rate, and pieces of different sizes cook at different rates. If, for example, two different-sized cuts of potato are boiled in the same pot, the larger of the two will be undercooked when the smaller one is done, and the smaller one will be overcooked when the larger one is done.

Many different cuts of foods are used in the many dishes you will be making. Each cut has a special name that communicates specific information about shape or size or both. Figure 3.15 shows some common cuts. You may recognize some of them already. As you pursue cooking, they will all become familiar. The range of sizes given for some of the cuts means simply that these are the sizes to which the term applies. It does not mean that a batch of French fries, for example, can vary in size from 3/8 to 1/2 inch (0.75–1 cm). They must all be the same.

The essence of good cutting is to make smooth, clean cuts of food, with all pieces equal in size and shape for even cooking. A clean cut is one that is crisply cut, with a sharp knife and good cutting technique. Clean and even cutting is the foundation of good vegetable preparation.

What is true of vegetables is true also of meats and fruits. Cubes of meat for a stew or slices of apple for a pie should be cut with the same care and precision as the vegetables that are to be served at the table. These foods, too, must cook evenly, to the same degree of doneness.

PROCESSING

Processing includes all the things done to get foods ready for cooking and serving. In some kitchens, more time and labor may be spent in processing than in the cooking itself. Cleaning and cutting, of course, are major processing activities. In addition, there are many specific processes and techniques that figure in the pre-preparation of many different kinds of foods.

PUTTING THINGS TOGETHER

Let us look first at some processing terms and techniques that have to do with putting ingredients together.

- **Mix** To combine ingredients in such a way that the parts of each ingredient are evenly dispersed in the total product
- **Blend** To mix two or more ingredients so completely that they lose their separate identities
- **Bind** To cause a mixture of two or more ingredients to stick together as a homogeneous product, usually by adding a binding agent
- **Beat** To move an implement back and forth to blend ingredients together or to achieve a smooth texture (Figure 3.16a)

- **Whip** To beat with a rapid lifting motion to incorporate air into a food (Figure 3.16b)
- **Fold** To mix a whipped ingredient lightly with another ingredient or mixture by gently turning one over and under the other with a flat implement (Figure 3.16c).

The first of these terms, *mix*, is a general term that includes the other five, which refer to specialized kinds or ways of mixing. Mixing also includes less specialized processes of combining, such as stirring together chicken, celery, and mayonnaise to make a chicken salad.

Blending is a specific kind of mixing in which ingredients are indistinguishably merged. Milk and ice cream are blended to make a milk shake. The yolks and whites of eggs are blended to make an omelet.

Binding is a process that gives permanence to a blend. Blending is a mechanical mixing, and some blends may not stay blended. To make them cohere, or stick together, as a homogeneous product—one that is the same throughout—you can add a binding agent to hold them together. The binding agent usually changes the texture, too, by thickening the product. Some binding agents, such as starches, require cooking the blend together with the binding agent. Others, such as gelatin, simply require mixing and chilling.

Beating is a particular way of mixing. Beating is sometimes a way of getting lumps out of a product. Getting rid of lumps in this way is actually another aspect of mixing, since what you

Figure 3-16 BEAT, WHIP, FOLD

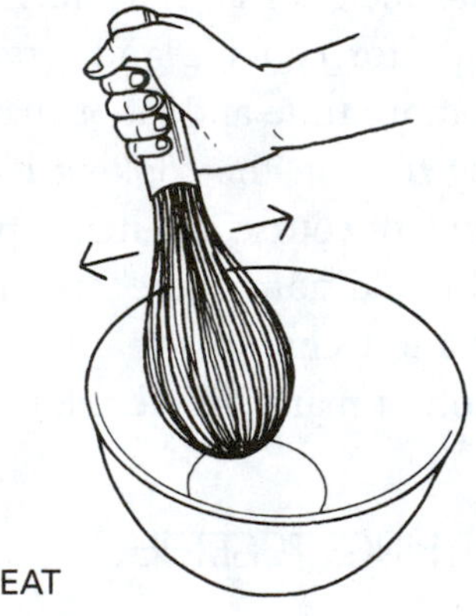

a. BEAT

a. Beating uses a back-and-forth motion of the utensil to mix or smooth out a product.

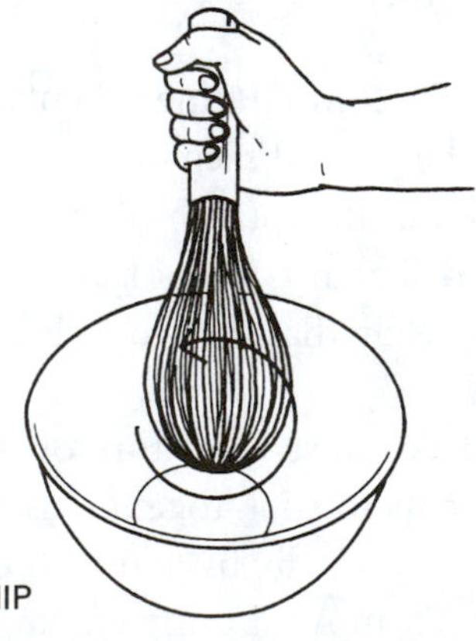

b. WHIP

b. Whipping uses a rapid beating stroke with a lift to it to incorporate air. The back-and-forth motion becomes circular.

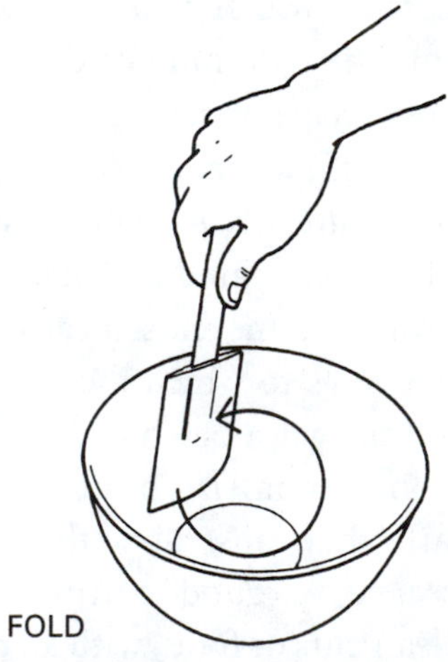

c. FOLD

c. Folding uses a continuous slow circular stroke that scoops up the product from the bottom and spreads it gently over the top.

are doing is breaking up the lumps and blending their contents into the product.

Whipping is a particular way of beating in which you mix air into a food so evenly that it stays there as part of the product. When you "beat" egg whites for a meringue, you are really whipping them.

Folding is a special technique for handling a whipped product so as to retain the air you have whipped into it. You would fold whipped egg whites into a mixture to make a soufflé, or dry ingredients into a sponge cake batter, for example, or whipped cream into a gelatin mixture to make a Bavarian cream.

Figure 3.17 illustrates some of the hand tools used in putting things together. Bowls are indispensable all-purpose utensils; stainless steel is the material of choice since it is light in weight and impervious to acid. Whips are used to beat, whip, and blend liquids and semiliquids; a mixture that is too thick will become enmeshed in the wires. Rubber spatulas are often used in folding, and

Figure 3-17 MIXING TOOLS AND UTENSILS

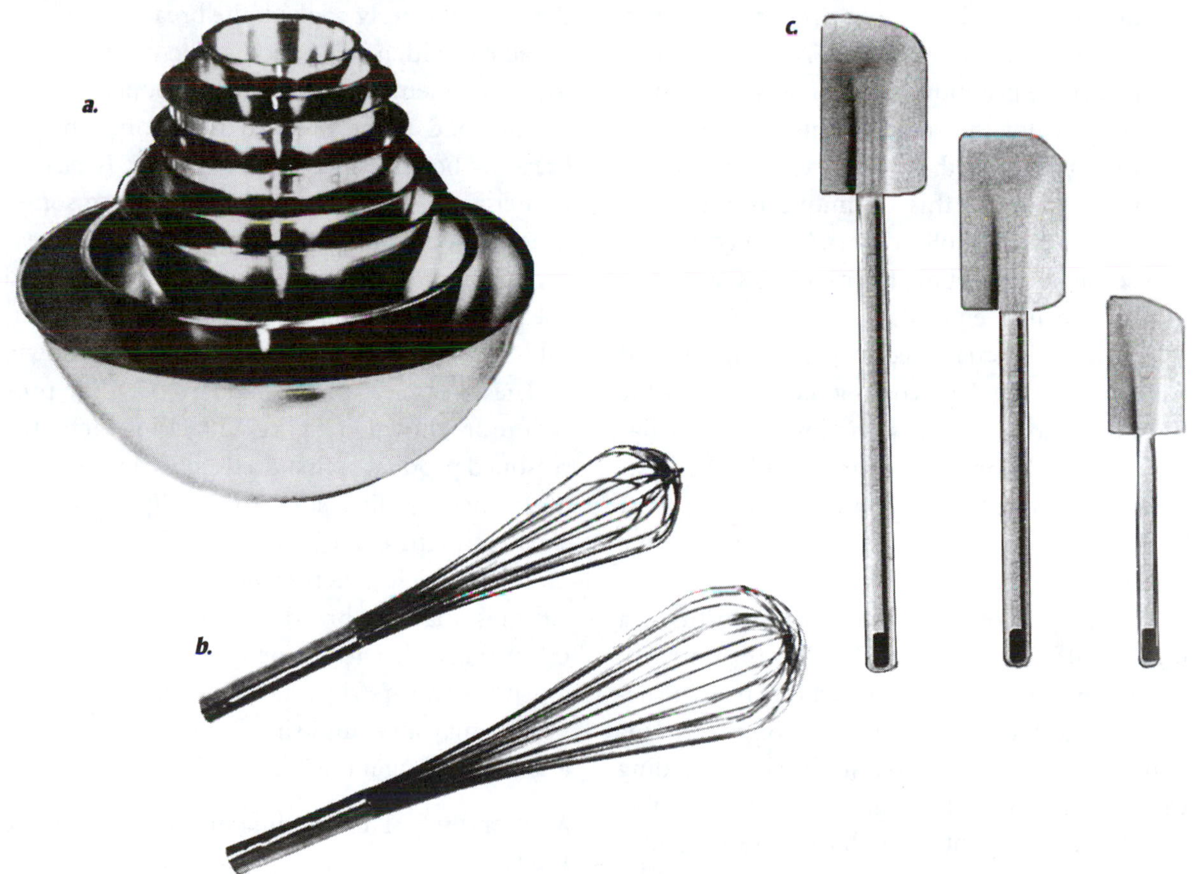

a. Round-bottomed stainless steel bowls. (Photo courtesy Bloomfield Industries.) ***b.*** Wire whips. (Photo courtesy Intedge Industries, Inc.) ***c.*** Rubber scraper/spatula. (Photo courtesy Rubbermaid Commercial Products.)

they are invaluable in scraping out the contents of containers. Mixing is also done by machine; the **power mixer** is one of the major workhorses of the quantity kitchen.

COATING

The term **coating** refers to covering a food with a layer of crumbs, meal, flour, or other fine substance before cooking it. There are several different ways of coating a food, notably dredging, breading, and battering. Let us examine these one at a time.

Dredging means passing a food through a fine dry or powdery substance in order to coat it. A number of different substances can be used—flour, cornmeal, almonds, and others. The key to dredging is not the substance used to coat but the way it is applied. Another term used commonly to describe this technique is rolling. A recipe may read, "Roll in flour," or in cornmeal, and so on. After rolling, the excess is shaken off, to produce an even coat.

Dredging is often used to prepare meats and fish for sautéing. The coating adds color to the finished product and is sometimes used for flavor, as with almonds or cornmeal. It is often seasoned. A dredged food cannot be held but must be cooked at once or the dry coating will become moist and soggy.

Dredging is often confused with dusting—a totally different process. Outside the kitchen, dusting is lightly removing particles from a surface. In the kitchen, it is just the opposite: It is lightly adding particles to a surface by sprinkling them on gently. In baking, we dust a worktable with flour to prevent a dough from sticking. And we dust corn fritters, French toast, and waffles with powdered sugar, mostly for appearance and for taste. Dredging is also confused sometimes with breading. It is, in fact, the first step of the breading process.

Breading is a three-step process of coating a food with crumbs or meal. It is applied to many kinds of foods—meats, vegetables, fish, poultry, croquettes. Breaded items are often baked or fried.

The coat of breading around a food does a number of things. It transmits heat from the fat to the food and keeps the food from absorbing the fat (the breading will absorb some fat). It forms a shield that helps the food stay moist and also allows the food to be seasoned without harm to the fat. It produces a crisp and crunchy texture that contrasts pleasantly with the softness of the food. Properly cooked, the breading adds an attractive golden color and its own pleasant taste to complement the taste of the product.

The food to be breaded is seasoned before breading begins, since there is no way to season it afterward. Seasoning and flavoring are sometimes added to the breading, but they will season or flavor only the breading and not the food itself. In addition, the seasonings may be harmful to the cooking fat, causing it to break down.

The three steps of the standard breading procedure are shown in Figure 3.18. Using tongs, the seasoned product is first dredged in flour (which helps the breading stick), then dipped in **egg wash** (a mixture of eggs and liquid), and then in crumbs (which give breading its golden color). Crumbs may be bread crumbs, cornmeal, or crushed cereal. The breaded items are then set in a pan to await refrigeration or final cooking.

This may all sound simple. But problems can arise in cooking if the breading is not done right.

✗ **Problem:** The breading may not stick to the food.

✓ **Solution:** To be sure the breading will stick, always follow these steps carefully:

Figure 3-18 STANDARD BREADING PROCEDURE

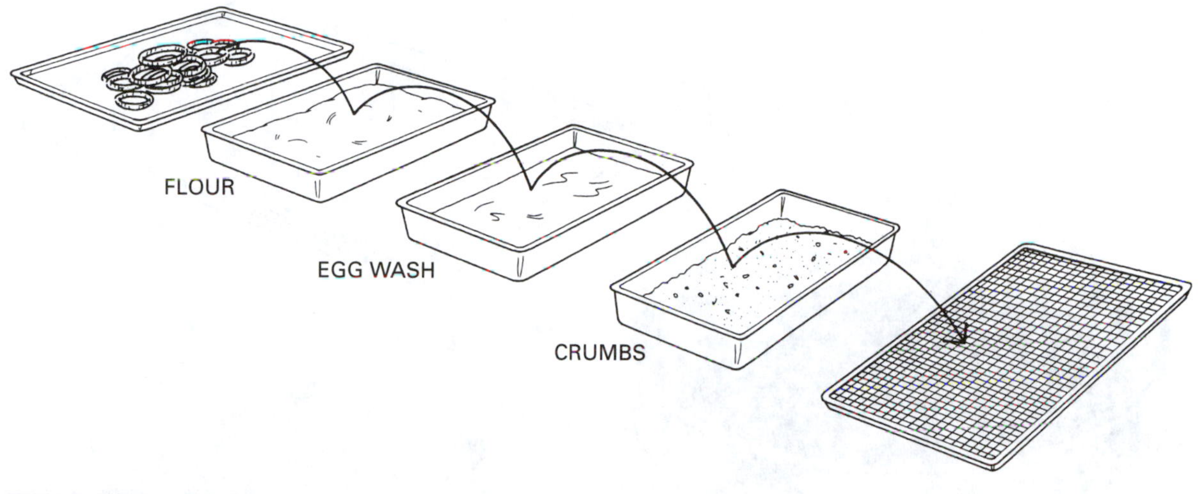

The right hand deals with the flour and crumbs. The left hand deals with the egg wash.

1. Dry the excess moisture from the food so the flour will stick to it readily.
2. Pass it through the flour, making sure it is completely covered; then shake off the excess. This gives a dry, even coat for the wash to stick to.
3. Dip it in egg wash. Again, make sure it is completely covered; then drain off the excess. This gives a wet, even coat for the crumbs or meal to adhere to.
4. Put the food in the crumbs, coat it completely, and shake off the excess.

A product carefully breaded in this fashion will not shed its coat in cooking.

✗ **PROBLEM:** The breading may cook golden brown before the product inside is cooked.

✓ **SOLUTION:** If the product is one that requires more than a short cooking time, precook it prior to breading. Chicken breasts may be precooked before breading.

✗ **PROBLEM:** The breading may crack during frying.

✓ **SOLUTION:** The breading will indeed crack if eggs alone are used. An egg wash, however, is not just beaten eggs; it is the eggs plus a liquid, usually in a ratio of 2 parts egg to 1 part liquid by volume. The milk or water that is added to the eggs will eliminate cracking.

✗ **PROBLEM:** The finished product may have a ragged appearance or have dark spots marring its golden coat.

✓ **SOLUTION:** You can achieve a uniformly good appearance by always using dried crumbs that are very fine. They will adhere evenly and cook evenly. Toasting or drying bread, crushing it, and running it through a screen (Figure 3.19a) makes fine crumbs.

The first time you attempt to bread something, you may find that your hands are getting as fully breaded as the product, and that you are getting egg wash in the crumbs and crumbs in the flour,

Figure 3-19 EQUIPMENT USED IN BREADING

These items also have many other uses. ***a.*** Fine-mesh strainer. (Photo courtesy Lincoln Manufacturing Company.) ***b.*** Sheet pans, full and half size. (Photo courtesy Commercial Aluminum Cookware Company.)

and that your temperature is rising. The secret of successful technique is to keep one hand dry for the flour and crumbs and to use the other hand only for the egg wash. If you are working from left to right, keep your right hand dry. If you go from right to left, keep your left hand dry. You should be wearing gloves.

In spite of good technique, your flour, egg wash, and crumbs may invade the wrong containers after a time. Then you can sift the flour, strain the wash, and sift the crumbs to restore them. Otherwise, your breading may lump.

Place your breaded items neatly on a sheet pan (Figure 3.19b) or rack in a single layer, so that they do not sweat or become soggy or stick to one another. If you must stack breaded items, put wax paper between the layers.

Breaded items may be prepared in advance of cooking and held in the cooler or frozen for future use. They should not be held at room temperature because they are likely places for bacterial growth. Very moist items, such as raw oysters or clams, should not be held because the breading will become soggy in no time.

A third way of coating a food to be cooked is dipping it in batter, or **battering.** A **batter** is a semiliquid—too stiff to be called a liquid and too fluid to be called a solid. It is often used with chicken, fish, and vegetables.

A batter usually consists of an egg-and-liquid mixture thickened with flour to achieve a smooth, rich consistency. Cornstarch may be added to batter to give a crisp and shiny finish coat, or a leavener (such as baking powder or beaten egg whites) may be added to make the product lighter. A recipe is given in Chapter 16.

The food to be cooked is battered by dipping it in the batter just before cooking. For good results, it is often dredged in flour first to give the batter a dry surface to adhere to.

The term battering is often confused with breading. Battering is used for the same kinds of foods as breading and performs the same functions, but the tastes and textures are different. Battered products cannot be held; they must be cooked immediately.

PRECOOKING AND PARTIAL COOKING

Processing often includes cooking. Depending on the food and the dish in which it is to be used, the cooking can be either total or partial.

In many instances, a food must be totally cooked before it is used in a dish—for example, the chicken for a chicken salad, the macaroni for macaroni and cheese, the hard-cooked egg in a Thousand Island dressing. Precooking may be carried out by any cooking process appropriate to the food.

Partial cooking refers to any cooking process that is stopped before the product reaches doneness. Any cooking method can be used. Common cooking methods used to partially cook foods include boiling (called **parboiling** when used to partially cook a food), steaming, and deep-frying.

Another method, called blanching, also partially cooks foods. **Blanching** means to drop a food briefly into boiling water (generally less than a minute) and then plunge it into cold water to stop the cooking. Raw vegetables are commonly blanched to kill the enzymes in them. Enzymes in vegetables cause them to discolor and also to deteriorate quicker. Vegetables to be used in a raw vegetable platter are blanched to improve their color and maintain their freshness longer. Blanching actually makes most vegetables much brighter in color.

Partial cooking is done for several reasons. It may be necessary in order to use the food in a recipe. For example, if a recipe calls for chopped tomatoes without skins, you can easily remove the tomatoes' skins by blanching them. Partial cooking may be a way of bringing a food to an equality with others, such as partially cooking a carrot that is going to share a soup with quicker-cooking celery and tomatoes. It may be a technique of preparing a food somewhat short of doneness in order to hold it for finish cooking. This is often done to save time during the serving period, when partially cooked foods may be finish-cooked quickly in batches as needed.

Partial cooking is also done to extend the **shelf life** (safe keeping time) of many items. Potatoes, for example, when peeled, deteriorate rapidly. Partial cooking slows deterioration and enables them to be stored in the cooler or freezer to prevent loss.

MARINATING

Another prepreparation process, marinating, has produced some of the most famous dishes in the world—sauerbraten from Germany, chicken tandoori from India, beef teriyaki from the Far East, shish kebab from the Near East. **Marinating** is soaking a food in a seasoned liquid (called a **marinade**) or applying a dry marinade, also called a **dry rub,** to add flavor or to tenderize it or both.

Liquid marinades are made from many ingredients, ranging from sour cream to peach brandy, depending on the particular flavor the cook wants to add to the dish. Vegetables, fruits, and meats are marinated with an infinite number of flavor combinations. The cook's choice will be guided by the preferences of the clientele.

A typical formula for a liquid marinade would be oil, flavor builders, and acid. Each of these ingredients has a specific purpose. The oil is a vegetable oil, used to help hold natural juices in the meat to avoid loss of the meat's own flavor. Flavor builders are such tastemakers as onion, garlic, spices, and herbs. The choice depends on the specific flavors desired. Acids, such as vinegar, lemon juice, or wine, are used to tenderize meats and poultry by breaking down connective tissue. Fish is naturally tender, so fish marinades are used for only a brief time to add flavor.

Marinating with a liquid can take a matter of minutes or it can take several days. It depends on the purpose and on the nature and size of the product. Cubes of meat for shish kebab need not be marinated as long as a pot roast. Game might be marinated a day or more because it lacks tenderness. Sauerbraten is sometimes marinated a week or longer. Whatever the length of time, it must be taken into account in planning for precooking readiness.

Marinating must be done in a container that is impervious to acid, such as stainless steel or glass. Don't marinate food in an aluminum container, because the aluminum will react with the acid in the marinade. Foods must be completely covered in marinade and kept refrigerated at proper temperatures. Finally, never use a marinade as a sauce unless you boil it for several minutes to kill any bacteria.

In addition to liquid marinades, there are dry marinades. A dry marinade is made of herbs and spices (and other seasonings), sometimes moistened with a little oil, and rubbed (or patted) on the surface of meat, poultry, or fish. Meat or poultry may be scored to allow the rub to penetrate more. The food is then refrigerated (to allow the flavors to be absorbed) and then cooked either with the rub still in place or with it scraped

Recipe 3-1 RUBS

a. Latin American Rub

YIELD: ***1 cup (250 mL)***

4 Tb	**ground cumin**	**60 mL**
4 Tb	**chili powder**	**60 mL**
2 Tb	**ground coriander**	**30 mL**
1 Tb	**cinnamon**	**15 mL**
1 Tb	**brown sugar**	**15 mL**
2 Tb	**salt**	**30 mL**
1 Tb	**red pepper flakes**	**15 mL**
2 Tb	**ground black pepper**	**30 mL**

1. Place all ingredients in a small bowl and stir well.
2. Store covered at room temperature.

b. West Indian Rub

YIELD: ***1 cup (250 mL)***

3 Tb	**curry powder**	**45 mL**
2 Tb	**ground cumin**	**30 mL**
2 Tb	**ground allspice**	**30 mL**
3 Tb	**paprika**	**45 mL**
2 Tb	**ground ginger**	**30 mL**
1 Tb	**cayenne pepper**	**15 mL**
2 Tb	**salt**	**30 mL**
2 Tb	**ground black pepper**	**30 mL**

1. Place all ingredients in a small bowl and stir well.
2. Store covered at room temperature.

c. Far East Rub

YIELD: ***1 cup (250 mL)***

4 Tb	**five-spice powder**	**60 mL**
4 Tb	**onion powder**	**60 mL**
2 Tb	**ground cloves**	**30 mL**
2 tsp	**garlic powder**	**10 mL**
2 Tb	**salt**	**30 mL**
2 Tb	**sugar**	**30 mL**
2 tsp	**ground white pepper**	**10 mL**
2 tsp	**ground coriander**	**10 mL**

1. Place all ingredients in a small bowl and stir well.
2. Store covered at room temperature.

off. Dry rubs are popular with meat, poultry, or fish that are grilled, broiled, or pan-fried. Some examples of dry rubs are given in Recipe 3.1.

HOLDING AND STORAGE

Now, what do you do with all the foods you have cleaned, cut up, breaded, partially cooked, pre-cooked, marinated, and otherwise preprepared while you are prepreparing other products? You hold or store them.

The terms holding and storage are often used interchangeably, but they actually have distinct meanings. Both refer to the keeping of food products, but the keeping is for different lengths of time and different purposes. **Holding** is the keeping of a food product for a short period before its intended use at a specific time. **Storage** is the keeping of a food product for future use for an unspecified period of time.

HOLDING

Holding usually applies to a food that has been partly or fully processed. For most foods, it is a matter of hours or minutes, though it may extend 24 hours or longer for such items as gelatin salads and hard-cooked eggs. Most foods are held right in the kitchen in equipment designed for this specific purpose. Foods may be held either cold or hot, a major difference between holding and storage.

Foods that are held cold may be fully prepared dishes ready for service, such as salads or cold hors d'oeuvres. Or they may be partially processed items awaiting further processing or cooking, such as peeled vegetables and fruits or breaded items or partially cooked foods awaiting finish cooking, or almost anything in process of preparation. Such products are held in the refrigerator or in special cold-food holding boxes, such as the airline caterer uses to deliver cold food to the plane.

Processed foods to be held should be well covered or wrapped to prevent their absorbing odors and flavors from other foods. They should be held at temperatures above or below the temperature danger zone (40–140°F). As you know, sanitation codes require cooked foods in refrigerators to be covered and separated from raw foods to avoid cross-contamination.

How long you can hold a processed food depends on the product and the processing. Good production planning will help you keep holding time to a minimum.

Peeled vegetables and fruits present special holding problems unless they are partially cooked. Most of them discolor rapidly when exposed to air. Potatoes are a familiar example. Eggplant probably holds the record for quick color change: The first slice of an eggplant can discolor before you cut the last one. Apples, peaches, pears, bananas, and avocados are among the fruits that behave this way.

Two things can be done to prevent discoloring:

- Rinse with an ascorbic acid solution or citrus fruit juice (for fruits only) before holding. A tablespoon of lemon juice to a quart of water will do the trick.
- Hold in water, immersing completely.

The best way to eliminate problems with peeled products is to schedule production carefully. Do not peel items far in advance of further processing or use. Refrigerate until used.

Fully prepared foods to be served hot must be held either below or above danger zone temperatures—that is, either in the refrigerator if serving time is hours away or in special hot-food holding equipment if serving time is approaching.

Several types of equipment keep foods hot for service. The **steam table** (Figure 3.20) is probably the most familiar. At the bottom of the steam table is water, which is heated to boil. The resulting steam keeps the food in the pans warm. The steam table forms the hot-food portion of a cafeteria serving line. Foods are placed into hotel pans, also called counter or steam table pans, that fit right into the steam table wells. Some operations use a dry service counter that heats electrically.

Another holding device is the **bain-marie** (ban-ma-ree). This hot-water bath is kept at a thermostatically controlled 180°F (82°C) to keep pots of sauce, soup, or stew above the bacterial growth range but not hot enough to cook them further and cause evaporation. Typical bain-marie pots are illustrated in Figure 3.21. Whereas steam tables tend to be used most often in the serving area, bain-maries are used more in the production area.

Today's kitchens also have **heated cabinets,** which are like ovens set at low heat. Similar to other hot-holding equipment, heated cabinets will not heat the food, but will, when preheated,

Figure 3-20 STEAM TABLE AND PANS

Hot foods are kept hot with steam from below. Pans of various sizes and depths fit the openings in the table exactly. An unused opening is covered, so that the heating temperature is maintained below the food. (Photo courtesy The Vollrath Company.)

Figure 3-21 BAIN-MARIE POTS

(Photo courtesy The Vollrath Company.)

maintain for short periods the temperature of the food as it was when it was placed in them. Heated cabinets may be mobile carts and trucks or stationary. They may even be built in between a cooking and serving area with doors on both sides, so foods are passed directly through to the serving area.

Other devices such as the **chafing dish** and the overhead **infrared lamp** keep hot foods hot on the buffet and on the kitchen serving line (Figure 3.22).

Most hot foods hold well on the steam table and in chafing dishes if treated properly. This means that moist foods must be kept moist and crisp foods crisp. To hold rice on a steam table, for example, put a thin layer of butter in the bottom of the pan before you put the rice in. This keeps the rice from drying out. Any moist food should have a source of continuing moisture or fat during its stay in a chafing dish.

Crisp foods, on the other hand, must be protected from moisture. Never cover a pan of fried chicken or any deep-fried food; it will quickly lose its crunch and become soggy.

STORAGE

Storage—keeping foods for future use for unspecified periods of time—may apply to products of any kind, raw, processed, or fully cooked.

The three main kitchen storage areas are the dry storage area, the refrigerator, and the freezer. The latter two are referred to collectively as cold storage.

The **dry storage area** is typically a clean, cool, dry, shelf-lined place near the receiving area. It is kept at 60 to 70°F (15–21°C) with humidity between 50 and 60 percent. The types of foods requiring this kind of storage include:

- Unopened canned and bottled goods
- Rice, dried beans, and peas
- Flour, cereals, and other grains
- Sugar, salt, dried herbs, and spices
- Breads
- Oils and shortenings

Dry foods should be stored off the floor. Containers should be clean and closed or tightly covered to prevent contamination from dust, insects, and rodents. New products are always

Figure 3-22 HOT-FOOD BUFFET SERVICE

a.

b.

a. A chafing dish with a hot-water insert and a cover keeps moist foods hot. Mini-burners maintain temperature. (Photo courtesy Legion Utensils Company.) ***b.*** Overhead heat lamps on this buffer server supplement heat from below. (Photo courtesy Crescent Metal Products.)

placed either behind or under existing supplies of the same product to ensure that the oldest will be used first. This is called **rotating stock** and is standard practice in all storage. Dating stock as it is shelved aids in efficient rotation and use.

A refrigerator, known in everyday terms in the kitchen as a **cooler,** holds and stores foods at temperatures of 32 to 40°F (0–4°C). There are many forms—walk-in, often referred to simply as "the walk-in," reach-in, pass-through—and many sizes.

The purpose of keeping foods in a cooler is to prevent bacterial growth and to maintain the texture, size, and weight of foods until use. Three factors in addition to temperature play a part: humidity, air circulation, and cleanliness. Since the texture, size, and weight of foods are greatly affected by their water content, the relative humidity in a cooler is usually 80 to 85 percent to keep the foods from drying out. Air circulation, provided by fans in all but smaller coolers, maintains even temperature and humidity throughout. Cleanliness is essential to prevent spoilage.

Ideal storage temperatures vary depending on the product. Fresh milk should be stored at 33 to 41°F (1–5°C). Meat products can be stored at temperatures between 32 and 41°F (0–5°C). Poultry can be stored at even cooler temperatures—between 30 and 36°F (−1–2°C). Seafood is more perishable than meat or poultry and should be stored at about 30°F (−1°C). Fresh produce does better at a warmer temperature of 41°F (5°C) so that there is no chance of freezing. Large operations will have separate refrigerators to maintain appropriate temperatures for different products.

Produce that has had no processing goes into the cooler for storage. Fruits and vegetables normally arrive cooled, packed in cartons or crates. These should be emptied promptly and the produce repacked into perforated plastic containers. Such containers assure good air circulation, which prolongs freshness. The repacking allows you to check product quality right down to the bottom of the crate or carton. Don't forget that just one rotten apple can spoil many others!

Meats, seafood, and poultry, both processed and unprocessed, should be covered or wrapped well to prevent drying. Store raw and processed products separately (see Chapter 2). Label with name, date, and quantity, and rotate the stock.

Storage of meats may play an important role in the cook's day-to-day food handling, not because of any special requirements but because of the high cost of meat. Losses from improper handling or storage are prohibitively expensive.

Cooked-on-premises foods of any kind must be stored separately from raw foods or commercially processed foods. Foods being held during prepreparation follow the same rules: Refrigerate covered and store separately.

It is important to keep the cooler door closed at all times—to keep the temperature constant, the air humid, and the circulation effective. For similar reasons, do not put large amounts of hot foods in a cooler but cool them quickly, using an ice bath, to room temperature first. Check temperatures when placing anything in the cooler and report variations to your supervisor.

The freezer is a special refrigerator kept at 0°F (−18°C) or below. The typical freezer is used primarily for storing foods already frozen, not for freezing from scratch. Freezing large quantities of foods takes special equipment and techniques.

Sometimes, partially cooked and otherwise processed foods are frozen to prepare for large banquets or to prevent high loss from spoilage. Most foods that have had some processing have a limited shelf life in the cooler—hours or days at most. The freezer can extend shelf life by weeks or months.

But using the freezer to extend shelf life is something you should do only if you must. Though the typical kitchen freezer will freeze foods, they do not keep as well as commercially frozen foods. Furthermore, freezing makes demands on the equipment that may affect its performance.

To freeze products properly, you must cover them tightly or, preferably, wrap them in plastic and/or foil to prevent **freezer burn**—white spots having off flavors and a pulpy texture that comes from loss of moisture. Label each item with name of product, date, and quantity. Package meat to be frozen in sensible units. Thawing a 50-pound pack of ground beef in a hurry can be frustrating. Avoid the necessity of freezing meats by good production planning.

Open the freezer door only when you must and never leave it open. It is essential to maintain a constant freezer temperature in order to preserve product quality. Never use the freezer to cool down a large pot quickly. Check the temperature whenever you put something in or take something out and report to your supervisor any reading varying from 0 to −10°F (−18 to −23°C).

KEEPING FOODS SUCCESSFULLY

We will have more to say about holding, storage, and shelf life in the chapters on specific kinds of foods. In the meantime, let us summarize the keys to successful holding and storage in the following rules:

- Know the product and its shelf life.
- Store and hold at safe temperatures—below 40°F or above 140°F (below 4°C or above 60°C).
- Cover or wrap all foods.
- Store and hold in clean, odor-free areas.
- Store raw, processed, and cooked foods separately.
- Label stored foods with name, date, and quantity.
- Rotate stock.
- Plan production carefully to minimize holding.

PLANNING YOUR OWN PRODUCTION

The overall task of planning the day's production is carried out by management. For their place in the scheme of things, cooks rely on the plans management has formulated. A **production worksheet** developed by the manager or supervisor becomes the tool of communication.

Production worksheets contain assignments for each cook. They may vary in format but they always include all the information necessary for production—the food, the quantity (usually given in number and size of portions), and the time. They will also contain any additional information that varies from day to day, such as place needed and style of service in an operation having several dining rooms. Figure 3.23 shows an example of a production worksheet.

Another common method of communicating production needs is the **function sheet,** sometimes called an event order. It is an order form for one-time special events, such as banquets and receptions, at which a specific group of guests is served a specific menu at a specific time and place. A completed function sheet contains all the data the facility needs to put on the party, including the information necessary for kitchen production.

Figure 3.24 is a typical function sheet. Notice the many kinds of information it includes. Not all of it is pertinent to the individual cook. Sometimes, you must look carefully for the facts that are important to you:

- Number of people
- Date of service

Figure 3-23 A PRODUCTION WORKSHEET

Production Sheet

Department Salad Date 4/15

Product	Number Portions	Portion Size	Type Function	Time Needed
tossed salad	200	6 oz	banquet	7:00 PM
shrimp cocktail	200	4 oz	banquet	7:00 PM
thousand island	200	1½ oz	banquet	7:00 PM
cocktail sauce	200	1 oz	banquet	7:00 PM
Plus daily setup for a la carte --- 250 lunch --- 325 dinner				

Special Instructions
Dressings and sauces to be added by waiters before service.

- Time of service
- Place of service
- Style of service
- Menu
- Special instructions

This method of communication is often used in hotels, clubs, and restaurants where special events are booked frequently. A copy of the original is given to each cook or department (and sometimes to both), so that nothing is garbled as

Figure 3-24 A FUNCTION SHEET

Event Order

Person Making Reservation: D. Jones Date: 3/11

Address: 3311 Park Ave

Date of Event: 4/15 Time of Event: 7:30

Type of Service: banquet Guarantee: 200

Billing Address: 3311 Park Ave Price/Person:

Room or Place of Event: Regency Person in Charge: D. Miller

Menu	Room Setup
Shrimp cocktail — Tossed salad Thousand island dressing — Roast sirloin of beef Berny potato Buttered asparagus — Orange sherbet Rolls Coffee Iced tea Open bar after dinner for meeting	 N Head Table 10 10 10 10 10 10 10 10 10 10 10 10 10 10 10 10 10 10 10 10
	Special Instructions and Equipment
	1) Have podium and sound equipment at head table. 2) Room decoration supplied by Jones Florist 3) Have two portable bars available for service during meeting after dinner. Should be available at 8:15. 4) Price $25.00/person + 16% grat. + tax Drinks $3.00 ea.

Items to be prepared by the salad department have been circled for attention.

it passes through channels, which can happen with verbal instructions or hand-copied information. The items the department or individual is responsible for may be underscored or circled.

The individual function sheet will not give you your schedule for a given production period. You may have to combine it with other instructions.

STEPS IN PLANNING

Even though worksheets may be supplied, each worker's setup—mise en place—is an individual responsibility. So is organizing one's own time in order to complete assignments and meet deadlines. The cook's part in precooking readiness, then, means setting up for maximum efficiency. Only if you spend time getting ready for a job can you do the job effectively.

There are several steps essential to a good production plan:

1. Gather all your information together. You need to know what is required in the way of products, amounts, preparation methods, equipment, style of service, and times needed.
2. Determine what supplies you need and how much you need of each and make out your requisition for the day.
3. Divide your tasks into subtasks and arrange these roughly in the order in which you will carry them out.
4. Working backward from your deadline for each product, make out a time schedule for your subtasks. Rearrange the order of subtasks if necessary.

PLANNING A STATION SETUP

A **station** is any area set up with supplies and equipment in order to complete a production job. It may be a fixed station such as a broiler station or a grill. It may be a temporary station such as two tables put together at which several people are preparing salads in assembly-line fashion. It may be an area of variable size that includes the slicer and the counter beside it. It may simply be the place you put your cutting board and the parsley you are going to mince and the dish to put it in as you mince it.

Any place in the kitchen that is set up to complete a particular task is a work station as long as it is so set up. The term station is also used, as you know, to describe specific areas of a particular kitchen layout—the salad station, the sauce station, the vegetation station, and so on.

Where and how you set up a work station depends on the specific task. You may set up several times in the course of one production assignment. If you are doing canapés, for example, you may set up once to make croutons, several times to make different spreads, again to make garnishes, and a last time to assemble the canapés on trays. Clearly, there is no one right way to set up that would satisfy all tasks.

There are, however, certain common elements in any setup that you must handle well in order to achieve efficiency. The two main considerations are:

- The flow of supplies from raw materials to finished product
- The motions you will make in production

In planning the flow of supplies, you need to establish a layout that includes an area for supplies, an area in which to work, a holding area, and a means of keeping these areas free of waste and dirty dishes. In à la carte cooking, you may also need a dish-out area. In a fixed production station such as a grill, these areas are already laid out. In other situations, you may lay out your own. In either case, you need to arrange your supplies and movable equipment in these areas in such a way that the supplies can flow into production and out again as finished products with a minimum of motion, like an assembly line in a factory.

In thinking through the motions you will make, consider both your hands and your body. You want to make as few movements as possible, reach as short a distance as possible, and use both hands cooperatively (each hand must know what the other is doing). Your body motions should be smooth, comfortable turns, with no bending or reaching in uncomfortable or tiring postures and no running back and forth. All your motions should expedite the flow of supplies.

To set up for slicing salami, for example, you will plan your supply area on the right side of the slicer, so that you can pick up your salami and place it on the slicer with a minimum of motion. To plan the salami arrangement, you need to decide where and how you will remove the casing, whether you will slice the whole salami or cut it in half first, and whether you will need both hands to place the salami on the slicer. Your work area will include the slicer itself plus a stack of trays for receiving the slices. Beyond this, you need a holding area for filled trays. To plan this holding area, you must know whether your slices go into someone else's production or into the cooler, and you must decide how to get them there with a minimum of time and motion. Your total setup will vary with the counter space available, the amounts needed, and the flow of the product after it leaves you. Figure 3.25 shows one solution.

To set up for making sandwiches in quantity, you have a whole series of supplies and motions to deal with and a large number of finished products to be plated, wrapped, or held. Again, your supplies and equipment must be arranged for a smooth flow. But before you can do this, you need to think through your motions very care-

Figure 3-25 FLOW OF SUPPLIES IN A PRODUCTION STATION

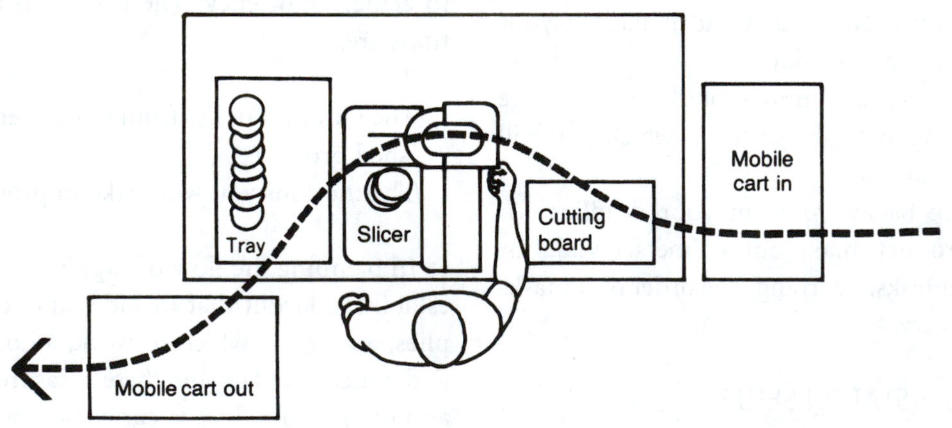

In this setup for slicing salami, the flow of supplies goes from the mobile cart on the right containing whole salamis, to the cutting board, where the salami is cut in half and the casing removed, to the slicer, to the holding tray, then to another mobile cart and out to another phase of production.

fully. What are the basic motions of making a sandwich? Will you use fewer motions if you make one sandwich at a time or several? If several, how many? Can you break down the motions into logical steps? How far can you reach to scoop up the filling or put a finished sandwich on a tray? How can you plan your motions so that you can use both hands to best advantage? How will you slice, plate, or wrap the sandwiches? How will you set up your supply and holding so that the bread stays moist and the tuna salad cold?

Sandwich production has been studied by efficiency experts and there are standard solutions for such problems. One of these is illustrated in Figure 3.26.

Setups for simple tasks are simple to plan, and if you keep in mind the two essentials—supply flow and motions of production—they will become almost automatic. In more complicated assignments that are new to you, the planning of your setup is well worth a detailed analysis of the task. The time you take to make a good plan will be saved in efficient production. In working out complicated or unusual setups, you can call on the experience of your supervisor for suggestions.

SETTING UP FOR À LA CARTE COOKING

In à la carte cookery, setting up is the key to production success or failure. A good setup depends on essentially the same elements and procedures as any other setup:

1. Efficient station layout for supplies, cooking, holding, and dish-out
2. Knowledge of production requirements
3. Analysis of the task and the motions necessary to complete the task in actual production
4. Efficient setup of supplies and equipment to facilitate these motions

Let's take a specific fixed station as an example and see how it can be set up to handle a hypothetical production requirement. Figure 3.27 is the broiler station of a steakhouse where several kinds of steaks—New York strips, filets, and top sirloins—are cooked à la carte to the specification of each guest. The workload is 350 to 400 steaks over a 3-hour period.

Step 1 is to examine the station layout. It is a fixed reality. Fortunately, the layout of this facility is an efficient arrangement that allows the supplies to flow smoothly from supply area (refrigerator) to work area (broiler) to holding area to dish-out. The cook's body motions can be limited to smooth turns to left or right. You will not need to cross your own path as you use different areas. You are in luck. In many facilities, stations were originally laid out for a different production goal. When the goal changes, the station has outlived its own efficiency, but the cook has to work with what is there.

Step 2 is to determine production requirements. Using your mental checklist, you establish the following:

- Product: 3 kinds of steaks (top, filet, strip) × 5 degrees of doneness = 15 possibilities for any one order
- Amount: 350–400 total
- Preparation method: grill
- Equipment: grill, refrigerator, tongs, plates for dish-out, area for holding until pickup
- Style of service: à la carte (random ordering)
- Times needed: random

Step 3 is to analyze the task and the motions of production.

Figure 3-26 HOW TO MAKE 24 SANDWICHES AT A TIME: MAXIMUM PRODUCTION WITH MINIMUM MOTION

a. Cut packages in half. Place cut side down on tray, leaving bread in wrappers until needed.

b. Taking four slices of bread in each hand, lay out two rows across of four slices each, a row at a time, dropping off the center slices first. Then pick up four more slices in each hand and complete two more rows for a square of 4 × 4 slices.

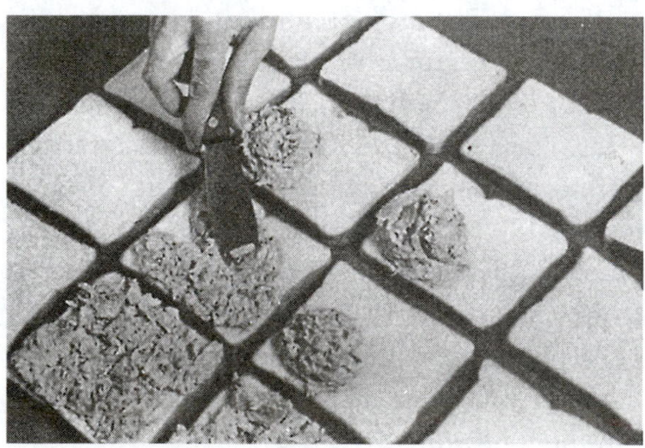

c. Place a scoop of sandwich filling in upper right corner of each of the eight center slices (left-handers place in upper left corner). Spread with S motion.

d. Using both hands, close sandwiches with bread slices from outside rows.

Repeat Step *b*, placing the center slices on top of the completed sandwiches; then repeat Steps c and d. Then do Steps *b*, *c*, and *d* again, so that you end with four stacks of three sandwiches each.

e. Cut each stack of sandwiches diagonally with a single downward stroke of the French knife. Steady the stack with your thumb and forefinger straddling the knife.

(Photo *c* by Patricia Roberts. Remaining photos and sandwich method courtesy American Institute of Baking.)

Figure 3-27 BROILER STATION FOR COOKING STEAKS TO ORDER

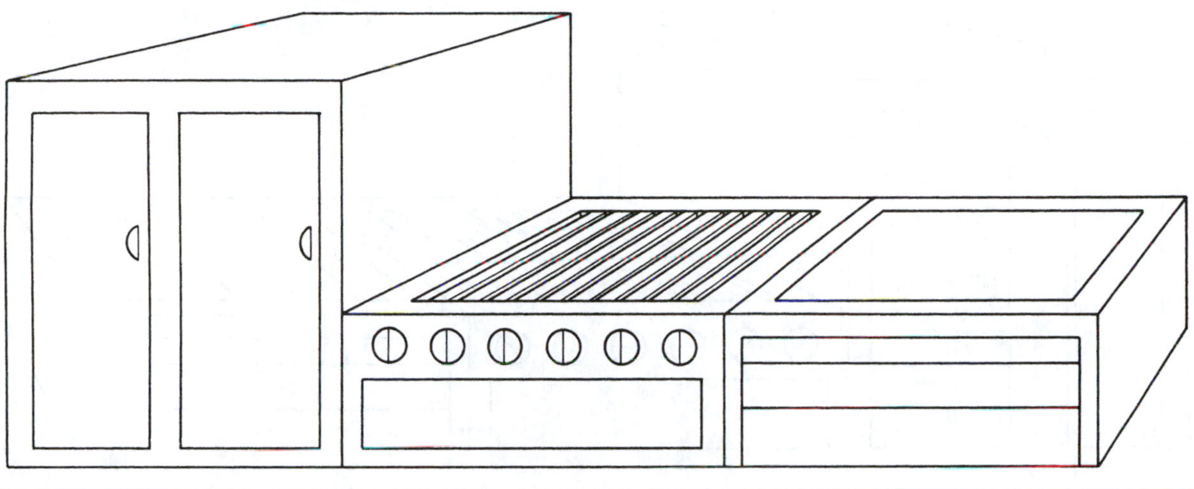

The flow of supplies moves from refrigerator (left) to grill to holding area (right).

The task is to cook the right kind of steak at the right time to the right degree of doneness and deliver it to the right order—400 times. As you can see, there are several real problems:

- Random timing of orders
- Random selection of products
- Varying degrees of doneness
- High volume

You cannot precook. You cannot time the cooking. It is out of the question to keep track of each individual order. The task is complicated.

Now, look at the motions of production. Reduced to their minimum, these are, for each order:

1. Remove steaks from supply area and put them on the grill.
2. Cook them.
3. Remove them from the fire and hold for pickup.
4. Serve them.

The motions of production are simple.

Step 4 is to set up supplies and equipment for efficiency. Efficiency = minimal error = the right kind of steak at the right time to the right degree of doneness for the right customer.

The secret is to set up so that all the cook has to do is concentrate on cooking steaks. No keeping track of which is which and for whom and when. There is a way to do this. If you divide the supply area into kinds of steaks, and the broiler and holding area into degrees of doneness, and place the steaks accordingly in each area, you don't have to keep track of anything. There will always be a steak of the right kind and doneness ready for pickup. It may not be the very steak you put on the fire when the order came in, but that does not matter.

Figure 3.28 shows the setup of each area. Here is the way you will use it. In the refrigerator, you separate the three kinds of uncooked steaks. There is no need to look around for a particular kind; you know exactly where it is. You put the highest-demand item in the easiest area to reach. This setup means that when a table order comes in you can simply reach in the refrigerator and

 SETUP FOR PRODUCTION

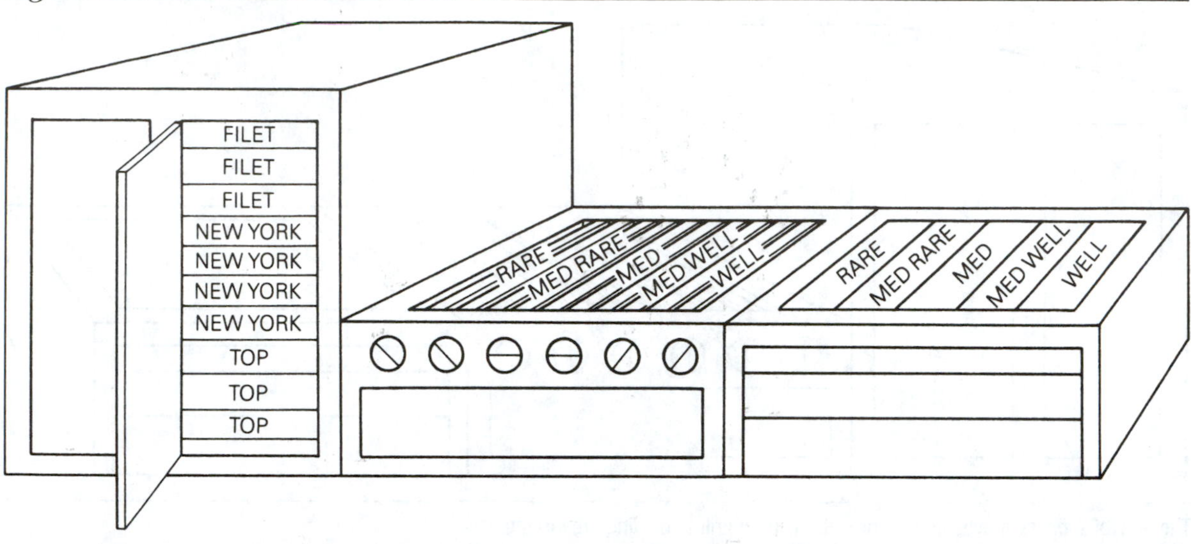

In the refrigerator, steaks are arranged on trays according to type, with the most ordered steak in the easiest-to-reach position.

On the broiler, degrees of doneness go in order from rare to well done. Note that the two left-hand controls are set at high for the rare steaks, the two middle controls are on moderate settings, and the right-hand controls are set on low for slow cooking of medium-well and well-done steaks. The system can work with any number of controls from two on up.

On the holding area, degrees-of-doneness areas are laid out in the same order. First-off-the-fire steaks are placed in the front of their appropriate row, with others lined up behind. Steaks are plated in first-in, first-out order when the server picks up.

get out the right kinds of steaks—two strips, one top, four filets, or whatever the order is—and put them on the fire.

You divide the broiler into five areas, one for each degree of doneness. You set the temperature controls for one end of the broiler on high heat for the rare steaks, the controls for the other end of the broiler on low heat for the well-done steaks, and the middle controls on moderate heat for medium steaks. You lay out your areas accordingly, with the medium rare between the high and moderate heats and the medium well between moderate and low. Now all you have to think about is putting each steak ordered on the right area of the grill as soon as it is ordered.

You cook all the steaks on the rare area to rareness, all the steaks on the medium area to medium, and so on. You do not need to keep track of the orders; whatever was ordered will be ready when the server comes to pick it up. You do not need to keep track of the kinds of steak; you can identify them by sight at pickup time. You just cook each steak on the broiler to the right degree of doneness for its broiler area, determining doneness by the feel method.

You also divide the holding area into degrees of doneness, arranged in the same order as the areas of the broiler. As each steak reaches the right degree of doneness for its area on the grill, you place it in the corresponding doneness section of the holding area. Within each section, you place the steaks in the order in which they are finished, so that the first steak done is the first served.

Any à la carte station has similar problems of random ordering, random timing, holding, and dish-out. Every station must be set up with the same attention to flow of supplies and economy of movement. In addition, many stations require considerable prepreparation. This is part of setting up the station, so that only finish cooking and assembly remain to be done in production. Whatever the station, the way you set it up—your mise en place—will determine whether you have smooth sailing or kitchen chaos.

SUMMING UP

Prepreparation means preparing everything ahead that can be done ahead, so that the final cooking at service time can be done without delay. Everything ready and in place—mise en place—is the goal.

The many tasks of prepreparation revolve around the cleaning, cutting, and processing of raw products. They require skill with the knife and careful operation of the kitchen's powerful machines as well as the ability to choose the right tool for the task. They also require knowing the precise meanings of kitchen terms and learning the techniques of blending, beating, whipping, folding, dredging, dusting, breading, battering, marinating, blanching, parboiling, and many more.

Holding and storage of preprepared foods constitute a critical stage of preparation for reasons of both sanitation and product quality. Successful holding of prepared products requires the correct use of holding equipment and, above all, the maintenance of safe temperatures.

The key to carrying out production tasks successfully is careful organization—finding out exactly what is needed, planning it carefully, and setting up your own mise en place. Not only do really skillful cooks know how to produce a quality product, they can do it with a minimum expenditure of time, motion, materials, and energy because they know how to organize their work. Some of the greatest achievements of great chefs and managers have stemmed from their ability to organize well prior to cooking. This is the essence of precooking readiness.

The Cook's Vocabulary

bain-marie
batonnet
batter, battering
beat
bind
blanching
blend
boning knife
breading
chafing dish
chop
coating
concasser
cooler
cut
dice (small, medium, large)
dredging
dry rub
dry storage area
egg wash
émincer
finish cooking
fold
freezer burn
French knife
function sheet

guiding hand
heated cabinet
holding
infrared lamp
julienne
marinade
marinating
mince
mise en place
mix
parboiling
paring knife
partial cooking
paysanne
peeler
power mixer
prepreparation
processing
production worksheet
purée
rotating stock
rough prep (prepping)
router
shelf life
slice
slicer
station
steam table
steel
stone (whetstone)
storage
tang
tourné
trueing the edge
utility knife
whip

Review Questions

Answer each question in complete sentences. Read each question carefully and make sure you answer all parts of the question. Organize your answer into more than one paragraph when appropriate.

1. Discuss the meaning and importance of mise en place and describe how you would apply it in preparing a specific recipe (pick one from this book).
2. How do cleaning procedures differ in preparing leafy vegetables, soft or fragile vegetables, and hard vegetables? Explain why.
3. Discuss the proper techniques in using the French knife and in sharpening and trueing knives.
4. Name the basic cuts with their dimensions and discuss the importance of careful, precise cutting.
5. Distinguish among the following terms: mix, blend, bind, beat, whip, and fold.
6. Describe the standard breading procedure and explain the differences between it and other coating procedures.
7. Within a cafeteria, where might you find a steam table, a bain-marie, a chafing dish, and an infrared lamp.
8. List six rules for keeping foods successfully.
9. To set yourself up to prepare anything in the kitchen, what questions should you consider.

Chapter 4

COOKING, EQUIPMENT, AND MEASUREMENT

Cooking is one of those everyday marvels like television and flying and the weather that are so commonplace no one thinks twice about how remarkable they are. Cooking makes all sorts of interesting transformations in raw foods to whet the appetite, delight the taste buds, and nourish the body. It softens some foods—the celery stalk, the potato, the grain of rice. It makes others firm—the egg, the cake batter, the meringue. It enlarges some things, such as popcorn, popovers, and soufflés; deflates some (spinach, for one); and makes others disappear altogether, like a liquid left forgotten on a hot burner or the alcohol in cherries jubilee.

Cooking changes colors—turns the brown lobster red and the red meat brown—and the green vegetable, too, if you cook it too long—and it changes butter from yellow to brown to black. It can bind foods together, as it does in sauces and cream soups and croquettes. It can break foods down—curdled milk, overheated hollandaise. It tenderizes flesh or toughens it, depending on how it is done. It can thin gelatin and thicken broth, liquefy fat and crystallize maple syrup. It makes some foods more nourishing by making their nutrients more available to the body, yet it can destroy other nutrients, such as vitamins. It can make foods safer to eat by killing disease-producing organisms. It does remarkable things with taste—blends and mellows flavors, heightens them, sometimes transforms them entirely, sometimes ruins them by burning, scorching, or just plain cooking too long.

How do such things happen? This chapter will lay the foundations for understanding at least some of them. We will also give you some nuts-and-bolts information about cooking equipment, weights, measures, and temperatures.

After completing this chapter, you should be able to:

- Define cooking and describe the three ways in which heat is transferred to a product.
- Explain how heat affects such food substances as proteins, carbohydrates, fats, vitamins, minerals, and water.
- Name and describe the various moist-heat and dry-heat cooking methods.
- Identify the major pieces of cooking and processing equipment, pots, pans, hand tools, and small equipment, and explain when each is used.
- Measure by weight, volume, or count.

- Use equivalent measures.
- Recognize common abbreviations in recipes.
- Measure temperatures.
- Recognize basic metric measurements.

THE COOKING PROCESS

The changes just mentioned all come about through a single process—applying heat over a period of time. That is what cooking is: bringing about a change in a food product by the application of heat over a period of time. The overall purpose of cooking is to make the food more edible. Speaking in the language of the kitchen, we say we are increasing its palatability.

Notice that two things are necessary in cooking to bring about change: heat and time. You will find that many specific cooking techniques have to do with the interplay of these two factors: the length of time and the degree of hotness, or the temperature.

When we talk about cooking temperature, we are usually talking about the temperature of the cooking medium—the fat in the fry kettle, the air in the oven, the water in the pot. The real purpose, of course, is to raise the temperature of the food itself to the point where the desired change will take place. This is what takes time. The lower the temperature of the cooking medium, the longer it takes to bring about change.

HOW HEAT AFFECTS FOOD

In addition to temperature and time, the makeup of the food itself is a determining factor in the changes cooking brings about. Foods are made up of varying combinations of the following components:

- Carbohydrates
- Fat (and fat-related substances)
- Proteins
- Vitamins and minerals
- Water
- Pigments and flavors

Each of these components, except pigments and flavors, is a nutrient. **Nutrients** are the nourishing substances in food that provide energy (measured in calories) and promote the growth, maintenance, and health of your body. One of the goals of good cooking is to conserve the nutrient values of foods.

These different components of foods react in certain distinctive ways to the heat of cooking. If you understand these reactions, you can control the changes and obtain the results you want.

CARBOHYDRATES

Carbohydrates include starches, sugars, and fiber. They are found mainly in plant foods such as cereal grains, vegetables, dried beans and peas, and fruits; in products made from cereal grains such as flours and cornstarch; in milk; and in refined sugar products such as granulated sugar and sugar syrups.

Nutritionally, starches and sugars are the body's main sources of energy. Those from whole foods (foods as we get them from nature), such as fruits and vegetables, contain many other nutrients, while foods high in refined sugar are often said to contain "empty calories." Empty calories means that these foods contribute few nutrients for the number of calories they contain. On the menu, starches and sugars appear in appetizers as soups, in entrées as pasta, in side dishes as vegetables, in desserts as puddings, to give a few examples.

In cooking, heat affects the three types of carbohydrates in different ways. With starches, the most important change that heat brings is **gelatinization.** This is the process by which dry starch granules (flour, cornstarch, etc.) absorb moisture in the presence of heat, thickening and binding the food with which they are mixed. This is an important part of making soups and sauces, and it also plays a role in baking. You will understand gelatinization better when we deal with these products. Acid can affect this process, too: Adding lemon juice, tomato, or wine can result in a thinner product unless it is added at the end after gelatinization is complete.

The most important change heat brings to sugar is **caramelization.** High temperatures will cause chemical changes in sugars that alter their flavor and color, turning them brown. The heat must be dry: If water is present, the sugars will dissolve, and because they are then limited by the boiling point of water they cannot reach high enough temperatures to caramelize until most of the water has evaporated.

Sugar can be caramelized by itself, or the sugar contained in a food product can be caramelized, as in the browning of baked goods and the caramelization of sugar in browned onions and hash brown potatoes. Similar browning occurs in meats seared or sautéed at high temperatures.

Fiber is the substance that gives structure and texture to fruits, vegetables, and grains. The effect of heat on fiber in the presence of moisture is to soften it. This will make it more palatable, up to a point. However, a certain firmness of texture is often desirable. One of the marks of the skilled cook is the ability to produce the exact texture desired in cooked fruits, vegetables, and such starchy foods as pasta and rice.

Besides heat, sugar and baking soda can also affect fiber. Whereas sugar tends to keep fiber firm, baking soda makes fiber mushy. This is why baked apples made with sugar keep their shape better than those made without sugar, and also why vegetables cooked with baking soda become very soft.

FATS

The word **fat** is truly an all-purpose word. We use it to refer to the excess pounds we carry, the blood component that seems to cause heart disease, foods such as butter and margarine, and the nutrient that provides energy to the body and plays an essential role in its functioning. But fats can also be health hazards. Too much fat in the diet, especially saturated fat (animal fats, butter, whole milk), is associated with two health problems: heart disease and cancer.

Fats and oils contain more fat than any other foods. A fat is typically solid at room temperature, while an oil is liquid at the same temperature. Solid fats include butter, margarine, and shortening. Oils are generally extracted from vegetables such as soybeans, corn, olives, and nuts. Fat is also found in meats, poultry, seafood, dairy products, nuts and seeds, egg yolks, sauces, condiments, baked goods, desserts, and snack foods.

As temperatures increase, fats will eventually break down—undergo chemical change. This change becomes visible when they begin to smoke. The smoke point differs for different kinds of fats. Most fats can reach much higher temperatures than water can. The fat in the fry kettle often cooks at 375°F (191°C), whereas water does not go above its boiling point of 212°F (100°C).

In foods, fats enhance taste, flavor, aroma, crispness (especially in fried foods), juiciness (especially of meat), and tenderness (especially in baked goods). Fat provides a smooth texture and a creamy feeling in the mouth. Eating a meal with fat makes you feel full because fat delays the emptying of the stomach.

PROTEINS

Proteins are an essential part of all living cells found in animals and plants. The protein found in animal and plant foods is such an important substance that the term "protein" is derived from the Greek word meaning "first." Nutritionally, proteins are the major building and maintenance materials of the body.

Protein is found in both animal and plant foods, although it is more plentiful in animal foods, including meat, poultry, seafood, dairy products, and eggs. Of the plant foods, grains, legumes, and nuts have more protein than vegetables and fruits.

In cooking, heat causes proteins to **coagulate**—that is, to become firm, join together. You can see this happen before your eyes if you fry an egg over low heat: The transparent liquid becomes white and opaque as the heat reaches it. If you cook it too long or at too high a temperature, it toughens—becomes too firm. The same thing happens when you cook meat: As the temperature of the product increases, the protein firms. Overcooking will make the meat tough.

If you heat milk too rapidly or too long, its protein will coagulate into a solid (called curds) and separate from the liquid (called whey), and we say it has curdled. This will spoil your soup, sauce, or custard. Cheese, which is made from milk curd, reacts to high or prolonged heat by quickly becoming tough, stringy, and unmanageable.

Connective tissue in meats is formed of certain kinds of protein that are naturally tough. The type known as collagen can be broken down and changed into gelatin by cooking at low temperatures with moisture. Acids can also soften meat fibers to some extent, as in marinating (Chapter 3). On the other hand, acid can reinforce the coagulation process. Adding vinegar to the water in which eggs are poached makes a firmer, more compact, and shapely product.

VITAMINS AND MINERALS

Vitamins and **minerals** are minute components in food that are essential for growth and good health. Some vitamins and minerals are easily lost in cooking. Some vitamins and all minerals are water soluble and may be thrown out with the cooking liquid. Some vitamins are also sensitive to high or prolonged heat. Minimizing nutrient loss during cooking is among the most challenging of cooking problems. Cooking methods that cook fast and use little or no water (such as steaming) are good choices to retain nutrients.

WATER

Water is the major ingredient in most foods. Fresh raw meats, fruits, and vegetables are at least 70 percent water; some fruits are as much as 96 to 98 percent water. The water in a food contains much of its flavor and many of its nutrients.

The effect of heat on the water in foods is very important in cooking them and in the finished product. The water in a food does a good deal of the cooking by conveying heat throughout the product. Moisture also helps to soften certain tough connective tissues in meat, as noted earlier.

On the other hand, the heat of cooking causes the product to lose moisture, and with it can go flavor, nutrients, and the moist, tender texture that makes food appetizing.

PIGMENTS AND FLAVORS

Heat also brings about chemical changes that affect both color and flavor in foods. This becomes a problem particularly in cooking vegetables. Good cooking techniques can help to retain the natural colors and flavors in foods, as we shall see later.

We will examine all these effects of heat on foods as we discuss the preparation of various food items in later chapters.

HEAT TRANSFER

How does the cook apply heat to a food to raise its temperature and bring about change? Heat can be transferred to food in three ways: by conduction, by convection, and by radiation.

CONDUCTION

Conduction is the transfer of heat from something hot to something touching it that is cooler. For example, heat from the fire passes to a pot; the pot conducts heat to liquid contained in it; the heated liquid conducts heat to any food submerged in it—a vegetable, an egg, a lobster.

Conduction also takes place within food: The eggshell in the hot liquid conducts heat to the egg; the outer portions of the egg—or of any food—conduct heat to adjacent portions, so that heat is transferred continuously within it. The fat in the fryer conducts heat to the breading, which conducts heat to the breaded food. The larger the product, the longer it takes for heat to be transferred to the center.

CONVECTION

Convection is the spread of heat by a flow of hot air or steam or liquid. This flow may be either natural or mechanical. In a pot of liquid, for example, the liquid at the bottom nearest the fire is heated first. As it is heated, it becomes lighter and rises to the top. The cooler, heavier liquid sinks down, becomes heated in turn, and rises. In this way, a naturally circulating current of hot liquid is set up throughout the pot. The same kind of natural convection current occurs in the air of an oven or in the steam of a covered pan or steamer.

In mechanical convection, the circulation of the heated air or steam or liquid is maintained mechanically. In a convection oven, for example, fans force the heated air to flow to and around the food, and vents carry off the cooler, moister air. When the term convection is used in the kitchen, it usually refers to this type of convection.

RADIATION

Radiation is the transfer of heat through energy waves radiating directly from a heat source to the food, in the same way that your skin is sunburned by the sun's rays. In radiation, the food to be cooked is exposed directly to the energy waves from the heat source. Two kinds of radiation in the commercial kitchen include **microwave radiation** and **infrared radiation.**

Inside the microwave oven is a magnetron that converts electrical power into high-frequency energy waves called microwaves. These waves penetrate the food placed in the oven, causing the water molecules in the food to vibrate. This creates heat and cooks the food without heating the oven itself. Although heat is produced directly in the food, microwave ovens do not cook food from the inside out. Microwaves penetrate the food only about 2 inches (at best) so the outside layers get hot first. The center of the food cooks by conduction of the heat from the outside to the inside. Microwaves penetrate the food to the depth of about half an inch on dense foods and up to two inches on liquids.

Infrared radiation is given off by an electric element or a gas-heated element, as found in some broilers and grills. The elements become so hot that they give off infrared radiation, which actually cooks the food.

Probably the most important consideration in applying heat in cooking is whether the heat is moist or dry. Cooking methods in which heat is provided by water-based liquids or steam are called moist-heat methods. The remaining methods are called dry-heat methods because water is not the vehicle providing the heat. Dry-heat methods use hot air, hot metal, hot fat, or radiation to cook foods. The type of method used has a profound effect on what happens during cooking and how the product turns out.

In this chapter, we will examine both groups of cooking methods and define precisely the term that is attached to each individual method. Only when you learn a term's exact meaning can you translate it into action properly.

MOIST-HEAT COOKING

All moist-heat cooking methods involve water, a water-based liquid, or steam as a vehicle of heat transfer. Among these methods are boiling, simmering, poaching, steaming, and braising.

COOKING IN THE POT: BOILING, SIMMERING, POACHING, REDUCING

Several methods of cooking take place in a pot of liquid. They stem from the ancient practice of cooking over the open fire—in the primitive cook's clay pot; the earthen, bronze, and silver vessels of the Greeks and Romans; the medieval iron pot hung on a hook in the fireplace; the great cauldrons of manor and castle with legs to straddle the fire. Consider the following definitions:

Boil To cook food submerged in a boiling liquid or to cook the liquid itself at a boil. A boiling liquid is in turmoil, its surface agitated and rolling. Water and most other cooking liquids, except liquid fat, boil at 212°F (100°C) at sea level.

Simmer To cook food submerged in liquid just below a boil or to cook the liquid itself, at temperatures of 180°F (85°C) to just short of the boiling point. A simmering liquid has bubbles floating slowly from the bottom to the surface. There is some action in the liquid, but it is not agitated, as in a boil, and the surface is fairly quiet.

Poach To cook food submerged in liquid at a temperature of roughly 160 to 180°F (71–82°C). A liquid at this temperature will have bubbles on the bottom of the pot, but they will tend to stay there and not disturb the body of the liquid.

In all these methods, the temperature range is the most important factor. You don't measure the temperature; you tell how hot it is by the way the liquid behaves. Figure 4.1 shows the characteristic behavior patterns.

Above sea level, the temperature of water at the boiling point drops in proportion to the altitude, at a rate of 1°F for every 550 feet above sea level (1°C for every 300 meters). This means that it takes longer to cook something at a boil in the mountains than it does at a seaside resort. Poaching and simmering temperatures will also produce more action in the water at high altitudes than at sea level.

Figure 4-1 POACH, SIMMER, BOIL

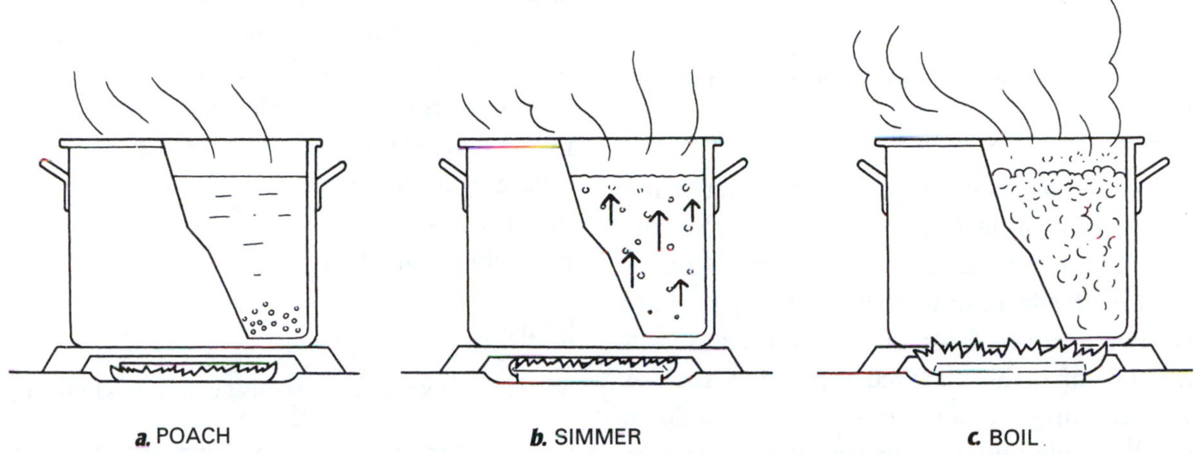

a. Bubbles on the bottom of a pot of liquid that is otherwise calm indicate a temperature suitable for poaching. **b.** Bubbles rising from the bottom, barely breaking the surface, indicate simmering temperatures. **c.** A liquid that is agitated throughout and has a vigorously bubbling or rolling surface is at the boiling temperature of 212°F (100°C).

Turning up the heat does not make a boiling liquid any hotter at any altitude. The boiling point is the temperature at which the liquid turns to vapor, and boiling it harder simply makes it evaporate faster.

Boiling is seldom used as a cooking method, except for starches and certain vegetables. The lower temperatures and gentler action of simmering and poaching produce much better results and give the cook greater control. The boiling point, however, is very useful. It is customary in many instances to bring a liquid to a full rolling boil and then turn the heat down until the liquid reaches the desired degree of action. The rolling boil does two things: It brings the full pot to the same temperature throughout, and it provides a point of departure from which to turn the heat down to maintain a lower temperature. Sometimes, getting the right degree of action in the pot takes several adjustments. Adding a food to the liquid lowers the temperature and the action, and heavy pots and electric heating coils respond slowly to change.

Many foods are cooked at a simmer—vegetables, shellfish, stews, soups, sauces. Poaching is used for shelled eggs and the delicate flesh of fish, which cook quickly even at low temperatures and retain their shape better in a calm liquid. Boiling is used mainly for pastas; with this product, the vigorous action of the liquid keeps the strands of pasta from sticking together.

Boiling and simmering are also used as processing techniques for partial cooking. The last chapter discussed two such techniques—blanching and parboiling. Each are done at a simmer. Though blanching begins at a boil, the entry of the food to be blanched reduces the temperature immediately. A food to be parboiled may be started in cold water and brought to a simmer or it too may be plunged into boiling water and the heat adjusted to maintain a simmer.

Still another technique that uses boiling or simmering is reducing:

Reduce To boil or simmer a liquid down to a smaller volume.

In reducing, the simmering or boiling action causes some of the liquid to evaporate. The purpose may be to thicken the product or to concentrate the flavor or to do both. A soup or sauce is often simmered for one or both reasons. A mixture of highly flavored ingredients such as wine or vinegar and spices may be boiled down to a few tablespoons of concentrated flavor to be added to a sauce—one of the few uses of boiling. The resulting product is called a reduction. Sauces are often thickened by reducing rather than by thickening agents.

STEAMING

The steam or vapor created by a boiling or superheated liquid captured in an enclosed space provides another moist-heat cooking method.

Steam To cook foods by exposing them to steam, either with or without pressure.

Steaming is a good method for cooking vegetables; it helps them retain flavor, color, texture, and nutrients.

In this method, steam is the heat conductor. When steam is under pressure, the temperature is hotter than a water-based liquid can ever be. Water will not get hotter than 212°F (100°C) no matter how hard you boil it. But steam under pressure of 5 psi (pounds per square inch) reaches 225°F (107°C) or more, and at 15 psi, it will be 250°F (121°C). Therefore, steam cooking under pressure is considerably faster than cooking in liquid. Also, keep in mind that steam carries more heat than boiling water, so it cooks quicker.

Food may also be steamed when it is tightly wrapped so that it cooks in steam made by its own water content. Steaming a food wrapped in foil or parchment paper is referred to as **en papillote** (on pap-eeyote). Fish are sometimes steamed this way. A "baked" potato wrapped in foil is also steamed—cooked by its own moisture.

BRAISING

Still another kind of moist-heat cooking is braising.

Braise To cook food until tender with a small amount of liquid in a covered container, usually after browning.

Braising falls somewhere between simmering and steaming. Up to two-thirds of the food is immersed in liquid. The rest is bathed in hot, vapor-filled air inside the pot. Steam, condensation, hot air, and simmering liquid all play their part. In the braising of some poultry and fish dishes, no liquid is added, and the foods steam in their own moisture and the moisture of other ingredients, such as vegetables.

Braising is particularly appropriate for less tender cuts of meat because long cooking with moist heat can soften tough meats, bringing many flavorful meats within the range of palatability. Stews, pot roasts, and sometimes vegetables are among the dishes prepared this way. Meats are usually browned first; vegetables may, or may not, be lightly sautéed first. Braising may be done in a covered container in the oven, on the range, or in a covered steam-jacketed kettle or tilting fry pan.

THE MANY ROLES OF LIQUIDS

In all the moist-heat methods of cooking, the moisture or liquid does a great deal more than simply conduct heat to a product. It interacts with the food being cooked in ways that can influence the final taste and texture. It softens not only the collagen of meats but the cellulose of vegetables. On the other hand, moist heat can have negative effects. It can rob vegetables of vitamins, flavor, and color unless carefully managed, and it can leach flavor from meats. If you cook a turkey wrapped in foil, it will be practically tasteless.

A cooking liquid can play an important part in the flavor of a dish. You can enhance the flavor of a product by adding herbs and spices and wine to the cooking liquid, as in simmering shrimp and poaching fish and chicken. If the liquid is to become part of the finished dish, as it does in soups and sauces, you build in the flavor very carefully to produce the final taste you want.

Vegetables and meats will give up flavor to liquid in which they are cooked. You can often use the liquid as stock in making a sauce or a soup. Many dishes depend for their success on the right balance between liquid and product, the length of time they stay together, and the right temperature for bringing about a happy ending.

DRY-HEAT COOKING

Dry-heat cooking methods transfer heat without the use of water or steam. They rely on hot air, radiation, hot metal, or hot fat.

COOKING WITH HOT AIR OR RADIANT HEAT

Consider the following definitions:

Bake To cook by heated air in an enclosed area, usually an oven. The term typically applies to pastries, cookies, breads, certain vegetables, and casseroles. It does not apply to braised dishes that are cooked in the oven in covered containers.

Roast To cook by heated air, usually in an enclosed space such as an oven or barbecue pit (note the similarity to baking). The food is not covered.

The term roasting nearly always refers to meats, poultry, and fish. Some oven-cooked meats are said to be baked—ham, fish, meat loaf—though the cooking method is the same as roasting. Meats and poultry are normally roasted on a rack to allow for maximum air circulation and to avoid having the meat cook in its own juices. Foods being roasted need to be turned around in the oven from time to time to allow for more even cooking. Most ovens have spots where they are cooler (usually by the door) and spots where they are hotter (usually in the back).

Roasting also applies to cooking on a revolving spit before an open fire, hardly a common method in industry today but the way everything was roasted for several thousand years. Spit-roasting is a radiant-heat method.

Barbecue A special dry-heat method in which heat is created by a wood fire at the bottom of an oven or barbecue pit.

In commercial kitchens, wood fires are not exactly practical, so some cooks use smoke ovens. Smoke ovens are conventional ovens with a special component that heats wood chips so they smoke, but don't burn. Foods cooked in smoke ovens can't truly be considered barbecued, but it's almost impossible to taste the difference.

Broil To cook with radiant heat from above.

Broiling is a high-heat cooking method that cooks foods quickly. Steaks, chicken, fish, and certain vegetables (such as onions, zucchini, and tomatoes) are all foods that are commonly broiled. Broiling can be tricky, because the heat is quite intense. Thick pieces of food need to be cooked further from the heat than thin pieces so as not to overcook the outside. Thin pieces cook quickly, especially those that are to be cooked rare, and can be placed closer to the heat. Like the oven, the broiler must be preheated.

Grill To cook on an open grid with heat from below, also a radiant-heat process.

Grilling is often incorrectly called broiling. Figure 4.2 illustrates the difference between the two processes.

Figure 4-2 BROIL, GRILL

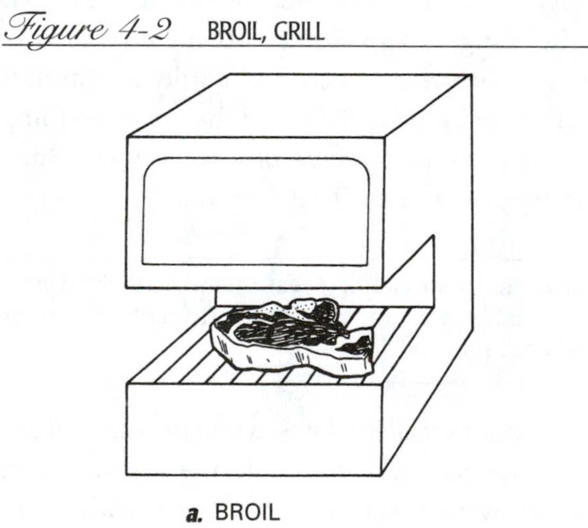

a. BROIL

a. Cooking by direct heat from above is broiling.

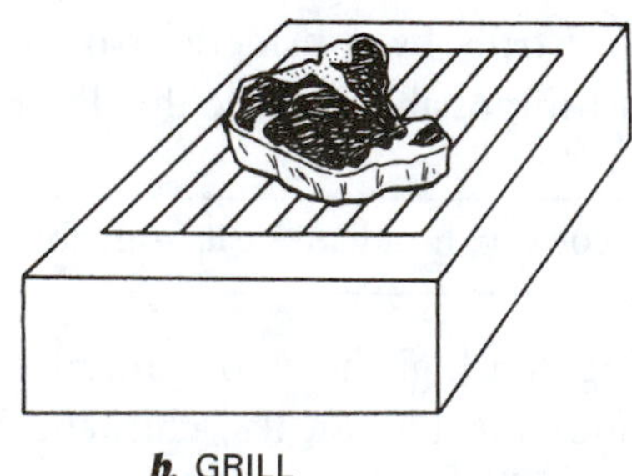

b. GRILL

b. Cooking by direct heat from below is grilling.

The term grill is also loosely used to mean cooking such items as hamburgers or pancakes on a griddle, which is often called a grill. This method of cooking is not grilling in the true sense. Many cooking professionals refer to cooking on a griddle as **griddling.**

Pan-broil To cook uncovered in a sauté pan or skillet without adding any fat or liquid. Fat is drained off as it accumulates.

Pan-broiling is similar to griddling, except that it is done in a sauté pan or skillet.

Dry-heat methods are used when some drying action is desired, as in baking, or when the effect of a moist environment is not needed or wanted, as in the cooking of tender, flavorful meat or poultry. Large tender cuts of meat and tender whole birds are usually roasted. Steaks and chops are usually broiled; chicken and some kinds of fish also broil well. Broiling or grilling are often the methods of choice for quick cooking of poultry, fish, and tender meats.

COOKING WITH FAT

The cooking methods generally called frying are classified as dry-heat methods. To fry is to cook food in hot fat. It includes the following methods:

Sauté To cook food quickly in a small amount of hot fat in a pan over high heat.

Pan-fry To cook food in a small to moderate amount of fat in a pan over moderate heat.

Deep-fry To cook food submerged in hot fat.

At first glance, you might think that frying is a moist-heat method, since the medium that conducts heat to the food is a liquid. Fat, however, does not contain moisture. Moreover, it does not interact with the food in the way that liquids do in moist-heat cooking. Fat may become part of a finished product by being absorbed in the food's coating, but in good fat cookery the temperature is kept hot enough for the food to cook quickly with a minimum of fat absorption. A greasy product is never desirable.

Frying in all its forms is a quick cooking process suitable for small tender foods, such as eggs, fish, chicken pieces, chops, and soft vegetables, or for foods partially cooked by some other method, such as deep-fried potatoes or croquettes made from cooked chicken. It is not a suitable method for large products or foods needing long, slow cooking.

Now, let's look at the ways in which the various frying methods differ.

Deep-frying, pan-frying, and sautéing differ in the amount of fat used. In deep-frying, the food is totally surrounded by hot fat. In pan-frying, a small to moderate amount of fat is used. In sautéing, little fat is used.

In deep-frying, the food is exposed to heat on all sides at once and cooks quickly and evenly. In pan-frying and sautéing, it must be turned or flipped to expose all sides to the hot fat.

Pan-frying differs from sautéing in several ways. One is a time and temperature difference: Sautéing is done quickly at high heat, while pan-frying uses moderate heat and slower, more deliberate cooking. Another difference is that pan-frying is generally used for larger pieces of food such as fish fillets or chicken pieces, while sautéing cooks smaller, equal-sized pieces of food, such as thin slices of veal or beef or vegetables, in a smaller amount of fat.

Perhaps the most interesting difference is that pan-frying is a quiet process that takes little of the cook's attention, and sautéing is an active process demanding the cook's full participation. To pan-fry, the cook places the foods in the hot fat and they cook by themselves until they are ready to be turned. To sauté, the cook adds the foods to sizzling fat and then shakes the pan back and forth vigorously to keep them in motion. By

Figure 4-3 PAN-FRY, SAUTE

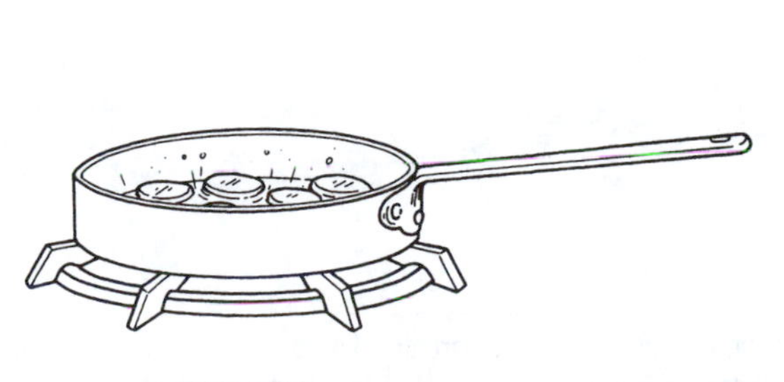

a. PAN-FRY

b. SAUTÉ

a. Pan-fried foods are cooked quietly and fairly slowly in fat over moderate heat. ***b.*** Sautéed foods are flipped quickly in hot fat.

using long strokes that send the food pieces to the far rim, the cook can flip them over with a slight upward movement. Figure 4.3 shows the difference in the two methods. (The French word *sauter* also means to leap, jump, hop, skip.) Both sautéing and pan-frying are often used as partial-cooking processes.

Dry-sauté To cook food quickly with little or no added fat in a pan over high heat.

To dry-sauté, a nonstick pan is often used. If a nonstick pan is not used, you may wipe the pan lightly with oil. Dry-sautéing has become popular as a way to lower fat in the finished product.

Sear To expose the surfaces of a piece of meat to extreme heat before cooking at a lower temperature. Searing (sometimes called browning) can be done in a hot pan in a little oil or in a hot oven.

Searing, like blanching and parboiling, is a partial-cooking process rather than a cooking method. Meats are often seared in a small amount of hot fat before braising. This process falls somewhere between pan-frying and sautéing. If the pieces are small, such as those for making a stew, the sautéing technique may be used. Larger pieces of meat are turned once with tongs or a spatula; this would be a form of pan-frying, though the heat is higher than usual. Searing is done to give color and sometimes to produce a distinctive flavor.

Another instance of partial cooking in fat is **sweating.** To sweat is to cook slowly in fat over low or moderate heat without browning, sometimes with a cover on the pan. Flavorful foods such as onions, celery, mushrooms, ham, and herbs are frequently sweated to bring out their flavors before they go into the making of a stock, soup, or sauce.

Another cooking method that resembles sautéing is **stir-frying.** Bite-sized ingredients, such as chicken and vegetables, are cooked over high heat in a small amount of oil, usually in a bowl-shaped pot called a wok, although any heavy skillet can be used. The food is tossed with utensils rather than being "jumped" and is cooked until crisp-tender.

MICROWAVE COOKING

Microwave cooking is not a cooking method, but rather a cooking tool (Figure 4.4). The cook does not cook the foods; the equipment does the cooking. The cook simply uses the equipment correctly. Although the microwave can be used to cook almost any food, it is used primarily to reheat prepared foods and thaw frozen foods. In today's kitchen, the microwave is often used to heat or reheat individual or small portions of

Figure 4-4 A MICROWAVE OVEN

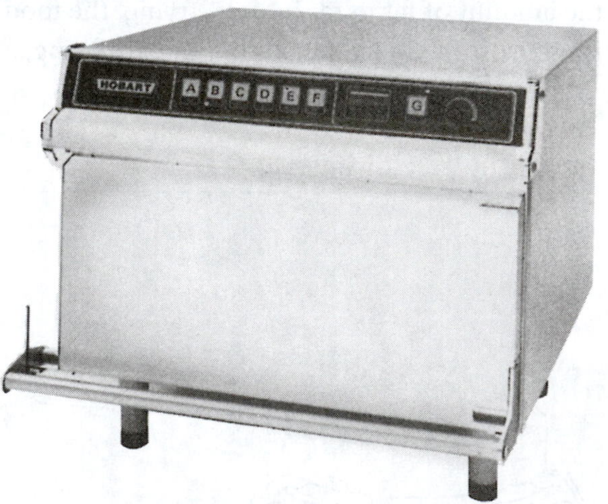

In the microwave oven, electronic tubes produce microwaves that penetrate the food and generate heat inside the food itself. This high-speed oven is used mainly to defrost, reheat, or reconstitute previously prepared foods. (Photo courtesy Hobart Corporation.)

food. For example, individual servings of items such as stew or vegetables may be brought up to serving temperature in the microwave rather than sitting in a steam table during service (and possibly being overcooked). The microwave is also used as an accessory to other forms of cooking—melting butter and chocolate or heating milk without scorching, for example. Using the microwave for large quantities of food has never been practical, mainly because it requires much more time.

As in conventional cooking, there are several factors that influence microwave cooking times. These include size (larger foods take longer), shape (thin foods cook quicker), density (porous foods cook quicker), volume (as volume increases so does cooking time), and type of ingredients (foods with much water or fat cook quicker). Microwaves penetrate the food to the depth of about half an inch on dense foods and up to two inches on liquids.

Tips for successfully using microwaves are listed in Figure 4.5.

INDUCTION COOKING

The technology for **induction cooking** was discovered many years ago, in 1831 to be precise, by the physicist Michael Faraday. Let's take a look at an induction burner unit to understand how this type of heat transfer, which has been popular for many years among chefs in Europe, works. The surface of the burner is made of tempered ceramic or glass, with a circle marked to indicate where to place a pot or pan. Underneath the surface, electricity runs through an inductor coil, which converts the electrical current into a magnetic field. When a magnetic surface (such as a stainless steel pan) is placed above the magnetic field, the molecules in the pan become excited and heat up instantly.

One of the major advantages of induction cooking is that the burner itself does not heat up, only the pan and its contents. Therefore, induction equipment does not heat up the kitchen, making for a more comfortable working environment. Also, induction equipment does not cause burns or accidental fires because there are no flames or hot surfaces. With a cool surface, food spills are easy to clean up because they don't cook onto the burner. Compared to gas, an induction burner can actually heat food more quickly and the controls allow for precise temperature settings.

Induction technology is available in commercial range tops, griddles, fryers, and portable burners. Induction equipment is more expensive than traditional equipment, but prices are expected to decrease as more foodservices start using it.

To successfully use induction ranges, you must use magnetic pots and pans. Stainless steel, enameled steel, iron or cast iron pots and pans work fine. Aluminum and copper pieces will not work unless fitted with a stainless or iron steel base.

COOKING EQUIPMENT

RANGES

To start with, let us look at **ranges,** since a great deal of moist-heat cooking takes place on them. The range has been called the jack-of-all-trades, the workhorse, the backbone of the kitchen. Here you can boil, simmer, poach, braise; you can make stocks, soups, sauces, stews. You can also cook by several dry-heat methods, and you can warm, heat, and hold foods already cooked.

Figure 4-5 TIPS FOR MICROWAVE COOKING

1. Use a thermometer to verify the food has reached a safe temperature.
2. Unless your microwave has a rotating turntable, you will need to turn the food, or stir it, at least once to ensure even cooking.
3. When you defrost food in the microwave, cook it immediately as defrosting often starts cooking the edges of the food.
4. The size and shape of your microwave container is important. Foods cook more evenly in round dishes than in square or rectangular containers. Also, the thickest part of the food (which will require the most cooking) should be turned to the outside to absorb the most microwaves.
5. When heating precooked foods, cover them to keep moisture in and provide even cooking. If using plastic wrap, make sure it does not touch the food because it can melt in contact with hot foods, and dangerous chemicals can get into the food as well. Paper towels and waxed paper can also be used to cover dishes.
6. Use only containers and products that have been approved for microwave use.
7. Whenever you cover foods, make sure there is some room for excess steam to escape such as by lifting a corner. Never put sealed containers into the microwave.
8. The most common problem with the microwave is overcooking of foods. One reason for this problem is that when you take a food out of the microwave, it continues to cook. This time is called **standing time.** Make sure you watch your timing carefully, keeping in mind that cooking continues after the microwave stops.
9. Food in the middle of a dish will heat slower than food at the edge of a dish, so put slower-heating foods around the edges. Also, with casseroles or vegetables, heap more of the food at the edge of the dish, and less in the middle, so it heats more evenly.
10. Use oven mitts to remove heated food from the microwave. The container usually gets hot.
11. Thaw frozen foods using a defrost cycle or low power. Do not use full power because the defrosting will be uneven and parts of the food will cook while other parts are still frozen.
12. Sliced, cooked meats reheat best when they are covered with sauce or gravy. Otherwise, they become dry.
13. Do not overcook potatoes because they can dry out and catch fire.
14. You can use aluminum foil within many of the newer microwaves to shield parts of food from being heated. (Microwaves do not penetrate aluminum foil.) Use foil only as directed in your microwave guide. When using foil, keep it at least 1 inch away from the sides of the oven.

Figure 4-6 RANGES

a.

b.

a. The open-top range has open burners, individually controlled. You put your pot or pan on the burner directly over the heat source and adjust cooking temperature by turning the heat up or down. (Photo courtesy Vulcan-Hart Corporation.) ***b.*** The flat top (or hot top) on the left side of this range has continuous metal plates that are heated from underneath. You put your pots and pans on the hot plates. Different parts of a flat-top range are usually set at different temperatures (low, moderate, high). You adjust cooking temperature by moving what's cooking from one place to another.

On the right side, the fry top, or griddle, often mistakenly called a grill, has a continuous smooth, slick surface on which such foods as eggs, pancakes, hot dogs, and hamburgers are fried directly (no pans)—a dry-heat method. The top must be kept oiled, or seasoned. Different parts of this range can also be set at different temperatures. (Photo courtesy Garland Commercial Industries.)

Figure 4.6 shows common types of ranges. The open-top range in Figure 4.6a has **open burners.** Open gas burners or electric coils are specifically sized for single pots or pans and are the most popular range top.

Hot tops (also called **flat tops,** as pictured in Figure 4.6b) are ranges with large, flat metal heating surfaces where any combination of pots and pans can be used, and more cooking space is available. Hot tops have either a constant heat across the entire surface or a graduated heat top. The graduated heat top has ring burners (you can see the outlines of the ring burners), which are very hot in the center and cooler at the edges. The center of the ring burner can be used for boiling, while the edges are best for simmering. The range featured in Figure 4.6b has a hot top to the left and a griddle top (or **fry top**) on the right. Griddles are popular for cooking pancakes, eggs, grilled sandwiches, hamburgers, and hot dogs.

Traditionally, turning on the ranges was the first thing done by the first person entering the kitchen. In these times of conserving resources, this is not often done. But remember that the flat top and the griddle need preheating before use.

The most important thing about cooking on a range is knowing your own equipment. This comes from operators' manuals and from experience.

OVENS

The oven is another kitchen workhorse. It is an enclosed space inside of which heated air does the cooking. Newer types of ovens heat food through the use of infrared heat or microwave radiation. In addition to roasting and baking, you can use an oven to sear, braise, stew, poach, simmer, melt, toast, defrost, warm, heat, and hold.

There are many types of ovens. **Range ovens** are part of the range unit. They contain adjustable wire racks on which to set pans. Using a **stack** or **deck oven** as shown in Figure 4.7a, you place your pans directly on the bottom of the oven, called the oven deck. These ovens are typically installed one on top of another in a stack and are from 8 to 15 inches high.

In **convection ovens** (Figure 4.7b), a fan or blower forces heated air to circulate throughout the oven. The constant even distribution of hot air cooks foods faster and at lower temperatures. For most cooking, the temperature of the convection oven must be set from 25 to 50°F (14–28°C) lower than a conventional oven. A problem that sometimes occurs in convection cooking is drying out of certain foods, so it's best to check the manufacturer's recommendations carefully for cooking foods properly.

Figure 4-7 OVENS

a. The stack (or deck) oven is an enclosed space 8 to 15 inches high, in which you put your pans directly on the oven bottom, or deck. The ovens are typically installed one on top of another in a stack. (Photo courtesy Vulcan-Hart Corporation.)

b. In the convection oven, a fan or blower forces heated air to circulate throughout the oven. The constant even distribution of hot air cooks foods at lower temperatures, often faster, and with less fuel that a conventional oven. Follow the operator's manual, not the recipe, for temperature settings and cooking times. (Photo courtesy Vulcan-Hart Corporation.)

The **combination steamer oven** (also called the combi oven—see Figure 4.8) is a relatively new piece of equipment that has impacted on commercial cooking techniques. This interesting piece of equipment can be operated in three different ways:

1. As a convection oven
2. As a convection steamer
3. As a high-humidity oven (when you use both the convection oven and convection steamer modes)

When using the dual mode, you combine force-air convection and steam to provide a moist heat that reduces the drying of foods. This combination mode is especially wonderful for producing juicy meats, fluffy breads and rolls, and reheating foods. Many kitchens have been buying combi ovens in an effort to save money by buying one piece of equipment to do two, even three, jobs.

When you use an oven such as the ones just described, there are a few simple things to remember.

- Preheat, allowing plenty of time.
- Keep the door closed. Every time you open it, the temperature drops, and the longer it is open, the more the oven cools. This can prolong cooking time, interrupt the cooking process, and cause cakes to fail and soufflés to fall.
- Load ovens carefully with space between items for air circulation.

Slow cook-and-hold ovens use low-temperature cooking, a common cooking practice many years ago in Colonial America, primarily to cook meats. When cooked in this manner, meats are juicy and do not shrink as much as in conventional ovens. The typical roasting temperatures for meats are low, between 200 and 225°F (93–107°C). Some of these ovens also use a fan to circulate the air gently throughout the oven. When the meat is cooked, the oven can maintain it at a holding temperature of 140 to 160°F (60–71°C).

Figure 4-8 COMBINATION STEAMER OVEN

(Photo courtesy Blodgett Combi.)

A **microwave oven** is illustrated in Figure 4.4. The inside space of a microwave generally allows one to two dinner plates. You can control the amount of cooking a food receives by the length of time the microwave cooks and the power level at which it cooks. For example, to cook two servings of frozen peas, you may program the microwave to cook at full power for 3 minutes. Microwave ovens vary in power from about 500 to 2000 watts. A 2000-watt microwave will cook the peas much quicker at full power than a 1200-watt microwave at full power.

Other specialized types of ovens include the following:

- **Revolving** or **reel ovens** are large ovens with something like a Ferris wheel inside them that holds pans. The pans revolve around the oven, making for even heating. Reel ovens are common in bake shops and high-volume production kitchens.
- **Smoke ovens** are conventional ovens with a special component that heats wood chips so they smoke, but don't burn. Smoked foods, such as mesquite chicken, are popular and quite flavorful.
- **Infrared** or **reconstituting ovens** produce strong infrared heat to reconstitute frozen foods quickly.

STEAM EQUIPMENT

The **steam-jacketed kettle** (steam kettle for short) is just what the name implies. It is a kettle surrounded on the bottom and sides with a hollow jacket that fills with steam when turned

Figure 4-9 SUPPLEMENTING THE RANGE

a. The tilting fry pan cooks large quantities of many foods usually prepared on the range in small quantities. It is shown here in its tilt position. For cooking, of course, the pan is level. (Photo courtesy General Electric Company.) ***b.*** Steam-jacketed kettles come in sizes ranging from 1 quart to 200 gallons (1–800 L). The one of the top is stationary, with a spigot at the bottom for emptying. The one on the bottom tilts to pour out its contents like a pitcher. You can control the heat in a steam kettle by opening and closing the steam valve. (Photos courtesy Groen Division, Dover Corporation.)

on (see Figure 4.9b). Steam transfers heat to the bottom and sides of the kettle, which then heats the product inside more quickly and evenly than does a pot on a range, where the heat is only on the bottom. You can use the steam kettle for boiling, simmering, poaching, and braising and for making such finished products as soups, sauces, stews, and puddings.

Steam kettles vary in capacity from 1 gallon to many hundreds of gallons. Some steam kettles are small enough to tilt with a lever or wheel; they are called **tilt** or **trunnion kettles** (Figure 4.9b). Kettles that can't tilt are emptied using a spigot at the bottom of the kettle.

In addition to steam-jacketed kettles, many kitchens have steam cookers. Steam cookers are divided into two categories: **pressure steamers** and **pressureless** or **convection steamers.** Pressure steamers use steam that is under pressure to cook foods. As already discussed, pressure steamers cook faster than pressureless steamers. A typical pressure steamer is illustrated in Figure 4.10.

The pressureless steamer does not use steam under pressure, but simply directs jets of steam at the food. It is not as fast as the pressure steamer, but it is more easily controlled and is safer overall.

Steaming is an excellent method for cooking many vegetables; it helps them retain flavor, color, texture, and certain vitamins and minerals. You can also cook rice, pasta, and some other foods, but nowadays its primary use is to cook vegetables.

Steam is a serious burn hazard if not used properly, so it is important for you to learn the correct operating and safety procedures. Never open the door of a pressure steamer until the pressure reading goes down to 0. (Convection steamers can be opened at any time.) Open steamer doors slowly and vent the steam away from your body. Learn thoroughly all operating and safety procedures.

Figure 4-10 PRESSURE STEAMER

This cabinet (compartment) steamer cooks food at a pressure of 13 psi (90 kPa). Foods are spread in large shallow pans, and tiny jets of superhot steam are directed at them for extra-speedy cooking. Different kinds of steamers require different cooking times for the same product, so you must follow the manufacturer's instructions. (Photo courtesy Garland Commercial Industries.)

BROILER AND GRILL

Broilers and **grills** are used to cook the same kinds of foods; the difference is the location of the heat source. The broiler's heat source is above the food; the grill's heat source is below the food (Figure 4.2).

An overhead broiler and a grill are illustrated in Figure 4.11. You will use these pieces of equip-

Figure 4-11 BROILERS

a. In the overhead broiler, you put the food *under* the fire, either on a rack or in a pan. The handles at right control distance from the fire. (Photo courtesy Vulcan-Hart Corporation.) ***b.*** On the grill, you set food *over* the fire, directly on a grate. Different parts of the grill can be set to different temperatures; you can have one section hot for cooking rare steaks quickly and another section cool for steaks well done. (Photo courtesy Garland Commercial Industries.)

ment to cook steaks, chops, poultry, hamburgers, seafood, and many other foods. A small overhead broiler known as a **salamander** is common in restaurant kitchens for quick glazing and browning of a product that is already cooked. The salamander is usually mounted over the range, as shown in Figure 4.6b.

With broilers and grills, there are two ways to control the cooking temperature. You can move the cooking surface toward the heat source or away from it (not all grills can do this), or you can turn the heat up or down. Whether using a broiler or grill, you must watch the foods closely as they cook so they do not overcook and burn. Like other cooking equipment, preheat this equipment before use.

GRIDDLE

A **griddle** is a flat, heated surface that is usually surrounded by a grease trough that drains into a receptacle. Griddles are used to cook pancakes, eggs, grilled sandwiches, hamburgers, and hot dogs. As we have already seen, a griddle may be part of a range. They are also available as separate units.

The griddle surface must be carefully cleaned and maintained. During cooking, keep the cooking surface scraped and wiped clean at all times. Also, keep the grease trough and receptacle clean. The surface can be polished with a griddle stone or griddle cloth. To maintain a nonstick surface, you must condition the griddle by applying a thin layer of oil and then turning up the heat to 400°F (200°C) and wiping clean.

TILTING FRY PAN

The **tilting fry pan,** also called a **tilting skillet** or **tilting brazier,** is a large, shallow pan with a continuous heat source (Figure 4.9a). It plays many roles. At a higher temperature setting, it is a great big fry pan and griddle. With lower heat and its cover down, you can convert it into a brazier. Or fill the uncovered pan with water, set the heat to maintain a simmer, and you have a perfect egg poacher. It can also be used as a stockpot, steamer, or steam table. Its name comes from the fact that it tilts for emptying and draining.

DEEP-FAT FRYER

The **deep-fat fryer,** also called the deep fryer or simply the fryer, has the single function of cooking food submerged in hot fat. It is used to cook many kinds of foods, from French-fried potatoes to doughnuts. The deep fryer is found in almost every kind of kitchen (Figure 4.12).

Deep fryers are available in countertop models or floor-mounted models, which have a much larger capacity. Some models are equipped with auto-lift so the baskets lift out when the food is fully fried. **Pressure fryers** have a fry pot similar to a basic fryer, but with a lid that seals it. Pressure fryers cook foods faster, and perhaps yield a moister product as well.

The deep fryer is a piece of equipment you must learn to know well and treat with respect. Hot fat is highly flammable, and a grease fire is difficult to deal with. Knowing how to use the deep fryer includes knowing how to take care of

Figure 4-12 THE DEEP FRYER

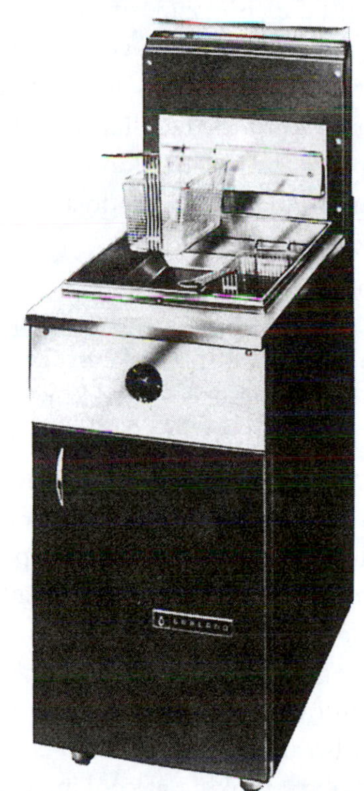

This typical deep fryer has a compartment, or kettle, in which fat is heated. Wire baskets fit into the compartment and hold food in the hot fat while it cooks. They are then raised for draining. (Photo courtesy Garland Commercial Industries.)

Figure 4-13 HOW TO CARE FOR FAT IN THE FRYER

Keeping fat for the deep fryer ready for cooking takes a special kind of care that goes on before, during, and after cooking.

To begin with, you must use the right kind of fat. A suitable fat is one that is odorless and tasteless and can withstand the continuous high temperatures needed without smoking or breaking down—that is, changing in chemical structure. Animal fats (meats, fish, poultry, butter) and olive oil are unsuitable because they have distinctive tastes and they smoke at low temperatures. Most vegetables oils are not stable enough. The best fats are certain vegetable oil products that have been specially processed to increase their stability. Such fats are hydrogenated, meaning that extra hydrogen has been added to their chemical structure to make them more stable.

Even a good fat is easily broken down by carelessness in use or storage. Breakdown can be caused by overheating or by exposure to salt, water, and crumbs. When fat breaks down, it cooks poorly, tastes bad, and must be discarded. Have you ever tasted rancid or fishy-flavored fried foods at a fly-by-night snack shack or a roadside greasy spoon?

If you take good care of it, fat will stay fresh and can be used several times. Care pays off, since good cooking fat is very expensive. Here are some important rules of care:

- Heat fat very gradually to cooking temperature. Do not let the temperature go above 200°F (100°C) until the fat all around the heating element is liquid.
- Keep salt, water, and loose crumbs away from the fryer. Drain wet foods such as potatoes before frying. Bread products with care for a firm coat. Skim off crumbs that surface during cooking.
- Fry just prior to service.
- Fry foods at an appropriate temperature: 350–375°F (175–190°C) works for most foods.
- Don't overload the baskets.
- Strain fat at least once a day, more often if volume is heavy. Use a special fat strainer or several layers of cheesecloth or a paper filter in a china cap or strainer. More and more fryers are built with self-cleaning devices.
- Add fresh fat after each day's use—more often if needed—to replace fat absorbed by foods during frying. The fresh fat helps to maintain the quality of the fat as a whole. Daily fat replacement should total 20 percent or more of the total amount. This continuing replacement is known as fat turnover. But . . .
- Do not add good fat to bad fat. It will not restore quality. Add fresh fat only to fat in good condition. Throw bad fat out.
- If fat breaks down, replace it entirely. Be alert to these signs of breakdown: off flavors (taste fat daily); smoking at cooking temperatures; yellow foam while cooking (good fat produces clear, distinct white bubbles).
- Periodically remove the fat and clean the fryer.
- Store fats and oils, covered, in a cool, dark dry place.

its fat, which is not discarded after use but can be reused with proper care. Figure 4.13 is worth your close attention. Review it again when you start to cook.

PROCESSING EQUIPMENT

The following pieces of equipment are useful for mixing and cutting. Any of these machines can be monsters and should be treated with suitable respect and dread. An accident with a machine is always serious. Before you attempt to use any machine, you must do three things:

1. Attend a demonstration and lecture on its use.
2. Study the manufacturer's instructions thoroughly.
3. Use the machine only under supervision until your instructor or supervisor is satisfied that you know what you are doing.

MIXER

The **mixer** (Figure 4.14) is one of the major workhorses of the quantity kitchen. Mixers come in various sizes—the size tells you how many quarts the bowl will hold. Smaller machines may fit on top of a worktable, whereas larger machines are bolted to the floor. Mixers can perform many tasks using a variety of mixing attachments:

- The **paddle** is the most useful and versatile of the mixer's accessories. It is used for general mixing jobs such as mashing potatoes and making cookie and cake batters.
- The **whip** is used to whip eggs, make salad dressings, and whip cream.
- A **dough arm** mixes and kneads yeast doughs.

You can also use the mixer's motor to run these attachments: a food grinder, a slicer/shredder, and a dicer.

For efficiency, and above all for safety, follow the manufacturer's instructions carefully. Use the right attachment for the job, the right size bowl, and the right motor speed for the task. Stop the motor while you are scraping the bowl or handling the product. Don't leave the machine running unattended.

SLICER

For slicing, the **food slicer** (Figure 4.15a) is superior to hand cutting in many instances. It gives you slices of uniform thickness and is therefore very useful in producing a standardized portion. It is used most frequently for slicing meats, cheese, and vegetables in quantity. A dial is used to adjust the thickness of the slices. As a safety precaution, when the machine is not being used, this dial is set to 0 so the blade does not stick out.

With some models, you have to manually move the carriage back and forth to slice meats. Other models run automatically. Fully automatic slicers have a motorized carriage that automatically moves the food to be sliced over the blade repeatedly.

As you can imagine, the slicer can be a very dangerous piece of equipment. Before turning it on, make sure it has been assembled correctly and all guards are in working order. Use the guards properly and always keep your hands away from the moving blade. Never walk away from an automatic slicer while it is running. Before cleaning, unplug the slicer.

FOOD CHOPPER

The **food chopper** (Figure 4.15b), usually called the **buffalo chopper,** uses revolving knives to

Figure 4-14 THE MIXER

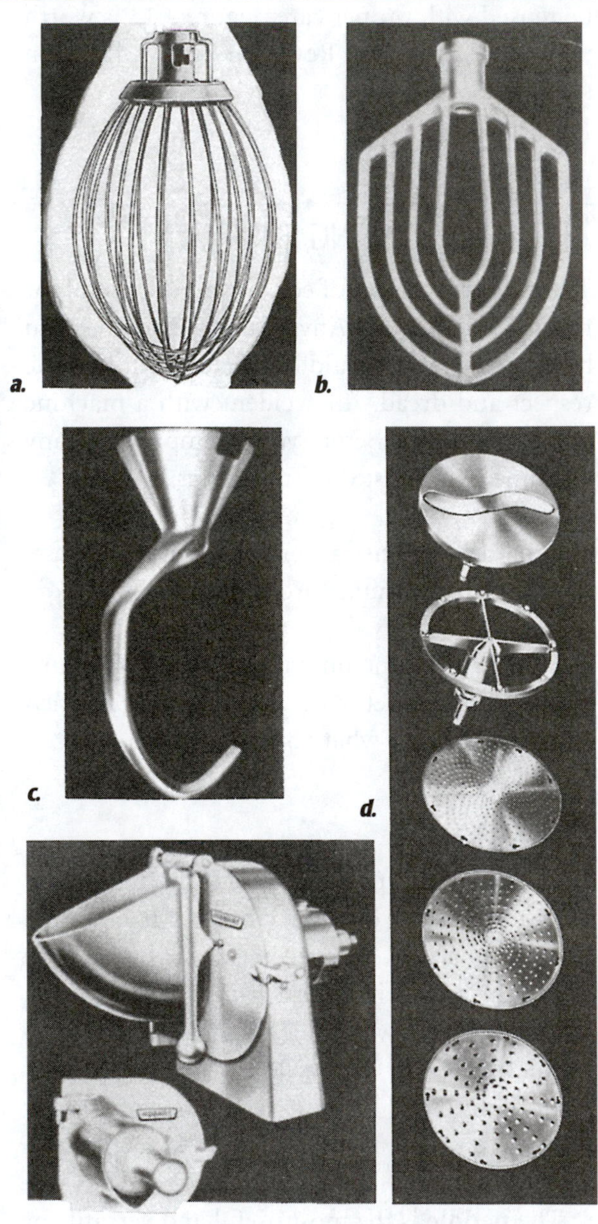

This 60-quart (56 L) mixer stands on the floor. It uses a wire whip (***a***) to whip eggs, make salad dressings, and whip cream. It uses a paddle (***b***) for heavier tasks such as cake and cookie batters and mashed potatoes. A special dough hook (***c***) mixes bread doughs. Special attachments will (***d***) grate and slice, (***e***) grind, and (***f***) dice. (Photos courtesy Hobart Corporation.)

cut, chop, and grate various food items. The knives are located under a cover that functions like a guard. A revolving bowl carries the food item to the blades. The degree of fineness is determined by the number of times the ingredients go under the knife blades. The food chopper can process such items as vegetables, nuts, meats, and bread crumbs with speed. For even chopping, place the food all at once in the bowl and then turn the machine on.

Figure 4-15 CUTTING EQUIPMENT

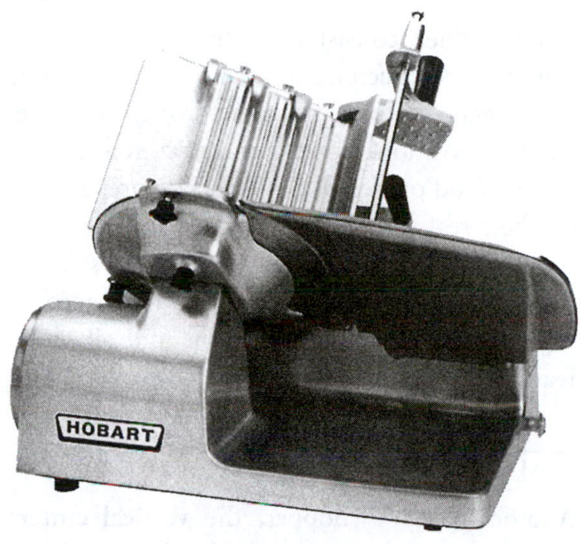

a. (left) The typical slicer has a sharp blade that whirls at high speed. The food to be sliced is placed on the carriage, which moves across the rotating blade and back again. You must use the end weight—not your hand—to feed the food. The whirling blade is quite capable of amputating your finger.

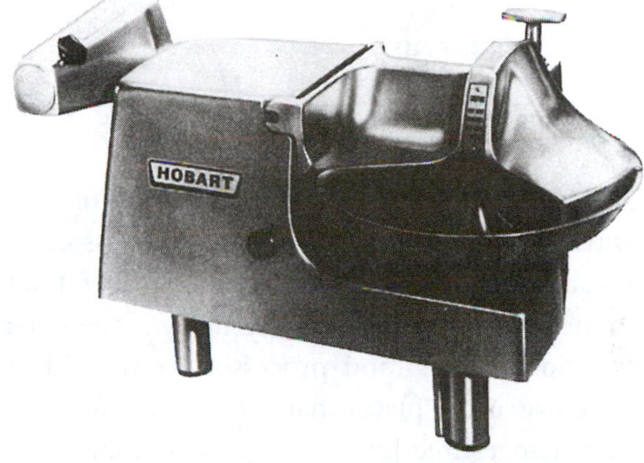

b. (above) In the food chopper, the knives are set vertically under the hood, and the bowl revolves to carry ingredients under the knives. It feeds in the foods automatically and needs no assistance from hands or implements.

c. The vertical cutter/mixer is a large-quantity, high-speed giant blender.

d. The grinder cuts up foods by forcing them through holes in cutting plates. (Photos courtesy Hobart Corporation.)

Follow the manufacturer's instructions and never reach under the cover/guard while the chopper is on. Blades make no distinction between an onion and a human hand.

FOOD PROCESSOR

The **food processor** (Figure 4.16) is one of the most versatile pieces of processing equipment and can perform many different types of cuts with speed and consistency. Food processors in the commercial kitchen are much larger than home processors, but perform many of the same functions. Most food processors come with a dozen or more plates that can be used for slicing, dicing, shredding, making julienne cuts, and more. When consistency is important, a continuous-feed machine is used. The continuous feed ejects the cut product through a chute, which is positioned over a pan or container. Using the food processor for vegetable preparation can be a real time-saver.

Figure 4-16 FOOD PROCESSOR

(Courtesy Robot Coupe U.S.A.)

As with other processing equipment, safety is paramount. Processors should be used according to manufacturers' directions and all safety features fully utilized.

VERTICAL CUTTER/MIXER

Another type of chopper, the **vertical cutter/mixer (VCM),** uses whirling knives in an enclosed bowl (Figure 4.17c). Think of it as a super-high-speed blender. It can cut up your salad greens in 5 seconds and will reduce them to soup if you run it a few seconds too long. As the name implies, this machine can also be used as a mixer for such things as dough and mayonnaise.

POTS, PANS, HAND TOOLS, AND SMALL EQUIPMENT

It's twice as hard as stainless steel, it conducts heat 28 times faster than glass, and it's nonstick for life. What is this product? It's anodized aluminum, just one of the many new inventions that have revolutionized the pots-and-pans industry. Whatever material is chosen, high-quality pots and pans should distribute heat evenly and uniformly so there are no hot spots, which burn food, or cold spots, which undercook food. Two factors will determine if your pots and pans will cook evenly:

- *Type of material used.* Each material used to make pots and pans transfers heat at different rates.

- *Thickness of the material.* A thick-bottomed pot cooks more evenly than a thin-bottomed pot. Thick-bottomed cookware is, of course, heavier and usually more expensive.

Each type of material used to make pots and pans has its own characteristics.

Aluminum is the most common material in most kitchens. One reason that it is so popular is that it is an excellent heat conductor. Aluminum is also lightweight, which makes it easy to handle and not too expensive. However, because aluminum is a soft metal, it can be damaged by rough treatment. Another concern is that it reacts with some foods, particularly high-acid foods, so aluminum should not be used for long cooking of high-acids foods, such as tomatoes, or for storing any foods. Aluminum also discolors light-colored foods, such as eggs and white sauces.

A newer product, called **anodized aluminum,** removes many of these concerns. Pots and pans made of anodized aluminum have a harder, more scratch-resistant surface. It does not react with acidic foods or discolor light foods. Food barely sticks on the hard, smooth surface, so it is easier to clean.

Stainless steel is popular for holding and storing containers, rather than pots and pans, because it does not react with any foods or discolor light foods. Stainless steel pots and pans have a major limitation: Stainless steel is a poor conductor of heat. This doesn't mean that there are no stainless steel pots and pans; there are, but most of them have aluminum or copper bottoms. Stainless steel is much more durable than aluminum, and its finish is hard and tough.

Copper is an excellent conductor of heat, especially for range cooking. Copper cookware must be lined with tin or stainless steel because copper reacts with many foods to create toxic substances. Copper pans are not very common also because they are very expensive and require much care.

Cast iron pots and pans have been around for many years. Cast iron is strong, inexpensive, and it's an even conductor of heat, but it requires a lot of care to prevent rusting. It can't be washed with strong detergents or scoured, and it must be wiped dry and conditioned with oil to prevent rusting.

Many pots and pans are available with **nonstick coatings** to which most foods won't stick. They have become popular not only because they are easier to clean, but because they allow for cooking with little or no fat. But you have to take good care of nonstick coatings: They can be scratched by sharp or rough-edged kitchen tools or abrasive scouring pads. Manufacturers recommend using plastic or wooden utensils (not metal) with nonstick pots and pans.

POTS AND PANS

Figures 4.17 and 4.18 illustrate typical pots and pans. You should learn to know each kind by name. But don't be inhibited by the name. Don't think, for example, that you have to have a brazier for braising, or that you can't do anything but braise in it. Use logic; think of what you are going to use it for. Choose a pan size appropriate to the amount of food you are going to put in it and to the cooking process you intend to use.

Stockpots are large pots for making stocks or soups. They are tall and narrow so that a large amount of simmering liquid will offer only a small surface for evaporation.

The **double boiler** is used for cooking or holding foods at low temperatures. You put the food

Figure 4-17 POTS AND PANS FOR THE RANGE

a. Stockpots are tall and narrow so that a large amount of simmering liquid will offer only a small surface for evaporation. (Photo courtesy Commercial Aluminum Cookware Company.) ***b.*** Straight-sided pans (double-handled saucepot, long-handled saucepans) are easiest for mixing and blending, as in making sauces. (Saucepot and deep saucepan courtesy Commercial Aluminum Cookware Company; shallow saucepan courtesy Lincoln Manufacturing Company.) ***c.*** The brazier, also called a rondeau, is designed for long, slow cooking on the back of the range or in the oven. (Photo courtesy Commercial Aluminum Cookware Company.) ***d.*** The double boiler is used for cooking or holding foods at low temperatures. You put the food in the top part and boiling water in the bottom. (Photo courtesy Commercial Aluminum Cookware Company.)

Figure 4-18 PANS FOR THE OVEN

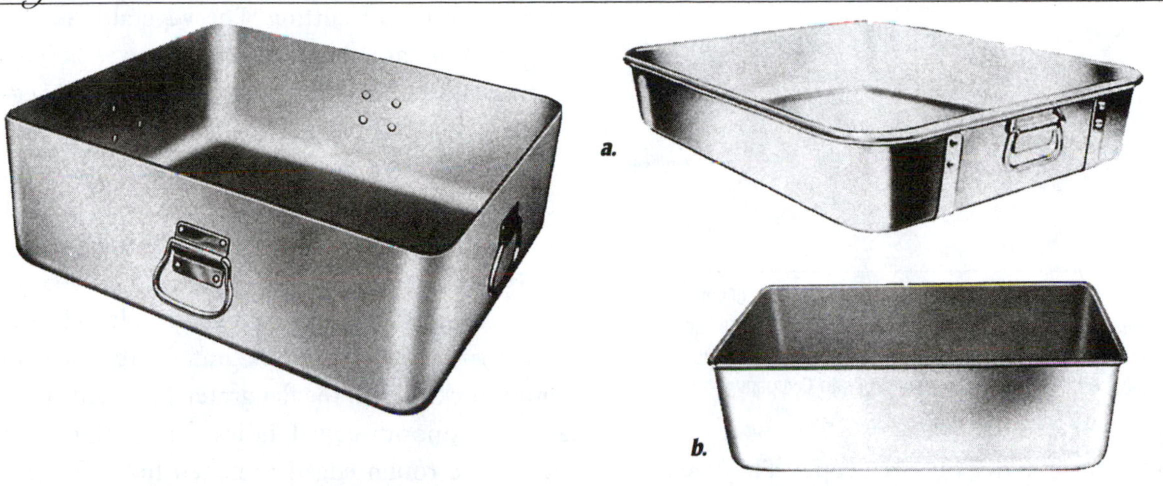

a. Roasting pans are shallow for even heat distribution, but deep enough to hold juices. Choose a pan slightly larger than the roast. (Photos courtesy Lincoln Manufacturing Company.) ***b.*** A loaf pan can cook a meat loaf or a loaf of bread with equal ease, as well as elegant foods like pâté en croûte. (Photo courtesy Wear-Ever Aluminum, Inc.)

in the top part and boiling water in the bottom. It is a convenient way to cook foods that can't be cooked over direct heat.

Saucepots are round pots of medium depth with two handles. Compared to the stockpot, they are shorter, which makes it easier to mix and blend. Saucepots are used for making soups, sauces, stews, and any liquids.

The broad and shallow **brazier** is designed for browning meats and long, slow cooking on the back of the range or in the oven. It is ideal for making stews and braised meats.

Next come the workhorses of range cooking: **saucepans** and **sauté pans.** Saucepans are simply small saucepots with one long handle instead of two. The sides of the saucepan are generally straight, but they can be slanted. Likewise, sauté pans may be straight sided or slope sided. Sauté pans are wide and shallow and are used for sautéing, frying, browning, and making egg dishes.

Most pans have flat bottoms for even contact with the range surface. A few are made with slightly rounded bottoms designed to fit the contour of the open gas burner. It's important not to try to cook with a round-bottomed pan on an electric burner or a flat-top range. You would get your direct contact with the heat in only one spot, and the food there would scorch or burn while the rest of it scarcely heated at all.

Next come pans that are used in the oven, steam table, or bain-marie. **Roasting pans,** used to roast meat and poultry, are shallow for even heat distribution, but deep enough to hold juices. A **loaf pan** is much smaller and can cook a meat loaf or a loaf of bread with equal ease. **Sheet pans,** which measure 18 × 26 inches (46 × 66 cm), are very versatile and can be used in both the kitchen and the bakery. They are used to bake cookies, cakes, rolls, and some breads, as well as roast and broil meats, poultry, and seafood. **Bake pans** are also rectangu-

Figure 4-19 STEAM TABLE AND PANS

Hot foods are kept hot with steam from below. Pans of various sizes and depths fit the openings in the table exactly. An unused opening is covered, so that the heating temperature is maintained below the food. (Photo courtesy The Vollrath Company.)

lar like sheet pans, but are deeper. They are used for general baking.

Ovenware must withstand high oven temperatures without warping. Be careful not to substitute a lighter-weight utility pan for the roasting pan. They may be similar in shape and size, but a warped utility pan could produce a disaster in a hot oven. As with range top pots and pans, choose a pan size appropriate to the amount of food to be roasted or baked.

Steam table pans, also called **hotel pans** or **counter pans,** are used to hold foods in the steam table and to cook foods in the oven or steamer (Figure 4.19). The standard steam table pan is 12 × 20 inches (325 × 530 mm), and fractions of this size (half pan, quarter pan, and so on) are also used. **Bain-marie inserts** are used to hold foods in the bain-marie. Instead of being rectangular like steam table pans, bain-marie inserts are round and tall and available in a variety of capacities (Fig. 3.21).

HAND TOOLS AND SMALL EQUIPMENT

Figure 4.20 and 4.21 show some of the hand tools and small equipment used in the commercial kitchen. Knives fit into this category as well; they were discussed in Chapter 3. Additional hand tools are used for cutting. The **vegetable peeler** (Figure 3.1) has a double blade that swivels. This feature allows it to efficiently peel fruits and vegetables with little waste. The sharp tip can be used to remove potato eyes, bruised spots, and so on. Stainless steel peelers are the best. Replace your peeler when it gets dull—it can't be sharpened.

Graters are wonderful when you need to shred and grate foods such as vegetables, cheese, and citrus rinds. Metal box graters are easier on your knuckles than the flat graters. One side usually has smooth-edged holes for grating; two sides have rough-edged punched holes for ripping foods, such as lemon peel, into small bits. The fourth side has a diagonal slit for slicing foods.

A **zester** has tiny, sharp-edged holes that are useful for cutting orange, lemon, or lime peel. The advantage of using a zester, rather than a knife, is that the zester does not cut into the white pith attached to the peel, which is bitter.

A **melon ball scoop,** or **ball cutter,** is used to cut fruits, and some vegetables, into ball shapes. The **pastry wheel** is a round rotating blade on a handle that is used to cut pizza and rolled-out dough. The **bench scraper,** or **dough knife,** is used particularly by the baker to cut pieces of dough and scrape down wooden worktables.

Figure 4.21 illustrates some of the hand tools used in putting things together. **Bowls** are indispensable all-purpose utensils; stainless steel is the material of choice since it is light in weight and impervious to acid. **Rubber spatulas** are often used in folding, and they are invaluable in scraping out bowls.

Whips are used to beat, whip, and blend liquids and semiliquids. There are **heavy whips** and **balloon whips** (also called **piano wire whips**). Heavy whips have fewer wires than balloon

Figure 4-20 COOKING IMPLEMENTS AND UTENSILS

a. Spoons: slotted, perforated, solid. (Photo courtesy The Vollrath Company.) ***b.*** Tongs. (Photo by Patricia Roberts.) ***c.*** Colander, used to drain liquid from foods. (Photo courtesy Lincoln Manufacturing Company.) ***d.*** China cap, or chinois, used to strain liquids into another container. (Photo courtesy Lincoln Manufacturing Company.) ***e.*** Offset spatula, used to turn foods in frying. (Photo courtesy Lincoln Manufacturing Company.)

Figure 4-21 MIXING TOOLS AND UTENSILS

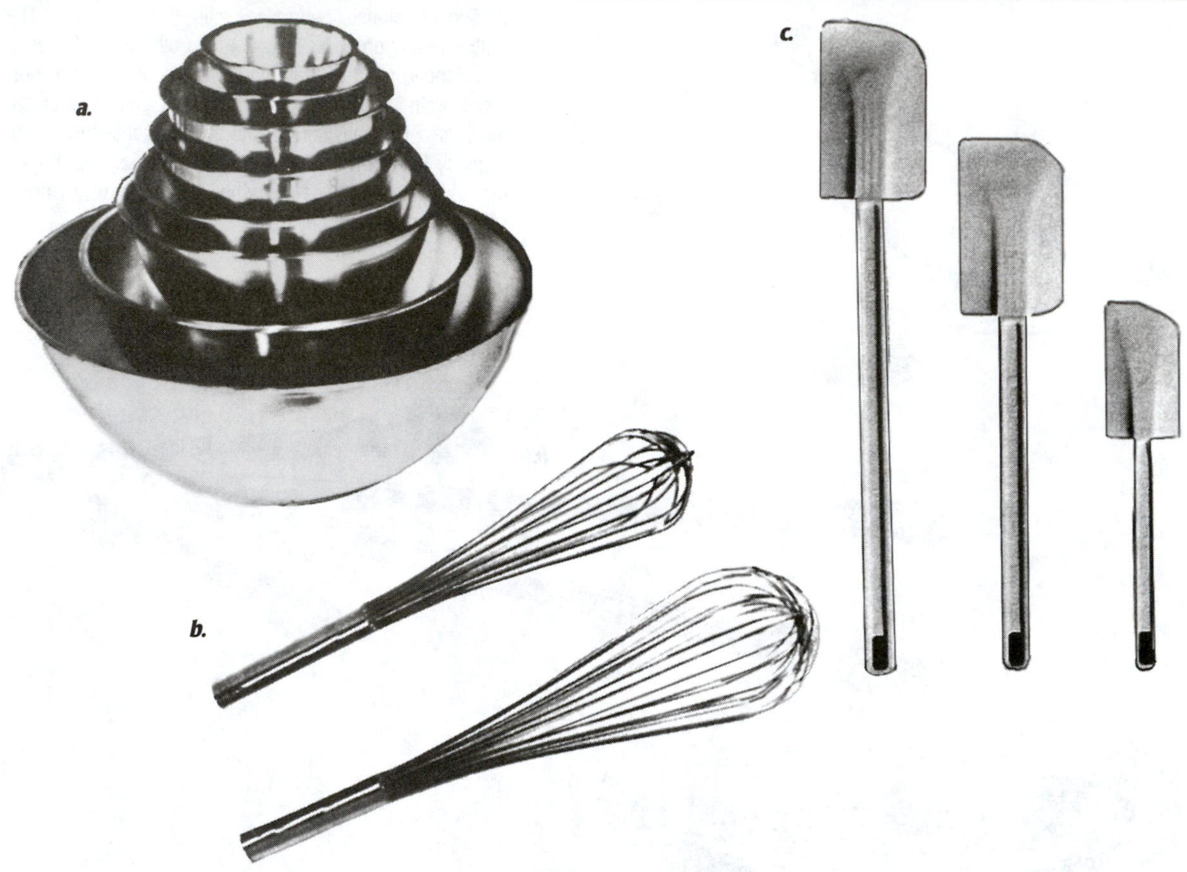

a. Round-bottomed stainless steel bowls. (Photo courtesy Bloomfield Industries.) ***b.*** Wire whips. (Photo courtesy Intedge Industries, Inc.) ***c.*** Rubber scraper/spatula. (Photo courtesy Rubbermaid Commercial Products.)

whips, but, as the name implies, these wires are much more heavy duty and can be used for general mixing. Balloon whips have many flexible wires and are best for whipping thinner and lighter liquids such as egg whites or cream.

Other useful equipment in this category include the following:

- **Colanders** are used to drain liquid from foods.
- A **china cap,** or **chinois,** is used to strain liquids into another container.
- **Tongs** are used to grip or pick up ice or small pieces of food.
- A **cook's fork** is used to lift and turn meat, and hold meat still while it is being carved.
- An **offset spatula** is used for turning food during cooking. The blade is offset so that it slides easily underneath food.
- A **straight spatula** is used for spreading icing on baked goods and for scraping bowls.
- A **sandwich spreader** is a short spatula that is used to spread fillings and spreads to make sandwiches.

- A **skimmer** is used to remove grease or other ingredients of stocks, soups, and other liquids.
- A **sieve** is used to sift flour and other dry ingredients.
- A **pastry brush** is used to brush something, such as a glaze, onto food.

MEASUREMENT

HOW QUANTITIES ARE MEASURED

Recipes may communicate quantities of ingredients in three different ways: by number (count), by volume, and by weight. These methods of communication represent three different systems of measurement. Number is measured by counting items. Volume is measured in utensils of the necessary sizes. Weight is measured with scales.

NUMBER. Ingredients that come in fairly uniform sizes are sometimes measured and expressed in numbers—6 apples, 3 eggs, 1 radish. In Figure 5.5, a recipe for cream of cauliflower soup, you see amounts of several ingredients expressed in numbers—2 celery ribs, $^1/_2$ bay leaf, $^1/_2$ garlic clove, and so on. Numbers are often used as measures of quantity where exact proportions are not of critical importance. It is quicker and easier to count than it is to weigh and measure.

Numbers are also used where units of food will remain identifiable in the end product. For example, a recipe for 50 stuffed avocado halves would specify 25 avocados.

VOLUME. On the other hand, a recipe for an avocado dip might call for a quart (liter) of mashed pulp rather than a certain number of avocados, since these fruits can vary greatly in size and yield. A quart (liter) represents a way of measuring quantity by volume—that is, by the amount of space it occupies. Units of volume measurement are teaspoons, tablespoons, fluid ounces (often called simply ounces), cups, pints, quarts, and gallons. Common metric measures of volume are milliliters and liters. Figure 4.22 shows typical volume measures for large and small amounts.

Figure 4-22 VOLUME MEASURES

a. Liquid measures come in sizes from pint to gallon (500 mL–4 L). Gradations are not labeled, so you have to know equivalents. (Photo courtesy Lincoln Manufacturing Company.) **b.** Measuring spoons range from $^1/_4$ tsp to 1 tablespoon (1–15 mL). They are used mostly for measuring herbs and spices. Fill them full and then level with a straight edge. (Photo courtesy Foley Manufacturing Company.)

Volume is used mainly to measure liquids, or fluids, since measuring a liquid is easier than weighing it. In our soup recipe, the quantities of stock and cream are expressed in volume. The pinch of herb or spice is also an expression of volume, though it is not an exact unit of measurement and doesn't apply to liquids. The fluid equivalent of a pinch is a dash.

Table 4-1 COMMON LADLE AND SCOOP SIZES

Common Ladle Sizes

1 oz = 1/8 C	30 mL
2 oz = 1/4 C	50 mL
4 oz = 1/2 C	125 mL
6 oz = 3/4 C	200 mL
8 oz = 1 C	250 mL

Portion Scoops and Capacities

Number[a]	*Level Measure*	*Ounces*	*Milliliters*
6	2/3 C	6	165
8	1/2 C	4	125
10	3/8 C	3–4	100
12	1/3 C	2 1/2–3	80
16	1/4 C	2	60
20	3 Tb	1 3/4–2	50
24	2 2/3 Tb	1 1/2–1 3/4	40
30	2 Tb	1–1 1/2	35

[a]Scoop number indicates approximate number of portions in level quart or liter.

Figure 4-23 PORTION MEASURES

a. Portion scoops are precisely sized for portion control. The number on each scoop indicates the number of scoops in a quart or liter.

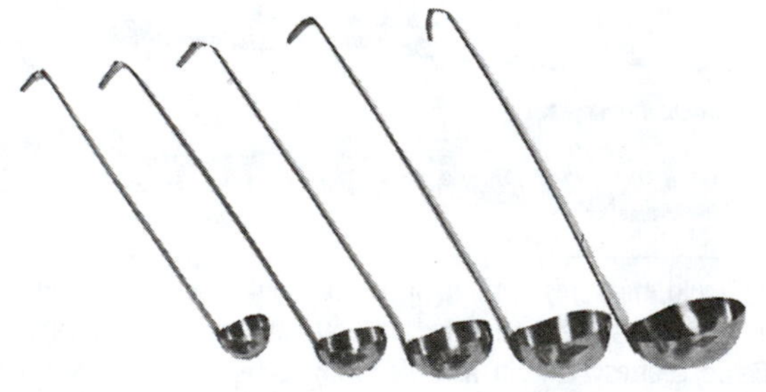

b. Ladles are also used for portioning. They are sized in ounces or milliliters for serving liquids such as soups and sauces. (Photo courtesy Intedge Industries, Inc.)

Volume is also used to measure portion sizes for serving finished items. For this purpose, special utensils are used, such as those pictured in Figure 4.23. Portion scoops (Figure 4.23a) are used for such foods as meat and potato salads, cottage cheese, and sandwich fillings. Ladles (Figure 4.23b) measure out liquids such as soups, sauces, and salad dressings. Some common ladle and scoop sizes are given in Table 4.1.

WEIGHT. Weight is usually used for solids, especially where exact quantities are of critical importance. Its units of measurement are pounds and ounces (grams, milligrams, and kilograms in metric). Weight is a much more precise measurement than number, because many products vary in size. Weight is also more precise than volume for solid ingredients. A cup of flour will vary in amount depending on whether it is sifted or unsifted. A cup of brown sugar will have more or less sugar according to how firmly it is packed. A quart of potatoes will be a variable amount according to how finely chopped the potatoes are. But a pound or a kilogram of any product is always the same amount of that product no matter how much space it occupies.

Where ratios or proportions of ingredients are of critical importance, quantities of solids are usually expressed entirely in weight. This is particularly true in baking. Even eggs and egg whites are listed in terms of pounds and ounces rather than numbers because eggs vary slightly in size.

Various kinds of scales are used to measure weight. Two spring scales are illustrated in Figure 4.24, and a baker's scale is pictured in Chapter 16. If a container is used to hold the ingredient being weighed, the weight of the container must be subtracted from the total weight.

EQUIVALENTS. It is important, in working with recipes, to be thoroughly familiar with all the units of measurement. It is also important to know the equivalents of each unit in terms of the others. You will be using such information constantly.

A basic table of units of measure is given in Table 4.2. The information on volume is expanded in Table 4.3 to show the equivalent of each unit of volume in terms of all the others. If you want to turn one unit of measure into another—fluid ounces into quarts, for example—read across the table from 1 fluid ounce to the figure below Quarts. To find out how many of one unit are contained in another—such as the number of tablespoons in a quart—read down the column headed Tablespoons to the figure in the 1 quart line. The table will even tell you how many gallons there are in a teaspoon.

Figure 4-24 SPRING SCALES

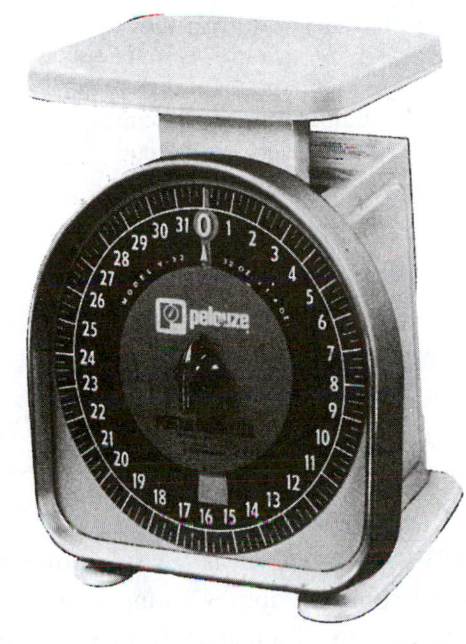

a. A spring scale with $^{1}/_{4}$-ounce markings.

b. A spring scale with 5-gram markings. (Photos courtesy Pelouze Scale Company.)

Table 4-2 UNITS OF MEASURE

less than 1/8 teaspoon	=	pinch/dash
3 teaspoons	=	1 tablespoon
2 tablespoons	=	1 fluid ounce
8 fluid ounces	=	1 cup
16 tablespoons	=	1 cup
2 cups	=	1 pint
2 pints	=	1 quart
32 fluid ounces	=	1 quart
4 quarts	=	1 gallon
8 pints	=	1 gallon
16 ounces	=	1 pound
1000 milliliters	=	1 liter
1 pound	=	454 grams
1000 grams	=	1 kilogram

ABBREVIATIONS. It is also important to know the common abbreviations for each unit of measurement (Table 4.4). If you mix up tsp and Tb, you may have a disaster. Some measures have more than one abbreviation. The ones we use in this text are given first in the table.

Although it is important to know the number of tsp in a Tb and the number of Tb in a C, these familiar household measures are used very little in industry. The amounts cooked make them impractical. It is best to begin thinking and cooking in terms of ounces and pounds and quarts and gallons (or grams and kilograms and liters and milliliters if you have converted to the metric system).

Two other abbreviations sometimes appear with an ingredient quantity in a recipe—AP and EP. **AP** stands for **"as purchased"** and **EP** stands for **"edible portion."** Thus, if a recipe lists "5 lb potatoes AP," it means whole unpeeled potatoes. If it says "5 lb potatoes EP," it means peeled potatoes. You can readily see that an EP potato will weigh less than an AP potato.

THE METRIC SYSTEM

The units of weight and volume that we use in the United States are not used in other countries. Most of the world uses the metric system.

You may run into recipes using the metric system, perhaps in Canadian and European publications. Someday, we will probably all be cooking in metric units. Meantime, it is useful to know metric terms and equivalents and be able to translate them into the units of measurement for which our equipment is designed.

The metric system is simple and logical. It is based on the decimal system. You are familiar with this system through our money, in which units are decimal parts or multiples of a basic unit, the dollar. A penny is 0.01 dollar, a dime is 0.10 dollar, and so on.

Table 4-3 VOLUME EQUIVALENTS

		Teaspoons	*Tablespoons*	*Fluid Ounces*	*Cups*	*Pints*	*Quarts*	*Gallons*		*Milliliters (rounded)*
1 teaspoon	=	1	1/3	1/6	1/48	1/96	1/192	1/768	=	5
1 tablespoon	=	3	1	1/2	1/16	1/32	1/64	1/256	=	15
1 fluid ounce	=	6	2	1	1/8	1/16	1/32	1/128	=	30
1 cup	=	48	16	8	1	1/2	1/4	1/16	=	250
1 pint	=	96	32	16	2	1	1/2	1/8	=	500
1 quart	=	192	64	32	4	2	1	1/4	=	1000 (1 liter)
1 gallon	=	768	256	128	16	8	4	1	=	4000 (4 liters)

Table 4-4 ABBREVIATIONS

teaspoon = tsp or t	milliliter = mL
tablespoon = Tb, Tbsp, or T	liter = L
cup = C or c	gram = g
fluid ounce = fl oz	kilogram = kg
pint = pt	
quart = qt	
gallon = gal or G	
ounce = oz	
pound = lb	

The metric system of measurement applies the decimal system to weight, volume, and other systems of measurement such as length, distance, and area. Units of measurement are decimal parts or multiples of 10 of a basic unit. Here are four useful prefixes to remember:

kilo- = 1000
deci- = 1/10
centi- = 1/100
milli- = 1/1000

METRIC WEIGHT. The basic unit of weight is the gram. In the kitchen the units of weight used are the gram (abbreviated g) and the kilogram (abbreviated kg and pronounced kill-o-gram), sometimes shortened to kilo. A kilogram is 1000 grams.

- A gram is 0.035 ounce. (There are about 28 grams in 1 ounce.)
- A kilogram is 2.2 pounds.

In translating a recipe from metric weight to U.S. weight, these are your multipliers. You multiply each ingredient as you do in converting a recipe from one quantity to another.

Here is a recipe in which metric measures are converted to pounds:

Ingredient	*Metric*	*Multiplier*	*U.S.*
Lima beans	15 kilograms	× 2.2	= 3.0 pounds
Mushrooms	4 kilograms	× 2.2	= 8.8 pounds
Shallots	500 grams (0.5 kilograms)	× 2.2	= 1.1 pounds
Butter	1 kilogram	× 2.2	= 2.2 pounds

The scales in Figure 4.24 show metric and U.S. measures of weight.

METRIC VOLUME. The basic unit of volume is the liter (abbreviated L and pronounced lee-ter). The liter is also the basic kitchen measure. You may also meet the deciliter (dL, pronounced dess-a-leeter) and the milliliter (mL, pronounced mill-a-lee-ter) in recipes. The deciliter is 1/10 liter and the milliliter is 1/1000 liter.

- A liter is 1.056 quarts (just a little more than 1 quart).
- A deciliter is 100 milliliters or about a half cup.
- A milliliter is 0.001 quart or 0.034 fluid ounce.

If you wanted to convert a recipe from metric volume to U.S. volume, these would be your multipliers.

CONVERTING TO METRIC MEASURE. To convert from U.S. measure to metric measure, you use the same process as in converting from metric to U.S. measure.

- A pound is 0.454 kilogram.
- An ounce is 28.35 grams.
- A quart is 0.946 liter.
- A fluid ounce is 29.57 milliliters or 0.3 deciliter.

You can use these as your multipliers.

In real life, you will seldom have to convert a recipe from one measuring system to another. The recipes in this book provide both U.S. and metric quantities. The metric quantities given in this book are rounded off and are not as precise as the U.S. quantities. Do not use a mixture of the two systems.

MEASURING TEMPERATURE

Another form of measure that has two standards is temperature, which expresses the intensity of heat. Again, the United States uses one standard, the Fahrenheit scale, and the rest of the world uses another, the Celsius scale, also called the centigrade scale.

On the Fahrenheit scale, the freezing point of pure distilled water is 32° and its boiling point is 212° at standard atmospheric pressure. On the Celsius scale, the freezing point of pure distilled water is 0° and the boiling point is 100° at standard atmospheric pressure. One Celsius degree equals 1.8 Fahrenheit degrees.

Temperatures can be converted from one scale to the other by using the following formulas:

$$C = 5/9(F - 32)$$
$$F = 9/5C + 32$$

In other words, to find degrees Celsius, start with degrees Fahrenheit, subtract 32, and multiply by 5/9. To find degrees Fahrenheit, start with degrees Celsius, multiply by 9/5, and add 32.

Suppose, for example, you want to find the Celsius equivalent of a simmering temperature of 185° F:

$$C = 5/9(F - 32)$$
$$185 - 32 = 153$$
$$5/9 \times 153 = 85°C$$

Or suppose your room thermometer reads 25°C and you want to find the Fahrenheit equivalent:

$$F = 9/5C + 32$$
$$9/5 \times 25 = 45$$
$$45 + 32 = 77°F$$

Celsius temperatures are coming into common use, so it is wise to become familiar with them. Learning to think in Celsius terms is even better than translating from one system to the other.

Temperature, as you know, is measured with thermometers. A thermometer is an instrument that measures the intensity of heat and reads it out on a Fahrenheit or Celsius scale.

We use thermometers for many purposes. We can check the operation of thermostatic controls on our equipment: The thermometer in Figure 4.25a can be placed in a refrigerator or freezer to check the readings of the equipment's own gauges. Similarly, the thermometer in Figure 4.25b will check out the fat in the deep fryer.

Another very important type of thermometer indicates the internal temperature of foods being cooked or held. A meat thermometer is an indispensable cooking tool: It measures the internal temperature of meats as they cook so that you know when they reach the right degree of doneness. With the testing thermometer, you can determine the temperature of anything you want to test. It is especially handy for finding out whether foods being held for service are in the safe zone.

Thermometers are key features of the cook's domain. Learn how to interpret what they tell you, check them regularly on your equipment, and use them intelligently in cooking and holding foods.

Figure 4-25 TEMPERATURE MEASURES

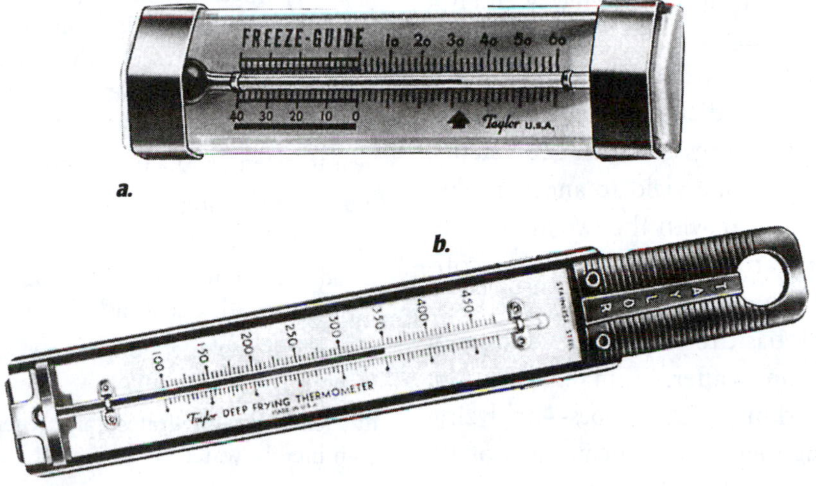

a. A thermometer for indicating temperature in a refrigerator or freezer. ***b.*** A thermometer for testing the temperature of the fat in the deep fryer.

SUMMING UP

Cooking is a way to change plain raw foods into delectable dishes that please the customer, supply the schoolchild with energy, and help to make the patient well. The way we bring about such changes is to apply heat to foods over a period of time. We can do this in a number of ways.

Heat is applied by being transferred from something that is hot to something that is not. There are three methods of heat transfer: conduction, convection, and radiation. Often, more than one process is involved.

Heat brings about change in foods by affecting the various substances of which they are made—the proteins, carbohydrates, fats, water, and minute substances that provide their flavor and color. It can also determine whether the vitamins and minerals present in raw foods are passed on to the diner or lost along the way. You will understand better how all this works as you learn more about specific foods and how to cook them in chapters to come.

The many ways of transferring heat are divided into moist-heat and dry-heat methods, depending on whether or not moisture is the vehicle of heat transfer. Moist-heat methods include boiling, simmering, poaching, steaming, and braising. Dry-heat methods depend on hot air, radiation, or fat for heat transfer; they include baking, roasting, broiling, grilling, barbecuing, deep-frying, pan-frying, and sautéing.

Many times, cooking terms defy precision and usage crisscrosses accuracy, as with broiling for grilling and grilling for cooking on a griddle. There is the backyard barbecue, a good American term for a process that is not truly barbecuing; it is either grilling over coals or roasting on a spit with a barbecue sauce brushed on the meat. If you have ever attended a corn roast, you know that the corn and potatoes are not really roasted. If you've been to a real clambake, you know the clams are not actually baked. You may work in kitchens that use terms in their own way and not as we have defined them.

In order to understand and follow recipes, you must know how ingredients are measured, the various quantity measures and their equivalents, and how to convert one yield to another. You should also be familiar with the two systems of measuring temperature and know how to convert from one to the other.

This chapter is basic to your understanding of everything that comes after. From this point on, you will be working with recipes—analyzing them, converting them, using them, most of all, to understand what takes place when you put a group of ingredients together and cook them in a certain way. Learn to make recipes your tools, not your masters. Learn measures and equivalents; they, too, are indispensable kitchen tools.

Come back and reread this chapter after you have engaged in battle with some recipes in the kitchen, and you will discover new insights.

The Cook's Vocabulary

as purchased (AP)

broiler, salamander

caramelization

coagulate

cooking with fat: sauté, dry-sauté, pan-fry, deep-fry, sear, stir-fry

deep-fat fryer, pressure fryer

dry-heat cooking: bake, roast, barbecue, broil, grill, pan-broil, griddle

edible portion (EP)

grill

en papillote

gelatinization

hand tools and small equipment: vegetable peeler, grater, zester, melon ball scoop or ball cutter, pastry wheel, bench scraper or dough knife, bowls, rubber spatula, whips (heavy, balloon), colander, china cap or chinois, tongs, cook's fork, offset spatula, straight spatula, sandwich spreader, skimmer, sieve, pastry brush

heat transfer: conduction, convection, radiation

induction cooking

materials for cooking equipment: aluminum, anodized aluminum, stainless steel, copper, cast iron, nonstick coating

moist-heat cooking: boil, simmer, poach, steam, braise

nutrients: carbohydrates, fat, proteins, vitamins, minerals, water

ovens: range oven, convection oven, stack or deck oven, combination steamer oven, slow cook-and-hold oven, microwave oven, revolving or reel oven, smoke oven, infrared or reconstituting oven

pots and pans: stockpot, double boiler, saucepot, brazier, saucepan, sauté pan, roasting pan, loaf pan, sheet pan, bake pan, steam table pans (counter or hotel pans), bain-marie inserts

processing equipment: mixer (paddle, whip, dough arm), food slicer, food chopper or buffalo chopper, food processor, vertical cutter/mixer

radiation: microwave, infrared

ranges: open burners, hot tops or flat tops, fry top

reduce

standing time

steam equipment: steam-jacketed kettle, tilt or trunnion kettle, pressure steamer, pressureless or convection steamer

sweat

tilting fry pan, tilting skillet, tilting brazier

Review Questions

Answer each question in complete sentences. Read each question carefully and make sure you answer all parts of the question. Organize your answer into more than one paragraph when appropriate.

1. List the important substances of which foods are made, and discuss how cooking affects them.
2. Name and describe the three ways in which heat is transferred to a product and give examples of each.
3. Discuss the differences between the two types of cooking methods and give examples of each type. What methods would be suitable for cooking small tender cuts of meat? Vegetables? Cakes?
4. Discuss the need for caring for the fat used in the deep fryer and cite several things you should and should not do to keep it fresh.
5. What equipment would you choose in preparing the following: pot roast, 50 pounds of broccoli, poached eggs, meat loaf, baked ham, hamburgers, French fries, pancakes? Explain why in each case.
6. Discuss the three methods used in measuring ingredients. Give examples of types of foods appropriate to each method.
7. Explain why it is helpful to know equivalents in converting recipes. Give examples from your own experience of mistakes in using equivalents and what happened as a result.
8. What are the basic units of measurement in the metric system?

Chapter 5

MENUS, NUTRITION, AND RECIPES

A ***menu*** *is a list of the dishes* offered for service at a meal. The menu means different things to different parts of the foodservice establishment. To the production worker, it is a brief description of work to be done. To the guest, it is a written presentation of available foods from which to choose. To the operation, it can be the difference between success and failure.

For each menu item, there is one or more recipes. **Recipes** are communication tools, abbreviated ways of passing information from one person to another. A recipe tells the cook what ingredients are needed to make a given dish and gives instructions about how to make it. It tells the person who buys the food what products must be on hand for each menu item the establishment serves. Recipes give the manager essential information for figuring food costs and keeping them from getting out of hand. The typical foodservice kitchen revolves around recipes that have been standardized for its menu.

But one thing a recipe does not communicate very well is how to become a good cook. Some people think that following a recipe is all there is to cooking. Many cooks simply follow one recipe after another for all their cooking lives. If a recipe is mislaid, they can't make the dish. If they don't have all the ingredients on hand, they are lost. They do not really understand what they are doing.

Learning to cook by following one recipe after another is like learning English by reading the dictionary. You could memorize the meanings of all the words in the book, but you would never know how to put them together to make meaningful sentences. In the same way, you could know dozens of recipes by heart and make them over and over, and never understand how the ingredients function together to make a dish, or why a certain product turns out well one time and poorly the next.

This chapter will look at how to plan and evaluate menus, the basics of nutrition, and both sides of recipes—their indispensable roles in the kitchen and the pitfalls of trying to learn to cook from them. It will suggest a more meaningful approach to recipes than the one-ingredient-after-another point of view of most cookbooks. You will see how to look at ingredients in terms of what they do in a recipe and how they relate to one another. We will introduce you to the concept of cooking with your senses and your common sense.

After completing this chapter, you should be able to:

- Explain why the menu is called the core of the foodservice operation.

- List five types of menus.
- Discuss five considerations for planning menus.
- Discuss the various aspects of menu balance.
- Cost out menus and recipes.
- Identify major nutrients, their functions, and food sources.
- Define a standardized recipe and cite reasons for its use.
- Understand the concepts of recipe structure and ingredient roles.
- Convert a recipe to a larger or smaller yield or a different portion size.

MENUS

Each foodservice facility has its own special menu or group of foods, chosen to fill its own needs and objectives. The hospital, the quick-service franchise, the resort hotel, the luxury dining room, and the little Italian restaurant on the corner have widely differing menus because their purposes are different. The menu expresses the character of an operation; it builds its reputation, good or bad.

The menu is the point of departure for all aspects of the business, the core around which everything revolves. It controls the purchasing and production; it provides the framework for the budget; it generates the income. In a new operation, it determines the equipment and its layout and may even determine whether a bank will finance the project.

Because of its central importance, today's successful menu is a carefully researched document prepared by management. There is as much input from the business side of the operation as from the food specialist, sometimes more.

Today, a menu reflecting only the skills of the chef is a chancy document. The chef's input is important, but it is only one consideration among many. A commercial operation will consult specialists in cost control, marketing, and customer appeal. A hospital operation must have input from nutritionists and the medical staff. The apparently simple choice of what to cook for dinner is a vastly complex and intricately balanced decision.

Even a simple menu planned by the most skillful of menu writers is a venture into the future, like opening a new play on Broadway. Until it has been offered to the people it is designed to please, no one knows exactly how well it will all work. The proof of this pudding is literally in the eating.

Most new menus have some rough spots in the beginning. Customer response may be better than anticipated for some items and not as good for others. Food cost and availability of supplies can change overnight. One small menu change may require several others. The skilled person who originally wrote the menu watches it closely during its early days in action, analyzing the problems and continuing to make adjustments. Over a period of time, the rough spots are smoothed out and a final document represents the essence of the establishment

Though each menu is unique, the way each establishment goes about its menu writing is not so very different from one operation to another. There are certain questions all must ask and answer. If they don't, they don't last long.

Here are the most important questions to be raised and answered in the development of a successful menu:

- Type of menu
- Menu structure
- Clientele: its needs, tastes, and willingness to pay

- Menu balance
- Nutrition
- Portion size
- Availability of products, equipment, and production skills
- Profitability

These and other considerations, such as style of service and number of people to be fed, are all interdependent. Each must be considered in relation to the others in order to achieve a workable menu. As we focus on each one in turn, you will begin to see how difficult it is to isolate any one from the others.

TYPES OF MENUS

There are many types of menus, and they can be categorized in different ways. Menus can be categorized based on the regularity with which the menu items are offered. Think of the quick-service restaurant discussed in Chapter 1, the menu is the same every day. This type of menu is called a **static menu** (Figure 5.1a), because it changes only infrequently. If you think of a school's cafeteria menu, it changes from week to week. This type of menu is called a **cycle menu** (Figure 5.1b). The cycle menu is a carefully planned menu for a set period of time, such as 4 weeks. Every day during the 4 weeks, the menu is different. At the end of the 4-week cycle, the menu repeats itself (in other words, it goes back to the menu on the first day of the cycle).

As you can imagine, it would get boring over time to choose your lunch every day from a static menu. The cycle menu would definitely offer more variety. And, indeed, the cycle menu is generally used in foodservices that feed a relatively captive audience, such as school students, hospital patients, and employees.

In addition to static and cycle menus, there are also **market menus,** which are based on product availability. Some chefs change their menu frequently, even daily, to take advantage of fresh foods at the market. A menu that changes daily is called a **du jour menu.**

Menus can also be categorized by the extent of selection the customer has. A **selective menu** allows the customer to choose what he or she wants. Most menus are selective to some extent, although there are some circumstances under which menus are **nonselective**—such as airline feeding or some nursing homes. Nonselective menus usually offer a list of alternatives in the event a customer does not want the preselected menu items. Some menus combine aspects of both selective and nonselective menus and are called **semiselective menus.** For example, a family-style restaurant may offer a variety of entreés that come with standard side dishes (they can't be selected).

Finally, menus can be categorized by pricing. In an **à la carte menu,** menu items are priced separately. In a **table d'hôte menu,** a complete meal is offered at a set price. A menu with some characteristics of both these menus is a **semi à la carte menu,** which has some separately priced items along with a set price for an entrée and its accompaniments.

MENU STRUCTURE

Whatever the meal or the menu type, there is a common method of constructing a menu. The offerings are grouped into the courses in which the meal is to be served, and the courses are listed in order of service. The customer selects one item per course.

The typical American dinner, and sometimes lunch, menu consists of three courses: appetizer,

New England Summer Seafare

Appetizers

Little Necks on Half Shell

Snail Salad — Shrimp Cocktail

Chowders

New England Clam Chowder
Cup — Bowl

Rhode Island Clam Chowder
Cup — Bowl

Hot Entrees

English Style Fish & Chips
Cole Slaw

New England Fish Cakes, Tomato Sauce
Baked Macaroni Au Gratin

Broiled Halibut Steak
Maitre D' Hotel

Baked Stuffed
Quahog

"Land Lubbers" Feature

Broiled Chopped Beef Steak, Sauteed Mushrooms

From the Grill

Toasted Clam Roll
Tartar Sauce

Fishwich, Steak Roll
Tartar Sauce

Grilled Delmonico on Torpedo
(Sauteed Onions, Peppers, or Mushrooms)

Sandwich Board

Tuna Salad Sandwich — Shrimp Salad Roll — Langostino Salad Roll

Standard Daily Menu Items Also Available

Figure 5-1b MENU

Menu

	SUNDAY	MONDAY (LABOR DAY)	TUESDAY	WEDNESDAY	THURSDAY	FRIDAY	SATURDAY
SOUP	BROCCOLI	SPINACH	CREAM OF TOMATO	BEEF VEGETABLE	CREAM OF CHICKEN	MANHATTEN CLAM CHOWDER	FRENCH ONION
GRILL	Chef's Choice	-----	Open Face Tuna Melt/Pumpernickle	Meatball Hoagie	Italian Hoagie	Chili Dog	Chef's Choice
ENTREE	Country Pork Chop	-----	Beef Stroganoff	Salisbury Steak w/mushroom gravy	Manicotti	Eggplant Parmesan	Pizza Rounds
LITE ENTREE	-----	Bar-B-Q Chicken	Cheese Ravioli	Chicken Piccata	Pork Cutlet w/ Burgundy Wine Sauce	Seafood & Pasta	--------
BLUE PLATE SPECIAL	-----	-----	Beef Stroganoff with noodles and Peas & Onions	Salisbury Steak with mashed potatoes and vegetable	Manicotti and Zucchini	Seafood & Pasta w/ small salad	--------
COLD PLATTER	-----	Cream Cheese with Nuts & Honey on Date Nut Bread	Tuna Salad	Egg Salad Stuffed Tomato	Cheese Vegetable Platter	Chicken Salad on Croissant	--------
VEGETABLE	String Beans	Cauliflower & Fresh Carrots	Confetti Corn	Breaded Green Peppers & Mushrooms	Glazed Beets	Creole Tomatoes	French Style Green Beans
VEGETABLE	Corn on the Cob		Peas & Onions	Collard Greens	Breaded Zucchini Sticks	Hot Cinnamon Applesauce	Succotash
STARCH	Brown Rice	Curried Rice	Buttered Noodles	Mashed Potatoes	Shoe String Fries	Baked Potato w/ cheese & bacon	Hash Browns

Figure 5-1b (Continued)

Menu

	SUNDAY	MONDAY	TUESDAY	WEDNESDAY	THURSDAY	FRIDAY	SATURDAY
SOUP	JULIENNE VEGETABLE	TOMATO RICE	BEEF BARLEY	SNAPPER	COLD FRUIT SOUP	NEW ENGLAND CLAM CHOWDER	CHICKEN GUMBO
GRILL		BAR-B-Q Hot dogs Hamburgers Bar-B-Q Chicken	Grilled Cheese w/ Bacon & Tomato	Reuben	Bacon Double Cheeseburger	Buffalo Wings	
ENTREE	Pot Roast Au Jus	Meatloaf	Sweet & Sour Pork	Basket of Fried Chicken	Macaroni & Beef Casserole	Macaroni & Cheese	Lemon Chicken
	Chicken Chow Mein						Turkey Divan
LITE ENTREE	-----	Presby Fishcake	Vegetable Lasagna	Vegetarian Special	Chicken Kebob on rice	Flounder Almondine	--------
BLUE PLATE SPECIALS	-----	Meatloaf, rice, 1 vegetable	Vegetable Lasagna w/small salad	Basket of Fried Chicken w/fries	Chicken Kebob/ rice, sm fruit soup	Buffalo Wings & small macaroni	--------
COLD PLATTER	-----	Pasta & Cheese	Cottage Cheese & Fruit	Sliced Roast Beef Platter	Cold Chicken Platter	Chef's Salad	--------
VEGETABLE	Broccoli	Peas/Onions	Broccoli Spears	Stewed Tomatoes	Baby Carrots & Zucchini	Yellow Squash	Peas
VEGETABLE	Carrots	Buttered Beets	Whole Baby Carrots	Lima Beans	F.F. Onion Rings	Green Beans	Yam Patties
STARCH	Rice	Brown Rice	Baked Potato	Shoestring Fries	Rice Florentine	Mashed Potatoes	Brown Rice

soup, or salad; entrée (main dish); and dessert. Desserts often include fruit, cheeses, or sweets. In more formal meals, the first course may include two or three of the following: appetizer, soup, or salad (served in this order, never all at once). According to European tradition, the salad is usually served after the entrée, before dessert. The purpose of this practice is to cleanse the palate and refresh the appetite before dessert.

CONSIDERING THE CLIENTELE

The people to be served are the most important consideration in menu design. They are, after all, the reason for each operation's existence.

In some types of operations, you know quite well whom you are serving. A hospital serves patients, staff, and sometimes visitors. A club serves a membership with fairly predictable tastes. A school cafeteria serves students with limited time and money and hearty appetites. A highway restaurant serves travelers in a hurry. A big-city hotel serves conventions, expense-account executives, and potential big spenders. A quick-service restaurant serves individuals and families in search of a fast meal.

In each operation, the particular clientele dictates certain things about the menu. For example, in the hospital the primary consideration is the health of the patients. The menu must provide for three meals a day of a nutritionally balanced diet, with special versions for special needs—low-fat, low-sodium, and so on. The menus for staff and visitors will probably be spin-offs from the general patient menu. Although the patient may not have a choice of foods, the menu is still intricate in design because of the variety of special needs. In addition, the menu offerings change from one day to the next, so that the patients won't get tired of the food.

A menu for a school cafeteria, as another example, would typically be a low-budget, nutritionally balanced meal consisting of foods most students like—nourishing foods easily served and quickly eaten. Specific offerings would depend on whether you were serving persons less than 3 feet tall, or college athletes in training, or middle-school students in their hungry years.

The most successful restaurant dinner menus contain a variety of selections, including dishes of proven popularity. A choice between old favorites and unusual dishes—foods the diners would not cook themselves—makes it a pleasure for customers to plan their own menus for the evening.

Most customers, in fact, tend to be comfortable and happy with foods they understand and are used to. The new cook must remember this. New cooks have a tendency to try to make their mark in history by giving birth to a new dish—something different and unusual. This can get out of hand. Never forget that you are in a service industry. Your responsibility is to give the customers what they want. Set aside your personal tastes and dreams of glory and learn to know the customer who is paying for your food.

Customer tastes may be motivated by needs, habits, ethnic traditions, and regional preferences. Working people may need fast foods because of limited time, or heavy foods because of physical labor and hearty appetites. Temperature and seasons of the year affect customer preferences. Cold weather requires more hot dishes on the menu, hot weather more cold dishes.

Different foods are in demand in different areas of the country. In the Southwest, people lean toward spicy foods such as chili; in the Northeast, they prefer blander flavors. Seafood is popular on both coasts; roast meat and potatoes and apple pie are chosen by Middle America. City tastes are different from small-town tastes, though the quick-service franchises are making us all more and more alike.

The cook as well as the menu writer must understand the styles and tastes of various dishes in different areas. Chili does not mean the same thing to a Texan and a Midwesterner. Milk shakes get thicker the farther west you go. You must take great care not to disappoint the customer's expectations.

Perhaps the most important thing about the customer is the amount of money he or she is willing to spend. This immediately puts brackets around the kind of food the menu will feature. The family cafeteria does not have lobster and beef tenderloin on its menu, nor dishes requiring the salaries of highly skilled cooks. The federal school lunch program requires a certain amount of protein in a lunch that typically sells for over a dollar, thus reducing its menu choices to a very small number of entrée foods with inexpensive vegetables and fruits. At the other end of the scale, the well-heeled customer will demand every dollar's worth and expects a menu worthy of its high price tag in product quality, cooking skills, and presentation. Such customers will not come back unless they have experienced something on the menu worth remembering.

BALANCING THE MENU

Once the menu planner has established the type of menu, the menu structure, and the clientele, the next thing is to think in terms of specific dishes. The balancing of a menu is in essence the selection of its dishes in relation to one another. This requires a knowledge of what foods go well together.

There are several aspects of menu balance. There is the balancing of heavy foods with light foods, of spicy with bland, of light with dark, of soft with crispy or chewy. There is the blending and contrasting of colors. There are some foods that go well together for no observable reason, and some that do not, also for no apparent reason. There is nutritional balance. There is the goal of total satisfaction: A guest prefers to feel pleasantly satisfied, neither stuffed nor starved.

The successful balancing of a meal depends to a great extent on the amount of selection allowed the guest. In a nonselective menu, it is possible to balance everything that requires balancing. Thus, a hospital having a nonselective menu can provide a nutritionally balanced diet for its patients because it feeds them three meals a day. Hospitals that offer a limited selection of foods can offer alternative choices that fill the same nutritional needs. The nonselective menu can also balance tastes, textures, colors, and heavy and light foods. This is a matter for intensive study in preparing an elaborate banquet menu.

At the opposite extreme is the menu on which everything is à la carte—individually priced and individually ordered. Here the menu planner has no control over what the customer will put together to make a meal. The most the menu writer can do is to offer selections that make it possible—even probable—that the customer will put together a meal with balance.

In between is the menu that precombines certain parts of the meal for the diner. Its entrées, for example, are carefully combined with accompaniments for a good balance of tastes, textures, colors, and so on. The guest may then select from the appetizers, soups, and desserts offered. Usually, the salad is planned in relation to the entrées, with the dressing the only selection to be made.

Let's look more closely at some of the elements of balance.

TASTE. You want a certain amount of contrast in tastes so that one food enhances another. Here are some specific rules.

- Balance spicy foods with something bland. Notice that the hot curries and the heavily spiced foods of some Far Eastern cuisines are usually served with plain rice.
- Balance bland foods with something flavorful or spicy. A meal of roast veal, plain rice, and boiled zucchini would put the taste buds to sleep.
- Do not repeat items in the same meal. If tomato soup is served, don't serve tomato sauce or a tomato vegetable dish.
- Avoid serving foods of similar tastes together. Cauliflower, broccoli, cabbage, and turnips, for example, all belong to the same group of tastes.
- Avoid more than one fried item on the same plate. This is a matter of both taste and texture. Fried foods tend to have a similarity of taste when eaten together. The exception to this rule of menu planning is the popular fried-fish platter of the seafood restaurant.

TEXTURE. With texture, too, balance means contrast. Every food combination should have something you can get your teeth into, but not everything should be chewy.

- Balance soft foods with something crisp or chewy and vice versa.
- Don't serve cream soups with sauce-based entrées.
- Don't serve sauces on breaded items. The sauce will spoil the texture of the breading. If sauce must be served, put it under the breaded item.
- In general, serve one starch. Starches are similar in texture; they are also universally heavy.

These rules do not apply, of course, to situations in which the customers choose their own food combinations. A cafeteria line will offer several starches, and you might find a cream soup and a sauce-based entrée on the same à la carte menu along with other selections.

COLOR. Color in itself and the balancing of colors served together should be planned right into the menu.

- Put bright-colored foods on the menu. Don't depend on the cook's garnish for sprucing up a plate.
- Choose foods with color contrast for service together.
- Don't serve all dark or all light foods. The veal–rice–zucchini meal mentioned earlier would put the eyes as well as the taste buds to sleep. Pot roast and gravy served with beets wouldn't be too great to look at, either.

The foods served together on a plate should have a balance between light and heavy items. There should also be an alternation of light and heavy from one course to the next—light soup, heavy entrée (clear soup with prime rib, for example); heavy soup, light entrée (cream soup with broiled fillet of sole).

The balancing of light and heavy foods is more than a convention dictated by tradition. The light food complements the heavy one when they are eaten together—like peanut butter and jelly. Balance also contributes to the pleasant feeling of satiety—not stuffed, not starved—that the diner should have at the end of the meal. It is doubtful that anyone could complete a 12-course dinner if the courses were not well balanced.

On an à la carte menu, it is impossible to balance courses for the guest. But the menu can and should be written so that guests can achieve such a balance in their selections. A banquet menu, and any other nonselective menu, should observe this balance of courses.

Menus should also display a balance in terms of nutrition. Nutrition is discussed in detail in a few moments.

It is in the balancing and pairing of foods in menu writing that knowledge of foods and cooking is most important. Though the menu may not be left to the cook to write, it must certainly have input from the kitchen.

PORTION SIZES

Not only the nature of the dishes on the menu but also the sizes of the portions must be established as part of the menu writing. Fixed and appropriate portion sizes are important for many reasons. From the guests' point of view, a good balance of the amounts of different foods is important to enjoyment of the meal. They may not be aware of portioning—portion sizes are seldom mentioned on the menu card, except for steaks. But a diner may be unhappy if there is too much gravy and not enough meat in an order of pot roast, or if the fruit salad–sandwich luncheon plate is mostly peanut butter sandwich with a dab of salad. There is also the subtler measure of how the customer feels at the end of the meal. Suitable portion sizes can help to avoid the extremes of stuffed and starved.

Some restaurants offer a choice of portion sizes for the entrée, with a corresponding difference in price. Some also offer smaller-sized portions for children. Many operations serve larger portions than they need to, and food is left uneaten on the plate. Food thrown away is profit thrown away. Smaller portions would have filled the need as well. Some restaurants will give customers doggy bags for taking home the food they can't finish. This shouldn't be necessary if the menu is well planned, though there may be customers who consider it a plus.

Portion sizes are important to plate layout. One more asparagus spear on the plate, or a smaller ear of corn, or a little more shrimp on a little less rice may make all the difference.

To purchasing and production, specific portion sizes are absolutely essential. They determine amounts of foods to be purchased and produced. The kitchen would be chaos without them.

Established portion sizes also make it possible to figure costs accurately and set suitable prices of individual dishes and the menu as a whole, as you will see shortly. Changing portion size is also one way of adjusting a cost/price ratio that is off balance, though it is not always the best way.

Finally, established portion sizes provide the basis for portion control. We discussed in the previous chapter how important this is in the management of both quantity and cost.

There are no absolute rules for portion sizes for every food and every menu. But there are some guidelines for quantities that represent general acceptability. Table 5.1 gives you suggested portion sizes for various foods. Notice that many portion sizes vary according to the meal, the course, or the time of day. A luncheon filet of beef, for example, would be 4, 5, or 6 ounces, whereas a dinner portion would range from 6 to 8 ounces. Sometimes restaurants will offer extra-large portions as a special feature, such as a 12- or 16-ounce steak on a steakhouse menu.

PRODUCTION CAPABILITY

In choosing specific dishes, the menu writer must consider another set of questions. Can each

Table 5-1 COMMON SERVING PORTIONS[a]

Breakfast		
Eggs	2–4 oz (1–2 eggs)	50–125 g
Meat	2–4 oz	50–125 g
Fruit	$^1/_2$–1 C	125—250 mL
Cereal	$^3/_4$–$1^1/_2$ C	175 mL
Juice	$^1/_2$–1 C	125–250 mL
Bread	1–2 slices	(30–60 g)
Lunch		
Soup	6–8 oz	175–250 mL
Salad	4–8 oz	125–250 g
Salad dressing	1–2 oz	25–50 mL
Main dish	4–6 oz	125–175 g
Starch	3–4 oz	75–100 g
Vegetable	3–4 oz	75–100 g
Sauce	1–2 oz	25–50 mL
Bread	1–2 slices	30–60 g
Dessert	2–4 oz	50–100 g
Dinner		
Soup	8–12 oz	250–375 mL
Salad	4–8 oz	125–250 g
Salad dressing	1–2 oz	25–50 mL
Main dish	6–8 oz	175–250 g
Sauce	1–2 oz	25–50 mL
Starch	3–4 oz	75–100 g
Vegetable	3–4 oz	75–100 g
Bread	1–2 slices	30–60 g
Dessert	2–4 oz	50–125 g

[a]Quantities given reflect general practice. Specific needs will vary.

dish be produced successfully, and can they all be produced successfully together? Three things must be available: the products, the equipment, and the production skills.

The menu planner must establish that the products to be used are readily available in the area. Though a restaurateur may have a burning desire to open a great seafood restaurant in a small Midwestern town, it could be difficult to get fresh seafood at realistic prices.

Many foods are perishable and seasonal. When such items are being considered, it is essential to make sure they are continuously available. Fresh fruit and vegetables make good menu items, but it may be difficult to serve fresh strawberry shortcake in January at a reasonable price.

Unless you can make a product exactly as it is stated on the menu, don't state it. Seasonal foods should be added to a printed menu in the form of a flyer or insert that can be removed when the product is not available.

The proposed menu must be reviewed, item by item and as a whole, in the light of the equipment and labor it takes to prepare it. In a new operation, there is the option of designing the kitchen to accommodate the menu. In an existing kitchen, the menu must be producible with the existing equipment. An establishment will often attempt a menu item that is too difficult to produce profitably with limited equipment. If you are given the responsibility of selecting items for a menu, be sure you can make them readily with the equipment you have.

The professional skill level of an operation is just as important to menu writing as its equipment capability. Complicated dishes that require special skills fit only in operations that have the personnel with these skills. An added consideration in any operation is the spread of the workload among employees to take maximum advantage of the work hours available.

PROFITABILITY

The final test of a menu, profitability, tells us whether a menu item can be produced within the budget guidelines set by management. In a nonprofit operation, the cost of all the food on the menu must be within the limit of so much per person, or per meal, or whatever standard management has set. In a commercial operation, the menu must maintain the minimum spread between food cost and sales—at menu prices the customer is willing to pay. No sales, no restaurant. Sales but not enough profit, no restaurant. The unskilled menu writer can write himself or herself right out of a job.

Before a menu can be launched, then, both the individual dishes and the menu as a whole are carefully costed to make sure they can be served within the guidelines. Costing a menu means figuring the raw-food cost of each product as served.

When you are planning a menu, there are two ways of working with menu costs. You can find out what you will be able to spend first and then pick menu items you can produce for that price, or you can decide on specific items you think will fall within the guidelines and then check them out.

Suppose you have been given a **food cost percentage** of 30 percent of menu price and a sales price limit of $5.95. To find out how much you can spend, you multiply the price by the percentage:

$5.95, rounded to	$6.00	menu price
	× $0.30	desired food cost percentage
	$1.80	food cost allowance

This means that the cost of raw food must not exceed $1.80 to stay within budget.

Or you can figure it the other way around. Take the raw-food cost of the dish as served and divide it by the cost percentage, and you come up with the necessary menu price:

$$\frac{\text{Cost}}{\text{Percentage}} = \frac{\$1.80}{0.30} = \$6.00 \qquad \text{menu price}$$

Because raw-food prices fluctuate constantly, menus are costed and recosted frequently. Consider the following menu:

Tossed salad
Thousand Island dressing
Onion soup
Prime rib au jus
Baked potato
Pineapple sorbet

To cost this menu, you begin by computing separately the portion (EP) cost of each item. You do this by costing the recipe for each dish, using the procedure illustrated in Figure 5.2. You figure the EP cost of each raw ingredient in a given dish, add these costs together, and divide the total by the yield to determine the individual portion cost for that dish. When you have the cost for each dish, you add these costs together to determine the total cost of this meal for one person. For example,

Tossed salad	$0.25
Dressing	$0.10
Onion soup	$0.35
Prime rib	$4.50
Baked potato	$0.24
Sorbet	$0.75
	$6.19

To establish a tentative menu price for this dinner, you would divide the total cost of the dinner by the cost percentage as you did for the single dish:

$$\frac{\text{Cost of meal}}{\text{Food cost percentage}} = \frac{\$6.19}{0.30} = \$20.63 \qquad \text{menu price}$$

This might be translated into a typical menu price of $19.99. Such a price would include a small allowance for cost changes.

Figure 5-2 HOW TO COST A RECIPE

1. Find the as-purchased (AP) cost of each ingredient.
2. Convert the recipe amount of the ingredient and the AP amount to the same unit of measure. Usually you would convert the AP unit of measure (e.g., gallons, below) to the recipe unit of measure (e.g., pints). Occasionally you would do it the other way around (e.g., numbers of eggs to dozens).
3. Find the cost of 1 unit by dividing the AP cost by the number of units.
4. Find the recipe cost of the ingredient by multiplying the cost of 1 unit by the number of units the recipe calls for.
5. Find the total cost of the recipe by adding up all the ingredient costs.
6. Find the cost per portion by dividing the total recipe cost by the number of portions (yield).

For example:

THOUSAND ISLAND DRESSING

YIELD: ***1 qt (1 L) or 32 1-oz (30-g) portions***

Ingredients	*Step 1* *AP Cost*	*Step 2* *Unit Conversion*	*Step 3* *Unit Cost*	*Step 4* *Recipe Cost*
$1^1/_2$ pt mayonnaise	5.21 per gal	1 gal = 8 pt	$\frac{5.21}{8} = 0.651$	0.651 × 1.5 = 0.977
$^1/_4$ pt chili sauce	3.57 per #10 can	1 can = 6 pt	$\frac{3.57}{6} = 0.595$	0.595 × 0.25 = 0.149
$^1/_4$ pt catsup	3.29 per #10 can	1 can = 6 pt	$\frac{3.29}{6} = 0.548$	0.548 × 0.25 = 0.137
6 eggs	0.91 per dozen	6 eggs = $^1/_2$ doz	0.91	0.91 × 0.5 = 0.455
2 oz onions	0.11 per lb	1 lb = 16 oz	$\frac{0.11}{16} = 0.007$	0.007 × 2 = 0.014
2 oz dill pickles	0.99 per lb	1 lb = 16 oz	$\frac{0.99}{16} = 0.062$	0.062 × 2 = 0.124

Step 5: TOTAL RECIPE COST: 1.856

Step 6: $\frac{\text{cost of recipe}}{\text{number of portions}}$ $\frac{1.856}{32}$ = 0.058 COST PER PORTION

The actual pricing of a menu includes many factors besides cost/price ratios, and the cost/price ratio used here is an arbitrary example of a budget goal. The whole subject of pricing is complicated and well beyond the scope of this text. What is important for you at this point is to grasp the mechanics of costing and pricing and to understand their importance as tools in menu development.

Costing a menu or a dish is also used as a tool of cost control to determine whether costs and prices are maintaining the minimum spread necessary to successful operation. Suppose, for example, that the menu we have been costing is one you have been serving at a price of \$15.95, and you are recosting the menu to see if your cost/price budget ratio of 30 percent is holding. To find the current percentage, you divide the cost by the price:

$$\frac{\text{Current menu cost}}{\text{Current sales price}} = \frac{\$5.44}{\$15.95} = 0.341 \text{ or } 34.1 \text{ percent}$$

Your costs, you find, have risen above the 30 percent of sales that was your target.

When such changes occur, management may decide to raise the menu price, or to make changes in menu ingredients to reduce food costs, or to let the cost/price ratio rise. Sometimes popular high-priced items are allowed to rise above an overall cost/price percentage goal because their dollar return is high. A best-selling steak whose cost/price ratio is 45 percent still brings in more dollars than an inexpensive chicken dish with smaller sales at a 30 percent cost/price ratio. The right decision depends on the circumstances. The important thing to realize is that costing a menu and looking at cost in relation to dollar sales will give the facts needed to make the decision.

You can see that the costing of menus is an essential ingredient in the success of an operation. You can also see that the process does not end once the menu is written. In commercial

Figure 5-3 MENU EVALUATION

1. Does the menu meet the food habits and preferences of the customers?
2. Do the menu items look appealing and taste good?
3. Are nutritious menu items available?
4. Is there a balance of color in the menu items?
5. Is there a balance of texture—soft and crisp versus firm-textured foods?
6. Is there a balance of shape, with different-sized pieces and shapes of foods?
7. Are flavors varied?
8. Are the food combinations acceptable?
9. Are cooking methods varied?
10. Can each menu item be prepared properly by the staff?
11. Is there enough equipment to produce this menu?
12. Is the food cost appropriate for the prices being charged?
13. Are any of the menu items too labor intensive for the price being charged?
14. Are the raw ingredients all available to make this menu?

menus, the pricing is as important as the costing. Successful menus stay within budget guidelines, and successful pricing includes allowances for cost changes.

You can see, too, by this time, why menu writing is not left entirely to the chef, no matter how skilled that chef may be in the kitchen.

A final consideration when planning menus is nutrition, our next topic. Before jumping ahead, review Figure 5.3. It is a checklist you can use to evaluate your menu that ties together everything we have discussed.

NUTRITION

Nutrition can be defined as a science that studies nutrients in foods and in the body, and how these nutrients are related to health and disease. Nutrition also examines the processes by which you choose what to eat and the balance of foods in nutrients in your diet. It is very important to understand basic nutrition concepts because nutrition is an important consideration when planning menus, particularly for populations such as children, the elderly, and healthcare patients with special nutritional needs.

Let's start by looking at the characteristics of a nutritious diet. A nutritious diet is:

1. Adequate
2. Moderate
3. Balanced
4. Varied

Whereas an adequate diet provides enough of the essential nutrients and calories, a moderate diet avoids excessive amounts of calories and any particular food or nutrient. In the case of calories, consuming too many leads to obesity. One of the best ways to have an adequate and moderate diet is to choose nutrient-dense foods. **Nutrient-dense foods,** such as broccoli, contain many nutrients for the calories they provide.

Next, you need a balanced diet. A balanced diet does not overemphasize certain foods at the expense of others. For example, if you drink a lot of soft drinks, you may not be drinking much milk, a rich source of the mineral calcium. In a well-balanced diet, protein should provide 10 to 15 percent of the calories, carbohydrates 50 to 55 percent, and fats not more than 30 percent. Vitamins, minerals, and water contribute no calories but are essential to growth and health.

Finally, you need a varied diet—in other words, one that includes many different foods. A varied diet is important because it is more likely to ensure that you get the essential nutrients in the right amounts.

As mentioned in Chapter 4, food contains about 50 nutrients that can be arranged into six groups:

1. Carbohydrates
2. Fat
3. Proteins
4. Vitamins
5. Minerals
6. Water

Most foods are a mixture of these nutrients.

Carbohydrates include sugars, starches, and fibers. **Sugar** occurs naturally in fruits and milk and in refined forms, such as table sugar or corn syrup. Refined sugars are found in soft drinks, cakes and other bakery products, candies, syrup, jams and jellies, and other sweetened foods. Refined sugar is unusual in that it is pure carbohydrate and contains no other nutrients. Although refined sugar seems to be responsible for only one health problem (causing cavities in your teeth), foods high in refined sugars, such as many cakes, contribute calories without providing much in the way of other nutrients.

Grains, such as wheat, corn, rice, rye, barley, and oats, are rich sources of **starch.** Grains are used to make flour, breakfast cereals, and pastas. Besides grains, starches are also found in potatoes, vegetables, and dried beans and peas. Most starchy foods contain little or no fat.

Like starch, **fiber** is found abundantly in plants, especially in the outer layers of cereal grains and the fibrous, chewy parts of fruits, dried beans and peas, vegetables, nuts, and seeds. Fiber is not found in any animal products (such as meat, milk, or eggs). What's different about fiber is that it can't be broken down or digested in your digestive tract, like sugars and starches, so it passes through the stomach and intestines unchanged and is excreted. Fiber has many healthy effects; it helps prevent constipation, may lower your blood cholesterol level, and helps you feel full after a meal.

The *fat* in your diet is both visible and invisible. When discussing fats, many people think only about the visible fats—butter, margarine, oils—in their diet. But much of the fat in your diet comes from less visible sources—the fatty streaks in meat, the fat under the skin of chicken, the fat in milk and cheese, the fat in many snack foods and desserts. By contrast, fruits and vegetables (except avocados and olives), cereal grains, flour, pasta, breads, and most cereals have little or no fat.

There are three types of fats in foods:

1. **Saturated fats.** These are found mostly in animal foods such as meats, milk, eggs, and cheeses (unless they are made to contain no fat).
2. **Monounsaturated fats.** These are found in plant oils such as olive oil, peanut oil, and canola oil.
3. **Polyunsaturated fats.** These are found in greatest amounts in safflower, corn, soybean, cottonseed, sesame, and sunflower oils. Nuts and seeds also contain polyunsaturated fats.

Recommendations suggest limiting your saturated fat intake, because a high saturated fat intake leads to high blood cholesterol levels, an important risk factor for heart disease. In recent years, research has shown that monounsaturated fat probably helps keep cholesterol levels down.

Cholesterol is a fatlike substance that the human body needs, but too much of it is not desirable. Cholesterol is found only in foods from animal sources. Plant foods, such as grains, fruits, or vegetables, do not contain cholesterol.

Fat and cholesterol have been associated with two health problems: heart disease and cancer. The higher your blood cholesterol level, the greater is your risk or chance of developing the most common form of heart disease. To prevent high blood cholesterol levels (and perhaps some forms of cancer), it is best to have a diet with a moderate amount of fat and low amounts of saturated fat and cholesterol. Since fat, saturated fat, and cholesterol tend to go together in the same foods, lowering your intake of these nutrients is not too confusing.

Proteins are an essential part of all living cells found in animals and plants. Nutritionally, proteins are the major building and maintenance materials of the body. Protein is found in both animal and plant foods, although it is more plentiful in animal foods, including meat, poultry, seafood, dairy products, and eggs. Of the plant foods, grains, legumes, and nuts have more protein than vegetables and fruits. Protein is very important because it builds and maintains the body.

Vitamins and *minerals* are essential in small quantities for growth and good health. If you have too little of a vitamin or mineral, it may lead to a deficiency disease. Neither vitamins nor minerals contain calories, as do carbohydrates, fat, and protein.

Vitamins are classified according to how soluble they are in fat or water. Fat-soluble vitamins (A, D, E, and K) generally occur in foods containing fat. Water-soluble vitamins include vitamin C and the B-complex vitamins.

Sodium is a mineral that is often overconsumed. This creates a problem for people who have high blood pressure and are sodium sensitive, meaning that excess sodium will increase their blood pressure. The major source of sodium in the diet is salt and processed foods, such as salted snack foods, canned vegetables and soups, frozen dinners, and many luncheon meats.

Deny someone food and he or she can live on for weeks. But death comes quickly, in a matter of a few days, if you deprive a person of *water.* Nothing survives without water, and virtually nothing takes place in the body without water playing a vital role. A little more than half your body weight is water. You need between 8 and 10 cups of fluid every day.

To plan menus with good nutrition in mind, consider the following **Dietary Guidelines for Americans:**

1. Eat a variety of foods.
2. Balance the food you eat with physical activity—maintain or improve your weight.
3. Choose a diet with plenty of grain products, vegetables, and fruits.
4. Choose a diet low in fat, saturated fat, and cholesterol.
5. Choose a diet moderate in sugars.
6. Choose a diet moderate in salt and sodium.
7. If you drink alcoholic beverages, do so in moderation.

Also, use the **Food Guide Pyramid** (Figure 5.4) for guidance.

RECIPES

A recipe is a bridge between someone who knows how to make a certain dish and someone who wants to make it. Ideally, the teacher and the would-be cook would be in the same place at the same time, but that is not always possible. Since food preparation is ongoing and universal, a permanent, universal method of communication is needed. This is the written recipe—a set of directions for making a dish or product. The directions give the reader two things: the ingredients needed and instructions for combining them to make the finished product.

THE STANDARDIZED RECIPE

Written recipes are often developed for use in a particular operation to record the way in which that establishment makes the various dishes it serves. This kind of recipe is called a **standardized recipe.**

The typical standardized recipe lists the ingredients in order of use, states the amount of each ingredient required to make a certain number of servings of a certain size, and gives instructions for putting the ingredients together to make the dish. The number and size of servings are listed on the recipe as the yield.

The recipe is written for numbers of servings commonly used in the operation. Many establish-

Figure 5-4 THE FOOD GUIDE PYRAMID—A GUIDE TO DAILY FOOD CHOICES

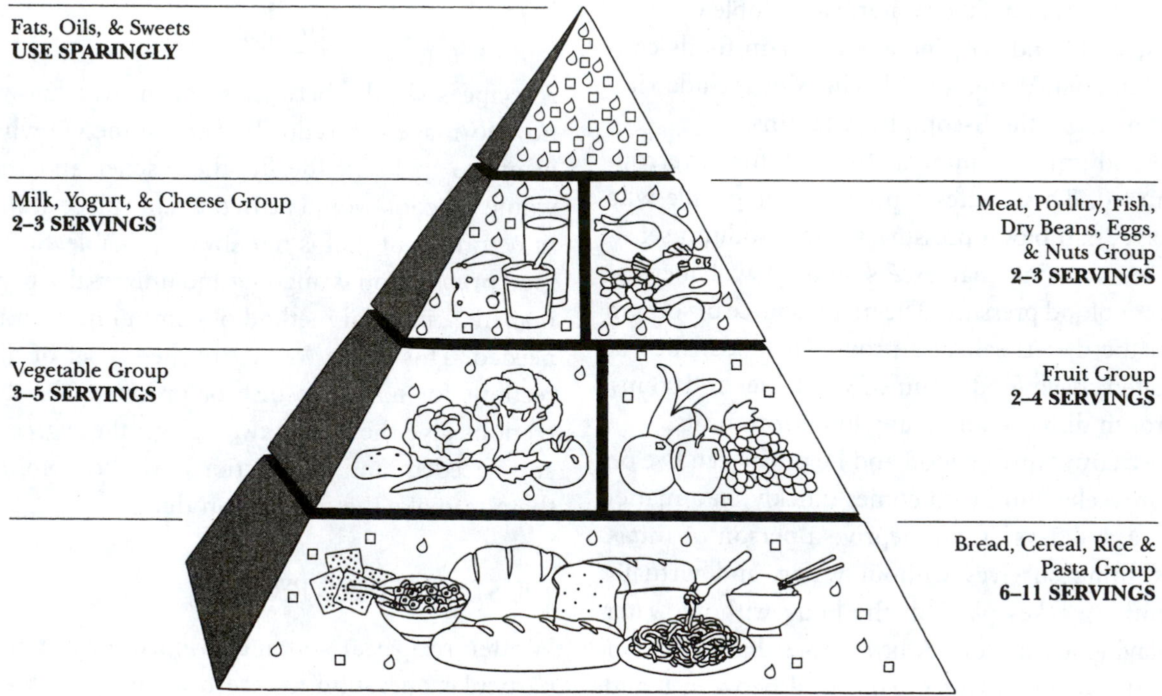

Looking at the Pieces of the Pyramid

The Food Guide Pyramid emphasizes foods from the five major food groups shown in the three lower sections of the Pyramid. Each of these food groups provides some, but not all, of the nutrients you need. Foods in one group can't replace those in another. No one of these major food groups is more important than another—for good health, you need them all.

(From U.S. Department of Agriculture and the U.S. Department of Health and Human Services.)

ments write recipes for 25 or 50 servings. In some, the recipe may also be figured for larger yields, such as 100, 500, or 1000 servings. The serving dish, garnish, and plate layout are often specified. Sometimes, the card has a picture of the dish in color.

A standardized recipe applies only to one operation. Many people have the mistaken idea that a standardized recipe contains a foolproof set of ingredients, amounts, and instructions that will work every time in every kitchen for every cook. There is no such thing. If you transplant a recipe standardized for one kitchen to another kitchen and another set of cooks, it may work or it may not. If it works in the new kitchen after thorough testing of a small amount, it may be extended to larger yields and adopted as the operation's standardized recipe. If it doesn't work, that kitchen may make adjustments in the recipe to fit its equipment and its cooks and its clientele and to achieve the precise yield and quality standards required. When all the necessary adjustments are incorporated, it then becomes a standardized recipe for that operation.

FUNCTIONS OF STANDARDIZED RECIPES. The standardized recipe is useful in several ways. For one thing, it helps to assure that a product offered by the establishment is consistent from one cook to another. A customer who brings friends in to taste a well-remembered mushroom soup won't find the soup of memory gone and a new cook making a very different product. The new cook can refer to the standardized recipe, and it will indicate the special things that give that particular mushroom soup its character. Each establishment's standardized recipes are records of dishes that have proved to be successful for that operation.

Another function of standardized recipes is to provide a basis for cost analysis. Accurate costs per serving can be projected and analyzed from the precise data the recipes contain. Many standardized recipes have the cost data recorded on the recipe card. Some establishments keep their standardized recipes on a computer, where changes in ingredients and costs can easily be kept up to date. When cost problems occur—when food costs run higher than projected—the quantities and costs of items being used can be compared to the quantities and costs that should have been used, in order to see what is wrong and how to correct it.

With computers in wide use, the standardized recipe is playing an ever more important role in making an inefficient industry more efficient. Good standardized recipes coupled with the computer enable management to control expenses or costs even before they are incurred. Current market prices, availability, and alternate ingredients are programmed into the computer so that costs can be determined instantly before food products are bought and used. Before the computer, figuring costs with a pencil or a calculator took hours and was seldom done. Thus, the standardized recipe is one of management's most useful tools for achieving profitability, and profitability is the one essential in the commercial kitchen—something the cook must never forget.

Standardized recipes are also highly useful to the person who orders supplies or makes purchasing forecasts. A person planning a banquet can quickly figure what is needed to serve the expected number of diners because the items, quantities, and yields are right there in the recipe.

Standardized recipes are especially valuable in hospital kitchens, where cooks must follow the recipes to the letter. The amount of salt or butter in a portion of food may be critical for a patient on a special diet. Bakers, too, use standardized recipes because a tiny variation in the ratios of ingredients can make the finished product a total failure. Operations requiring penny-by-penny cost control, such as many public-school foodservices, depend heavily on standardized recipes. And many large institutional foodservices find that standardized recipes carefully worded for the low-skill worker help to keep labor costs down yet still produce good, consistent results.

In an efficient operation, each standardized recipe is checked periodically to ensure that it reflects current kitchen practice, or that current kitchen practice follows the recipe, whichever is more important. Changes in practice are noted on the card, so that it remains an accurate master record of that dish for that establishment.

You can readily see that the standardized recipe is an essential industry tool. But learning to cook by following such a recipe one ingredient at a time is not the best way to do it. The standardized recipe was written as a record, not as a teaching tool. How good is a recipe—any recipe—at telling you how to make a dish you have never made before?

To answer this question, let's examine a typical recipe for a classical cream soup (Figure 5.5). It is not a standardized recipe because it is not designed to be used in a particular operation. It is the kind of recipe you find in dozens of books.

Figure 5-5 A TYPICAL RECIPE
Cream of Cauliflower Soup

Yield: ***20 6-ounce servings***

Ingredients	*Amounts*	*Method*
butter	6 oz (175 g)	Cook vegetables, herbs, and spices in butter for 5 minutes.
cauliflower	1 head	Blend in flour and cook for 10 minutes over low heat.
celery, diced	2 ribs	Add stock and blend well. Cook over low heat for 20 minutes.
leek, diced	1	Blend in hot cream. Season with salt and pepper. Strain and
onion, diced	1	serve.
parsley, diced	few stems	
bay leaf	1/2	
clove	1	
garlic	1/2 clove	
rosemary	pinch	
thyme	pinch	
peppercorns, crushed	pinch	
flour	6 oz (175 g)	
stock	1 gal (4 L)	
cream	1 pt (500 mL)	
salt	1 Tb (15 mL)	
pepper	1 tsp (5 mL)	

If you gave this recipe to 20 beginning cooks, they might very well turn out 20 different soups.

How can this be? The recipe gives specific ingredients. It specifies exact quantities. It states exact cooking times. It spells out each step in the cooking process. How can anything go wrong?

The fact is that, in cooking, there are many variables, and these variables practically guarantee a variety of results unless you understand how to deal with them. Many recipes give rigid instructions about things that vary from one kitchen to another, from product to product, from person to person.

For example, no two ranges perform in exactly the same fashion. No two heads of cauliflower are exactly alike. No two products of any kind are exactly alike, no two utensils, no two cooks. You yourself are not likely to turn the flame of the gas burner to exactly the same height two days in a row. Even the weather, the altitude, and the kitchen temperature can change things.

The recipe, in trying to ensure a standard result by specifying cooking times, actually guarantees a variety of results because of all the variables. Different pots of soup prepared by different people on different equipment do not cook in exactly the same length of time. One cook's soup will evaporate more than another's, so the two soups will not have the same taste and texture and will not need the same amount of salt.

Perhaps the most common and most serious variable is cooking time. The recipe in Figure 5.5 tells you to cook the vegetables and herbs in butter for 5 minutes and to blend in flour and cook for 10 minutes over low heat. The conscientious, unsuspecting recipe follower will go on cooking it for 10 minutes no matter what. But cooking times vary widely, and unless the cook understands what is supposed to be happening, disaster may follow.

COOKING WITH YOUR SENSES. In this book, the recipe instructions will seldom specify cooking times. Instead, they will give you a time range as a guideline, but they will hardly ever tell you to cook something for a specific number of minutes or hours. Instead, they will give you observable checkpoints such as "when it thickens," or "when it begins to produce an aroma," or "it should feel firm to the touch," or "until no starch taste remains." These checkpoints will usually be more accurate and realistic than exact times, because they adapt to all the variables and avoid the difficulty of measurement.

Many professional cooks use guidelines like these. They don't time things, except in a general way. They know how something is supposed to look, feel, smell, and taste as it develops into a dish, and they take action accordingly.

Admittedly, descriptive guidelines in a set of instructions, no matter how carefully worded, can be somewhat imprecise in communicating exactly what is going on. They may not mean much to you until you see something cooked and cook it yourself. Then, you, too, will get the feel, the look, the taste, and the smell of it, and you will really be cooking.

USING PRECISE TERMINOLOGY. In order to cope with another variable—the meanings of words to the reader—the instructions in this book are built around the precise use of terms as they are defined in Chapters 3 and 4. Other terms, added as we go along, are incorporated into recipe instructions in the same way. Often, such a term avoids a long, involved instruction giving directions on time, temperature, and method. The term sauté, for example, tells you to flip briefly, at a hot temperature, in a small amount of fat. The term communicates all this simply and precisely.

STRUCTURE AND FUNCTION IN A DISH. Most recipes list the ingredients in order of use. Let's take the ingredients from the soup recipe in Figure 5.5 and rearrange them according to their function in the soup. Then they will begin to make sense. What do we mean by "their function in the soup"?

Any dish created in the kitchen has certain qualities. It has a **major flavor**—beef, or mushroom, or asparagus, for example. It has a **body**—that is, it has substance and volume. It has a **texture**—thin or thick, smooth or coarse, crunchy, creamy, chewy, and so on. To create these qualities in a dish, you use certain ingredients.

In our soup, the cauliflower provides the predominant flavor. That is its function in the dish. The liquids provide the body; that is their main function. The flour and butter, cooked together, thicken the soup to provide its characteristic texture; that is their function. These ingredients play the major roles in the dish; they are the stars of the show.

Then, there is the cast of supporting characters in this soup: the celery, onion, leek, parsley, herbs, spices, and seasonings. They assist the major ingredients but never upstage them. Their function is to build up, blend, enhance, enrich, or accent the flavor, body, and texture provided by the stars.

Figure 5.6 groups the recipe's ingredients according to the roles they play. This format helps you to see the role of each ingredient and understand how they all fit together. Keep in mind when using the recipes in this book to look for the ingredients that provide the major flavor, body, and texture and the supporting ingredients that build flavor.

RATIOS AND PROPORTIONS. Another thing that the traditional recipe format does not

Figure 5-6 DIAGRAM OF FIGURE 5.5
Cream of Cauliflower Soup

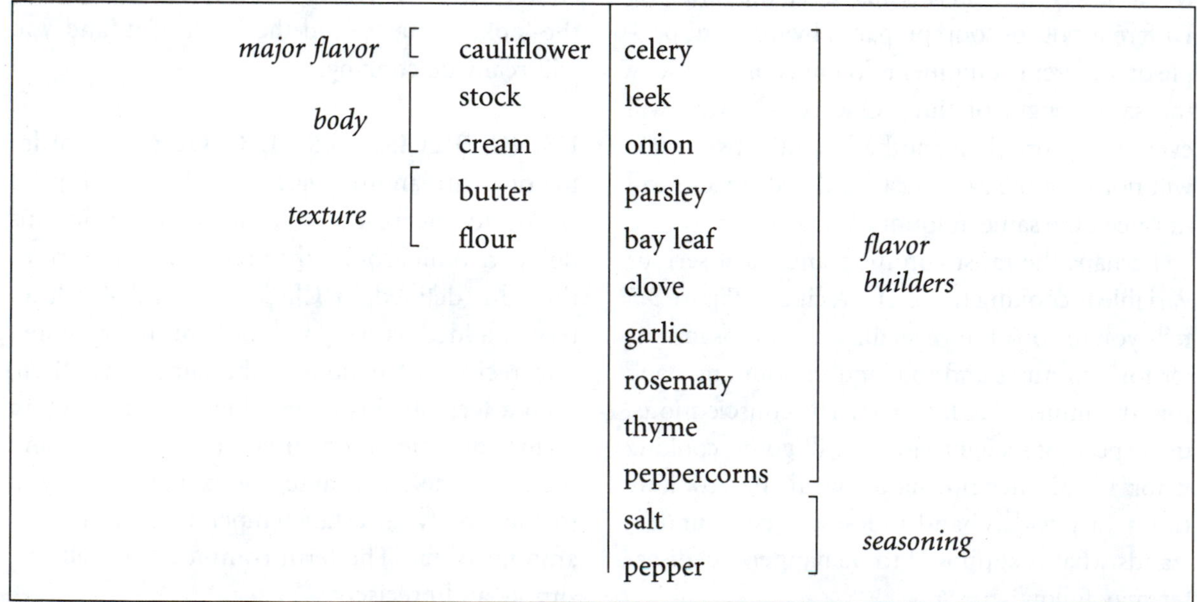

Figure 5-7 RECIPE IN T FORMAT

Cream of Cauliflower Soup

YIELD: *1 gallon (4 liters) = 20 6-ounce servings*

major flavor	1 lb	cauliflower	500 g	2	celery ribs	*flavor builders*
body	1 gal	stock	4 L	1	leek	
	1 pt	cream	500 mL	1	onion	
texture	6 oz	butter	175 g	few	parsley stems	
	6 oz	flour	175 g	1/2	bay leaf	
				1	clove	
				1/2	garlic clove	
				pinch	rosemary	
				pinch	thyme	
				pinch	peppercorns, crushed	
					salt	*seasoning*
					pepper	

communicate is the ratios and proportions, or relationships, among ingredients. Let us add quantities to the ingredients in Figure 5.7 and see what emerges.

Probably the first thing you notice in Figure 5.7 is that there are large quantities of the major ingredients and very small quantities of the supporting ingredients. This is hardly surprising in view of their functions in the recipe.

If you look more closely at the left-hand side, you can see some basic quantity relationships among the various major ingredients: 1 pound of cauliflower to 1 gallon of stock; 3/4 pound of flour–butter thickener to 1 gallon of stock. (Or, in metric, 500 grams of cauliflower to 4 liters of stock to 350 grams of thickener makes 4 liters of soup.) If you examine the right-hand side, you can see that there are specific relationships among the various supporting ingredients. There are further relationships among each supporting ingredient and the quantities of major ingredient and finished soup. Half a bay leaf to a pound of cauliflower to a gallon of soup. One onion. One clove.

It is the proportions of ingredients to one another that make the dish what it is. This is the way many professionals approach their cooking. They think of ingredients in groups according to their functions and memorize the basic proportions. They refer to the recipe card for quantities and yields and the special variations practiced by the kitchen where they work. When using the recipes in this book, consider the proportions of major ingredients to supporting ingredients and of single ingredients to each other.

Figure 5-8 CONVERTING A RECIPE

Ingredients	*20 Servings (yield given)*	*× 5 =*	*100 Servings (yield desired)*	*or × 0.5 or 1/2 =*	*10 Servings (yield desired)*
Flour	6 oz		30 oz = 1 lb 14 oz		3 oz
Cauliflower	1 lb		5 lb		1/2 lb
Stock	1 gal		5 gal		1/2 gal
Cream	1 pt		5 pt = 2 1/2 qt		1/2 pt
Butter	6 oz		30 oz = 1 lb 14 oz		3 oz
Flour	6 oz		30 oz = 1 lb 14 oz		3 oz
Celery	2 ribs		10 ribs		1 rib
Leeks	1		5		1/2
Onions	1		5		1/2
Parsley stems	few		5 × few = handful		1–2
Bay leaf	1/2		2 1/2		1/4
Clove	1		5		1/2
Garlic	1/2 clove		2 1/2 cloves		1/4 clove
Rosemary	pinch		5 pinches		1/2 pinch
Thyme	pinch		5 pinches		1/2 pinch
Peppercorns	pinch		5 pinches		1/2 pinch
Salt	to taste		to taste		to taste
Pepper	to taste		to taste		to taste

RECIPES AS BASIC PATTERNS. A recipe is what you make of it. As you study cooking, much of your success will depend on how you are able to use a recipe. If you follow it blindly step by step without understanding, you will be a slave to it. If you see it as a blueprint for the construction of a dish, it can open doors for you. When you understand its pattern and master the techniques required, you can make the dish in any quantity with or without a recipe. You can also apply the pattern and proportions to similar products. Thousands and thousands of recipes are really variations of a few basic patterns, which makes the whole world of cooking very simple.

CONVERTING RECIPES

Another recipe-related skill you need to develop is changing the amounts of ingredients to produce a larger or smaller yield. Equivalents, as discussed in Chapter 4, are indispensable when it comes to increasing or decreasing a recipe to produce a larger or smaller amount. This process usually involves translating some units into others, such as pounds to ounces or quarts to gallons, or vice versa.

To produce a different amount of the same product, you must keep the proportions of ingredients the same or you will not get the same product. Figuring the amounts of ingredients in the correct proportions for a different number of servings is called **converting the recipe.**

Converting a recipe is really very simple. Everything stays in the correct proportions if you multiply every ingredient by the same number. To find what number to use, you divide the amount you want by the amount the recipe yields. The answer will be a number larger than 1 if you are increasing and smaller than 1 if you are decreasing.

To see how this works, let's take as an example our cauliflower soup recipe. Figure 5.8 lists the ingredients in that recipe in Column 1. Column 2 lists the amount of each ingredient for 20 6-ounce portions (yield given). Suppose we want to make 100 6-ounce portions (yield desired, Column 3). (To keep this example simple, we have omitted the metric figures, but metrics work in exactly the same way.)

Step 1 is to find the multiplier. To do this, you divide the number of portions desired (100) by the number of portions given:

$$\frac{100 \text{ portions desired}}{20 \text{ portions given}} = \frac{100}{20} = 5 \quad \text{(multiplier)}$$

Step 2 is to multiply the amount of each ingredient by your multiplier—in this case 5—to give you the amount you need for 100 portions:

$$1 \text{ lb cauliflower} \times 5 = 5 \text{ lb}$$
$$1 \text{ gal stock} \times 5 = 5 \text{ gal}$$

and so on. Multiplying the amount of each ingredient in Column 2 by 5 gives you the amounts in Column 3.

Column 4 shows the same recipe converted to 10 servings. The multiplier is determined in the same way:

$$\frac{10 \text{ portions desired}}{20 \text{ portions given}} = \frac{10}{20} = 0.5 \text{ (or } ^1/_2)$$

Notice that, in Column 3, equivalents have been used to convert such amounts as 30 ounces and 5 pints to units of measurement you would use if you were actually going to make the dish. In practice, you would also convert such amounts as 5 pinches to something more practical. You might guesstimate a quantity equal to 5 pinches. If you were going to make the larger quantity regularly, you might establish an exact amount by using a measured amount each time until you achieved a taste identical to that of the smaller recipe. You would record this tested and proved amount on your standardized recipe.

It is a good idea to look at your ingredient amounts when you have finished a conversion to see whether they make sense. It is easy when multiplying to slip in an extra digit by mistake. You might end up with 100 celery ribs instead of 10.

Another factor that is important in converting recipes is the way the yield is expressed. It may be in gallons or in 6-ounce servings and you may want 8-ounce servings. In such cases, you must first use your equivalents to convert the yield desired and the yield given to the same unit (i.e., a gallon or an 8-ounce serving) so that you can divide one by the other in order to find your multiplier.

For example: Your recipe yields 1 gallon. You want 80 8-ounce servings. You can choose an 8-ounce serving as your unit of measurement and convert 1 gallon into 8-ounce servings. Thus,

$$1 \text{ gal} = 128 \text{ oz}$$

$$\frac{128 \text{ oz}}{8 \text{ oz per serving}} = 16 \text{ servings}$$

Or you can convert 80 8-ounce servings into gallons:

$$80 \text{ 8-oz servings} = 640 \text{ oz}$$

$$\frac{640 \text{ oz}}{128 \text{ oz per gal}} = 5 \text{ gal}$$

$$\frac{5 \text{ gal desired}}{1 \text{ gal given}} = \frac{5}{1} = 5 \qquad \text{(multiplier)}$$

Or perhaps you have a yield of 20 6-ounce servings and you want 60 8-ounce servings. Here again you use equivalents to convert the yield to a common unit and then proceed as before:

$$60 \text{ servings} \times 8 \text{ oz} = 480 \text{ oz desired}$$

$$20 \text{ servings} \times 6 \text{ oz} = 120 \text{ oz given}$$

$$\frac{480 \text{ oz desired}}{120 \text{ oz given}} = \frac{480}{120} = 4 \qquad \text{(multiplier)}$$

Converting by multiplying seems simple and straightforward on paper, but in actual cooking problems do occur. Not all recipes increase and decrease well. Recipes that are converted by small amounts usually work all right. When a recipe is converted to very large numbers, problems can arise.

For example, a recipe for 4 people converted to 500 can run into trouble. Not all ingredients multiply well. Some problem items are eggs, thickening agents, and seasonings. Some foods, such as soufflés and some kinds of sauces, do not adapt well to large-quantity production because of mixing, cooking, and equipment limitations. You might have to make a smaller quantity several times.

Experienced cooks are aware of such problems and allow for them in preparation. They make adjustments by feel and note them on standardized recipes for future use.

SUMMING UP

Though each menu is unique, the way each establishment goes about its menu writing is not so very different from one operation to another. There are certain questions all must ask and answer, such as type of menu, menu structure, clientele, menu balance, nutrition, portion size, profitability, and availability of products, equipment, and production skills. These and other considerations, such as style of service and number of people to be fed, are all interdependent. Each must be considered in relation to the others in order to achieve a workable menu.

It is very important to understand basic nutrition concepts because nutrition is an important consideration when planning menus, particularly for populations such as children, the elderly, and healthcare patients with special nutritional needs. Food contains about 50 nutrients that can be arranged into six groups: carbohydrates, fat, protein, vitamins, minerals, and water. It's important to know the basic functions and sources of these nutrients.

A recipe is an abbreviated way of communicating the necessary information for making a dish. A standardized recipe is one written for use in a given operation specifying exactly how a certain dish is made in that operation. The standardized recipe has many roles. It helps the cook to maintain consistency of product. It provides the data for cost analysis, thus helping to control costs and assure profitability. It provides essential data for purchasing and planning for future needs.

A standardized recipe applies to one operation only; it is not a universal key to making a given dish anywhere, any time, by anybody. Many uncontrollable variables complicate the picture: differences in equipment, differences in cooks, differences in products, differences in temperature, and differences in understanding and communication. A written recipe cannot substitute for understanding the structure of a dish, the roles and relationships of its ingredients, and what is supposed to happen in the making.

Converting recipes is really quite simple—that is, once you know the multiplier. Use this skill to increase or decrease yields with confidence that the product will be just right.

The Cook's Vocabulary

à la carte menu
body
cholesterol
converting the recipe
cycle menu
Dietary Guidelines for Americans
du jour menu
fats: saturated, monounsaturated, polyunsaturated
fiber
food cost percentage
Food Guide Pyramid
major flavor
market menu
menu
nutrient-dense foods
nutrition
recipe
selective, semiselective, nonselective menus
semi à la carte menu
standardized recipe
starch
static menu
sugar
table d'hôte menu
texture

Review Questions

Answer each question in complete sentences. Read each question carefully and make sure you answer all parts of the question. Organize your answer into more than one paragraph when appropriate.

1. Describe four different types of menus. In which type of foodservice would each be appropriate?
2. Bring in a menu from a place you like to eat. Which type of menu is it? Does it meet the needs of the clientele?
3. List major menu planning considerations.
4. List the six groups of nutrients, foods they are found in, and their functions.
5. Why doesn't the same recipe always produce the same product in any kitchen for any cook? Cite instances from your own experience in which a recipe produced different results. Can you think of still other factors that might affect the outcomes?
6. What is meant by the structure of a dish? If you can, give examples of two or more finished dishes that have the same basic structure.
7. Explain why it is helpful to know equivalents in converting recipes. Give examples from your own experience of mistakes in using equivalents and what happened as a result.
8. Take a recipe from a cookbook and double the yield, triple the yield, and halve the yield.

Chapter 6

BUILDING FLAVOR, BODY, AND TEXTURE

There are two different kinds of cooking. One is the cooking of foods that are so good in themselves that nothing need be added—the baked potato, the stir-fried vegetables, the grilled chicken breast. All you have to do to such a food is cook it properly.

The other kind of cooking is the blending together of several foods to make another kind of food—a soup, a sauce, many kinds of main dishes. This kind of cooking requires an understanding of how such foods are built.

The process is something like the building of a house. There is a plan. Raw materials are put together according to this plan. Because of the way everything is combined, the finished product is more than just the raw materials added together. It has its own identity. The house has its own shape, size, and style. The dish has its own flavor, body, and texture.

The raw materials the cook uses to build flavor in soups, sauces, and entrées are spices, herbs, vegetables, meat, and bones. For body, you add a liquid. For texture, you use another set of raw materials called thickening agents, which are mostly starches or starch–fat combinations.

In this chapter, we'll see how the cook puts together raw materials to build flavor, body, and texture. We'll also take a close look at the whole subject of flavor, the ingredients used to season and flavor, and how to use seasonings to bring out the natural flavors of foods.

After completing this chapter, you should be able to:

- Understand and explain the concepts of building flavor, body, and texture in a dish.
- Describe how to prepare a sachet, an onion piqué, and basic and white mirepoix.
- Describe how to prepare good-quality white, brown, and vegetable stocks, and explain their uses and how they differ.
- Know how and when to use convenience products in making stocks.
- Explain how to build texture in a liquid using various types of thickening agents.
- Explain the differences among seasoning, flavoring, and flavor building.
- Use seasonings to bring out the natural flavors of foods.

BUILDING FLAVOR: FLAVOR BUILDERS

Flavor is the way a food tastes. A carrot has a carrot flavor, an onion has an onion flavor, chicken tastes like chicken, and a stew is a blend of meat and vegetable flavors. People who like to analyze flavor will point out that there are only four basic tastes: sweet, sour, bitter, and salt. When you eat, these tastes combine with the aromas perceived by your nose to produce the flavor of the food you are eating.

Cooks do not think in terms of flavor analysis. They are concerned with the totality of flavor perceived by the diner. They know how a dish is supposed to taste, and they build toward that taste each time they make that dish.

In building foods, the cook works with two kinds of flavors, predominant flavor and support flavor. Just as a building has a major structural element, such as wood, concrete, or steel, a dish can have a major material in its construction, such as beef, onion, or asparagus. It may not be the major material in terms of volume (celery soup, for example, has far less celery than it has liquid), but it is the material that determines the character of the dish. This major material, or main ingredient, will contribute the predominant flavor—**major flavor**—of the dish.

Other ingredients may be added in the cooking to enhance the flavor of the main ingredient. We call these flavor builders, and the kind of flavor they provide is what we call support flavor. The flavor builders should never be allowed to overwhelm the predominant flavor. A good understanding of the relationships between predominant and support flavors is one of the most important keys to successful cooking.

The basic flavor builder in soups and sauces is a flavored liquid known as **stock.** Stock itself has a predominant flavor that comes from bones, and it has support flavors that come from flavor builders.

Let us look at some of the flavor builders commonly used in making stocks, soups, and sauces. Several standard groupings are used in professional cooking: mirepoix, bouquet garni, sachet, onion piqué, and the group of herbs and spices used with a mirepoix in making stock.

MIREPOIX

The group of flavor builders known as a **mirepoix** (meer-pwah) is a combination of rough-cut vegetables—onion, carrot, celery, and sometimes leek. A standard flavor builder for stocks, it is also used in soups, sauces, and braised dishes, and it is often added to the pan liquids from roast meat if a sauce is to be made from them. Mirepoix was named for a French general. Though this custom of naming foods after the cook's master or the king's mistress can be confusing until you get used to it, it also lends color to the kitchen. "Mirepoix," once you've mastered it, is much more interesting than "cut-up vegetables."

Standard ratios of ingredients for a basic mirepoix are 50 percent onion, 25 percent carrot, and 25 percent celery. These proportions will yield a balanced blend of flavors. Thus, if a recipe specifies a pound (500 g) of mirepoix, you know it means:

8 oz (250 g) onion
4 oz (125 g) carrot
4 oz (125 g) celery

This would be enough for 1 gallon (4 L) of flavorful stock. It is important to maintain these ratios so that no one ingredient will become a predominant flavor and spoil the stock, soup, or sauce. Leeks, if they are available, may be used to replace some of the onion and enhance the flavor blend.

Mirepoix ingredients are chosen not only for flavor but for color. Carrots and the skins of onions will lend their color to the liquid in which they are cooked. This can be an asset in most stocks and sauces, but it may spoil the appearance of a fish stock or a white sauce. So we have a variation of the mirepoix, called white mirepoix, which omits the carrots. Some chefs replace the carrots with parsnips and then add mushrooms and leeks for additional flavor. Some chefs simply prefer to use just mushrooms and leeks in place of the carrots.

For a darker mirepoix, tomatoes are sometimes added for more color and flavor, in a ratio of 2 oz (60 g) to 1 lb (500 g) mirepoix. Tomatoes have a very strong flavor that can easily take over if too much is used. Also, too much tomato may make a brown stock cloudy.

The following guidelines will give you the most flavor and the best flavor from a mirepoix of any kind:

- Use only good-quality products.
- Thoroughly wash all products, especially the leek, which is usually very sandy. To clean it well, cut it in half lengthwise and rinse thoroughly under running water.
- Cut all vegetables the same size. The size of the pieces will vary according to use. If you are going to cook them a long time, as in making a stock, you will cut them in 1- to $1^1/_2$-inch (2.5–3 cm) pieces so that their flavor will not be exhausted before the stock is finished. If the cooking will be brief, as in making a sauce from pan juices or a cream soup, you will cut them much finer—say small dice. This will expose more vegetable surface to the liquid and draw out more flavor in the allotted time. Whatever the size, the pieces should be roughly equal so that all the ingredients will cook at the same rate.
- Keep the ratios of ingredients carefully balanced.
- If the mirepoix is going to be cooked a long time, use low heat to avoid a bitter flavor.

But vegetables are only half the flavor-building story for stocks, soups, and sauces. Most of the time, the mirepoix vegetables are accompanied by certain herbs and spices that enhance the flavor blend. Some cooks consider these to be part of the mirepoix and some don't, since they may vary with the product being made. To avoid confusion, we will use the term mirepoix to refer to the vegetables alone.

For making stock, the standard group of herbs and spices that goes with the mirepoix consists of bay leaf, thyme, parsley, clove, and peppercorns. In this book, we refer to them as stock herbs and spices. Recipe 6.1 lists the amounts

Recipe 6-1 BASIC MIREPOIX WITH STOCK HERBS AND SPICES

YIELD: ***Approximately 1 pound (450 g)***

8 oz	**onions**	**250 g**
4 oz	**carrots**	**125 g**
4 oz	**celery**	**125 g**
5–6	**parsley stems**	
$^1/_2$	**bay leaf**	
$^1/_2$ tsp	**thyme**	**2 mL**
2	**cloves**	
5–6	**peppercorns**	

1. Wash onions, carrots, celery, and parsley stems.
2. Chop onions, carrots, and celery into $1–1^1/_2$ in. (2.5–3 cm) pieces. For use in fish stock, cut pieces smaller than 1 in. (2.5 cm).
3. Use vegetables, herbs, and spices as directed in stock recipe.

Per pound:		Carbohydrates:	33 g
Calories:	164	Cholesterol:	0 mg
Fat:	1 g	Fiber:	9 g
Protein:	4 g	Sodium:	144 mg

suitable for making a gallon (4 L) of any kind of stock. In this recipe, they appear alongside the standard mirepoix so that you can begin to think of these proportions as going together.

Another combination of herbs (usually fresh) and vegetables is the **bouquet garni** (boo-kay gar-nee—literally, garnished bouquet). This term originally referred to sprigs of herbs—parsley, thyme, and bay leaf—tied together with a string, which, in turn, was tied to the handle of the stockpot. When cooking was done, the herbs could easily be pulled out of the pot. Sometimes, a celery rib, cut in half, was added to the bouquet. The herbs were placed in the trough of one half and covered with the other half, and the string was tied tightly around the celery, as in Figure 6.1a.

Today, the term bouquet garni is used in several different ways. For some cooks, it always means those three specific herbs—parsley, thyme, and bay leaf—used together but not necessarily tied together if the liquid they are enriching is to be strained. More commonly, bouquet garni includes parsley stems, thyme sprigs, bay leaf, leeks, celery, and sometimes carrots. Yet another usage of the term refers (incorrectly) to tying dried herbs and spices in cheesecloth. This is more properly called a sachet.

Because there are so many versions of the bouquet garni, we avoid this term in recipes in order to prevent confusion. If you run into the term as you pursue cooking, you will be wise to find out exactly what people mean when they use it.

A **sachet** (sa-shay—French for a small bag) is any mixture of herbs and spices tied in a square of cheesecloth. It is used in making soups and sauces when the product is not strained, as well as in braised dishes. The string that ties the sachet is usually tied to the handle of the stockpot

Figure 6-1 FLAVOR BUILDERS

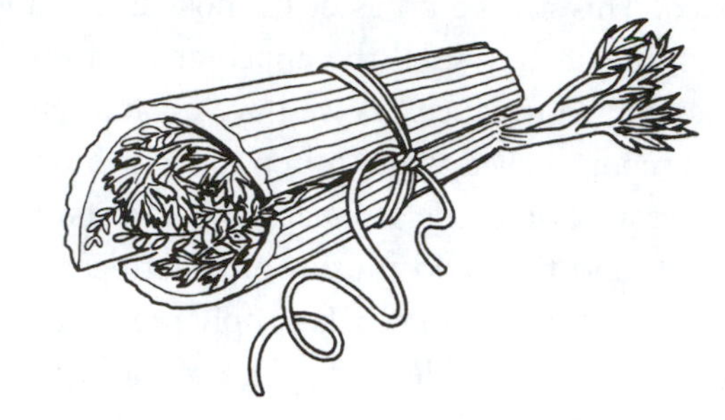

a. A bouquet garni readied for the pot in classical fashion.

b. A sachet is a cheesecloth bag filled with herbs and spices.

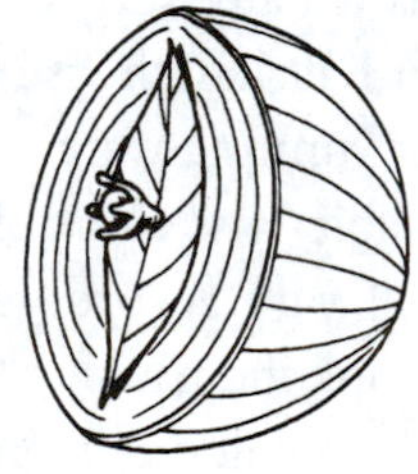

c. An onion piqué is a peeled or unpeeled onion half with a bay leaf affixed to it with a clove.

so that it can easily be removed and discarded. Figure 6.lb illustrates the sachet. Its typical ingredients are parsley stems, thyme, bay leaves, peppercorns, cloves, and perhaps garlic.

An **onion piqué** (pee-kay) is another technique for adding certain flavor builders in making a stock or sauce. The flavor builders are onion, bay leaf, and clove. The technique is to attach the bay leaf to the onion by using the clove as a nail (Figure 6.lc). It is another way of keeping the flavor builders together for easy removal. Usually, the onion is peeled, to be used in flavoring a light or white sauce without adding color. If color does not matter, you can use the onion with the skin on.

An interesting way of using an onion to build flavor and color in a dark stock or sauce is to caramelize it. To understand how this works, you must understand the onion. The onion has a high sugar content. This contributes two good things: a pleasant sweet flavor and a tinge of caramel color. To coax these out of the onion, cut the onion in half crosswise and place the cut surface on a hot griddle. This will caramelize the sugar and fill the kitchen with a heavenly aroma. You then add the onion to the liquid, cut side down, and the caramelized sugar dissolves as the half onion floats around, adding flavor and especially color to the liquid.

BUILDING BODY: STOCKS

A stock is a flavored liquid that is used in making soups and sauces. Stock functions as the body of the finished soup or sauce and also as a flavor builder. The French call stock *fond de cuisine* (fawn da kwee-zeen), meaning base of cooking, which describes its role exactly.

What do we mean by body? **Body** is two things—physical substance and strength of flavor.

A stock provides the physical body of a soup or sauce. The physical body of an entrée may be solid food such as meat or vegetables, or it may be a combination of solid food and sauce.

Body in the sense of strength of flavor is a less tangible quality. We speak of a light-bodied soup or a rich, hearty soup, a light wine or a full-bodied wine. If a liquid tastes watery or flavorless, we say it is lacking in body. Body, then, refers to the amount of flavor—its strength or richness. Even a solid food can be said to lack body if its taste has been cooked away and its flavor is pallid.

Stocks are made by simmering water, bones, and flavor builders together for hours (Figure 6.2). As they simmer, the flavor-producing substances are extracted from the bones and flavor builders and dissolve in the water. The resulting liquid product is the stock. **Gelatin** is also drawn from the bones, a major source of body. Though it may be imperceptible in a hot stock, gelatin causes the stock to thicken or jell when chilled.

To say it a little differently, the way to build a stock is to take water, a flavorless liquid, and give it body with a predominant flavor and support flavors. The predominant flavor of a stock will come from the major ingredient. There are several different predominant flavors for stocks:

Figure 6-2 MAKING STOCK

This is a white stock simmering on the range. Notice the tall, narrow shape of the pot, the ratio of bones to water, the mirepoix floating on top, the quiet surface with bubbles rising, indicating that the temperature is just right.

chicken, beef, veal, fish, and vegetable. Of these, the meat flavors come from bones. The support flavors for stocks come from a mirepoix coupled with stock herbs and spices.

There are various types of stocks: white stocks, brown stocks, fish stocks, and vegetable stocks. Although they may differ in their ingredients and procedures, they are all made by simmering water, flavor builders, and sometimes bones.

White stocks are made by simmering chicken, beef, or veal bones in water with flavor builders. White stock should be relatively colorless, except for chicken stock, which may be slightly yellow.

Brown stocks are made like white stocks, except that the bones (generally beef or veal) and mirepoix are browned before using. This results in a rich dark-brown stock. Tomato products may also be used.

Fish stock is made like a white stock, simply using fish bones and/or crustacean shells. Fish stock cooks very quickly, in about 30 to 45 minutes.

Vegetable stock is made without any animal products. Vegetables, herbs, and spices are simmered in water. Wine may be added. Vegetable stock is important for the preparation of many vegetarian dishes.

GENERAL GUIDELINES

In building a good stock, you need to know the nature of the product you are aiming for. Here are the principal measures of stock quality:

- A good stock is fat-free.
- A good stock is clear—translucent and free of solid matter.
- A good stock is pleasant to the senses of smell and taste.
- A good stock is flavorful, but the flavor is neutral. The flavor of the main ingredient, though predominant, is not overpowering. No one flavor builder is identifiable over the flavor of the main ingredient.

And here are some very important guidelines to observe in making stock:

- Use good raw bones—bones that are pleasant smelling and fresh. They should be cracked or cut up crosswise to expose the marrow. If using beef or veal bones, shank and knuckle bones are preferred. If using chicken bones, choose bones from the neck and back. If using fish bones, choose bones from lean fish (such as flounder or sole). Any large bones should be cut into pieces 3 to 4 inches (7–10 cm) long.
- Use fat-free bones. Fat will produce grease in the stock, spoiling its flavor and appearance.
- Start with cold liquid. Bones are naturally filled with blood and other impurities. These impurities will dissolve in cold water, and then as the stock is heated, they will become solid and rise to the surface (where you can skim them off). Therefore, a cold-water start will produce a clear stock, whereas starting with hot water will produce a cloudy one.
- For a white stock, some chefs blanch the bones first to remove some of the impurities and, therefore, make the stock very clear. To blanch bones, they are placed in cold water that is turned to high heat. As soon as the water boils, the impurities are skimmed off and the water is drained. Other chefs prefer not to use this process as they feel it also removes some important flavors.
- Use a tall, narrow pot to minimize evaporation. A certain amount of flavor is lost in evap-

oration, and the rate of evaporation depends on the surface area of the liquid.

- After bringing the cold water to a boil, reduce the heat to a simmer (about 185°F or 85°C). Keep the cooking temperature below the boil. It takes long, slow simmering to extract the flavors you want from the bones and flavor builders. Too high a temperature will increase evaporation and loss of desirable flavors. It will also break down vegetable textures, producing undesirable flavors and a cloudy stock.
- **Skim** occasionally—that is, remove the impurities that rise to the surface, using a skimmer or ladle. Figure 6.3 illustrates the technique.
- Do not salt the stock because it will usually be further cooked, in a sauce or soup, for example. As a stock is cooked further, it **reduces,** meaning its volume decreases because of evaporation. A stock that tastes lightly salted when prepared will taste much saltier as it is further cooked and reduced in volume.
- If you add kitchen scraps to stock, make sure they are clean and wholesome.
- Strain the stock by passing it through a china cap lined with several thicknesses of dampened cheesecloth. The straining is relatively simple. Ideally, the stockpot will have a spigot at the bottom. If it does, simply open the spigot and strain the liquid through a fine china cap and cheesecloth into a clean storage pot. If there is no spigot, carefully pour the liquid from the pot through the strainer—using proper safety precautions—or dip it out of the pot with a ladle.
- Cool the stock quickly and store it properly. To cool quickly (Figure 6.4), place the pot of stock on a rack in the sink and surround it

Figure 6-3 SKIMMING WITH A LADLE

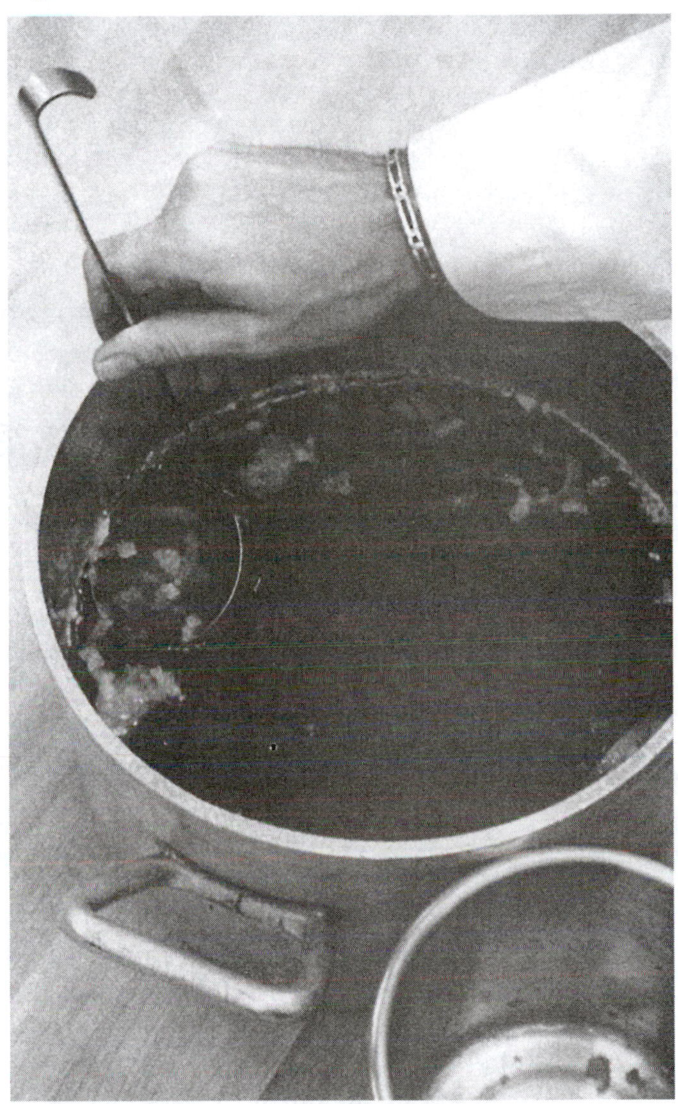

First, move the underside of the ladle bowl rapidly around in a circle in the center of the surface. This will send the gray scummy particles toward the sides of the pot. Then, tipping the ladle toward the side of the pot, run the lip of the ladle under the scum as shown, taking as little as possible of the liquid underneath. Empty the ladle into the bowl that you have set next to the pot. (Photo by Patricia Roberts.)

Figure 6-4 HOW TO COOL A LARGE POT OF LIQUID

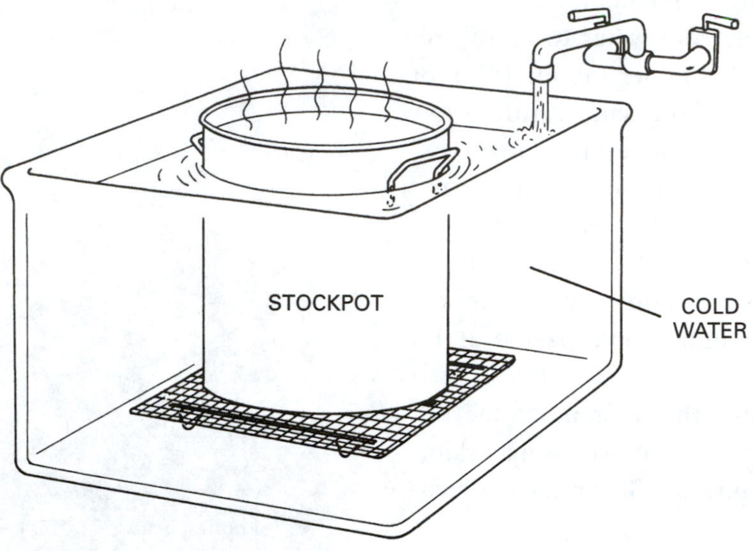

Stir occasionally to cool it evenly.

with ice water or cold running water, stirring occasionally. This will cool the stock evenly instead of leaving a warm core where bacteria can develop quickly. Cover the stock after it is cool but never while it is cooling. A cover will slow the cooling and increase the health hazard.

- A stock's shelf life is no more than 3 to 5 days in the cooler. Stocks can be frozen without loss of quality. However, it is safest and most practical to make no more than you will use in a few days. The amounts and kinds of stock you make will be determined by the soups and sauces on your menu and the number of people you expect to serve.
- Degrease the finished stock—that is, remove the fat from the surface. The most effective method is to chill the stock and remove the layer of fat that congeals on top. If you must use the stock immediately, you can skim the hot fat off the top with a ladle or blot it with a clean cloth containing ice cubes.

WHITE STOCKS

Here is a list of the most common white stocks and their ingredients. Their French names (in parentheses) are given because you may encounter them in the kitchen or the cookbook. The pronunciations given are common in American kitchens; the true French pronunciations are untranslatable.

- Veal stock (*fond blanc*—fawn blahnk): veal shank bones, water, mirepoix, stock herbs and spices
- Chicken stock (*fond de volaille*—fawn da vol-eye'): chicken bones, water, mirepoix, stock herbs and spices
- Fish stock (*fond de poisson*—fawn da pwa-

sone'): fish bones, heads, tails, water, light mirepoix, lemon, stock herbs and spices.

- Ordinary white stock: veal, beef, or chicken bones, or combinations of bones, water, mirepoix, stock herbs and spices

Recipe 6.2 provides a formula that can be used to make any white stock (except fish stock) simply by changing the kind of bones. White stocks made from this formula are the basis for many dishes in the kitchen. The dish you are going to serve will dictate the kind of stock you make.

Fish stock has some special requirements, as you can see in Recipe 6.3. It uses a light mirepoix, for color reasons, and it has a much shorter cooking time. Because of the short cooking time, less liquid will evaporate, so you need less to begin with. You cut the mirepoix finely so that maximum flavor will be extracted in the short time the stock cooks.

Recipe 6-2 WHITE STOCK

YIELD: ***Approximately 1 gallon (4 L) or 16 cups***

4 oz	**onions**	**125 g**
4 oz	**carrots**	**125 g**
4 oz	**celery**	**125 g**
5 lb	**bones, chicken, veal, or beef**	**2.5 kg**
5 qt	**cold water**	**5 L**
5–6	**parsley stems**	
1/2	**bay leaf**	
2	**cloves**	
1/2	**tsp thyme**	**2 mL**

1. Chop onions, carrots, and celery into 1–1 1/2-in. (2.5–3 cm) pieces.
2. Put bones in a tall pot or steam kettle and cover with cold water. (Blanch bones first if desired.)
3. Bring to a simmer and skim.
4. Add remaining ingredients in sachet and return to a simmer.
5. Simmer 3–4 hours for chicken stock, 6–8 hours for veal or beef stock.
6. Strain and degrease.
7. If the stock is to be refrigerated, cool down in a water bath first.

Per cup:		Carbohydrates:	0 g
Calories:	6	Cholesterol:	6 mg
Fat:	0 g	Fiber:	0 g
Protein:	1 g	Sodium:	10 mg

Recipe 6-3 FISH STOCK

YIELD: ***Approximately 1 gallon (4 L) or 16 cups***

5 lb	**bones, heads, and tails of dover sole or other flatfish**	**(2.5 kg)**

Light mirepoix:

3 oz	**onions**	**90 mg**
3 oz	**leeks**	**90 mg**
3 oz	**celery**	**90 mg**
1 gal	**water**	**4L**
1/2 tsp	**thyme**	**2 mL**
1/2	**bay leaf**	
5–6	**parsley stems**	
1/2–1 Tb	**lemon juice**	**10–15 mL**
1 C	**wine**	**250 mL**

1. Wash bones, heads, and tails.
2. Chop onions, leeks, and celery into 1/2 in. (1 cm) pieces.
3. In a stockpot or steam kettle, cover bones, heads, and tails with cold water.
4. Bring to a simmer and skim.
5. Add mirepoix, thyme, bay leaf, and parsley stems in a sachet. Add lemon juice and wine. Return to a simmer.
6. Simmer 30 to 45 minutes.

Per cup:		Carbohydrates:	1 g
Calories:	10	Cholesterol:	1 mg
Fat:	0 g	Fiber:	0 g
Protein:	0 g	Sodium:	1 mg

Some dishes may call for a strong stock. You can strengthen a stock in either of two ways: You can increase the usual ratio of solid ingredients to liquid at the start, or you can reduce the strained finished stock through further simmering. Both methods will give you a stronger flavor—more body, in other words.

Recipe 6-4 BROWN STOCK

YIELD: ***Approximately 1 gallon (4 L)***

5 lb	**beef or veal bones**	**2.5 kg**
8 oz	**onions**	**250 g**
4 oz	**carrots**	**125 g**
4 oz	**celery**	**125 g**
5 qt	**cold water**	**5 L**
5–6	**parsley stems**	
1/2	**bay leaf**	
2	**cloves**	
1/2 tsp	**thyme**	**2 mL**
5–6	**peppercorns, crushed**	

1. Brown bones in a hot oven (400°F/200°C).
2. When bones are golden brown, add mirepoix and brown.
3. When the onion is brown and lightly caramelized and the bones are dark brown, remove from oven and pour off any remaining fat.
4. Add cold liquid (about 1/4 of total) to deglaze pan.
5. Transfer everything to a stockpot and add the remaining cold liquid.
6. Bring to a boil and skim. Add parsley stems, bay leaf, cloves, thyme, and peppercorns in sachet.
7. Reduce to a simmer. Simmer for 6–8 hours, skimming occasionally.
8. Strain and degrease.

Per cup:		Carbohydrates:	0 g
Calories:	12 g	Cholesterol:	10 mg
Fat:	1 g	Fiber:	0 g
Protein:	1 g	Sodium:	1 mg

BROWN STOCKS

Recipe 6.4 gives you a basic formula for any brown stock made from any types of bones. As you can see by reading the instructions, brown stocks are more complicated to make than light stocks, but the techniques are worth learning. Not only do they make good stocks, they are also important in other areas of cooking. The procedures of browning bones, adding flavor builders, and then simmering in a liquid are used in making many sauces and meat dishes.

The technique known as **deglazing**—adding cold liquid to the hot pan (Step 4)—is also used in making sauces and meat dishes. Any browned bits of food sticking to the pan are scraped up and added to the liquid.

VEGETABLE STOCKS

Because vegetable stocks do not include animal products, they do not contain gelatin, which contributes to body. A vegetable stock may be made mostly from one vegetable for a single purpose. For example, you might make a broccoli stock for use in cream of broccoli soup. To make broccoli stock, you would add a little bit of some neutral vegetables, such as celery, to the broccoli. In addition, you would use herbs and spices and maybe some wine. Vegetable stock may also be made using a variety of vegetables, as in Recipe 6.5, and then used in a variety of vegetarian dishes.

Vegetable stocks are usually made from trimmings that would otherwise be discarded, such as the tough portions of asparagus stalks. You simmer these in water until they are cooked through—no longer. Longer cooking will cause

Recipe 6-5 VEGETABLE STOCK

YIELD: ***1 gallon (4 L)***

1 lb	**leeks, chopped**	**450 g**
1 lb	**onions, chopped**	**450 g**
2 lb	**celery, chopped**	**900 g**
2 lb	**tomatoes, chopped**	**900 g**
2 lb	**carrots, chopped**	**900 g**
1 lb	**mushrooms, sliced**	**450 g**
4	**bay leaves**	
2 Tb	**garlic, chopped**	**30 mL**
2 Tb	**black peppercorns, cracked**	**30 mL**
2 Tb	**white peppercorns, cracked**	**30 mL**

1. Place all ingredients together in a large stockpot and simmer for 2 hours.
2. Strain through cheesecloth in a china cap.

Per cup:		Carbohydrates:	3 g
Calories:	18	Cholesterol:	0 mg
Fat:	0 g	Fiber:	0 g
Protein:	0 g	Sodium:	8 mg

unwanted flavor changes and loss of good flavor through evaporation. Dark green leafy vegetables, in particular, develop a disagreeable flavor when overcooked. Cooking times for vegetable stock vary from 30 to 45 minutes.

For a neutral-tasting vegetable stock, avoid strong-flavored vegetables such as cauliflower, brussels sprouts, and artichokes. Also, if you want the stock to be clear, avoid starchy vegetables such as potatoes, because they make the stock cloudy.

GLAZES

Glazes are basic preparations in classical cookery and are the forerunners of today's convenience products. They are simply stocks reduced to a thick, gelatinous consistency. Meat glaze, or *glace de viande* (vee-end), is made from brown stock. *Glace de volaille* is made from chicken stock, and *glace de poisson* is made from fish stock.

To prepare a glaze, you reduce stock over moderate heat, frequently skimming off the foam and impurities that rise to the top. When the stock has reduced by about half, strain it through cheesecloth into a smaller heavy pan. Place it over low heat and continue to reduce until the glaze will form an even coating on a spoon. Cool, cover, and refrigerate or freeze.

Small amounts of glazes (remember, they are very concentrated!) are used to flavor sauces. They can also be added to soups to improve and intensify flavor. However, they cannot be used to recreate the stock from which they were made; the flavor is not the same after the prolonged cooking at higher temperatures.

CONVENIENCE BASES

Concentrated convenience bases are widely used. When added to water, they produce flavored liquid similar to stocks. In view of the time and labor required in making stocks, convenience products are widely used in making soups and sauces, and the stockpot is seen in fewer and fewer kitchens.

The results vary widely, partly because of the bewildering variety of products on the market and partly because they are often misused. Few of them can function as instant stocks. They are more successful as flavor boosters. Compare the taste of a convenience base prepared according to instructions with the taste of a stock made from scratch and you will see why. Many bases have a high salt content and other seasonings and preservatives. This gives them strong and definite tastes that are difficult to work with in building subtle flavors for soups and sauces.

Among the many bases available, take care to choose the highest-quality products, though these are expensive. Look for those that list beef, chicken, or fish extract as the first ingredient (not salt!). If you must use a base as a stock, try simmering with a mirepoix, stock herbs and spices, and a few bones to improve flavor. Strain before using in a recipe.

Cooking without fresh stock means using your head. There is no one all-purpose stock substitute. If a recipe calls for stock, you will have to analyze the role the stock is to play in that recipe and choose the type of convenience item accordingly. Use with caution and taste the product as you go. Remember that salt is the major ingredient in nearly every base and adjust the amount of salt in your recipe. Follow the package instructions for the mechanics of using the convenience product and the proportion of water to be added; different brands and types have different requirements. Consider, too, that water alone can sometimes be a substitute body builder. Let your head, your taste buds, and your conscience be your guides.

You will understand all this a good deal better when you learn more about how stocks function in the making of soups and sauces. Then you will see why it is important to know how stock is made even if you never make it outside the laboratory. It will give you a basis for choosing the right convenience item for the right purpose and using it intelligently for optimum results. Convenience products are not foolproof substitutes. If anything, they require more sophisticated cooking knowledge than cooking from scratch.

The importance of good stocks and good flavor builders cannot be overemphasized. If a good building is to be built, good building materials are a must.

BUILDING TEXTURE: THICKENING AGENTS

All food products have texture, a natural texture granted by Mother Nature. It may be thick or thin, rough or smooth, coarse or fine. The natural texture of a product may not be the most desirable serving texture for a finished dish, so the cook may create another texture. One measure of a cook's skill is the ability to create proper texture in such dishes as sauces and soups.

The creation of texture in cooking usually means making a thin food thicker. This is accomplished with a group of products known as thickening agents. Thickening agents increase the viscosity of a liquid, or, simply stated, make it harder to pour.

Many foods have been used in this role over the years. In medieval times, bread crumbs were added to meat juices to make them thick enough to eat with the fingers. (The French essayist Montaigne confessed to eating so fast he sometimes bit his fingers.) Almonds ground to a paste were added to thicken sauces. In Creole cooking, powdered sassafras leaves were borrowed from the Indians to make a dark-green spicy thickener known as filé (fil-lay′ or fee-lay′). Eggs, arrowroot, gelatin, tapioca, cornstarch, flour, potatoes, and rice have all been used as thickeners.

Thickening can be achieved in two ways: naturally and by using **thickening agents.** Natural thickening means using a high-starch food such as potato, rice, beans, or dried peas as an integral part of a dish. As these products cook, their starch content is released into the liquid surrounding them, causing it to thicken, while their flavor is added to the dish. Natural thickening is used mostly in soups, and the thickener is usually the major flavor ingredient. Natural thickening also occurs when you simmer a sauce, because, as it simmers, it reduces and becomes thicker.

The second way to thicken means adding a thickening agent, an ingredient whose primary function is to thicken. Starches are excellent candidates for thickeners, because starch granules, when heated with liquid, will absorb moisture, swell, and become jellylike. This process, known as gelatinization, was discussed in Chapter 4. For a smoothly thickened product, the starch granules must be evenly dispersed in the liquid and evenly heated, so that the swelling will take place at an even rate and lumps will not form.

ROUX

Of the fat–flour group, the single most important one for the beginning cook to master is **roux** (roo). Roux is a one-to-one ratio by weight of fat and flour blended and cooked over low heat. The definition is broad: Any fat can be used to make a roux. **Clarified butter** (butter with its water and milk solid content removed), butter, or margarine are the best choices whenever possible. Many fats will impart their own distinct flavor to a product, thus limiting the versatility of the roux. Consider bacon drippings, for example. Think what they would do to a cream of asparagus soup! On the other hand, vegetable oil can act as the fat in roux; however, it adds no flavor to the product so it is not often used.

There are several kinds of roux:

- **White roux** is cooked until the mixture is foamy and begins to have a chalky look. When made with butter, it has a pale yellow color.
- **Blond roux** is cooked somewhat longer, until the roux is blond in color, or slightly darker than white roux.
- **Brown roux** is cooked until the color is brown and the taste is nutty.
- **Dark-brown** or **"black" roux** is cooked even further, until the roux is deep brown in color with a strong aroma.

To make a roux, you melt the fat in a heavy-bottomed pan over moderate heat and stir in the flour to make a smooth, lump-free paste. Once the roux is smooth, cook the roux to the desired degree of doneness. For brown roux, lower the heat once the roux is smooth. It takes only minutes. Simple.

Simple, that is, once you have mastered the technique. There are several tricky parts:

- One is smoothing out the roux when you add the flour to the fat. This takes good agitation with a whip and persistence. Eventually, the lumps will go. They are tiny clumps of dry flour surrounded by granules that have begun to swell. Agitation breaks these lumps apart and releases the dry flour before the surrounding granules gelatinize.
- Another tricky point is recognizing the degree of doneness you want when you have reached it. This comes with experience. The neat trick here is to cook it long enough without overcooking. Not only do color and flavor change with prolonged cooking, but the roux begins to lose its thickening power, and by the time you have reached the brown-roux stage the loss is considerable.
- On the other hand, undercooking has its hazards, too. The roux must cook until the flour is fully cooked and no starch taste remains. The flour is at least partly cooked by the time the roux reaches the foamy stage. It cooks further when added to a liquid. The mixture must

come close to the boiling point before the flour reaches its full thickening power. To ensure complete cooking, test-taste the thickened liquid and simmer it until all raw-flour taste is gone.

- Be careful not to brown the roux if you don't want brown roux. The taste is permanent. You can brown it with too hot a fire as well as by cooking it too long.

Adding the roux to the product is tricky, too. Do not try to combine hot roux with a hot liquid (or cold roux with a cold liquid), as you will be rewarded with little hard lumps and bumps that your whip may not succeed in breaking up. The easiest way is to remove your hot roux from the heat and let it cool for a few minutes. Add part of your liquid cold (make sure it's not ice cold), once again stirring the lumps out vigorously until you have a smooth blend. Then you can add the remaining liquid hot, with no complications. The blend will be thin, but it will thicken again as you gradually return the soup or sauce to a boil, and then simmer for at least 20 minutes to get rid of the flour taste (stir occasionally during this step). No lumps, no bumps. Figure 6.5a shows the two steps.

It is also possible to add cold roux to a hot liquid over heat a little at a time, agitating vigorously with a whip so that the roux melts and softens easily without lumping (Figure 6.5b). Simmer the sauce until the roux has thickened it appropriately and the starchy taste is gone.

A good white roux is smooth and pleasant tasting but for the most part uncommitted in flavor—that is, it has no taste that will conflict with or modify the taste of another food with which it is combined. White roux is the most widely used of the three types. It creates texture for many soups, sauces, stews, soufflés, and other entrées.

Brown roux is strong in flavor and will carry a definite taste to the final dish. It has less thickening power than a light roux, so more must be used to produce the same texture. Brown roux is used for brown sauces.

BEURRE MANIÉ

A thickening agent that is similar to roux is **beurre manié** (burr man-yay)—literally, worked butter. The ratio of fat to flour is the same, but the fat is butter and the method of preparation is different. The flour and soft butter are kneaded together to the consistency of paste, and the mixture is not cooked before use. Today, margarine is often used in place of butter because of cost and health considerations.

To use beurre manié to thicken, you pinch a small piece off, whip it into simmering liquid until it disappears, and keep repeating the process until the liquid reaches the consistency you want. Then you cook the thickened liquid a few minutes more until no raw-flour taste remains. A day's supply of beurre manié may be made ahead, kept in the cooler, and used as needed.

STARCH-AND-WATER THICKENERS

The starch-and-water thickeners (called **slurries**) are simpler to understand and use than the starch-and-fat thickeners. The general steps for using a starch, such as cornstarch, include the following:

1. Mix the starch with cold water. The amount of cold water should be about one to two times the volume of the starch.
2. Make sure the liquid you want to thicken is at a low boil or simmer.
3. Slowly add the starch-and-water mixture, whipping vigorously to prevent lumping and burning the bottom of the pan.

Figure 6-5 COMBINING ROUX AND LIQUID

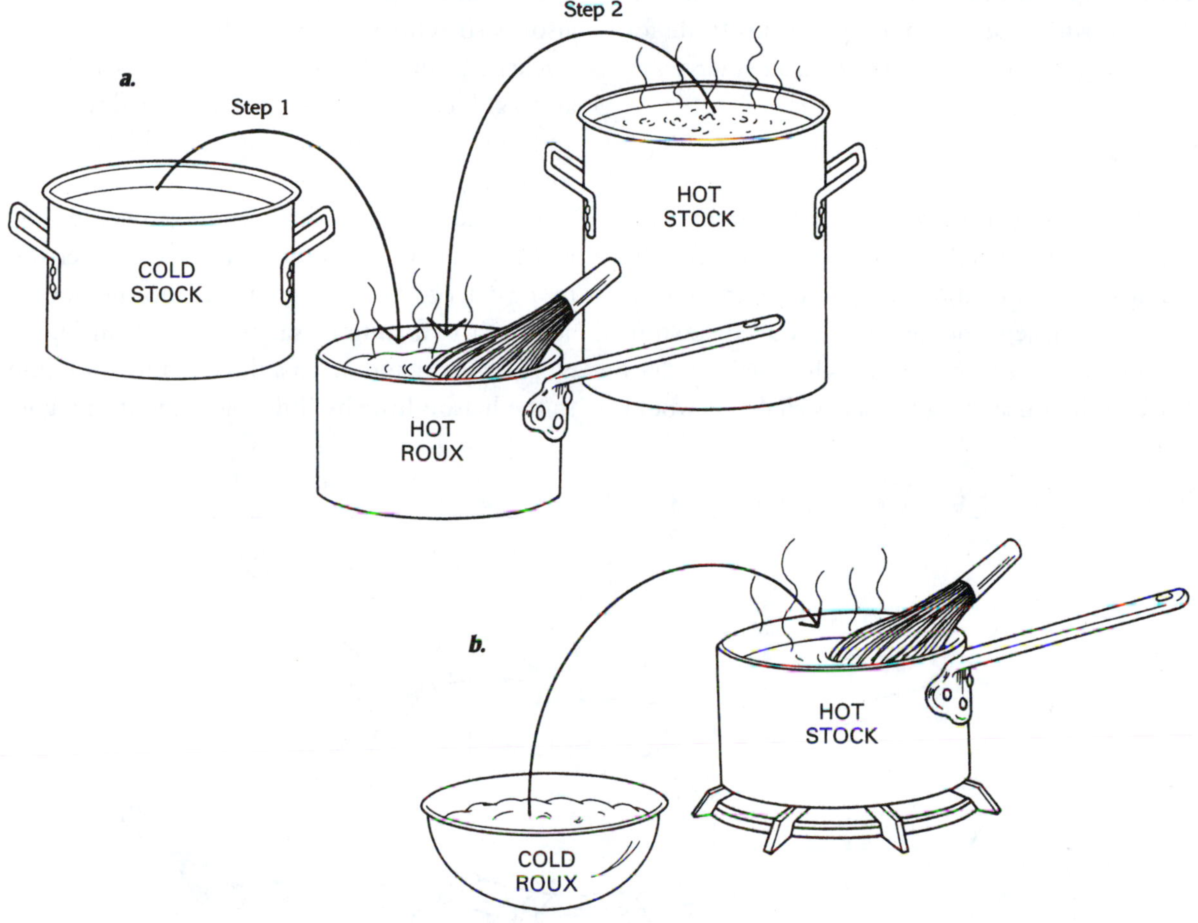

a. When you have *hot* roux, combining it with liquid is a two-step process. In Step 1, you add part of your liquid, *cold,* to the hot roux, blending it in with a whip. In Step 2, you blend in the rest of the liquid, *hot.* ***b.*** When you have *cold* roux, you can combine it with a *hot* liquid over heat, by blending it in with a whip a little at a time. Do not try to combine hot roux with a hot liquid or cold roux with a cold liquid.

4. Return the liquid to a boil. Cook until the product is of the appropriate thickness and the starchy taste is gone.
5. Products thickened with slurries may become thin if held for too long, so keep an eye on them.

Cornstarch, arrowroot, rice flour, potato starch, and many name-brand combination starch products are among the available thickeners that can be used in this way. Arrowroot gives an even clearer product than cornstarch and thickens at a lower temperature as well, but cornstarch is still used more frequently because it is much less expensive.

Flour is another starch that can be dispersed in water and used to thicken, but it must be cooked longer than the other starch mixtures to get rid of its raw taste. The flour–water mixture, called a **whitewash,** is not a good substitute for roux for general use. Use it only in an emergency.

LIAISON

Another product commonly referred to as a thickening agent is the **liaison** (lee-ay-zon). A liaison is a combination of egg yolks and cream used to thicken and to give a velvety texture to soups and sauces. Although a liaison does thicken, its thickening power is slight. It would take a ridiculous number of eggs to provide the same thickening power as a pound of roux. A liaison also refines and smooths the texture of a thickened liquid by binding and gives it flavor and a golden color. It is generally added to soups and sauces that have already been thickened by something else.

A liaison is made by blending together egg yolks and heavy cream in a ratio of 2 parts cream to 1 part egg yolk by volume. The method of adding it to a soup or sauce is shown in Figure 6.6. First, you add up to a third of the hot liquid to the liaison little by little, blending it in vigor-

Figure 6-6 TEMPERING A LIAISON INTO A LIQUID

a. The first step is to add up to a third of the hot liquid gradually to the blended egg yolks and cream, whipping it vigorously. ***b.*** The second step is to add this mixture to the remainder of the hot liquid, again whipping vigorously.

ously with a whip. This is known as **tempering.** Its purpose is to raise the temperature of the liaison (especially the egg) closer to the temperature of the hot liquid. If this were not done, the hot liquid would cause the egg yolk to coagulate (become solid), spoiling everything. The second step is to add the liaison mixture to the remainder of the hot liquid.

In contrast to the starchy thickeners, the liaison requires great care and patience. Egg yolks will coagulate at temperatures well below the boiling point. This creates problems in both preparation and holding of anything to which a liaison is added. For this reason, the liaison is always added to the finished product shortly before use.

Although the liaison is not used as much today as it once was, tempering—the technique of combining eggs and hot liquids—applies in other areas of cooking, especially in the making of desserts.

VEGETABLE PURÉES AND CRUMBS

Purées of cooked vegetables have become popular as thickeners in part because they are much lower in fat than thickeners such as roux. To make a brown gravy, for example, you might thicken a reduced beef stock with a purée of carrots, onions, and parsnips. High-starch vegetables are especially good at thickening. They include potatoes, sweet potatoes, yams, parsnips, winter squash, pumpkin, corn, and peas. Cooked legumes (dried beans and peas) may also be puréed to help in thickening. The types of vegetables or legumes you choose will depend on the color and flavor you want in the final product.

Crumbs, made from breads, crackers, cereals, cookies, and cakes, can also be used to thicken soups or sauces in which smoothness is not important. When using crumbs, the starch is already cooked so the product will thicken at once. The flavor of the crumbs should match the product they will be used in. For example, crumbs made from gingersnap cookies may be used in some dessert sauces.

SEASONINGS, FLAVORINGS, AND FLAVOR BUILDERS

Cooks have at their disposal a splendid array of food products that have pleasing and distinctive tastes and some that have the ability to enhance the tastes of other foods. Among these are wines and spirits, extracts and oils, condiments, spices, herbs, and seasonings. These are the secret ingredients in the secret recipes we are always hearing about.

There are three distinctly different ways of using these products: seasoning, flavoring, and flavor building. Let us explore these concepts further.

Seasoning is the addition of substances that heighten the taste of a food without altering that taste or adding their own flavors. Such substances are called seasonings. They will bring out the rich flavors hidden in a bland, unseasoned stock or make a cream of chicken soup taste more like chicken. Whenever possible, they are added at the end of the cooking, after the product is complete in every other respect. They are added earlier to such solid foods as meats and vegetables, however, to give the seasonings time to penetrate and bring out their flavor.

Flavoring, on the other hand, is the addition of a product for the purpose of adding its own distinctive flavor to the final dish. It is the blending of one flavor into another in such a way that the two complement each other but retain their own identity. A good example of flavoring is the addition of sherry wine to consommé as it is almost ready to serve. The basic consommé flavor then has a perceptible taste of sherry. Most flavorings, except sherry as in our example, are added at the beginning of cooking to allow enough time for the heat to release their flavors.

Flavoring and seasoning are often confused. Whereas flavoring makes a change in the taste of the dish by adding a new flavor, seasoning brings out the flavor that is already there.

Flavor building is different from both seasoning and flavoring in that it is an integral part of the cooking process. Flavor builders are cooked right into the dish, so that their separate flavors merge with the total flavor. This, for example, is what happens to the mirepoix when you make stock. In flavor building, the added flavor is not perceived separately, whereas in flavoring it is easily recognizable. In seasoning, the added product is not perceived at all.

With these differences in mind, let's look more closely at each process in turn and at the kinds of products that function as seasonings, flavorings, and flavor builders.

SEASONING AND SEASONINGS

Seasoning is one of the most important processes in the entire field of cooking. Everything else you learn about cooking can be futile if you do not master seasoning. It is the finish work of cooking and, like finish work in any trade or profession, it is a measure of the cook's skill. Skill in seasoning is the ability to use seasonings to bring a food to its peak of flavor, its ultimate in taste.

What are these miracle workers that can make a food taste more like itself? They are three familiar everyday products. Salt and pepper are standard seasonings for all foods and all cooks. Fresh lemon juice may or may not be used, depending on the cook and the dish. The kind of pepper used may also vary from one cook to another.

Seasonings are limited to these three or four because they alone enhance a food's flavor without altering it. Used in the right quantities, they do not add their own flavors to a food. If you can taste any one of them, you have added too much of it.

SALT. A crystalline substance mined from the earth or extracted from brine, salt is cheap and plentiful. In other times and places, it was often scarce and valuable and was sometimes used as money. It was used for centuries to preserve meats and fish, and the cook's chief concern with it was not how much to add but how to get rid of the taste.

Salt is essential to health, and the desire for it is said to be a natural instinct in both humans and animals. But the amount of salt essential to health is far less than we Americans habitually consume. Fortunately, habits are changing, and the trend is toward less use of salt and more interest in natural food flavors.

There is only one rule to follow in seasoning with salt: Do not overuse it. Once a dish is too salty, there is no way to correct it. It is far better to undersalt than to risk a salty flavor. For one thing, the heavy hand of an insensitive diner can spoil your finest creation. For another, customers who must watch their salt intake for health reasons will certainly not come back if they can taste the salt in your food.

Most table salt in the United States is **iodized salt,** meaning that iodine (a nutrient) has been added to it. The iodine does not cause any change in taste or its ability to be used in cooking. Iodine has been added to salt for many years because it is an easy way to ensure that we get enough of this valuable nutrient. Iodized salt is very fine grained because it contains additives that keep it from clumping. **Sea salt** is made, as its name implies, from sea water. Its texture may be fine, like table salt, or coarse, like kosher salt. **Kosher salt** is a coarse-grained salt that contains no additives. It is about half as salty as table salt.

PEPPER. Like salt, pepper was scarce in other times and places and was used as money. Taxes, ransoms, dowries, and bribes were often paid in peppercorns. The barbarians who conquered Rome demanded, among other things, 3000 pounds of pepper as tribute. Pepper even changed the course of history: Columbus was looking for pepper when he sailed west to the East and discovered America instead.

Pepper comes in three forms: black, white, and green. White and black pepper both come from the oriental pepper plant. Black pepper is the dried unripe berry; white pepper is the kernel of the ripe berry. Green peppercorns are picked before ripeness and preserved.

Black pepper comes in three forms: whole black peppercorns, crushed peppercorns, and table-ground pepper. Whole pepper is used as a flavor builder during cooking, as in making stocks. Crushed black pepper can function as a flavor builder during cooking, as well, or it can be added as flavoring to a finished dish. Many Americans enjoy the flavor contrast of fresh crushed peppercorns straight from the pepper mill on a crisp green salad. It can also be used in cooking meats in a combined role of flavor builder/major flavor/flavoring, as in pepper steak.

Table-ground black pepper is pepper ground fine enough to be shaken from a shaker on the dining table. Some cooks use it as a seasoning, but its flavor has the sharpness of the unripe berry from which it comes, and it is difficult to use it without conveying this flavor to the food.

The flavor of ground black pepper is characteristic of certain cuisines and certain parts of the country. Cooks catering to these clienteles are likely to add this flavor as they season the food. One way to be sure of pleasing everybody is to season for natural flavor and allow the guest to add the extra black pepper flavor at the table.

As a seasoning, black pepper is used only in dark-colored foods; it spoils the appearance of light-colored foods. **White pepper** is used in light-colored foods because its presence is concealed. White pepper comes in two forms: whole peppercorns and ground white pepper. White peppercorns are used in the same ways as black peppercorns.

Ground white pepper is a good pepper for all-around seasoning. It blends imperceptibly into white dishes both in appearance and in flavor, and it has the strength necessary to season dark dishes. Ground white pepper is chosen by most good cooks as the true seasoning pepper. It is seldom used as a table pepper, as it is expensive.

Green peppercorns are preserved either by packing them in liquid (such as vinegar or brine) or by drying them. They are used in white tablecloth (luxury) restaurants to complete certain recipes.

RED PEPPER. **Red pepper,** also called **cayenne,** is completely unrelated to white or black pepper. It comes from dried pepper pods. It is quite hot and easily overdone. Used with restraint in soups and sauces, it can add a spicy hotness. When used without as much restraint, it creates the hot flavor of many foods from Mexico and India.

FRESH LEMON JUICE. Lemon juice is seldom called a seasoning, and yet its use as a seasoning is not unusual. Many recipes call for small amounts of lemon juice. When it is used with restraint to spark the flavor of the dish itself and the lemon flavor cannot be perceived, lemon juice is a seasoning. Many chicken and veal dishes, sauces, and cream soups such as asparagus, mushroom, cauliflower, and broccoli can be enhanced by seasoning with fresh lemon.

HOW TO SEASON. Seasonings must be added in suitable proportions in order to bring out the flavor of a food without adding their own. There are no rules for defining "suitable proportions" because every product is slightly different every time you make it. The process is one of trial and error, or, more accurately, trial and taste. Add, taste, adjust, taste, adjust, taste, until your product has reached its best possible flavor.

A standardized recipe will often give specific quantities of seasonings. These represent the carefully measured trial-and-taste process of the skilled cook who standardized the recipe. They are very useful as seasoning guidelines if used with caution. It is a good idea, if you are working with such a recipe, to start with amounts somewhat below those specified, and then taste, adjust, taste to refine the final flavor.

Figure 6-7 EQUIPMENT FOR SEASONING A LIQUID

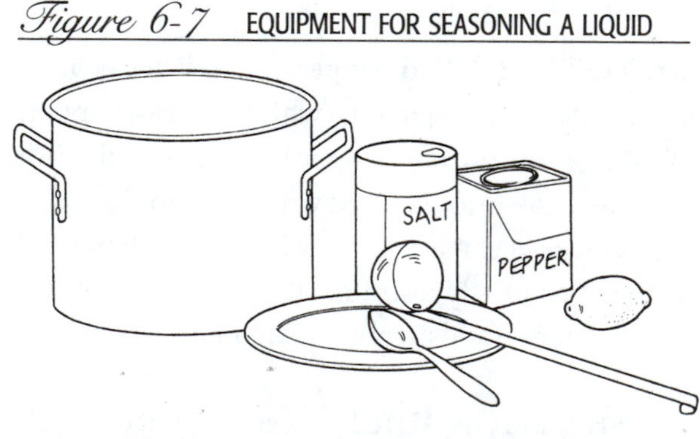

Ladle a little liquid onto the plate for quick cooling. Taste from the plate.

Figure 6.7 shows the equipment needed for seasoning a hot liquid: small plate, ladle, spoon, and seasonings. The plate is for cooling the hot liquid quickly. You ladle a small amount onto the plate and taste with the spoon. It is important not to put into the pot any implement that may be contaminated in the tasting process.

The basic rules for seasoning are the two you are already aware of:

1. Do not overseason. You should not be able to taste the seasoning itself.
2. Seasoning a liquid is an end cooking process.

The second rule has several corollaries:

- When a liquid product is to be reduced in volume, season after reduction, not before.
- When a liquid product is to act as a base for another, do not season it at all. Season the new product when it is finished.
- When a product cannot be seasoned after cooking, season before cooking. This applies to solid products such as meats, which will not absorb seasonings after cooking.

Some cooks misuse as seasonings products that change the taste of the food or impose their own tastes. For this reason, many potentially good dishes never reach their peak of flavor. Many potentially good cooks never quite make it for the same reason. Recipe books can add to the problem. "Season the sauce with sherry," a recipe will say, or "Season to taste with garlic salt and oregano." Here is a confusion of seasoning with flavoring, or of seasonings with flavor builders, or of one term with another, and more than likely a confusion of tastes in the products being seasoned.

It is important to use as seasonings only the products you know will do the job. Other products can be used to change taste but not to perfect taste that is already there. Let us therefore add a third basic rule of seasoning:

3. Season only with true seasonings—products that will heighten flavor without changing it or adding their own taste.

We noted earlier that true seasoning skill is the ability to use seasonings to bring a food to its ultimate in taste. The goal is the food's own flavor—the way a food "ought" to taste. The instrument you use to achieve this goal is your own sense of taste.

Your first step in mastering seasoning is to train your own sense of taste. You may be making many dishes you have never tasted before. You need to learn what each dish tastes like when made by a good cook. Then, when you make the same product, you will have an idea of what taste to aim for in seasoning.

In addition, you can sharpen your own sensory awareness. Experiment with seasonings and become aware of their effects on flavor. Start working with very small amounts of seasonings until your product tastes good. Then try a little more. It may taste even better or it may be ruined. But you won't recognize its ultimate flavor until you've gone beyond it.

But, you may say, people's tastes differ. Indeed, they do. This is why the word "ought" is in quotes. Who decides? Do you please the good cook whose product you first tasted, the customer, or yourself?

The answer is that you strive to please the customer. To do this, you must learn to know the customer's taste in tastes. Every culture has preferences in food taste. Every area of the country has preferences. Southerners, for example, like heavily seasoned dishes. Parts of the Midwest and North prefer mild or subtly seasoned foods. You can learn to know your customers' tastes by watching their reactions to the foods you serve. Knowing customer tastes is one of the most important skills a cook can develop.

Then, you must put aside your personal preferences and give the customers what they want, not what you want them to have. It is not easy to learn this—to use your own sense of taste to season to someone else's taste. It takes experience and practice.

Making a food taste the way a customer expects it to taste is seasoning at its indispensable minimum. Making that same food taste better than the customer's highest expectations is achieving the ultimate in taste. Foods with the ultimate in flavor are bound to have come-back appeal.

FLAVORING AND FLAVORINGS

Flavoring adds a complementary flavor to a dish at the end of its preparation. It creates a blend in which both the original flavor and the added flavor are identifiable, as in the addition of black pepper to a green salad. Most flavorings are products with distinctive tastes, capable of holding their own in a dish.

ALCOHOLIC BEVERAGES. For example, wines, liqueurs, brandy, Cognac, and other spirits are often added as flavorings at the end of cooking. Sherry is a popular American flavoring for sauces. Wine or brandy is often poured over a dish and flamed—set afire—at the time of service. This adds some flavor but is done more for show.

In such dishes as sauces, wines and spirits may be added during cooking to become part of the total flavor. They are then flavor builders rather than flavorings. The same product can play one role in one dish and a different role in another dish.

GRATED LEMON AND ORANGE RIND. Grated rind of fresh citrus fruits such as lemon and orange is often added to a sauce or used in baking. Only the colored outer portion, called the **zest**, is suitable; it contains flavorful oils. The white beneath it is acid and has a bitter taste.

EXTRACTS AND OILS. Extracts and oils from aromatic plants are used in small quantities primarily in the bakeshop—extracts of vanilla, lemon, and almond; oils such as peppermint and wintergreen.

VINEGARS. Various types of vinegars can add flavor to a wide variety of dishes from salads to sauces. They have a light, tangy taste and add flavor without fat. Popular vinegars include wine vinegars (made from white wine, red wine, rosé wine, rice wine, champagne, or sherry), cider vinegar (made from apples), and balsamic vinegar. Balsamic vinegar, a dark-brown vinegar with a rich sweet–sour flavor, is made from the juice of a very sweet white grape and is aged for at least 10 years. Vinegars can also be infused, or flavored, with all sorts of ingredients, such as chili peppers, roasted garlic, or any herbs, vegetables, and fruits. These types of vinegars are called flavored, or infused, vinegars. For example, lemon vinegar works well in salad dressings and cold sauces.

FLAVORED OILS. Like vinegar, oils can be infused with ingredients such as fresh herbs, ground spices, and fresh roots. Small amounts of flavored oils can add much flavor to sauces or can even be used alone as a sauce for both hot and cold foods. To make a flavored oil, place the ingredient into a bland oil such as canola, corn, or safflower oil until the oil has taken on the desired flavor.

CONDIMENTS. **Condiments** are highly flavored bottled sauces that are added to a dish as flavorings after the cooking is complete, usually by the diner. Among these are catsup, soy sauce, chili sauce, taco sauce, salsa, prepared mustard, prepared horseradish, chutney, hot pepper sauce, pickle relish, and Worcestershire sauce (Worcestershire is pronounced wuss′-ter-sheer; wuss rhymes with puss). Generally speaking, condiments are served at the table and are not used in the kitchen, but, occasionally, one is used in flavoring a cooked food or cold sauce. Soy sauce is used particularly in oriental cooking, as both flavoring and flavor builder. Worcestershire sauce is used as a flavoring in gravies and salad dressings.

ONIONS AND THEIR RELATIVES. Onions and their cousins—garlic, scallions, leeks, shallots, and chives—are a special category of flavorings that add strong and distinctive flavors and aromas to both cooked and uncooked foods. These bulbous plants of the lily family arrive in the kitchen whole and fresh rather than dried and powdered, though some are available in dried forms. We use them in greater quantity, except for garlic, than the "pinch" or the "few" that is our limit on most herbs and spices. Figure 6.8 illustrates this family.

The *onion* is the scaly bulb of an herb used since ancient times and grown the world over, the most common and most versatile flavor builder in the kitchen. You already know the onion well. Raw, it adds a pungent flavor to salads and cold sauces. Cooked, it has a sweet, mellow, come-on flavor that blends with almost any-

Figure 6-8 THE ONION FAMILY

(Clockwise from top): leek, green onion, chives, shallot, red onion, yellow onion, white onion, garlic. (Photo by Patricia Roberts.)

thing. Cooked onions are also served as a vegetable. Although dried minced onions and onion powder are available, they do not substitute well for fresh onions as tastemakers.

Garlic, the bulb of a plant of the same family, is available as cloves (bulblets), as a powder, or in juice form, with the fresh clove having by far the best flavor. Garlic is used as a flavor builder in stocks, stews, and sauces and as an uncooked flavoring in salads and salad dressings. It has been used for centuries not only for its pungent flavor but as a medicine and tonic.

Chives are another bulbous herb of the onion family, the only one whose leaves rather than bulb are eaten. Chives are usually used raw, since most of their flavor is lost if they are cooked. They are clipped from the plant and added, minced, to cold foods and sauces just before service. Minced chives are also marketed in freeze-dried and frozen form.

The *leek*, a mild-flavored relative of the onion, has a cylindrical bulb. It is the partner of the onion in the mirepoix. Leaves and all are used in stocks, but for soups most of the green is cut off because it seems to develop a bitterness. Boiled leeks are very popular as a vegetable in France, where they are known as the poor man's asparagus. The leek's triumph is the cold soup known as vichyssoise (veeshe-swahz), which was created in an American kitchen by the famous French chef Louis Diat.

The *scallion* is a young onion, also known as a green onion or spring onion. It has a mild flavor as onions go. Minced or sliced, it is added to salads, tops and all. It can pinch-hit in cooking for the full-grown onion, and its green top, minced, can substitute for chives in an emergency.

The *shallot* (shall′-et or sha-lot′) is a cluster of brown-skinned bulblets similar to garlic. It is somewhere between garlic and onion in both size and flavor but is milder and more delicate than either. If browned, it acquires a bitter flavor. One thinks of shallots with wine cookery, with mushrooms in a marvelous stuffing called duxelles, and with special butters.

HERBS AND SPICES

In today's kitchen, herbs and spices are usually flavor builders. A few can be flavorings, and a few can also play the part of a major flavor, as hot peppers do in Mexican cuisine and curry powders do in many oriental dishes. When properly used, they can help the cautious cook; when misused, they can hurt the careless cook. **Herbs** are the leafy parts of certain plants that grow in temperate climates. **Spices** are the roots, bark, seeds, flowers, buds, and fruits of certain tropical plants. Figure 6.9 shows a number of herbs and spices.

Whether you are using an herb or a spice, they must be used in small amounts and carefully coordinated with other ingredients, or their flavor will take over. Herbs and spices are available in dried form. Many herbs are also available fresh.

Figure 6-9 HERBS AND SPICES

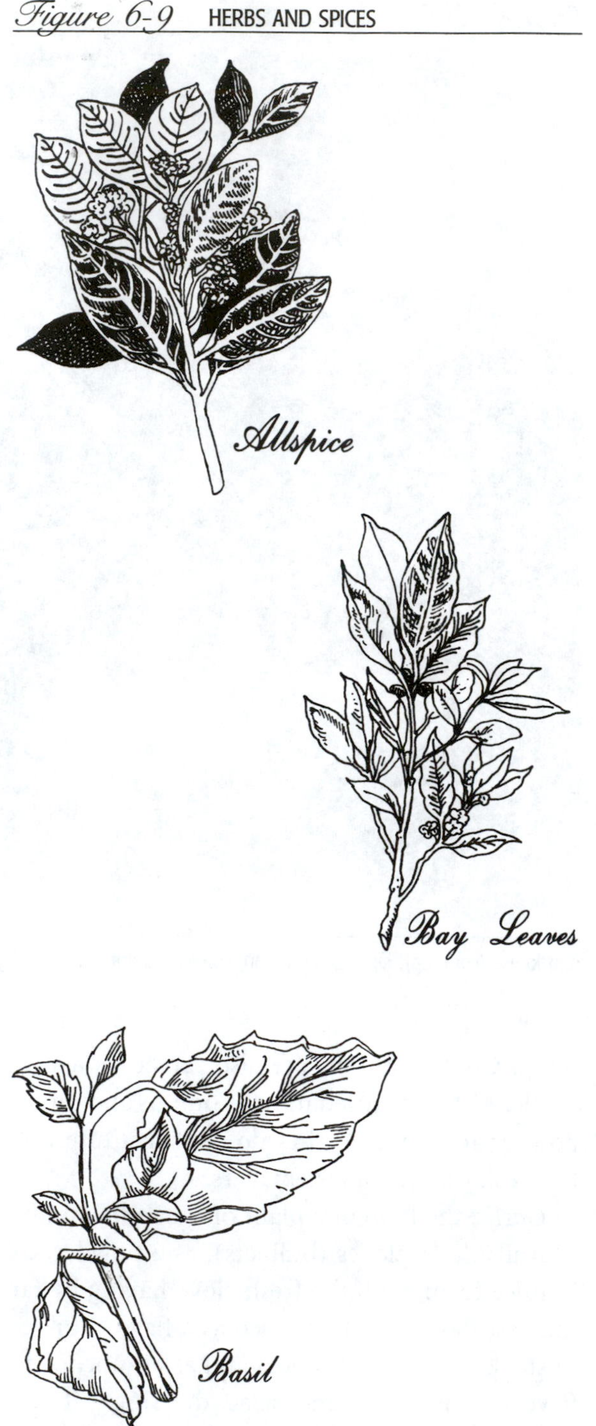

(Courtesy American Spice Trade Association.)

Figure 6-9 (Continued)

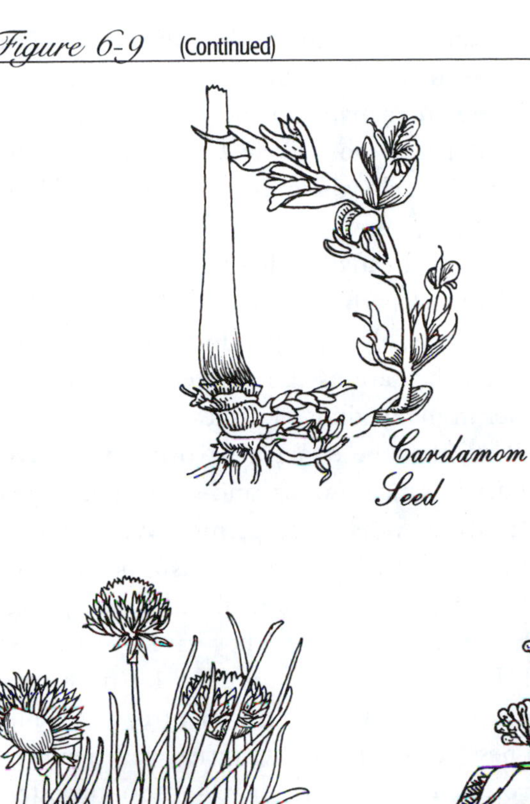

In medieval Europe, spices were among the most important ingredients in cookery. In a large household, the grinding of spices was a full-time job performed by a person known as a powder beater. Pepper, cinnamon, ginger, and cloves were imported at great cost from the Far East and used to mask the taste of rancid or salty meats. Garden herbs like parsley, sage, rosemary, and thyme (pronounced time) were used for flavoring and also for the medicinal properties they were believed to have.

The real purpose of herbs and spices is not to rescue, remedy, flavor, or season, but to build. Spices and herbs are basically flavor builders. You have seen some of them in action in this role in making stocks. This is their proper use in cooking; they should be cooked with the dish as it is being made so that their flavors blend smoothly with the others in the dish. With some exceptions, they should never be added raw to a food at the moment of completion.

Dried herbs and spices should be kept dry in tightly closed containers, and, when stored in a cool, dry place, spoilage is not a problem. One factor limits their shelf life: Over a period of time, they lose strength and thus their power to do the job. Most spices and herbs, once opened, hold well up to six months; they then lose flavor rapidly and by the time they have been opened a year the loss is appreciable. As a rule of thumb, discard an opened container more than a year old. It is a good idea to date the container when you open it. It is also wise to buy a container size you will empty within six months.

Learning to identify the innumerable different herbs and spices requires a keen sense of taste and smell. Simply looking at them is not enough. Taste them, smell them, feel them, use them. The key to most of them is their aroma, for in their aroma is about 60 percent of their flavor. Their aromatic quality not only adds flavor to the food as it is eaten but heightens the anticipation of the diner as the food is being cooked and served.

There are many, many herbs and spices. Let's look at those most likely to be found in the kitchen. To help you understand them, we'll sort them into groups.

You are already familiar with the first group, the five stock herbs and spices—parsley, bay leaf, clove, thyme, black pepper. Indispensable to any kitchen, they are used separately as well as together in many kinds of dishes.

Parsley can be either a flavoring or a flavor builder in sauces, soups, and stews. Fresh parsley is also a widely used garnish. With its dark-green flat or curly leaves, it has a pleasant appearance and a light, sweet flavor. Dried parsley flakes are also available. They have a very different flavor and cannot substitute for fresh parsley in most recipes. Fresh cilantro, also called Chinese parsley, is another variety with a piquant flavor, often used in Asian and Southwestern cooking. It is the plant from which coriander seeds derive.

Bay leaf is used as a flavor builder in dishes made with liquids: soups, sauces, stews, and braised and poached meats. It is generally used whole and removed before service, since it retains its tough, brittle texture even after long cooking. Bay leaf comes from the sweet bay or laurel tree, the same tree whose fresh leaves crowned the winners in the original Olympic Games.

One or two *cloves* accompany a bay leaf in many a simmering pot. Whole cloves are also, in greater numbers, stuck into ham and pork as it cooks and used in sauces, braised meats, and marinades. A dried tree bud shaped like a nail, the clove gets its name from the French word for nail, *clou*. Ground cloves are used in baking and in sweet desserts as they have a sweet flavor.

Thyme has a strong and pungent flavor that calls for sparing use. Powdered thyme is an ingredient of many soups, sauces, and meat and poultry dishes.

Finally, *black pepper* is the only spice that can function in all three taste-making roles—seasoning, flavoring, and flavor building.

Now, let's look at nine herbs and spices that are used as often for their distinctive flavors as for general flavor enrichment. As a flavor builder, each goes beyond the subtlety of the stock herbs and spices and gives a definitely different support flavor—even though you can't single it out from the flavor of the dish as a whole. Used in quantities large enough to taste, they become major flavors rather than flavor builders. Several of them can also be used as flavorings.

Basil, oregano, and *tarragon* are available fresh and also come in the form of crushed dried leaves. They look somewhat alike, but their tastes, however, are very different.

Basil (bay-sul or baz-ul) has a warm, sweet flavor that is welcome in many soups, sauces, entrées, and vegetables such as tomatoes, peas, eggplant, and squash. It blends especially well with tomato. Like many other herbs, it has a symbolism: In India, it expresses reverence for the dead; in Italy, it is a symbol of love.

Oregano (a-reg′-a-noh) belongs to the same herb family as basil, but it makes a very different contribution to a dish—a strong bittersweet taste and aroma you may have met in spaghetti sauce. It is used in many Italian and Mexican dishes.

Tarragon (tair′-a-gon) has a flavor that is somehow light and strong at the same time. It tastes something like licorice. Its flavor is most closely associated with tarragon vinegar and with béarnaise (bare-naze or bay-ar-nez) sauce, although it is also used in poultry and fish dishes, as well as salads and salad dressings.

Rosemary, like bay leaf, is used in dishes where a liquid is involved—soups, sauces, stews, braised and poached foods. The leaf of an evergreen shrub of the mint family, it has a pungent flavor and fragrance. Fresh or dried, it looks and feels like pine needles. Rosemary is a traditional symbol of fidelity and remembrance.

Powdered sage comes from the dried leaves and stems of the sage plant. It is used to flavor sausage and stuffings for poultry, fish, and pork. Sage complements pork beautifully. The velvet-leaved plant was traditionally valued highly as a guarantor of good health. "Why should a man die whilst sage grows in his garden?" goes a medieval saying.

Dill and *mustard* have flavors that will be very familiar to you: dill as in pickle and mustard as in hot dog. Fresh or dried dill leaves, often called dill weed, are used in soups, fish dishes, stews, salads, and butters. Whole dill seed is used in some soups and sauerkraut. Dry mustard, a powdered spice made from the seed of the mustard plant, comes in two varieties: white or yellow and brown. The brown has the sharper and more pungent flavor. Both kinds are used to flavor sauces and entrées. Prepared mustards are also made from both kinds. The mustard flavor is especially popular with ham.

Paprika is another powdered spice that comes in two flavors, mild and hot. Both kinds are made from dried pods of the same pepper family as red pepper and cayenne, and they look something like the seasoning peppers, but they do not do the work of seasonings. Hungarian paprika is the hot spicy one; Spanish paprika is mild in flavor and its red color has lots of eye appeal. Hungarian paprika is used to make goulash and other braised meats and poultry. Paprikas are sensitive to heat and will turn brown if exposed to direct heat.

Still another branch of this same pepper pod family gives us chili peppers, the crushed or dried pods of several kinds of Mexican peppers. Colors range from red to green and flavors from mild to hot. Chili peppers are used in Mexican cuisine and in the spice combination called chili powder.

Several spice blends are available. Two of them are standards in any kitchen. *Chili powder* is one, with a spice called cumin (coo-min) predominating. Other more familiar ingredients may be garlic, chili pepper, black pepper, oregano, and clove. Chili powder varies from mild to hot. It is used, of course, in chili, where it functions as a major flavor, and in Mexican and Southwestern dishes.

Curry powder is a blend of up to 20 oriental spices. In India, where it originated, cooks blend their own curry powders, which may vary considerably. In the United States, curry powder comes premixed in various blends from mild to hot. Curry powders usually include cloves, black and red peppers, cumin, garlic, ginger, cinnamon, coriander, turmeric (which provides the characteristic yellow color), and sometimes other spices.

A group of powdered sweet aromatic spices from the tropics are used frequently in baking and in dessert cookery and, occasionally, in sauces, vegetables, and entrées. Among these are *cinnamon, nutmeg* and its counterpart *mace,* and *ginger.* Cinnamon comes from the dried bark of the cinnamon or cassia tree, nutmeg and mace from the seed of the nutmeg tree, and ginger from the dried root of the ginger plant.

In hot foods, the nutmeg flavor goes well with potatoes and spinach and some kinds of veal dishes, and it gives the French béchamel sauce its

Figure 6-10 TIPS FOR USING HERBS AND SPICES

1. Use only good-quality herbs and spices.
2. Store dried herbs and spices in cool, dry areas away from light and moisture, which deteriorate them at a faster rate.
3. Fresh herbs can be washed, dried, and kept in the refrigerator for one week in an air-tight container.
4. Dried herbs and spices need heat to release their flavors. Think of their nature and you will see the reasons why. They are uncooked. They are demoisturized. They need cooking to mellow their raw taste and moisture to bring out their full flavor, and time for both things to happen. If you add them raw to a dish, you are adding undesirable raw, dry flavors. Adding dried rosemary to a finished soup, for example, is like adding a mouthful of pine needles. Fresh herbs should be added later in the cooking.
5. Also, keep in mind that ground herbs and spices release their flavors quicker than whole. Whole herbs and spices are excellent in long-cooking dishes such as stews because they take longer to release their flavor. Wrap whole herbs and spices in a cheesecloth or muslin bag for easy removal and add at the beginning of the cooking process.
6. Overcooking of products with herbs and spices can result in flavor loss. The kitchen may smell wonderful, but the food is losing its flavor.
7. If adding herbs and spices to cold foods such as salads and dressings, allow at least several hours for the flavors to develop.
8. Dried herbs and spices are much stronger than fresh ones. A useful formula is: About 3 teaspoons fresh herbs = 1 teaspoon dried.
9. Pair intense herbs, such as tarragon and rosemary, with richly flavored foods.
10. Taste foods while they are cooking and before serving so you can adjust the seasoning.

distinctive taste. Mace, a somewhat paler alternative to nutmeg, has a similar flavor. Cinnamon and ginger are used in oriental dishes. Cinnamon is available also in sticks. They make good swizzlers for hot buttered rum or after-dinner coffee.

Mint is a sweet herb, with the familiar flavor you meet in toothpaste and chewing gum. Mint is available in two varieties: spearmint or peppermint. The flavor of a mint sauce offers a refreshing complement to lamb. Fresh mint makes a good flavoring and garnish for certain fruits and vegetables and iced tea.

In fact, many fresh herbs are available today, and their use is more and more common. When replacing dried herbs with fresh in a recipe, use three times as much. The dried herbs are three to four times as potent as fresh herbs because the aromatic oils have been concentrated in the drying. You should also add fresh herbs later in the cooking because they turn brown when cooked too long. Always taste carefully as you add, just as you do in seasoning.

Seeds of various herbs are used whole in baking and in salad dressings—the dark-brown, crescent-shaped caraway seed; the round, blond sesame seed; the blue-black seeds of the poppy flower. Seeds have the added advantage of textural interest as well as flavor.

This minicatalog of herbs and spices is not meant to be memorized and then forgotten. Come back to it as a reference as you cook with flavor builders and flavorings, along with Figure 6.10 and Tables 6.1 and 6.2, and again later as you begin to develop dishes on your own. Use it as a resource for experiment. Variety, as the old saying goes, is the spice of life.

Table 6-1 HERB AND SPICE EQUIVALENTS

Spice	*Teaspoons per Ounce*	*Spice*	*Teaspoons per Ounce*
Allspice	14	Mixed pickling spice	17
Anise	14 1/2	Mustard	14 1/2
Basil	35	Nutmeg	12 3/4
Bay leaves	136 leaves	Oregano	26
Caraway seed	9 1/2	Paprika	13 1/2
Cardamom seed	14 1/2	Parsley	50
Cayenne pepper	14 1/2	Pepper, black	15 1/4
Celery seed	14	Pepper, white	13 1/4
Chili powder	11 1/2	Red pepper	14
Cinnamon	17 1/2	Crushed red pepper	16
Cloves	14 1/2	Poppy seed	11 1/4
Coriander	14	Poultry seasoning	14
Cumin	14	Rosemary	35
Curry powder	12 1/2	Saffron	35
Dill	14	Sage	22
Fennel	14	Savory	18 3/4
Fenugreek	14	Sesame seed	14
Ginger	14	Tarragon	50
Mace	14	Thyme	20 1/4
Marjoram	19 1/2	Turmeric	12
Mint	50		

Table 6-2 HERB AND SPICE REFERENCE CHART

Product	*Description*	*Product Notes*
Allspice (spice)	Dried, dark-brown berries of an evergreen tree.	Clove-like flavor, but smoother, mellower; undertones of cinnamon, nutmeg, hence name; also called "pimento."
Anise seed (herb seed)	Small, gray–brown seeds of plant of the parsley family.	Licorice-like flavor. Its oil is heavily used used for licorice flavoring, though true licorice is from the roots of another plant.
Star anise (spice)	Large, brown, star-shaped fruit of an evergreen tree. Each point contains a seed; whole fruit is used.	Anise-like flavor. Old-time pickling favorite.
Basil (herb)	Bright-green leaves of an herb of the mint family.	Special affinity for tomato-flavored dishes; currently enjoying fastest popularity growth of an herb.
Bay leaves (herb)	Large, olive-green leaves of the sweet-bay or laurel tree.	An important product; only dried herb to come in original, whole-leaf form. Also "laurel."
Caraway seed (herb seed)	Hard, brown, scimitar-shaped seeds of an herb of the parsley family.	The seed of "seeded rye bread"; essential in liqueur kummel; German sauerkraut favorite.
Cardamom seed (spice)	Pod and dark-brown seeds of a plant of the ginger family.	Scandinavian bakery goods; Indian foods; worldwide biggest use is in Middle East coffee.
Celery seed (herb seed)	Tiny brown seeds of the smallage, or wild celery plant.	Strong celery flavor; heavy use in salad dressings, sauces, vegetable cocktails.
Chervil (herb)	Lacy, fern-like leaves of a plant of the parsley family.	Much like parsley, but sweeter and more aromatic; anise-like fragrance with slight pepper flavor.
Chives (herb)	Tubular green leaves of a member of the onion family.	Normally freeze-dried to protect fragile quality and vibrant green color; product is tiny lengths of tubular shoots.
Cinnamon/ cassia (spice)	Bark of various evergreen trees of the cinnamomum family.	Two main types: Zeylanicum (Ceylon) is tan colored, thin bark, mild, sweet flavor. Cassia is reddish brown, thicker bark, strong cinnamon flavor, most popular in U.S.
Cloves (spice)	Dried, unopened flower buds of an evergreen tree.	Intriguing, nail-like shape makes exotic garnish. Ground cloves very strong flavored.

Table 6-2 (Continued)

Product	Description	Product Notes
Coriander leaves (herb)	Green leaves of a plant of the parsley family.	Most frequently called "cilantro." Strong, exotic flavor, associated with Mexican food.
Coriander seed (herb seed)	Small, round, buff-colored seeds of the coriander plant.	Mild, delicately fragrant aroma with lemony/sage undertone.
Cumin seed (herb seed)	Small, elongated, yellowish-brown seeds of a plant of the parsley family	Also "comino." The aromatic flavor note in chili powder and essential in curries.
Dill seed (herb seed)	Small, oval-shaped, tan seed of a member of the parsley family.	Principal flavor of dill pickles, also used in dips, sauces, sausages.
Dill weed (herb)	Green, feathery leaves of the dill plant.	Dill weed is much used in sauces for fish, cheese dips, salads, dressings.
Fennel seed (herb seed)	Small, yellowish-brown, watermelon-shaped seeds of a member of the parsley family.	Anise-like flavor. The distinctive note note in Italian sausages (both sweet and hot).
Fenugreek seed (herb seed)	Very small, reddish-brown seeds of a member of the pea family.	Pleasantly bitter flavor with curry-like aroma. Essential in curry powder; basis of imitation maple.
Ginger (spice)	Dried roots (rhizomes) of a member of the zingiber family.	Root pieces are called "hands." Smooth, straw-colored ones have been peeled, bleached.
Mace (spice)	Lacy, scarlet-colored aril (orange when dried) that surrounds the seed of the nutmeg fruit.	Flavor is stronger than nutmeg. Ground mace is often chosen for light-colored products, such as pound cake.
Marjoram (herb)	Grayish-green leaves of a member of the mint family.	A cousin of oregano but with milder, sweeter flavor.
Mint flakes (herb)	Dark-green leaves of either the peppermint or spearmint plant.	Spearmint is the mint usually packed as mint flakes for retail and foodservice; peppermint is also available to industrial customers.
Mustard seed (spice)	Tiny yellow or brownish seeds of a member of the cabbage family.	Yellow (or white) seeds have sharp bite, but no aromatic pungency. Brown (and oriental) seeds are aromatically pungent as well as biting (i.e., Chinese restaurant mustard).
Nutmeg (spice)	The brown seed of the fruit of an evergreen tree.	Of the two sources, Indonesian and West Indian compare favorably in aroma, but higher fixed oil in the W.I. restricts its use in some applications.

(*Continued*)

Table 6-2 (Continued)

Product	Description	Product Notes
Oregano (herb)	Light-green leaves of member of the mint family.	Two distinct types: Mediterranean (Italian/Greek foods); Mexican (chili, Mexican, TexMex foods).
Paprika (spice)	Powder milled from the flesh of pods of certain capsicum plants.	Extractable color is principal evaluation of paprika. Flavor can range from sweet-mild to mildly pungent.
Parsley (herb)	Bright-green leaves of parsley plant.	About 12 pounds of de-stemmed parsley leaves are required to make one pound of parsley flakes.
Black peppercorns (spice)	Dried, mature berries of a tropical vine.	The whole dried berry (peppercorn) is used for black pepper.
Chili pepper (spice)	Large, mildly pungent pods of Anaheim (or "California-type") peppers and the newer "6–4" variety (New Mexican type).	Spice industry reserves "chili peppers" for these mild pods; "chilies" for the hot little pods (see Red Pepper).
Green peppercorns	Immature berries (dried or freeze-dried) of the pepper vine.	Pepper berries are picked while still green, resulting in somewhat milder flavor.
Pink peppercorns	Dried, red berries of a shrub-like evergreen of the Anareardiacease.	No relation to black pepper. Proper label is Rose Baises (Red Berries).
Red pepper (spice)	Dried fruit (pods) of various small, hot peppers. Whole pods are called "chilies."	"Red pepper" is today's industry designation for any ground hot pepper product. "Cayenne" is being phased out.
White peppercorns	Light tan-colored seed of the pepper berry from which the dark outer husk has been removed.	White pepper has the heat but not the total bouquet of black. Often chosen for light-colored soups, soups, sauces.
Poppy seed (herb seed)	Tiny, gray–blue seeds of the poppy plant.	The same plant produces opium and morphine, but the seeds have no drug significance.
Rosemary (herb)	Green, needle-like leaves of a shrub of the mint family.	Rosemary and lamb are closely associated, but it's also important in Italian herb blends, sauces and salad dressings. Has natural antioxidant properties.
Saffron (herb)	Dried flower stigmas of a member of the crocus family.	By the pound, our most expensive spice, but a pinch does so much flavoring and coloring that it is not prohibitive.

Table 6-2 (Continued)

Product	Description	Product Notes
Sage (herb)	Long, slender leaves (silver–gray when dried) of a member of the mint family.	Three types: "Cut" is used for end products where sage should show. "Rubbed" is minimally ground and coarsely sieved to a fluffy consistency. "Ground" is sieved to a fine degree.
Savory (herb)	Small, brownish-green (when dried) leaves of a summer savory—a member of the mint family.	So good with green beans, its German name translates to "bean herb." Also in poultry seasoning and other herb blends.
Sesame seed (herb seed)	Small, oval, pearly white seeds of a member of the Pedaliacae family.	Also "benne." Needs toasting or high heat of baking to develop its nutty flavor.
Tarragon (herb)	Slender, dark green leaves of a member of the aster family.	Distinctive for its hint of anise flavor. Hallmark of béarnaise sauce, salad dressings, vinegars.
Thyme (herb)	Grayish-green leaves of a member of the mint family.	One of the strongest herbs. Manhattan-style clam chowder and innumerable herb blends.
Tumeric (spice)	Orange colored roots (rhizomes) of a member of the ginger family.	Provides color for prepared mustards, curry powder, mayonnaise, sauces, pickles, relishes.

SOURCE: American Spice Trade Association. (Reprinted with permission.)

SUMMING UP

In Chapter 5, we talked about the structure of a dish—its flavor, body, and texture. This chapter has dealt with the materials and techniques for building each element of the structure.

To build flavor in stocks, the cook uses bones, mirepoix, and herbs and spices. The mirepoix is a standard combination of flavorful vegetables, which is usually used with a standard combination of herbs and spices to flavor stocks. Stocks, in turn, are used to build flavor in soups and sauces.

To build body in soups and sauces, the cook makes stocks from water, bones, mirepoix, and herbs and spices, building flavor at the same time. Different types of stocks (white, brown, fish, and vegetable) have their own special ingredients, techniques, and uses in soups and sauces. Stocks may be turned into glazes by reducing meat, chicken, or fish stocks until they coat the back of a spoon. Glazes are used mainly to add flavor and texture to sauces. In today's kitchen, convenience bases often replace stock made from scratch, but they must be chosen with care and used with understanding.

To build texture, the cook uses thickening agents. Natural thickeners are high-starch foods that often function as the major ingredient in a dish, providing flavor and character as well as thickening. Artificial thickeners are starch products whose primary function is to thicken. They include fat–flour combinations—roux and beurre manié—and starch–water thickeners made with cornstarch, flour, arrowroot, or various name-brand starch combinations. Vegetable purées and crumbs can also be used successfully to thicken.

Another texture builder is the liaison, made of egg yolks and cream. It is used to thicken, although it doesn't thicken very much, and also to refine and smooth the texture of already thickened products.

In addition to a food's own taste, the cook has available many strong-flavored ingredients that are used in minute amounts in producing flavorful and distinctive dishes. These special ingredients are used in three ways: to season, to add a specific flavor accent, or to build a total flavor that supports or enriches a dish's major flavor.

In seasoning, the added products—salt, pepper, and fresh lemon juice—bring out the food's own flavor. The taste of a seasoning should not be perceived at all in the finished dish. The art of seasoning depends on the cook's sensory awareness, knowledge of tastes, and experience.

In flavoring, the product added brings its own distinctive flavor to complement the major flavor of the dish so that both are perceived separately. Flavorers commonly used are wines and spirits, grated rinds of citrus fruits, extracts and oils, condiments, onions, and other members of the onion family.

In today's kitchen, herbs and spices are usually flavor builders. A few can be flavorings, and a few can also play the part of a major flavor.

Flavor builders, stocks, and thickening agents are the building materials for endless numbers of menu items. The final dish can be only as good as the flavor, body, and texture built with these materials. As Escoffier said of one of them, "If one's stock is good, what remains of the work is easy; if, on the other hand, it is bad or merely mediocre, it is quite hopeless to expect anything approaching a satisfactory result."

The Cook's Vocabulary

beurre manié
body
bouquet garni
clarified butter
condiment
deglazing
flavor
flavor building
flavoring
gelatin
glaze
herbs
liaison
major flavor
mirepoix
onion piqué
pepper: black, white, green
red pepper (cayenne)
reduce
roux: white, blond, brown, dark brown or black
sachet
salt: iodized, sea, kosher
seasoning
skim
slurry
spices
stocks: white, brown, fish, vegetable
tempering
thickening agent
whitewash
zest

Review Questions

Answer each question in complete sentences. Read each question carefully and make sure you answer all parts of the question. Organize your answer into more than one paragraph when appropriate.

1. What roles do mirepoix, bouquet garni, sachet, and onion piqué play in producing flavor?
2. Discuss the differences in the procedures for making light stocks and dark stocks.
3. Describe the techniques used when combining:
   a. Roux with liquid
   b. Beurre manié with liquid
   c. Starch thickeners with liquid
   d. A liaison with liquid
4. Describe the differences in seasonings, flavorings, and flavor builders. Name some ingredients that might be used in each role.
5. Suggest some guidelines for developing seasoning skill.

Chapter 7

SOUPS

Nothing begins a meal better than a cup of steaming-hot soup. Soup teases and yet soothes the appetite. The tempting aroma of broth and herbs makes the diner look forward with relish to a pleasant experience.

Soup may also be a main course, or it may be a pick-me-up between meals. In today's health-oriented society, the coffee break has become a soup break for many people, and soup is a popular late-night snack. Soup-and-sandwich is a typical midday meal. Some people even like hot soup for breakfast.

What is soup? It is so familiar it is almost hard to define. Let us say that soup is a flavored, seasoned liquid, usually cooked, that is served as a dish in itself.

There are many, many different kinds of soups. To classify them according to flavor would be like measuring wealth in pennies—we would spend a great deal of time counting. But if we look at soup textures, and if we examine the methods of achieving different textures, we find that most soups group themselves naturally into three categories:

- Unthickened soups, also known as clear soups
- Naturally thickened soups
- Starch-thickened soups, also called cream soups

Of course, there are a number of specialty soups that don't fit well into any of these categories.

We are going to look at the different categories of soups and the ways they are made, and you will see how to make many different soups from a few basic formulas. We will also consider some well-known specialty soups, as well as some soups that are served cold. Soup cookery will introduce you to many different cooking techniques. Once you learn to cook all kinds of soups, you will have mastered the basics of many other dishes.

After completing this chapter you should be able to:

- Understand and explain the structure of clear soups, naturally thickened soups, and cream soups.
- Understand and explain how to use purées, roux, beurre manié, and liaisons successfully to produce specific soup textures.
- Identify well-known specialty soups.
- Explain how to prepare cold soups.
- Choose appropriate soup ingredients.
- Hold and store soups to maintain quality and avoid bacterial growth.

CLEAR SOUPS

Most unthickened soups are translucent; that is, they allow light to pass through. Because of this quality, they are known as **clear soups.** The simplest clear soup is **broth** or **bouillon,** a clear soup without any solid ingredients. It is made from simmering meats and/or vegetables.

The kinds of clear soups you find on the typical menu add a great variety of ingredients to good stocks to make a great variety of good clear soups. Let us look at several of the most popular ones.

ONION SOUP

First, we will look at a great favorite, onion soup, and see just how it is prepared. Figure 7.1 shows what it takes to make it, and Recipe 7.1 shows its structure and the way you put it all together.

Here, by adding a flavor-determining ingredient and some supporting herbs and spices to the stock, we have created another soup. It is a simple soup because of the limited number of ingredients. Yet even the simplest soup requires a certain skill—to produce the flavor, texture, aroma, and appearance the diner expects.

As you can see from the recipe, the structure of the soup is simple. The onions provide the major flavor and the stock provides the body. Onions and stock together create an interesting texture that is thin yet has substance. The flavor-building herbs and spices enhance the major flavor without imposing their own tastes. You tie them in a piece of cheesecloth to make a sachet so that you can remove them before serving the soup.

To cut the onions julienne, you cut the peeled onions in half lengthwise and slice them thin. As they cook, the layers will separate into individual strips. The onions should be cooked long enough to caramelize the sugar in them so that they are golden throughout, but there should be no dark-brown edges. Nor should

Figure 7-1 ONION SOUP

Onions, stock, and flavor builders make an easy, inexpensive, flavorful clear soup. The onions are cut julienne.

Recipe 7-1 ONION SOUP

YIELD: ***Approximately 1 gallon (4 L) or 16 8-oz (250 mL) portions***

2 lb	**onions, julienne cut**	**1 kg**
	butter or oil for sautéing	
$^3/_4$ gal	**dark stock**	**3 L**
$^1/_4$	**bay leaf**	
$^1/_2$	**clove**	
3–4	**peppercorns**	
	pinch rosemary	
	pinch thyme	

1. Sauté the onions in butter or oil until onions are golden.
2. Add stock and sachet containing remaining ingredients. Simmer until onions have thoroughly flavored stock and are cooked through but still retain their shape.
3. Remove sachet and season soup to taste.

Per serving:		Carbohydrates:	5 g
Calories:	37	Cholesterol:	6 mg
Fat:	2 g	Fiber:	1 g
Protein:	1 g	Sodium:	2 mg

Recipe 7-1a FRENCH ONION SOUP

To Recipe 7.1, add:

4 oz	**soft butter or margarine**	**125 g**
3 oz	**grated parmesan cheese**	**90 g**
16	**bread or roll slices, $^1/_4$–$^1/_2$ in. (0.5–1 cm) thick**	

1. Blend butter/margarine and cheese to make a paste; spread on bread slices.
2. Bake at 350°F (180°C) until dry and brown, or brown lightly in salamander or broiler.
3. At service, float 1 crouton on each portion.

Per serving:		Carbohydrates:	17 g
Calories:	178	Cholesterol:	20 mg
Fat:	10 g	Fiber:	2 g
Protein:	5 g	Sodium:	294 mg

Recipe 7-1b ONION AND ALMOND SOUP

To Recipe 7.1, add:

4 oz	**sliced blanched almonds**	**125 g**
1 tsp	**ground cumin**	**5 mL**
16	**croutons**	
$^1/_3$ C	**sliced almonds, toasted**	**75 mL**

1. In blender, grind almonds fine.
2. Gradually add 4 oz (125 mL) soup; process until smooth and milky. Add cumin to produce a balance of flavors.
3. Add almond mixture to soup; heat to holding temperature.
4. At service, float 1 crouton topped with 1 tsp (5 mL) toasted almonds on each portion.

Per serving:		Carbohydrates:	8 g
Calories:	101	Cholesterol:	0 mg
Fat:	7 g	Fiber:	2 g
Protein:	3 g	Sodium:	24 mg

they be overcooked in the simmering. They should be tender but still retain their shape. This may take anywhere from 45 seconds to 15 minutes depending on the quantity and other variables.

The seasonings should bring out the maximum flavor of the ingredients. A well-made onion soup is clear and flavorful with a rich, appetizing aroma.

You can turn this simple soup into another simple soup by topping it with a special crouton—a slice of bread with a butter–cheese spread baked or broiled until crisp and brown (Recipe 7.1a). Or you can turn the basic soup into a more sophisticated soup by adding special flavorings, as in Recipe 7.1b. It gives you a good example of how flavorings function in a dish. The result is a balance in which the onion, almond, and cumin are individually perceptible while blending harmoniously.

VEGETABLE SOUPS

Going back to broths or stocks as our point of departure, we can take our soup making one step farther and add to a broth or stock not just one major vegetable flavor but several. Almost any number of vegetables (and sometimes meat, poultry, or starches) can be combined with different-flavored broths or stocks to create a great variety of clear vegetable soups.

Recipe 7.2 is one example. Examining it carefully, you will see that it is made with several vegetables having different textures and different cooking rates. Yet, to make a good vegetable soup, all the ingredients must be done—fully done but not overdone—and must reach doneness at the same time. This is why it is put together the way it is.

Notice that, to produce the most flavor and the best texture for the ingredients, several different cooking processes are used. The herb and vegetable flavor builders are **sweated** (cooked in a small amount of fat over low heat) to get a nice blend of flavors before the stock is added. The carrots are parboiled before being added to the soup, so they will reach doneness at the same time as the other vegetables. The soup is simmered to achieve doneness with a minimum of flavor loss through evaporation. The tomatoes are poached last in the hot liquid to avoid overcooking.

Here are the guidelines for combining different stocks and different vegetables successfully:

- Begin with a well-flavored stock or broth.
- Know what flavors complement each other.
- Know the rates at which different foods cook.
- Do not overcook.
- Cut vegetables uniformly and large enough to be identified, but small enough to fit in a spoon.

Recipe 7-2 VEGETABLE SOUP

YIELD: ***1 gallon (4 L) or 16 8-oz (250 mL) portions***

1/2 lb	**onions, diced**	**250 g**
1/2 lb	**celery, diced**	**250 g**
1/2 lb	**carrots, diced**	**250 g**
1/2 lb	**potatoes, diced**	**250 g**
1/4	**bay leaf**	
1/2	**clove**	
1/2	**garlic clove**	
	pinch rosemary	
	pinch thyme	
3–4	**peppercorns**	
	butter/oil	
3/4 gal	**stock**	**3 L**
1/2 lb	**tomatoes, peeled, seeded, chopped**	**250 g**

1. In a stockpot, sweat onions, celery, carrots, potatoes, and sachet (bay leaf, clove, garlic clove, rosemary, thyme, and peppercorns) in butter/oil until onions are translucent.
2. Add stock and simmer until celery is about half done.
3. Simmer until all vegetables are done to al dente stage.
4. Add tomatoes and heat through.
5. Remove sachet and season soup to taste.

Per serving:		Carbohydrates:	7 g
Calories:	57	Cholesterol:	4 mg
Fat:	3 g	Fiber:	1 g
Protein:	1 g	Sodium:	37 mg

Although flavor and taste are to some extent a matter of opinion, certain flavor combinations seem to be universally pleasing—chicken and celery, for example, or beef and tomato. Certain spices and herbs blend well with certain stocks—chicken and clove, fish stock and lemon, beef and thyme.

Knowing the rates at which different foods cook comes best through experience. Feel their texture, cook them, and taste them. Here are some general groupings:

- Hard vegetables such as carrots and raw green beans take longest to cook. They should be parboiled before being added to a soup in the making.
- Soft vegetables such as tomatoes, greens, and canned vegetables take the shortest time, or no time at all, and should be added late in the cooking.

In between are the medium vegetables, such as potatoes, celery, turnips, and frozen vegetables. They can be cooked right in the soup during the soup making.

Do not overcook! "Done" for vegetables is firm to the bite, a texture known as *al dente.* Al dente vegetables will keep their separate flavors and their bright, attractive colors along with their pleasant texture.

There is a common and persistent belief that soup should be cooked for long periods of time to extract flavor from the ingredients. Although prolonged cooking does extract flavor, what is added to the soup is lost to the individual vegetables. Some vegetables change flavor as well as color when they are overcooked. And much flavor can be lost through evaporation.

A more logical approach than prolonged cooking is to simmer the soup just to doneness. Whether you hold it for service hot or cold, flavors will continue to blend and be released by the vegetables within. In the perfect vegetable soup, you should be able to taste the individual flavors and, at the same time, the blended flavor of the soup as a whole.

Meat, rice, pasta, barley, and many other products can be added to a vegetable soup. Many such ingredients are cooked separately and added to the soup at the end of the cooking process. One reason for doing this is to maintain the soup's clarity. Starchy foods such as cereals and pastas will cloud the liquid in which they are cooked without contributing flavor in the process.

The minestrone in Recipe 7.3 is a case in point: The spaghetti and beans are precooked and added at the end. This well-known Italian specialty is a hearty soup thick with ingredients, yet it is still a clear soup. The liquid has not been thickened and it is still translucent.

CONSOMMÉ

Many clear soups use an enriched stock called consommé (con-sum-may) as the body liquid in preference to a simple stock. **Consommé** is also a clear soup in itself and a very important one. It has a rich color and a hearty flavor that give it top rank among clear soups.

Historically, the making of a perfect consommé was a measure of a cook's skill. A perfect consommé has two outstanding qualities: clarity and strength of flavor. These two measures of quality are achieved by using a rich and full-flavored stock and by a process known as **clarification**—the removing of particles in a stock by a special cooking process. At the same time that the stock is being cleared, flavor is being added to it to make the consommé. It may be made from any kind of stock, though chicken and chicken and beef consommé are very common.

Making consommé is a long and exacting process. Recipe 7.4 gives you a modern version of the classical method.

In Step 1, you combine lean ground beef, mirepoix and other flavor builders, egg whites, and possibly an acid ingredient (such as tomato products) to make a mixture called **clearmeat.** This is what is going to clarify the stock and add

Recipe 7-3 MINESTRONE

YIELD: ***1 gallon (4 L) or 16 8-oz (250 mL) portions***

3 fl oz	**olive oil**	**100 mL**
12 oz	**onions, sliced thin**	**375 g**
4 oz	**celery, small dice**	**125 g**
4 oz	**carrots, small dice**	**125 g**
$1\frac{1}{2}$ tsp	**garlic, chopped**	**8 mL**
4 oz	**potatoes, small dice**	**125 g**
4 oz	**cabbage, shredded**	**125 g**
4 oz	**zucchini, medium dice**	**125 g**
12 oz	**crushed tomatoes**	**375 g**
3 qt	**white stock**	**3 L**
$\frac{1}{2}$ tsp	**basil**	**2 mL**
1 lb	**white beans, canned and drained**	**450 g**
8 oz	**cooked pasta, small shape**	**250 g**
3 Tb	**chopped parsley**	**45 mL**
salt to taste		
pepper to taste		
6 Tb	**grated Parmesan cheese**	**90 mL**

1. Heat the oil in a stockpot over medium heat.
2. Add the onions, celery, carrots, garlic, and potatoes. Sweat them until the onion is translucent.
3. Add the cabbage and zucchini and sweat for 3 more minutes.
4. Add the tomatoes, stock, and basil. Simmer until vegetables are al dente.
5. Add the beans and cooked pasta. Bring the soup to a boil.
6. Add the parsley. Season to taste with salt and pepper.
7. Add the Parmesan cheese just prior to service.

Per serving:			
Calories:	120	Carbohydrates:	14 g
Fat:	6 g	Cholesterol:	1 mg
Protein:	4 g	Fiber:	3 g
		Sodium:	114 mg

some flavor as well (except for the egg whites—their job is strictly to clarify). Chill it thoroughly.

In Step 2, you slowly add the cold stock to the clearmeat. The cold liquid will dissolve proteins in the meat.

In Step 3, you heat and stir the mixture gently, keeping the clearmeat moving so it doesn't stick to the pot.

In Step 4, as the stock approaches a simmer, bits of clearmeat move slowly toward the surface, absorbing particles from the stock as they rise, in other words, clarifying it. The egg white and dis-

Recipe 7-4 BEEF CONSOMMÉ

YIELD: ***1 gallon (4 L) or 16 8-oz (250 mL) portions***

1 lb	**lean ground beef**	**450 g**
8 oz	**egg whites**	**250 g**
8 oz	**canned crushed tomatoes**	**250 g**
Mirepoix:		
8 oz	**onions, small dice**	**250 g**
4 oz	**celery, small dice**	**125 g**
4 oz	**carrots, small dice**	**125 g**
6	**parsley stems, finely chopped**	
	pinch thyme	
$\frac{1}{2}$	**bay leaf**	
2	**cloves**	
$\frac{1}{2}$	**tsp crushed peppercorns**	**2 mL**
5 qt	**beef stock, cold**	**5 L**

1. Mix thoroughly all ingredients except stock in a stockpot. Refrigerate for 30 minutes.
2. Slowly add cold stock, stirring gently to combine.
3. Over moderately low heat, bring to a simmer, gently moving clearmeat to keep it from sticking to bottom of pot.
4. When it simmers, stop stirring and reduce at once to a low simmer.
5. Simmer slowly without stirring for about $1\frac{1}{2}$ hours until full flavored and clear.
6. Strain the consommé through a china cap lined with cheesecloth.
7. Degrease thoroughly and season to taste.

Per serving:			
Calories:	29	Carbohydrates:	2 g
Fat:	0 g	Cholesterol:	10 mg
Protein:	5 g	Fiber:	0 g
		Sodium:	20 mg

solved meat proteins begin to coagulate and gather up all the particles from the stock as they rise. The acid of the tomato helps in the coagulation process, too. When the clearmeat reaches the top, it forms a mass called a **raft.** At this point, all stirring stops. These critical stages of clarification are shown in Figure 7.2.

As the soup simmers (Step 5), flavor is extracted from the raft to give the soup its double strength. It is literally being beefed up. At the same time, the stock is further clarified as convection currents in the simmering pot carry particles upward to cling to the bottom of the raft.

When the consommé has reached its full flavor and clarity (1 to 2 hours of simmering after the raft has formed), it is strained through a double thickness of dampened cheesecloth in a china cap (Step 6). Be sure to remove any traces of fat from the surface of the consommé as well.

Here are the important guidelines for making consommé:

- Use cold stock.
- Use low heat throughout.
- Do not allow the clearmeat to stick to the bottom of the pot. Stir in the beginning.
- Keep the liquid quiet. Do not boil.
- Do not stir after the raft has formed.
- Do not disturb the raft.
- Measure cooking time from raft formation.
- Judge doneness by clarity and flavor. Adjust seasonings.
- Strain carefully, keeping the raft intact.

VERSATILITY IN CLEAR SOUPS

Stocks, bouillons, and consommés are points of departure for countless clear soups. Following the basic patterns and methods of the soups we have examined, you can make hundreds of different soups by adding almost any ingredients that are compatible in flavor—vegetables, meats, cereal products, croutons, dumplings, stuffed pastas, and so on.

The amounts of ingredients and the size of the pieces depend on the cook's intent. You can use flavorful foods as major flavors, as we do in our onion and vegetable soups, cooking them right

Figure 7-2 CLARIFYING STOCK TO MAKE CONSOMMÉ

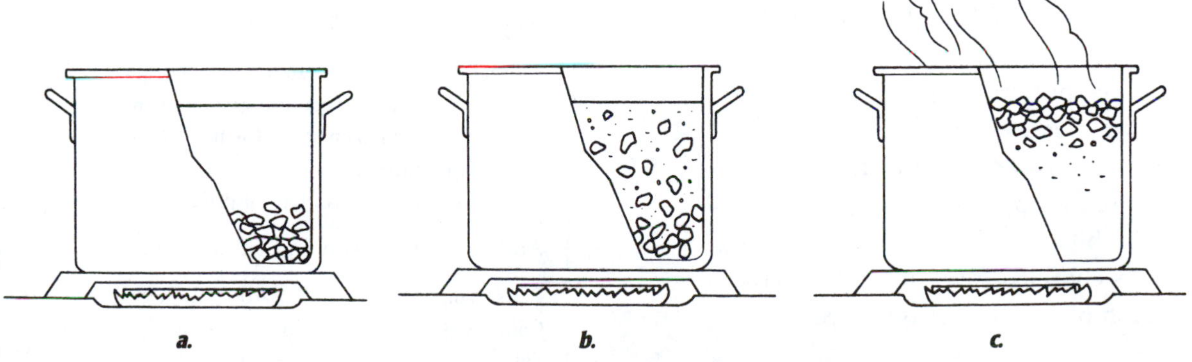

a. Clearmeat is placed in the bottom of a stockpot, cold stock is added, and the pot is placed over a low fire. ***b.*** As the temperature approaches a simmer, bits of clearmeat move slowly toward the surface, absorbing particles from the stock as they rise—clarifying it. ***c.*** The clearmeat forms a raft at the surface. Simmering extracts its flavors, strengthening the stock to produce consommé.

in the soup so that they enrich the liquid. Or you can use the same ingredients as a garniture to complement or contrast with the basic bouillon or consommé, enhancing its flavor and appearance rather than changing it. In this case, you would use them in small amounts and cut them very fine.

A garniture is a specific way of transforming a single basic dish into many different dishes. It is a term often confused with garnish.

Garnish Something edible added to a finished dish entirely for eye appeal, such as a sprig of mint or parsley beside a lamb chop or a cherry in the center of a grapefruit half. A garnish may be eaten but that is not its purpose.

Garniture Something edible added to a finished dish for eye appeal, flavor, and often textural contrast, such as croutons added to a bowl of soup. A garniture becomes part of the dish and is eaten with it.

Examples of items that can serve as a garnish or garniture include the following:

Homemade seasoned croutons
Fried wontons
Fried tortilla strips or chips
Ramen noodles
Roasted or grilled thinly sliced vegetables
Chilies
Flavored butter
Grated cheese
Sour cream or crème fraîche
Flavored whipped cream
Bacon bits
Finely chopped fresh or toasted herbs
A dash of spices or seasonings

With a garniture, you can turn a consommé, whether bought or made, into any number of classic clear soups. Add a garniture of vegetables brunoise for a consommé brunoise (Recipe 7.4a). Julienne of fresh spinach turns it into consommé florentine.

In each case, the flavor of the garniture is an essential part of the soup, and the name of the garniture becomes the name of the soup. In the world of cooking, there are hundreds of special garnitures. Their names mean the same thing the world over, providing a universal language of cookery. Florentine, for example, always includes spinach, whatever the basic dish. Printanière is always diced spring vegetables.

Recipe 7-4a CONSOMMÉ BRUNOISE

To 1 gallon (4 L) finished consommé, add:
1 pt vegetables brunoise 500 mL

Parboil vegetables separately in a little consommé. Add 2 Tb (25 mL) per portion when served.

Per serving:			
Calories:	38	Carbohydrates:	4 g
Fat:	0 g	Cholesterol:	10 mg
Protein:	5 g	Fiber:	0 g
		Sodium:	21 mg

Recipe 7-4b CHICKEN CONSOMMÉ

In Recipe 7.4, make the following changes:
Add $^1/_2$ lb (250 g) ground raw chicken.
Substitute chicken stock for beef stock.
Omit tomatoes.
Add $1^1/_2$ oz (50 mL) lemon juice.

Add ground chicken and lemon juice in Step 1.

Per serving:			
Calories:	25	Carbohydrates:	1 g
Fat:	0 g	Cholesterol:	8 mg
Protein:	4 g	Fiber:	0 g
		Sodium:	20 mg

The crouton that turns a simple onion soup into a French onion soup is also a garniture. So is the Parmesan cheese added to the minestrone.

You can do other things with consommé besides adding garnitures. Enrich it with sherry just before service time for a consommé au sherry in which two complementary flavors are evident. Add gelatin to the consommé and serve it jellied and well chilled on a hot summer evening.

You can make a chicken consommé by making a few changes in the basic consommé recipe (Recipe 7.4b). Add tomatoes to the chicken consommé to make consommé madrilène. These are all examples of how a single dish can be turned into dozens of others.

All the soups we have been discussing are clear soups, no matter what is added. The liquid has not been thickened and it is still translucent.

Whatever the ingredients and however they are used, the same few rules apply to all clear soups. Use flavor combinations that go well together, add raw ingredients in order of their cooking times, and do not overcook.

NATURALLY THICKENED OR PURÉE SOUPS

The next step in our venture toward mastery of soupology is to learn how to create a heavier texture. The simplest way to do this is to purée the ingredients that give a particular soup its character and blend them back into the liquid. This gives us our second category of soups—**naturally thickened soups,** also called **purée soups.**

The texture of the naturally thickened soup is thick and slightly rough or coarse to the tongue, as compared with the clear soup and the cream soup. The soup may vary greatly in consistency depending on the intent of the cook, the taste of the diner, or the use to which it is put. If served as an appetizer, it may be no thicker than cold whipping cream, but a meal-in-itself luncheon serving might be much thicker. Naturally thickened soups appeal to the hearty appetite and are likely to have more of a peasant quality than the consommés and creams, though vichyssoise does honor to the most elegant table.

Purée soups have a range of textures, from a smooth, glossy, and elegant purée to hearty and chunky soups in which the ingredients are left whole or only a portion of them is puréed. Usually, such soups are made with starchy ingredients—beans or potatoes—and some of the starch is dispersed in the liquid during cooking, providing natural thickening even though the solid ingredients are not puréed.

HOW TO MAKE A NATURALLY THICKENED SOUP

The making of purée soups is not very different from the making of clear soups, except for the puréeing process. Flavor is built with familiar flavor builders, using familiar techniques, and the cooking process is the same. But the requirements of thickening with a purée call for some special attention. Consider the recipe for potato and leek potage (Recipe 7.5). Figure 7.3 shows the ingredients.

You can see at a glance that preparation of this soup is not at all complicated. The one critical step is Step 4. At this point, a good soup is assured if you understand doneness. "Done" for this soup is when the potatoes have been cooked 100 percent but still retain their shape—slightly past al dente but not mushy. If they are not fully cooked, they will not thicken the soup properly. If they are overcooked, flavor is lost. Doneness is even more important for the naturally thick-

Recipe 7-5 POTATO AND LEEK POTAGE

Yield: ***1 gallon (4 L) or 16 8-oz (250 mL) portions***

2 oz	**butter**	**60 g**
$^1/_2$ lb	**onions, small dice**	**250 g**
$^1/_2$ lb	**leeks (white and pale green only), $^1/_8$-in. (3 mm) slices**	**250 g**
$^3/_4$ gal	**white stock**	**3 L**
2 lb	**peeled potatoes, medium dice**	**1 kg**
$^1/_2$	**bay leaf**	
1	**clove**	
4–5	**peppercorns, crushed**	
1 C	**heavy cream**	**250 mL**
	Salt and pepper to taste	

1. Heat butter in a stockpot over a moderately low heat.
2. Add the onions and leeks. Sweat until onions are translucent.
3. Add the stock, potatoes, and sachet with bay leaf, clove, and peppercorns.
4. Simmer until the potatoes are done. Remove the sachet.
5. Purée ingredients and blend them back into the liquid.
6. Bring the soup back to a simmer.
7. Season and adjust the texture. If too thick, add stock or cream. If too thin, reduce by simmering. If desired, heat the cream and add to soup just prior to service.

Per serving:		Carbohydrates:	16 g
Calories:	144	Cholesterol:	28 mg
Fat:	9 g	Fiber:	1 g
Protein:	2 g	Sodium:	41 mg

ened soup than it was for the clear soup. The time range is broad, but it should take well under an hour.

Any thickened soup may need some adjustment of texture (Step 7) as one of the finishing touches. To thin, add an appropriate liquid—for this soup, light stock or extra cream. To thicken, simmer the soup until it reaches the consistency desired. Seasoning (Step 7) always follows as a last step because thinning and thickening will change the proportions of seasoning to liquid.

You can turn this delicious hot soup into vichyssoise by chilling it and adding a garniture of chives (Recipe 7.5a). Or make another hot soup by adding another major flavor as in Recipe 7.5b.

Many recipes for naturally thickened soup call for the ingredients to be cooked until they fall completely apart into the soup. But to do this would require the cook to choose one of two undesirable alternatives: to increase the heat to cause boiling or to cook for a much longer time. Both would increase evaporation of good food flavor and reduce the yield.

Not every vegetable makes a successful purée soup. Generally speaking, high-starch vegetables work best. Among the most common in addition to the potato are the dried legumes: split peas, lentils, and the various beans—lima, red kidney, white or navy, pinto, black, and others. The cook is not limited to these vegetables, but they are starchy enough to be good natural thickeners.

Vegetables that don't work well as thickeners are those having little or no starch and those whose strong flavors create an undesirable taste when used in the volume necessary to thicken a soup. Examples of these are celery and onion. Such vegetables are often used as flavor builders and puréed along with the main ingredient. Tomato makes a good purée soup, but it has too strong and acid a flavor to be used alone as a thickener. It is usually combined with another purée or made into a cream soup.

The basic method of soup making given for the potato and leek potage can be used for any starchy vegetable, with some modifications. One

Figure 7.3 POTATO AND LEEK POTAGE

Potatoes, leeks, and onions provide flavor and texture for a hearty potage.

is that most dried vegetables need to be soaked several hours or overnight in water or stock. Use about a gallon of liquid to a pound of vegetables and keep them in the cooler while they are soaking. Cook them in the same liquid, adding more if necessary to cover. A shortcut is to boil them for 2 minutes and then let them soak for an hour. You can cook split peas and lentils without soaking. You can even cook beans without soaking, but it will prolong the cooking time.

Recipe 7-5a VICHYSSOISE

To recipe 7.5, add 8 oz (250 g) minced fresh chives. Adjust seasoning when cold.

You can use a mirepoix for added flavor. Smoked meat is another welcome flavor builder. You can simmer a ham bone in the pot along with everything else. You can chop bits of the meat and blend them into the final soup along with the puréed vegetables, or you can sauté finely diced smoked meat and blend it in shortly before service.

Recipe 7.6 is an example of how it all goes together. To render the fat from the bacon in Step 2 means to heat the bacon until the fat separates from the connective tissue.

Dried vegetables may take longer to reach doneness than potatoes. Again, the range is broad: Soaked split peas will probably take less than an hour and navy beans may take three. The

Recipe 7-6 NAVY BEAN SOUP

YIELD: ***1 gallon (4 L) or 16 8-oz (250 mL) portions***

1 lb	dried navy beans	450 g
2 oz	bacon, diced	60 g

Mirepoix:

4 oz	onions, small dice	125 g
2 oz	celery, small dice	60 g
2 oz	carrots, small dice	60 g
1 gal	white stock	4 L
2	garlic cloves	
1	bay leaf	
	pinch thyme	
	pinch crushed peppercorns	
1	ham hock	
1 pt	canned crushed tomatoes with juice	500 mL

1. Wash and pick over beans; soak overnight in 3 qt (3 L) water or stock.
2. Cook the bacon in a stockpot to render the fat.
3. Add mirepoix ingredients to bacon fat and sweat until the vegetables are almost tender.
4. Add the stock, sachet (with garlic cloves, bay leaf, thyme, and crushed peppercorns), ham hock, and beans and simmer until the beans are tender.
5. Add the tomatoes and reheat to a simmer; remove from heat.
6. Remove ham hock and sachet.
7. Purée the soup.
8. Bring the soup back to a simmer. Adjust to desired texture by adding stock or water if too thick.
9. If desired, dice meat from hock and return to soup.
10. Season to taste.

Per serving:		Carbohydrates:	20 g
Calories:	136	Cholesterol:	6 mg
Fat:	3 g	Fiber:	8 g
Protein:	9 g	Sodium:	240 mg

others fall somewhere in between. The test of doneness is the same—slightly past al dente but not mushy. Too thick a consistency can be adjusted by adding stock, water, or cream. If the texture is too thin, adjust by simmering.

VERSATILITY IN PURÉE SOUPS

You can make many other purée soups from a simple one by adding different garnitures. This is how vichyssoise is made, as we've already observed. You can also make the potato and leek potage into new soups by adding potatoes cut in different shapes, or chopped parsley, or diced bacon. Combining garnitures will create still other soups, each with its own distinctive flavor. You can do the same thing with other potages.

You can make other soups from legumes by adapting the navy bean soup recipe as in Recipe 7.6a. You can also substitute any other dried bean for the navy bean and follow the recipe exactly.

Another way to create different soups is to combine purées. Potage mongole is made by combining purée of split peas with puréed tomatoes and stock (Recipe 7.6b).

Recipe 7-6a SPLIT PEA SOUP

In Recipe 7.6, make the following changes:
Substitute split peas for navy beans.
Omit tomatoes.

1. Follow instructions, omitting Step 5.
2. Simmer until peas are tender.

Per serving:		Carbohydrates:	18 g
Calories:	131	Cholesterol:	6 mg
Fat:	3 g	Fiber:	8 g
Protein:	9 g	Sodium:	145 mg

Recipe 7-6b POTAGE MONGOLE

To 2 qt (2 L) split pea soup (Recipe 7.6a), add:

1 qt	**stock**	**1 L**
1 qt	**tomato purée**	**1 L**
$^{3}/_{4}$ pt	**green peas, diced carrots, diced leeks, parboiled**	**400 mL**

1. Blend stock with tomato purée. Stir into hot soup.
2. Reheat to serving temperature.
3. Serve each portion with $1^{1}/_{2}$ Tb (25 mL) mixed vegetables.

Per serving:		Carbohydrates:	26 g
Calories:	167	Cholesterol:	6 mg
Fat:	3 g	Fiber:	10 g
Protein:	11 g	Sodium:	172 mg

CREAM SOUPS

Of the three classes of soups, **cream soups** require the most effort and the greatest skill. Texture in the clear soups and potages was achieved naturally and simply. The smooth, creamy texture of cream soups is achieved through the use of thickening agents. A cream soup, then, is defined as a soup made with a thickening agent.

Cream or milk adds to the smoothness and flavor of a cream soup; it also adds a lot of confusion in classifying soups. It is not cream that makes a soup a cream soup; it is the creamy consistency produced by thickening with starch.

Cream soups consist of three main elements: liquid, one or more flavor-determining ingredients, and thickening agent. Flavor builders may also be used, and seasonings are added at the end of the cooking. Most cream soups are thickened with a flour–butter thickening agent, either roux or beurre manié.

There are two methods of making a good cream soup. In the first method, you start making the soup by making roux, introducing flavor-determining ingredients and flavor builders into the roux-making process. Then, you add the liquid and complete the cooking. We'll call this the roux method.

In the second method, you start making the soup by cooking the flavor-determining ingredients and flavor builders in the liquid. You add a thickener, such as roux, beurre manié, or other starch, toward the end of the cooking. Beurre manié is the thickener most commonly used, so we'll call this the beurre manié method. Figure 7.4 illustrates the differences between the two methods.

A close examination of a soup made by the two methods will give you a better understanding of the methods and the special techniques involved in each.

THE ROUX METHOD

In Recipe 7.7, you will see that the roux forms the base to which the liquid is added. This is a traditional method of soup cookery going back perhaps 200 years. It involves a number of critical matters of technique.

In Steps 2 and 3, the roux must be well blended so that all the flour is evenly dispersed, and the heat must be low so that the roux does not brown. If you get a brown-flour taste in a cream soup, it is going to taste brown no matter what you do to it. At this point, the roux should look like wallpaper paste with lumps of vegetables in it.

In Step 4, the abrupt temperature change "breaks" the roux, or stops the thickening action, and the roux dissolves readily in the cold stock with

Figure 7.4 TWO WAYS OF MAKING A CREAM SOUP

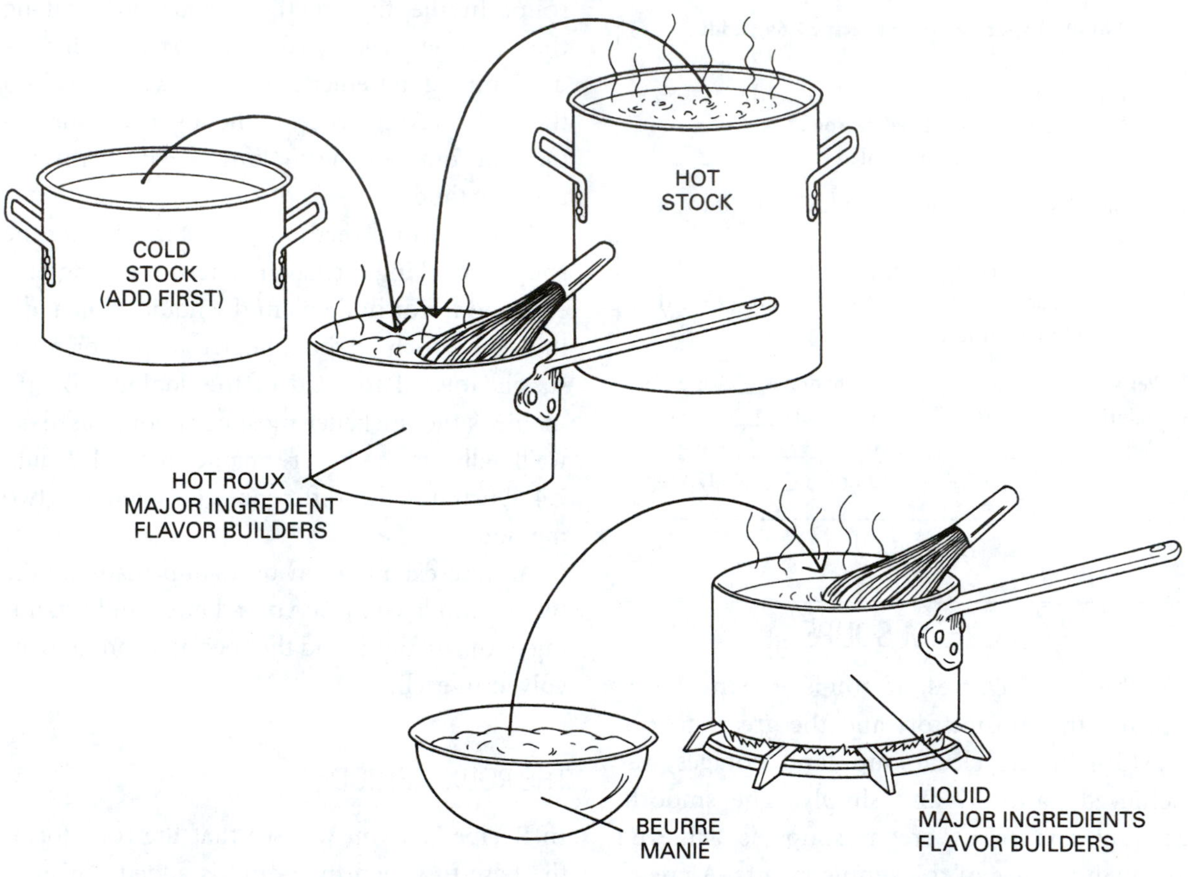

a. In the roux method, you add the liquid to the hot roux at the beginning of the cooking. ***b.*** In the beurre manié method, you add a cold thickener to the hot liquid toward the end of the cooking.

the help of some vigorous blending. It is at this point that the ultimate texture of the soup is determined. It is important to use cold liquid to dissolve the hot roux. If you add hot stock to hot roux, little balls of roux that won't dissolve are likely to form. Although you can strain these out of the final soup, their thickening power is lost and the soup will be thinner than it was supposed to be.

After a successful Step 4, Step 5 is no problem. The hot stock blends right in. The thin liquid of Step 5 thickens as it nears the boiling point. After it has thickened, add the cream or milk (Step 6). If you add milk sooner, it may curdle.

Simmer the soup until done. "Done" is the point at which the soup reaches the taste and texture the cook is aiming for. The broccoli should be completely cooked and the liquid should have the desired broccoli taste. Cooking time will average 30 minutes. It may take more time or less, depending on quantity and other variables.

The texture of the liquid should be smooth, its consistency slightly thicker than that of ordinary

Recipe 7-7 CREAM OF BROCCOLI SOUP (ROUX METHOD)

YIELD: ***1 gallon (4 L) or 16 8-oz (250 mL) portions***

Light mirepoix:

3 oz	**onions**	**90 mg**
3 oz	**leeks**	**90 mg**
3 oz	**celery**	**90 mg**
6 oz	**butter**	**175 g**
6 oz	**flour**	**175 g**
1 gal	**white stock**	**4 L**
$1^1/_2$ lb	**broccoli, chopped**	**750 g**
1 pt	**light cream or milk, hot**	**500 mL**
	salt to taste	
	white pepper to taste	
$^1/_2$ pt	**small broccoli florets, parboiled**	**250 mL**

1. Over moderate heat, sweat mirepoix in butter until flavors are blended and ingredients give off an aroma.
2. Reduce heat and add flour, blending to make roux.
3. Cook roux until light and foamy.
4. Remove from heat. Add 1 qt (1 L) cold stock to dissolve roux.
5. Return to heat and add remaining stock, hot, and broccoli, stirring until thickened.
6. When thickened, blend in cream or milk. Simmer until done.
7. Strain through a china cap lined with cheesecloth. Adjust texture as necessary. Season to taste.
8. Add 1–3 tsp (5–15 mL) broccoli florets to each portion when served.

Per serving:		Carbohydrates:	13 g
Calories:	193	Cholesterol:	43 mg
Fat:	15 g	Fiber:	2 g
Protein:	4 g	Sodium:	790 mg

Recipe 7-7a CREAM OF MUSHROOM SOUP

Substitute 1 lb (450 mg) mushrooms, chopped, for broccoli.
Add 2 Tb (25 mL) lemon juice.

Sweat mushrooms and lemon juice with mirepoix. Proceed as in Recipe 7.7.

Per serving:		Carbohydrates:	12 g
Calories:	189	Cholesterol:	43 mg
Fat:	15 g	Fiber:	1 g
Protein:	3 g	Sodium:	780 mg

whipping cream. The texture may be thinned by adding cream or stock in Step 7 after straining. It may be thickened by blending in beurre manié.

Does this all sound complicated? It is. But this is a technique you will use over and over, so learn it well.

THE BEURRE MANIÉ METHOD

The beurre manié method is simpler. In this method, everything is added to the liquid, as shown in Recipe 7.8. There are only a few points of possible difficulty:

Recipe 7-7b CREAM OF CHICKEN SOUP

Substitute 1 gal (4 L) strong chicken stock for 1 gal white stock (4 L).
Omit broccoli.
Add 4 oz (125 g) cooked chicken, julienne or small dice.

Proceed as in Recipe 7.7. Add chicken at end and heat through.

Per serving:		Carbohydrates:	12 g
Calories:	199	Cholesterol:	49 mg
Fat:	15 g	Fiber:	1 g
Protein:	5 g	Sodium:	784 mg

Recipe 7-8 CREAM OF BROCCOLI SOUP (BEURRE MANIÉ METHOD)

YIELD: ***1 gallon (4 L) or 16 8-oz (250 mL) portions***

$1\frac{1}{2}$ lb	**broccoli, chopped**	**750 g**
$\frac{1}{2}$	**bay leaf**	
1	**clove**	
1 gal	**white stock**	**4 L**
1 pt	**heavy cream**	**500 mL**

Beurre manié:

6 oz	**flour**	**175 g**
6 oz	**butter**	**175 g**
	salt to taste	
	white pepper to taste	
$\frac{1}{2}$ pt	**small broccoli florets, parboiled**	**250 mL**

1. Simmer broccoli, bay leaf, and clove in stock and cream until broccoli is al dente and liquid is full flavored.
2. Thicken with beurre manié to consistency desired.
3. Simmer until no starch taste remains.
4. Strain through a china cap lined with cheesecloth. Season to taste.
5. Add 1–3 tsp (5–15 mL) broccoli florets to each portion when served.

Per serving:		Carbohydrates:	11 g
Calories:	231	Cholesterol:	64 mg
Fat:	20 g	Fiber:	2 g
Protein:	3 g	Sodium:	693 mg

- In Step 1, it is important to use heavy cream. Neither milk nor light cream nor half-and-half will stand up to the simmering.
- In Step 2, the beurre manié must be added a little at a time and blended in well each time with a whip until no lumps remain.
- After the final addition, the soup must continue to simmer a few minutes to cook the flour in the beurre manié (Step 3).

Final success depends on skillful seasoning to bring out the maximum flavor of the main ingredient (Step 4).

You can see that the beurre manié method is much simpler than the traditional method. With fewer ingredients and fewer steps, preparation time is shortened and less attention is needed during cooking.

The newer method with its fewer ingredients produces a singleness of flavor that makes a refreshingly distinctive soup. In the older method, the blended flavor base created by the mirepoix makes a delicious soup but tends to give all cream soups a common flavor.

Both cream soup methods may be used with almost any vegetable as a main ingredient. The usual ratio is $1\frac{1}{2}$ to 2 pounds (750–1000 g) of vegetable to 1 gallon (4 L) of stock. For a strong-flavored vegetable, less may be used. In making cream soup by the roux method, you can sweat the major vegetable along with the mirepoix for fuller flavor. If you make mushroom soup this way, you need more butter because the mushrooms soak it up (Recipes 7.7a and 7.8a).

A few special cream soups are made with stock alone as the flavor-determining ingredient—cream of chicken, for example. Such a soup is made by either method, using an extra-rich stock

Recipe 7-8a CREAM OF MUSHROOM SOUP

Substitute 1 lb (450 g) mushrooms, chopped, for broccoli.

Proceed as in Recipe 7.8.

Per serving:		Carbohydrates:	10 g
Calories:	225	Cholesterol:	64 mg
Fat:	20 g	Fiber:	1 g
Protein:	2 g	Sodium:	682 mg

Recipe 7-8b CREAM OF CHICKEN SOUP

Substitute 1 gal (4 L) strong chicken stock for 1 gal white stock.
Omit broccoli.
Add 4 oz (125 g) cooked chicken, julienne or small dice.

Proceed as in Recipe 7.8. Add chicken to soup after seasoning to taste. Heat through.

Per serving:		Carbohydrates:	8 g
Calories:	220	Cholesterol:	68 mg
Fat:	20 g	Fiber:	0 g
Protein:	2 g	Sodium:	685 mg

and adding a garniture of chicken meat cut julienne or diced (Recipes 7.7b and 7.8b).

A liaison may be added to any cream soup for the ultimate in texture, using the technique illustrated in Figure 6.6. But liaisons are tricky: They must be added to the hot soup without letting the egg cook in the process. After the liaison is added, the soup must not be allowed to reach the boiling point, nor does it hold well. A liaison must therefore be added just before serving time.

Success with a liaison is not as easy to measure as failure. If failure is the outcome, the soup will have scrambled egg yolks floating on top. Success will be a velvety texture known best to the educated palate of the diner in the very expensive à la carte restaurant. Because of holding problems with liaisons, they are impractical for everyday use.

QUALITY MEASURES FOR CREAM SOUPS

Whatever the method, the finished cream soup should be smooth to the tongue and free from lumps, with a consistency no thinner than that of fresh, cold whipping cream. It may be somewhat thicker if desired, but it should pour readily in a smooth, free-flowing fashion.

A good cream soup looks very smooth. It has gloss and color, the latter deriving from the flavor-determining ingredient.

Its flavor is that of the major ingredient subtly enriched by the supporting flavors. The latter will modify the major flavor more in the soup made by the first method, but in either soup no supporting flavor should be identifiable. There should be no taste of roux or flour.

The soup should be seasoned to bring out the maximum flavor, but no taste of seasonings themselves should be detectable.

CREAM SOUP VERSATILITY

Like the other kinds of soups, cream soups take readily to garnitures as a method of creating new varieties. A simple cream of chicken is transformed by a garniture of asparagus tips and diced chicken. Add a garniture of cheese straws to a cream of chicken and it becomes crème Monaco. The garniture is always added as close to serving time as possible so that it remains distinct from the body of the soup and retains its own texture.

Cream soups need not always be served as the smooth finished dish we have been describing. Instead of straining the vegetables out, you may leave them in the liquid and serve a hearty soup more like a potage in spirit. This is often done with mushroom soup. In this version of a cream soup, if you make it by the beurre manié method, you would use a sachet for your flavor builders.

Still another way to vary a cream soup is to purée the ingredients. Since this will thicken the soup, you will need to adjust the texture with cream or stock, seasoning to taste after the liquid is added.

SPECIALTY SOUPS

The many soups discussed thus far come mostly from classical European cuisine and are common throughout the world. They fall neatly into our three soup categories. Now, we come to some exceptions that use many of the same techniques and methods, but they create their own categories. Each of these **specialty soups** has a characteristic set of ingredients, or flavor, or texture, or method of cooking. Often, they grew up outside the classical kitchen in some particular part of the world and became famous because they were so good. Usually, they began as a meal in a pot using local ingredients. Most of them remain associated with their place of origin.

AMERICAN SPECIALTY SOUPS

Chowders are an American contribution to soup cookery, though they are said to have originated in the fishing villages of Brittany, where successful fishing expeditions were celebrated by cooking a huge communal pot of fish and vegetables. Whatever their origin, the chowders we know today come from the East Coast, where fish and clams are plentiful.

Chowders are basically chunky, hearty soups of fish or vegetables, with a large proportion of solid ingredients served in the liquid. They usually have quite a bit of potato. Many chowders are either cream soups or purée soups. Thick or thin, they typically use milk as the liquid. Manhattan clam chowder is an exception; it substitutes tomatoes for milk. There is much controversy between New Englanders and New Yorkers over which is the true clam chowder. A bill was once introduced in the Maine state legislature to make it illegal to put a tomato into clam chowder.

The New England clam chowder in Recipe 7.9 is a roux-thickened soup. In the recipe, you will recognize many techniques used for cream soups. Fat from salt pork substitutes for butter in the roux. The liquid is clam juice plus fish stock. The straining step for cream soups is eliminated, and the milk is added at the end. After

Recipe 7-9 NEW ENGLAND CLAM CHOWDER

YIELD: ***1 gallon (4 L) or 16 8-oz (250 mL) portions***

1 qt	**canned clams with juice**	**1 L**
2 qt	**juice from clams plus fish stock or water**	**2 L**
1 1/2 lb	**potatoes, small dice**	**750 g**
4 oz	**salt pork, small dice**	**125 g**
8 oz	**onions, small dice**	**250 g**
4 oz	**flour**	**125 g**
1 qt	**milk, hot**	**1 L**
1/2 pt	**light cream, hot**	**250 mL**

1. Drain clams, reserving clams and juice separately. Add fish stock or water to clam juice to total 2 qt (2 L).
2. Cook potatoes separately in boiling water to cover until al dente.
3. In a stockpot, render salt pork. Add onions and sweat until translucent.
4. Add flour and make roux.
5. Add 1 pt (500 mL) cold clam juice/water; then 3 pt (1500 mL) hot clam juice/water. Simmer until thickened and no starch taste remains.
6. Stir in milk, cream, potatoes, and clams. Reheat to a simmer than remove from heat. Do not boil.
7. Season to taste.

Per serving:		Carbohydrates:	19 g
Calories:	176	Cholesterol:	25 mg
Fat:	9 g	Fiber:	1 g
Protein:	6 g	Sodium:	205 mg

the milk is added, the soup must not be allowed to boil or it may scorch or curdle.

Black pepper is traditional in this chowder—an exception to the rule of using white pepper in a light-colored dish.

Gumbos are another American specialty, native to Louisiana. Creole versions, developed in New Orleans, blended the culinary heritage of the French and Spanish upper classes with local ingredients such as seafood and hot peppers and contributions from native Indians and slave cooks from Africa. New Orleans gumbos have a certain city sophistication. Another type of gumbo, made by the Cajuns of southwest Louisiana, is country food, stemming from the hearty meal-in-a-pot fare that French Acadian fishermen and farmers developed after fleeing British rule in Canada in the 1700s. Bringing with them a French peasant heritage, they, too, used local ingredients and borrowed from the Indians.

The typical gumbo is so crowded with meat or fish and vegetables that the liquid plays a minor role. Among its distinctive ingredients are brown roux, hot pepper, tomatoes (in New Orleans), okra, and filé—ground sassafras adopted from the Indians. Both okra and filé have a slight thickening effect. Creole cooks generally use okra but not filé, and Cajun cooks generally use filé but not okra.

A **bisque** (pronounced bisk) is a cream soup made with shellfish. The bisque made its appearance in nineteenth-century Europe and has been adopted as a regional specialty in parts of the United States where shellfish are plentiful. You'll find lobster bisque in New England and crayfish bisque in Louisiana. The bisque is a smooth, rich, hearty soup that is expensive to prepare. The traditional finished soup is thickened by two methods—puréeing the fish flesh

Recipe 7-10 SHRIMP BISQUE

YIELD: ***Approximately 2 quarts (2 L) or 10 6-oz (200 mL) portions***

1 oz	**butter**	**30 g**
4 oz	**onions, brunoise**	**125 g**
2 oz	**carrots, brunoise**	**60 g**
2 oz	**celery, brunoise**	**60 g**
1	**bay leaf**	
2	**whole cloves**	
1/2	**lemon, sliced thin**	
1 1/2 qt	**water**	**1.5 L**
1 lb	**shrimp, raw in shell**	**450 g**
8 oz	**roux**	**250 g**
1 qt	**milk, hot**	**1 L**
1 pt	**cream, hot**	**500 mL**
2 oz	**sherry or brandy**	**50 mL**
	salt to taste	
	white pepper to taste	

1. Over moderate heat, sweat onions, carrots, and celery in butter in a stockpot. Add bay leaf, cloves, lemon, and water.
2. In another pan, sauté shrimp until shells are lightly browned.
3. Deglaze pan with a little of the liquid and return to stockpot along with shrimp.
4. Simmer until shrimp flesh is pink and firm.
5. Strain, reserving liquid.
6. Peel and devein shrimp and chop coarsely. Reserve.
7. Cook roux until light and foamy.
8. Remove from heat. Add reserved liquid to dissolve roux.
9. Return to heat and stir until thickened.
10. When thickened, blend in milk and cream. Simmer until done.
11. Add sherry. Adjust texture and season to taste.
12. Add coarsely chopped shrimp at time of service.

Per serving:		Carbohydrates:	11 g
Calories:	219	Cholesterol:	48 mg
Fat:	15 g	Fiber:	1 g
Protein:	9 g	Sodium:	158 mg

and thickening with a roux. The bisque in Recipe 7.10 is a somewhat simplified version: It does not purée the shrimp but leaves them coarsely chopped, providing a different texture.

Notice that the extra flavor contained in the shrimp shells is extracted in Step 2. This is similar to sweating the vegetables in Step 1: The higher heat of sautéing brings out the maximum flavor from the ingredients. The coarsely chopped shrimp are added at service time to avoid overcooking during holding.

NATIONAL SOUPS

There are many individual soups associated with particular countries. **Borscht** (pronounced borsh) is a Russian or Polish soup, a thin soup made with beets and other ingredients in many versions. In addition to beets, it usually contains cabbage and an acid ingredient such as vinegar, which keeps the beets from losing their red color. Sour cream is another typical ingredient, either blended into the soup or used as a garniture.

The best-known Italian soup is **minestrone,** an unthickened soup full of vegetables and pasta that can easily be a meal in itself. As we saw earlier (Recipe 7.3), minestrone is made using familiar techniques such as sweating the flavor builders and adding ingredients according to their cooking times. Some of the ingredients that make this a typically Italian soup are the olive oil, garlic, zucchini, tomatoes, some type of bean, the pasta, and the Parmesan cheese.

Mulligatawny is a famous soup that represents a culture of the past: It came from British India. It is a curry-flavored chicken soup, lightly thickened with roux, containing diced chicken meat, often rice, and sometimes tart apples. Some versions even include vegetables. It is easily made using the roux method for cream soups.

Spain is famous for olla podrida (ah-la padree′-da or ohl-ya pa-dree′-da) and gazpacho (gah-spah-cho). Olla podrida, often called the Spanish national soup, resembles an unthickened stew of meats and vegetables, always including Spanish sausage and chickpeas. In its full-scale version, it is an entire feast.

Gazpacho, another Spanish soup, is better known in this country and far more easily made. It originated as a salad composed of marinated leftover vegetables. An exception to the usual concept of soup, it is an uncooked purée thickened with bread crumbs and served cold.

By looking at the ingredients in Recipe 7.11, you can see clearly the salad origin of this soup. The bread crumbs not only thicken it slightly but help to bind the oil, which normally tends to separate from water-based liquids.

Bouillabaisse (boo-yah-bess) is a fish soup or stew in a class by itself and a meal in itself. One legend says that Venus, the goddess of love, invented the dish to put her husband into a sound sleep so that she could pursue her pleasures unhindered. Legend aside, bouillabaisse comes from Provence in southern France and originated as a simple Mediterranean fisherman's soup.

From the point of view of soup cookery, bouillabaisse is unique in that it does not use stock but creates the stock as the soup is made. Ideally, six or more kinds of fish and shellfish are cooked together in a tall pot with olive oil, flavor builders, water, and sometimes white wine. Leeks or onions, tomatoes, saffron, garlic, and some milder vegetables and herbs blend with the main ingredients to give this dish its distinctive flavor.

Recipe 7-11 GAZPACHO

YIELD: ***1 gallon (4 L) or 16 8-oz (250 mL) portions***

$2^1/_2$ qt	canned tomatoes, chopped	2.5 L
$1^1/_2$ lb	peeled cucumbers, chopped	750 g
12 oz	onions, chopped fine	375 g
6 oz	seeded green peppers, chopped fine	175 g
1 pt	tomato juice or cold water	500 mL
3 oz	fresh bread crumbs	90 g
3	garlic cloves, puréed	
4 fl oz	red wine vinegar	125 mL
5 fl oz	olive oil	150 mL
	salt to taste	
	pepper to taste	
	lemon juice to taste	

Garniture:

2 oz	onions, small dice	60 g
2 oz	peeled and seeded cucumbers, small dice	60 g
2 oz	seeded green peppers, small dice	60 g

1. Purée in a blender all ingredients except salt, pepper, lemon juice, and garniture. Or pass everything but olive oil, salt, pepper, lemon juice, and garniture through a food mill; gradually whip in oil.
2. Season to taste with salt, pepper, and lemon juice. Chill.
3. Mix garniture ingredients together. When served, add 1 Tb (15 mL) garniture to each portion.

Per serving:		Carbohydrates:	13 g
Calories:	144	Cholesterol:	0 mg
Fat:	9 g	Fiber:	2 g
Protein:	3 g	Sodium:	737 mg

The fish in true French bouillabaisse are local Mediterranean fish most Americans have never heard of, such as rascasse, chapon, conger eel, and red mullet. Each Mediterranean village has its own version of bouillabaisse, Paris has still another, and rivalry is intense. A similar dish can be made in this country with lobster and shrimp and various kinds of American fish.

COLD SOUPS

Many cold soups, such as melon soup, are indeed specialty soups. However, some cold soups, such as cold cream of cucumber soup, are simply cold versions of clear, naturally thickened, or cream soups.

Cold soups can make a refreshing hot-weather meal or the first course of an elegant dinner or luncheon. Fruit soups are often served at breakfast in some European countries. Such soups make appropriate items for brunch, which combines two meals in one.

Cold soups may belong to any of the three classes of soups discussed so far, or they may take off in a new direction as gazpacho does. You have already seen how a hearty potato and leek potage can be transformed into an elegant vichyssoise (Recipe 7.5a). The same thing can be done with cream soups by chilling and blending in a little cream. Or use a pound of peeled and seeded cucumbers in either cream soup formula, chill the finished soup, blend in cream or sour cream and a tablespoon of dill, and you have a delicate, refreshing summer soup. Mulligatawny is another cream soup sometimes served cold, with the chicken meat diced as a garniture.

Borscht can be served hot as a thin soup, or you can turn it into a naturally thickened cold soup. Purée it in a blender after cooking and serve it chilled with a teaspoon of sour cream on each portion—a beautiful sight.

Some soups are only served cold and are not related to cooked soups at all. The fruit soup in Recipe 7.12 is an example. It is cooked only to thicken it with cornstarch and then to blend the flavors. Cooking also helps the sugar to dis-

Recipe 7-12 FRUIT SOUP

YIELD: ***1 gallon (4 L) or 16 8-oz (250 mL) portions***

$1\frac{1}{2}$ oz	cornstarch	50 g
$1\frac{1}{2}$ qt	cold water	1.5 L
$1\frac{1}{2}$ qt	orange juice	1.5 L
8 oz	drained sweet pitted cherries	250 g
8 oz	drained canned sliced peaches	250 g
12 oz	mandarin oranges with syrup	375 g
3 oz	seedless raisins	90 g
4 oz	sugar	125 g
3 oz	lemon juice	100 mL

1. Mix cornstarch with a small amount of the cold water.
2. In a stockpot, bring orange juice and remaining water to boiling point. Blend in cornstarch mixture. Simmer until thickened. Adjust texture (texture will be somewhat thicker when cold).
3. Add all remaining ingredients and simmer until flavors are blended (5 minutes or so).
4. Adjust tartness to taste with sugar or lemon juice.
5. Chill.

Per serving:		Carbohydrates:	32 g
Calories:	128	Cholesterol:	0 mg
Fat:	0 g	Fiber:	1 g
Protein:	1 g	Sodium:	3 mg

solve and plumps the raisins. The amount of lemon juice needed will depend on how sweet or tart the other flavors are. You might consider the lemon as a seasoning as well as a flavorer.

Cold soups often need extra seasoning. Taste buds do not pick up flavors as readily in chilled foods, and there is less aroma. So taste and season carefully.

Cold soups are always served ice cold in chilled cups. The soup cup may be embedded in a dish of crushed ice, a style of service known as suprême (soo-prem).

SELECTING INGREDIENTS, HOLDING, AND STORING

SELECTING THE RIGHT STOCK

The choice of stocks open to the soup cook includes every stock in his or her repertoire. Many soups may be made using any of several different stocks, and using different stocks may be one way of making different soups from the same recipe. In other situations, the use of different stocks may simply have a subtle effect on flavor and color.

How do you choose a stock for a given soup? You must always consider two qualities of the stock, color and taste, in relation to the color and taste of the soup you are going to make.

The color of the stock should harmonize with the color of the soup. Cream soups and potages whose major ingredients are light in color are made with light stocks. Darker cream soups and potages and even clear soups may use the darker stocks. A good example of a soup that uses dark stock is onion soup. Most American versions of onion soup are quite dark in color and have a strong beef flavor. Beef and chicken stocks are often used together for onion soup in a one-to-one ratio.

But you cannot choose a stock on the basis of color alone. Taste is equally important, and the taste must not compete with the soup's predominant flavor. Chicken stock is suitable in color for any light cream soup or potage, for instance, but it can create problems of flavor. A cream of mushroom soup made with chicken stock would taste more like a cream of chicken soup with mushrooms added for a garniture. A light stock made from veal bones or a vegetable stock made from mushroom pieces would be more appropriate. It goes without saying that a fish stock would not be used for any soup but fish.

Taste selection has its positive side, too. You may want to use a specific stock flavor subtly as a flavor builder. As you become really expert at creating soups, you will begin to think in these terms.

Because the liquid or stock plays such an important role in a soup, it is important to use care and thought in its selection.

Now, suppose your particular kitchen does not make stock, as is so often the case nowadays. What will you use for stock—for the body of the soup?

The kind of soup you make will determine the kind of stock you must create. If you need a meat-flavored stock, you can make one using a base. Start making your soup with water in place of stock as the body ingredient, and add the base toward the end of the cooking, using taste as your guide.

For a clear vegetable soup, when you want a stock for general flavor support rather than specific meat flavor, use a small amount of base. Add it by taste at the end of the cooking until you get the general support flavor you want, but stop before you can taste the base itself. Since every base and every bouillon powder is different, it is impossible to give proportions.

SELECTING MAJOR INGREDIENTS

The ingredients used in soups should be fresh and high in quality. Some of them may be leftovers in the sense of trimmings from products used in preparing other dishes—bones, celery tops, mushroom stems and peelings, parsley stems—or products whose shape or size or color caused them to be rejected for some other use, or the remaining half of a package opened and half used. But they should not be warmed-over foods cooked for another purpose or another day. The flavor has already gone into another product, and everyone will know it.

Canned vegetables have similar drawbacks when used for soups. (Tomatoes and beets are exceptions.) Whatever happens to raw vegetables during cooking that puts flavor into the soup has already happened to the canned vegetable before the soup making begins. In addition, the canned vegetable has already undergone the texture and flavor changes that come from the overcooking necessary to can foods safely. Frozen vegetables are often used and are somewhat better than canned since they are only partially cooked, but they are no substitute for fresh.

HOLDING AND STORING SOUPS

Just as the ingredients should be fresh, so should the soup itself be freshly made. Each day's supply will usually be made in the morning for the entire day. It should be stored in the refrigerator and heated for service in small amounts as needed.

Soups awaiting service should be held in a bain-marie or steam table at or above 140°F (60°C), above the bacterial growth range but not hot enough to cook further. Heat additional amounts quickly on the range as needed. In this way, you can avoid overcooking caused by prolonged holding.

Stir the soup occasionally. During lulls in service, you should put a cover on the pot to prevent evaporation, which will affect not only the texture but also the yield. You can correct the texture with stock or cream if it becomes too thick. Check the seasoning if you add anything and adjust it if necessary.

When storing a soup for later use, treat it as you would a stock: Put it in the cooler at 40°F (4°C) or below. Do not cover it while it is cooling, but do keep it covered during storage. Clear soups can be stored for a day or two without problems, but cream soups need special care: Cover them with plastic wrap right on the surface of the soup after they have cooled to refrigerator temperature.

SUMMING UP

Soup is an appetizing and relatively inexpensive way to open a meal or to make a meal. Soups fall naturally into three classes: clear or unthickened soups, naturally thickened soups (potages), and cream soups, thickened with starches. Nearly all of them are based on stocks and take off from there in all directions.

Of the unthickened soups, consommé is a star performer and is famous as the classical clear soup from which many other classical soups are made. Other familiar unthickened soups are vegetable soup and onion soup, each capable of many variations. Soup quality depends on the cook's skill in combining flavors and in cooking the ingredients to retain both form and texture.

Naturally thickened or purée soups are made with such ingredients as potatoes and legumes, which lend their natural texture to thicken the soup. In smooth soups, these ingredients are puréed and blended with the liquid. In some soups made from legumes, the vegetable is left whole or only a portion is puréed. These are hearty soups with a country or peasant quality.

Cream soups are made with artificial thickeners. The major flavor ingredients are simmered in stock either after thickening (the roux method) or before thickening (the beurre manié method). A liaison may be used to perfect the texture.

The techniques for making these three types of soups are also used in making many specialty soups such as the regional and national soups that originated as meals in a pot. Among these are bouillabaisse, chowders, gumbos, and such national soups as borscht and minestrone. Still another type is the cold soup of the summertime menu, which may be made as a thin soup, a purée, a cream soup, or something entirely different based on fruit juice or buttermilk.

Soup puts together in the kitchen all the things we have been discussing in previous chapters. Once you can make soups, you have learned to use techniques and concepts that appear and reappear in other areas of the kitchen. You have met all kinds of thickeners—roux (white roux, brown roux), beurre manié, purées, cornstarch, liaisons, and bread crumbs. You have discovered a great deal about flavor building, texture, seasoning, doneness, cooking times and cooking methods, garnitures and garnishes, patience and the pleasures of success. You may also have learned more than you care to know about overcooking, undercooking, lumping, burning, too much celery, too much salt—the lessons of culinary disaster sometimes linger longer than the triumphs.

Soup making offers possibilities often overlooked by restaurants. Not only does soup bring a good price on the menu, it can be made for a good price. Trimmings, scraps, and water, put together with tender loving care, can create an outstanding soup du jour (soup of the day) for pennies a portion.

"All it takes is a little barter, a little scavenging, a little kitchen thievery, if you will," says one exuberant soup-and-vegetable cook. "I beg ham bones from the garde manger, trade soup bases for fresh mushrooms from the saucier, pick over everybody's cooler for a little of this and that, and then I create!" No other dish can be made for so little and possess so much.

The Cook's Vocabulary

bisque
borscht
bouillabaisse
broth, bouillon
chowder
clarification
clearmeat
clear soup
consommé
cream soup
garnish
garniture
gazpacho
gumbo
minestrone
mulligatawny
purée or naturally thickened soup
raft
specialty soup
sweat

Review Questions

Answer each question in complete sentences. Read each question carefully and make sure you answer all parts of the question. Organize your answer into more than one paragraph when appropriate.

1. Discuss the differences in procedures in making the three classes of soup. Which techniques provide the textures desired in each one?
2. What role does each of the following ingredients play in producing a consommé: egg whites, mirepoix, lean meat, tomato product, stock?
3. Using the description of mulligatawny soup, develop a recipe including ingredients and procedures.
4. What extra steps and ingredients would you add to a cream soup to serve it "en suprême"?

Chapter 8

SAUCES

The mystique surrounding sauce cookery has been cultivated for centuries by chefs of the European tradition. Only cooks with years of experience were allowed to learn the secrets hiding under enigmatic names having nothing to do with the nature of the sauces. Small wonder that sauce making has not flourished in the home kitchen, and that for many people sauce is synonymous with catsup and Worcestershire. It is time to tear away the veil and expose the real simplicity of sauce cookery.

A **sauce** is a seasoned liquid, usually thickened, that enhances a dish. The making of sauces has much in common with the making of soups and stocks. Historically, sauces, like soups, originated in the pot in which meat or game or fowl was cooked over the open fire. The juices from the cooking were thickened in medieval times with bread crumbs or pounded almonds so they would stick to the meat or the sop of bread. Later, starch-thickened sauces were developed as part of the more delicate classical cuisine. Inventing a sauce became a fashionable way of inventing a new dish.

For so many years, it was thought that the classical French sauce families were all a new cook needed to learn. While they still need to know the basics of these classic sauces, many new sauce-making techniques have taken hold. One of the reasons for new types of sauces, such as reduction sauces, is that many of the French sauces used immoderate amounts of butter, cream, and other fats. As Americans became more health conscious, chefs started experimenting successfully with new sauces that were lower in fat. In this chapter, we will discuss classic sauces, as well as contemporary sauce-making techniques.

The presentation of sauced foods has also changed. Instead of covering a food with sauce, a contemporary chef is likely to ladle a bar of sauce across the food or pool the sauce on the plate and serve the food on top, revealing rather than concealing its natural appeal.

After completing this chapter, you should be able to:

- Identify classical sauce families, describe or diagram their structure, and explain the relationship between basic and finished or small sauces.
- Describe or demonstrate how a reduction is used in sauce making.
- Explain the nature of an emulsion and describe or demonstrate how to emulsify butter and egg yolks.
- Describe or demonstrate how to adjust sauce texture and how and when to season a sauce.

- Describe or demonstrate how to make compound butters.
- Hold and store sauces to maintain quality and sanitation.

THE PERFECT SAUCE

The quality of a sauce is judged by its flavor, its strength, and its texture. Its strength derives from the quality of its basic stock. Its texture is determined by cooking technique—the skillful use of the thickening agent and the liaison, the careful straining and the final adjustment of sauce consistency. Its flavor comes from stock, flavor builders, and flavorings, and it is perfected by seasoning.

A good sauce is smooth and velvety in texture with no lumps. It has an appropriate color as well as gloss and a fluid appearance: "It must seem vaguely in motion even after it has been poured," wrote the master chef Louis De Gouy. It is thin enough to pour easily but thick enough to stay with the food it accompanies. There is no sign of fat, no taste of fat or flour. It is warm and inviting, never cold, set, or solid. It has a subtle bouquet or aroma suggesting the pleasure to come. Its flavor enhances the flavor of the food with which it is served, complementing or contrasting but never dominating. Whether delicate or strong, it tastes very special.

CLASSICAL SAUCES

The hundreds of sauces of classical cuisine all stem from a few basic sauces. Because of these relationships, the **basic sauces** are often known as **mother sauces** or **leading sauces.** Although each basic sauce is different from the others in important ways, they all have a common structure: They are all built from a liquid that is turned into a sauce by using a thickening agent (Figure 8.1).

Figure 8.2 shows how each basic sauce is made and in which sauce family it belongs. It also gives you clues to some of the differences between the various families. **White sauces** are made from either **béchamel** or **velouté.** Béchamel is made from milk with roux as the thickening agent. The velouté sauces are made with light stocks (meaning chicken, veal, and fish) thickened with roux. The basic **brown sauces—espagnole** and **fond lié**—are made from dark stocks thickened with brown roux or cornstarch. **Tomato sauce,** the basic **red sauce,** is made from light stock and tomatoes and possibly thickened with roux. The basic **butter sauces, hollandaise** and **béarnaise,** use melted butter as the liquid and egg yolks as the thickener.

A basic sauce is not usually a finished product. It is a base for a **small** or **finished sauce,** a sauce made by adding one or more ingredients to a basic or leading sauce. To make a small sauce from a basic sauce, then, you add flavoring and

Figure 8-1 FINISHED SAUCE STRUCTURE

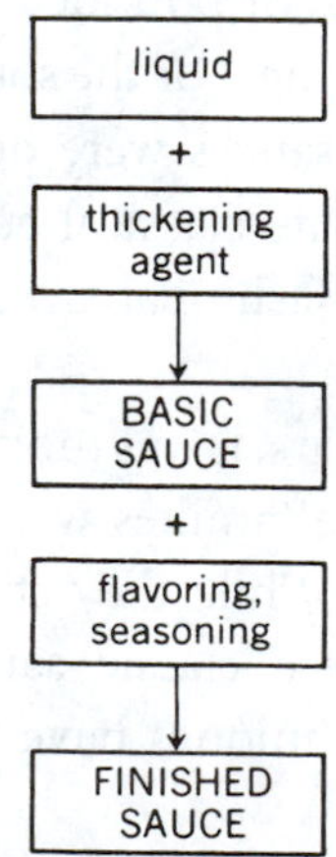

Figure 8-2 BASIC SAUCE STRUCTURE

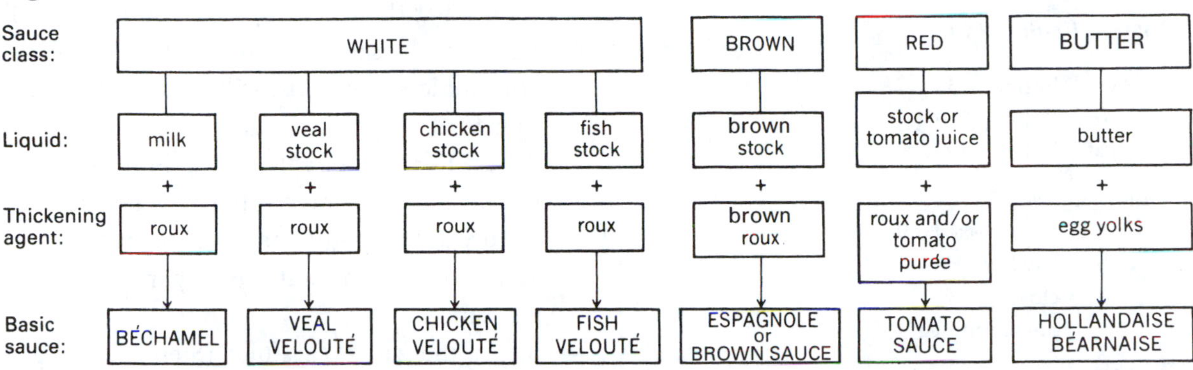

seasoning or seasoning alone. That is all there is to the structure of a sauce. Master sauce structure well, and you will have learned the first secret of sauce cookery.

In a large operation serving European cuisine, the saucier, or sauce cook, makes up large batches of basic sauces at a time, according to menu needs. The stocks will have been made the day before, or several days before. Once the basic sauces have been prepared, the cook can make one, ten, or twenty different finished sauces from each basic sauce, in the quantities needed that day.

Now that you have seen what these sauces have in common, let's look at each sauce family separately. What gives each class of sauce its individuality, and how is it made?

WHITE SAUCES

BÉCHAMEL SAUCE. Béchamel is the starting point for many small sauces in this category. The elegant name for this simple sauce comes from a French nobleman who was lord steward of the royal household of Louis XIV. He was not a cook but a financier; he did not invent the sauce; nor was it made then as it is now. It was probably seventeenth-century kitchen politics that immortalized Louis de Béchamel in this creamy sauce. A glance at Figure 8.2 shows that most of the sauces use stock as the liquid. Béchamel is different: It uses milk—a good, rich, flavorful stock made by the cow with no effort on the cook's part.

Béchamel is an easy sauce to make if you deal with the milk properly. In other contexts, cooking with milk can pose problems. If milk by itself is overheated, the protein in it may scorch (burn) or the milk may curdle, separating into solid protein curds and a watery liquid called whey. However, you will not run into these problems in making béchamel if you make it properly—over low heat. Do not allow the milk to reach the boiling point until after you have incorporated it into the roux. The roux keeps it from separating. For extra security, you can make the sauce in a double boiler.

Recipe 8.1 shows you how to make a basic béchamel sauce. Do the instructions sound familiar? A basic white sauce is made using the traditional techniques for making cream soups. As in the soups, there are several critical points:

- Make a good, well-blended white roux, cooked until it looks foamy and begins to

Recipe 8-1 BASIC BECHAMEL SAUCE

Yield: ***1 gallon (4 L)***

8 oz	**butter**	**250 g**
8 oz	**flour**	**250 g**
1 gal	**milk**	**4 L**

Onion piqué:

1	**small peeled onion**
1/2	**bay leaf**
1	**clove**
	pinch nutmeg

1. Melt butter in a heavy-bottomed pan; add flour, blending to make roux.
2. Cook roux until light and foamy. Remove from heat.
3. Add cold milk (about 1 qt or 1 L); blend until smooth.
4. Return to heat and blend in remaining milk, hot, stirring constantly until thoroughly combined.
5. Cook over low heat, stirring occasionally with whip, until sauce is thickened.
6. Add onion piqué and nutmeg and simmer 30–45 minutes, stirring occasionally.
7. Adjust texture as necessary.
8. Strain through a china cap lined with cheesecloth.

Note: Some cooks omit the onion piqué and nutmeg, simmering the sauce only until no starch taste remains. This makes a bland, neutral basic sauce.

Per ounce:		Carbohydrates:	3 g
Calories:	39	Cholesterol:	8 mg
Fat:	2 g	Fiber:	0 g
Protein:	1 g	Sodium:	30 mg

lighten (Steps 1 and 2). Be careful not to brown it.

- Add cold milk to the hot roux and blend it well (Step 3).
- Simmering the sauce with the flavor builders (Step 6) will enrich the sauce and spark the general flavor without adding a specific taste. (Note that the onion is peeled so that it will not color the sauce.) If you do not use the flavor builders, you must still simmer the sauce to get rid of the starch taste.
- Adjust the texture with hot milk if the sauce has become too thick (Step 7). Checking the texture at this point and adjusting it as necessary should be an automatic part of making any sauce.
- Strain the sauce carefully (Step 8), using a china cap lined with dampened cheesecloth for a smooth, velvety texture. The extra refinement of texture can make the difference between an ordinary sauce and an extraordinary one.

Some cooks use a slightly different method by adding scalded milk (milk heated to just below the boiling point) to roux that has been cooled for a minute or two. The mixture is whisked vigorously while the milk is slowly added to the roux.

Master the techniques of making a basic sauce with roux, and you will have learned the second secret of sauce cookery. It should not be difficult after your experience with cream soups.

There is one major difference between a cream soup and a basic white sauce. The soup is a finished product; the basic sauce is not. You want the sauce's flavor to be uncommitted, so that you can go in any flavor direction you wish when you use it to make finished sauces. For this reason, you do not use specific flavors in a basic sauce, as you do in a cream soup. For the same reason, you do not season a basic sauce. Seasoning belongs only to finished sauces.

Your choice of seasonings may be made from the basic three: salt, pepper (white or cayenne for a white sauce), and fresh lemon juice. Your purpose is, as always, to bring out the natural flavor,

Recipe 8-1a CREAM SAUCE

YIELD: ***5 cups (1.25 L)***

1 qt	**basic béchamel sauce from Recipe 8.1**	**1 L**
$^1/_2$–1 C	**cream, hot**	**125–250 mL**
	salt to taste	
	white pepper to taste	

1. Blend sauce and cream.
2. Simmer until flavors are blended.
3. For a finished sauce, season to taste with salt and white pepper.

Per ounce:		Carbohydrates:	2 g
Calories:	43	Cholesterol:	12 mg
Fat:	4 g	Fiber:	0 g
Protein:	1 g	Sodium:	22 mg

considering both the sauce itself and the dish it is to enhance. Nutmeg is commonly used to season béchamel sauce.

Recipe 8.1b, Mornay Sauce, is an example of a finished sauce from basic béchamel. This cheese sauce can be used in casseroles or to complement and add variety to vegetables. When cooking with cheese, keep the heat low and do not leave the sauce over heat any longer than necessary. Too much heat will cause the proteins in the cheese to become tough and stringy, and its butter fat may even separate out. Recipe 8.1a, Cream Sauce, is made simply by adding hot cream to the béchamel.

Recipe 8-1b MORNAY SAUCE

YIELD: ***5 cups (1.25 L)***

1 qt	**basic béchamel sauce from Recipe 8.1**	**1 L**
4 oz	**Swiss-style cheese, grated**	**125 g**
2 oz	**Parmesan cheese, grated**	**60 g**
	hot milk as needed	
	salt to taste	
	white pepper to taste	

1. Over low heat, stir in cheeses just until melted.
2. Adjust texture with hot milk as necessary.
3. Season to taste with salt and white pepper.

Per ounce:		Carbohydrates:	2 g
Calories:	42	Cholesterol:	9 mg
Fat:	3 g	Fiber:	0 g
Protein:	2 g	Sodium:	53 mg

Béchamel is used in almost every type of kitchen. It is as useful to the casserole cookery of the low-budget cafeteria as it is to the continental cuisine of the most expensive restaurant. Béchamel-based sauces usually accompany vegetables or eggs and occasionally meats. Heavier versions having a higher proportion of roux to milk ($1^1/_2$ lb or 750 g roux to 1 gal or 4 L milk) are used in making thickened cooked dishes such as mousses, soufflés, and croquettes.

Béchamel is also used to make cream soups. Sweated vegetables are combined with the basic sauce and simmered until done. The sauce is then thinned with hot milk and finished with cream. This was a classical way of making a cream soup, and a very logical one when you already had a pot of basic béchamel in the bain-marie.

VELOUTÉ SAUCES. The three velouté sauces are more accurately classified as blond sauces because, in classical cuisine, they were made with pale or blond roux and light stocks. In the modern kitchen, either a white or a blond roux may be used. The stock also adds a touch of color. Yet both in structure and in method these sauces are so similar to béchamel that they are sometimes all lumped together as white sauces.

The mother sauces in this group are the three veloutés—veal, chicken, and fish. The name velouté (ve-loo-tay) is the French word meaning

Recipe 8-2 BASIC VELOUTÉ SAUCE (VEAL, CHICKEN, OR FISH)

Yield: ***1 gallon (4 L)***

8 oz	**butter**	**250 g**
8 oz	**flour**	**250 g**
1 gal	**stock (veal, chicken, or fish)**	**4 L**

1. Melt butter in a heavy-bottomed pan over low heat; add flour, blending to make roux.
2. Cook roux until light and foamy. Remove from heat.
3. Add cold stock (about $^1/_4$ of total amount); blend until smooth.
4. Return to heat and blend in remaining stock, hot, stirring constantly until thoroughly combined. Bring to a boil and then reduce to a simmer.
5. Simmer 45–60 minutes, stirring occasionally.
6. Adjust texture as necessary with stock.
7. Strain through a china cap lined with cheesecloth.

Per ounce:		Carbohydrates:	2 g
Calories:	22	Cholesterol:	4 mg
Fat:	1 g	Fiber:	0 g
Protein:	0 g	Sodium:	18 mg

velvety, an apt characterization of a sauce that feels like velvet to the tongue and taste buds.

Making a basic velouté follows the same pattern as making a basic béchamel, as you can see by comparing Recipe 8.2 with Recipe 8.1. The major difference is the use of stock rather than milk. A good flavorful stock is the key to a good velouté. The sauce does not need added flavor builders because the flavor is already in the stock. The longer the sauce is simmered, the more flavor it develops. Evaporation concentrates the flavor, and when you adjust texture by adding more stock, you add more flavor, too.

Veal, chicken, and fish veloutés are all made by the same method. The only difference is the kind of stock used. The kinds of veloutés the cook makes on any given day will be determined by the dishes the finished sauces are to accompany—veal velouté with veal, chicken with chicken, fish with fish.

Small sauces based on veloutés take off from the mother sauce in the same way the small white sauces do. They are made by adding flavoring, seasoning, or textural ingredients to a basic velouté. In each case, the added ingredients determine the special character of the finished sauce.

Recipes 8.2a and 8.2b are examples of sauces derived from veloutés. Allemande (alla-mahnd) sauce (Recipe 8.2a) is a veal or chicken velouté enriched with a liaison and a touch of lemon. It is often used as a basic sauce in the same way

Recipe 8-2a ALLEMANDE SAUCE

Yield: ***5 cups (1.25 L)***

1 qt	**basic velouté sauce (veal or chicken) from Recipe 8.2**	**1 L**

Liaison:

2	**egg yolks**	
$^1/_2$ C	**light cream**	**125 mL**
1 Tb	**lemon juice**	**15 mL**
	salt to taste	
	white pepper to taste	

1. Simmer velouté to reduce it slightly.
2. Beat the egg yolks and cream together to make a liaison. Use a stainless steel bowl.
3. Slowly add a little of the hot velouté to the liaison in the stainless steel bowl. This will temper the liaison. Slowly add the tempered liaison back into the saucepan.
4. Reheat to just below a simmer. Season and strain through a china cap lined with cheesecloth.

Per ounce:		Carbohydrates:	1 g
Calories:	29	Cholesterol:	7 mg
Fat:	2 g	Fiber:	0 g
Protein:	1 g	Sodium:	25 mg

Recipe 8-2b SUPRÊME SAUCE

YIELD: ***5 cups (1.25 L)***

1 qt	**chicken velouté from Recipe 8.2**	**1 L**
$^1/_2$ pt	**heavy cream**	**250 mL**
1 oz	**butter**	**25 g**
	salt to taste	
	white pepper to taste	
	lemon juice to taste	

1. Simmer velouté in a saucepan until reduced by one-fourth to $1^1/_2$ pt (750 mL).
2. Slowly add a little of the hot sauce to the cream in a stainless steel bowl. This will temper the cream. Slowly add the tempered cream back into the saucepan.
3. Simmer until flavors are blended.
4. Off heat, swirl in butter. Season and strain through china cap lined with cheesecloth.

Per ounce:		Carbohydrates:	1 g
Calories:	43	Cholesterol:	13 mg
Fat:	4 g	Fiber:	0 g
Protein:	0 g	Sodium:	29 mg

that cream sauce is. In this case, seasonings are omitted. Poulette sauce is allemande made with mushrooms.

Suprême sauce (Recipe 8.2b) is chicken velouté enriched with cream. Like allemande, it is sometimes used as a basic sauce, as in ivory sauce, which has meat glaze added, and in aurora sauce, which adds tomato paste and is finished with butter. In these two small sauces, color as well as flavor is important. The meat glaze produces a beautiful ivory color, and the tomato is meant to create the color of a rosy dawn (French *aurore,* meaning dawn). Aurora can also be made from a basic velouté.

Note the tempering of the cream in making suprême sauce. This is the same technique as tempering a liaison: You stir up to a third of the hot sauce into the cream to bring it gradually to the sauce's temperature. If you shocked it by adding it cold to the hot sauce, it might curdle.

Notice also that in making suprême sauce you simmer the basic sauce to reduce it. This is to allow the cream to be added without making the sauce too thin. You reduce the sauce by one-fourth (half a pint—250 mL) because that is the amount of cream you are adding. In making allemande sauce, you also reduce the basic sauce slightly for the same reason. You do this before adding the liaison because you cannot simmer it afterward.

Notice that you reduce first and season last. If the process were reversed, you would have too much seasoning. Seasoning in sauce cookery, as with soups, is always an end process.

A white wine sauce (Recipe 8.3), made from a basic fish velouté, presents a more complex

Recipe 8-3 WHITE WINE SAUCE

YIELD: ***1 quart (1 L)***

$^1/_2$ C	**fish stock**	**125 mL**
4 oz	**dry white wine**	**125 mL**
1 oz	**mushrooms**	**25 g**
2–3	**peppercorns, crushed**	
1 qt	**fish velouté**	**1 L**
$^1/_2$ pt	**cream**	**250 mL**
	salt to taste	
	white pepper to taste	

1. Combine stock, wine, mushrooms, and peppercorns in a saucepan.
2. Simmer until volume is reduced by two-thirds or more to about $2^1/_2$ oz (75 mL).
3. Add velouté to reduction in pan, blending well. Blend in cream.
4. Simmer sauce to desired consistency.
5. Strain.
6. For a finished sauce, season to taste.

Per ounce:		Carbohydrates:	2 g
Calories:	47	Cholesterol:	12 mg
Fat:	4 g	Fiber:	0 g
Protein:	1 g	Sodium:	36 mg

Figure 8-3 INGREDIENTS FOR WHITE-WINE-SAUCE REDUCTION

These high-flavor ingredients are blended and concentrated by cooking them down to a fraction of their original volume. This reduction is then added to the basic sauce.

technique of dealing with sauce texture by concentrating a great deal of flavor in a small volume. It uses a combination of flavor ingredients (Figure 8.3) cooked together to blend and concentrate their combined flavor. This is known in sauce making as a **reduction.**

Examine the procedures in the recipe closely to see how the reduction is done. In Steps 1 and 2, ingredients of the reduction, chosen for their specific flavors, are cooked together to blend and concentrate these flavors. A maximum of total flavoring is thus added to the basic sauce with a minimum of liquid (Step 3). Step 4 is then an adjustment of texture, and Steps 5 and 6 finish off the sauce.

The reduction was a favorite technique of the classical French chef for concentrating a great deal of flavor in a small volume. "When the stock is reduced to a coating on the bottom of the pan . . . " reads a Carême recipe for a brown sauce.

There is a standard ratio of basic sauce to reduction to cream that will enable you to make enriched sauces without a written recipe once you know the ingredients. Use 4 parts sauce to 1 part reduction liquid (measured before reduction). If the reduction contains more than one liquid, use equal parts of each. To complete the formula, add 1 part cream. Thus, our white wine sauce recipe calls for 1 quart (1 L) of basic sauce to $^{1}/_{2}$ pint (250 mL) of reduction liquid composed of 4 ounces (125 mL) of fish stock and 4 ounces (125 mL) of wine, with $^{1}/_{2}$ pint (250 mL) of cream to complete the formula. Figure 8.4 may help you to visualize the proportions.

Figure 8-4 STANDARD RATIO OF BASIC SAUCE TO REDUCTION TO CREAM

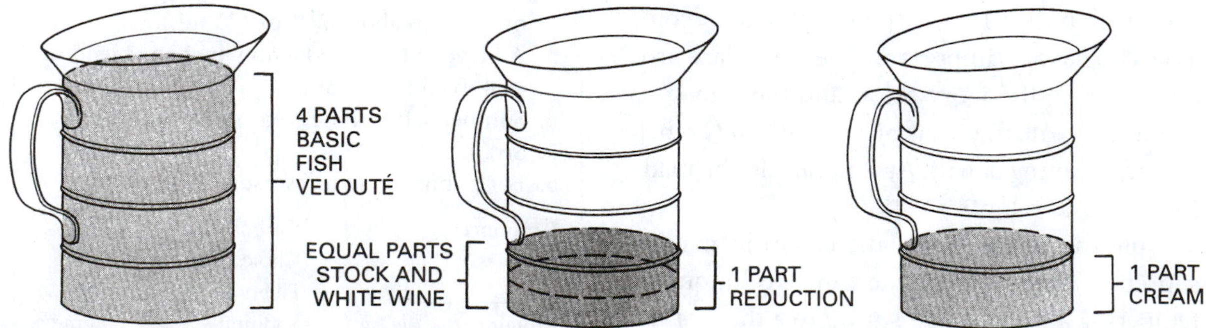

When you put the sauce together and reduce it to the right consistency, you will end up with the same amount of sauce you started with before adding the reduction and cream.

The white wine sauce given here can play the role of a basic or mother sauce for many small sauces, or it can be a finished sauce in its own right. The cook will season it or not depending on its role.

BROWN SAUCES

Brown sauces use dark stock as their liquid base. They are thickened with brown roux or cornstarch. They use more ingredients than the white and blond sauces, they take more time, and they may seem more complicated, but they are probably less difficult to make.

Recipe 8.4 gives a recipe for basic brown sauce or espagnole, but today this name is commonly used for any basic brown sauce. What you are doing with this recipe is enriching a stock by cooking it again with additional ingredients and turning it into a sauce at the same time by reducing and thickening it. Espagnole is a sauce that is rather light in texture but rich brown in color and hearty in flavor.

Another type of brown sauce, known as **fond lié** (fawn lee-ay), is made by thickening a dark stock with cornstarch. Sometimes, it is made like the classical espagnole, with bones and flavor builders and long simmering, but is thickened with cornstarch at the end. Sometimes, it is simply dark stock reduced by half and then thickened with cornstarch. Sometimes, it is simply a dark stock thickened with cornstarch. It is a sauce with a beautiful sheen and an almost transparent quality. Fond lié is seldom made as a basic sauce, but it is made when pan juices from cooked meats are turned into finished sauces, as we will see in Chapters 10 and 11.

Recipe 8-4 BASIC BROWN SAUCE OR ESPAGNOLE

YIELD: ***1 gallon (4 L)***

8 oz	**butter**	**250 g**

Mirepoix:

1 lb	**onions, medium dice**	**450 g**
8 oz	**carrots, medium dice**	**250 g**
8 oz	**celery, medium dice**	**250 g**
8 oz	**flour**	**250 g**
6 qt	**brown stock**	**6 L**
8 oz	**tomatoes or tomato purée**	**250 g**
$^1/_2$	**bay leaf**	
$^1/_4$ tsp	**thyme**	**1 mL**
5–6	**parlsey stems**	

1. Melt butter in a stockpot and cook mirepoix until it is golden brown and onions are caramelized.
2. Add flour and stir to make a roux. Cook until roux is brown with a nutty aroma.
3. Add $1^1/_2$ qt ($1^1/_2$ L) of cold stock to the stockpot, stirring well. Add remaining stock and tomato, stirring while you bring the sauce to a boil.
4. Reduce heat and add sachet with bay leaf, thyme, and parsley. Simmer until the sauce is reduced to 1 gallon (4 L)—about $1–1^1/_2$ hours. Skim surface frequently.
5. Strain through china cap lined with cheesecloth.

Per ounce:		Carbohydrates:	2 g
Calories:	25	Cholesterol:	5 mg
Fat:	2 g	Fiber:	0 g
Protein:	1 g	Sodium:	22 mg

Often, a basic brown sauce is enriched still further with additional stock before being used to make small or finished sauces. This makes another sauce known as **demiglace** (demi-glass or demi-glaze). As Recipe 8.4a shows, it is half brown sauce and half dark stock, reduced by half. The procedure is simple though time consuming. The sauce must be skimmed often as it reduces and strained

Recipe 8-4a DEMIGLACE

Yield: ***1 gallon (4 L)***

1 gal	**brown sauce**	**4 L**
1 gal	**brown stock**	**4 L**

1. Combine sauce and stock in a heavy stockpot.
2. Simmer, skimming frequently, until reduced to 1 gallon (4 L).
3. Strain through a china cap lined with cheesecloth.

Per ounce:		Carbohydrates:	2 g
Calories:	25	Cholesterol:	0 mg
Fat:	2 g	Fiber:	0 g
Protein:	1 g	Sodium:	27 mg

through cheesecloth like other fine sauces. The result is a rich, robust sauce, one used so often to make small sauces that Escoffier called it a "*grande sauce de base.*" The brown sauces obviously have more strength and flavor built into them than the more delicate white sauces. Brown sauces go well with red meat and some kinds of game.

Basic brown sauces, however hearty, remain uncommitted as long as they are unseasoned. Any of them can be finished by seasoning or can be made ahead in quantity and used as the basic sauce for any number of different finished sauces.

Most finished brown sauces have added flavor ingredients. Recipes 8.4b to 8.4d offer some typical examples. Mushroom sauce contains mushrooms, shallots, and sherry. Marchand de vin (wine merchant) combines demiglace with a reduction of red wine and shallots. These two are typically served with beef. Robert (roh-bare) is the sauce for grilled pork chops or roast pork. If you add a julienne of sour pickles at serving time, you will turn robert into charcutière sauce.

Notice the use of a flavor reduction in marchand de vin sauce and the reducing of the white wine in robert sauce. Notice also the technique of simmering a sauce to adjust texture as well

Recipe 8-4b ROBERT SAUCE

Yield: ***1 quart (1 L)***

4 oz	**minced shallots**	**125 g**
1 oz	**butter**	**30 g**
1/2 pt	**white wine**	**250 ml**
1 qt	**demiglace**	**1 L**
1 tsp	**dry mustard**	**5 mL**
1 Tb	**lemon juice**	**15 mL**
	salt to taste	
	pepper to taste	

1. Sweat shallots in butter until aroma is apparent.
2. Add white wine; reduce by two-thirds.
3. Add demiglace; simmer until flavors are blended.
4. Strain through a china cap lined with cheesecloth.
5. Blend mustard with lemon juice and stir into sauce.
6. Season to taste with salt and pepper.

Per ounce:		Carbohydrates:	3 g
Calories:	39	Cholesterol:	2 mg
Fat:	3 g	Fiber:	0 g
Protein:	1 g	Sodium:	35 mg

Recipe 8-4c MUSHROOM SAUCE

8 oz	**sliced mushrooms**	**250 g**
2 oz	**minced shallots**	**50 g**
1 oz	**butter**	**30 g**
1 qt	**demiglace**	**1 L**
2 oz	**sherry**	**50 mL**
	salt to taste	
	pepper to taste	

1. Cook mushrooms and shallots in butter until golden.
2. Add demiglace. Simmer until flavors are blended.
3. Add sherry. Season to taste.

Per serving:		Carbohydrates:	3 g
Calories:	37	Cholesterol:	2 mg
Fat:	3 g	Fiber:	0 g
Protein:	1 g	Sodium:	34 mg

Recipe 8-4d MARCHAND DE VIN SAUCE

6 fl oz	**red wine**	**175 ml**
2 oz	**minced shallots**	**60 g**
1 qt	**demiglace**	**1 L**
	salt to taste	
	pepper to taste	

1. Boil red wine with shallots until reduced by two-thirds, to about 3 fl oz (100 mL).
2. Add demiglace. Simmer to desired texture.
3. Strain through a china cap lined with cheesecloth.
4. Season to taste with salt and pepper.

Per serving:		Carbohydrates:	3 g
Calories:	30	Cholesterol:	0 mg
Fat:	2 g	Fiber:	0 g
Protein:	1 g	Sodium:	28 mg

as to blend and enhance flavors. There is an interesting variation of the usual pattern in robert sauce: The mustard and lemon are added after the sauce is strained. The slight graininess of the mustard accents the bite of its flavor, and you don't want to lose any of it. The finished mushroom sauce is not strained at all, and the mushrooms become part of the dish to which the sauce is added.

Quality standards for finished brown sauces are the same as those for the other roux-based sauces. The quality of the stock makes all the difference in a brown sauce. The sauce flavor should be hearty, the color a rich brown, and the aroma enticing. Salt and white pepper are standard seasonings, with other peppers used judiciously. As always, seasoning is an end process.

RED SAUCES

The red sauces are tomato based, and the stock is really subordinate to the juices of the tomato in both the flavor and the body of the sauce. There are two types of red, or tomato, sauces: those that are roux based (which are rarely made nowadays) and those made without roux. The latter depend for their thickening on careful reducing through simmering, as well as the thickness of the tomato purée or paste (see Recipe 8.5). Simmering is always done with a low heat because tomato sauce scorches easily. Various flavor ingredients can be added to tomato sauce to make a variety of finished sauces (see Recipes 8.5a–8.5c).

Recipe 8-5 TOMATO SAUCE

YIELD: ***Approximately 1 gallon (4 L)***

$2^1/_2$ lb	**onions, small dice**	**1.25 kg**
1 Tb	**puréed garlic**	**15 mL**
1 C	**minced parsley**	**250 mL**
2 fl oz	**olive oil**	**60 mL**
6 lb	**canned tomatoes, chopped (1 #10 can)**	**3 kg**
2 C	**tomato paste**	**500 mL**
1–2 tsp	**basil**	**5–10 mL**
1–2 tsp	**oregano**	**5–10 mL**
1	**bay leaf**	
	sugar to taste	
	salt to taste	
	pepper to taste	

1. In a heavy pot, sweat onions, garlic, and parsley in oil until onions are translucent.
2. Blend canned tomatoes and tomato paste. Add to onion mixture.
3. Add basil, oregano, and bay leaf. Cover pot and simmer 1–2 hours over low heat, or simmer, covered, in 350°F (180°C) oven to prevent scorching.
4. Strain through a china cap lined with cheesecloth.
5. If too thick, adjust texture with white stock. If too thin, reduce by simmering uncovered.
6. For a finished sauce, add sugar, salt, and pepper to taste.

Per ounce:		Carbohydrates:	2 g
Calories:	15	Cholesterol:	0 mg
Fat:	0 g	Fiber:	1 g
Protein:	0 g	Sodium:	37 mg

Recipe 8-5a SPANISH SAUCE

Yield: ***6 cups (1.5 L)***

6 oz	**onions, small dice**	**175 g**
4 oz	**green peppers, small dice**	**125 g**
2 Tb	**olive oil**	**30 mL**
2	**garlic cloves, puréed**	
4 oz	**mushrooms, sliced**	**125 g**
1 qt	**tomato sauce**	

Sachet:

1 bay leaf
pinch thyme
pinch crushed peppercorns
salt and pepper to taste
hot pepper sauce to taste

1. Sweat onions and green pepper in oil.
2. Add garlic and mushrooms. Cook until garlic aroma is evident.
3. Add tomato sauce and sachet. Simmer until flavors are blended.
4. Remove sachet. Season to taste with salt, pepper, and hot pepper sauce.

Per ounce:		Carbohydrates:	2 g
Calories:	17	Cholesterol:	0 mg
Fat:	1 g	Fiber:	1 g
Protein:	0 g	Sodium:	25 mg

A good tomato sauce should be full bodied, full flavored, and hearty. The mother sauce must be smooth and free of lumps, but it need not attain the velvet smoothness of the other classical sauces. Many of the small sauces, being unstrained, deliberately have a certain country quality in keeping with their origins and uses. All the tomato sauces should be free of sharp, bitter, or scorched flavors.

Recipe 8-5b CREOLE SAUCE

Add to Spanish Sauce Recipe 8.5a:

4 oz	**celery, small dice**	**125 g**

Add celery to onions and green pepper in Step 1.

Per ounce:		Carbohydrates:	2 g
Calories:	17	Cholesterol:	0 mg
Fat:	1 g	Fiber:	1 g
Protein:	0 g	Sodium:	26 mg

Recipe 8-5c PORTUGAISE SAUCE

Add to 1 qt (1 L) unseasoned Spanish sauce Recipe 8.5a:

1 lb	**tomatoes, concassé**	**450 g**
2–4 Tb	**minced parsley**	**25–50 mL**
	salt and pepper to taste	

1. Combine Spanish sauce and tomatoes. Simmer until reduced by one-third.
2. Stir in minced parsley. Season with salt and pepper to taste.

Per ounce:		Carbohydrates:	2 g
Calories:	19	Cholesterol:	0 mg
Fat:	1 g	Fiber:	1 g
Protein:	0 g	Sodium:	27 mg

BUTTER SAUCES

Butter sauces cover a large spectrum of possibilities, from simple melted butter to the complexities of the two mother sauces: hollandaise (hol-un-daze) and béarnaise (bare-naze or bay-er-nez). In an era when every continental chef worth his title was a master of sauce cookery, an Italian visitor to England reported that the English had 60 religions but only one sauce, and that sauce was melted butter. Today, melted butter, though not a sauce from one of the major sauce families, is often used in various forms to enhance a dish in the same way a true sauce is used.

Butter is a fat that comes from the milk of the cow (or the goat or the sheep or the buffalo). It is contained in the creamy part of the milk in the form of minute globules of oil suspended in emulsion with water. In butter making, the liquid is churned until the emulsion breaks; then the butter particles are gathered together and the liquid is drained off. You can see how this butter–water emulsion breaks if you overbeat whipping cream; it will separate abruptly into butter and a watery liquid.

Salt is added to butter during processing. It is possible to buy unsalted butter, called **sweet butter.** This butter is very desirable for making sauces as well as for most other cooking uses.

Margarine, a butterlike fat made from hardened vegetable oils, is cheaper than butter and similar in taste. Most margarines will perform like butter in making sauces. However, to be sure of the best-tasting sauce, it is wise to use butter or, for economy, half butter, half margarine. Margarine used alone is never a substitute for butter.

Let's start off our discussion with the simple butters and compound butters (Figure 8.5) and then move on to the more complicated leading sauces: hollandaise and béarnaise.

SIMPLE BUTTERS. A **simple butter** is one that contains nothing but butter; it has no added ingredients. The differences between one simple butter and another come from the way each is affected by heat. Heat will change the consistency of butter. It can change the taste and color as well.

Butter solidifies at cool temperatures, softens at room temperatures, melts when exposed to heat, and burns when exposed to extreme heat. All these reactions to temperature change are exploited by the cook as assets. They may also be liabilities, and the beginning cook needs to learn how to work with them.

Figure 8-5 SIMPLE AND COMPOUND BUTTERS

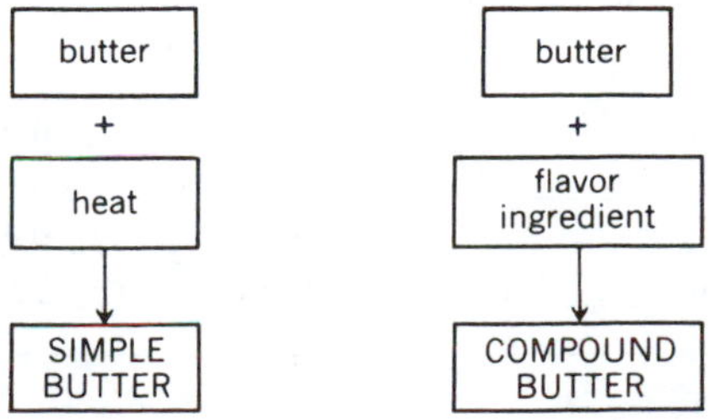

butter + heat → SIMPLE BUTTER

butter + flavor ingredient → COMPOUND BUTTER

There are statistics on the melting, browning, and burning temperatures of butter, but they won't mean as much to you as getting the feel of butter in action with heat. How does it behave when it sits for a while in a warm room? How does it look and act in the pan as it melts, as it browns, as it burns? How quickly do the changes take place? How high have you turned the burner? Only your own experience can answer these questions, since every range is different and every set of circumstances is different, and every pan and possibly every pound of butter.

The simplest simple butter is melted butter, often called **drawn butter** (*beurre fondu* in French). Used to enhance a food, it is merely poured over the fish or vegetable or whatever, or served on the side in a small dish. **Clarified butter** is also used in this way and in sautéing, since it does not burn as easily as whole butter. Butter is at least 80 percent fat, with a residue of milk solids, water, and salt. Since we do not want the residues in a butter sauce, we clarify the butter by melting it over low heat. When butter is melted, it separates. All the pure butterfat rises, and all the water, salt, and solid residues settle to the bottom. Then, we skim off the foam that floats on the melted butter and carefully pour off the liquid butterfat, leaving the water and solids behind. A pound of whole butter (454 g) will yield about 12 ounces (350 mL) of liquid butterfat, or clarified butter.

This clarified butter is what you use to make a butter sauce. Removing the solids raises the smoking point, so clarified butter does not burn as easily as whole butter. Without the water and milk solids, the sauce will have a creamier texture. Clarified butter is a major ingredient in hollandaise and béarnaise.

When whole melted butter is allowed to cook gently, the solid residues will brown, changing both the color and the flavor of the butter. Butter cooked to a golden brown is known as **brown butter** (*beurre noisette* in French, pronounced burr nwah-zet). It is used most often for fish and vegetables. When lemon juice and chopped parsley are added at the time of service, the combination is referred to as à la meunière (ah la mun-yair), meaning "in the style of the miller." The lemon juice and chopped parsley are usually placed directly on the fish or vegetable because adding them to the hot butter causes spattering.

When butter is cooked until it is dark brown or just short of burned, it becomes **black butter,** or *beurre noir* in French. It is usually flavored with vinegar by pouring the black butter on the food, deglazing the pan with the vinegar, and then pouring the vinegar on the food.

Adding ingredients at the time of service takes the last two butters out of the category of simple butters, strictly speaking. However, they are more closely related to simple butters than to anything else because of the way they are made.

COMPOUND BUTTERS. Compound butters are easy to understand, simple to make, convenient to have on hand, and delicious. Like simple butters, they are not true sauces but they often play the role of a sauce. They differ from simple butters in two ways: They are a blend of butter and one or more additional ingredients, and no heat is used in the making.

A **compound butter** is made by blending together softened butter and puréed or finely chopped ingredients. It is usually made in quantity in the mixer. It may then be spread in a long sheet pan, chilled, and cut into serving-size blocks. Or it can be rolled in paper in the shape of a long tube, chilled, and sliced in serving portions. Either way, it can be frozen and brought out to be used as needed. Place a piece of the compound butter on a hot steak and it melts, transforming the steak. Twenty different butters on twenty steaks will give you twenty different-tasting dishes.

Compound butters are also used on other meats and on fish, vegetables, and eggs. They are frequently used to finish a white or brown sauce, meaning that a piece of the butter is swirled in the hot sauce at the last minute before serving (**monter au beurre**), much as a garniture is added to a soup. Compound butters are also often used in their softened state as spreads for canapés or for croutons such as those for French onion soup (Recipe 7.1a).

Maître d'hôtel butter (Recipe 8.6) is one of the most frequently served compound butters. You will probably notice its similarity to that served à la meunière, but it is most often made cold and either served cold as a spread or placed

Recipe 8-6 MAITRE D'HÔTEL BUTTER

YIELD: *Approximately 1 pound (450 g)*

1 lb	**butter, softened**	**450 g**
2 oz	**minced parsley**	**50 g**
1½ oz	**lemon juice**	**45 mL**
	pinch white pepper	

1. Beat the butter at low speed using an electric mixer until it is smooth and fluffy.
2. Add the remaining ingredients and thoroughly blend in.
3. Roll the butter in parchment or wax paper to make a roll 1 in. (2.5 cm) thick. Chill.
4. For service, cut into ½ in. (1 cm) slices.

Per ounce:		Carbohydrates:	0 g
Calories:	100	Cholesterol:	60 mg
Fat:	23 g	Fiber:	0 g
Protein:	0 g	Sodium:	220 mg

on hot food at service time. Many other butters are made in the same way using other flavorings. Anchovies, shallots, shrimp, garlic, glazes, and herbs are only a few of the possibilities.

You can use maître d'hôtel and other compound butters like mother sauces and make other butters from them, or you can make the other butters from scratch. It will depend on your menu and production needs.

A good compound butter is well blended and has the definite taste of the major ingredient added to the butter. It should not be bland; it should taste piquant, rich, and memorable.

HOLLANDAISE AND BÉARNAISE. Unlike most of the classical sauces, the creamy thick texture of hollandaise and béarnaise derives from an **emulsion** of butter and egg yolks. You can see these differences in structure clearly by referring back to Figure 8.2.

The preparation techniques for these sauces are also very different. The sauces made with thickening agents depend heavily on the cooking process. The butter sauces are scarcely cooked at all, but what cooking there is is critically important. So is the technique of creating the emulsion—getting the ingredients to go together by beating them at a temperature falling within a narrow range.

The differences in techniques may be summed up by saying that the ingredients of these mother sauces are whipped together at a warm temperature, while those of the thickening-agent sauces are simmered together at a higher temperature.

The making of these sauces depends entirely on the unique characteristics of the two major ingredients, egg yolks and butter. The egg yolk plays the key role. You have met the egg yolk in the liaison, and you know that handling eggs with care does not always refer to keeping their shells from breaking. Two peculiarities of egg yolks are important in making butter sauces and require careful handling. One is the low coagulation temperature of the yolk; the other is the yolk's capacity as an emulsifier.

Coagulation, as you know, is the process of firming, solidifying, or coming together in a mass that takes place as the egg is heated. The coagulated egg is, in a word, cooked. Egg yolks coagulate somewhere between 144 and 158°F (62–70°C). If they are mixed with liquid food products, they include these products in the coagulation process, or bind them. This is a major purpose of the liaison, as we saw in Chapter 6.

Adding things to eggs raises the coagulation temperature somewhat, but at higher temperatures the egg yolk will break away from the other products, solidifying separately and losing its ability to bind. This is similar to the curdling of overheated milk. Thus, the right temperature becomes very important in the making of a sauce in which the egg yolk is the vehicle. It must be hot enough to begin coagulation, to thicken or firm the egg yolk slightly, but not hot enough to harden it and shut out the butter.

The second characteristic of the egg yolk, its talent for emulsifying, or forming an emulsion, is what makes the butter sauces possible. The liquid yolk can hold tiny droplets of liquid butter in suspension: That is, once they are dispersed in the yolk, it will keep them apart. The result is a thickened semiliquid of incredible smoothness.

This remarkable quality of the egg yolk is one that the cook must treat with tender loving care. The yolk can emulsify only a little oil at a time and that little bit must be evenly dispersed before the yolk can handle more. There is a limit, too, to its total capacity. Too much, too fast, too little beating, and the droplets of oil will coalesce—run together—and the emulsion will break.

The art of making these sauces, then, is being able to work with the unique qualities of the egg yolk to create a stable emulsion of yolk and liquid butter.

The two mother butter sauces, hollandaise and béarnaise, are both made the same way. There are two differences between them: The reductions are different, and the hollandaise is strained but the béarnaise is not. By closely examining the hollandaise recipe (Recipe 8.7), you can grasp the basic principles of both sauces.

Each step in the making of a butter sauce is critical:

- In Step 1, the reduction must be sufficiently reduced. If there is too much liquid, the egg yolks will not foam or thicken properly in Step 5.
- In Step 2, the reduction must be cooled. If it is too hot, it will cook the egg yolks in Step 4 and the sauce is lost then and there.
- In Step 3, the clarified butter must be warm but not hot. If it is too hot, it will cook the egg in Step 7. If it is not warm enough, it will tend to solidify and form larger droplets than the egg yolk can handle, and emulsification will not take place.
- In Step 4, the round-bottomed bowl (Figure 8.6) is essential so that every bit of egg yolk can be picked up by the whip. The bowl must be stainless steel to avoid any reaction with the acid in the reduction. If you are making a large quantity, you will use the bowl of the mixer. The reduction is strained at this point because it is much simpler to strain than the finished sauce.
- Step 5 is one of the two most critical steps. You want the eggs to cook slightly and evenly. If you undercook them, you are going to wind up with a watery sauce. If you overcook them, you will have lumps of cooked egg in the sauce that won't form an emulsion with the butter. You must whip steadily so that the cooking is even. The mixture will have reached the right degree of thickness when it becomes foamy,

Recipe 8-7 HOLLANDAISE SAUCE

YIELD: ***Approximately 1 pint (500 mL)***

1 Tb	**lemon juice**	**15 mL**
1 Tb	**distilled vinegar**	**15 mL**
1 Tb	**distilled white wine**	**15 mL**
1 Tb	**shallots**	**15 mL**
1/2	**bay leaf**	
2	**parsley stems**	
2	**peppercorns**	
12 fl oz	**clarified butter**	**350 mL**
4–5	**egg yolks**	

1. Cook the lemon juice, distilled vinegar, white wine, shallots, bay leaf, parsley stems, and peppercorns together until the liquid is reduced by 80 percent.
2. Cool the reduction.
3. Warm the clarified butter.
4. Place the egg yolks in a round-bottomed stainless steel bowl and add the reduction, straining it into the bowl.
5. Heat the egg yolk–reduction mixture over hot water or in a bain-marie, whipping steadily, until the mixture is foamy and slightly thickened.
6. Remove the bowl from the hot water.
7. While whipping the egg yolk–reduction mixture constantly, slowly add the warm clarified butter.
8. When half the butter has been added, adjust the texture with a few drops of warm water.
9. Continue slowly whipping in the remainder of the clarified butter.

Per ounce:		Carbohydrates:	0 g
Calories:	210	Cholesterol:	124 mg
Fat:	23 g	Fiber:	0 g
Protein:	1 g	Sodium:	225 mg

Figure 8-6 THICKENING THE EGG YOLKS

a. For a small amount of sauce, you can whip the yolks by hand in a round-bottomed bowl over hot water.

b. For a large amount of sauce, whip the yolks in the mixer bowl in the hot water of the bain-marie. (Photo by Patricia Roberts.)

lightens in color, increases in volume, and shows a slight but perceptible thickening.

- Step 6 stops the cooking action at this very critical point. If you are using the mixer, put the bowl in place and begin whipping, using medium speed. If you are making the sauce by hand, move your bowl to a worktable. A damp cloth under it will help it to stay put as you beat, so that you don't need a third hand.
- Step 7 is the other most critical step. It is at this point that the emulsion is created. The two essentials here are to keep the whipping constant and to add the warm butter slowly (Figure 8.7)—very, very slowly at first. After an emulsion is started—a smooth thickening process that is easy to recognize—the butter can be added a bit more quickly. Never add it faster than it can be absorbed.
- In Step 8, the few drops of water increase stability and improve texture. Step 9 finishes the basic sauce.

If your butter has not cooled too much, the egg yolks will be able to handle all the butter with no problem. The yolk of a large egg will

Figure 8-7 WHIPPING IN THE BUTTER

Add the clarified butter very, very slowly in a thin, steady stream while whipping on medium speed. (Photo by Patricia Roberts.)

emulsify about 3 ounces (90 mL) of clarified butter. Smaller eggs will handle proportionately less. This is why the proportions in the recipe call for 4 or 5 yolks to 12 ounces (350 mL) of butter: The number you use will depend on their size.

If your emulsion begins to break during Step 7—that is, if the yolks and butter begin to separate—there are several kinds of first aid you can apply:

- You can use more egg yolks in another bowl and beat the broken sauce little by little into the fresh yolks. This is the best possibility.
- You can put an ice cube in the center of the bowl and keep beating in the same spot. The quick temperature change may cause things to happen: The sauce will either re-form or break completely.

Hollandaise is the sauce toward which most young culinarians feel the greatest awe. Actually, if the rules are followed carefully, it is not hard to make. Sometimes, students who do not know that it is supposed to be a difficult sauce have no trouble at all, while some who have been bombarded with directives and cautions have problems. So relax as you work and enjoy seeing hollandaise appear before your very eyes.

Just don't neglect it. Once you have begun to make it, you are committed to giving it your full attention. There is no way you can make a butter sauce and do something else at the same time.

Many of today's kitchens no longer bother with a reduction but use the simplified version given in Recipe 8.8. Although this recipe makes a good sauce, it does not have the richness of flavor of the traditional formula. The same guidelines apply when heating the egg yolks and incorporating the butter.

Recipe 8-8 HOLLANDAISE SAUCE—CONTEMPORARY VERSION

YIELD: *Approximately 1 pint (500 mL)*

4–5	**egg yolks**	
1 fl oz	**cold water**	**30 mL**
1 lb	**butter, clarified**	**450 g**
$1^1/_2$ fl oz	**lemon juice**	**50 mL**
	salt and cayenne to taste	

1. Whip together egg yolks and cold water in a stainless steel bowl until thoroughly blended.
2. Over hot water, continue to whip until thick and creamy.
3. Off heat, whip in butter slowly and gradually. Add lemon juice as needed when mixture becomes too thick.
4. For a finished sauce, season to taste with lemon juice, salt, and cayenne.

Per ounce:		Carbohydrates:	0 g
Calories:	209	Cholesterol:	124 mg
Fat:	23 g	Fiber:	0 g
Protein:	1 g	Sodium:	221 mg

In comparing the two hollandaise recipes, you may notice that the butter in Recipe 8.7 is given as "clarified butter" and the butter in Recipe 8.8 is given as "butter, clarified." These terms make an important point. "Clarified butter" is butter measured after clarifying. "Butter, clarified" is butter measured before clarifying, which will, of course, be a larger amount than you will have left to blend with the egg yolks.

Béarnaise sauce is made in exactly the same way as hollandaise except that the reduction is somewhat different. The béarnaise reduction is heavily flavored with tarragon, and the ingredients are finely minced or crushed since it is not strained. This makes it look quite different from hollandaise, whose creamy appearance is unbroken by any speck of herb or spice. Compare the

Recipe 8-8a MOUSSELINE SAUCE

YIELD: ***Approximately 3 cups (0.75 L)***

To recipe for hollandaise, add:

3/4 C	**heavy cream, whipped**	**175 mL**

Carefully fold whipped cream into sauce until thoroughly combined. Season to taste.

Per ounce:		Carbohydrates:	1 g
Calories:	178	Cholesterol:	98 mg
Fat:	19 g	Fiber:	0 g
Protein:	1 g	Sodium:	152 mg

reduction in the béarnaise recipe (Recipe 8.9) with the hollandaise reduction in Recipe 8.7.

Béarnaise sauce is often made by simply adding tarragon to hollandaise. This is not, however, a true béarnaise, for the tarragon does not cook together with the other flavor builders, and, as a result, the sauce has a raw taste. Nor do the other herbs make an appearance in the final sauce, as they do in a true béarnaise.

Béarnaise and hollandaise are, as we have noted, mother sauces, and the formula we have given for hollandaise is for a basic sauce. Making finished sauces from a basic butter sauce is similar to making a finished sauce from any other basic sauce. You can make a finished hollandaise by seasoning it. Or you can make an-

Recipe 8-8b DIVINE SAUCE

YIELD: ***Approximately 1 pint (500 mL)***

1/2 C	**hollandaise sauce**	**125 mL**
1/2 C	**chicken velouté**	**125 mL**
1/2 C	**heavy cream, stiffly whipped**	**125 mL**
	salt and pepper to taste	

1. Blend hollandaise and velouté.
2. Fold in whipped cream.
3. Season to taste with salt and pepper.

Per ounce:		Carbohydrates:	1 g
Calories:	58	Cholesterol:	17 mg
Fat:	6 g	Fiber:	0 g
Protein:	0 g	Sodium:	97 mg

Recipe 8-9 BÉARNAISE SAUCE

YIELD: ***Approximately 1 pint (500 mL)***

1 Tb	**lemon juice**	**15 mL**
1 Tb	**distilled vinegar**	**15 mL**
1 Tb	**distilled white wine**	**15 mL**
1 Tb	**tarragon**	**15 mL**
1 Tb	**shallots**	**15 mL**
1/2	**bay leaf**	
2	**parsley stems**	
2	**peppercorns**	
12 fl oz	**clarified butter**	**350 mL**
4–5	**egg yolks**	

1. Cook the lemon juice, distilled vinegar, white wine, tarragon, shallots, bay leaf, parsley stems, and peppercorns together until the liquid is reduced by 80 percent.
2. Cool the reduction.
3. Warm the clarified butter.
4. Place the egg yolks in a round-bottomed stainless steel bowl and add the reduction.
5. Heat the egg yolk–reduction mixture over hot water or in a bain-marie, whipping steadily, until the mixture is foamy and slightly thickened.
6. Remove the bowl from the hot water.
7. While whipping the egg yolk–reduction mixture constantly, slowly add the warm clarified butter.
8. When half the butter has been added, adjust the texture with a few drops of warm water.
9. Continue slowly whipping in the remainder of the clarified butter.

Per ounce:		Carbohydrates:	1 g
Calories:	260	Cholesterol:	134 mg
Fat:	29 g	Fiber:	0 g
Protein:	1 g	Sodium:	281 mg

Recipe 8-9a CHORON SAUCE

YIELD: ***Approximately 1 pint (500 mL)***

To recipe for basic béarnaise, add:

2 Tb	**tomato paste**	**30 mL**
	salt and pepper to taste	

Blend tomato paste into béarnaise. Season to taste with salt and pepper.

Per ounce:		Carbohydrates:	1 g
Calories:	260	Cholesterol:	134 mg
Fat:	293 g	Fiber:	0 g
Protein:	1 g	Sodium:	282 mg

other sauce by adding something else—another flavor-building reduction, a special ingredient for flavor or texture, a garniture.

Mousseline (moos-a-leen) sauce, for example, is hollandaise combined with whipped cream and seasoned (Recipe 8.8a). Maltaise (moltez) sauce is hollandaise flavored with orange juice and grated orange rind. Girondin (zheeron-dan) sauce is hollandaise with prepared mustard; powdered mustard would make it aegir (ay-zheer) sauce. And so on.

Small sauces are made from béarnaise in the same way. Add the flavor and color of tomato paste to béarnaise for choron (sho-rawn) sauce (Recipe 8.9a). Stir a little melted meat glaze into béarnaise to make a rich-tasting foyot (foy-oh) sauce. As with the other sauce families, seasoning is always an end process. For seasoning a hollandaise, cayenne is usually the pepper of choice, along with lemon and salt.

Another way to create different sauces is to combine sauces from different classes. For example, you can add a reduction of brown sauce and red wine to béarnaise to make medici (med-a-chee) sauce (Recipe 8.9b). Or you can fold together chicken velouté, hollandaise, and stiffly whipped cream to make divine sauce (Recipe 8.8b). Combine béchamel or velouté, hollandaise, and whipped cream in equal parts for a royal sauce for glazing. There is no end to the possibilities, once you know how everything works.

There are, however, limits to what you can do with the texture of a butter sauce. You can thin it with a reduction. But because of the egg, you can't thicken it by cooking it down, as you can with a roux-thickened sauce. For this reason, in making finished sauces, keep in mind the final texture you are striving for. Reductions must be reduced accordingly. And the critical temperature must always be kept in mind, lest the egg be cooked or the emulsion broken at the last minute.

The practice of cooking and holding these egg-containing sauces at or below 140°F (60°C) suggests some serious safety considerations. First, be sure you use bowls and utensils that are absolutely clean. Second, make sure the eggs you use are clean and high-quality. Third, hold hollandaise sauce for no more than one hour and make sure you hold it in a stainless steel (not aluminum) container. Finally, don't mix hol-

Recipe 8-9b MEDICI SAUCE

YIELD: ***Approximately 1 pint (500 mL)***

To recipe for basic béarnaise, add:

2 fl oz	**brown sauce**	**60 mL**
2 fl oz	**red wine**	**60 mL**
	salt and pepper to taste	

1. Reduce brown sauce and red wine by two-thirds.
2. Blend in béarnaise. Season to taste.

Per ounce:		Carbohydrates:	1 g
Calories:	264	Cholesterol:	139 mg
Fat:	29 g	Fiber:	0 g
Protein:	1 g	Sodium:	285 mg

landaise you have already made into freshly made product.

A good hollandaise or béarnaise sauce is ultrasmooth and light in texture, similar to lightly whipped cream. It is barely pourable, yet it looks and seems fluid. It has a high gloss but never a greasy look. There is no hint of solidified butter, no bit of cooked egg, no tendency to separate or break. You taste the butter but it is not an oily taste. You know the egg is there but the sauce does not taste eggy. Its flavor will vary from delicate to robust according to the flavoring ingredients. Color will vary, too, for the same reasons.

Practice is the only way to master the use of such special products as egg yolks and butter. Overcook eggs, undercook them, burn some butter, experience failure and success, but master these basics. The rewards will amaze you.

PURÉE SAUCES

The sauce families discussed so far derive from the classical or grande cuisine of nineteenth-century European cooking. Heavy, smooth, and rich, they are traditionally ladled on foods to mask or cover them completely, exciting the appetite with their lavish appearance and refinement of texture.

The trend today is away from the heavy roux-based sauces and toward preserving and enhancing the natural flavors and colors of fresh ingredients. Rather than covering foods with rich, heavy sauces, the emphasis is on the taste and appearance of the food itself. In sauce making, this has meant a great change in the techniques of thickening. Instead of roux, followers of the new style use other classical techniques to thicken their sauces. Among these techniques are using purées.

As you have seen in Chapters 6 and 7, purées are cooked or raw foods that have been processed to a thick consistency. They can be used to thicken soups or sauces. **Coulis,** a French term, refers to a sauce made of a purée of vegetables or fruits. A vegetable coulis, such as bell pepper coulis, can be served hot or cold to accompany entrées and side dishes. Fruit coulis is usually served cold as a dessert sauce. Recipes 8.10 and 8.11 provide examples.

Recipe 8-10 YELLOW BELL PEPPER COULIS

YIELD: ***2 cups (500 mL)***

2	**yellow bell peppers, chopped**	
$^1/_2$	**mild green chile, seeded and finely chopped**	
1 Tb	**chopped mixed fresh herbs, such as parsley, thyme, and rosemary**	**15 mL**
$1^1/_4$ C	**vegetable stock**	**300 mL**
2 Tb	**dry white wine**	**30 mL**
$^1/_2$ tsp	**salt**	**2 mL**
$^1/_4$ tsp	**pepper**	**1 mL**
1 Tb	**cornstarch**	**15 mL**
	salt and pepper to taste	

1. Put all ingredients except cornstarch into a saucepan and bring slowly to a boil.
2. Once it boils, reduce heat and simmer 10 minutes, stirring from time to time. Remove pan from heat and let cool.
3. When mixture is cool enough to handle, purée until smooth using a blender or food processor. Put sauce into another saucepan.
4. Mix cornstarch with 2 Tb (30 mL) water.
5. Stir cornstarch mixture into pepper sauce and heat gently until sauce thickens, stirring constantly. Simmer 3 minutes. Remove pan from heat and adjust seasoning.

Per ounce:		Carbohydrates:	2 g
Calories:	8	Cholesterol:	0 mg
Fat:	0 g	Fiber:	0 g
Protein:	0 g	Sodium:	229 mg

Recipe 8-11 PLUM SAUCE

YIELD: ***About 2 cups (500 mL)***

12 oz	**fresh plums**	**375 g**
1	**orange, zest and juice**	
$^1/_4$ C	**sugar**	**60 mL**
$^1/_2$ tsp	**cinnamon**	**2 mL**
1 Tb	**brandy**	**15 mL**

1. Halve and pit plums.
2. Bring plums in $^2/_3$ C water slowly to a boil. Next, reduce heat, cover, and simmer until plums are soft, stirring from time to time.
3. When mixture is cool enough to handle, purée plums and liquid until smooth using a blender or food processor.
4. Put sauce into another saucepan and add orange zest, orange juice, sugar, cinnamon, and brandy. Mix well. Simmer for 2–3 minutes.

Per ounce:		Carbohydrates:	9 g
Calories:	39	Cholesterol:	0 mg
Fat:	0 g	Fiber:	1 g
Protein:	0 g	Sodium:	2 mg

A vegetable coulis is often made by cooking the main ingredient, such as tomatoes, with typical flavoring ingredients, such as onions and herbs, in a liquid such as stock. The vegetable and flavorings are then puréed, and the consistency and flavoring of the product are adjusted. A vegetable coulis can also be made by cooking the vegetable and flavorings in oil until the proper consistency is reached.

The texture of a vegetable or fruit coulis is quite variable, depending on the ingredients and how it is to be used. A typical coulis is about the consistency and texture of a thin tomato sauce. The color and flavor of the main ingredient should stand out.

A vegetable or fruit coulis, since it is made with little or no fat, is considered a healthier choice than many of the classical sauces that use much fat.

SALSA AND RELISH

Salsas and relishes are versatile, colorful, low-fat sauces. You have probably already tasted tomato salsas—they are chunky and full of tomatoes, chili peppers, onion, garlic, cilantro, and possibly other ingredients. Tomato salsas are common in Mexican and Southwestern cooking.

Salsas and **relishes** can be defined as chunky mixtures of vegetables and/or fruits and flavor ingredients. They may feature ordinary ingredients, such as tomatoes, and sometimes not so ordinary ingredients, such as papaya or jicama. Served cold, they are used as sauces for meat, poultry, and seafood.

Since salsas and relishes contain little or no fat, they rely on intense flavor ingredients, such as cilantro, jalapeño peppers, lime juice, and

Recipe 8-12 SALSA

YIELD: ***$1^1/_2$ cups (375 mL) or 6 servings***

1 C	**tomato sauce**	**250 mL**
1 Tb	**chili peppers, finely chopped**	**15 mL**
$^1/_4$ C	**green pepper, finely chopped**	**60 mL**
2 Tb	**onion, finely chopped**	**30 mL**
1	**clove garlic, minced**	
$^1/_4$ tsp	**oregano leaves, crushed**	**1 mL**
	pinch cumin	

1. Mix all ingredients thoroughly.
2. Chill before serving to blend flavors.

Per serving:		Carbohydrates:	4 g
Calories:	16	Cholesterol:	0 mg
Fat:	0 g	Fiber:	1 g
Protein:	1 g	Sodium:	247 mg

Recipe 8-13 ZUCCHINI RELISH

Yield: ***2 quarts or 32 servings***

$2^1/_2$ C	**zucchini, sliced**	**625 mL**
1 C	**onion, chopped**	**250 mL**
$^1/_2$	**green pepper, sliced**	
$^1/_2$ C	**vinegar**	**125 mL**
$1^1/_2$ C	**sugar**	**375 mL**
$^1/_4$ tsp	**dry mustard**	**1 mL**
1 tsp	**cornstarch**	**5 mL**
$^1/_2$ tsp	**celery seed**	**2 mL**
$^1/_4$ tsp	**turmeric**	**1 mL**
$^1/_2$ tsp	**mustard seeds**	**2 mL**
	pinch pepper	

1. Using food processor, chop zucchini, onion, and green pepper fine.
2. Boil vinegar, sugar, and remaining ingredients. Stir to dissolve sugar.
3. Add chopped vegetables and simmer 30 minutes.
4. Remove from heat and chill.

Per serving:		Carbohydrates:	10 g
Calories:	39	Cholesterol:	0 mg
Fat:	0 g	Fiber:	0 g
Protein:	0 g	Sodium:	1 mg

lemon juice. Salsas and relishes, with their many colors, flavors, and textures are a thoroughly contemporary addition to sauces. See Recipes 8.12 and 8.13 for sample recipes.

PAN GRAVY

Pan gravy is just what its name implies: It is a sauce made in a pan from the juices or drippings of the items cooked in the pan. The steps to make pan gravy are as follows:

1. Remove the cooked meat or poultry from the pan.
2. Add mirepoix to enrich the pan juices (if it was not already done during the roasting process) and cook until it is brown and most of the liquid in the pan has evaporated.
3. Pour off the fat and use it as the fat for the roux.
4. Deglaze the pan with an appropriate stock. Deglazing incorporates the fond—the pan drippings and the bits of food clinging to the pan bottom.
5. Add enough stock to make the proper amount of gravy. Bring to a simmer.
6. Make a roux, cool it slightly, and beat it into the stock to thicken.
7. Simmer until done, about 20 minutes. Strain the gravy and season to taste.

Another way to make a gravy, such as brown gravy, is thicken a reduced beef stock with a purée of carrots, onions, and parsnips. High-starch vegetables are especially good at thickening. They include potatoes, sweet potatoes, yams, parsnips, winter squash, pumpkin, corn, and peas.

SAUCES FROM CONVENIENCE PRODUCTS

All kinds of convenience sauce products are available—paste and powder bases, concentrated sauces needing only to be thinned, and finished sauces. They have the advantage of saving both time and labor and are widely used for these reasons, especially in kitchens where low budgets prevail and the staff is not skilled in sauce making.

Some of the convenience items, especially those for basic sauces, can be turned into very good products if properly chosen and properly used. Avoid any with a high salt content and follow the directions on the package, since different items are reconstituted differently. As with the stock substitutes, you must determine for each product just how it fits into the overall sauce-making process, and then carry the process forward accordingly. For example, be sure you don't try to make a basic sauce using a convenience product intended to produce a finished sauce.

Do not be deceived, however, by the words "quick and simple." You have to use judgment and care to achieve a sauce from a convenience product that is as good as a sauce made from scratch. The knowledge and experience you gain in making sauces from scratch will be invaluable in working with convenience products and in setting standards for convenience sauces.

SUMMING UP

The hundreds of sauces of classical cuisine all stem from a few basic sauces, known as mother sauces or leading sauces. The sauces deriving from them, called small or finished sauces, are made by adding specific flavoring ingredients to the basic mother sauces.

All the basic sauces are similar in structure. Their body is a liquid. Their texture is provided by a thickening agent. Flavorings and seasonings complete the finished sauces.

The white sauces, with béchamel as the mother sauce, are made with milk and roux. The blond sauces, or veloutés, are based on veal, chicken, or fish stock combined with white or blond roux. The brown sauces are made from dark stock thickened with brown roux or cornstarch. The red, or tomato, sauces use stock or tomato juice as their liquid. The classical tomato sauce is thickened with roux, but many American versions are thickened by reducing and puréeing. The butter sauces are thickened by emulsifying liquid butter in egg yolks. Butter is also used in the role of a sauce, both alone and in the form of compound butters piquantly flavored and placed cold on hot dishes to melt and enrich.

Today's sauces also include more than the triumphs of the past. Nouvelle followers are bringing new tastes and textures to sauces by using such classical techniques as reducing and puréeing to thicken. New and unusual flavor combinations are appearing, and sauced dishes are being presented in fresh new ways.

Many sauces today are made from convenience products; in fact, most kitchens use such products in one way or another. They can be successful when they are selected with concern for quality ingredients and a low salt content and are used with the understanding of how they fit into sauce-from-scratch procedures.

In today's restaurants, sauces are a very successful yet simple way of offering a menu with great variety. They are a means of presenting a single product such as veal or steak in a number of different ways, each sauce blending its special flavor with the flavor of the meat to create a distinctively different dish. There is no need to associate the perfect sauce with the expensive commercial restaurant and the extended menu. Sauce of one kind or another is invaluable in the low-budget operation. Whatever the setting, the use, or the price tag, the quality of the sauce can make or break the dish.

Now, you know all about the basic secrets of sauce cookery—the structure of sauces, the making of roux, the liaison, the seasoning, the reduction, the emulsion, the puréeing. But mastery of sauce cookery requires one more secret that no text or teacher can supply, and that is practice.

The Cook's Vocabulary

basic, mother, or leading sauce
brown sauces: espagnole, fond lié
butter sauces: hollandaise, béarnaise
compound butters: maître d'hôtel butter
coulis
demiglace
emulsion
finished sauce
monter au beurre
pan gravy
red sauces: tomato sauce
reduction
relish
salsa
sauce
simple butters: drawn butter, clarified butter, brown butter, black butter
sweet butter
velouté sauces: veal, chicken, fish
white sauces: béchamel, velouté

Review Questions

Answer each question in complete sentences. Read each question carefully and make sure you answer all parts of the question. Organize your answer into more than one paragraph when appropriate.

1. Compare sauce making with soup making: consider structure, technique, versatility, holding, and storing.
2. After reading and reviewing this chapter, draw a chart on your own that shows the basic sauces and one small sauce for each basic sauce.
3. In what types of operations would you make sauces from scratch, and in what types would you use convenience products? Are there operations that would use no sauces at all? If so, give examples.
4. Do you think it is important to learn how to make sauces from scratch even if you never have to make them? Defend your answer.
5. Discuss the various ways of controlling texture in different kinds of sauces. Is it always possible to adjust a sauce that is too thin or too thick? Explain.
6. Define the key terms in this chapter that were new to you.

Chapter 9

VEGETABLES, GRAINS, AND PASTA

When it comes to vegetables, the average restaurant menu has undergone a remarkable change in the last dozen or so years. The once-prevailing side dish of overcooked green beans has given way to a great variety of well-prepared, well-presented vegetables accompanying entrées, acting as entrées, gracing salad bars, serving as appetizers, and being used as garnishes to make exceptional plate presentations.

Much of this change has come in response to consumer interest. People of all ages are paying increasing attention to fitness and health and are eating more vegetables and cutting down on meats and sweets. Vegetables have far fewer calories, more vitamins and minerals, and more fiber—all important to good looks and well-being. It has also become clear that a diet high in vegetables (and fruits) is associated with a lower risk of cancer. Properly prepared, vegetables are attractive to the eye and they taste good.

Good vegetable preparation is not the easiest of kitchen assignments. It takes product knowledge plus an understanding of how cooking can affect the product and an alertness to the sensory cues of doneness. It takes timing and practice.

After completing this chapter, you should be able to:

- Explain the effect of an acid or alkaline medium on color in vegetables.
- Discuss the nutritional importance of vegetables and explain how to retain nutrients in cooking.
- Choose cooking methods appropriate to different vegetables and describe or demonstrate their use.
- Cite the major holding and production problems for vegetables and suggest ways of overcoming them.
- Distinguish the major types of legumes and describe the general procedure for cooking them.
- Distinguish the major types of rice and describe ways to cook them.
- Distinguish the major types of pasta and describe how to cook fresh and dried pastas.

ABOUT VEGETABLES IN GENERAL

Defining vegetables seems almost as unnecessary as defining your hands. Potatoes, carrots, onions, broccoli, and cabbage are household words. We all know what vegetables are. It is fortunate we do, because it is rather hard to define them precisely.

Vegetables are the edible parts of certain plants. They may be roots, tubers, bulbs, stems, leaves, flowers, fruits, seeds, or pods. As a group, they are high in vitamins and minerals. They are also important sources of dietary fiber. A few of them—the dried beans and peas (also called legumes)—contain significant amounts of high-quality protein, a factor of importance to vegetarians. The other vegetables are low in calories, a feature that appeals to anyone trying to lose weight. But the vitamin and mineral content of all vegetables is what makes them an essential part of a balanced diet for everyone (see Table 9.1). In addition, vegetables offer far more than just vitamins and minerals—researchers have identified dozens of disease-fighting chemicals, called **phytochemicals,** in plant foods. The bright-yellow vegetables (carrots, winter squash, for example) and the deep-green leaves and flowers (broccoli, spinach, artichoke) are especially important.

Vegetables have been on the menu for centuries. The lentil was a staple of the Egyptian diet; onions, cabbage, and mushrooms were also eaten. The Greeks and Romans added broad beans, carrots, cucumbers, lettuce, squash, broccoli, asparagus (for the rich only), garlic, and other vegetables. It is said that the Romans ate cabbage to avoid getting drunk and to cure hangovers.

But vegetables were very unpopular in medieval Europe. They were thought to cause "wind and melancholy." Only cabbage and the onion family were grown, mostly for soup. Dried peas provided pease porridge hot, cold, and nine days old, if we can believe the nursery rhyme. Garlic was eaten to ward off the plague.

Columbus and other explorers took back to Europe the corn, potatoes, squash, tomatoes, peppers, and beans they found the Indians cultivating in the Americas. Some of the strange vegetables caught on, notably the hot peppers. Some didn't. But gradually people began to regard vegetables in general in a more favorable light. Vegetables became fashionable and played an important part in the developing French cuisine.

Until the development of refrigerated transportation in the twentieth century, fresh vegetables were available only in the summer near where they were grown. Today, we can get almost any vegetable we want at almost any time of the year.

Vegetables come into the kitchen in three market forms—fresh or raw, frozen, and canned. Of the three, fresh vegetables produce the best finished dish in flavor, texture, appearance, and nutritive value. But they have their drawbacks. The labor cost is high; they are very perishable. The market product varies seasonally, even daily at times, and the price fluctuates, too.

Many frozen vegetables can be almost as good as fresh ones. They have several advantages: They save preparation time and labor, they are available year-round, and they yield a standard finished product. One of their major disadvantages is that most lack the crunchiness of fresh produce; in other words, they tend to have a softer texture.

Canned vegetables are the most convenient, the least attractive, and very high in sodium. Like frozen vegetables, they yield a standard product.

In cooking the different market forms, you have to consider the degree to which they are already cooked. Fresh vegetables are, of course, totally uncooked. Frozen vegetables have been partially cooked before freezing, to avoid deterioration during storage. Canned vegetables have been completely cooked; in fact, they have been unavoidably overcooked by the prolonged high temperatures of the canning process. To cook each market form, you simply take it where it stands—raw, partially cooked, or overcooked—and bring it to doneness.

Fresh vegetables are cooked from scratch. Frozen vegetables should be cooked from their

Table 9-1 SELECTED NUTRIENTS IN FRUITS AND VEGETABLES

Vegetables $^{1}/_{2}$ ***Cup Cooked***	***Vitamin A***	***Vitamin C***	***Fiber***	***Cruciferous***
Asparagus		■	■	
Beans, green			■	
Bok choy	●	■	■	✓
Broccoli	■	●	■	✓
Brussels sprouts		●	■	✓
Cabbage		■	■	✓
Carrots	●		■	
Cauliflower		●	■	✓
Chili peppers ($^{1}/_{4}$ cup)	●	●		
Corn			■	
Dried peas and beans			●	
Eggplant			■	
Green pepper		●		
Greens[a]	●	■	■	
Lettuce (1 cup fresh)				
Spinach	●	■	■	
Romaine	■			
Red and green leaf	■			
Iceberg				
Okra			■	
Peas, green			■	
Potato (1 medium baked)		■	■	
Spinach	●		■	
Squash, winter	●		■	
Sweet potato	●		■	
Tomatoes (1)	■	■	■	
Zucchini			■	

■ These selections supply at least 25 percent of the U.S. RDA for vitamins A and C or at least 1–3 grams of dietary fiber per serving.

● These selections supply at least 50 percent of the U.S. RDA for vitamins A or C or at least 4 grams of dietary fiber per serving.

[a]Values are averages calculated using beet and mustard greens, swiss chard, dandelion, kale, and turnip greens. These foods are part of the cruciferous family.

frozen state, except for spinach and other greens and various kinds of summer squash, which are practically solid blocks of ice. These should be thawed in the cooler before cooking. Canned vegetables are merely heated to serving temperature since they are already cooked beyond doneness. Heat them in their own liquid, using only enough to cover them.

Any market form can be cooked by any cooking method, observing the guidelines for the particular vegetable. The only thing you have to be careful of in following recipes is to remember degrees of doneness in substituting one market form for another, especially if the recipe specifies a cooking time. Doneness is not a matter of time but of texture, as we shall see.

When you buy fresh vegetables and fruits from the vendor, they are called produce. Once in the kitchen, they become different things to different cooks. In the cold preparation area, or pantry, they are raw materials for salads and other cold foods. To the soup cook and the sauce cook, they are flavor-determining ingredients or flavor builders, to be orchestrated along with stocks and thickeners and spices into composite blends of foods. To the vegetable cook, the vegetable is a dish in its own right. In this chapter, we will talk about vegetables as seen by the vegetable cook—as dishes prepared to be served with the main entrée or as the main entrée.

VEGETABLE CHARACTERISTICS AND COOKING

COLOR IN COOKING

There are several characteristics of vegetables that influence the way we cook them. One of these is color. No matter what color a raw vegetable is, we want to preserve as much of that color as possible.

Vegetables may be grouped by color into four categories:

- Red: beets, red cabbage, red beans
- Green: green beans, lima beans, broccoli, asparagus, peas, artichokes, okra, brussels sprouts, spinach, parsley, green peppers, greens (mustard, turnip, and so on)
- Yellow: carrots, rutabaga, winter squash, yams, sweet potatoes, corn, tomatoes
- White: potatoes, green cabbage, turnips, celery, summer squash, cauliflower, onions, mushrooms, cucumbers, zucchini

These colors come from substances in vegetables known as **pigments.** Certain pigments react to heat, acid, or alkali during cooking, undergoing chemical changes that cause a vegetable to change color. It is important to know which pigments are susceptible to color change and how to deal with them in cooking.

RED VEGETABLES. The pigments in red vegetables are known as **anthocyanins.** These pigments are red in an acid medium but will change to blue or purple in an alkaline medium. They are also water soluble and can be drawn out of the vegetable into the cooking liquid. Although tomatoes are red in color, they are classified with the yellow and orange vegetables because their pigment is more closely identified with these vegetables.

Cooking red vegetables in an acid medium intensifies their red color. Vegetables themselves contribute acid to the cooking medium. To preserve the color, red vegetables such as beets should be cooked in a covered container to keep the acid from evaporating. Beets should be cooked unpeeled, to keep the red pigment in the beet instead of letting it leach into the water. You will see these rules illustrated in Recipe 9.1.

Some water supplies are alkaline and may stay on the alkaline side during cooking in spite of the added vegetable acids. In an alkaline medium, red cabbage will not only lose its redness but will turn purple, blue, and green. A small amount of vinegar, wine, or lemon juice in the water will maintain its red color. For example, in Recipe 9.2, red cabbage is cooked covered (braised) with apples, wine, and vinegar providing extra acid.

GREEN VEGETABLES. The pigments in green vegetables are known as **chlorophyll.** Their reaction to acids and alkalis is just the opposite of the red pigments' reactions. They tend to lose their brilliance as their acids are released into the cooking water and may turn an olive green, a very drab color. They keep their color best in a slightly alkaline solution. Therefore, they should be cooked uncovered to allow their acids to evaporate. By cooking them in extra water (more than just enough to cover), you help dissolve plant acids and therefore retain color.

You might think that since you can add lemon juice to maintain an acid solution for red vegetables, you should be able to add baking soda to create an alkaline solution for green ones. Not so! If color were the only quality desired, this approach would be fine. However, baking soda has other less desirable effects. It tends to destroy such nutrients as vitamins. It also makes the vegetables mushy and sometimes adds a bitter taste.

Recipe 9-1 BOILED FRESH BEETS

YIELD: ***12 4-oz (100 g) portions***

3 1/2 lb	**AP fresh beets**	**1.5 kg AP**
3 oz	**butter**	**90 g**
	salt and pepper to taste	

1. Wash beets well. Trim stems 2–3 in. (4–6 cm) above beets.
2. Place in boiling salted water to cover.
3. Return to a simmer, cover pot, and simmer until tender (about 30–60 minutes).
4. Drain and rinse in cold water. Peel and cut into uniform slices.
5. Heat in butter and season with salt and pepper.

Per serving:		Carbohydrates:	9 g
Calories:	92	Cholesterol:	16 mg
Fat:	6 g	Fiber:	2 g
Protein:	2 g	Sodium:	131 mg

Recipe 9-2 BRAISED RED CABBAGE

YIELD: ***12 4-oz (125 g) portions***

3 lb	**AP red cabbage**	**1.5 kg AP**
1/2 lb	**onions, small dice**	**250 g**
3 oz	**vegetable oil**	**90 g**
1/2 lb	**apples, peeled, cored, 1/2-in. (1 cm) dice**	**250 g**
2 oz	**sugar**	**60 g**
1/2 C	**red wine**	**125 mL**
1 fl oz	**cider vinegar**	**30 mL**
1 1/2 C	**light stock or water**	**375 mL**
	salt and pepper to taste	

1. Core cabbage and shred coarsely (1/4–1/2 in. or 0.5–1 cm).
2. Sweat onions in oil until translucent.
3. Add remaining ingredients, adding stock or water last. Make sure liquid is about 1 in. (2 cm) below level of cabbage.
4. Cover with parchment paper and simmer until al dente (about 20 minutes).
5. Season to taste. Hold in braising liquid; serve with slotted spoon.

Per serving:		Carbohydrates:	28 g
Calories:	183	Cholesterol:	0 mg
Fat:	8 g	Fiber:	6 g
Protein:	2 g	Sodium:	20 mg

The slightest overcooking will also make green vegetables turn from bright to olive green. This is true not only in boiling but in other cooking methods, too. The dark color of canned green vegetables comes from the prolonged cooking at high temperatures during the canning process.

Green vegetables cooked for only 5 to 7 minutes will usually retain their brilliant natural green. This is another argument for al dente vegetables.

YELLOW AND ORANGE VEGETABLES. The pigments in the yellow vegetable group are called **carotenes.** There are several types, ranging from the yellow of corn to the orange of carrots to the red of tomatoes. Yellow vegetables do not suffer color loss in either acid or alkaline solutions. Some of them can lose color from overcooking, however. You can see this in the tired carrot that has been used in making stock.

WHITE VEGETABLES. The pigments in white vegetables are known as **flavones.** They remain white in acid but turn yellow in an alkaline medium, so a bit of lemon juice or a cover on the pot is in order. Acid tends to toughen vegetables, so keep the amount small.

For white vegetables, too, time is an enemy to quality with all cooking methods. White vegetables turn gray when overcooked and develop an undesirable taste. They should be cooked as quickly as possible and only until barely tender.

FLAVOR

Many flavor-producing substances are lost through evaporation or by being dissolved in the cooking water and then discarded. This means that a boiled vegetable should be cooked as quickly as possible, in as little water as possible, and in a covered pot if color will not be affected. Above all, it should not be overcooked. The longer the cooking, the more flavor goes into the liquid or into the air.

Not only does overcooking produce flavor loss, it often creates flavor change. Some vegetables take on new, undesirable flavors when overcooked. Members of the cabbage family—cabbage, turnips, cauliflower, brussels sprouts, broccoli—will develop a strong acrid taste and unpleasant smell if overcooked, owing to chemical changes. These vegetables will taste best when cooked quickly, with the cover off the pot to allow evaporation of the strong-flavored substances. For the red and white family members, this practice conflicts with covering the pot to maintain an acid solution. A little lemon juice or vinegar or another cooking method may solve this problem.

TEXTURE

Vegetables can be grouped roughly into three textural classes: hard, soft, and starchy. As you discovered in making soup, cooking times vary according to texture. Soft vegetables cook quickly; hard and starchy vegetables take longer.

Textural change is a primary purpose of cooking vegetables, and achievement of good texture is a primary goal. Many vegetables are palatable only if softened by heat and if other tenderizing chemical changes take place. But we want to carry these changes only so far. Good texture for a vegetable is, as you know, **al dente**—firm to the bite, pleasantly crunchy, crisp-tender—which again means do not overcook.

In addition, we want to preserve the vegetable's own texture as much as possible. Remember that an acid cooking medium toughens the vegetable and an alkaline medium softens it.

The degree of firmness desired varies from one vegetable to another. Green beans are firmer than squash. A good boiled potato is firmer than a good baked potato. If a vegetable can be eaten raw, undercook it slightly for the best texture.

We want the vegetable to reach the diner still in that firm but tender textural state, appetizingly hot but without further cooking. This is a challenge, since the vegetable continues to cook while being held for service. For this reason, it is desirable to cook vegetables as close to serving time as possible and in as small quantities as possible, so that they may be replenished frequently with a freshly cooked supply.

Some people do not like al dente vegetables and will leave them uneaten or send them back to the kitchen as "underdone." It is quite possible that they have never eaten any but overcooked vegetables. If a majority of your customers prefer such disasters, you will just have to store what you are learning here in the back of your mind and, as in Rome, do as the Romans do.

NUTRIENTS

Vegetable nutrients can easily be lost in cooking. Many vitamins and minerals are water soluble, some are destroyed in alkaline solutions, and some are heat sensitive and may be destroyed by either high heat or prolonged cooking.

No one cooking method will conserve all the nutrients. In boiling, you lose some that dissolve in the cooking liquid and some that are destroyed by heat. Steaming retains some nutrients better than boiling does, but some nutrients are lost: The shorter cooking time of steaming saves some nutrients, but the higher heat destroys others. Braising uses little liquid and low heat but has a long cooking time. Frying has a short cooking time but high temperatures. Baking unpeeled vegetables retains most nutrients, but the prolonged high heat destroys vitamins that lie close to the skin. So there is no one ideal method.

There are, however, ways to keep nutrient losses to a minimum. The one rule that applies to all methods is: Do not overcook. This cuts down on all types of nutrient loss. A second general rule is to cook as close to serving time as possible. During holding, nutrients continue to disappear through exposure to air, and keeping vegetables hot for service continues to cook them slightly.

Some special rules for boiling will keep nutrient loss for that method at a minimum. One rule is to use no more liquid than necessary—just enough to cover so all pieces cook evenly. There are two exceptions to this rule: You may want to use extra liquid for green vegetables (to retain a vibrant green color) and strong-smelling vegetables (to help them lose some of their strong flavors). Another rule is to keep the liquid slightly acid when cooking red and white vegetables. Also, avoid additives such as baking soda for green color. A fourth rule is to have the liquid boiling before adding the vegetable and simmer the vegetable (boiling is really a bit of a misnomer). A hard boil will cause rapid evaporation and may also break the vegetable pieces, causing additional leaching of nutrients. Most vegetables should be cooked at a simmer until done.

Preparation of raw vegetables can also affect the nutritive value of the cooked product. In many vegetables, the vitamins are near the skin, so as little flesh as possible should be cut away in peeling. Nutrients also leach out of cut surfaces. This means that the larger the cut surface, the greater the nutrient loss in cooking. There are many times, however, when flavor, appearance, cooking time, or the requirements of a garniture will dictate the way a vegetable is cut.

When nutrition conflicts with flavor, appearance, or production needs, the choice will be made according to circumstances and the clientele being served. The hospital may choose nutrition; the continental restaurant may choose flavor and appearance. The goal should be the most of everything for everybody.

Actually, the things that make for good flavor, texture, and appearance tend to be the same things that conserve nutrients. One thing is certain: The nutrients are more likely to be eaten if the vegetable looks and tastes good.

QUALITY STANDARDS

Vegetable quality begins with the arrival of produce in the kitchen. Raw vegetables should be properly stored, refrigerated and covered (Chapter 3), and promptly used. The exceptions to this rule are potatoes, onions, and winter squash. They should be stored in a dry, cool storage area. Exposure to air alters flavor and texture and causes nutrient loss. The same considerations apply to holding vegetables preprepared for cooking.

Prepreparation should be scheduled as close to cooking time as possible. Raw vegetables should be thoroughly cleaned and crisply cut in uniform pieces, not only for even cooking but also for appearance on the diner's plate.

Cooked vegetables should have the same fresh, bright colors they had before they were cooked. Their flavors should be equally fresh; they should make a fresh-from-the-garden impression on the tongue and taste buds.

Most vegetables should be cooked to al dente doneness—pleasantly crunchy, never overcooked. The few that are served soft—sweet and white potatoes, winter squash, eggplant, legumes—should be tender throughout, but not soggy or mushy.

When served, all vegetables should be well drained and arranged attractively on the plate. Remember that they are meant to enhance the foods they are served with and often play the visual role of garnishes. Any seasonings and/or sauces should be appropriate to the vegetable and used lightly.

Vegetables should be chosen for both color and flavor in relation to other menu items—blending, complementing, or contrasting in a pleasing fashion. Though selection may not be the cook's job, if you keep in mind their menu role you will probably do a better job of cooking: You will concentrate on maintaining and enhancing the qualities they were chosen for.

METHODS OF COOKING VEGETABLES

Not all methods of cooking adapt well to all vegetables and not all vegetables adapt well to all methods of cookery. The cook's choice of methods will be those that best suit equipment and production needs and, at the same time, give each vegetable perfection in the customer's eyes.

The most common methods of vegetable cookery are:

- Steaming
- Boiling
- Sautéing
- Pan-frying
- Stir-frying
- Braising
- Baking
- Roasting
- Broiling
- Grilling
- Deep-frying

STEAMING

Steaming is a wonderful method to cook vegetables quickly and, at the same time, retain nutrient and color. To steam, you place the cleaned and prepared vegetables evenly in pans, usually without water. The vegetables should be put in shallow layers. Perforated steam table pans should be used unless you want to retain the cooking liquid (then use solid pans). The cooking is very quick; the higher the pressure, the quicker. It is so quick, in fact, that most vegetables can be steamed in small quantities as needed for service. Some vegetables can be steamed in serving pans, thus requiring less handling than most other methods. Others cook better in perforated pans where the steam can circulate all around them.

Steamed vegetables cook so quickly that it is easy to overcook them, spoiling color, flavor, and texture and causing some nutrient loss. To avoid overcooking, follow the timing charts that apply to your own equipment.

Among vegetables that turn out well when steamed are artichokes, asparagus, broccoli, brussels sprouts, cabbage, carrots, cauliflower, green beans, lima beans, onions, potatoes, rutabagas, summer squash, tomatoes, turnips, and zucchini. Some vegetables don't allow steam to circulate through them as well, so they cook unevenly. These include whole-kernel corn, peas, spinach, and puréed squash.

BOILING

To boil vegetables, add them to a pot of lightly salted boiling liquid (1 tsp salt per gallon). Use just enough liquid to cover the vegetable (Figure 9.1), but you may want to use more liquid for green vegetables and strongly flavored vegetables. Bring it back to a boil as quickly as possible and simmer it to al dente doneness, being careful not to overcook. Cover the pot to speed up cooking, unless you are cooking green vegetables or strong-flavored vegetables. You can add herbs and spices (preferably fresh) for flavor.

Drain the vegetable as soon as cooking is complete. It cannot be held in hot liquid or it will go on cooking. If you avoid overcooking and use the right amount of liquid—no more than necessary—you will produce flavorful, good-looking vegetables.

You can serve plain boiled vegetables garnished or ungarnished; many are eye-pleasing in themselves. Or you can do other things with

Figure 9-1 BOILING A VEGETABLE

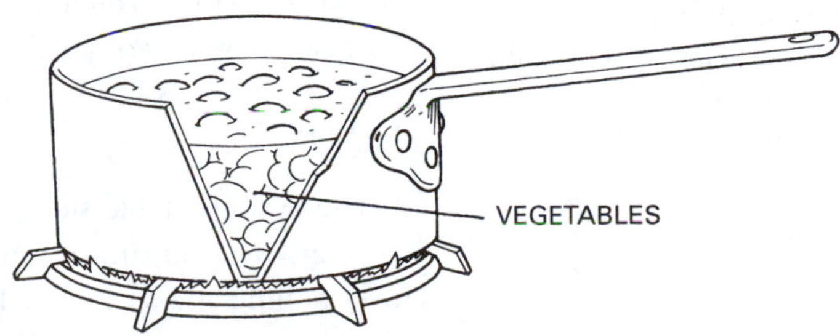

Use only enough hot liquid to cover the vegetable. This minimizes nutrient loss.

them to make them more glamorous. The recipes will give you some ideas.

SAUTÉING, PAN-FRYING, AND STIR-FRYING

Flipping a partially cooked vegetable in a little hot fat in a pan is a tasty way of finish cooking it. Some cooks prefer to steam or boil vegetables, followed by cooling right away under cold water. When needed, they are lightly sautéed, which also reheats them, then served.

The glazed carrot recipe (Recipe 9.3) illustrates another use of sautéing. The butter and sugar plus the high heat of sautéing add a shiny coat of glaze to the vegetable. You can use the same recipe to prepare turnips, pearl onions, or parsnips. Recipe 9.4 uses sautéing to combine two vegetables having different cooking times.

Recipe 9-3 GLAZED CARROTS

YIELD: ***12 3-oz (100 g) portions***

3 lb	**AP carrots**	**1.5 kg AP**
2 oz	**butter**	**60 g**
1 oz	**sugar**	**30 g**
	salt and white pepper to taste	
1 oz	**chopped parsley**	**30 g**

1. Wash, peel, and trim carrots. Cut into uniform pieces—$^1/_8$-in. (3 mm) diagonal slices.
2. Add to boiling water. Cook at a low boil until al dente. Drain.
3. Melt butter in a sauté pan. Add carrots; sprinkle with sugar, salt, and pepper. Sauté until carrots are lightly golden and glazed.
4. Adjust salt and pepper to taste. At service time, garnish with parsley.

Per serving:		Carbohydrates:	14 g
Calories:	92	Cholesterol:	10 mg
Fat:	4 g	Fiber:	3 g
Protein:	1 g	Sodium:	79 mg

Recipe 9-4 SAUTÉED SUMMER SQUASH AND TOMATOES

YIELD: ***12 4-oz (125 g) portions***

3 lb	**AP yellow squash or zucchini**	**1.5 kg AP**
2 oz	**butter**	**60 g**
$^1/_2$ lb	**tomatoes, canned, drained, diced, or fresh peeled, seeded, chopped**	**250 g**
	salt and white pepper to taste	

1. Wash squash, trim ends, and cut into 3/8-in. (8 mm) diagonal slices.
2. Melt butter in a sauté pan. Sauté squash until half cooked.
3. Add tomatoes and continue sautéing until both vegetables are al dente.
4. Season to taste with salt and pepper.

Per serving:		Carbohydrates:	9 g
Calories:	54	Cholesterol:	10 mg
Fat:	4 g	Fiber:	2 g
Protein:	2 g	Sodium:	102 mg

Sautéing, pan-frying, and stir-frying are very similar, yet each has its differences. Whereas sautéing is done quickly in a small amount of fat, pan-frying uses more fat and generally takes longer (the heat is also lower). Stir-frying is just like sautéing except that instead of moving the pan to stir the food, you use utensils. When pan-frying, you don't have to stir the food constantly, you simply turn the vegetables over at least once during cooking. Whichever method you choose, you can cook raw or partially cooked vegetables.

BRAISING

Cooking a vegetable slowly, covered, in a small amount of liquid affords some distinct advantages over boiling and steaming. The flavorful juices of the vegetable are not lost; the liquid remaining when it is done (if any) can be reduced or thickened and served with the vegetable. Braising is often done in the oven, with the vegetable covered and with stock, water, wine, or any combination as the liquid. The vegetable may first be cooked in fat before the liquid is added. Particularly suitable for braising are brussels sprouts, cabbage, celery, leeks, endive, fennel, lettuce, mushrooms, onions, potatoes, summer squash, and zucchini.

Braised vegetables typically have added ingredients, as in Recipe 9.2. Like this red cabbage dish, they often begin with flavor builders sweated or sautéed in fat.

BAKING AND ROASTING

Such vegetables as winter squash, potatoes, eggplant, onions, and tomatoes, which can be cooked in their skins, adapt very well to cooking by dry heat in an oven. Baking retains more vitamins and minerals than most cooking methods. Several of these vegetables are high in starch, and the dry heat of the oven gives them a suitable texture.

Two baked tomato dishes are given in Recipes 9.5 and 9.5a. Winter squash can be baked in cut halves, buttered, and flavored with ingredients usually associated with the bakeshop—cinnamon, nutmeg, and brown sugar (Recipe 9.6). Baked potatoes will be discussed in detail shortly.

Baking is also used to make vegetable casseroles. A casserole is a dish in which one or more cooked foods are combined with a sauce and heated together in the oven. Usually, the dish is covered with bread crumbs and butter and sometimes cheese, and the topping is lightly browned in the salamander or under the broiler. This is known as **gratinéing,** and the dish is said to be **au gratin.**

Such a dish can be made in individual casseroles or it can be baked in hotel pans and cut into portions for serving. Recipe 9.7 is a master recipe for many different kinds of vegetable casseroles. You can substitute broccoli, brussels sprouts, celery, leeks, or cooked diced potatoes, omitting the lemon juice in all cases. Be sure the vegetables are thoroughly drained so that the cooking liquid will not dilute the sauce. A casserole is one way of avoiding some of the problems of holding vegetables for service.

Roasted vegetables are cooked in the oven as are baked vegetables. The difference between roasted and baked vegetables lies in the kinds of

Recipe 9-5 TOMATOES CLAMART

YIELD: ***12 portions (1 half tomato each)***

6	**whole fresh tomatoes**	
	oil as needed	
12 oz	**cooked peas, seasoned**	**375 g**
4 oz	**bread crumbs**	**125 g**
2 oz	**melted butter**	**60 g**

1. Wash tomatoes.
2. Core tomato stems. Cut tomatoes in half crosswise and scoop out pulp and seeds, leaving outer flesh intact.
3. Place halves cut side up on lightly oiled baking sheet.
4. Fill with peas; top with bread crumbs; drizzle with melted butter.
5. Bake at 350°F (180°C) until tomatoes are heated through and bread crumbs are golden.

Per serving:		Carbohydrates:	12 g
Calories:	94	Cholesterol:	10 mg
Fat:	4 g	Fiber:	2 g
Protein:	3 g	Sodium:	120 mg

Recipe 9-5a TOMATOES FORESTIÉRE

In Recipe 9-5, make the following change:

Replace peas with 6 oz (175 g) mushrooms, sliced, sautéed, in Step 4.

Recipe 9-6 BAKED WINTER SQUASH

YIELD: ***4 servings***

1	**large acorn or small butternut squash**	
1 Tb	**margarine or butter**	**15 mL**
3 Tb	**brown sugar**	**45 mL**
1/4 tsp	**cinnamon or nutmeg**	**1 mL**

1. Cut squash in half lengthwise. Remove seeds. Place in a baking pan.
2. In a sauté pan, melt margarine or butter over moderately low heat. Add brown sugar and cinnamon or nutmeg.
3. Pour sauce into cavity of each squash. Cover and bake at 350°F (175°C) for 45–60 minutes, or until tender.

Per serving:		Carbohydrates:	5 g
Calories:	28	Cholesterol:	0 mg
Fat:	1 g	Fiber:	1 g
Protein:	0 g	Sodium:	13 mg

Recipe 9-7 CAULIFLOWER AU GRATIN

YIELD: ***12 4-oz (125 g) portions***

3 lb	**cauliflower florets**	**1.4 kg**
3 C	**mornay sauce**	**750 mL**
1 oz	**bread crumbs**	**30 g**
1 oz	**melted butter**	**30 g**

1. Wash cauliflower.
2. Cook cauliflower in boiling water with lemon juice until barely tender. Drain well.
3. Place in buttered hotel pan or individual casseroles and cover with sauce.
4. Sprinkle with bread crumbs and melted butter.
5. Bake in 350°F (180°C) oven until thoroughly heated (about 15–20 minutes).
6. Place under salamander or broiler until top is lightly browned.

Per serving:		Carbohydrates:	12 g
Calories:	173	Cholesterol:	25 mg
Fat:	12 g	Fiber:	2 g
Protein:	7 g	Sodium:	343 mg

Recipe 9-8 ROASTED VEGETABLES

YIELD: ***8 servings***

2 C	**carrots, thickly sliced**	**500 mL**
2 C	**parsnips, thickly sliced**	**500 mL**
2 C	**rutabagas, peeled, cut in half, and thinly sliced**	**500 mL**
2 C	**sweet potatoes, peeled, cut in half, and thickly sliced**	**500 mL**
1 C	**turnips, peeled and cut into medium rounds**	**250 mL**
1 C	**onions, cut into wedges**	**250 mL**
1/4 C	**olive oil**	**60 mL**
	salt, garlic powder, and fresh ground pepper to taste	

1. Place the prepared vegetables in a bowl and toss with olive oil and seasonings.
2. Transfer to a roasting pan.
3. Cook at 400°F (200°C) for 1 hour, tossing every 15 minutes. Vegetables are done when tender. If not tender enough after 1 hour, allow another 15 minutes' cooking time.

Per serving:		Carbohydrates:	24 g
Calories:	161	Cholesterol:	0 mg
Fat:	7 g	Fiber:	5 g
Protein:	2 g	Sodium:	34 mg

vegetables used and the amount of time in the oven. Onions and root vegetables are frequently roasted (see Recipe 9.8). First, they are oiled or buttered, then roasted in the oven until the exterior of the vegetable browns and caramelizes. Roasted vegetables, such as onions, have a sweet, complex taste. Roasting does not work as well for other vegetables, such as most green vegetables, because the heat would destroy their color.

BROILING AND GRILLING

Some quick-cooking vegetables can be completely cooked by either broiling or grilling.

These vegetables include eggplant, mushrooms, onions, tomatoes, peppers, and zucchini. To broil or grill them, slice the vegetables (not thinly), brush or drizzle with melted butter or olive oil, and cook until lightly browned. Many other vegetables can be partially cooked using another cooking method, then browned for a minute or two under the broiler.

Recipe 9.9 is an example of broiled tomatoes, a delicious and handsome addition to a plate. If you add 4 oz (125 g) Parmesan cheese to the mixture in Step 4, you will be making Parmesan broiled tomatoes.

Recipe 9-9 BROILED TOMATOES PROVENÇALE

YIELD: ***12 portions (1 half tomato each)***

6	**whole fresh tomatoes**	
	oil as needed	
	salt and pepper to taste	
6 oz	**bread crumbs**	**175 g**
1	**garlic clove, puréed**	
1 Tb	**minced parsley**	**15 mL**
1 tsp	**basil or oregano**	**5 mL**
1/4 tsp	**thyme**	**1 mL**
2 oz	**melted butter**	**60 g**

1. Wash tomatoes.
2. Core stems from tomatoes. Cut in half crosswise and squeeze out seeds.
3. Place on lightly oiled baking sheet. Season with salt and pepper.
4. Mix bread crumbs, garlic clove, minced parsley, basil or oregano, thyme, and melted butter to make the topping.
5. Press a thin layer of topping to cover top of each tomato half.
6. Bake in 350°F (180°C) oven until heated through (about 5–10 minutes).
7. Place briefly under salamander until topping is lightly golden.

Per serving:		Carbohydrates:	10 g
Calories:	85	Cholesterol:	10 mg
Fat:	5 g	Fiber:	1 g
Protein:	2 g	Sodium:	121 mg

DEEP-FRYING

Most vegetables that are deep-fried are breaded or battered first; the potato is an exception. Most vegetables can be breaded or battered and fried. Quick-cooking vegetables (such as onion rings, mushrooms, peppers, and zucchini) do not need to be precooked before frying. Other vegetables (such as broccoli, carrots, cauliflower, and green beans) need to be precooked before deep-frying. Vegetables that are too small to be individually breaded or battered can be mixed with a batter and dropped by spoonfuls in the fryer. This type of product is called a **fritter.**

Cooking in the deep fryer is simplicity itself if you follow these rules:

- Cut uniform pieces for even cooking.
- Partially cook hard vegetables.
- Bread carefully for a complete, even coat with no loose crumbs. Season before breading or after removing from the fryer. Do not season uncoated foods; the salt will break down the fat.
- Be sure the fat is at the right temperature before immersing the food. If the temperature is too low, the food will absorb too much fat. If it is too high, the food may be overbrowned on the outside and undercooked on the inside. Vegetables cook well at 350°F (177°C).
- Do not overload the fryer. Fill baskets only one-half to two-thirds full. Overloading will cool the fat, prolong the cooking, and produce greasy foods. Partly filled baskets allow you to shake the food occasionally to keep the pieces from sticking together.

- When the food is golden brown, lift the basket out of the fat and drain a minute or so over the kettle. Drain further on absorbent material if necessary.
- Serve immediately.

These rules apply equally well to deep-frying of all foods.

Fried eggplant (Recipe 9.10) provides the contrast of soft and crunchy textures in one flavorful dish. You can substitute zucchini batonnets, small whole mushrooms, onion rings, or cauliflower florets. Recipe 9.10a shows the versatility of a deep-fried vegetable: You can put it together with other ingredients to create a variety of dishes. This eggplant Parmesan recipe is an easy way of preparing this popular vegetable dish, often used as a vegetarian entrée.

Recipe 9-10 FRIED EGGPLANT

YIELD: ***12 4-oz. (125 g) portions***

$3^1/_4$ lb	**eggplant**	**1.6 kg**

Breading:

3 oz	**flour**	**90 g**
$^1/_2$ tsp	**salt**	**2 mL**
$^1/_4$ tsp	**white pepper**	**1 mL**
1 C	**egg wash**	**250 mL**
$^1/_2$ lb	**bread crumbs**	**250 g**
	oil for frying (as needed)	

1. Wash eggplant; cut crosswise into $^1/_4$-in. (5 mm) round slices or French fry cuts. Hold in ice water.
2. Drain the eggplant and pat dry with towels.
3. Set up 3 pans for breading: flour with salt and pepper, egg wash, and bread crumbs. Bread.
4. Pan-fry the eggplant in $^1/_4$ in. (5 mm) oil in a heavy skillet or sauté pan until browned on both sides. Or deep-fry at 350°F (180°C) until golden brown and tender. Drain well on absorbent paper.

Per serving:		Carbohydrates:	22 g
Calories:	245	Cholesterol:	53 mg
Fat:	16 g	Fiber:	3 g
Protein:	5 g	Sodium:	218 mg

Recipe 9-10a EGGPLANT PARMESAN

To finished eggplant, add:

3 C	**tomato sauce**	**750 mL**
4 oz	**Parmesan cheese, grated**	**125 g**
8 oz	**mozzarella cheese, grated**	**250 g**

1. Spread a $^1/_4$-in. (5 mm) layer of tomato sauce in a hotel pan or individual casseroles.
2. Place a layer of eggplant on sauce; then add another layer of sauce. Sprinkle with a layer of Parmesan and mozzarella cheeses.
3. Continue layering, ending with sauce and cheeses.
4. Bake in 350°F (180°C) oven until thoroughly heated and cheese is melted (about 15–25 minutes).

Per serving:		Carbohydrates:	27 g
Calories:	359	Cholesterol:	75 mg
Fat:	23 g	Fiber:	4 g
Protein:	13 g	Sodium:	834 mg

SEASONING, FLAVORING, AND VEGETABLE VERSATILITY

If seasonings have not been added during cooking, season to taste before service. If seasonings have been added, check and adjust before serving. Don't forget fresh lemon or vinegar as a seasoning, but don't add this acid to a green vegetable during cooking.

When you add flavors to vegetables, compatibility is important. Table 9.2 suggests flavors that go well with specific vegetables. It is by no

Table 9-2 FLAVORINGS AND COMBINATIONS FOR VEGETABLES

Food	*Flavoring and Combinations*
Asparagus	Lemon juice, mustard sauce, mushrooms
Broccoli	Lemon, orange, nutmeg, ginger, garlic powder, sesame seeds, almonds, shallots
Green beans	Dill, basil, garlic, tarragon, caraway seeds, sesame seeds, mushrooms, celery, onions, shallots, garlic, almonds
Lima beans	Oregano, thyme, corn, onion, mushroom
Brussel sprouts	Dill, cheese
Cabbage	Caraway seed, dill, mustard seed, tarragon, curry powder, celery seeds with dill, nutmeg, carrots, onion
Carrots	Cinnamon, nutmeg, ginger, brown sugar, mint, orange, brown sugar, dill, tarragon, peas, celery
Cauliflower	Dill, nutmeg, mustard seeds, curry powder, peas, Parmesan cheese
Corn	Chili powder, cumin, dill, onion, sweet or hot peppers, cheese, lima beans
Cucumber	Garlic, dill, tarragon, mint
Eggplant	Oregano, garlic, tomato, Parmesan cheese
Mushrooms	Dill, nutmeg, lemon, peas, spinach, green beans
Peas	Rosemary, sage, mint, basil, dill, carrots, potatoes, water chestnuts
Potatoes	Dill, onion, parsley, caraway, nutmeg, chives
Spinach	Garlic, nutmeg, mushrooms
Squash, summer	Mint, tarragon, basil, oregano, garlic, cinnamon, tomatoes, carrots, onions, Parmesan cheese
Squash, winter	Cinnamon, nutmeg, brown sugar, allspice, orange, apples
Sweet potatoes	Cinnamon, clove, brown sugar, nutmeg, orange, apples, shallots
Tomatoes	Basil, bay leaf, garlic, rosemary, tarragon, bell peppers

means a complete list, but it includes many combinations that are generally well liked.

Remember, when adding flavorings, that they should never drown out the vegetable's own taste but should simply provide an interesting accent. Remember, too, that dried herbs and spices should be cooked with the product, not sprinkled on like seasonings at the end. Fresh herbs, on the other hand, should be added near the end of cooking for their distinctive tastes.

Certain vegetables may be combined with others for variety and interest. Mushrooms go well with beans, peas, or squash. Tiny whole onions also go well with these vegetables. Lima beans and corn are served together as succotash. Carrots and peas are often partners. The vegetables should be cooked separately and mixed near the end of cooking.

Combining vegetables often involves more than one cooking method, as when boiled or steamed vegetables are finished by sautéing. Recipe 9.11 follows parboiling with sweating in butter to combine three vegetables in an interesting mix of flavors. You can vary the flavor mix by substituting mint or chervil for lettuce.

Sauces, dressings, and garnitures are other methods of adding variety and attractiveness to vegetables, as you have seen in a number of recipes. Hollandaise is often served with asparagus, cauliflower, or broccoli. Spinach, peas, and

Recipe 9-11 PEAS FRANÇAISE (FRENCH GREEN PEAS)

YIELD: ***12 4-oz (125 g) portions***

4 oz	pearl onions	120 g
8 oz	lettuce, shredded	250 g
2 oz	butter	60 g
$2^1/_2$ lb	frozen or parboiled fresh green peas	1 kg
$^1/_2$ Tb	sugar	7 mL
	salt and white pepper to taste	

1. In a sauté pan, sweat onions and lettuce in butter until onions are translucent.
2. Stir in peas and sugar and cook until peas are al dente.
3. Season with salt and white pepper to taste.

Per serving:		Carbohydrates:	15 g
Calories:	115	Cholesterol:	10 mg
Fat:	4 g	Fiber:	6 g
Protein:	5 g	Sodium:	123 mg

green beans are enhanced by cream sauce or a hot vinaigrette sauce of vinegar, oil, and spices. Garnitures of minced hard-cooked egg, grated cheese, sliced almonds, or pimientos are often added to various vegetables. A dollop of sour cream is a standard garniture for baked potato, often topped with chopped chives or crisp crumbled bacon. Sour cream is also good with beets and spinach.

HOLDING AND PRODUCTION PROBLEMS

Whatever the vegetable, market form, cooking method, or dish, the cook faces problems in getting vegetables onto the diner's plate at their peak of goodness. At holding temperatures, the vegetables go on cooking. Within a very short time—20 minutes to half an hour—most of them change flavor, lose their bright, attractive colors, become mushy, and lose nutrients. If the cook prepares a large amount at once, all but the first few portions will be overcooked before they can be dished out.

BATCH COOKING

In many production situations, the problems can be solved by **batch cooking,** also called **stagger cooking,** fresh or frozen vegetables in small quantities as needed, using quick-cooking methods such as steaming under pressure or microwaving. Whereas steaming a full pan of vegetables every 15 minutes may work in a hospital kitchen that serves 300 meals in an hour, a restaurant may microwave single portions as needed. In this way, production stays just ahead of service.

PARTIAL COOKING

This method of vegetable preparation was widely practiced in large-volume operations until the pressure steamer came along and speeded up vegetable cooking. With this method, vegetables in large quantities are precooked to 50 to 75 percent of doneness. They are then quick-chilled with ice, either by plunging them into ice water or by plunging ice into the cooking pot. The icy bath must lower the temperature to below 40°F (4°C) within several minutes. This stops the cooking, preserves the color and texture, and allows the vegetables to be held in the cooler for two or three days. They can be finish-cooked quickly when and where they are needed for service, using any desired cooking method. Often, they are finished by sautéing or microwaving. Flavoring and seasoning can be added at this time.

This method of production spreads the use of cooks and equipment efficiently over the time available. It puts any vegetable within minutes of doneness so that the finish cooking can be staggered as needed without dependence on one type of equipment. Or thousands of portions can be preprepared at one central location and distributed to several kitchens for finish cooking and service.

This two-step method allows vegetables to be stored at a stage of doneness in which color and texture are intact, instead of held for service at a doneness that deteriorates rapidly to unacceptability. Wherever and however they are finish-cooked, the cook has control of that last critical percentage of the cooking process. You can send to the table vegetables that are fresh in color, al dente in texture, and full of flavor because they are freshly done in spite of the large quantities required.

Not all vegetables are suitable for partial cooking. The hard vegetables are the ones for which it is most useful. Soft vegetables reach doneness so quickly it would be a waste of time to precook them. They should simply be batch-cooked as needed. Most starchy vegetables should be cooked without interruption until done, even though they do not cook quickly. The potato is an exception; it can often be treated as a hard vegetable.

THE POTATO

Americans are often said to be meat-and-potato eaters, and the reputation is well founded. Potatoes are served three times a day in this country in all forms. Most cooks learn more ways to cook potatoes than any other vegetable.

Potatoes adapt to more styles of cooking than any other vegetable. They are baked, fried, pan-fried, boiled, braised, steamed, sautéed, mashed, and hashed. Successful cooking depends in part on choosing the right potato for the cooking method.

The many varieties of potato divide into waxy types and nonwaxy or mealy types. **Mealy** (or **starchy**) **potatoes** are high in starch and low in sugar. They are best for French-fried, mashed, and baked potatoes, as well as for potato-thickened soups. You can purchase two types of starchy potatoes: the attractive, long *russet* or *Idaho potato,* which is used almost exclusively for baking; and the *all-purpose* or *chef potato,* which has an irregular shape. The all-purpose potato is less expensive than the russet and tends to be used to make puréed or mashed potatoes.

Waxy potatoes, also called **new potatoes,** are high in sugar and low in starch. They are better for dishes requiring a firm potato that will hold its shape when cooked, such as stews, boiled potatoes, pan-fried potatoes, and potato salad.

Storage temperatures can alter the starch/sugar ratio over a period of time. Potatoes kept under refrigeration will increase in sugar in relation to starch. Potatoes kept at room temperature will undergo the opposite change. Optimum storage temperature for stability is about 60°F (16°C). Most operations use potatoes heavily and buy frequently, so starch and sugar changes are seldom a problem.

Potatoes have more nutrients than they are generally given credit for. In addition to starch and sugar, they contain appreciable amounts of vitamin C, many B vitamins, and many minerals. Many people think of potatoes as fattening, but they have far fewer calories than imagined. It is the foods (usually fats) we add to them and the fat we fry them in that add the calories.

A quick glance at a culinary dictionary shows hundreds of recipes for potatoes. Yet beneath the variety is simplicity. Most of them are cooked by everyday cooking methods but they are often specially cut or shaped or breaded or dressed and given a special name. The cooking methods for potatoes are basically the same as for other vegetables, with a little twist here and there, and with certain methods more commonly used than others.

BOILING AND STEAMING

Boiled or steamed potatoes can be served as is, but are generally seasoned and/or flavored with a variety of ingredients, such as butter and parsley, before serving. They are boiled or steamed just like other vegetables, except that boiled potatoes are started in cold water (for more even cooking), but never cooled off in cold water (it makes them soggy).

Boiled or steamed potatoes are the basis for making potato purée, which can, in turn, be used to make mashed or whipped potatoes, duchesse potatoes, and potato croquettes. To make potato purée, boil or steam starchy potatoes to doneness. Make sure they are well drained before using a food mill or mixer to purée.

For traditional mashed potatoes, beat the potato purée in the mixer with butter, light cream, milk, salt, and pepper. The butter and cream should be added only after all lumps have disappeared.

Recipe 9-12 MASHED POTATOES

YIELD: ***8 servings***

	salt as needed	
2 lb	**potatoes, peeled and quartered**	**900 g**
$^1/_3$–$^1/_2$ C	**milk**	**85–125 mL**
$^1/_4$ C	**margarine or butter**	**60 mL**
	salt and pepper to taste	

1. Boil salted water (1/2 tsp or 2 mL salt to 1 C or 250 mL water).
2. Add potatoes and cook until tender, about 20 to 25 minutes. Drain.
3. Leave potatoes in pan over low heat to dry them out.
4. Mash potatoes until no lumps remain. Beat in milk in small amounts. Add margarine or butter, salt, and pepper. Beat vigorously until potatoes are light and fluffy.

Per serving:		Carbohydrates:	15 g
Calories:	124	Cholesterol:	2 mg
Fat:	6 g	Fiber:	2 g
Protein:	3 g	Sodium:	75 mg

Recipe 9-13 DUCHESSE POTATOES

YIELD: ***25 3-oz (100 g) portions***

5 lb	**peeled potatoes, chopped**	**2.5 kg**
3 oz	**melted butter**	**50 g**
	nutmeg, salt, and white pepper to taste	
6	**egg yolks**	

1. Simmer potatoes until tender in lightly salted water to cover.
2. Drain and put back on low heat to dry, stirring constantly to avoid burning, or dry in low-heat oven, stirring frequently.
3. Purée potatoes and blend in melted butter.
4. Flavor with nutmeg and season with salt and pepper to taste.
5. Beat in egg yolks all at once.
6. Fill plain-tipped pastry bag with mixture. Pipe out desired shapes onto sheet pans.
7. Just prior to service, place in hot oven until lightly browned.

Per serving:		Carbohydrates:	18 g
Calories:	118	Cholesterol:	58 mg
Fat:	4 g	Fiber:	2 g
Protein:	2 g	Sodium:	33 mg

Figure 9-2 THE VERSATILE MASHED POTATO

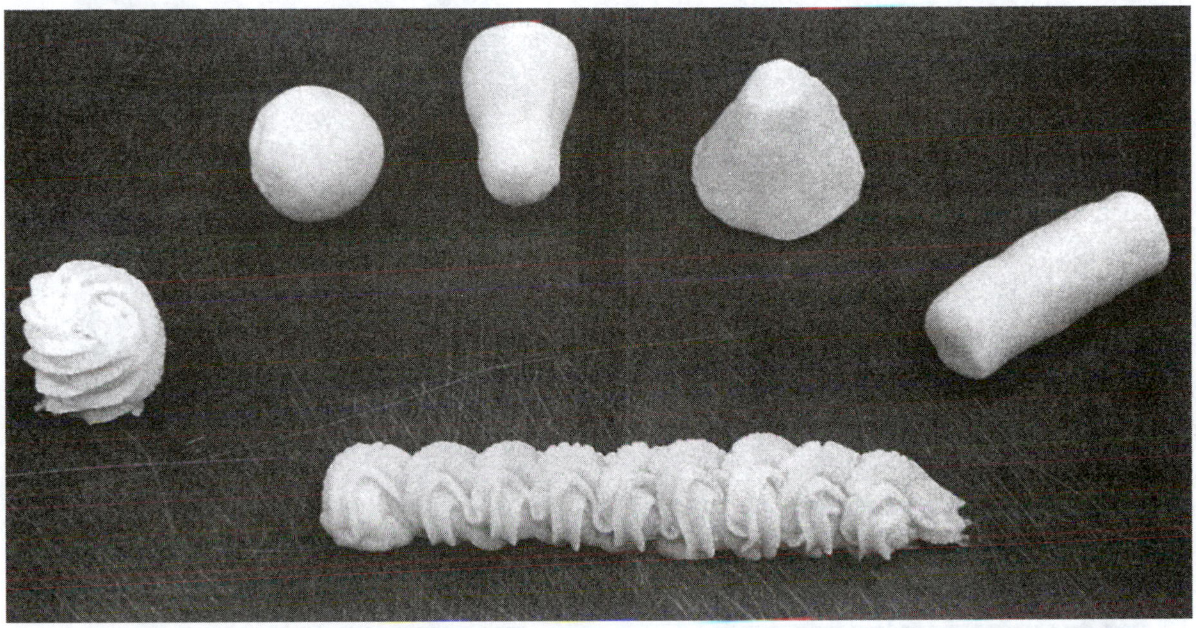

On the left is a duchesse potato. Next are a potato berny and a potato William ready for breading. The two on the right are croquettes, also ready for breading. Down center stage is a potato border. All came from the pastry bag.

The croquettes and the berny and William potatoes are chilled and then smoothed by hand. After breading, they will be deep-fried. The duchesse potato and the border will be glazed in the salamander. (Photo by David Mizer.)

Good mashed potatoes, whether made from scratch (see Recipe 9.12) or convenience products, are smooth, free from lumps, fluffy, and mealy. Plain mashed potatoes are moist and thick enough to hold their shape but not so thick that they break apart in chunks. In color, they are creamy white with no hint of gray.

Many establishments use instant mashed potatoes to save the time and cost of preparation. To prepare, follow the instructions on the package. Sometimes, prepared instant potatoes are blended with mashed potatoes made from scratch for volume serving, as for banquets when a great quantity is needed at once.

Potato purée, when mixed with egg yolks and butter, becomes a versatile potato mixture called **duchesse potatoes** (Recipe 9.13). The duchesse mixture is piped through a pastry bag to make the shape called for in a particular dish—round, pyramid, cork-shaped, pear-shaped, crescent, whatever. Figure 9.2 illustrates some of these shapes. Figure 9.3 shows you how to use a pastry bag. Recipes 9.13a and 9.13b show how to use duchesse potatoes to make such classical potato dishes as dauphine potatoes (Recipe 9.13a) and potato croquettes (Recipe 9.13b), which are both deep-fried.

DEEP-FRYING

Made-from-scratch French fries (Recipe 9.14) are prepared by a two-step process, following the gen-

Figure 9-3 HOW TO USE THE PASTRY BAG

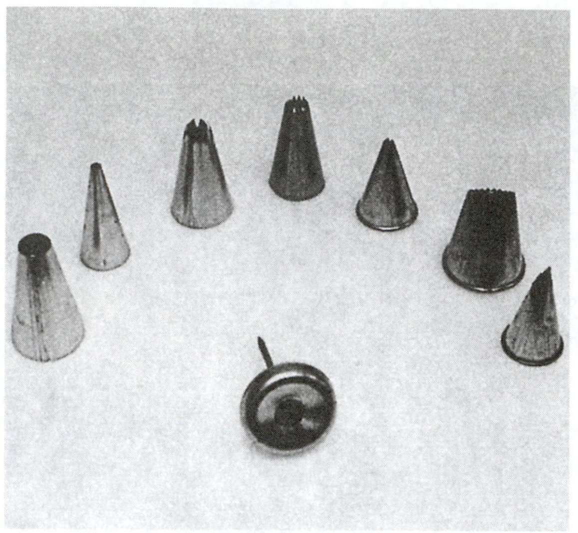

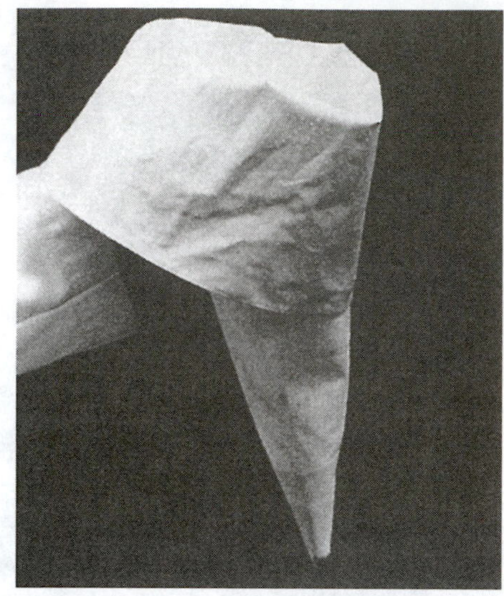

a. The pastry bag is a plastic or canvas funnel used to force a soft mass of food into decorative shapes through a pastry tube, or tip, fitted into its small end. An assortment of tubes with different openings make different patterns as the food is forced through.

b. Here is the bag itself, fitted with a tip and ready to be filled. About a third of the top is folded over into a collar. One hand, under the collar, holds the bag open for filling.

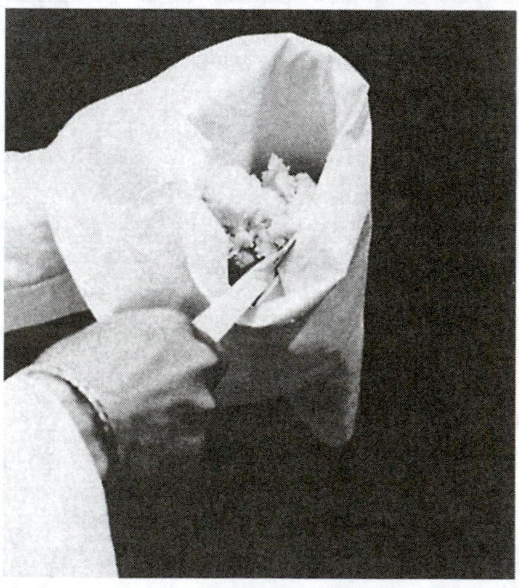

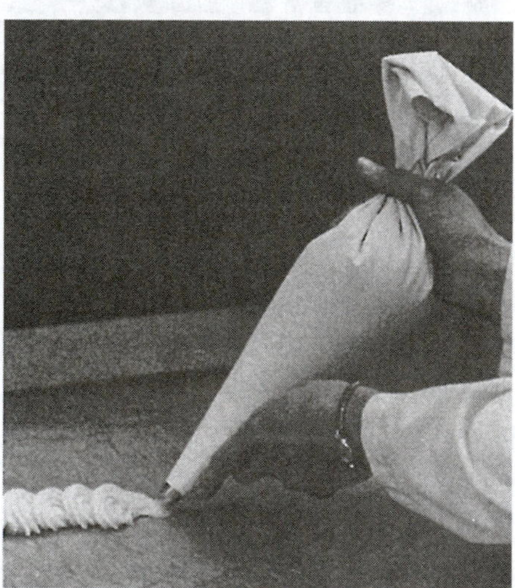

c. The other hand fills the bag, pushing the food down to make a continuous mass with no air pockets. (Fill only enough to handle easily—about one-third full for beginners.) The collar is then turned up, the food is given a final firming down from the outside, and the bag is grasped firmly at the top of the food mass.

d. Here is the bag in action. One hand squeezes the bag down from the top while the other guides the movement of the tip and steadies it. A good product comes from good coordination of pressure and movement. The two hands must work together. The whole process is called piping.

The third and fourth shapes in Figure 9-2 were made by pyramiding the potatoes and shaping by hand. The second and fifth shapes are also hand-finished. The duchesse potato and the border are just as they came from the bag. (Photos by Patricia Roberts.)

Recipe 9-13a DAUPHINE POTATOES

Yield: ***10 portions (2–3 pieces each)***

2/3 lb	**pâte à choux**	**325 g**
2 lb	**duchesse mixture**	**1 kg**

1. Fold pâté à choux into potatoes until thoroughly blended.
2. Fill plain-tipped pastry bag with mixture.
3. Hold over 350°F (180°C) deep fat. Force out potatoes, cutting 2-in. (5 cm) lengths with a knife and letting them drop into fryer.
4. Fry until golden. Drain on absorbent paper.

Per serving:		Carbohydrates:	16 g
Calories:	149	Cholesterol:	96 mg
Fat:	8 g	Fiber:	1 g
Protein:	2 g	Sodium:	103 mg

Recipe 9-13b POTATO CROQUETTES

Yield: ***25 portions (2–3 pieces each)***

5 lb	**duchesse potato mixture**	**2.5 kg**

Breading:

6 oz	**flour**	**175 g**
1 tsp	**salt**	**5 mL**
1/2 tsp	**white pepper**	**2 mL**
2 C	**egg wash**	**500 mL**
1 lb	**bread crumbs**	**450 g**

1. Using plain-tipped pastry bag, pipe long strips of duchesse mixture on sheet pans dusted with flour.
2. Cut strips into 2-in. (5 cm) lengths. Chill.
3. Set up 3 pans for breading: flour with salt and pepper, egg wash, and bread crumbs.
4. Bread strips.
5. Deep-fry at 350°F (180°C) until golden brown. Drain on absorbent paper.

Per serving:		Carbohydrates:	33 g
Calories:	191	Cholesterol:	59 mg
Fat:	5 g	Fiber:	2 g
Protein:	5 g	Sodium:	131 mg

Recipe 9-14 FRENCH FRIES

Yield: ***15 4-oz (150 g) portions***

10 lb	**AP potatoes**	**4.5 kg AP**
	salt to taste	

1. Wash and peel potatoes.
2. Cut into strips 3/8 in. × 3/8 in. × 4 in. (8 mm × 8 mm × 10 cm) or cut julienne for alumette (shoestring) potatoes.
3. Deep-fry at 325°F (180°C) until nearly tender. Drain on absorbent paper and refrigerate.
4. At service time, finish deep-frying at 350°F (180°C) until golden brown. Drain, salt, and serve immediately.

Per serving:		Carbohydrates:	36 g
Calories:	280	Cholesterol:	0 mg
Fat:	14 g	Fiber:	2 g
Protein:	4 g	Sodium:	191 mg

eral rule for deep-frying of hard vegetables. You partially cook or blanch them first (at a lower-than-normal frying temperature), cool them, and then finish-cook them in the deep fryer in small quantities as needed. This allows them to cook slowly and cook through. If the fat is too hot, the outside of the potato will brown before the middle gets hot enough to cook. French fries are not salted until cooking is complete, since they are not breaded and the salt would break down the fat.

A variation on the basic French fry will produce a crisp home-style potato chip (Recipe 9.15). Cut the potatoes on the slicer, then soak the slices in ice water to firm them and to remove some of the starch so they will crisp better when they cook. The cold water also keeps them white while being held. Notice that you cook these French fries only once. These chips will retain their texture better than other types of French fries.

Recipe 9-15 HOME-STYLE POTATO CHIPS

Yield ***15 4-oz (150 g) portions***

10 lb	**AP potatoes**	**4.5 kg AP**
	salt to taste	

1. Wash and peel potatoes.
2. Slice potatoes crosswise 1/8–1/16 in. (2–3 mm) thick (paper thin).
3. Cover with ice water for 30 minutes. Drain and dry thoroughly.
4. Deep-fry at 350°F (180°C). Drain, salt, and serve immediately.

Per serving:		Carbohydrates:	36 g
Calories:	309	Cholesterol:	0 mg
Fat:	17 g	Fiber:	2 g
Protein:	4 g	Sodium:	268 mg

Most kitchens do not make French fries or potato chips from scratch. Instead, they purchase frozen French fries in a variety of shapes and sizes (see Figure 9.4). Frozen fries are partially cooked, like other frozen vegetables, and are simply given the second half of the two-step treatment before service.

Whether made from scatch or from frozen, a good French fry is golden brown, cooked through, nongreasy, crisp on the outside, mealy tender on the inside, and hot when served. It holds poorly, becoming moist soggy on the inside while the outside becomes shriveled and dull.

As mentioned, duchesse potatoes and potato croquettes complete their cooking in the deep-fat fryer. Deep-fried duchesse potatoes or croquettes are golden brown and crisp on the outside with a soft yellow–white center. A duchesse mixture may be piped as a decorative border to an individual entrée or presentation platter and glazed under the broiler. In this form, it has a light-brown glossy crust atop a soft-textured interior.

BAKING

The baked potato (Recipe 9.16) is a truly American dish. A good baked potato is fluffy, white, and mealy, almost dry. To produce such potatoes, you rub the scrubbed, dry skins with oil (unless you want the skin to be more tender) and pierce the ends with a fork or snip them off altogether. Piercing or snipping the ends allows the potatoes to let off steam. You then bake them in a hot (400°F/200°C) oven until they are cooked through.

Holding baked potatoes is a problem. They take so long to cook that batch cooking is not often practical, and any baked potato will deteriorate: It loses its fluffy mealiness and becomes moist and soggy, and its white color turns to yellow, gray, and even black. An hour of holding should be the limit.

Some operations solve the holding problem with the microwave. Potatoes are oven-baked to three-fourths of doneness and then refrigerated. Cooking is completed as needed in small quantities in the microwave in a matter of minutes.

Some cooks like to wrap their potatoes in foil before baking. Potatoes baked in foil tend to be moist and soggy because they are steamed in their own moisture. Some people think that a foil-wrapped baked potato looks more attractive on the plate than the bumpy, eye-pocked skin of the vegetable itself. However, many diners prefer a nicely browned skin and baked interior to a plate of aluminum foil.

Recipe 9.16a offers a delicious way of dressing up the plain baked potato.

Figure 9-4 THE VERSATILE FRENCH FRY

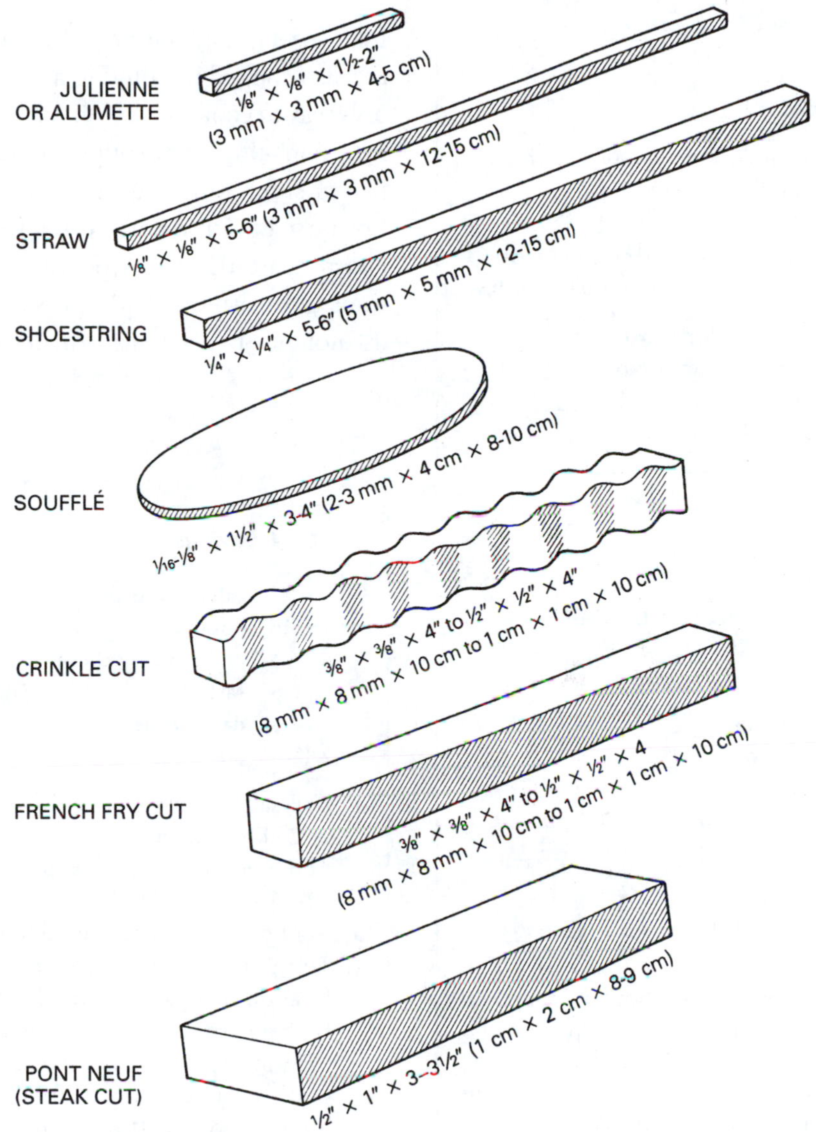

Cut potatoes in different shapes, fry them in the deep fryer, and you have several different potato dishes.

SAUTÉING AND PAN-FRYING

The procedures for sautéing and pan-frying potatoes are basically the same as for other vegetables. Popular dishes in this category include hash brown potatoes (Recipe 9.17) and potato pancakes.

Truly, the possibilities for presenting eye-appealing and palate-pleasing potato dishes are limited only by imagination and sometimes cost.

Recipe 9-16 BAKED POTATO

YIELD: ***12 portions***

12 baking potatoes
oil as needed

1. Wash potatoes well. Pierce ends with fork so steam can escape.
2. Oil potato skins lightly.
3. Place on a sheet pan and bake in 400°F (200°C) oven until done (about 60 minutes).

Per serving:		Carbohydrates:	51 g
Calories:	220	Cholesterol:	0 mg
Fat:	0 g	Fiber:	5 g
Protein:	5 g	Sodium:	16 mg

Recipe 9-16a STUFFED BAKED POTATO

YIELD: ***12 portions***

12	**baking potatoes**	
	oil as needed	
2 oz	**butter**	**60 g**
$^1/_2$ C	**light cream or milk, hot**	**125 mL**

1. Wash potatoes well. Pierce ends with fork so steam can escape.
2. Oil potato skins lightly.
3. Place on a sheet pan and bake in 400°F (200°C) oven until done (about 60 minutes).
4. Cut a lengthwise slice off each potato and scoop out pulp.
5. Purée pulp with butter and cream. Season to taste with salt and white pepper.
6. Pipe back into shells with pastry bag with star tip.
7. Place potatoes on a sheet pan and bake in 400°F (200°C) oven until thoroughly heated.

Per serving:		Carbohydrates:	51 g
Calories:	273	Cholesterol:	17 mg
Fat:	6 g	Fiber:	5 g
Protein:	5 g	Sodium:	59 mg

LEGUMES

Like vegetables, **legumes** (dried beans and peas) are also cooked in liquid in a pot. In fact, it is the only way to cook them. You have met legumes before in making purée soups. Cooking them is similar to simmering vegetables, but legumes must first be soaked in water in order to rehydrate them and prepare them for cooking. The only exceptions to this rule are split peas and lentils, which do not need to be soaked. Before soaking any

Recipe 9-17 HASH BROWN POTATOES

YIELD: ***4 servings***

	salt as needed	
$1^1/_2$ lb	**potatoes**	**700 g**
2 Tb	**onion, finely chopped**	**30 mL**
$^1/_2$ tsp	**salt**	**2 mL**
	dash pepper	
2 Tb	**oil**	**30 mL**

1. Boil salted water ($^1/_2$ tsp or 2 mL salt to 1 C or 250 mL water).
2. Add potatoes and cook until tender, about 20–25 minutes. Drain.
3. Cool potatoes. Shred enough to measure 4 C.
4. Toss potatoes, onion, salt, and pepper in bowl.
5. Heat oil in a pan over moderate heat.
6. Pack potato mixture in a pan, leaving a $^1/_2$-in. (12 mm) space around the edge.
7. Cook over low heat until bottom crust is brown, about 10–15 minutes.
8. Cut potato mixture into quarters and turn over.
9. Add oil if necessary. Cook until brown, about 10–15 minutes longer.

Per serving:		Carbohydrates:	22 g
Calories:	162	Cholesterol:	0 mg
Fat:	7 g	Fiber:	3 g
Protein:	3 g	Sodium:	295 mg

legume, they must be washed carefully and picked over to remove any foreign particles.

DRIED BEANS

Dried beans are among the oldest of foods and today are considered an important staple for millions of people. Beans were once considered to be worth their weight in gold—the jeweler's "carat" owes its origin to a pealike bean found on the east coast of Africa. Beans also once figured very prominently in politics. During the age of the Romans, balloting was done with beans. White beans represented a vote of approval, and dark beans meant a negative vote.

Many varieties of beans are used on menus. Here are some popular varieties and their uses.

- Black beans have an oval shape and a black skin. They are popular in thick soups and in oriental and Mediterranean dishes.
- Black-eyed peas are small, oval shaped, and creamish white with a black spot on one side. They are often used in main dishes. Black-eyed peas are really beans.
- Garbanzo beans (also called chickpeas) are nut-flavored and commonly pickled in vinegar and oil for salads. They are round, beige and yellow in color, and hard in texture.
- Kidney beans are large and have a red color and kidney shape. They are popular for chili con carne and add zest to salads, soups, and Mexican dishes.
- Navy beans include Great Northern and other beans. They are used in soups, salads, casseroles, and baked beans.
- Pinto beans are of the same species as kidney beans. Beige-colored and speckled, they are used in salads, refried beans, and chili.

Table 9.3 describes additional types of beans.

Soybeans are a very important dried bean that was first domesticated in China 3000 years ago. The Chinese call it the "yellow jewel" or the "great treasure" for several reasons. Soybeans are easy to farm, and the plants do not deplete the soil. They are inexpensive to buy, contain the most and best quality protein of all legumes, and are a very versatile food. When merely boiled, however, they have a strong taste with a metallic aftertaste. This is perhaps the reason soybeans have been used to make a wide variety of products such as **tofu.** Tofu is made in a process similar to making cheese. It is white in color and bland in taste but readily picks up other flavors.

Table 9.4 shows the nutritional profile of cooked dry beans. Dry beans are:

- High in complex carbohydrates
- High in fiber
- A good protein source
- Low in fat
- Cholesterol free
- Rich in potassium, iron, and folate
- A good source of other vitamins and minerals
- Low in sodium

Because of the protein content in legumes, they are often combined with rice in vegetarian dishes. For example, beans and rice each contain certain kinds of protein that the other lacks, so when combined they supply the complete protein needed in a sound diet. An example of such a dish is given in Recipe 9.18. This is a regional dish from Cajun cuisine that is very popular in the Southwest. Use the cayenne and Tabasco with caution! Cajun cooking is very spicy.

To cook dried beans, use 2 to 3 quarts of stock or water to a pound of dried vegetables, and soak them in it overnight. If you don't have the time

Table 9-3 COOKING INFORMATION FOR LEGUMES

Bean, Pea, or Lentil	Size/Shape/Color	Flavor	Soaking Required	Cooking Time	Cups Liquid for Cooking	Yield[a]	Uses
Black beans (turtle beans)	Small, pea-shaped, black	Full, mellow	Yes	$1^1/_2$ hours	4	2	Mediterranean cuisine, soups (black bean soup), chilis, salads, with rice
Black-eyed peas (cowpeas, black-eyed beans)	Small, oval, creamy white with black spot	Earthy, absorb other flavors	No	50–60 minutes	3	2	Casseroles, with rice, with pork, Southern dishes
Chickpeas (garbanzo beans, ceci beans)	Round, tan, large	Nutty	Yes	$2^1/_2$ hours	4	4	Salads, soups, casseroles, hors d'oeuvres, hummus and other Middle East dishes
Fava beans, whole	Large, round, flat, off white or tan	Full	Yes	3 hours	$2^1/_2$	4	Soups, casseroles, salads
Great Northern beans	Large, oval, white	Mild	Yes	$1^1/_2$ hours	$3^1/_2$	2	Soups, casseroles, baked beans, and mixing with other varieties
Kidney beans	Large, kidney-shaped, red or white (red is much more common)	Rich, meaty, sweet	Yes	$1–1^1/_2$ hours	3	2	Chili, casseroles, salads, soups, a favorite in Mexican and Italian cooking

Lentils	Small, flat, disk-shaped, green, red, or brown, split or whole	Mild, earthy	No	30–45 minutes	2	$2^1/_4$	Soups, stews, salads, casseroles, stuffing, sandwiches, spreads, with rice
Lima beans	Flat, oval, cream or greenish, large or baby size	Large—full Baby—mild	Yes	$1^1/_2$ hours (large) 1 hour (baby)	2	$1^1/_4$	Soups, casseroles, side dishes
Navy beans (pea beans)	Small to medium, round to oval, white	Mild	Yes	$1^1/_2$ hours	3	2	Baked beans, soups, salads, side dishes, casseroles
Peas, split	Small, flat on one side, green or yellow	Rich, earthy	No	30 minutes	3	$2^1/_4$	Soups, casseroles
Peas, whole	Small-medium, round, yellow or green	Rich, earthy	Yes	40 minutes	3	$2^1/_4$	Soups, casseroles, Scandinavian dishes
Pinto beans	Medium, kidney-shaped, pinkish brown	Rich, meaty	Yes	$1^1/_2$ hours	3	2	A favorite for chili, refried beans, and in other Mexican cooking
Pink beans	Medium, oval, pinkish brown	Rich, meaty	Yes	1 hour	3	2	Popular in barbecue style dishes
Soybeans	Medium, oval-round, creamy yellow	Distinctive	Yes	$3^1/_2$ hours or more	3	2	Soups, stews, casseroles

[a]From 1 cup of uncooked bean, pea, or lentil.

Table 9-4 NUTRITIONAL PROFILE OF COOKED DRY BEANS AND LENTILS (1 CUP)

Nutrient	*Cooked Dry Beans*	*Cooked Lentils*
Calories	230 calories	231 calories
Protein	16 g	18 g
Fiber	9 g	10 g
Fat	1.5 g	Trace
Cholesterol	0	0
Sodium	10 mg	4 mg
Iron	5.4 mg	6.6 mg
Zinc	2.1 mg	2.5 mg
Folate	63 μg	358 μg
Magnesium	92 mg	71 mg
Copper	0.5 mg	0.5 mg
Manganese	1.0 mg	1.0 mg
Potassium	620 mg	731 mg

to soak overnight, add them to boiling water and boil them for 2 minutes, then soak for 1 hour. Always discard the soaking water before cooking. Next, simmer (don't boil—they may toughen) the beans until they are done throughout but firm enough to hold their shape (see Table 9.3 for how long this takes). Partially cover the pot during cooking. For extra flavor, you can cook them with smoked meat or a ham bone and flavor builders.

DRY PEAS AND LENTILS

Dry peas are a versatile food that add variety to meals. They may be green or yellow, whole or split (in half). Split peas are probably more popular—they are used in soups, salads, pilafs, main dishes, and appetizers. Whole peas need to be soaked before cooking; split peas can skip soaking.

The *lentil* is an old-world legume that is disk shaped and about the size of a pea. Thousands of years old, lentils were perhaps the first of the convenience foods—they cook in only 20 to 30 minutes (no soaking required!). Lentils come in different colors, such as greenish-brown, pink, or yellow. They are an excellent partner with many foods. They make excellent side dishes and go well in soups, stews, sauces, stuffings, and salads. Lentil purée is used in dips, spreads, Mexican dishes, and vegetable fillings. Take a look at Recipe 9.19 for an example.

GRAINS

The full name for grains is cereal grains. Cereal grains are the seeds of cultivated grasses such as wheat, corn, rice, rye, barley, and oats, among others. All cereal grains have a large center area high in starch known as the **endosperm.** At one end of the endosperm is the **germ,** the area of the kernel that sprouts when allowed to germinate. The **bran** covers both the endosperm and

Recipe 9-18 RED BEANS AND RICE

YIELD: ***4 servings***

1/2 C	**onions, chopped**	**125 mL**
1/2 C	**celery, chopped**	**125 mL**
1	**clove garlic**	
2 Tb	**margarine or butter**	**30 mL**
14 oz	**kidney beans, cooked**	**425 g**
2 C	**rice, cooked**	**500 mL**
1 Tb	**chopped parsley**	**30 mL**
	salt and pepper to taste	

1. Sauté onion, celery, and garlic in margarine or butter until tender. Remove garlic.
2. Add remaining ingredients and simmer for 10 minutes.

Per serving:		Carbohydrates:	66 g
Calories:	286	Cholesterol:	0 mg
Fat:	2 g	Fiber:	11 g
Protein:	12 g	Sodium:	191 mg

Recipe 9-19 LENTIL BURRITOS

YIELD: ***8 burritos***

1 C	**lentils**	**250 mL**
2 C	**water**	**500 mL**
$^{1}/_{2}$ C	**onions, minced**	**125 mL**
1	**clove garlic, minced**	
$^{1}/_{2}$ tsp	**ground cumin**	**2 mL**
	dash hot pepper sauce	
1 C	**mild taco sauce**	**250 mL**
1 C	**zucchini, chopped**	**250 mL**
1 C	**bell peppers, chopped**	**250 mL**
4 oz	**shredded cheese**	**125 g**
8	**flour tortillas**	

1. Place washed lentils in a saucepan with water, onion, garlic, cumin, and hot pepper sauce. Heat to boiling, cover, reduce heat, and simmer 10–12 minutes or just until lentils are tender.
2. Drain, if necessary. Toss lentils with taco sauce, zucchini, pepper, and cheese.
3. Spoon about $^{1}/_{2}$ cup (125 mL) lentil mixture down center of each warmed tortilla. Roll up and serve.

Per serving:			
Calories:	209	Carbohydrates:	32 g
Fat:	5 g	Cholesterol:	8 mg
Protein:	10 g	Fiber:	4 g
		Sodium:	196 mg

the germ. The seed contains everything needed to reproduce the plant: The germ is the embryo, the endosperm contains the nutrients for growth, and the bran protects it.

Most grains undergo some type of processing or milling after harvesting to make them cook more quickly and easily, be less chewy, and lengthen their shelf life. Grains, such as oats and rice, have an outer husk or hull that is tough and inedible, so it is removed. Other processing steps might include polishing the grain to remove the bran and germ (as in making white flour), cracking the grain (as in cracked wheat), or steaming the grain (as in bulgur) to shorten the cooking time. The processes of rolling or grinding a grain, such as oatmeal, also shorten the cooking time.

Whenever the fiber-rich bran and the vitamin-rich germ are left on the endosperm of a grain, the grain is called a whole grain. Examples of whole grains include whole wheat, whole rye, bulgur (whole wheat grains that have been steamed and dried), oatmeal, whole cornmeal, whole hulled barley, and brown rice. If the bran and germ are separated (or mostly separated) from the endosperm, the grain is called refined or milled. For example, whole wheat flour is made from the entire kernel of wheat, and wheat flour, usually called white flour, is made only from the endosperm.

Unfortunately, refined grains lose most of their fiber, oil, B vitamins, and some protein that were in the germ and bran. Whole grains are always a more nutritious choice and are:

- Low or moderate in calories
- High in starch and fiber
- Low in fat
- Moderate in protein
- Full of vitamins and minerals

To make up for some of the nutrition lost in processing, white flour is enriched with thiamin, riboflavin, niacin, folate, and iron.

Most grains are cooked by stirring into a boiling liquid, reducing the heat to a simmer, covering, and cooking until the liquid is absorbed. Table 9.5 summarizes the cooking information for each grain. Recipes 9.20 and 9.21 are examples of recipes highlighting grains. The following section will give more specific information on rice, a very popular grain.

Table 9-5 COOKING INFORMATION FOR GRAINS

Grain	Appearance	Flavor	Soaking Required	Cooking Time	Cups Liquid for Cooking	Cups Yield[a]	Uses	Storage
Barley, pearl	White–tan	Mild, nutty	No (but will reduce cooking time)	35–40 minutes	3	$3^1/_2$	Soups, casseroles, stews, cooked cereals, side dishes, pilafs	Air-tight container—6–9 months at room temperature
Barley, whole hulled	Brownish-gray	Nutty, chewy	Yes	60–90 minutes	3	4	Same as above	Air-tight container—1 month at room temperature, 4–5 months in refrigerator
Buckwheat, whole white	Brown–white	Mild	No	20 minutes	2	$2^1/_2$	Side dishes	Air-tight container—1–2 months, better stored in refrigerator
Buckwheat, roasted (kasha)	Brown	Distinct, nutty, chewy	No	10–15 minutes	2	$2^1/_2$	Soups, side dishes, salads, pilaf, stuffing, hot cereal	Same as above
Corn, whole hominy	Yellow or white	Sweet, creamy texture	No	$2^1/_2$–3 hours	$2^1/_2$	3	Soups, stews, casseroles, hot cereal, puddings, baked goods	Air-tight container—1 month at room temperature, 5 months in refrigerator
Corn, hominy grits	Whitish-gray	Distinct	No	20–25 minutes	4	3	Hot breakfast cereal	Air-tight container, many months at room temperature
Millet	Bright gold color, small	Like corn, crunchy	No	30–35 minutes	2	3	Soups, casseroles, meat loaves, porridge, croquettes, pilaf, salads, stuffing, side dishes	Air-tight container, 6 months at room temperature
Oats, steel-cut	Off-white	Mild, pleasant	No	45–60 minutes	2	2	Hot cereal	Air-tight container—1 month at room temperature, 6 months in refrigerator
Rice, regular-milled long grain	White	Mild	No	15–20 minutes	2	3	Side dishes, casseroles, stews, soups, stuffing, salads	Air-tight container—many months at room temperature

Rice, regular-milled, medium or short grain	White	Mild	No	20–25 minutes	$1^1/_2$	3	Same as above	Same as above
Rice, parboiled	White	Mild	No	20–25	$2–2^1/_2$	3–4	Same as above	Same as above
Rice, brown	Tan–brown	Nutty	No	40–50 minutes	$2^1/_2$	4	Same as above	Air-tight container—1 month at room temperature, 6 months in refrigerator
Rice, wild	Dark brown	Nutty	No (but rinse it)	30–45 minutes	3	$3^1/_2$–4	Side dishes, stuffing, casseroles	Air-tight container—many months at room temperature
Rice, basmati	White	Nutty, spicy	Yes (rinse also)	25 minutes	$1^1/_2$	3	Side dishes, casseroles	Air-tight container—1 month at room temperature, 6 months in refrigerator
Rye, whole berries	Brown, oval	Distinct rye flavor	No	$1^1/_2$ hours	3	3	Hot cereal, side dishes	Air-tight container—1 month at room temperature, 5 months in refrigerator
Wheat, bulgur	Dark brown	Nutty	No	20–25 minutes	$2^1/_2$	2	Salads, soups, breads, desserts, with rice, meat dishes, in place of rice pilaf, stuffing	Air-tight container in cool place, or refrigerator for 5–6 months
Wheat, whole berries	Deep brown	Nutty, crunchy	Yes (1 cup to $3^1/_2$ cups cold water)	1 hour	3	2	Salads, meat loaves, croquettes, breads, side dishes	Air-tight container in cool place up to 1 month, up to 5 months in refrigerator
Amaranth	Golden	Mildly spicy, toasted sesame flavor	No	25 minutes	$2^1/_2$	$3^1/_2$	Hot cereal, pilaf, in baking, can be popped as a snack	Air-tight container, in cool place for many months, otherwise refrigerate for 5 months
Quinoa	Pale yellow	Nutty	No	12–15 minutes	2	$2^1/_2$	In place of rice	Air-tight container in cool place for 1 month, otherwise refrigerate for 5 months

Recipe 9-20 KASHA PILAF

YIELD: ***3 servings***

2	egg whites	
1/2 C	kasha	125 mL
2 tsp	oil	20 mL
1	rib celery, sliced thin	
1	small onion, coarsely chopped	
1 C	chicken stock	250 mL
	freshly ground black pepper and salt as needed	
1/4 C	toasted slivered almonds	60 mL

1. In a nonstick saucepan, beat the egg whites slightly.
2. Mix kasha with the whites. Stir frequently over medium heat until each grain is separate and dry. Remove from pan.
3. Add oil to the pan. When it is hot, add celery and onion and sauté over medium heat a few minutes until onion begins to soften and brown.
4. Add chicken stock, pepper and salt, and kasha. Reduce heat. Cover pan and simmer about 15 minutes, until kasha is tender.
5. Stir almonds into kasha and serve.

Per serving:		Carbohydrates:	26 g
Calories:	214	Cholesterol:	1 mg
Fat:	6 g	Fiber:	4 g
Protein:	13 g	Sodium:	315 mg

RICE

Rice was one of the earliest foods to be cultivated and is still the chief food eaten in most Asian countries. Rice is an excellent source of starch and only contains a trace of fat and no cholesterol. Brown rice, because it is a whole grain, contains more nutrients, including fiber, than white rices, which have the hull and bran removed. Most U.S.-grown and -processed white rice is enriched with iron, thiamin, riboflavin, and niacin, by applying a coating of nutrients. Table 9.6

Recipe 9-21 BULGUR WHEAT WITH TOMATO ONION AND MINT TABBOULEH

YIELD: ***12 servings (1/2 cup or 125 mL each)***

1/2 C	bulgur wheat	120 mL
1/2 C	finely minced onion	120 mL
1/2 tsp	minced garlic	2 mL
1/2 tsp	ground allspice	2 mL
1 tsp	fresh ground black pepper	5 mL
1 1/2 tsp	salt	8 mL
1/2 C	freshly squeezed lemon juice	120 mL
1/2 C	olive oil	120 mL
1 C	finely chopped, unpeeled, seeded tomato	250 mL
2 C	flat-leaf parsley, chopped	500 mL
1 C	scallions, chopped	250 mL
1/2 C	spearmint, chopped	120 mL
1	head leaf lettuce, washed and dried	

1. Soak the bulgur in 3 C (750 mL) water for 30 minutes. Scoop the wheat out of the water and squeeze it repeatedly to get the water out. Place in a bowl and set aside.
2. In another bowl, combine the onion, garlic, allspice, pepper, salt, and lemon juice. Stir well to dissolve the salt. Whisk in the oil to complete the dressing.
3. Add the tomato, parsley, scallions, and spearmint to the bulgur. Toss well with your hands, combining all the ingredients.
4. Add the dressing and stir well. Adjust the seasoning if necessary. The tabbouleh may need more salt, pepper, lemon juice, or olive oil. Chill at least 2 hours before serving and toss again just before serving. Portion tabbouleh into lettuce leaf cups to serve.

Per serving:		Carbohydrates:	13 g
Calories:	134	Cholesterol:	0 mg
Fat:	9 g	Fiber:	3 g
Protein:	2 g	Sodium:	310 mg

Table 9-6 NUTRITIONAL INFORMATION FOR COOKED LONG-GRAIN RICE (PER 1/2 CUP SERVING)

	Brown	*Regular-Milled White (enriched)*	*Parboiled (enriched)*	*Precooked White (enriched)*
Kilocalories	111	131	100	80
Carbohydrate (g)	23	28	22	17
Protein (g)	3	3	2	2
Total fat (g)	1	0.3	0.2	0.1
Saturated fatty acids (g)	0	0	0	0
Cholesterol (mg)	0	0	0	0
Fiber (g)	1.7	0.5	0.5	0.6
Sodium (mg)	3.0	2.0	2	2

compares the nutrient profiles of four different types of rice.

MARKET FORMS. Rices can be classified according to their grain type.

- **Long-grain rice** is three to five times as long as it is wide. The cooked grains are separate and fluffy and used in side dishes, entrées, salads, pilaf, and so on.
- **Medium-grain rice** is a little shorter and plumper than long-grain rice; after cooking, it is more moist, tender, and has a greater tendency to cling together than long grains. Both medium-grain and short-grain rice are a good choice for making dishes that are creamy, such as rice pudding, **risotto** (an Italian dish of rice cooked in butter and stock), croquettes, or salads.
- **Short-grain rice** is just a little longer than it is wide. The shorter the grain the more tender and clinging it cooks. The boiled rice used in Japanese cooking is short-grain rice.

In addition to classifying rice by its shape, you can also classify it by the degree of processing it has received.

- **Brown rice** is the least processed form of rice. The outer hull (it's inedible) is removed but it still retains the bran layers that give it the characteristic tan–brown color, nutlike flavor, and chewy texture. Brown rice takes much longer to cook than the white rices.
- **Regular-milled white rice** has had the outer husk removed and the layers of bran milled away until the grain is white.
- **Parboiled or converted rice** is specially processed before milling to retain most of the vitamin–mineral content. It is partially cooked with steam, dried, and then milled to remove the outer hull and bran. The parboiling process results in a rice product that is extra separate and fluffy and more nutritious than regular-milled white rice. Because of its excellent appearance, and also the fact that it holds up well in the steam table, it is the most widely used rice in the kitchen.
- **Precooked or instant rice** has been milled, completely cooked, and then dried. Preparation simply involves adding boiling water to rehydrate. Its texture is not as appealing as other rice, and, if overcooked or held too long, it becomes mushy.

There are also numerous specialty rices. For example, **basmati rice** is a flavorful variety of extra-long-grain rice with a nutty flavor that is popular with Indian food.

Wild rice is not a true rice but the seed of a grass that grows wild in the marshes of the Great

Lakes region. It was harvested exclusively by the Indians of the region, who traveled the marshes in canoes and shook off the ripe grains. It is often served combined with white rice, because it is so expensive. The two kinds of rice are cooked separately and combined after cooking.

COOKING RICE. The vegetable cook is responsible for rice preparation. The goal of rice cookery is a tender but al dente product in which each grain stands out separately and the whole is fluffy and moist but not sticky.

Before being cooked, some cooks like to rinse the rice to remove any excess starch that may make the rice stick together. Unfortunately, most white rices made in the United States have a coating of nutrients that rinse off in this process. If rice appears dirty, or it is from overseas, rinsing is necessary. Otherwise, you will have to find out what has been the practice in your particular kitchen.

Rice is always cooked in liquid. This can be done in different ways producing different textures. Various methods of boiling and steaming produce rices ranging from al dente to soft and moist. To boil or steam, rice is first cooked in about $1^1/_2$ to 2 times its volume of water. A small amount of salt and butter are also used. Put the rice, salt, and butter into the water and bring to a boil. Once boiling, reduce to a low heat, cover, and cook according to the package directions (or see Table 9.5). Most rices, except brown, are cooked in under 25 minutes. After bringing the rice and water mixture to a boil, you can finish the cooking in a moderate oven (375°F or 175°C) or in a steamer. The rice should be covered if cooked in the oven, but uncovered in the steamer.

Brown rice is cooked in the same ways as white rice, except that it requires more liquid—about 2 times its volume—and a longer cooking time—about twice as long.

Another method of cooking rice is referred to as the **pilaf method.** The pilaf method yields a flavorful al dente rice. It involves two steps, as shown in Recipe 9.22. First, the rice is sautéed in butter, margarine, or oil. Next, boiling liquid is added to the rice, and the liquid is brought to a boil and then cooked at a low heat either on the stove or in the oven. Liquids used with the method range from water to the best of stocks. The rice absorbs all the liquid, and the grains stand out separately, firm but tender. This method works best with parboiled long-grain rice.

Many combinations of meat or vegetables can be added to pilaf, such as cooked peas, sautéed mushrooms, dried ham or bacon, sliced green

Recipe 9-22 RICE PILAF

YIELD: ***12 4-oz. (125 g) portions***

1 oz	**butter**	**30 g**
3 oz	**onions, small dice**	**90 g**
1 lb	**rice, long grain**	**450 g**
1 qt	**boiling chicken stock**	**1 L**
	salt to taste	

1. Melt butter in a heavy saucepan and sweat onions until translucent.
2. Add rice and stir well to coat the rice with butter.
3. Add boiling chicken stock and return to a boil.
4. Season to taste with salt.
5. Cover and bake in 350°F (180°C) oven until liquid is absorbed and rice is tender (about 15–20 minutes).

Per serving:		Carbohydrates:	32 g
Calories:	164	Cholesterol:	5 mg
Fat:	2 g	Fiber:	1 g
Protein:	3 g	Sodium:	308 mg

Recipe 9-23 HERB–RICE BLEND

YIELD: *4 servings*

2 C	water	500 mL
1 C	rice, long grain	250 mL
1 tsp	beef base or bouillon cube	5 mL
1/2 tsp	dried rosemary	2 mL
1/2 tsp	dried marjoram leaves	2 mL
1/2 tsp	dried thyme leaves	2 mL
1 tsp	dried minced onion	5 mL

1. Boil water in a saucepan. Add all ingredients, cover, reduce heat to low, and cook for 15–20 minutes until liquid is absorbed.
2. Fluff with a fork and serve.

Per serving:		Carbohydrates:	37 g
Calories:	170	Cholesterol:	0 mg
Fat:	0 g	Fiber:	1 g
Protein:	3 g	Sodium:	218 mg

onions, pimientos, spinach, raisins, or chopped nuts.

Recipe 9.23 and Table 9.7 suggest different seasonings for a variety of rice dishes.

PASTA

When we hear the word pasta, we relate it quickly to Italian cuisine. Pasta has been eaten for over 5000 years and is very closely associated with Italian cooking. Owing to the influence of Italian cooks, Americans are eating more pasta than ever before.

ABOUT PASTA

Pasta, from the Italian word for paste, is an edible paste or dough made from flour and water that is rolled and cut into one of over 150 pasta shapes found in the United States (Figure 9.5). Pasta may be dried or fresh. Dried pasta includes both **macaroni** and **noodles.** Macaroni products are pastas made from flour and water. These include spaghetti, elbow macaroni, lasagne, ziti, and other shapes. Noodles, by law, are also made from flour and water, but must contain 5.5 percent egg solids. Noodles are usually flat, like a ribbon, and come in different widths.

Semolina is preferred for making dried pasta. Semolina is the roughly milled endosperm of a type of wheat called durum wheat. Durum wheat is known as a very hard wheat, meaning that it has a high protein content. Semolina is used almost exclusively for making pasta. Less expensive pasta products are made from a softer flour. High-quality pasta should be yellow in color, brittle, and hold its shape well when cooked. Poor-quality pasta is often a whitish-gray color and when it is cooked, it becomes soft and loses its shape.

Pastas are often dried when they arrive in the kitchen. There are exceptions. Ravioli is a soft dough, stuffed with a filling. It may be made in the kitchen or purchased readymade and frozen. Spaetzle and gnocchi are also soft pasta doughs.

Table 9-7 RICE SEASONINGS

Rice Dish	*Seasonings*
Rice pilaf	Coriander, curry powder, red pepper, saffron
Rice and vegetable casserole	Tarragon
Risotto	Nutmeg
Spinach risotto	Nutmeg, rosemary, bay leaf
Greek rice	Mint
White rice	Allspice, parsley, turmeric
Wild rice	Thyme

Figure 9-5 FORMS OF PASTA

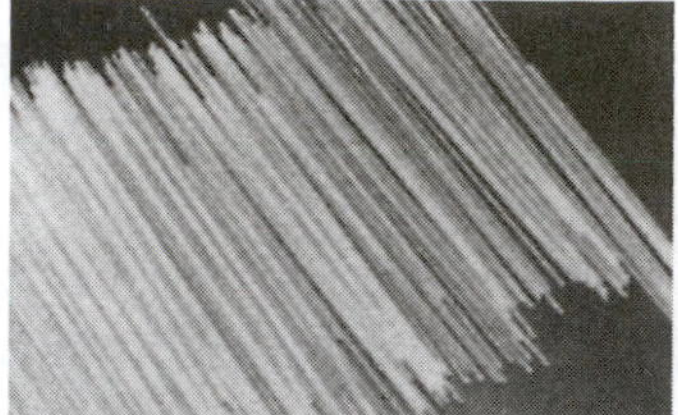

Spaghetti, Thin Spaghetti *(Spaghettini)*

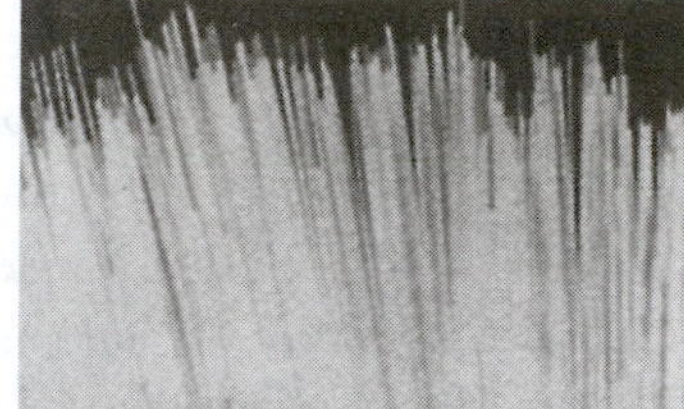

Vermicelli

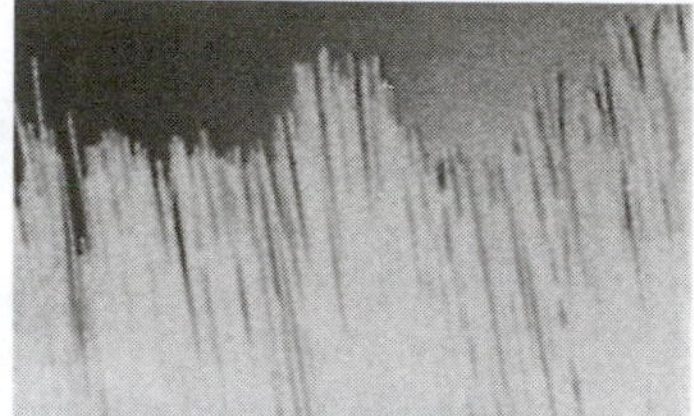

Angel Hair, Cappellini, Capelli Di Angelo

Ziti

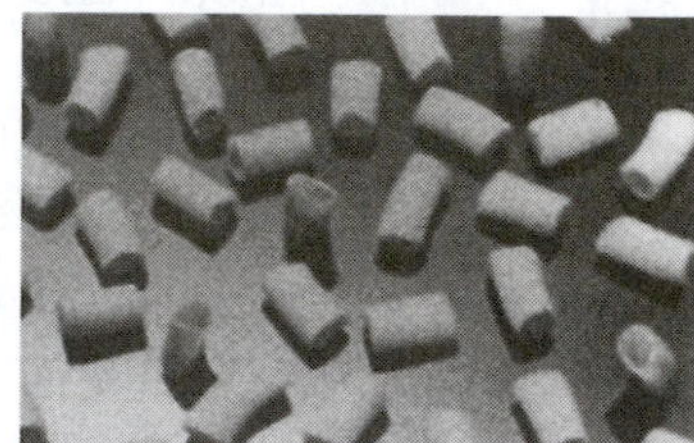

Rigatoni

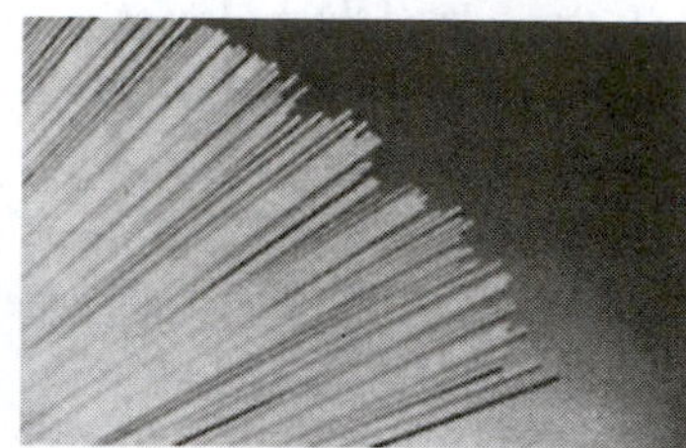

Linguine

Manicotti

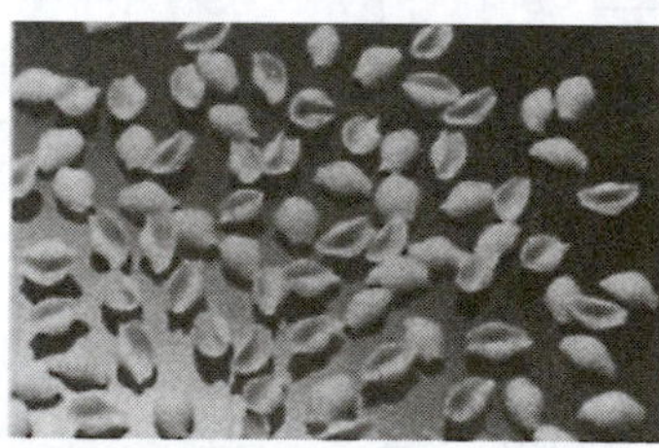

Shells, Seashells, Conchiglie *(Kon-KEEL-yeh)*

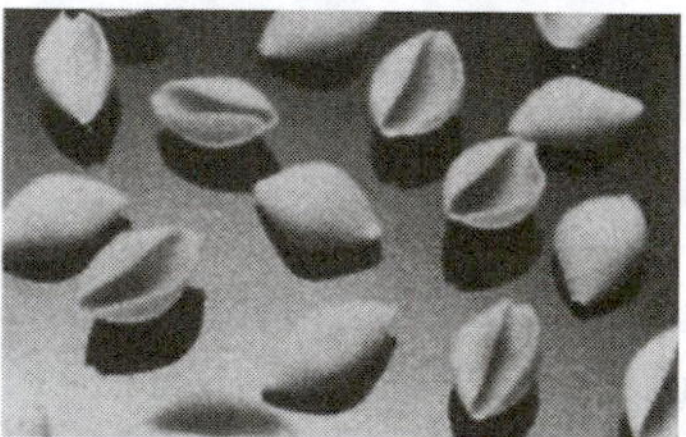

Jumbo Shells, Conchiglioni *(Kon-KEEL-yoni)*

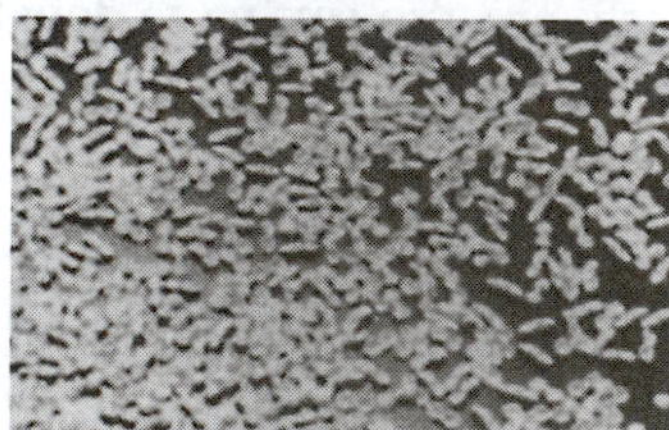

Bowties, Farfalle *(Far-FAH-leh)*
Larger size not shown

Lasagne

Rotelle, Rotini, Spirals, Twirls, Twists

Fusilli

Fettuccine

Mafalda

(Courtesy National Pasta Association.)

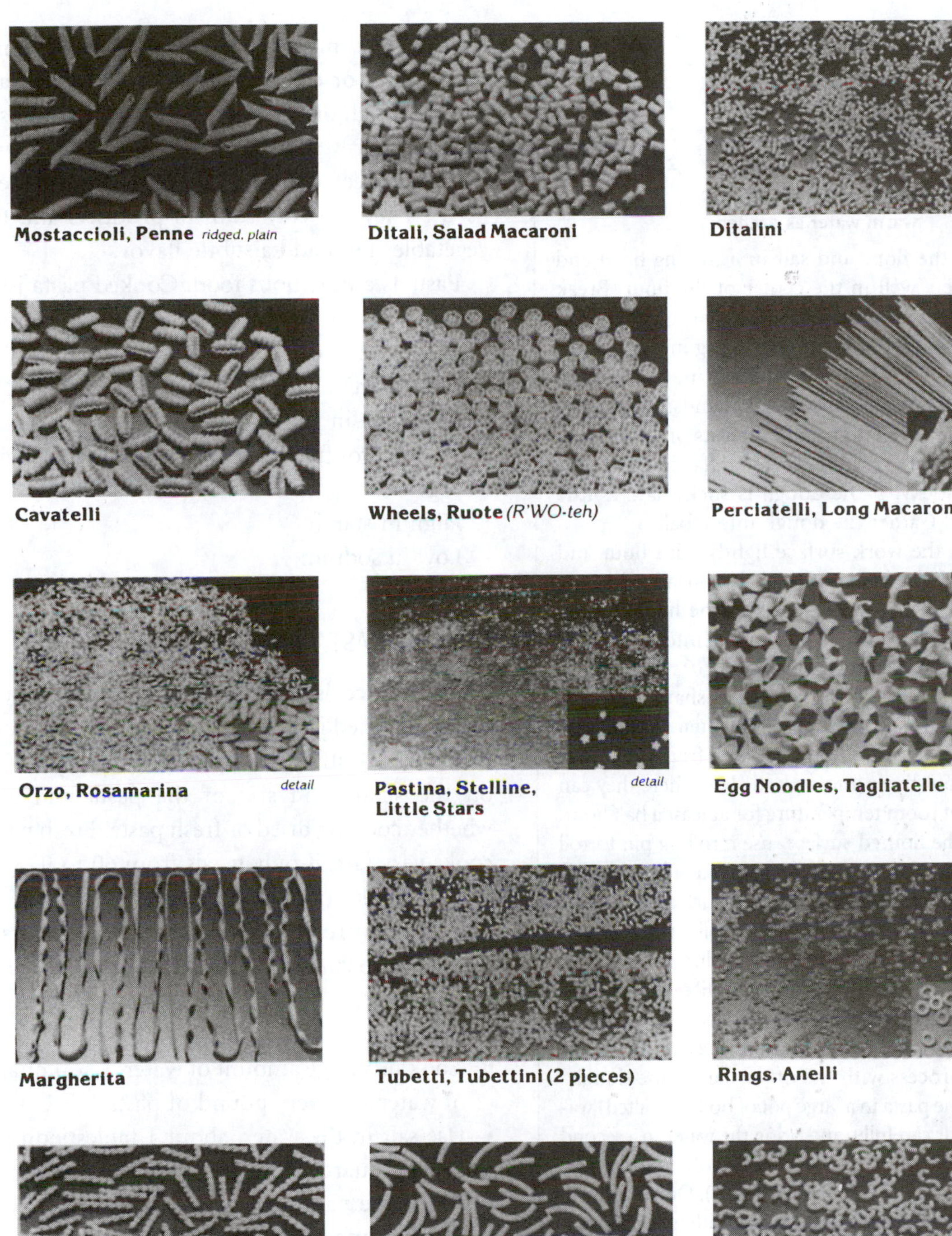

Mostaccioli, Penne *ridged, plain*

Ditali, Salad Macaroni

Ditalini

Cavatelli

Wheels, Ruote *(R'WO-teh)*

Perciatelli, Long Macaroni *detail*

Orzo, Rosamarina *detail*

Pastina, Stelline, Little Stars *detail*

Egg Noodles, Tagliatelle

Margherita

Tubetti, Tubettini (2 pieces)

Rings, Anelli *detail*

Gemelli

Mezzani

Elbow Macaroni

Recipe 9-24 FRESH PASTA

YIELD: ***6 servings***

3 C	**flour**	**750 mL**
1/2 tsp	**salt**	**2 mL**
3	**eggs, room temperature**	
	warm water as needed	

1. Mix the flour and salt in a mixing bowl and make a well in the center of the flour. Break the eggs into the well. With a fork, begin beating the eggs, gradually drawing in some flour. When all the eggs are mixed in, work in the remaining flour with your hands. If the mixture is stiff, add small amounts of water, a tablespoon at a time, to get a dry dough that is not sticky. If the dough is sticky, add a little flour. Gather the dough into a ball.
2. Dust the work surface lightly with flour and knead the ball of dough by pushing it away from you with the heels of the hand. Knead the dough until it is formed into a smooth, shiny, and elastic ball—about 10 minutes. Divide the dough in half with a sharp knife.

   Form into two balls and flatten slightly. Rub each ball with a little oil to keep from drying out and put them into a plastic bag where they can rest at room temperature for at least a half hour.
3. On the floured surface, use a rolling pin to roll the dough as thin as possible into a long rectangle. Sift a little flour over the surface, spreading it evenly with your hands. Roll up the dough from the long side, like a jelly roll. Cut the rolled-up pasta into 1/4-in. (5 mm) slices and quickly unroll the strips so that they do not stick together.
4. Place the strips on floured wax paper. Repeat the process with the other half of the dough.
5. Put the pasta in a large pot of boiling (salted) water, stir carefully, and bring the water to a second boil. At this point, taste a noodle to see if it is firm to the bite (or to your taste). Drain the noodles and serve immediately with your favorite sauce. Fresh pasta cooks in a matter of minutes.

Per serving:		Carbohydrates:	46 g
Calories:	270	Cholesterol:	105 mg
Fat:	4 g	Fiber:	2 g
Protein:	12 g	Sodium:	39 mg

Fresh pasta is made of flour and eggs and sometimes water or oil (see Recipe 9.24). It is available as dough or in shapes. Flavored pastas usually contain vegetables, such as red tomato, artichoke, beet, carrot, or spinach (only a little is used). They are very colorful products and the vegetables used add a subtle flavor.

Pasta is a nutritious food. Cooked pasta is:

- Moderate in calorie content
- Low in fat
- Moderate in protein
- Cholesterol free (except for pastas made with egg)
- High in starch
- Low in sodium

COOKING PASTA

Pasta, like rice, is prepared by the vegetable cook. Pasta is cooked in boiling water until al dente, or firm to the tooth. Cooking times vary depending on the shape and size of the pasta and also whether cooking dried or fresh pasta. Fresh pasta cooks very fast; it only needs from 60 to 90 seconds to cook once the water boils again.

The steps are not at all complicated. Here are a few simple rules you should learn for successful cooking:

- Cook in a large amount of water. Use 4 quarts of water for every pound of pasta.
- Use salt in the water, about 1 tablespoon for every 4 quarts of water.
- Submerge pasta in water that is already boiling, keeping the pieces separated as much as possible.
- Cook at a boil and stir several times to keep the pieces from sticking to the pan and to each other.

Recipe 9-25 FETTUCCINE ALFREDO

YIELD: ***12 5-oz (150 g) portions***

$1\frac{1}{2}$ lb	**fettuccine**	**700 g**
1 pt	**heavy cream**	**500 mL**
3 oz	**butter**	**300 g**
12 oz	**grated Parmesan cheese**	
	salt, black pepper, and nutmeg to taste	

1. Boil the fettuccine until it is slightly undercooked. Drain.
2. Over medium heat, simmer 1 C (250 mL) cream with the butter until slightly thickened, about 5 minutes.
3. Pour the butter/cream mixture over warm fettuccine and mix well. Add remaining cream and Parmesan cheese and mix well.
4. Add salt, pepper, and nutmeg to taste.

Per serving:		Carbohydrates:	9 g
Calories:	489	Cholesterol:	151 mg
Fat:	31 g	Fiber:	1 g
Protein:	19 g	Sodium:	621 mg

- Always cook al dente, or a little short of al dente if it is to be held. (The term al dente originated with the cooking of pasta.)
- Drain and rinse thoroughly with cold water until the rinse water runs clear. This stops the cooking process and is not necessary if the pasta will be served immediately.
- If held, coat lightly with oil to prevent sticking, refrigerate covered, and reheat in simmering water.

Learning to identify the point just under al dente is the most important part of cooking pasta. You can do this by pushing it against the side of the pot with a knife or spatula and feeling the delicate balance between resistance and give. Army cooks used to say that if you throw the pasta at the ceiling and it sticks, it's done, but feeling or tasting it is a more reliable test. When you are cooking a big kettleful of spaghetti, it is critically important to open the drain valve at the right time. You can ruin the spaghetti by being just a half minute late.

Pasta is usually served with a sauce that determines the character of the dish. It may be a simple tomato sauce to which various garnitures are added to make different dishes. Or it may be created especially for a given dish, as in Recipe 9.25. These dishes may be either served as an en-

Recipe 9-26 MANICOTTI

YIELD: ***12 portions (2 shells each)***

24 manicotti shells

Filling:

2 lb	**ricotta cheese**	**1 kg**
2	**eggs**	
1 lb	**spinach, cooked, well drained, chopped**	**450 g**
4 oz	**Parmesan cheese**	**125 g**
	salt and nutmeg to taste	
3 C	**tomato sauce**	**750 mL**
2 oz	**Parmesan cheese**	**60 g**

1. Cook manicotti shells in boiling salted water until al dente. Drain.
2. Mix filling ingredients together. Season to taste with salt and nutmeg.
3. Using a pastry bag with a plain tip, fill each shell and place on lightly oiled hotel pan.
4. Ladle sauce over shells and sprinkle with Parmesan cheese.
5. Bake in 350°F (180°C) oven until filling and sauce are thoroughly heated and cheese is golden (about 20–25 minutes).

Per serving:		Carbohydrates:	28 g
Calories:	294	Cholesterol:	77 mg
Fat:	13 g	Fiber:	2 g
Protein:	17 g	Sodium:	189 mg

trée or made in smaller portions and served as a first course preceding the entrée.

Each pasta shape is more appropriate for certain types of dishes.

- Elbow macaroni is good in salads and soups because it retains its shape.
- Tube pastas (such as elbow macaroni) or pastas with a hollow space, such as shells, work well with meat or vegetable sauces, as they trap the sauce in their spaces.
- Fresh pasta, because it is softer in texture and absorbs sauce more readily than dried, is better with a smooth, light sauce that coats the pasta evenly.
- Flat noodles are also better with smooth, light sauces.
- Delicate pasta should be served with delicate sauces. Hearty pasta is best with hearty sauces.

Recipe 9.26 illustrates yet another popular way of serving pasta. It is stuffed with a hearty filling and covered with a plain sauce. Many shapes of pasta are suitable for filling, and all kinds of fillings may be used. Here is another challenge to the cook's ingenuity.

SUMMING UP

The menu role of cooked vegetables is usually to accompany the entrée. Their function is to enhance the entrée by providing complementary flavors, textures, visual variety, and additional nutrients, especially vitamins and minerals.

Cooking vegetables is a real challenge to the cook because so many undesirable changes can take place if they are not cooked properly. Colors can change from bright green to olive drab, from white to yellow or gray, and from red to pink, purple, green, and even blue. Fresh flavors can fade or change to something entirely different and unpleasant. Textures can become soft and mushy. Nutrients can be lost. The one single all-embracing rule is: Do not overcook!

Because of these hazards of cooking, holding for service is a problem, since at safe temperatures vegetables go on cooking. To minimize these problems, you can cook vegetables in small batches as needed or partially cook them ahead and finish-cook them just before service.

Vegetable cookery utilizes nearly all cooking methods. The method should be suited to the vegetable. Often, the choice of method will solve the holding problem.

Vegetables are versatile. Besides the variety you can achieve with different cooking methods, you can combine vegetables, add flavoring ingredients, or add sauces, always keeping in mind the compatability of flavors, textures, and appearance. Properly cooked, vegetables are among the most attractive of foods on the plate, often taking the place of a garnish.

Legumes, cereal grains, and pasta, like vegetables, often supplement or become the entrée on the menu when combined with each other or other foods. This is especially true of pastas, which are only the beginning of many main dishes. Rice and pasta are not difficult to cook; the essentials are to follow the rules and to make accurate judgments about doneness.

The things you can do with 150 kinds of pasta boggle the mind. The same is true of rice. The same is true of vegetables.

Learn textures, tastes, and cooking methods. Learn what spices enhance what vegetables. Experiment. Use your imagination. You will be in good company. Some of today's best cooks are focusing their efforts on foods covered in this chapter and the good things that can be done with them.

The Cook's Vocabulary

al dente

au gratin

batch cooking, stagger cooking

duchesse potatoes

endosperm

fritter

germ

gratiné

legumes

macaroni

mealy or starchy potatoes

noodles

pastry bag

phytochemical

pigments: anthocyanins, chlorophyll, carotene, flavone

pilaf method

piping

rice: long grain, medium grain, short grain, brown rice, regular-milled white rice, parboiled or converted rice, precooked or instant, basmati, wild rice

risotto

semolina

waxy or new potatoes

Review Questions

Answer each question in complete sentences. Read each question carefully and make sure you answer all parts of the question. Organize your answer into more than one paragraph when appropriate.

1. Discuss the importance of color in cooking a vegetable. How would you maintain color when cooking cauliflower? Red cabbage? Spinach? Carrots?
2. Explain the problems in holding cooked vegetables for service and suggest ways to solve them.
3. To what extent are different market forms of vegetables (fresh, frozen, canned) already cooked? How do you deal with the differences when you cook them?
4. How does the potato differ from other vegetables? Give examples of 10 menu items that feature potatoes.
5. Explain briefly how legumes, grains, and pasta are cooked. Do their cooking methods have anything in common?
6. Discuss the menu roles of legumes, grains, and pasta.
7. Discuss any nutritional implications of entrées based on beef and entrées based on legumes, grains, and/or pasta.

Chapter 10

MEAT COOKERY

Meat cookery began in ancient China, so one story goes, when a young boy accidentally burned down his father's house and with it a litter of suckling pigs. Discovering the irresistible flavor of the burnt flesh, he and his father, and their neighbors, too, burned down their houses whenever they had a litter of pigs.

Spit-roasting of meat goes back to prehistoric times and carried right through to the days of Escoffier and beyond. In medieval times, the great banquet dishes were the whole ox, the wild boar, the boar's head (served with garlands and ushered in with trumpets), and the suckling pig spit-roasted over the open fire.

In the 1600s and 1700s, fresh meat became more available and a new cuisine emerged featuring a great variety of meat dishes. As classical cuisine developed, meat dishes multiplied through the use of different sauces and garnitures.

Today's American cook is the beneficiary of several revolutions in meat production—in feeding, transporting, preserving, aging, grading, and marketing. The United States is a world leader in the production of quality beef, pork, and veal, and one of the world's top consumers of meat.

Meat is by far the most expensive item the cook prepares. In almost every kitchen, the dollars spent on meat far exceed those spent on any other item. It becomes very important, then, to cook it well so that this high-cost menu item can pay its own way.

After completing this chapter, you should be able to:

- Choose appropriate cooking methods for different cuts of meat.
- Describe the different degrees of doneness in red meats and determine when the desired degree of doneness has been reached.
- Describe or demonstrate how to braise, simmer, broil, grill, pan-fry, sauté, and roast appropriate cuts of meat.
- Describe or demonstrate how to make sauces, gravies, and jus using cooking liquids, pan juices, and fonds.
- Handle and store raw and cooked meats properly.

ABOUT MEAT IN GENERAL

Meat is the flesh of domestic animals—beef and veal from cattle, pork and ham from hogs, lamb and mutton from sheep. Venison, hare, squirrel, and coon are also spoken of as meats, but, from a cook's point of view, they are **game** and do not belong in our discussion.

Another group of meats, known as **variety meats,** consists of such things as liver, kidneys, heart, tongue, and sweetbreads, which are organs of the animal. Meat mixtures such as sausage meat and cold cuts are also classified as variety meats.

Table 10-1 LEAN CUTS OF MEAT

Lean cuts of meat
BEEF
Top round (roasted for roast beef, cubed for kebabs, marinated to make London broil)
Eye of round (roasted for roast beef or braised for pot roast)
Tip round (cubed for kebabs)
Strip loin steak (broiled to make New York strip steak, club steak, and others)
Top sirloin butt steak (broiled to make sirloin steak, cubed for kebabs, or marinated to make London broil)
Flank steak (marinated and broiled to make London broil)
Tenderloin steak (broiled to make filet mignon)
PORK *(Each cut has less than 9 grams of fat per 3-ounce cooked serving)*
Boneless loin roast
Boneless rib roast
Center rib chop
Center loin chop
Top loin chop
Sirloin roast
Boneless sirloin chop
Tenderloin
VEAL
Almost all cuts are low in fat.
LAMB
Sirloin roast
Shank half of leg roast
Loin chops
Blade chops
Foreshank

Meat is a good source of many important nutrients, including protein, iron, copper, zinc, and many B vitamins. Meat is also a significant source of fat, saturated fat, and cholesterol. For health-conscious customers, the cook has a variety of lean cuts of meat to choose from (Table 10.1) that can be carefully trimmed of fat and cooked using a method that requires little or no fat.

The various kinds of meats are very individual in flavor, but their cooking is similar. Lamb is roasted the same way as beef. Veal stew, beef stew, and lamb stew all use the same techniques of cooking. For this reason, we do not need to talk about cooking each different kind of meat in turn. It makes more sense to talk about meats as a group, to look at the things about meat that affect the cooking, and to learn how to deal with them.

If you are going to get a good meat dish on the table, you need to know quite a bit about the raw product. What makes it tender? What makes it tough? How do you tell which is which, and how do you deal with it?

We'll talk about raw meats under the following broad topics. Each of them has a bearing on cooking methods and final product quality.

- Structure of meats
- Aging
- Inspection and grading
- Cuts of meat and how to use them
- Handling and storage

STRUCTURE OF MEATS

Meat is the muscle of the animal. The muscle is composed of fibers—tubelike strings held together by connective tissue. The texture of the fibers and the amount and kind of connective tissue determine the tenderness of the meat.

Young animals, females, and males castrated when young have finer muscle fibers and are therefore more tender. Uncastrated males and mature animals have coarser fibers and therefore less tender meat. The texture of the muscle fiber also varies from one part of the animal to another.

Connective tissue is a factor the cook does not have to cope with when cooking fish and poultry. In meat, it makes a big difference in what you choose to cook and how you choose to cook it. Connective tissue is tough. The more a muscle has been exercised and the older the animal, the more connective tissue there will be.

There are two kinds of connective tissue—**collagen** (kol′-a-jun), which is white, and **elastin** (ee-lass′-tun), which is yellow. Collagen can be tenderized by proper cooking. If cooked a long time at a low temperature by moist heat, it gradually breaks down and turns to gelatin and water. Meat cuts that are high in collagen, such as brisket, plate, and chuck, are therefore cooked by moist-heat methods. Cuts that are low in collagen and have fine-textured fibers, such as steaks and loin cuts, can be cooked by dry-heat methods.

Elastin remains tough no matter how it is cooked. The only way to deal with elastin is mechanically—by cutting it away or by grinding, for example. Ground beef, such as used to make hamburgers, is often made from tougher meats that need to be mechanically ground before they are tender enough to eat.

Fat in meat also differs from fat in poultry and fish. There is a fat layer all around the meat carcass (called *finish*) as well as fat distributed throughout the meat, called **marbling.** Fat in meat is associated with tenderness. It melts at low temperatures and encircles the muscle fibers, thus preserving their juices. Hot fat and hot juices cook the fibers to a moist tenderness.

AGING

Shortly after an animal is slaughtered, a stiffening of the muscles occurs called rigor mortis. In red meats, it takes three or four days for substances within the flesh called enzymes to soften the rigid muscle tissue. In white meats, there is little rigor and it disappears more quickly. The practice of holding meats long enough for enzymatic action to be effective is called **aging.** During aging, the meat is held at cool temperatures to prevent bacterial growth.

Meats that are not allowed time to soften are called **green meats.** Cooked green meat is tough. Since it usually takes several days for meats to reach the market, green meat is not a common problem.

Meats such as pork and veal are not aged beyond the time it takes for rigor to disappear. Red meats, on the other hand, can be aged for several weeks, allowing enzymatic action to increase tenderness and flavor. The difference is that red meats are protected from bacterial action by a layer of fat. Veal does not have much fat covering. Pork does, but pork fat quickly becomes rancid. Actually, both pork and veal are tender to begin with and do not need aging.

Figure 10-1 FEDERAL INSPECTION MARK

U.S.
INSPECTED
AND PASSED BY
DEPARTMENT OF
AGRICULTURE
EST. 38

The number refers to the establishment where the meat was inspected. (Courtesy USDA.)

Figure 10-2 FEDERAL GRADE SHIELDS

Federally graded beef, veal, and lamb are stamped with the appropriate quality grade shield. A meat grader rolls a choice veal carcass with the USDA shield. (Photo and shields courtesy USDA.)

There are a number of ways of aging meats. In frontier days, the hunter used to hang his kill on the back porch in cold weather and let it ripen. Today, meat carcasses may be similarly hung in coolers for three to six weeks with carefully controlled temperature, air flow, humidity, and bacteria-killing ultraviolet light. This method is known as **dry aging.** Dry-aged meats are a specialty product and cost more.

Most often, however, meat is Cryovac-aged, also called **wet aging.** In this process, the carcass is broken down into smaller cuts that are vacuum-packed in moisture–vapor-proof plastic bags and aged under refrigeration. The removal of oxygen reduces mold and bacterial growth and fat rancidity, while allowing enzymatic action to continue.

Aging does not affect quality grading, but it

can affect quality eating. It contributes to the tenderness and flavor that no grade stamp can guarantee.

INSPECTION AND GRADING

All meats must pass **inspections** for wholesomeness. They are inspected by the federal government if they are shipped interstate. If they are sold within the state where they are produced, they are inspected either by the state or by the federal government, whichever has the higher standard. Animals are inspected before slaughter and again after kill. An inspection mark (Figure 10.1) certifies that the meat is wholesome and has been processed under sanitary conditions.

Meats that pass inspection are usually graded, although **grading** is not required by law. Most meat sold to foodservice operations is graded by the U.S. Department of Agriculture (USDA) and bears its grade shield (Figure 10.2). USDA grade standards are based on the age of the animal, the amount of marbling in the meat, and the texture and color of the meat.

Pork is an exception to the grading found for beef, veal, and lamb. Because the quality of pork is very consistent, it is not graded for quality, but, instead, is graded for yield. Yield Grade 1 has more usable meat in proportion to fat than Yield Grade 5 (the lowest grade).

Meat grades are important to the cook because they influence the choice of cooking method. Higher grades are juicier and tenderer than lower grades. But a good cook can create a palatable dish from any grade of meat by choosing an appropriate way to cook it.

There are several grades of meats, but, from the kitchen standpoint, there are only a few of any importance. For beef, lamb, and veal, there are three primary grades.

Prime grade is the highest in quality as well as in price. Prime meat has a good-quality fat cover (thick, white, brittle), fine-textured flesh, and abundant marbling. Most prime cuts are both tender and juicy. Beef, veal, and lamb are available in prime, although the supply is quite limited.

Choice grade meat is high in quality. Most cuts are tender and juicy. Choice is the commonly used grade. It is usually in abundant supply, so the price is within reason.

The next grading level down is called **select** for beef and **good** for veal and lamb. Select or good grade meats may have lower-quality fat or less fat cover and less marbling than the two higher grades. The meat fibers are not always smooth and tender. Lack of fat and coarser flesh texture will not yield as tender and juicy a product as will choice and prime. The price is correspondingly lower.

CUTS OF MEAT AND HOW TO USE THEM

In addition to grade, the cook must consider the cut of meat to be cooked. The charts in Figure 10.3 show how the beef, veal, lamb, and pork carcasses are divided into **primal cuts**—large divisions or wholesale cuts. Figures 10.4 to 10.7 show how the primal cuts may be further divided into cuts of meat for cooking, and which common cooking methods are used for these various cuts.

Meat cuts fall neatly into three groups—tender, moderately tender, and less tender. Generally speaking, the tender cuts come from the part of the animal getting the least exercise. You can prove this for yourself by studying the charts. An exercised muscle has built up tough connective tissue while muscles that have been idle have remained fine grained with a minimum of connective tissue.

Figure 10-3 PRIMAL (WHOLESALE) MEAT CUTS

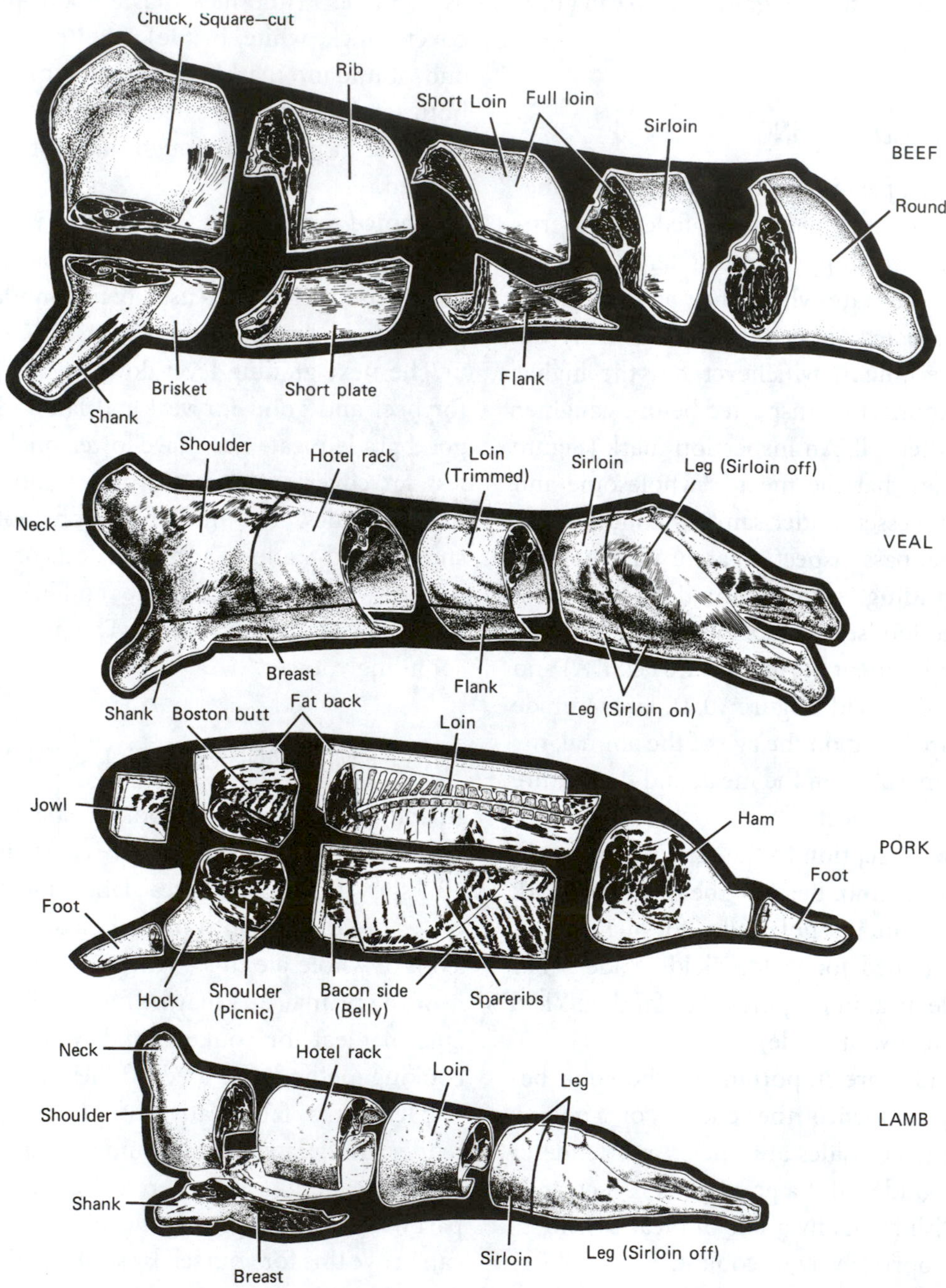

(Courtesy National Live Stock and Meat Board.)

Figure 10-4 THIS IS A SIDE OF BEEF—ONE-HALF OF THE ANIMAL CARCASS

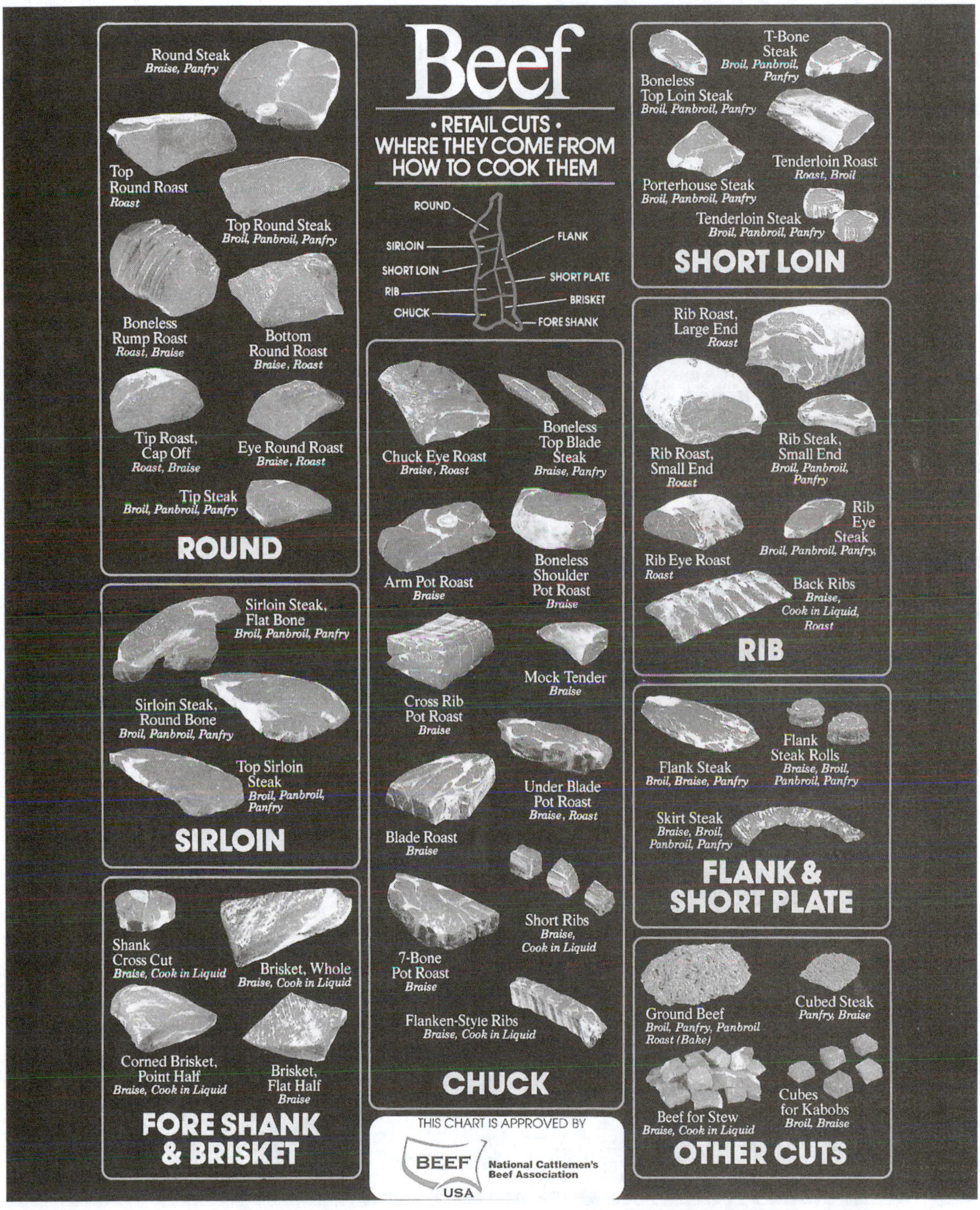

The large divisions (chuck, rib, round, and so on) are the primal cuts. They are broken down into smaller cuts according to how they will be used. The ones shown in this chart may be seen in the supermarket. For foodservice use, the primal cuts may be cut a little bit differently. (Reproduction courtesy of the National Cattlemen's Beef Association, © 1986.)

Figure 10-5 THIS IS A WHOLE VEAL CARCASS

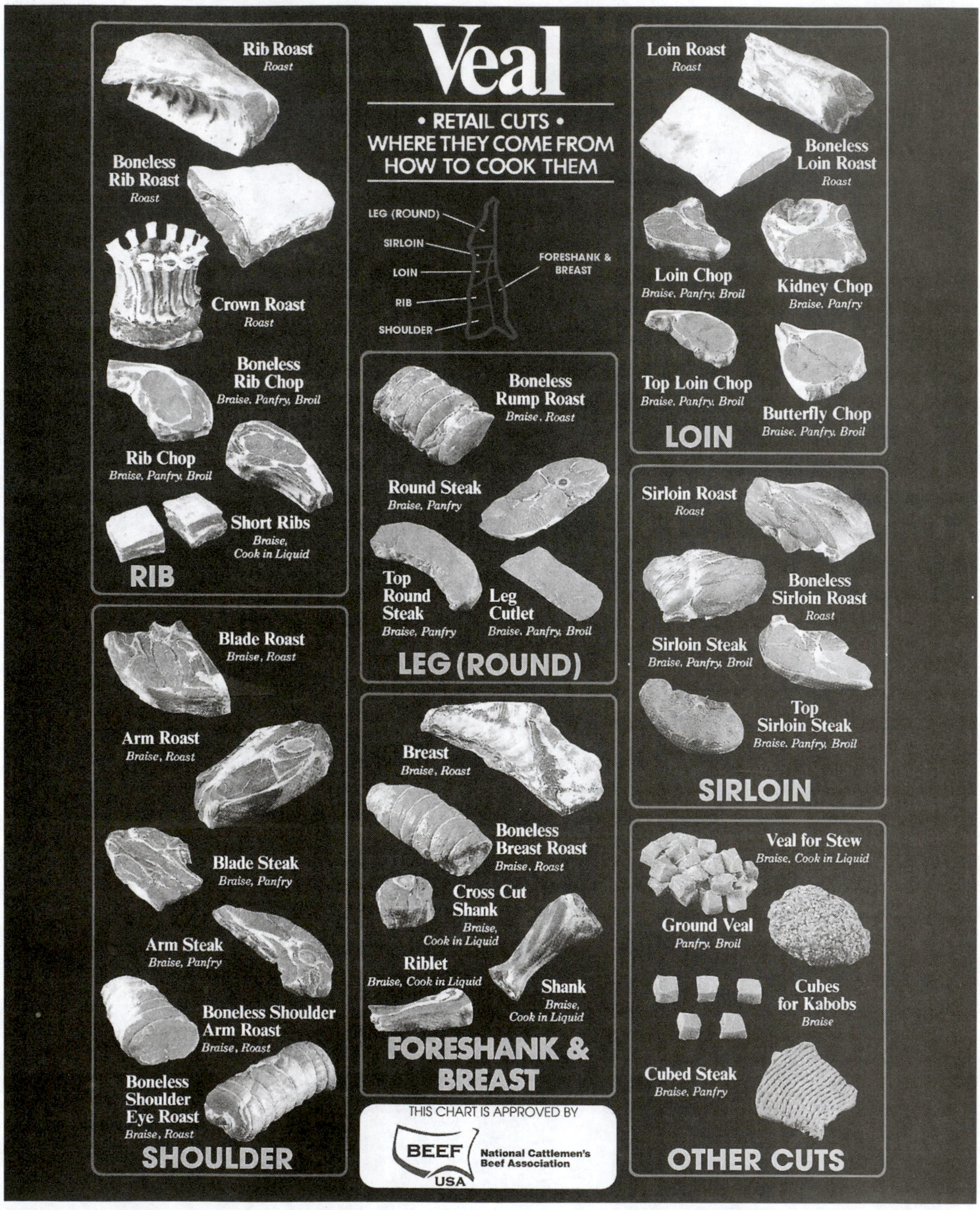

All of it is tender and can be cooked by any method. Foodservice operations use veal from all parts of the animal, though not always in the retail cuts shown here. (Reproduction courtesy of the National Cattlemen's Beef Association, © 1986.)

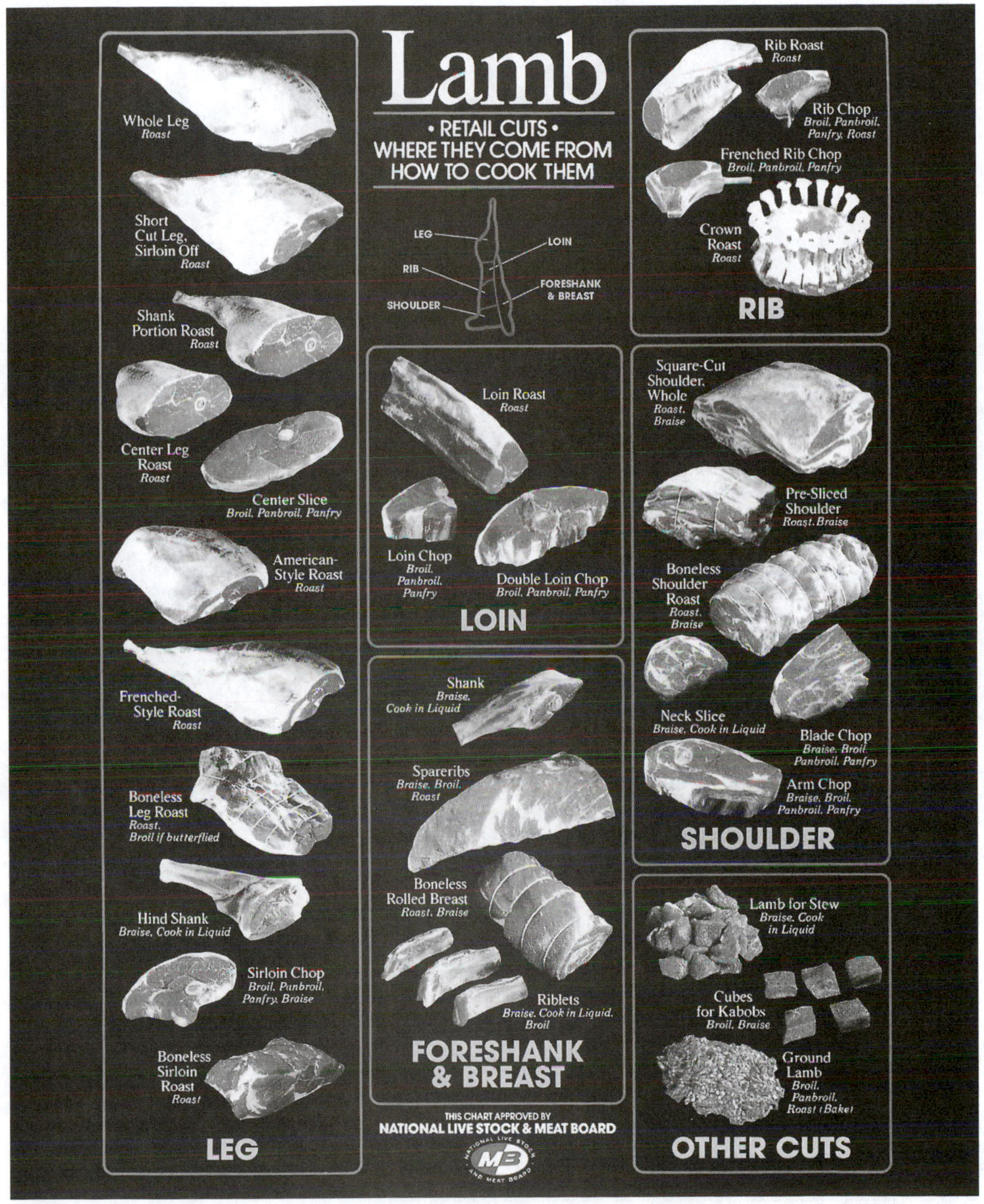

Almost all its meat is tender. Cuts most commonly used in foodservice establishments are loin chops for broiling, the leg for roasting, and the rib roast served as rack of lamb. (Reproduction courtesy of the National Cattlemen's Beef Association, © 1986.)

Figure 10-7 THIS IS ONE-HALF OF A HOG CARCASS

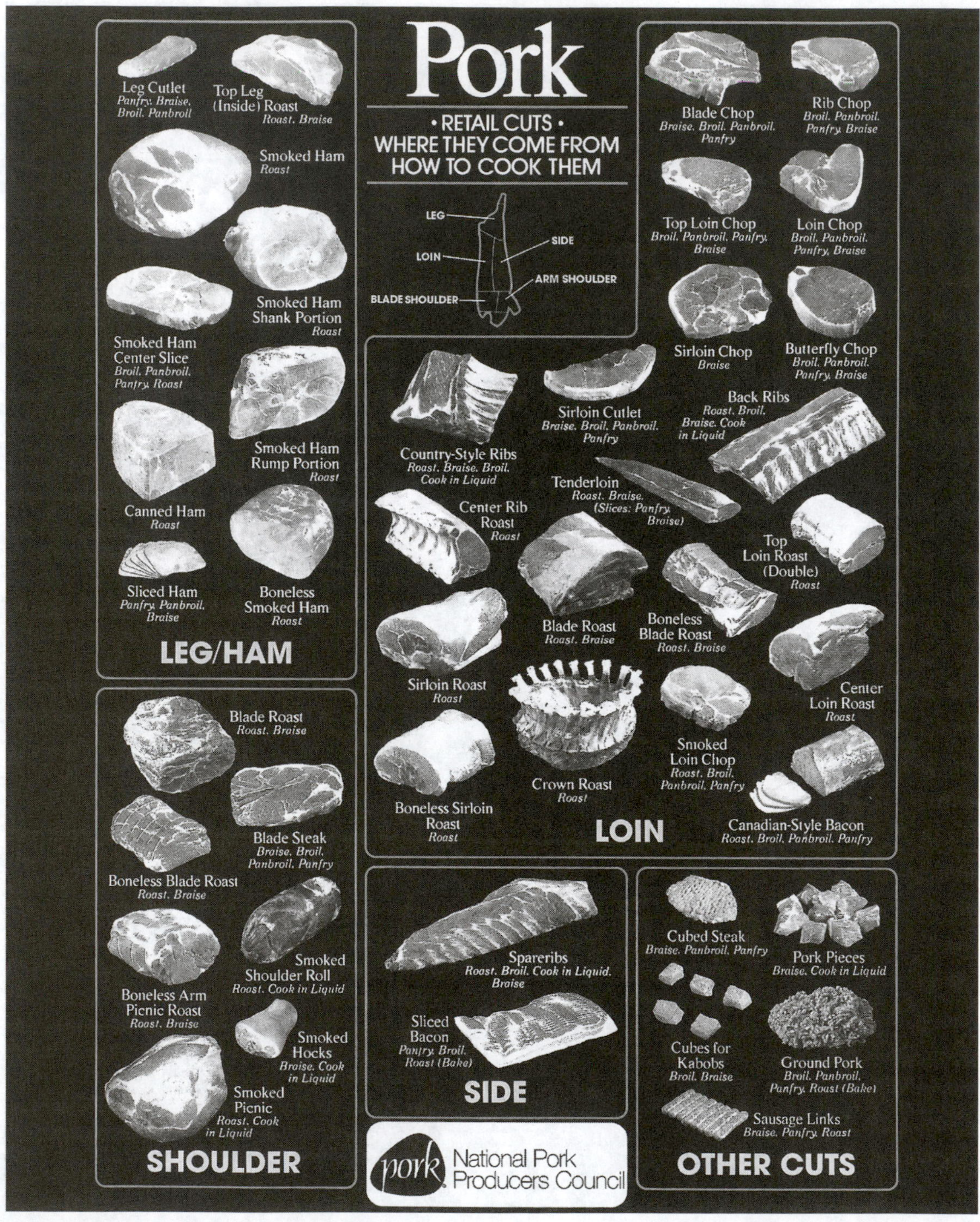

Almost all its meat is tender. The heavy layer of fat surrounding the lean flesh gives us bacon, salt pork, fatback, and lard. (Reproduction courtesy of the National Pork Producers Council, © 1986.)

Tender cuts include rib steaks and roasts and loin-cut steaks such as T-bone, sirloin, and tenderloin. Generally speaking, meat that touches the backbone is tender, suitable for steaks and quick cooking. You can cook the tender cuts by dry-heat methods in any grade.

Moderately tender cuts include rump, sirloin tip, chuck or shoulder, and top-round roasts, plus steaks cut from the round and chuck. You can cook any of these cuts from prime- and choice-grade meats by dry-heat methods, but the same cuts from a lower grade need moist-heat cooking.

Less tender cuts include shoulder, arm, flank, and brisket. These cuts need moist-heat cooking in all grades. Ground meats and cubed steaks can be cooked using dry or moist heat because they have been mechanically tenderized.

There are differences among beef, veal, pork, and lamb that need to be mentioned. Veal, pork, and lamb generally come from younger animals than beef. More cuts of veal, pork, and lamb can be cooked using dry heat than moist heat. In fact, only the following cuts of veal, pork, and lamb must be cooked by moist heat: shank, breast, brisket, and flank.

SMOKED AND CURED MEATS

Another market form of meat is the group of products that are **smoked** or **cured.** Smoking (exposing to a wood fire) and curing (exposing to heat or salt) serve the dual purpose of preserving meats from spoilage and adding flavor. Meats may be either cured or smoked or both.

Hams, shoulders, bacon, spareribs, loins, and sausages are among the pork products that arrive in the kitchen smoked or cured. Many are ready-to-eat items to be served either cold or hot.

Bacon arrives in kitchens in one of two ways: whole slab or sliced. The cook has to slice the whole slab bacon. Sliced bacon comes by the count—that is, so many slices to the pound. Common sizes are 18 to 22 slices to the pound. The larger the number the thinner the slice.

Ham is available in several market forms—cooked and uncooked, bone-in and boned, rolled and tied or canned. Most hams arrive in today's kitchen already cooked. Cooked hams come both bone-in and boned. Canned hams are boned and cooked and commonly come in two shapes. The pullman ham is rectangular and slices uniformly for easy preparation. The other common canned ham is pear shaped.

The distinctive flavor in a ham comes either from the curing method or from smoking. Most hams used today are cured but not smoked. Smoked hams cost more and are usually used only for specialty dishes. Cured uncooked hams, sometimes referred to as country hams, include the famous Smithfield ham from Virginia. These hams are dry-cured in salt, rubbed with a seasoned coating, smoked, and aged for up to two years. They must be soaked for 12 to 24 hours and scrubbed before cooking. Then they are roasted like any other raw meat.

Partially cooked hams usually carry the phrase "Cook before eating." Fully cooked hams are labeled "Ready-to-eat" or "Heat and serve." Many imported hams of high quality (and cost) are used for their specialized flavors—produced by different smoking and curing methods and ingredients. Danish hams, Westphalian hams from Germany, and prosciutto from Italy are some examples.

Smoked or cured sausages that originated in many different countries are now produced domestically as well as being imported. Among the choices are frankfurters, salami and summer sausages, braunschweiger (liver), bologna, pepperoni, and Thuringer. Some are smoked or cured but not fully cooked. Make sure you know which of these need to be cooked to safe internal temperatures.

Corned beef—usually cured from the brisket—smoked tongue, and dried, cured, and smoked sliced beef are also used in the kitchen. They should be refrigerated, but they have a slightly longer shelf life than fresh beef.

HANDLING AND STORING UNCOOKED MEATS

Meat used to be bought by the whole carcass, and each establishment butchered its own meat. Even today, a few large operations maintain their own butchers, but the practice is dying out in this country. Today, many establishments buy their meats in portion-controlled cuts ready for use.

It goes without saying that raw meats should be refrigerated. Meats that arrive in the kitchen wrapped in Cryovac should remain wrapped until use. Unwrapped meats should be stored loosely to allow good circulation of air. Air circulation will dry the meats to some extent. Although this may cause some shrinkage, it will retard bacterial growth, since bacteria thrive in moisture.

Fresh meats can stay in the refrigerator for up to five days, with a few exceptions: ground meat, stew meat, and variety meats. These products should be used within one to two days. If you must keep meats for any length of time, wrap them well and freeze them. But even in a freezer meats do not have an indefinite shelf life. Most fresh meats are best if not frozen for more than six months.

All smoked and cured meats should be refrigerated. The preservative processes do not substitute for refrigeration and cooking, but they do prolong shelf life. Canned ham must be refrigerated like any other ham.

UNDERSTANDING DONENESS IN MEATS

When cooking pork and veal, only one degree of doneness is acceptable—total cooking throughout the flesh. With beef and lamb, you will work with several degrees of **doneness.** This phrase refers not to degrees of temperature but to the changes in the physical state of the meat itself as it progresses from rawness to total doneness. It is true that degrees of temperature can be an index to degrees of doneness. But think of doneness first in terms of the meat itself.

DEGREES OF DONENESS FOR BEEF AND LAMB

Degrees of doneness apply to the cooking of beef and lamb. This is not to say that they must be cooked something less than well done, but that they can be. Pork and veal, as well as variety meats, are generally cooked well done for tenderness and taste. In the case of pork, there is also a health reason for well-done cooking. At one time, undercooked pork carried the parasite causing trichinosis. Though none has been found in federally inspected pork for many years, it is still safer to cook pork to temperatures that will kill the parasite.

Degrees of doneness may be described as follows:

- **Rare**: cool and red in the center
- **Medium rare**: slightly warm in the center, with deep-pink or pale-red center color
- **Medium**: warm and pink in the center
- **Medium well**: slightly hot and slightly pink in the center
- **Well done**: fully cooked, hot in the center with no pink, but still moist

As a meat progresses from rare to well done, the outside becomes brown and the meat shrinks somewhat and gradually becomes drier. A sixth degree of doneness—overdone or ruined—causes the meat to shrivel, dry out, and toughen.

Why varying degrees of doneness for beef and lamb? Cooked less than well done, they are juicier and possess a flavor many diners enjoy. Furthermore, a good cut of beef or lamb cooked less than well done is definitely more tender. If cooked all the way to doneness, it dries out and begins to toughen. Many restaurants will not guarantee the tenderness of steaks cooked beyond medium well. Notice that the relationship between tenderness and doneness in red meat is the reverse of this relationship in poultry and fish and in pork and veal. With these, the flesh is not tender until it is fully cooked. However, overdoneness is tough in all types of flesh.

Table 10-2 INTERNAL TEMPERATURES FOR DEGREES OF DONENESS

Meat	*Rare*	*Medium*	*Well Done*
Beef/lamb	140°F (60°C)	140–150°F (60–66°C)	160–165°F (71–74°C)
Pork	—	—	155°F (68°C)
Veal	—	—	160°F (71°C)
Ground beef	—	—	155°F (68°C)
Stuffed meats	—	—	165°F (74°C)

IDENTIFYING DONENESS

But enough about what and why. The next question is: How do you cook to the right degree of doneness and no more? There are three good methods for identifying the degree of doneness:

- Internal temperature
- Time/weight
- Feel

Let's examine these one at a time and then apply them to specific situations.

THE INTERNAL-TEMPERATURE METHOD. Table 10.2 shows the internal temperatures at which various meats reach various degrees of doneness. The only method for checking internal temperature is to insert a meat thermometer into the flesh with the point in the center of the meat. Many meat thermometers have doneness readings for different kinds of meats marked on the face or dial. Instead of relying on these numbers, consult a table (such as Table 10.2) or check your standardized recipe.

Achieving the right degree of doneness has one complicating factor known as **carryover cooking.** Simply stated, the inside of the meat goes on cooking after you remove it from the heat source. This happens through conduction of heat through the meat from outside to inside. Thus, the internal temperature will rise anywhere from 5°F (3°C) in small cuts to 25°F (15°C) in very large roasts after removal from heat for 15 to 30 minutes. The average rise is 10 to 15°F (6–9°C). Therefore, remove roasts from the oven when the temperature is about 10°F (6°C) below the desired number of degrees. The effects of carryover cooking will bring the temperature up to where you want it in about 30 minutes. Letting the roast rest also allows you to slice the meat with less loss of tasty juices.

Internal temperature is certainly the most accurate indicator of doneness, but you need to know the other two methods as well. Each one has its uses.

THE TIME/WEIGHT METHOD. According to the time/weight method, you achieve the degree of doneness you want by computing the time necessary to do the job and then cooking the meat for that length of time. To do this, you must know the time it takes for a pound of meat to cook at a given temperature to the degree of doneness you want. While charts are available with this type of information, they are useful in estimating cooking time, but doneness would still need to be assessed using either a thermometer or the next method.

THE FEEL METHOD. The use of feel as a check for doneness is just that. You feel for a particular texture that tells you what degree of doneness has been reached.

Meat as it cooks becomes firmer in texture. The more it cooks, or the closer it gets to well done, the firmer it gets. Well-done meat is firm to the touch; it resists pressure. Medium meat feels medium firm; there is some resistance to pressure but also some give. Rare meat feels soft; there is little resistance.

With practice, a cook can quickly learn to judge with reasonable accuracy the doneness of a steak, remembering that some carryover cooking will take place. A broiler cook with oversensitive fingers may dip them into a pot of ice water to keep them from being well done after 400 steaks.

WHICH METHOD WHEN? Just which method of checking for doneness is the best? What's best depends on the circumstances.

Internal temperature is certainly the most accurate test, but it may not always be the best method. Imagine a broiler cook trying to measure the internal temperature of 400 steaks to be cooked to different degrees of doneness in a one-hour period.

To make the matter simple, let's list the situations in which each method would be best and see just how to use it.

Internal temperature is best . . .

- When large pieces of meats are being roasted.
- When different meats and other products are being roasted at the same time in the same oven—for example, prime rib, leg of lamb, and turkey. Each kind must have its own thermometer.
- When large numbers of different-sized pieces of the same item are being roasted—say 20 prime ribs of varying size. In this case, you would stagger the thermometers according to the sizes of roasts as you do in poultry roasting. Place one in a small roast, one in a medium size, and one in one of the larger pieces. Then consider each thermometer as representing all roasts of a similar size. In this way, you can achieve consistency in doneness for all the meats.
- Whenever you can use it.

Time/weight is best . . .

- When all meats being roasted are similar in size and type, and your ovens have been time tested and calibrated so that you know they will perform according to the table you are using.
- When you also use a meat thermometer to verify doneness.

Feel is best . . .

- When small pieces of meat are being cooked—steaks or chops, for example.
- When different items are being cooked with the same equipment starting at different times—for instance, rare, medium, and well-

done steaks and some hamburgers, being cooked to order.

- When there is doubt about the accuracy of the first two methods. In this case, feel is a good final check. However, it is not an accurate substitute for either of the other methods. For example, as large roasts are roasting, they may feel firm to the touch. Allowed to stand, they will once again feel soft and you may find you are serving meat that is much less done than you intended.

It takes practice to learn how to choose the most appropriate method for each meat-cooking situation, and then how to put each method to work with accurate results. These are the keys to successful meat cookery. Good meat, the right cooking method, and the right degree of doneness are the three secrets of tenderness and flavor.

Anyone can put meat into an oven, but it takes a good cook to take it out at the right degree of doneness.

METHODS OF COOKING MEAT

Choosing the right method of cooking depends on the cut of meat you are going to use and the dish you are going to make.

The better cuts and higher grades of meat are cooked by dry-heat methods such as broiling and roasting and pan-frying. These meats are tender to begin with, and the cook's chief concern is to achieve the desired degree of doneness while preserving tenderness and flavor.

The less tender, less expensive cuts are cooked by moist-heat methods such as braising and simmering. The cook's goal here is to create tenderness, and the way to achieve it is to use moisture, low temperatures, and prolonged cooking. This combination of conditions breaks down tough connective tissues (collagen) while avoiding the toughening of muscle fiber that takes place at higher temperatures.

The choice between dry-heat and moist-heat methods is of the greatest importance. Roasting or broiling less tender cuts of meat would never make them tender, no matter how long you cooked them. Cooking a tender cut by braising or simmering would be wasting the very quality of instant tenderness that makes it so desirable.

Let's look at moist-heat cooking first.

BRAISING

Braising is a means of creating delicious dishes from less tender cuts of meat by cooking them covered in a small amount of liquid. The meats may be either bite-sized pieces, which become a stew, or larger pieces such as pot roasts, which are cooked whole. The latter are served sliced, often with a sauce made from the cooking liquid. All kinds of meats may be braised.

The meat is usually seared over high heat to brown it before the liquid is added and the pot is covered and the long, slow braising process begins. The braising can be done in a slow oven or over low heat on the range or in a covered tilting fry pan.

Testing doneness in a braised meat is rather different from the methods described earlier. Braised meat is done when it is tender, and the best way to test tenderness is by feel with a fork. When the prongs go into the meat easily and come out easily, the meat is done. Because of the slow moist cooking, you do not have to worry about releasing juices by probing with the fork. They have already blended with the liquid in the pot—and vice versa.

Even a braised dish can be cooked too long, so that tenderizing ceases and toughening begins. It is important to use the time guidelines given in recipes to start testing for doneness.

Pot roasts are among the most common of braised dishes. The label is not a cooking term but a dish name. A pot roast is not roasted; it is cooked in a pot. It is a large cut of meat cooked whole and sliced for service, but there its similarity to roasted meat ends. It is selected from less tender cuts of meat such as brisket or round, and slow moist-heat cooking makes its flavor very different from that of roasted meats. Recipe 10.1 makes a typical pot roast of beef.

When you examine the recipe, you can see that you are preparing two things at the same time, a meat and a sauce. The stock, thickening ingredients, and mirepoix are all sauce ingredients, and the proportions given represent the proportions for a good sauce.

In order to get the best interaction of meat and moisture during cooking, you need enough liquid to submerge half to three-fourths of the roast. The quantity required to do this will vary with the shape of the roast and the size of the pan.

Estimate the amount of sauce you need before you begin to cook, using pan capacity and roast size to make your judgment. You do not need to be exact. But if it is apparent that 2 quarts will be either far too much or far too little, decrease or increase the sauce part of the recipe. Remember also that you need a minimum amount of $1^1/_2$ to 2 ounces of sauce per serving. If this minimum threatens to submerge the whole roast, choose a larger pan.

Going back to the cooking instructions, you see that cooking begins with the high-heat process of searing. This is done mostly for color, both for the meat and for the sauce. It does not affect the meat texture or its juiciness. Notice that you do not season the meat before searing. This is because salt will draw out the meat juices and interfere with browning.

After browning the mirepoix, you add the

Recipe 10-1 POT ROAST

YIELD: ***12–15 4-oz (125 g) portions with 1 oz (30 mL) sauce each***

2 fl oz	**oil**	**60 mL**
5–6 lb	**rump roast**	**2.5–3.0 kg**

Mirepoix:

4 oz	**onions, medium dice**	**125 g**
2 oz	**celery, medium dice**	**60 g**
2 oz	**carrots, medium dice**	**60 g**
6 oz	**canned tomatoes**	**175 g**
2 qt	**brown stock**	**8 L**

Sachet:

1	**bay leaf**
1	**garlic clove**
6	**peppercorns**
	salt and pepper to taste

1. Heat oil on high in a brazier.
2. Sear roast on all sides until brown. Remove from pan.
3. Over a medium heat, sauté mirepoix until lightly caramelized.
4. Add tomatoes and enough stock to submerge half to three-fourths of the roast. Bring to a boil.
5. Add the sachet and rump roast.
6. Cover brazier and place in 300°F (150°C) oven for 2–3 hours until done.
7. Strain sauce, adjust consistency, and season to taste.
8. Slice meat across the grain. Serve sauce over meat.

Per serving:			
Calories:	310	Carbohydrates:	4 g
Fat:	15 g	Cholesterol:	90 mg
Protein:	36 g	Fiber:	0 g
		Sodium:	60 mg

tomato product and stock. After boiling this mixture, you return the meat to the pan, cover it, and simmer until done. In the final steps, you prepare a sauce/gravy from the braising liquid.

You can also prepare a pot roast by making the sauce first, then braising the meat in the sauce. It is a little messier, so many cooks prefer to make the sauce at the end.

Individual portions of meat may also be braised—for example, the chops in Recipe 10.2.

Recipe 10-2 BRAISED PORK CHOPS, SAUCE ROBERT

YIELD: *10 portions*

1/4 C	**oil**	**60 mL**
10 6-oz	**pork chops**	**175 g**
2 oz	**shallots, minced**	**60 g**
8 fl oz	**dry white wine**	**250 mL**
8 fl oz	**cider vinegar**	**250 mL**
1 1/2 pt	**espagnole**	**750 mL**
1 Tb	**mustard**	**15 mL**
	salt, pepper, and lemon juice to taste	

1. In a heavy sauté pan, heat oil over moderate heat.
2. Sear chops in oil until well browned. Remove chops and hold.
3. Sweat shallots in oil until translucent.
4. Deglaze pan with wine and vinegar, incorporating fond. Reduce liquid by half over high heat.
5. Stir in espagnole and mustard.
6. Season chops lightly and return to pan. Cover and cook at low heat until chops are tender.
7. Remove chops. Adjust sauce texture and seasoning as needed.
8. Strain sauce over chops.

Per serving:		Carbohydrates:	12 g
Calories:	379	Cholesterol:	89 mg
Fat:	19 g	Fiber:	0 g
Protein:	35 g	Sodium:	453 mg

The structure of this dish is very much like that of a pot roast simmered in its sauce: Meat is browned and then cooked slowly in a sauce that conveys delicious flavors to the meat and is served over the finished dish.

Many braised dishes are descended from the peasant's pot-on-the-fire and are made by the same methods as the first two recipes. Each region has its own variation. For example, in beef bourguignon, from the Burgundy region of France, julienne of salt pork provides the fat, red wine deglazes the pan, and the cubes of beef are simmered in the wine, fond, and demiglace. Mushrooms and pearl onions, cooked separately, complete the finished dish.

Notice how closely the method follows the making of the other braised dishes. Compare it also with the coq au vin (Chapter 11), a braised poultry dish. You will find striking similarities.

In Recipe 10.3, we have a braised dish that departs from the pattern we have observed so far: The meat is not browned before braising. It is simply simmered with flavor builders in a light stock until tender, then thickened with a white roux and enriched with a liaison. The liaison and the distinctive color elevate this classical dish to the level of elegance.

This dish may also be simmered uncovered if the level of the stock remains high enough to keep the meat surrounded with liquid. If frequent skimming is necessary, as it may be with veal, it is simpler not to replace the cover each time.

Many other meal-in-a-pot dishes may be made by braising or simmering cut-up meats, adding other ingredients, and serving them in the cooking liquid, thickened or unthickened. They may go by various names—stew, ragout, fricassee (usually white), navarin (a brown lamb dish), and so on depending on their origin and

Recipe 10-3 BLANQUETTE DE VEAU (VEAL IN WHITE SAUCE)

YIELD: ***10 5-oz (150 g) portions***

4 lb	**boneless veal shoulder or breast, 1-in. cubes**	**1.8 kg**
1 pt	**white stock**	**500 mL**
1	**onion piqué**	
Bouquet garni:		
1	**celery rib**	
$^1/_2$	**small carrot**	
5–6	**parsley stems**	
$^1/_2$ tsp	**thyme**	**2 mL**
1	**bay leaf**	
3 oz	**roux**	**90 g**
	salt, white pepper, lemon juice, and nutmeg to taste	

1. Blanch veal to improve appearance by covering with cold water, bringing to a boil, and then draining and rinsing the veal under cold water.
2. In another pot, cover the veal with stock. Add the onion piqué and bouquet garni.
3. Simmer the meat, covered, until tender—about $1^1/_2$ hours. Skim frequently.
4. Remove meat to another pan and keep warm.
5. Blend cold roux into the hot liquid to produce desired texture. Simmer to blend flavors and remove starch taste. Remove onion piqué and bouquet garni and discard.
6. Strain the sauce. Season to taste with salt, white pepper, lemon juice, and nutmeg.

Per serving:		Carbohydrates:	3 g
Calories:	257	Cholesterol:	142 mg
Fat:	13 g	Fiber:	0 g
Protein:	29 g	Sodium:	149 mg

their specific ingredients. You can make a family-style stew as you would a soup, first braising cubes of meat and then adding vegetables—carrots, celery, turnips, potatoes, and so on—in the order in which they will cook to doneness. Serve it in soup plates or bowls.

All these braised dishes are a way of turning less tender meats into delicious dishes through long, slow cooking with moist heat. You can even turn a braised dish into a pot pie by topping each serving with a pie crust.

SIMMERING

Lower grades and tougher cuts of meat are usually cooked by simmering. Low temperatures and longer cooking time in a moist medium tenderize their coarser fibers and their collagen. Beef brisket and the less tender variety meats, such as tongue, fall into this category. Cooking below the boiling point prevents shrinkage and toughening and minimizes flavor loss. The simmering of meat is similar to the poaching of fish or poultry, but meats need the slightly higher temperatures of simmering.

A typical example of a simmered meat is given in Recipe 10.4. You can see its similarity to the braising of a pot roast, but the meat is entirely covered with liquid, and no sauce is made from it. You can use the same recipe for such variety meats as tongue.

The small pot (Step 1) is efficient. Use water to cover, with $^1/_2$ to 1 inch (1–2 cm) above the meat to ensure that it remains submerged during the cooking.

In Step 2, adjust the amounts of the flavor builders in proportion to the amount of water you use. (You may notice that there is no salt in this recipe, since corned beef is well equipped with its own salt. For a fresh brisket, you would add an ounce or so of salt, or about 25 g.)

Cooking time (Step 3) may be a matter of hours. Test tenderness by fork or by feel. The meat will first become firm and rubbery; then it will feel less firm to the touch as it becomes tender to the bite.

Recipe 10-4 "BOILED" BRISKET

YIELD: ***16 4-oz (125 g) servings***

5 lb	**corned beef brisket**	**2.25 kg**
2 oz	**carrots, chopped**	**60 g**
2 oz	**celery, chopped**	**60 g**
4 oz	**onions, chopped**	**125 g**
4 oz	**leeks, chopped**	**125 g**
6	**parsley stems**	
$^1/_2$	**bay leaf**	
2–3	**cloves**	
5–6	**peppercorns**	

1. Place meat in a small pot and add enough cold water to cover it, plus $^1/_2$–1 in. (1–2 cm) more.
2. Bring to a boil and skim. Add flavor builders.
3. Reduce heat, cover, and simmer until tender when forked.
4. Slice thinly across the grain and serve hot.

Per serving:		Carbohydrates:	1 g
Calories:	285	Cholesterol:	111 mg
Fat:	20 g	Fiber:	0 g
Protein:	21 g	Sodium:	885 mg

Tender variety meats such as sweetbreads and brains are also simmered, but only briefly and for different reasons. They are blanched for a few minutes to firm them up so they can be skinned or otherwise handled. They are then usually finish-cooked by some other method, such as broiling or pan-frying.

BROILING AND GRILLING

We turn now to the dry-heat methods of cooking, suitable only for tender cuts of meat. Of these methods, broiling and grilling head the list in customer popularity. Almost every menu includes broiled or grilled meats, and many specialty restaurants such as steakhouses serve nothing else. The broiler station is one of the most common areas of specialization in the kitchen.

In broiling and grilling, degree of doneness is 95 percent of the game. You have tenderness to begin with, so the task is to produce the degree of doneness the diner orders and to recognize it when it is reached.

You already know how the various degrees of doneness are defined. (Let us hope the diner agrees with the definitions. Some diners have their own firm convictions about medium rare and medium well, which can cause frustration all around when cook and diner disagree.)

You know, too, how to determine doneness. Since you are usually broiling or grilling small pieces—steaks, chops, liver—you use the feel method.

How do you cook to the right degree of doneness? You season the meat and put it in the overhead broiler or directly on the grill. You cook it, touch-testing it frequently, until it feels like the degree of doneness you want. Then you turn it over, using tongs, and cook the other side the same way. Recipe 10-5 sums things up.

There are some fine points to the cooking:

- Always preheat the broiler or grill.
- Use lower temperatures for medium well and well done. Use higher temperatures for meats at the other end of the scale. You can control the temperature either by turning the heat up or down or by moving the meat toward or away from the heat source.
- Pay attention to the thickness of the cut. Thin cuts cook rapidly and thick cuts take longer.
- A grill marks the meat as it cooks. To make crisscross grid marks, place the meat on the grill diagonally. When you are halfway through cooking the first side, rotate it 60 to 90°. When you turn the meat over, the marked side becomes the presentation side (the side that will face the guest) of the finished product (Figure 10.8).

Recipe 10-5 BROILED LAMB CHOPS

Yield: *10 portions*

10 6-oz	**lamb chops, rib**	**175 g**
	salt and black pepper to taste	
	oil as needed	

1. Season the chops with salt and black pepper.
2. Brush lightly with oil.
3. Place on preheated broiler or grill.
4. When chops are one-quarter done, turn each one about 90° to mark the presentation side.
5. When chops are half done, turn with tongs.
6. Cook to desired degree of doneness.

Per serving:		Carbohydrates:	0 g
Calories:	305	Cholesterol:	82 mg
Fat:	25 g	Fiber:	0 g
Protein:	18 g	Sodium:	62 mg

Successful broiling and grilling take practice and learning from your mistakes. You have to become fairly expert before you can distinguish medium well and medium rare by feel. Mastery of rare, medium, and well done is more than enough for the beginning broiler cook.

A piece of meat that has been perfectly broiled will stand alone, but it can be enlivened by imaginative accompaniments. Try choosing contrasting or complementary flavors for broiled steaks, lamb chops, pork chops, or liver from the following list:

- Compound butters of various flavors
- Chutneys—sweet–sour preserves from east Indian cuisine
- Sautéed or puréed fruits such as apples or peaches
- Puréed vegetable or fruit sauces
- Marinated vegetables or relishes
- Mint sauce (for lamb)

Another way to add flavoring is to use hickory, mesquite, or other types of wood to impart their distinctive flavors to foods being grilled.

A few less tender cuts of beef may be broiled or grilled if marinated first to tenderize them. The tasty favorite known as **London broil** is made by marinating flank steak in a zesty marinade for several hours and then broiling quickly over high heat. The outside should be well browned and the inside rare. Medium rare is recommended for maximum tenderness and juiciness. Recipe 10.6 gives you a formula. Thick cuts of round or chuck steak can also be used successfully in this broiling method.

Figure 10-8 HOW TO MAKE GRID MARKS

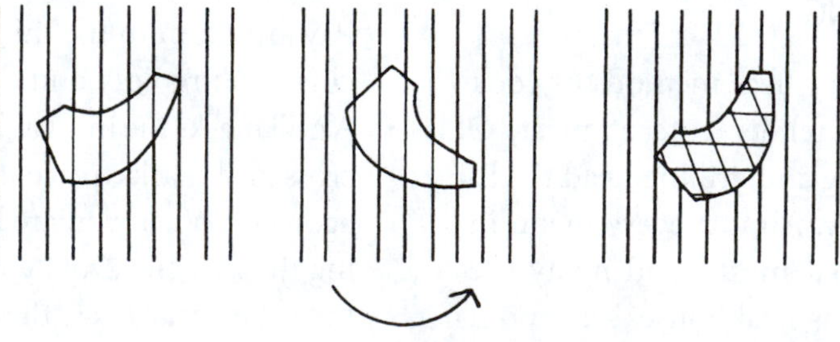

Recipe 10-6 LONDON BROIL (MARINATED FLANK STEAK)

YIELD: ***12 5-oz (150 g) portions***

Marinade:

$1^1/_2$ C	**oil**	**375 mL**
$^1/_4$ C	**lemon juice**	**60 mL**
1 tsp	**salt**	**5 mL**
1 tsp	**pepper**	**5 mL**
1 tsp	**fresh ginger**	**5 mL**
$^1/_2$ tsp	**thyme**	**2 mL**
5 lb	**flank steak**	**2.4 kg**

1. Combine marinade ingredients in shallow pan.
2. Add flank steaks to pan, coating all sides with marinade.
3. Marinate in refrigerator at least 2 hours, but not more than 9 hours.
4. Remove meat from marinade and place on preheated broiler or grill.
5. Cook quickly to desired doneness, about 3–5 minutes per side, turning once.
6. Slice across the grain in very thin diagonal slices.

Per serving:		Carbohydrates:	0 g
Calories:	194	Cholesterol:	47 mg
Fat:	9 g	Fiber:	0 g
Protein:	27 g	Sodium:	56 mg

SAUTÉING AND PAN-FRYING

Sautéing, a quick flip in a bit of hot fat, is usually a partial-cooking process, but it can be a finish-cooking process, too, for meats so thin they cook almost instantly, as you will see shortly. Pan-frying involves larger cuts of meat, more fat in the pan, a more moderate temperature, and a somewhat longer cooking time.

Meats that are pan-fried are tender cuts such as steaks, chops, cutlets, and sliced liver. Meats are often pan-fried without breading or dredging, but they are sometimes breaded or otherwise coated for variety and flavor.

Recipe 10.7 is a dish with a breading or coating. The coating allows you to season the meat before cooking, because it is not the meat that must brown but the coating. You can turn this simple dish into the elegant and famous Wiener schnitzel by topping each serving with an anchovy rolled around a caper on top of a peeled lemon slice and arranging chopped hard-cooked egg yolks, chopped hard-cooked egg whites, and parsley to accompany it.

The pepper steak in Recipe 10.8 also has a coating. You could not broil this steak without

Recipe 10-7 BREADED VEAL CUTLET

YIELD: ***10 portions***

10 6-oz	**veal cutlets**	**175 g**

Breading:

3 oz	**flour**	**90 g**
$^1/_2$ tsp	**salt**	**2 mL**
$^1/_4$ tsp	**white pepper**	**1 mL**
1 C	**egg wash**	**250 mL**
$^1/_2$ lb	**bread crumbs**	**250 g**
6 oz	**oil or clarified butter**	**175 g**

1. Flatten cutlets to $^1/_4$-in. (5 mm) thickness.
2. Set up breading station: flour with salt and pepper, egg wash, and bread crumbs.
3. Bread veal.
4. Heat oil or butter in a large sauté pan over moderate heat.
5. Pan-fry cutlets until coating is golden brown. Turn and cook other side until coating is golden brown and meat is tender.

Per serving:		Carbohydrates:	19 g
Calories:	460	Cholesterol:	140 mg
Fat:	29 g	Fiber:	0 g
Protein:	31 g	Sodium:	291 mg

Recipe 10-8 PEPPER STEAK

YIELD: ***1 portion***

1 Tb	**black pepper, coarse grind**	**15 mL**
1 8-oz	**boneless sirloin steak**	**250 g**
1 oz	**oil or clarified butter**	**30 g**
1 Tb	**minced shallots**	**15 mL**
1 fl oz	**red wine**	**30 mL**
2 fl oz	**demiglace or espagnole**	**60 mL**
	salt and lemon juice to taste	

1. Press black pepper into both sides of steak to coat evenly.
2. Heat oil or clarified butter in pan.
3. Sear both sides of steak.
4. Reduce heat and pan-fry to three-fourths of desired doneness. Remove and drain excess fat from pan.
5. Sweat shallots in remaining fat until translucent.
6. Deglaze pan with red wine, incorporating fond. Reduce liquid by half over high heat.
7. Blend in demiglace or espagnole. Return steak to pan. Simmer to blend flavors (about 5–10 minutes).
8. Remove steak to serving plate.
9. Strain sauce and season to taste with salt and lemon juice. Serve meat with sauce.

Per serving:		Carbohydrates:	4 g
Calories:	610	Cholesterol:	123 mg
Fat:	39 g	Fiber:	0 g
Protein:	53 g	Sodium:	505 mg

losing at least some of its peppery coat. Nor could you add a sauce made in the pan from its fond to intensify the flavor. This is a dish that is usually cooked to order. The techniques are familiar to you by now; the skills come with practice.

Recipe 10.9 illustrates how the simple techniques of pan-frying are adapted to another kind of meat, and how you can add complementary ingredients for a hearty and satisfying dish.

Turning from pan-frying to sautéing, let us look at the veal dish in Recipe 10.10. The veal slices are cooked quickly to maintain their delicacy and tenderness, using the sautéing technique. To make the sauce in the sauté pan, remove the meat once it's cooked. Keep it warm. Then deglaze the pan with wine, stock, or other liquids, and reduce the liquid. By swirling in butter, you have a butter sauce. Finally, adjust the consistency and seasonings.

Meats are seldom deep-fried. The one exception is cooked meats used in croquettes. This is not really a way of cooking meat but a way of

Recipe 10-9 CALF'S LIVER WITH ONION

YIELD: ***10 portions***

2 oz	**butter**	**60 g**
$1^1/_2$ lb	**onions, thinly sliced**	**750 g**
2–4 fl oz	**brown stock**	**60–120 mL**
10 5-oz	**slices calf's liver, $^1/_4$-in. (5 mm) thick**	**150 g**
	salt and pepper to taste	
2 oz	**flour**	**60 g**
2 fl oz	**oil**	**60 mL**

1. Melt the butter over moderate heat in a sauté pan. Add the onions and sweat until lightly golden.
2. Add enough stock to moisten and simmer briefly to blend flavors. Remove from heat and keep warm for service.
3. Season liver slices with salt and pepper and then dredge in flour.
4. In another pan, heat oil and pan-fry liver on both sides to desired doneness. Maintain moderate heat to avoid a hard crust.
5. Serve each portion with $1^1/_2$ oz (45 g) onions.

Per serving:		Carbohydrates:	18 g
Calories:	340	Cholesterol:	514 mg
Fat:	16 g	Fiber:	0 g
Protein:	30 g	Sodium:	202 mg

Recipe 10-10 VEAL FRANÇAISE (FRITTURA PICCATA)

YIELD: ***10 portions (2 pieces each)***

20 2-oz	**veal scaloppine**	**60 g**
	salt and pepper to taste	
2 oz	**flour**	**60 g**
2 fl oz	**oil or melted butter**	**60 mL**
1 C	**white stock**	**250 mL**
2 oz	**butter**	**60 g**
3 Tb	**lemon juice**	**45 mL**
1/4 C	**chopped parsley**	**60 mL**
10	**thin lemon slices**	

1. Flatten scaloppine to 1/4-in. (5 mm) thickness, taking care not to tear. Season with salt and pepper; dredge in flour.
2. Sauté in butter or oil until lightly golden on both sides (about 3–5 minutes). Remove to warm platter.
3. Drain excess fat from pan. Deglaze with white stock and reduce liquid by one-third.
4. Swirl in butter and cook until nut-brown. Stir in lemon juice.
5. Serve sauce over veal. Garnish with chopped parsley and lemon slices.

Per serving:		Carbohydrates:	5 g
Calories:	299	Cholesterol:	100 mg
Fat:	21 g	Fiber:	0 g
Protein:	22 g	Sodium:	326 mg

making a dish out of a meat that has already been cooked.

ROASTING AND BAKING

Roasting is a common method of meat cookery and a good one. Tender meats roast well to produce good dishes.

Roasting meat is very simple, so simple that the procedure is all contained in the first two steps of Recipe 10-11. Everything else has to do with making the jus to be served with the meat.

Notice that you do not season the roast. In a prime rib, it would be a waste of seasonings! Since it has a thick layer of fat on the top and sides and a layer of bones on the bottom, the salt would not penetrate to the meat except on the ends.

In other roasts, seasoning may be appropriate. If a surface is edible or servable, it should be seasoned. In most instances, an edible, servable surface will allow seasoning to penetrate the flesh to some extent and bring out the flavor of the meat. However, if a sauce is to be made from the

Recipe 10-11 ROAST PRIME RIB AU JUS

YIELD: ***18 6-oz (175 g) portions***

1 14-lb	**prime rib, oven ready**	**6.3 kg**
Mirepoix:		
8 oz	**onions, 1/2 in. (1 cm) chopped**	**250 g**
4 oz	**celery, 1/2 in. (1 cm) chopped**	**125 g**
4 oz	**carrots, 1/2 in. (1 cm) chopped**	**125 g**
2 qt	**cold stock**	**2 L**
	salt and pepper to taste	

1. Place meat thermometer in center of roast. Place roast in roasting pan.
2. Roast meat in a preheated moderate oven (350°F/180°C).
3. When meat reaches the desired internal temperature, remove it from the pan and let it stand.
4. Add mirepoix to pan and cook it in the fat until lightly caramelized.
5. Pour off fat, keeping mirepoix in pan.
6. Simmer liquid and mirepoix in pan until vegetables are fully cooked (about 20 minutes).
7. Strain and degrease the jus and season to taste.
8. Slice roast and serve au jus.

Per serving:		Carbohydrates:	0 g
Calories:	340	Cholesterol:	72 mg
Fat:	29 g	Fiber:	0 g
Protein:	19 g	Sodium:	55 mg

pan juices, salting the meat may make the drippings too salty to be used. Salt also interferes with browning by drawing the juices to the surface.

In the roast prime rib au jus, all logic tells us not to season. Let us go on to make the jus. The jus means the natural juices from the meat, enhanced with appropriate flavor builders and served over the meat—au jus.

In Step 4, you begin to make the jus by adding mirepoix to the pan. Notice that the mirepoix is added only after the roast is cooked. Some cooks like to roast the meat in a bed of mirepoix from the beginning. However, this adds no flavor to the roast, overcooks the mirepoix, and spoils the pan juices with the flavors of overcooked onion, celery, and leek.

When you first add the mirepoix to the roasting pan, it cooks briefly in the fat from the roast, since there is virtually no other liquid in the pan. In effect, you are sautéing the mirepoix as you do your flavor builders when you are making a soup or sauce.

Pouring off the fat in Step 5 is easy because it is the only liquid in the pan. The juices are neatly preserved in the crust on the bottom of the pan, and you recover them by deglazing in Step 6.

In deglazing, you add enough liquid to make the quantity of jus you want, allowing for 40 to 50 percent evaporation. Then you simmer it until the mirepoix has contributed its best flavors to the jus—up to about 20 minutes (Step 6). If necessary, you can add a little meat base to increase the quantity and flavor. Strained, degreased, and seasoned (Step 7), the jus is ready for the table at the same time as the roast.

The roast, meanwhile, has been standing—a necessary step. When first removed from the oven, it goes on cooking and its temperature continues to rise (carryover cooking). You must give it about 30 minutes to stop cooking so that the juices will settle before you carve it. If you cut it too soon, the juices shoot out under pressure and are lost to the meat forever.

The French term **au jus** refers to the manner of serving the meat—roast beef served with juice—and not to the juices themselves. You will hear people refer to these as "the au jus," pronouncing it "oh zhoos," "oh joos," and even "ah juice." The faulty usage and pronunciations jar the ears and sensibilities of people who know French, but the distortions are so common they have become part of the jargon of the trade in some places.

Another source of confusion is the meaning of the word prime in roast prime rib. It does not

Recipe 10-12 ROAST LEG OF LAMB

YIELD: ***12–16 4-oz (125 g) servings***

5–7 lb	**leg of lamb**	**2.7–3.1 kg**
	lemon juice as needed	
2 Tb	**chopped fresh parsley**	**30 mL**
1/2 tsp	**onion salt**	**2 mL**
1/2 tsp	**rosemary**	**2 mL**
1/2 tsp	**basil**	**2 mL**
1/2 tsp	**black pepper**	**2 mL**
2	**cloves garlic, puréed**	

1. Cut $^1/_2$-in. (12 mm) wide × 1-in. (25 mm) deep pockets in meat to put flavorings into.
2. Brush lemon juice on meat and into pockets.
3. Mix rest of ingredients and rub on meat and into pockets.
4. Roast meat, fat side up, on a rack in 325°F (165°C) oven to desired degree of doneness.
5. Cover meat with foil and let stand 15–20 minutes before slicing.
6. Serve sliced meat with au jus.

Per serving:		Carbohydrates:	0 g
Calories:	292	Cholesterol:	105 mg
Fat:	18 g	Fiber:	0 g
Protein:	28 g	Sodium:	75 mg

refer to the grade of meat, as many people assume. It applies rather to the cut of meat, a seven-rib cut from the forequarter.

Whatever you think it is and however you pronounce it, roast prime rib au jus is a dish of both substance and elegance that is simple to prepare—a good one to master.

Lamb, ham, pork, and veal, as well as other cuts of beef, are roasted the same way as prime rib, as seen in Recipe 10.12.

If you are going to roast a ham for a "baked ham" entrée, you need to know whether it is fully cooked, partially cooked, cured uncooked, or fresh uncooked. Fresh uncooked hams are easily identified: They are the color of pork and are treated like any other fresh pork roast. Any ham that is cured includes salt in the process, so no more is needed for seasoning.

HANDLING AND STORING COOKED MEATS

Meats reach their upper limits in quality as soon as cooking is completed. Ideally, service immediately follows readiness. Realistically, it may not. Two such situations are common in quantity production. One is leftover meats. The other is extremely large volume that cannot be handled all at once—a thousand steaks for a banquet, for example.

Any cooked meats that are to be served at a later time must be first quickly chilled to room temperature, then either covered or wrapped, and then stored in a cooler or freezer.

If you do not cool these products before covering or wrapping, you are inviting great losses from bacterial growth and spoilage. A warm, moist, enclosed place is the ideal breeding ground for bacteria that feed on meat. It is entirely possible that in a careless or slovenly operation the difference between profit and loss lies right here.

SUMMING UP

Since meat is the centerpiece of the menu in most foodservices as well as the most expensive item, it is critical for you to know how to cook it well. It is important to the budget, the balance sheet, and the customers. They are not likely to return if the meat is overcooked, undercooked, too salty, tasteless, tough, dry, or unattractive.

The two secrets of good meat cookery are knowing how to cook the different cuts of meats and being able to cook them to the right degree of doneness. The right degree of doneness for pork and veal, and for less tender cuts of beef and lamb, is well done—cooked through. Tender cuts of beef and lamb may be cooked from rare to well done according to customer preference. Generally, the less well done a steak, chop, or roast from a tender cut of beef or lamb, the more tender, juicy, and flavorful it is.

Many meat dishes include sauces that incorporate the fond from roasted, pan-fried, or sautéed meats or are made from liquids in which the meat was braised. In many braised dishes, meat and sauce are cooked together, enriched by the same flavor builders and enriching each other. Broiled meats can be served with a variety of accompaniments.

Meat cookery is a special skill but it is not complicated. If you know your product, choose the right cooking method, and cook to the right degree of doneness, you can hardly miss. At today's prices, you had better not.

There are many ways of creating different entrées with butters, sauces, marinades, dressings, garnitures, and special flavor combinations from cuisines of other countries. The techniques you have learned in this and earlier chapters put all kinds of meat dishes within your reach.

The Cook's Vocabulary

aging
au jus
carryover cooking
choice grade
collagen
cured
doneness
dry aging
elastin
game
grading
green meat
inspection
London broil
marbling
meat
medium
medium rare
medium well
pot roast
primal cuts
prime grade
rare
select or good
smoked
variety meat
well done
wet aging

Review Questions

Answer each question in complete sentences. Read each question carefully and make sure you answer all parts of the question. Organize your answer into more than one paragraph when appropriate.

1. Discuss the importance of meat on the menu and the role of meat cost in the profitability of an establishment.
2. Which primal cuts are naturally tender and why? How would you cook them? Which cuts are less tender and why? What are the best methods of cooking them?
3. Using Figures 10.4 to 10.7, list five cuts of meat from each figure and write down the suggested cooking method of each.
4. How can you tell when meat is done? What method would you use for steaks? For roasts? For braised dishes?
5. Suggest several ways of building in extra flavor when cooking meats.
6. What nutrients does meat contribute to the diet? Why do some people avoid eating it? Give an example of a lean cut of beef, pork, lamb, and veal.

Chapter 11

POULTRY COOKERY

A bird in the hand is worth two in the bush.

So goes the ancient proverb. You might say that poultry consists of birds in hand, since poultry is raised to be eaten. The two in the bush that the hunter hopes to bag are game.

Early human beings recognized the advantages of the bird in hand when they gave up nomadic life and settled down to raise their own food. Thousands of years ago, they tamed the jungle fowl of India, ancestor of today's chicken. Indians in ancient Mexico tamed the wild turkey.

By the time of the great Middle East civilizations, not only did the well-to-do have birds in hand but these birds were being specially fattened to satisfy gourmet tastes. "Fatted fowl" was part of the daily fare at King Solomon's court. Peacocks were raised in the Egyptian empire and geese were force-fed to produce foie gras (fwah grah), the fat goose liver that has remained a symbol of elegant cuisine.

Birds raised for today's market lead similarly restricted lives devoted to getting fat quickly. Confined in small cages and fed special diets, tender-fleshed chickens and ducklings are ready for market in a matter of weeks; turkeys in four to seven months. So efficient has the poultry industry become that these specially nurtured birds with flesh fit for a king's table are among the most economical of protein foods on the market. And they are universally popular. Americans eat billions of pounds of poultry in a year.

High popularity, high nutrition, and low price make poultry a good item on any menu, whether for the low-budget school or hospital or the profit-oriented restaurant. In addition, it is versatile. It adapts to almost any cooking method. Hundreds of different dishes can be made with it, from fast-food fried chicken to elaborate creations from classical cuisine and intriguing menu items from all parts of the world.

After completing this chapter, you should be able to:

- Identify the kinds and classes of poultry and suggest appropriate cooking methods for each.
- Discuss the handling and storage of fresh and frozen poultry and explain how to avoid the health hazards associated with poultry.
- Describe poultry in terms of menu uses, nutritional roles, and special cooking requirements.
- Describe or demonstrate how to roast, poach, sauté, pan-fry, deep-fry, broil, and braise various poultry dishes.
- Discuss the preparation of dressings and the hazards of cooking a stuffed bird.

ABOUT POULTRY IN GENERAL

The term **poultry** refers to edible birds domestically raised for human consumption. The word is often used loosely to include wild birds such as pheasant and wild duck. Such birds are hunted for sport and are more correctly classified as game. A few farm-raised game birds such as pheasant, squab, and quail are now on the market.

NUTRITIONAL PROFILE

Chicken and turkey are rich in protein, niacin, and vitamin B6. They are also good sources of vitamin B12, riboflavin, iron, zinc, and magnesium. Duck and goose are quite fatty, when compared to chicken and turkey, as they contain all dark meat. Light meat has less fat, and fewer calories, than dark meat. In chicken and turkey, light meat is found in the breast and wings, while dark meat is found in the legs. Dark meat is found in the muscles that are most active. Because chickens and turkeys do not generally fly, only their legs get much exercise so they have dark meat. Ducks and geese do fly, so their wings and breast, in addition to their legs, have dark meat.

In comparison to red meats, skinless light-meat chicken and turkey are comparable in cholesterol but lower in total fat and saturated fat (Table 11.1). If you compare the amount of fat in chicken to that found in turkey, you will no doubt be amazed. Chicken has about 50 percent more fat than turkey.

A significant amount of the fat in poultry is concentrated in the skin of the bird or just under it. This is why some dishes are served without the skin.

INSPECTION AND GRADING

All poultry shipped from one state to another must be inspected by an agent of the U.S. Department of Agriculture (USDA). The poultry must be processed under sanitary conditions and meet federal standards of wholesomeness. Approved poultry products carry the USDA mark of inspection (Figure 11.1).

State governments have similar regulations that vary from one state to another. Some cities also have regulations. A poultry product must meet whatever standard is highest—federal, state, or local—in the place where it is produced and the place where it is sold.

Table 11-1 NUTRITIONAL COMPARISON: BEEF AND POULTRY

Food Type (3 ounces, cooked)	*Saturated Fat (grams)*	*Dietary Cholesterol (milligrams)*	*Total Fat (grams)*	*Calories*
Beef, top round, broiled	3	73	8	185
Beef, whole rib, broiled	10	72	26	313
Chicken, light meat without skin, roasted	1	64	4	130
Chicken, light meat with skin, roasted	3	71	19	189
Ground turkey—breast meat only	<1	35	<2	130
Ground turkey (meat and skin), cooked	3	87	11	200

SOURCE: National Institutes of Health, 1994. *Step by Step: Eating to Lower Your High Blood Cholesterol.* NIH Publication No. 94-2920.

Figure 11-1 FEDERAL INSPECTION MARK AND GRADE SHIELD FOR POULTRY

(Courtesy USDA.)

Poultry is also graded for quality by the USDA. Grading is not mandatory, but much poultry is graded. There are three grades—A, B, and C, with A at the top of the scale. The factors that determine grade are conformation (shape of the carcass), fleshing (amount of flesh on the carcass), fat coverage, absence of pinfeathers, and freedom from damage such as skin tears, cuts, blemishes, and broken bones. Poultry graded by the USDA must carry the grade shield illustrated in Figure 11.1, with the appropriate grade, of course.

MARKET FORMS

There are different **kinds** of poultry, including chicken, turkey, duck, goose, guinea, and squab pigeon. Chicken is the most popular kind of poultry in the United States and a very versatile product. Turkey is the second most popular kind of poultry. Turkeys are generally larger than chickens. Unlike chicken and poultry, duck and goose contain much fat, due in large part to their dark meat.

Each kind of poultry is divided into **classes** that are based on age and tenderness (see Table 11.2). Age affects the tenderness of the bird and dictates the cooking method to use for maximum flavor and tenderness. Older birds need moist-heat cooking, such as simmering, steaming, or braising, to make them tender and develop their full flavor. Younger birds are naturally tender and can be cooked using almost any method.

In addition to knowing the kinds and classes of poultry, you need to know the **style** of the poultry, in other words, how much processing has taken place. Most foodservices use birds that are ready to cook, available either whole or as parts. Figure 11.2 shows the names of the various poultry parts.

HANDLING AND STORING POULTRY

Fresh poultry should be checked over upon delivery, even though it is inspected and graded, because of its very limited shelf life and potential health hazards. Poultry is a frequent carrier of salmonella and offers a good growth medium unless properly handled.

Fresh poultry should be delivered packed in shaved ice, and it should be kept on ice until used. Fresh poultry should have unblemished skin without feathers or bruises. The skin should be smooth, soft, and moist without any indication of slime. The color of the skin, which ranges from white to deep yellow, is not a measure of nutrition value, flavor, tenderness, or fat content. The color is determined by the breed of bird and its diet. Ideally, fresh poultry should be used within 24 hours of receiving.

Frozen poultry should be delivered at or below 0°F (−18°C). If you see much frozen moisture in the packaging, the product has likely been thawed and refrozen. Discolored patches on the skin indicate freezer burn.

With frozen poultry, the hazards lie not in storing but in thawing and in handling during

Table 11-2 POULTRY CLASSES

Kind/Class	*Age*	*Weight (pounds)*	*Cooking Method*[a]
Chicken			
Rock Cornish game hen	5–6 weeks	$^3/_4$–2	Roast, broil, grill
Broiler or fryer	9–12 weeks	$1^1/_2$–$3^1/_2$	Roast, broil, grill
Roaster	3–5 months	$3^1/_2$–5	Roast, stew
Capon	4–5 months	6–9	Roast
Turkey			
Fryer-roaster	Under 16 weeks	4–9	Roast
Young turkey	5–7 months	8–22	Roast, stew
Yearling	Under 15 months	10–30	Roast, stew
Duck			
Broiler or fryer duckling	Under 8 weeks	3–4	Roast, broil
Roaster duckling	Under 16 weeks	4–6	Roast
Other			
Young goose	Under 6 months	6–10	Roast
Young guinea (related to pheasant)	About 6 months	$^3/_4$–$1^1/_2$	Roast, sauté
Squab pigeon	3–4 weeks	$^3/_4$–$1^1/_2$	Roast, broil, grill, sauté

[a]These are common cooking methods used with each different class of poultry. All of the above birds are young and tender and can be cooked using any cooking method.

The following birds are mature and need moist-heat cooking to make them tender and develop their fuller flavor:

Chicken	Mature chicken, hen or fowl (sometimes called stewing chicken)
Turkey	Mature turkey
Duck	Mature duck
Goose	Mature goose
Guineas	Mature guinea
Pigeons	Pigeon

preparation. Many cooks fail to carry out these processes properly. Chapter 2 discusses the only safe ways to thaw out poultry. The best way is to thaw the frozen bird in the cooler, allowing **slack time**—that is, time for slow thawing. This may take as long as three to five days for large birds such as turkeys or one to two days for chickens. Always thaw in the original packaging.

All frozen poultry should be thawed before cooking. Once a bird is thawed, it should be treated as a fresh bird. A thawed bird should not be refrozen unless it has been cooked.

But the greatest health hazards in handling poultry occur during prepreparation. Any salmonella bacteria a bird carries will multiply at kitchen temperatures while it is being prepared for cooking. Furthermore, these bacteria are easily transferred to fingers, knives, cutting boards,

Figure 11-2 CUT-UP POULTRY

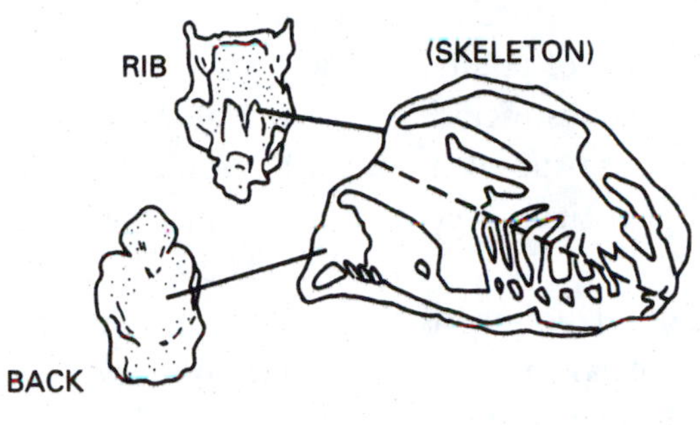

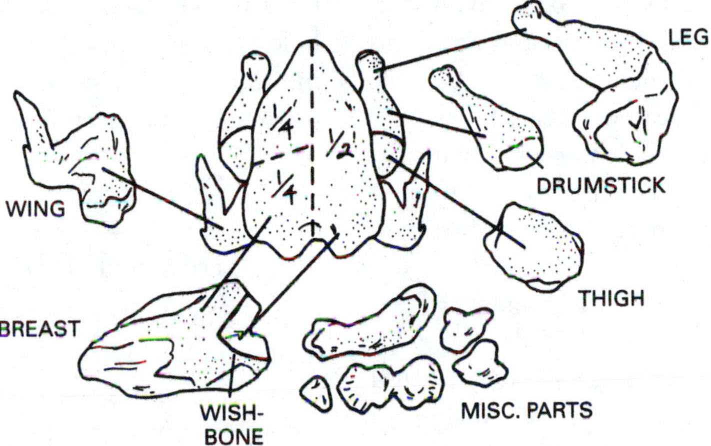

A whole bird may be broken down into halves, quarters, or parts.

towels, and anything else a raw bird touches. These items, in turn, may pass the salmonella along to contaminate other foods.

To prevent such bacterial growth and spread from developing into a full-blown episode of foodborne illness, the cook must take constant precautions. Hands must be washed and work surfaces and utensils must be sanitized as soon as preparation is complete, and the poultry must be either cooked immediately or returned to refrigeration. Large quantities should be prepared in small batches at a time and returned to refrigeration as completed. Poultry should be cooked to at least 165°F (74°C).

Improperly handled, poultry is one of the most hazardous foods in the kitchen. The poultry cook must think about this all the time and consciously follow all sanitary practices.

UNDERSTANDING DONENESS IN POULTRY

The cooking of poultry is challenging because there are so many ways it can be prepared. But whatever the kind, class, and cooking method, one concern must always remain uppermost in the cook's mind: doneness.

Poultry must always be cooked done. "Done" is the point at which the meat is cooked through but not dried out. A common pitfall of poultry cooking is the inability of the cook to distinguish between done and ruined. If a once-succulent breast of chicken tastes like rubber, it is overcooked.

A distinguishing characteristic of poultry is that, unlike beef, it contains **light meat** and **dark meat.** This affects how quickly the meat is done. Light meat cooks faster than dark meat, in large part because it contains less connective tissue. When cooking whole chicken or turkey, this means that the breast (light meat) will be done before the legs (dark meat) are done. Techniques for dealing with this problem, such as trussing, will be discussed in the roasting section. Keep in mind also that dark meat is fattier than light meat.

There are several indicators of doneness:

- Firmness of flesh. Underdone flesh will feel soft to the touch; done flesh will remain firm (but not hard) when pressed. On a whole bird, the leg and thigh are the best places for touch testing.
- Joints becoming loose. You can feel this by twisting the leg slightly.
- Flesh beginning to separate from the bone.
- In roasted poultry, clear, translucent juices inside the bird. Before doneness is reached, the juices will be opaque and brown.
- Internal temperature of 165 to 170°F (74–77°C). In roasting, use a meat thermometer in the thigh as this is the last part to become fully cooked. The thermometer should not touch the bone.

All these indicators can be used, depending on the cooking method. The degree of accuracy depends on the skill and experience of the cook. The thermometer is the safest and most accurate method.

For volume production, it may be difficult to use a thermometer for each of 40 or so birds, so random placing of a few is a good method. Birds should be grouped according to size, with a thermometer in one bird of each size.

One common method of testing doneness is definitely not recommended for a roasted bird, and that is to stick it with a meat fork. If you do this, the bird's good juices will run out of the holes you have punched. Poultry loses enough moisture in cooking without having the cook provide another avenue of loss.

METHODS OF COOKING POULTRY

Cooking methods suitable for poultry include all the methods there are. All kinds and most classes of poultry can be cooked by almost any method. Some common methods are:

- Roasting
- Broiling and grilling
- Sautéing
- Pan-frying
- Deep-fat frying
- Braising
- Poaching and simmering

ROASTING

Roasting is a way of cooking poultry that is near and dear to the American heart. Roast turkey on the Thanksgiving table is usually oven-roasted. It may also be smoked, barbecued, or spit-roasted. Whole young birds do very well in this dry-heat process because of their tender flesh and the protection of a layer of fat between it and the skin. The skin and fat form a coating that conserves the juices, thus keeping the flesh moist as it cooks.

The procedures for roasting poultry are the same for all kinds of birds, except for thing: cooking time. The larger the bird, the longer the cooking time.

Recipe 11.1 is a typical formula for roasting poultry. Let us review the basic steps.

In Step 1, the bird is washed inside and out to help reduce the number of harmful bacteria.

In Step 2, the seasoning is put inside the bird, not on the skin. Seasonings will not penetrate the skin, so there is no need to season the skin unless it is to be served.

Trussing the bird (Step 3) ensures even roasting. The object is to make the bird a solid piece by tying the legs and wings neatly to the body. Extended wings or legs will cook done before the breast is cooked, which means they will be overcooked when the breast is done. Trussing will

Recipe 11-1 ROAST CHICKEN

Yield: ***Approximately 10 4-oz (125 g) portions***

1 4–5 lb roaster chicken about 2 kg
salt, pepper, and oil as needed

1. Wash outside of chicken and its cavities.
2. Season inside of chicken with salt and pepper.
3. Truss the bird.
4. Oil chicken skin.
5. Roast back side down on rack in roasting pan at 325°F (165°C) until done.
6. Let chicken rest 15 minutes before carving.

Per serving:		Carbohydrates:	0 g
Calories:	265	Cholesterol:	121 mg
Fat:	15 g	Fiber:	0 g
Protein:	30 g	Sodium:	90 mg

prevent this and maintain uniform quality. Figure 11.3 shows a quick and easy method for trussing a bird.

Many turkeys come from the market with a wire clip holding the legs in place. These birds do not need trussing; just turn the wing tips under.

Step 4 is primarily for appearance. Oil added to the skin will give the roasted bird a golden-brown color. In addition, it will prevent the skin from cracking and blistering and will help to keep the flesh moist. Notice that the recipe makes no mention of basting the bird with water or stock. Basting is totally unnecessary. Worse, it introduces moisture into dry-heat cooking—not needed, not wanted. If basting is necessary, as it is for large turkeys, it's better to baste with fat about every half hour.

Roasting the bird back side down (Step 5) steadies it on the rack and gives the breast its crisp golden coat.

A bird should rest for a short time after cooking before it is carved (Step 6). This allows the juices to settle into the flesh, keeping it moist, instead of running out. Twenty to thirty minutes is enough for a large bird to rest. If poultry is to be stored after roasting, place it breast side down. This will keep the juices from draining away from the breast.

The temperature for roasting whole chicken given in this recipe (325°F or 165°C) is common, but higher temperatures, such as 350 or 375°F (175 or 190°C) can be used as well. When roasting chicken parts, use the higher temperatures—350 to 375°F (175–190°C)—so they cook quickly.

To cook whole chickens under 5 pounds (2 kg) or chicken parts, you can also start cooking them at a high temperature (450°F or 230°C) for 15 minutes and then reduce the temperature to

Figure 11-3 HOW TO TRUSS A BIRD

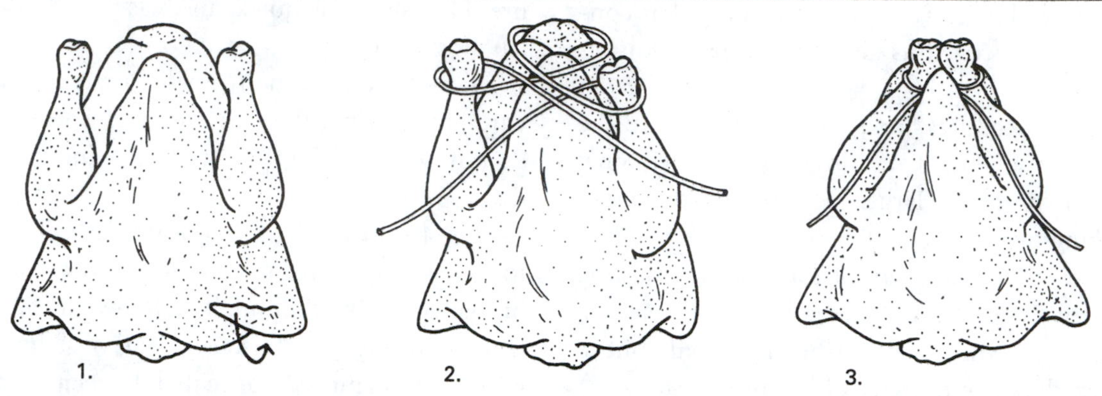

Step 1. Place the bird on its back with the neck toward you and tuck the wing tips under the V's of the wings, pointing them toward the tail. *Step 2.* Take a piece of butcher string about three times the length of the bird and loop it around the tail and under and over the ends of the legs. *Step 3.* Pull the legs together tightly, tuck the strings under the breastbone cartilage, and run the two strings toward you beside the thighs.

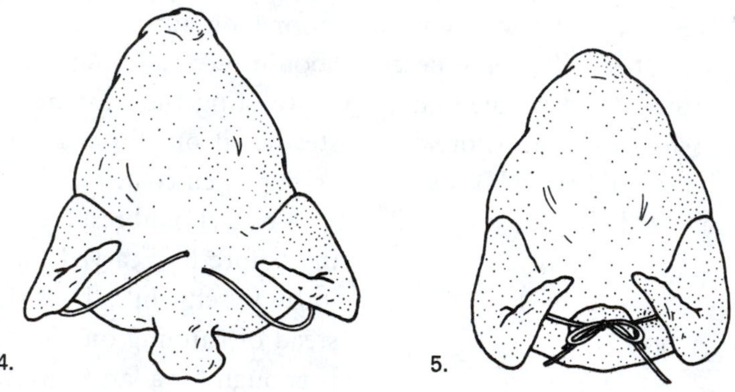

Step 4. Hook them through the V's of the wings and turn the bird over. *Step 5.* Tie the strings firmly just below the neck opening and tuck the neck skin under the string to close the neck cavity.

300 to 325°F (150–160°C) for the remainder of the cooking. The high initial temperature helps brown the chicken. This method, known as the **searing method,** is not necessary when roasting turkeys because the longer cooking time normally ensures that they will brown.

After you roast your chicken, you can combine the techniques of roasting and sauce making in an easy and tasty dish (Recipe 11.1a). The mirepoix is added in Step 2 to enrich the pan juices; it does not flavor the chicken meat. In Step 3, the pan is deglazed with brandy to capture all this rich flavor. Deglazing incorporates the fond—the pan drippings and the bits of food clinging to the pan bottom. The remaining steps of gravy making follow the usual sauce-making techniques.

You can apply both the roasting method and the sauce techniques to make a great variety of dishes. The well-known duckling à l'orange, for example, is made on the same pattern, using a brown sauce flavored with orange juice and caramelized sugar and enriched with the deglazed fond. Because the duck is so fatty, it is roasted at the high temperature of 425 to 450°F (220–230°C) for the first 15 minutes and then at 375°F (190°C) until done. This helps to render the fat from beneath the skin and produce a crisp covering that intensifies the special duck flavor.

Larger birds, such as whole turkeys, can also be cooked successfully at 325°F (165°C) or as low as 250°F (120°C). However, a temperature of 250°F (120°C) will require a good deal longer cooking time—enough longer, in fact, to put it out of reach of many kitchen schedules. It also raises food safety questions if you are cooking a whole stuffed turkey. The 325°F (165°C) temperature is the most logical for quantity cooking from the point of view of oven use. All meats and poultry for a given meal are often cooked at the same time in one or two ovens. A temperature that adapts to all kinds eliminates constant oven adjustment and production problems.

In addition to oven roasting, smoking and barbecuing are special methods of roasting poultry. The roasting process is the same as for ordinary oven roasting, except that the temperature is lower, the cooking time is therefore longer, and smoke is infused to give the flesh distinctive flavor. Spices are often added to the bird to create specific flavors.

Spit-roasting is another special method, used mainly for show. It requires special equipment but no special knowledge or technique. Small birds are trussed, oiled, and placed on spits that revolve before a hot fire. Basting with a spicy sauce is common.

In all these special roasting methods, the chief consideration is doneness. The tests for doneness are the same as those for conventional roasting.

DRESSINGS AND STUFFINGS. Roast poultry served with a dressing is a traditional American dish. A bird roasted whole seems to invite stuffing with a flavorful dressing. There is no question that this makes a tasty dish, but cooking stuffing in a bird is surrounded with question marks. Let us look first at the nature of dressings and then at the question marks that apply to cooking them inside birds.

A poultry dressing is usually made with a starch for body and texture, such as bread or rice

Recipe 11-1a ROAST CHICKEN WITH BRANDY SAUCE

YIELD: ***6–8 portions chicken; 1 pint (500 mL) sauce***

To Recipe 11-1 add:

1 lb	**mirepoix, 1/2" (1 cm) concassé**	**500 g**

Sauce:

1 oz	**brandy**	**25 ml**
3/4 pt	**chicken stock**	**375 mL**
2 oz	**beurre manié or roux**	**50 g**
1 oz	**heavy cream**	**25 mL**
	salt, white pepper as needed	

1. Complete Steps 1–4 of 11.1 and begin Step 5.
2. Forty-five minutes before you expect the chicken to be done, add mirepoix to pan.
3. Remove chicken when done. Pour off fat and deglaze pan with brandy. Add stock.
4. Thicken with beurre manié or roux to desired consistency. Simmer to blend flavors and remove starchy taste.
5. Add cream and simmer until hot. Strain. Adjust seasoning and texture as necessary. Serve each portion of chicken with 2 oz (50 mL) sauce.

Per serving:		Carbohydrates:	3 g
Calories:	316	Cholesterol:	131 mg
Fat:	19 g	Fiber:	1 g
Protein:	31 g	Sodium:	321 mg

(cornbread in the South), plus a flavor base of pan-fried onions and often celery with various spices and herbs such as thyme and sage. Some sort of fat and often stock are included to add moisture. Some cooks add eggs for binding. Many other things can be added—fruits, nuts, seafoods such as oysters or shrimp, tasty meats such as sausage or ham. Such additions can create many interesting flavors to complement the flavor of the bird itself.

A tasty product like this is called a **stuffing** if it is stuffed into a cavity in a bird, fish, meat, or vegetable. It is called a **dressing** whether it is stuffed into another food or is cooked and served separately. Recipe 11.2 gives you a basic formula.

Now, let us consider whether to roast such a dressing inside the bird following American family tradition or to bake it separately. From a production standpoint, it makes sense to stuff a bird only if it is to be presented whole and will hold enough dressing to accompany all the meat from the bird. This is generally true only of small birds intended to serve one or two persons.

The far more serious questions have to do with what happens in cooking a stuffed bird. Consider these important factors:

- Stuffing a bird will prolong its cooking time—by as much as an hour for a big bird.
- The temperature of the stuffing inside the bird will rise very slowly and it will remain in the ideal range for bacterial growth for most of the cooking period.
- The ingredients in the stuffing will undergo little or no cooking.

The primary problems come from improper handling and use of ingredients that pose health threats—specifically eggs and egg-based products that are used incorrectly and meats that are insufficiently cooked. The length of time it takes to bring a cold, thick mass of stuffing surrounded by a cold, thick mass of poultry flesh out of the bacterial growth range poses a real risk of foodborne illness. To give you a feeling of how easily the worst can happen, let us assume you are going to use Recipe 11.2 as a stuffing. The problems come up one after another like this:

- In Step 1, the vegetables are often undercooked. They will not cook any further inside the bird. Onions that are not properly cooked will give a bad flavor to the stuffing and may harbor bacteria that cause foodborne illness.

Recipe 11-2 BREAD DRESSING

YIELD: ***20 3-oz (100 g) portions***

1 lb	**onions, small dice**	**450 g**
1/2 lb	**celery, small dice**	**250 g**
6 oz	**butter or fat**	**175 g**
2 lb	**cubed bread**	**1 kg**
1 oz	**chopped parsley**	**30 g**
1 tsp	**sage**	**1 mL**
1–2 pt	**chicken stock, cold**	**0.5–1.0 L**
1 tsp	**salt**	**5 mL**
1/2 tsp	**black pepper**	**2 mL**

1. Cook onions and celery in butter or fat until vegetables are done.
2. Cool the cooked vegetables and add to the cubed bread in a bowl.
3. Add chopped parsley and sage.
4. Gradually add stock until the dressing is just moist. Toss to combine.
5. Adjust the seasonings with salt and pepper.
6. Bake in hotel pans at 350°F (180°C) about 1 hour.

Per serving:		Carbohydrates:	25 g
Calories:	194	Cholesterol:	19 mg
Fat:	9 g	Fiber:	2 g
Protein:	4 g	Sodium:	241 mg

- In Step 2, the vegetables are often added to the bread while still hot. They shouldn't be; they should be cooled to room temperature. This will help prevent spoilage if the product is to be stored. Keep it cool.
- In Step 4, if the stock is added hot so the bread will absorb it quickly and evenly, you are going to put warm or hot stuffing into a cold bird. Then, if the bird is stored for later roasting, the stuffing cools far too slowly while inside the bird. Or, if the bird is roasted right away, the stuffing starts out in the critical temperature range and stays there far too long. This is especially dangerous if the stuffing contains eggs.

The following rules will eliminate these problems:

- Combine the problem ingredients with starches at cool temperatures.
- Don't use eggs if you can do without them.
- If sausage or other meats are used, cook them fully before adding.
- Make stuffing only as needed, stuff only small birds, and cook immediately.

Dressing that is cooked separately cooks far more quickly and avoids the prolonged period of hazardous temperatures. Bake it in shallow pans so that all of it will make a quick trip through the danger zone.

If you do stuff a bird, put the stuffing loosely in the body and neck cavities. It expands during cooking, and if you pack it in, it will be heavy and soggy.

The stuffed birds in Recipe 11.3 are another way of preparing roast stuffed birds. They do not run the risks of foodborne illness because they are small and cook quickly and because the stuffing is already cooked and contains no problem ingredients. Again, the mirepoix is added to enrich the pan juices and does not flavor the meat of the birds.

Recipe 11-3 ROAST STUFFED ROCK CORNISH GAME HENS

YIELD: ***4 portions***

4	**rock Cornish game hens**	
	salt and pepper as needed	
Stuffing:		
1 pt	**cold cooked rice, pilaf style**	**500 mL**
2 oz	**chopped parsley**	**50 g**
4 oz	**pine nuts, toasted**	**125 g**
Mirepoix:		
4 oz	**onions, 1/2 in. (1 cm) chopped**	**125 g**
2 oz	**celery, 1/2 in. (1 cm) chopped**	**60 g**
2 oz	**carrots, 1/2 in. (1 cm) chopped**	**60 g**
1 pt	**chicken stock**	**500 mL**

1. Wash outside of game hens and inside cavities.
2. Season inside of game hens with salt and pepper.
3. Combine stuffing ingredients and stuff cavities loosely.
4. Truss birds.
5. Place mirepoix in pan. Set birds on rack above.
6. Roast in 350°F (180°C) oven until done.
7. Remove birds. Pour off fat and deglaze pan with stock. Strain.
8. Remove trussing strings and serve birds with pan juices.

Per serving:			
Calories:	831	Carbohydrates:	27 g
Fat:	48 g	Cholesterol:	337 mg
Protein:	67 g	Fiber:	2 g
		Sodium:	170 mg

BROILING AND GRILLING

Poultry can be broiled or grilled with great success. The fat tissue in poultry allows it to be broiled fairly slowly without drying out. Compared to meats, tender pieces of poultry are broiled at lower temperatures, but use the same procedures.

Recipe 11.4 gives you the basic method for broiling chicken. Put the chicken skin side down on the broiling rack to minimize loss of flavorful juices. The mechanics are simple, but you can run into hidden problems.

✗ **Problem:** The outside may cook done before the inside does.

✓ **Solution:** Use a lower temperature. You can lower it either by turning down the heat or by moving the cooking surface farther from the heat. Sometimes, it is useful to finish broiled poultry in the oven.

✗ **Problem:** The meat may stick to the grate of the broiler.

✓ **Solution:** Be sure to brush with butter or oil, maintain a moderate to low temperature, allow the meat to cook to the halfway point before attempting to move it or turn it, and keep the grate clean at all times.

A few more observations are in order:

- Seasoning is done before cooking.
- Coating the surface with butter will do three things: Prevent surface drying, add flavor, and keep the chicken from sticking. Oil may be used instead for cost reasons, but it will not add flavor.
- Using tongs for turning is a must. Or, more accurately, not using a fork is a must. Piercing the flesh with a fork will release the sealed-in juices.
- Brush with melted butter or oil during cooking.
- If you are grilling the chicken, you may move the skin side once to produce crisscross marks. (This technique is spelled out in Chapter 10.)

Once you get the feeling of the cooking temperature, you will find broiling a simple way to cook poultry, and the results are excellent.

Broiled chicken may be dressed up for variety and excitement. Chicken diable (deeah-bla, meaning devil) is one such variation. For chicken diable, the chicken is broiled until half done, then coated with mustard and bread crumbs, and broiled to doneness. You can also experiment with your own combinations of herbs, compound butters, or other flavorers to add zest to plain broiled or grilled chicken.

Recipe 11-4 BROILED HALF CHICKEN

Yield: ***1 portion***

salt and pepper as needed
1/2 chicken
melted butter or oil as needed

1. Sprinkle salt and pepper on chicken. Brush with melted butter or oil.
2. Put skin side down on a moderately hot broiler or grill.
3. Cook until half done and then turn, using tongs.
4. Finish cooking and serve.

Per serving:			
Calories:	331	Carbohydrates:	12 g
Fat:	8 g	Cholesterol:	123 mg
Protein:	50 g	Fiber:	0 g
		Sodium:	126 mg

SAUTÉING

Sautéing poultry has become quite popular, and understandably so. It is fast, gives the meat a nice brown color, adds only a little fat, and allows the cook to deglaze the pan to make a wide variety of sauces.

Recipe 11-5 SAUTÉED CHICKEN WITH CAPERS AND LEMON

YIELD: ***servings***

4	**chicken breast halves, boneless, skinless**	
	salt and white pepper as needed	
1 oz	**flour**	**30 g**
1 oz	**clarified butter**	**30 g**
4 fl oz	**white wine**	**125 mL**
2 Tb	**lemon juice**	**30 mL**
2 Tb	**capers**	**30 mL**

1. Season chicken breasts with salt and pepper. Dredge in flour.
2. Heat clarified butter in a sauté pan over moderate heat.
3. Sauté chicken breasts until half cooked and lightly browned. Turn over.
4. When chicken is done, remove from pan and keep warm.
5. Deglaze the pan with white wine and lemon juice. Reduce by one-half.
6. Add capers, heat through, and then pour sauce over chicken and serve.

Per serving:		Carbohydrates:	7 g
Calories:	258	Cholesterol:	93 mg
Fat:	10 g	Fiber:	0 g
Protein:	29 g	Sodium:	249 mg

To be sautéed successfully, the poultry must be small and preferably boneless. Boneless chicken breasts and slices of turkey breast work well. Before cooking, season the poultry and flour it and heat up the sauté pan. Place the meat presentation side down (it will be turned once) and don't overcrowd the meat in the pan or else it will cook in its own juices (as well as lower the cooking temperature). Large items can be started by sautéing and completed in the oven.

To make a sauce in the sauté pan, remove the meat once it's cooked. Keep it warm. In the drippings (remove any excess), sauté your flavor-builders—they may be onions, garlic, shallots, mushrooms, whatever the recipe calls for. Then deglaze the pan with wine, stock, or other liquids, and reduce the liquid. Add any ingredients that don't need much cooking. Finally, adjust the consistency and seasonings. Recipe 11.5 is an example.

PAN-FRYING

Pan-frying of chicken uses more fat than sautéing—you normally pan-fry in about $^1/_4$ to $^1/_3$ inch (1 cm) of fat. Low to moderate temperatures are necessary to keep the surface of larger pieces such as the breast and thigh from overbrowning before the center reaches doneness. Wings and drumsticks cook through more quickly. Recipe 11.6 gives you a step-by-step procedure for pan-frying poultry.

Recipe 11-6 PAN-FRIED CHICKEN

YIELD: ***4 portions***

1	**chicken, quartered**
	salt and pepper as needed
	milk and flour as needed
	oil as needed

1. Sprinkle the chicken pieces with salt and pepper.
2. Dip the chicken in milk.
3. Dredge the chicken in flour. Remove excess flour.
4. Heat oil (about $^1/_4$ in. or 5 mm deep) in a heavy skillet over moderately high heat.
5. Pan-fry chicken over moderate heat.
6. Brown on both sides; then lower heat and cook until done.

Per serving:		Carbohydrates:	10 g
Calories:	330	Cholesterol:	117 mg
Fat:	20 g	Fiber:	0 g
Protein:	26 g	Sodium:	21 mg

Sprinkling the seasonings on the chicken (Step 1) assures an even distribution of the seasoning on the bird. Many cooks season the flour and thus season and dredge the chicken at the same time. Although this may save time, it does not assure even seasoning. Salt is heavier than flour and will settle to the bottom of the dredging pan. Using just salt and pepper makes sense when you will be serving the chicken with a sauce; otherwise, you can also use herbs and spices.

Dipping the pieces in milk (Step 2) before dredging them in flour (Step 3) will assure that the flour sticks to the chicken to give it a golden-brown crust.

The use of oil instead of butter in Step 4 eliminates rapid browning or burning of the butter before the chicken reaches doneness. Cook both sides to a golden brown, then lower the heat and cook until done. Use tongs for turning. Test for doneness by feel.

For quantity production, pieces of poultry can be browned in the pan and then placed in an oven to cook through. This is a way of producing "fried" chicken in volume, often referred to as **oven-frying,** though it is actually baking. It is also a way of avoiding the pan-frying problem of overbrowning the surface of large pieces while cooking the center to doneness. Temperatures of 300 to 350°F (150–180°C) are appropriate for this type of cooking.

Many different entrées made with chicken breasts are cooked by pan-frying. In Recipe 11.7, the boneless breast of a half chicken, known on the menu as a **suprême** (sooprem), is breaded with a special coating and served with a garniture of brown butter and lemon. You can vary this basic formula with other coatings and garnitures to make other dishes.

In other pan-fried chicken entrées, the breasts (suprêmes) are stuffed before breading—with ham and cheese, for example, for chicken cordon bleu, or with other flavorful stuffings.

Recipe 11-7 CHICKEN SUPRÊME MILANESE STYLE

YIELD: ***10 portions***

Breading:

3 oz	**flour**	**90 g**
1/2 tsp	**salt**	**2 mL**
1/4 tsp	**white pepper**	**1 mL**
1 C	**egg wash**	**250 mL**
1/4 lb	**grated Parmesan**	**125 g**
1/4 lb	**bread crumbs**	**125 g**
10 5-oz	**chicken breasts, skinless and boneless**	**150 g**
1/4–1/2 C	**clarified butter**	**60–125 mL**
6 oz	**butter**	**175 g**
10	**lemon slices**	

1. Set up breading station with 3 pans: flour with salt and pepper, egg wash, and grated Parmesan with bread crumbs.
2. Bread chicken breasts. Chill.
3. Heat clarified butter in a heavy pan and cook breasts over moderate heat until chicken is done and coating is lightly brown.
4. Remove the chicken from the pan. Swirl in whole butter and make beurre noisette.
5. Serve chicken with sauce and lemon slice as garnish.

Per serving:		Carbohydrates:	13 g
Calories:	441	Cholesterol:	201 mg
Fat:	25 g	Fiber:	0 g
Protein:	39 g	Sodium:	644 mg

DEEP-FRYING

Deep-frying is a very common method of cooking poultry. It is not at all difficult and the product is very popular.

Two forms of poultry are deep-fried. One is chicken parts—chicken breasts or thighs, for example—that are either battered or breaded. The other is croquettes, which are made of cut-up cooked meats bound with a heavy béchamel sauce, shaped, and breaded.

Good frying temperatures usually range from 325 to 350°F (160–175°C). At these temperatures, small pieces pose no problem. Larger pieces may not reach doneness internally before the surface becomes too brown. To achieve doneness, you can finish-cook such pieces in the oven, as you may do with pan-fried chicken, especially when a large quantity is required. But if you want to limit your frying to a single step, the solution is to use only pieces small enough to cook to doneness in the fryer.

A typical recipe for croquettes is given in Recipe 11.8. You will recognize the flavor-building and body-building techniques from several earlier chapters, as well as the heavy béchamel from Chapter 8. The cooking may remind you of the potato croquettes in Chapter 9, though the preparation techniques are different. You may substitute other poultry for turkey, and you may use high-quality leftover meats.

Some specialty poultry dishes are deep-fried. One such dish is chicken Kiev (Recipe 11.9). The thinned-out breast meat cooks quickly. The meat and the breading seal in the butter even though it melts. This dish can also be pan-fried in clarified butter or oil to brown it quickly and then finished in the oven.

Like all other deep-fried foods, deep-fried poultry dishes should be served promptly. If they are held, their crust becomes soggy and loses all its charm.

BRAISING

In braised poultry dishes, the cut-up bird is cooked slowly in a small amount of liquid in a

Recipe 11-8 TURKEY CROQUETTES

YIELD: ***25 portions (2 2-oz/60-g croquettes each)***

8 oz	**celery, fine dice**	**250 g**
8 oz	**onions, fine dice**	**250 g**
12 oz	**clarified butter**	**375 g**
12 oz	**flour**	**375 g**
1 qt	**milk**	**1 L**
4 lb	**cooked turkey meat, small dice**	**1.8 kg**
2 oz	**parsley, chopped**	**60 g**

Breading:

8 oz	**flour**	**250 g**
2 tsp	**salt**	**10 mL**
1 tsp	**white pepper**	**5 mL**
2 C	**egg wash**	**500 mL**
$1^1/_2$ lb	**bread crumbs**	**750 g**
2 qt	**suprême sauce**	**2 L**

1. Sweat celery and onions in clarified butter until translucent.
2. Stir in flour and cook to make blond roux.
3. Add milk, stirring until smoothly blended with roux. Simmer to blend flavors and cook out starchy taste (about 10–15 minutes).
4. Add turkey and parsley. Season to taste with salt and pepper.
5. Cover loosely and refrigerate until firm (about 1–3 hours).
6. Using a No. 20 scoop, portion mixture into 50 2-oz (60 g) croquettes. Shape for uniform size and appearance.
7. Set up breading station with 3 pans: flour with salt and pepper, egg wash, and bread crumbs.
8. Bread croquettes.
9. Deep-fry at 350°F/180°C until golden brown. Drain on absorbent paper.
10. Serve with suprême sauce.

Per serving:			
Calories:	477	Carbohydrates:	38 g
Fat:	22 g	Cholesterol:	149 mg
Protein:	31 g	Fiber:	2 g
		Sodium:	821 mg

Recipe 11-9 CHICKEN KIEV

Yield: ***4 portions***

2	**garlic cloves, puréed**	
2 oz	**butter (room temperature)**	**60 g**
2 tsp	**minced chives**	**10 mL**
4 4-oz	**chicken breasts, boneless, skinless**	**125 g**

Breading:

3 oz	**flour**	**90 g**
1/2 tsp	**salt**	**2 mL**
1/4 tsp	**white pepper**	**1 mL**
1 C	**egg wash**	**250 mL**
1/2 lb	**grated Parmesan**	**250 g**
8 oz	**allemande sauce**	**250 g**

1. Combine garlic and butter. Form into 4 equal "fingers" about 2 × 1/2 in. (5 × 1 cm). Roll in chives. Chill.
2. Place chicken breasts skin side down between sheets of waxed paper. Flatten with mallett to 1/4 in. (5 mm) thickness.
3. Place a finger of butter in the center of each chicken breast. Roll breast to enclose butter, folding in ends to seal in butter completely.
4. Set up breading station: flour with salt and pepper, egg wash, and bread crumbs.
5. Bread chicken.
6. Deep-fry at 350°F/180°C until golden brown. Drain on absorbent paper.
7. Serve with allemande sauce.

Per serving:		Carbohydrates:	23 g
Calories:	695	Cholesterol:	320 mg
Fat:	39 g	Fiber:	1 g
Protein:	60 g	Sodium:	1029 mg

covered pot, usually with other ingredients that form part of the dish. Such dishes are descended from the peasant's pot-on-the-fire of ancient times, and the method was often used to cook a tough old bird that only slow, moist-heat cooking could tenderize. Contemporary cooks choose tender birds and use the method for other reasons. For one thing, braising produces a soft, moist texture. Even more important, it provides a method of flavoring the flesh by cooking it with flavorful ingredients such as wines, stocks, and flavor builders, which usually become part of a sauce served with the bird.

The typical braised poultry dish is really a two-step process in which the cut-up poultry pieces are first sautéed or seared before braising. Flavor builders are often cooked in the sauté pan and the pan is then deglazed with a liquid that becomes the body of a sauce. Everything is then cooked together with a cover on the pan, in a slow oven or over low heat on the range.

Reading through the steps in Recipe 11.10, you will see that this is exactly what happens when you make the famous French dish coq au vin. Not only are you cooking a chicken slowly with flavor builders to enrich its taste, the same ingredients are building the flavor and body of a sauce at the same time. This pattern of building a dish is a familiar one in braising.

Although there are many steps in this preparation, they are all familiar. You know about precooking such flavor builders as garlic, onions, and mushrooms to maximize their flavor contribution to the dish. You know about incorporating the pan scrapings (fond) into a liquid; you did this in making pan gravy. You also did this in making stocks in Chapter 6 when you deglazed the pan. You know about adjusting the sauce texture and seasoning; the sauce should be the consistency of espagnole. The only technique that may be new is searing. This is hotter and quicker than pan-frying. It is a partial-cooking process for browning the chicken, producing both color and flavor in the final dish. The braising step is, as you know, low-heat cooking in a covered pot. With chicken, it produces a melt-in-the-mouth product in which all flavors are blended.

Recipe 11-10 COQ AU VIN ROUGE

YIELD: ***4 portions (2 pieces chicken with 2 oz/50 mL sauce)***

1	**fryer, cut into 8 pieces**	
	salt and pepper as needed	
2 oz	**flour**	**60 g**
2 oz	**oil**	**60 g**
1–2	**garlic cloves, puréed**	
12	**pearl onions**	
7 oz	**mushroom caps, small or quartered**	**250 g**
	butter as needed	
1–2 C	**brown stock**	**250–500 mL**
$1^1/_2$ pt	**dry red wine**	**750 mL**

Sachet:

1	**parsley sprig**	
$^1/_2$–1	**bay leaf**	
$^1/_2$ tsp	**thyme**	**2 mL**
	salt and pepper to taste	

1. Season chicken parts and dredge in flour.
2. Heat oil over a moderately high heat in a sauté pan. Sear chicken on both sides until well browned. Remove from pan.
3. Reduce heat and cook garlic in fat until aroma is evident.
4. Add pearl onions to pan and cook until lightly caramelized on all sides.
5. Add mushrooms and cook until light golden, adding butter if necessary.
6. Stir in stock and wine, scraping with a wooden spoon to incorporate fond.
7. When the liquid simmers, return chicken to the pan.
8. Add sachet, cover pan, and simmer on range or in 350°F (180°C) oven until done—about 30–45 minutes.
9. Remove sachet. Degrease and adjust seasoning and texture of sauce as necessary.

Per serving:		Carbohydrates:	19 g
Calories:	575	Cholesterol:	110 mg
Fat:	28 g	Fiber:	2 g
Protein:	31 g	Sodium:	385 mg

You can also make coq au vin with white wine instead of red. It then becomes coq au vin blanc (white) instead of rouge (red).

POACHING AND SIMMERING

Poaching is used to cook tender pieces of poultry. Many cooks have a tendency to overcook the product. Poultry poaches very quickly. The chicken in Recipe 11.11 cooks done in less than

Recipe 11-11 POACHED BREAST OF CHICKEN

YIELD: ***10 portions***

	salt, pepper, and oil as needed	
10 6-oz	**chicken breasts, boneless, skinless**	**175 g**
1 qt	**chicken stock**	**1 L**
1 C	**white wine**	**250 mL**
1 C	**light cream**	**250 mL**
4 oz	**beurre manié or roux**	**125 g**
	salt and pepper to taste	

1. Sprinkle salt and pepper on the inside (the bone side) of each breast and tuck the edges under to make a compact piece.
2. Place the breasts close together in an oiled pan. Add enough chicken stock and wine to just cover chicken.
3. Bring to a simmer, cover, and poach until breasts are done (about 10 minutes).
4. Remove breasts from liquid.
5. Add cream to liquid and reduce by about one-third.
6. Thicken with beurre manié or roux to desired consistency. Cook until no starch taste remains.
7. Strain sauce. Adjust seasonings with salt and pepper.
8. Serve the breasts napped with the sauce.

Per serving:		Carbohydrates:	6 g
Calories:	344	Cholesterol:	137 mg
Fat:	13 g	Fiber:	0 g
Protein:	43 g	Sodium:	336 mg

Recipe 11-11a POACHED CHICKEN PRINCESSE

YIELD: ***10 portions***

To Recipe 11-11, add:

30 cooked asparagus spears

Place poached breasts on asparagus spears before napping with sauce in final step.

Per serving:		Carbohydrates:	8 g
Calories:	356	Cholesterol:	137 mg
Fat:	14 g	Fiber:	1 g
Protein:	44 g	Sodium:	340 mg

20 minutes. It is done when the flesh changes color and feels firm but not hard. When poached flesh is overcooked, it is dry, even though it has been cooked in liquid and even when it is covered with a sauce.

White wine is optional in poultry poaching. (If you omit it, you may need to increase the chicken stock to meet the guidelines.) The flavor builders given here are good ones but certainly not the only ones you can use. Different dishes may call for different flavor builders, different sauces, or additional ingredients.

Recipes 11.11a and 11.11b are adaptations of the basic recipe. Asparagus turns the dish into chicken princesse. The addition of spinach makes it florentine. If you add mushrooms to the sauce after straining, you will make it into chicken forestière—a familiar name by now.

Simmering is the method of choice for cooking tough birds for salad or cooked chicken dishes. The birds are placed in water or stock with a mirepoix and stock herbs and spices and are simmered until done—no longer (Recipe 11.12).

Recipe 11-11b POACHED CHICKEN FLORENTINE

YIELD: ***10 portions***

In Recipe 11-11, make the following changes:

Add 20 oz (625 g) spinach, cooked and buttered, hot.
Add 4–6 oz (125–175 g) mornay sauce, thick.
Omit beurre manié/roux.

1. Substitute mornay sauce for beurre manié/roux in Step 6.
2. Place breasts on bed of hot spinach.
3. Coat with sauce and glaze under salamander.

Per serving:		Carbohydrates:	11 g
Calories:	412	Cholesterol:	148 mg
Fat:	18 g	Fiber:	2 g
Protein:	47 g	Sodium:	414 mg

Recipe 11-12 SIMMERED CHICKEN

YIELD: ***Approximately 1 lb (450 g) meat***

1 3 lb	**broiler or fryer chicken, whole**	**1.5 kg**
Mirepoix:		
8 oz	**onions, chopped**	**250 g**
4 oz	**celery, chopped**	**125 g**
4 oz	**carrots, chopped**	**125 g**
1/2	**bay leaf**	
5–6	**parsley stems**	
1/2 tsp	**thyme**	**2 mL**
2	**cloves**	
7–6	**peppercorns**	

1. Place chicken in a stockpot with remaining ingredients.
2. Add water to cover.
3. Simmer until done (about 45–60 minutes), skimming as necessary.
4. Chill quickly. When chicken is cool enough to handle, remove skin, bones, and tendons. Cut meat into pieces of desired size and shape.

Per ounce:		Carbohydrates:	0 g
Calories:	310	Cholesterol:	111 mg
Fat:	18 g	Fiber:	0 g
Protein:	35 g	Sodium:	95 mg

Recipe 11-13 CHICKEN TETRAZZINI

YIELD: ***10 portions***

1 lb	**mushrooms, sliced**	**450 g**
2 oz	**butter**	**60 g**
1 pt	**chicken stock**	**500 mL**
2 oz	**roux or beurre manié**	**60 g**
$^1/_2$ C	**cream**	**125 mL**
1	**egg yolk**	
1 fl oz	**sherry**	**25 mL**
$1^1/_2$ lb	**boiled chicken meat, cut in strips $^1/_4 \times 2$ in. (0.5 × 4 cm)**	**675 g**
1 lb	**spaghetti or vermicelli, cooked**	**450 g**
8 oz	**Parmesan cheese**	**250 g**

1. Sauté mushrooms in butter until golden.
2. Add chicken stock and thicken with roux or beurre manié to make sauce.
3. Simmer until no starch taste remains.
4. Temper in liaison.
5. Add sherry.
6. Add chicken and heat, but do not boil.
7. Divide spaghetti into individual casseroles. Put chicken mixture in center and sprinkle everything with Parmesan cheese.
8. Gratiné under salamander or heat in oven until golden brown.

Per serving:		Carbohydrates:	29 g
Calories:	466	Cholesterol:	50 mg
Fat:	29 g	Fiber:	2 g
Protein:	19 g	Sodium:	705 mg

The usual tests for doneness are hard to practice on a big bird in a stockpot. One way is to remove the bird from the liquid and apply the touch test. If the breast feels firm, the bird is done. Another way is to test with a meat thermometer.

When you need to use the meat right away, remove the chicken from the broth and place it in the refrigerator, covered, until cold enough to handle. Strain the broth, cool it quickly, and refrigerate. If the cooked meat is not needed immediately, cool the pot quickly in cold running water with the bird in the broth, then refrigerate—bird, broth, pot, and all. This keeps the bird from drying out. The poaching liquid can be used to produce a sauce or to fortify a stock or a soup, since it has a great deal of flavor.

Notice that in this recipe the chicken is unseasoned. You leave the seasonings out of this preparation because you want the chicken to be uncommitted in flavor, just as you want a basic sauce to be uncommitted. You add your seasonings when you use the chicken in a dish, and you season according to the needs of that dish.

One such dish is given in Recipe 11.13. It is one of many casserole-type dishes you can make with chicken or turkey meat. Cooked chicken, in fact, has many menu uses, especially for luncheon or buffet service—chicken salad, chicken à la king, chicken pot pie. You cut your cooked meat as required by the dish you will make and season and flavor it accordingly.

In making the chicken tetrazzini, if you had a pot of chicken velouté on hand you would add it to the mushrooms in the pan in Step 2 in place of the stock and thickener. In a real life kitchen situation, a pot of velouté would probably be a part of your mise en place.

SUMMING UP

Poultry is one of the easiest foods to cook well, and one of the most widely used. It is a desirable menu item for just about any type of foodservice establishment. It is inexpensive, it is popular both for its taste and for its nutritional values, and it is versatile. It is at home in the fast-food operation in the form of fried chicken, and it is equally at home in the elegant restaurant, appropriately selected, cooked, sauced, and garnished.

Poultry adapts to all cooking methods. It may be roasted, poached, fried, sautéed, broiled, grilled, braised, or prepared by combining methods, such as frying/baking, poaching/baking, or sautéing/braising. The chief challenge to the cook is achieving the moist and tender quality that goes with the right degree of doneness—fully cooked but not overcooked.

The chief caution to bear in mind in working with poultry is the health hazards it poses if not handled properly. Every cook must take constant, scrupulous care to avoid cross-contamination and danger zone temperatures in preparing, holding, and serving poultry dishes.

If you want to venture beyond the usual American fare, you will find poultry a popular food in almost any country. Using your basic skills, try the popular Indian chicken tandoori, marinated in yogurt and braised or roasted; or the Spanish arroz con pollo, rice with chicken. But don't forget how good the simple dishes taste—plain broiled chicken, plain roast turkey—when they are cooked to perfection.

The Cook's Vocabulary

dark meat
dressing
light meat
oven-frying
poultry: kinds, classes, styles
searing method
slack time
spit-roasting
stuffing
suprême
trussing

Review Questions

Answer each question in complete sentences. Read each question carefully and make sure you answer all parts of the question. Organize your answer into more than one paragraph when appropriate.

1. List the kinds, classes, and styles of poultry.
2. Is all poultry inspected and graded?
3. In what ways are the cooking of poultry and the cooking of meat similar? In what ways are they different?
4. Give an example of a chicken dish prepared using each cooking method discussed in this chapter.
5. Suppose you want to prepare duckling à l'orange, chicken with dressing, and baked potatoes for the same meal. Can you do them all in the same oven? If not, what additional equipment will you need?
6. Give examples of several ways in which sauces are made for poultry dishes. Explain how they differ.
7. Of the poultry dishes discussed in this chapter, which, in your opinion, needs the most attention to avoid health hazards? What are the critical control points for this dish and how will you deal with them?

Chapter 12

FISH AND SHELLFISH COOKERY

What we think of as "fish" are more properly called fin fish. **Fin fish** obviously have fins, but they also have a skeleton. It is their internal skeleton that distinguishes them from **shellfish,** which wear their skeleton on the outside. Fin fish are smooth and slippery and swim about in fresh or salt water by moving their tails. Examples include flounder, salmon, and tuna. Shellfish, on the other hand, have hard outer shells. Examples include clams, oysters, crabs, lobster, and shrimp.

The cook who can prepare fish, shellfish, and sauces well has an inexhaustible source of entrées. They are quick and some are relatively inexpensive, yet they taste delicious, look elegant, and can command a good menu price. Both fish and shellfish also make good appetizers, soups, salads, sandwiches, casseroles, garnishes, and garnitures. Once you know the basic methods of cooking and the strengths and weaknesses of the product, all these uses are open to you.

After completing this chapter, you should be able to:

- Understand the special characteristics of fish and explain how these influence fish cookery.
- Describe the different market forms of fish and specify how to handle, store, and prepare each type for cooking.
- Select fish types and forms appropriate for broiling, baking, deep-frying, poaching, and pan-frying, and describe or demonstrate each process.
- Identify different kinds of shellfish and specify how to handle, store, and prepare each type for cooking.
- Understand and follow the basic guidelines for fish and shellfish cookery.

ABOUT FIN FISH AND SHELLFISH IN GENERAL

There is one thing very special about fish and shellfish, and that is their delicate and fragile quality. Fish and shellfish of all kinds have little or no connective tissue, which contributes to their natural tenderness. They have a high moisture content that evaporates readily, carrying much flavor away with it. The flavor is delicate; its texture is ultra-tender when properly cooked; its cooking time and shelf life are short. Some shellfish are not edible if they die before they are cooked.

You might expect fish or shellfish to have a strong and indestructible fishy taste, but, properly cooked, it tastes like a tender and delicately flavored dish. Fresh uncooked fish has a sweet and pleasant odor and does not smell fishy at all.

The tastes and odors we call fishy come primarily from fish and shellfish that are less than fresh.

Getting fresh fish and keeping it edible have always posed problems. Wealthy Romans raised their own fish in specially built reservoirs or had relays of slaves bring fish fresh from the sea in buckets of water. Medieval monasteries had their own ponds to supply live fish. A Portuguese abbey boasted of a trough running from a trout stream right into the kitchen, where a trapdoor could be opened to let in the day's supply. Problems of supply caused one famous tragedy: A fine chef named Vatel, supervising a banquet for Louis XIV, fell upon his sword and killed himself when the fish for the first course failed to arrive in time.

The railroad and the development of canning and refrigeration put most fish within the reach of most places by 1900. A man named Clarence Birdseye completed the process. Fishing through the ice in Labrador, he caught a fish that froze stiff in the cold air before he could get it off his hook. He discovered that such quick-frozen fish, when thawed and cooked weeks later, tasted as though they were freshly caught. In 1930, Birdseye launched the frozen-foods industry. Today, you can get almost any fish you want to cook—if not fresh, then frozen or canned.

NUTRITIONAL PROFILE OF FIN FISH AND SHELLFISH

Fish and shellfish are excellent sources of protein and are also:

- Relatively low in calories, fat, and saturated fat when compared to meat
- Low to moderate in cholesterol content
- Low in sodium (unless canned)
- A good source of certain vitamins (such as vitamins E, K, and niacin)
- A good source of certain minerals (such as iodine and potassium)

A fish is either lean or fat, but you can't tell which by looking at it. Fish do not have the kind of fat covering over the entire body that land animals do. For the most part, fat is distributed throughout the fish in the form of oil. In a few fish, such as salmon, you will find a layer running along each side. The percentage of fat in a fish may vary from 0.1 to 20 percent.

Table 12.1 lists some common fish and shellfish. You can see from the table that most fin fish and all shellfish are lean. Whether a fish is lean or fatty affects which cooking method you should choose. The type of fat found in these fish is rich in the health-promoting fatty acids (key components of fats) known as omega-3's. Fatty fish and shellfish are higher in omega-3's than lean fish, although lean fish contain some.

Table 12-1 FAT CONTENT OF FISH

Low-Fat Fish (fat content less than 2.5 percent)	*Medium-Fat Fish (fat content 2.5–5 percent)*	*High-Fat Fish (fat content over 5 percent)*
Cod	Bluefish	Albacore tuna
Croaker	Swordfish	Bluefin tuna
Flounder	Yellowfin tuna	Herring
Grouper		Mackerel
Haddock		Sablefish
Pacific halibut		Salmon
Pollock		Sardines
Red snapper		Shad
Rockfish		Trout
Sea bass		Whitefish
Shark		
Sole		
Whiting		

Shellfish got an unfair reputation in the past for being high in cholesterol. This was the result of outdated scientific methods that detected cholesterol-like substances as well as real cholesterol in shellfish, so cholesterol readings for many shellfish were mistakenly high. Certain shellfish—shrimp and crayfish—are higher in cholesterol than others, but a 3 1/2-ounce portion of either still has less cholesterol than one egg. Shellfish is also very low in saturated fat. Table 12.2 lists the nutritional profiles of common fish and shellfish.

Table 12-2 SEAFOOD NUTRITION CHART (BASED ON 3 1/2-OUNCE PORTIONS)

Species	*Calories*	*Fat (grams)*	*Saturated Fat (grams)*[a]	*Cholesterol (milligrams)*
FINFISH				
Carp, cooked, dry heat	162	7	1	84
Cod, Atlantic, cooked, dry heat	105	1	—	55
Grouper, cooked, dry heat	118	1	—	47
Haddock, cooked, dry heat	112	1	—	74
Halibut, cooked, dry heat	140	3	1	41
Herring, Atlantic, cooked, dry heat	203	12	3	77
Mackerel, Atlantic, cooked, dry heat	262	18	4	75
Perch, cooked, dry heat	117	1	—	115
Pike, northern, cooked, dry heat	113	1	—	50
Pollock, walleye, cooked, dry heat	113	1	—	96
Pompano, cooked, dry heat	211	12	5	64
Salmon, coho, cooked, moist heat	185	8	1	49
Salmon, sockeye, canned, drained solids with bone	153	7	2	44
Sea bass, cooked, dry heat	124	3	1	53
Smelt, rainbow, cooked, dry heat	124	3	1	90
Snapper, cooked, dry heat	128	2	—	47
Swordfish, cooked, dry heat	155	5	1	50
Trout, rainbow, cooked, dry heat	151	4	1	73
Tuna, bluefish, fresh, cooked, dry heat	184	6	2	49
Whiting, cooked, dry heat	115	2	—	84
SHELLFISH				
Clam, cooked, moist heat	148	2	—	67
Crab, Alaska king, cooked, moist heat	97	2	—	53
Crayfish, cooked, moist heat	114	1	—	178
Lobster, northern, cooked, moist heat	98	1	—	72
Oyster, eastern, cooked, moist heat	137	5	1	109
Scallops, raw	88	1	—	33
Shrimp, cooked, moist heat	99	1	—	195

[a]A dash (—) means less than 1 gram of saturated fat.
SOURCE: USDA.

FIN FISH

The varieties of fish being cooked and served in foodservices is astounding when you consider that only a few varieties, such as cod or flounder, were being served not that long ago. As a matter of fact, one of the concerns with serving fish has to do with selecting the ones that will work best for your clientele. Table 12.3 gives you the characteristics, availability, and market forms of over 20 varieties of fish. But before you order any in, you need to know how to handle and store them.

HANDLING AND STORING FIN FISH

The handling and storage of fish and shellfish are of great importance because of the delicate nature of the flesh and the short shelf life of fish products. The fragility of the flesh, the high moisture content, and the readiness with which the moisture evaporates—these characteristics underlie the handling and storing of fish.

In contrast to compulsory federal inspections of meat and poultry, fish and shellfish inspections are voluntary. Voluntary inspection is provided by the U.S. Department of Commerce. The "Packed Under Federal Inspection" mark is used on products that have been federally inspected. Voluntary quality grading is also available. The grades are A, B, and C. Figure 12.1 shows federal inspection and grading marks.

The less rigid inspection system for fish products means that the cook must take special responsibility for checking fish coming into the kitchen. The buyer for a foodservice establishment should specify inspected products when buying items for which inspection is available.

Fish and shellfish come into the kitchen fresh, frozen, and canned. Special considerations apply to each form.

FRESH FISH. Fresh fin fish should come into the kitchen really fresh—as soon as possible after catch and definitely within 24 hours. It is up to you to know quality and freshness.

Here are some measures of freshness:

- Tight scales
- Bright-pink to red gills

Table 12-3 GUIDE TO FISH

Name/Varieties	*Characteristics*	*Availability*[a]	*Market Forms*
Bluefish	Fatty flavorful fish, flesh turns from blue to gray when cooked, loose, flaky texture	Year-round	Whole, drawn, filleted
Cod	Lean, mild-flavored, moist fish with white, firm flake; most commonly used fish in the U.S.; scrod is a small, young cod	Year-round	Drawn, dressed, steaked, and frozen, breaded raw or cooked sticks and portions
Flounder (summer or fluke, winter, sand dab)	Lean fish with a white flesh, fine flakes, and mild, delicate flavor when cooked	Primarily July–December	Drawn, dressed, filleted, frozen, breaded raw or cooked fillets and portions
Grouper (red grouper)	Lean white fish similar in texture and flavor to red snapper	Year-round	Whole, steaked, filleted

Table 12-3 (Continued)

Name/Varieties	Characteristics	Availability[a]	Market Forms
Haddock	Lean fish with white, firm flake, delicate flavor, member of the cod family	Year-round	Drawn, dressed, filleted frozen, breaded raw cooked fillets, sticks, and portions
Halibut	Lean, white, mild-flavored fish	Primarily April–October	Whole, drawn, dressed, steaked, filleted
Mackerel (Spanish) mackerel, king mackerel)	Fat, firm flesh with rich flavor and slightly dark color	Almost year-round	Whole, drawn, dressed, steaked, filleted
Perch (ocean perch—redfish, freshwater perch—yellow)	Lean, mild-flavored white flesh with firm texture and fine flakes	Year-round	Whole, drawn, dressed, filleted, frozen, breaded raw or cooked fillets and portions
Pompano	Fatty fish with rich, well-flavored flesh, expensive	Year-round	Whole, filleted
Salmon (Atlantic, chinook, sockeye or red, coho or silver, chum, humpback or pink)	Pink-to-red flesh; fatty, strong-flavored fish with meaty texture	August–November	Dressed, steaked, filleted, frozen, canned, smoked
Shad	Fatty fish with rich sweet flavor, very bony	February–May	Whole, drawn, filleted, canned, smoked
Shark (mako, blue)	Like swordfish, except soft and a little moister, less expensive	Year-round	Steaked
Snapper (mangrove, silk, yellowtail)	Lean fish; firm, delicate, white flesh with large flakes; red skinned	Year-round	Whole, filleted
Sole (Dover, lemon or English, petrale)	Lean fish with white flesh, mild sweet flavor, member of the flounder family	Primarily July–December	Whole, filleted, breaded sticks and portions, stuffed
Swordfish	Fatty fish with firm dense texture; delicate flavor; expensive	Year-round	Steaks
Trout (lake, river, brook, rainbow)	Fatty fish with rich, fine-textured flavor; flesh may be white or pinkish-red	Year-round	Whole, drawn, filleted, steaked
Turbot (blue halibut, gray halibut, Newfoundland turbot, Greenland halibut)	Lean fish with snowy white, moist, finely textured flesh	July–November	Dressed, filleted filleted, frozen, smoked
Whitefish	Fatty fish with flaky, white flesh and slightly sweet flavor	Year-round	Whole, drawn, dressed, filleted, frozen, smoked

[a]Availability refers to buying fresh fish. Many types of fish are available year-round frozen or canned.

Figure 12-1 FEDERAL INSPECTION AND GRADING OF FISH

a. Each fish product processed under constant federal inspection is entitled to carry this seal. It certifies that the product is clean, safe, wholesome, properly labeled, and meets commercial standards of acceptability. ***b.*** This federal grade symbol indicates that the product meets not only all federal inspection standards but top quality standards for uniformity, appearance, and flavor as well. (Seal and symbol courtesy U.S. Department of Commerce, National Marine Fisheries Service.)

- Clear, almost transparent flesh, firm but elastic to the touch
- Firm adherence of flesh to bone
- Bulging, bright, shiny eyes with an expression of alarm
- Pleasant, sweet smell

As a fish ages, the gill area grays. Scales become loose. Eyes flatten and look dull and expressionless. The flesh is cloudy or milky and pulls easily from the bone. The fish develops a fishy smell.

It is also important for you to check the delivery to see that you get what you ordered. If you order red snapper, for example, and receive flounder instead, you may not be able to make the dish your menu calls for.

Fresh fish should be stored at 30 to 34°F (−1–1°C)—about 10 degrees cooler than most refrigerators. Fresh fish should always be stored on shaved or crushed ice in the cooler. The ice should be put in drip pans (pans with holes that fit into another pan) so that they do not stand in water as the ice melts. Change the ice daily, discarding the water. Proper storage keeps fish fresh longer and odor to a minimum. Whole fish can be placed directly on the ice; other forms of fish should be wrapped in moisture-proof packaging before icing.

How long fish will stay fresh cannot be stated in absolute terms. It depends on the species of fish, whether whole or portioned, the season of the year, and how it has been handled. Whole fish can generally last for three days if on ice (two days if not stored on ice). Other fish products can generally last for two days if kept on ice (one day if not stored on ice).

FROZEN FISH. Frozen fish products should be examined immediately to make sure they are solidly frozen when delivered. Then they should go right into the freezer, well wrapped to prevent freezer burn. The flesh of fish does not freeze at 32°F (O°C), the freezing point of water. Store it at O°F (−18°C) or below. Once thawed, fish should never be refrozen.

The safest and best method of thawing is to let the fish thaw at ordinary cooler temperatures. This may take some time, depending on the size of the frozen item, the temperature of the cooler, and other variables. A common practice is to move the fish from the freezer to the cooler the day before use.

Putting the frozen fish in hot water or soaking it in tepid water is the wrong way to thaw it. These methods encourage bacterial growth by raising the temperature of the fish. They also allow the flavor to drip away and sometimes cause partial cooking.

Another method of thawing is to put the product, in its original wrappings, under cold running water. This is better than soaking but not as safe and satisfactory as thawing in the cooler.

Whenever possible, do not thaw small pieces such as steaks and fillets. As fish thaws, it loses moisture and a great deal of flavor, so cook small pieces such as fillets up to 8 ounces (250 g) right from the frozen state. Once fish are thawed, you should treat them like fresh fish, which is what they are.

Many frozen fish products are available that fall into the category of convenience foods, meaning that they have been partly or completely prepared for cooking or service. They range from prebreaded fish fillets or shrimp to finished menu items such as sole florentine or lobster Newburg that need only to be heated. Such items are often manufactured to the buyer's specifications.

The cook's concern with convenience products is to handle and prepare them properly. Keep them frozen until use. Read the label to see exactly what the product is and how much preparation has been done: For example, is it raw or cooked? Then follow carefully all the standard guidelines for whatever cooking method is to be followed.

CANNED FISH. Canned fish should always be checked upon receipt to make sure there are no swollen or damaged containers. Swollen cans indicate spoilage. Damaged cans may have air leaks that allow the fish to spoil—and it will spoil quickly. Undamaged goods are kept in dry storage.

Once a can has been opened, its contents will keep two to three days in the cooler. Store the fish in a glass or plastic container, covered tightly so that it will not dry out and will not lend its special aroma to other foods.

MARKET FORMS OF FIN FISH

Fresh fin fish are available processed in several different ways. Figure 12.2 illustrates the different market forms.

- **Whole,** or **round,** fish are not processed. They are simply caught, iced, and delivered.
- **Drawn** fish are eviscerated (that is, relieved of their viscera or entrails—gutted), then iced and delivered.
- **Dressed** fish are eviscerated and scaled or skinned. They also have their head, tail, and fins removed.
- A **steak** is a crosscut of the body of a large dressed fish, such as salmon and halibut.
- A **fillet** or filet (both pronounced fil-lay) is a side of a fish that has been removed from the bones. It may or may still have its skin.
- **Sticks** are crosscuts of fillets.
- A **butterflied** fish consists of fillets from both sides removed together and still attached to one another.

PROCESSING WHOLE FISH

Although fish is usually bought in the market form in which it is to be used, it is still handy to know how to process a fish from the whole state. If you are going to do this, there are three things you must always keep in mind:

- Cut on a clean surface.
- Use clean knives.
- Clean everything thoroughly after cutting and before other food products are processed at the same station.

The reason for such care is that fish is easily contaminated, spoils quickly, and readily leaves behind these sanitary shortcomings along with its taste and its smell.

Fish have two kinds of bone structure, flat and round, as Figure 12.3 shows. The type of fish you have makes a difference in how you go about processing it, especially in filleting. **Flatfish** such as sole and flounder (Figure 12.3a) have four fillets, two on top and two on the bottom. **Round fish** (Figure 12.3b) have two fillets, one on each side. Figures 12.4 and 12.5 show how to fillet the two types of fish. A knife with a flexible blade is best.

Figure 12-2 MARKET FORMS OF FRESH FIN FISH

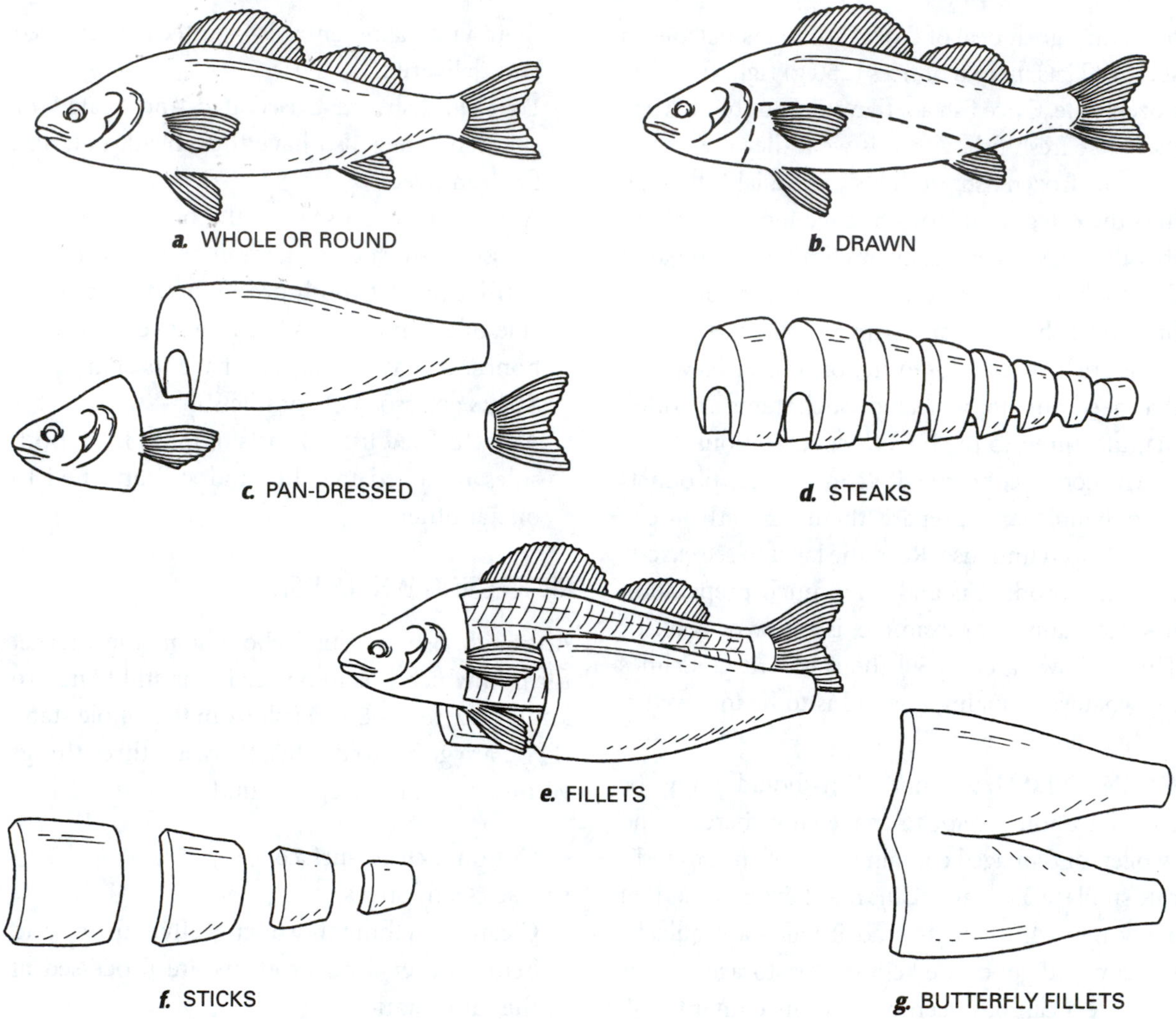

a. WHOLE OR ROUND

b. DRAWN

c. PAN-DRESSED

d. STEAKS

e. FILLETS

f. STICKS

g. BUTTERFLY FILLETS

Figure 12-3 BONE STRUCTURE OF FISH

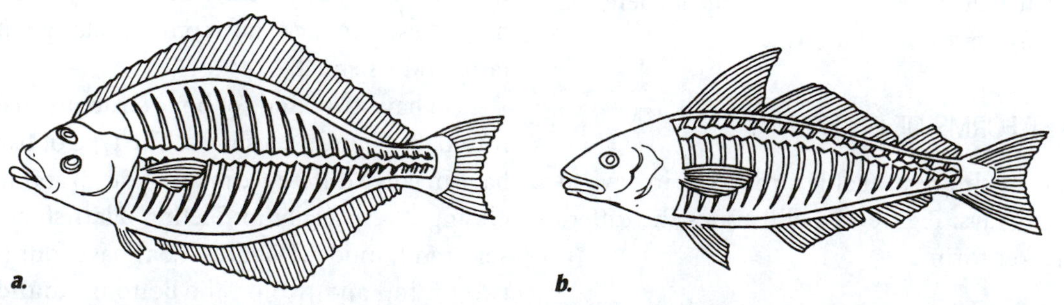

a. This bone structure is characteristic of flatfish, such as sole, flounder, and turbot. ***b.*** This bone structure is characteristic of round fish, such as trout and salmon.

Figure 12-4 HOW TO FILLET A FLATFISH

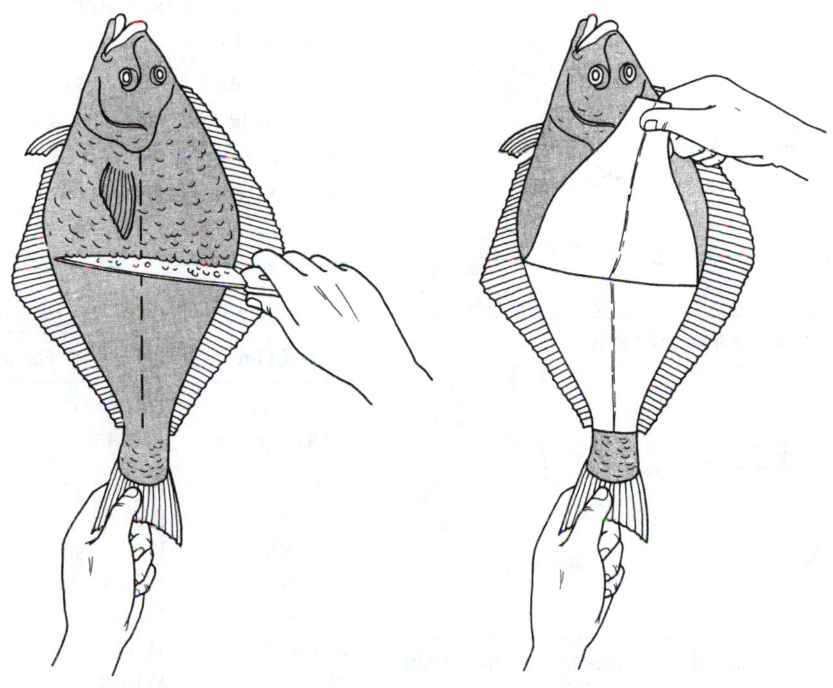

a. If skin is to be left on, scale it by rubbing a knife blade against the scales from tail to head until they flake off. ***b.*** To take the skin off, first cut through it near the tail. Hang onto the tail and pull the skin toward the head.

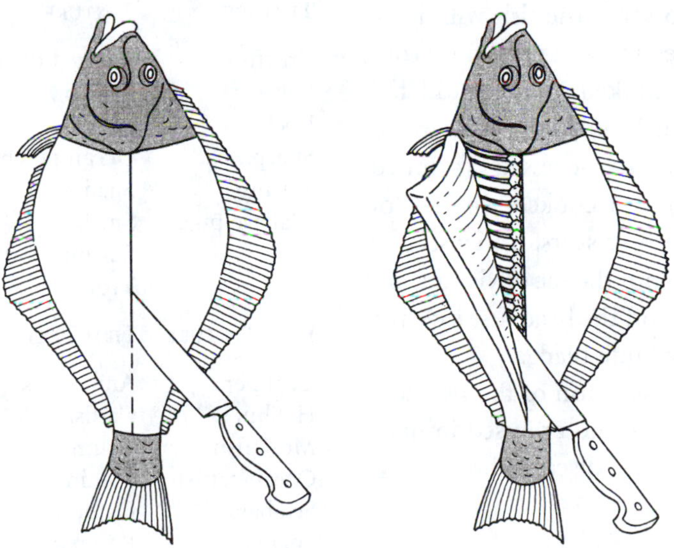

c. To remove the fillets, first cut along the backbone from head to tail. This is the bone running between head and tail along the middle of the fish. A line along the flesh parallels it exactly, so cut along this line. ***d.*** Holding the knife flat on the rib bones, cut outward to the edge of the fish. Repeat for the other three fillets.

Figure 12-5 HOW TO FILLET A ROUND FISH

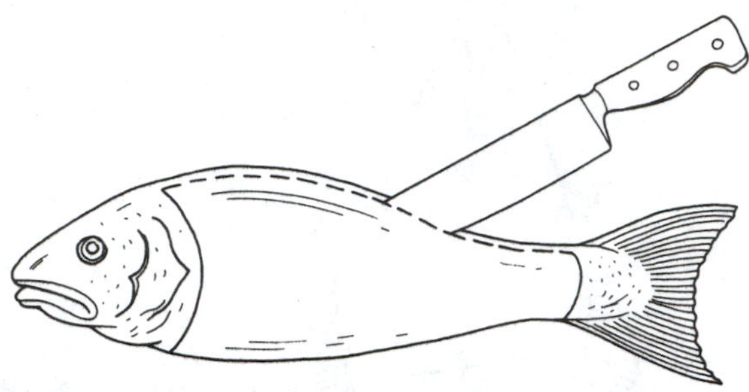

a. Cut along the backbone from head to tail.

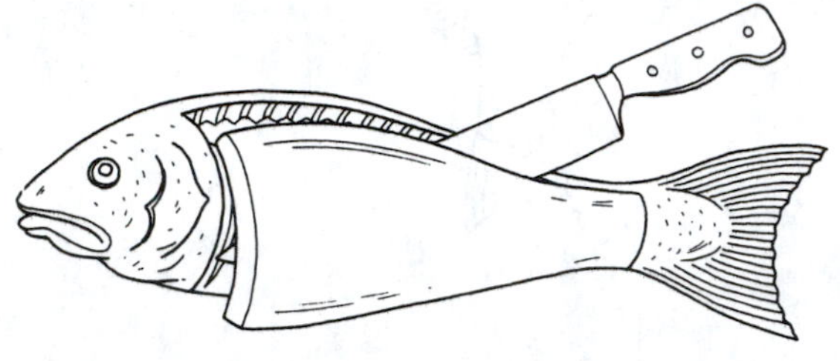

b. Cut down along the curve of the rib bones. Repeat for the other side.

How you intend to serve the fish will determine how much processing you must do. Trout, for example, is usually cooked with the head, tail, and skin left on and needs only to be eviscerated. Large fish are often pan-dressed (skinned, definned, eviscerated) and cooked whole. You can cut off the fins with scissors. To eviscerate, slit open the belly, pull out the sac of viscera, and clean the cavity. To cut off the head, use a cleaver or the big end of your knife blade.

The head, skin, and skeleton of the fish contain a great deal of flavor and are used in making fish stocks. Entrails are discarded.

COOKING FIN FISH

With fish, the basic flavor, body, and texture are built into the product by Mother Nature (see Table 12.4). The cook's job is to maintain and bring out the best that is there. This means to preserve fish's delicate flavor, fragile texture, succulence, and tenderness by careful cooking with a suitable method. Because it has a high and volatile moisture content, much of its flavor can evaporate or drip away.

Table 12-4 FLAVOR GUIDE TO FISH

Mild Flavor	*Moderate Flavor*	*Full Flavor*
DELICATE TEXTURE	**DELICATE TEXTURE**	**DELICATE TEXTURE**
Cod	Black cod	Bluefish
Crabmeat	Buffalo	Mussels
Flounder	Butterfish	Oysters
Haddock	Lake perch	
Pollock	Lingcod	
Scallops	Whitefish	
Skate	Whiting	
Sole		
MODERATE TEXTURE	**MODERATE TEXTURE**	**MODERATE TEXTURE**
Crayfish	Canned tuna	Canned salmon
Lobster	Conch	Canned sardines
Rockfish	Mullet	Mackerel
Sheepshead	Ocean perch	Smoked fish
Shrimp	Shad	
Walleye pike	Smelt	
	Surimi products	
	Trout	
FIRM TEXTURE	**FIRM TEXTURE**	**FIRM TEXTURE**
Grouper	Amberjack	Clams
Halibut	Catfish	Marlin
Monkfish	Drum	Salmon
Ocean catfish	Mahimahi	Swordfish
Sea bass	Octopus	Tuna
Snapper	Pompano	
Squid	Shark	
Tautog	Sturgeon	
Tilefish		

Fish cooks quickly and dries out quickly: As its muscle proteins coagulate, they become hard and chewy. Overcooking is the most common sin of fish cookery. Fish is done if it is opaque and gently firm (it should spring back quickly when touched). As fish cooks, its connective tissue, which is holding the fish together, starts to break down and the muscle starts to separate. Just as the muscle starts to naturally separate, a process called **flaking,** the fish is done. Some cooks prefer to stop the cooking process before the fish flakes (but after it has become opaque and firm) because of carryover cooking.

Small pieces of fish need special care, not only because of their fragility and quick cooking but because a single piece may not be the same size throughout. Thus, the thin tail of a fillet may dry out during cooking before the thickest part reaches doneness. To avoid this in poaching or baking, you can tuck the tail under to equalize the thickness (Figure 12.6a).

Another problem with fillets is their tendency to curl toward the dark, or skin, side of the fillet. One way of dealing with curling is to take advantage of it. This has led to several different ways of presenting the fish to the diner. In Figure 12.6b, the raw fillet (freshly thawed) is folded in thirds with its dark side in. The curling that takes place during poaching holds the fillet in shape. In Figure 12.6c, the fillet is rolled, dark side in, into a cylinder shape called a **paupiette** (pope-yet), usually fastened with string or a pick during cooking. You can put another kind of seafood inside, such as an oyster or a piece of lobster or fish meat. Each variation creates a new dish.

In the cooking of fish, seasoning has the same role as it does in meat and poultry. It brings out the food's natural flavors. For fish, one thing is common to all cooking methods—lemon. In fish cookery, lemon should become second nature, like putting on your shoes in the morning. Season with it, flavor with it, serve it with the fish. A traditional accompaniment, its sharp taste enhances the delicate, sweet fish flavor.

Almost any cooking method can be used for fish as a class, but few fish can be cooked by almost any method. The choice depends on the nature of the fish, and especially on whether it is fat or lean.

Figure 12-6 WAYS OF SHAPING FISH FILLETS

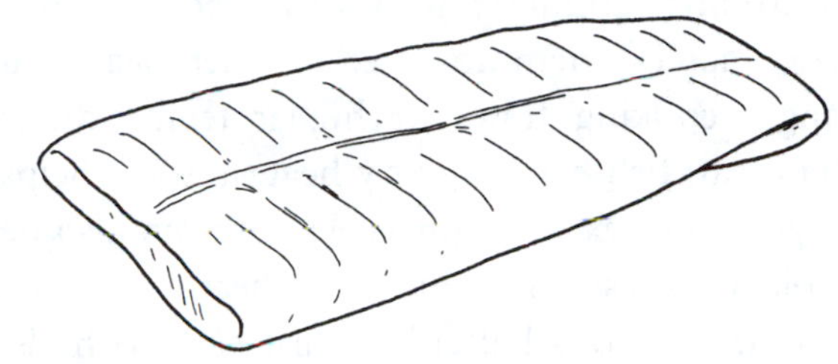

a. Tail folded under for even cooking.

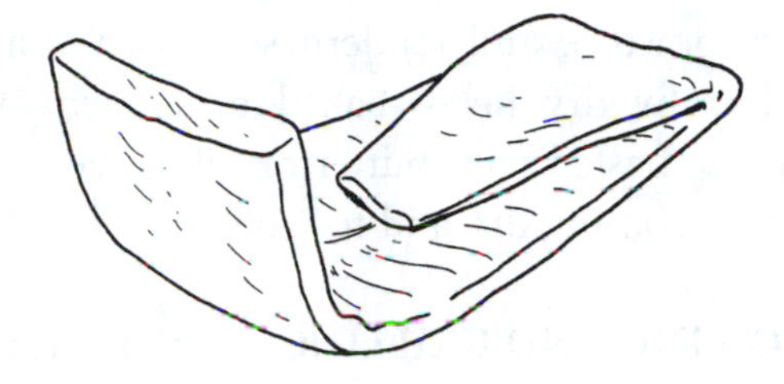

b. Folded in thirds.

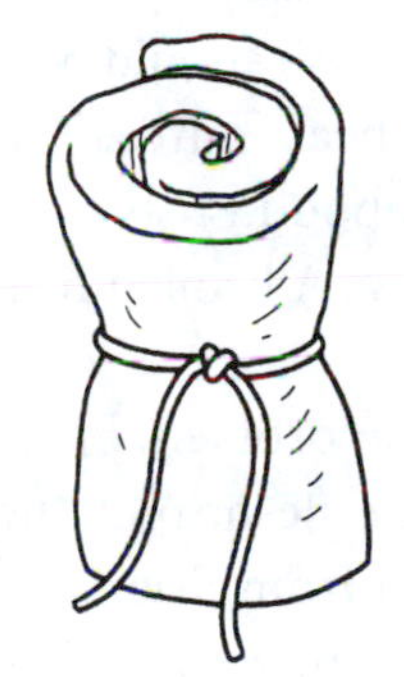

c. Rolled (paupiette).

Fat fish cook best by such dry-heat methods as broiling, grilling, and baking. Their fat content enables them to tolerate drier heat and longer cooking times or higher temperatures than lean fish can. The dry heat, in turn, helps to get rid of excess oiliness. Fat fish can also be cooked successfully using moist heat.

Lean fish cook better by moist-heat methods, such as poaching and steaming, or by cooking with fat. These methods enable them to retain their moisture and tenderness. If lean fish are cooked by dry heat—baked or broiled—they must be basted with butter or oil to keep them from becoming dry and tough.

BROILING AND GRILLING. Fish are usually broiled in an overhead broiler. This means that they are cooked quickly by direct heat at a high temperature. The fish should be 5 inches (12 cm) or less from the heat source. The high temperature, normally taboo in fish cookery, is offset by the quick cooking. A broiled fish cooks in a very few minutes.

Fat fish pose no problem in broiling. The high oil content in the flesh, plus the short cooking time, keeps them from drying.

Lean fish are not barred from broiling, but they require special care. A lean fish should be coated with melted butter or oil. Watch it closely: It cooks so fast it will dry out before you realize it. Here are the important steps:

- Use steaks or fillets.
- Season before broiling with salt and pepper (white pepper may be necessary).
- Coat fish, whether it's lean or fatty, with melted butter, or oil before cooking. This will help to counteract the drying effects of such high heat and also prevent sticking. For lean fish, you may dredge it first with flour before coating with butter or oil to get a brown crust. For fish that cook quickly, you may coat them with bread crumbs after coating with butter or oil. Since bread crumbs brown, and then burn, when exposed to too much heat, they should only be used when the cooking time is very short.
- Place thin fish on a greased pan, presentation side up. Place thick fish directly on the broiler rack presentation side down since they will be turned once during cooking.
- The skin may be left on a fillet to help hold it together, but only if it is attractive. If that's the case, the skin side can be the presentation side. When broiling fish with the skin on, you need to score the skin with diagonal slashes about $^{1}/_{4}$ inch deep, about 1 to 2 inches apart. This helps prevent the fish from curling during cooking.
- Preheat the broiler.
- Broil on one side unless the fish is thick, then turn once during broiling using a spatula.

Recipe 12-1 BROILED FISH FILLETS

YIELD: ***10 6-oz (175 g) portions***

10 6-oz	**fish fillets, cod or snapper**	**175 g**
2 fl oz	**melted butter or oil**	**60 mL**
	salt and pepper as needed	

1. Brush both sides of fillets with melted butter or oil.
2. Season with salt and pepper.
3. Place on a baking pan and broil at medium-hot temperature until gently firm. If very thick, turn once.

Per serving:		Carbohydrates:	0 g
Calories:	140	Cholesterol:	57 mg
Fat:	5 g	Fiber:	0 g
Protein:	22 g	Sodium:	133 mg

Recipe 12-1a BROILED FISH MAÎTRE D' HÔTEL

YIELD: ***10 6-oz (175 g) portions***

To broiled fish fillets from Recipe 12.1, add:

10 1/2-oz	**slices maître d'Hôtel butter**	**15 g**

Place 1 slice of butter on each portion immediately after removing from heat.

Per serving:		Carbohydrates:	0 g
Calories:	242	Cholesterol:	88 mg
Fat:	16 g	Fiber:	0 g
Protein:	22 g	Sodium:	250 mg

- Cook only until done. Fish is done when the flesh turns color and becomes opaque, when it springs back to the touch, and when it just starts to separate or flake.
- If using paprika, use it lightly. Otherwise, it will hide the true flavor of the fish.

Recipe 12.1 gives you a formula for broiled fish fillets. The cod or snapper fillets it calls for are fairly thick. You can substitute thinner fillets such as sole or flounder, but you must watch them carefully because they cook so fast.

Recipe 12.1a takes the formula one step further to produce a very tasty dish. You can substitute any other compound butter to produce a variety of broiled and grilled fish dishes. Rich butter sauces work well with lean fish. Vegetable coulis, salsas, and Creole sauce are flavorful, and healthful, accompaniments or sauces for a variety of fish.

Lean fish that are overcooked or held after cooking may curl or dry out. Flavor and appearance diminish with time, so timing of cooking in relation to service is of the utmost importance.

Sometimes steaks from such fat fish as salmon or swordfish are cooked on an open grill with heat from below, as in Recipe 12.2. For this method, oil or butter must be used to keep the fish from sticking to the grill. The steaks are turned to cook both sides. This type of broiling takes longer than cooking with heat from above. It requires skill to bring the steak to doneness while still keeping it moist and whole. Usually, the steak is marked with grid marks as well, a technique explained in Chapter 10.

These fish steaks may be served at once as they come from the grill, or they may be turned into many different dishes by adding sauces or garnitures. Recipe 12.2a is an example.

BAKING. Baking a fish in the oven, another dry-heat cooking method, is a good deal slower than broiling. Although the cooking temperature is much lower, the longer cooking time in the hot, dry air of the oven can cause lean fish to become too dry unless you take special care. So baking is usually more appropriate for fat fish than for lean fish.

Recipe 12-2 GRILLED FISH STEAKS

YIELD: ***10 6-oz (175 g) portions***

10 6-oz	**fish steaks**	**175 g**
3 fl oz	**melted butter or oil**	**100 mL**
	salt and pepper as needed	

1. Brush both sides of fish steaks generously with melted butter or oil.
2. Season with salt and pepper.
3. Place directly on medium-hot grill. Turn once. Fish is done when gently firm. If fish dries out during cooking, brush with melted butter or oil.

Per serving:		Carbohydrates:	0 g
Calories:	149	Cholesterol:	68 mg
Fat:	6 g	Fiber:	0 g
Protein:	22 g	Sodium:	145 mg

Recipe 12-2a GRILLED FISH STEAKS GRATINÉ

YIELD: ***10 6-oz (175 g) portions***

To grilled fish steaks from Recipe 12.2, add:

1–$1^1/_4$ pt	**royal sauce**	**500–600 mL**
1	**part velouté**	
1	**part hollandaise**	
1	**part whipped cream**	

Stripe steak with sauce. Place under salamander until lightly glazed.

Per serving:		Carbohydrates:	5 g
Calories:	376	Cholesterol:	123 mg
Fat:	28 g	Fiber:	0 g
Protein:	34 g	Sodium:	549 mg

Baking is a particularly easy way to prepare fish. Whole fish, whole stuffed fish, fillets, stuffed fillets, steaks, and chunks of fish may all be baked. To bake fish, do the following:

- Fat fish work best, but lean fish can be baked, too. Brush or dip either type of fish with melted butter or oil before cooking.
- Season before baking, using salt, pepper, and lemon. If the fish has not been skinned, season the inside of the fish.
- Place the fish in a well-oiled or buttered pan, presentation side up.
- Bake in a 350 to 400°F (180–200°C). Most fish can be cooked at the higher end of this range unless they are very large. Large fish should be baked around 350°F (180°C) so it bakes more evenly.
- Check the fish during cooking. Baste with melted butter or oil if it appears dry.
- Cook fish about 10 minutes per inch.

Recipe 12.3 is a good example of baking. It is important to keep an eye on the fish as it approaches doneness, so that it does not cross that line between tenderness and toughness. Baking small portions of fish is actually very quick, even though it is slower than broiling and grilling. The recipe can also be used for such other fish as cod, snapper, flounder, perch, haddock, and swordfish.

Sauce is often added after baking, as in Recipe 12.3a. It is one way of adding visual interest to a flat and colorless piece of fish, and it complements the delicacy of the fish's flavor. The paprika in Recipe 12.3 serves the same purpose. Be cautious in using paprika: Too much will mask the fish's flavor and lend a bitter flavor as well. Other appropriate sauces are Creole sauce and white wine sauce.

Another oven-cooked fish dish is one in which fillet portions are breaded as for frying, placed on heavily buttered sheet pans, brushed with butter on top, and then cooked in a hot oven (380–400°F or 190–200°C) until the crust is crisp. The fish stay moist under the protection of the breading, provided they are not cooked too long. This is a

Recipe 12-3 BAKED SEA BASS

YIELD: ***10 6-oz (175 g) portions***

10 6-oz	**portions fresh sea bass**	**175 g**
3 fl oz	**melted butter or oil**	**100 mL**
	salt, pepper, and paprika as needed	
	oil as needed	

1. Place sea bass portions on oiled baking sheet.
2. Brush fish with melted butter or oil.
3. Season fish with salt, pepper, and paprika.
4. Bake in 350°F (180°C) oven until done, about 10–15 minutes. If fish starts to dry out during cooking, brush with oil.

Per serving:		Carbohydrates:	0 g
Calories:	237	Cholesterol:	94 mg
Fat:	11 g	Fiber:	0 g
Protein:	34 g	Sodium:	194 mg

Recipe 12-3a BAKED SEA BASS PORTUGAISE

To baked sea bass from Recipe 12-3, add:

$1^1/_2$ pt	**portugaise sauce**	**750 mL**

Ladle sauce over sea bass after baking.

Per serving:		Carbohydrates:	5 g
Calories:	259	Cholesterol:	94 mg
Fat:	11 g	Fiber:	0 g
Protein:	35 g	Sodium:	468 mg

very good way of cooking fish for large-volume production. The result is like fried fish but it can be produced quickly in far greater quantities than it can by either pan-frying or deep-frying.

SAUTÉING AND PAN-FRYING. As with the cooking of meat, it is often difficult to draw a clear line between sautéing and pan-frying. Sautéing and pan-frying are common methods of cooking fish. The oil or butter aids in keeping the fish moist. Clarified butter works best, as it is less likely to burn. Lean fish do well with this style of cooking, especially if they are small whole fish or fillets. When sautéing or pan-frying fatty fish, be careful that you don't use too much fat and end up with a greasy product. Frozen fish should be thawed before cooking in a pan.

Fish to be sautéed or pan-fried are first seasoned and then dredged or breaded. The coating helps them keep their shape and moisture and gives them color. To ensure the flour or breading sticks to the fish, cooks sometimes dip the fish in milk first.

The fire under the pan is moderate, and the fish cook quickly. Small items can be cooked at a higher heat, whereas larger items should be cooked at a slightly lower heat to cook evenly.

Sautéed and pan-fried fish may be served without further elaboration, or they may be embellished in a number of ways. They often appear on the menu under the name à la meunière. This means they have been dredged in flour and pan-fried in brown butter, with fresh lemon and chopped parsley added at the end. You'll recognize this style from Chapter 8.

A closer look at a trout prepared à la meunière (Recipe 12.4) will not only explain this particular dish but give you a good grasp of the whole pan-frying process. Look closely at each step.

To season the trout (Step 1), you sprinkle salt, pepper, and lemon juice on the inside of the fish. A pan-dressed trout still has its head, skin, and tail, but its fins, bones, and entrails have been removed. The seasoning would not penetrate the skin to season the flesh.

Recipe 12-4 TROUT À LA MEUNIÈRE

YIELD: ***4 6-oz (175 g) portions***

4 6-oz	**trout, pan-dressed**	**175 g**
	salt, pepper, and lemon juice as needed	
1 oz	**flour**	**30 g**
2 oz	**clarified butter**	**60 g**
$^1/_4$ C	**lemon juice**	**60 mL**
2 Tb	**parsley, minced**	**25 mL**

1. Sprinkle trout inside with salt, pepper, and lemon.
2. Dredge trout in flour.
3. Sauté trout in clarified butter, turning once. Use care not to overbrown the butter.
4. Remove trout to serving plates. Add lemon juice and parsley to hot pan. Deglaze pan and cook mixture a few seconds.
5. Pour butter mixture over trout and serve at once.

Per serving:		Carbohydrates:	7 g
Calories:	366	Cholesterol:	131 mg
Fat:	21 g	Fiber:	0 g
Protein:	36 g	Sodium:	177 mg

Dredging the trout (Step 2) is no different from dredging other products. The only caution is to dredge just before cooking so that the flour does not have time to become soggy.

In Step 3, you use clarified butter as the fat, with a low heat to keep it from burning. For this dish, you want the butter to develop a golden-brown color during cooking (beurre noisette). Many sautéed or pan-fried dishes are prepared with half butter and half oil, which can be cooked over moderate heat without burning. Only use enough butter or oil to just cover the bottom of the pan. Always start to cook the fish with its presentation side down, because you will turn it once during cooking.

As the fish approaches doneness, the translucent flesh turns an opaque white. You can see this on the trout by examining the inside. When the flesh is all opaque and the texture is gently firm, the fish is done. If the texture becomes hard, the fish is overdone.

If you have a big fish and the butter is beginning to get too brown before the fish reaches doneness, you can put the whole pan in the oven for a few minutes. This will finish the cooking without further browning the butter. Then return the pan to the range and go on with Step 4.

The lemon juice in Step 4 is used to deglaze the pan and salvage all the flavorful buttery juices. The lemon and parsley contribute extra flavor. The parsley is added after the fish is cooked because it might burn if added sooner.

In Step 5, the butter is put back over the trout to add both flavor and moisture. If you don't like the vacant eye staring at you from the plate, you can cover it with a slice of lemon as a garnish.

Many other items can be sautéed and added to pan-fried fish, as is done in Recipes 12.4a and 12.4b. As usual, the name of the dish changes with each addition—à la belle meunière with the mushrooms, amandine with the almonds. Many other classical garnitures may be used. You can substitute other fish in the recipes—sole, flounder, perch, snapper, and other white fish.

At the other end of the scale of elegance and range of price, cooked fish may be mixed with duchesse potatoes and pan-fried as fish cakes for a delicious, luncheon dish (Recipe 12.5). This is a popular dish in some types of operations and a good way to use canned fish or high-quality leftovers. Crab cakes and codfish cakes make good regional house specialties, but any cooked fish may be used.

DEEP-FRYING. Lean fish adapt well to the deep-fry method. The chief reason is that when fish are deep-fried they are either battered or

Recipe 12-4a TROUT À LA BELLE MEUNIÈRE

To Recipe 12.4, add:

4 oz sautéed mushrooms 125 g

Add mushrooms to pan in Step 4 of recipe.

Per serving:			
Calories:	404	Carbohydrates:	8 g
Fat:	25 g	Cholesterol:	131 mg
Protein:	37 g	Fiber:	0 g
		Sodium:	178 mg

Recipe 12-4b TROUT AMANDINE

To Recipe 12.4, add:

4 oz sliced or slivered almonds, toasted 125 g

Add almonds to pan in Step 4 of recipe.

Per serving:			
Calories:	532	Carbohydrates:	13 g
Fat:	36 g	Cholesterol:	131 mg
Protein:	42 g	Fiber:	3 g
		Sodium:	180 mg

Recipe 12-5 FISH CAKES

YIELD: ***25 5-oz (150 g) portions (2 cakes)***

4 oz	**green peppers, chopped**	**125 g**
4 oz	**onions, chopped**	**125 g**
2 Tb	**oil**	**30 mL**
4 lb	**fish, cooked and flaked**	**2 kg**
4 lb	**duchesse potatoes**	**2 kg**
	salt, pepper, and nutmeg to taste	

Breading:

6 oz	**flour**	**175 g**
1 tsp	**salt**	**5 mL**
1/2 tsp	**white pepper**	**2 mL**
2 C	**egg wash**	**500 mL**
1 lb	**bread crumbs**	**450 g**
	oil as needed	

1. Sauté green peppers and onions in oil.
2. Mix well-sautéed vegetables, fish, and potatoes.
3. Season to taste with salt, pepper, and nutmeg.
4. Shape into 2 1/2-oz (75 g) patties and chill until firm.
5. Set up breading station and bread fish cakes.
6. Pan-fry fish cakes in oil over moderate heat until well browned and heated through. Drain well on absorbent paper.

Per serving:		Carbohydrates:	28 g
Calories:	240	Cholesterol:	85 mg
Fat:	6 g	Fiber:	2 g

breaded, which helps to retain their moisture and flavor. For the same reason, fat fish are not suitable for deep-frying; their fat would be retained and they would taste oily and fishy.

To deep-fry:

- Use small lean fish or portions: shrimp, scallops, clams, oysters, fish sticks, fillets; portion-sized pieces of large lean fish.
- Season with salt, pepper, lemon.
- Bread or batter to protect the fish from the heat of the fryer and to give it a lightly browned, crisp coating.
- Deep-fry at 350°F (175°C) in good-quality oil until golden brown. Do not overcook.
- Serve at once.

Fish should be fried separately from other foods.

Recipe 12.6 is a well-known deep-fried fish dish—a seafood platter. Any combination of fish and shellfish may be used. The platter should in-

Recipe 12-6 SEAFOOD PLATTER

YIELD: ***10 7–8-oz (200–250 g) portions***

Breading:

6 oz	**flour**	**175 g**
1 tsp	**salt**	**5 mL**
1/2 tsp	**white pepper**	**2 mL**
2 C	**egg wash**	**500 mL**
1 lb	**bread crumbs**	**450 g**
10	**shrimp, medium size, peeled and deveined**	
20	**oysters**	
10 2–3 oz	**fillets (sole, cod, or catfish)**	**50–75 g**
20–30	**clams**	
10 oz	**tartar sauce**	**300 g**
10 oz	**cocktail sauce**	**300 g**
10	**lemon halves**	

1. Set up breading station and bread all fish items thoroughly.
2. Deep-fry at 350°F (180°C) until golden brown, as close to service time as possible.
3. Arrange on each platter 1 shrimp, 2 oysters, 1 fillet, 2–3 clams.
4. Add sauces in individual cups. Garnish with lemon halves.

Per serving:		Carbohydrates:	50 g
Calories:	655	Cholesterol:	222 mg
Fat:	36 g	Fiber:	2 g
Protein:	33 g	Sodium:	914 mg

clude at least four kinds of fish. The variety offered in a single dish is part of its appeal. Notice that it is served with cold sauces and lemon.

Deep-frying is one of the most popular methods of fish cookery in America today. It is fast and efficient, it is easily mastered by most cooks, and it yields a tasty product.

POACHING. Poaching a fish means cooking it in a flavored liquid at temperatures of 160 to 180°F (71–82°C). A moist-heat method, it is most commonly used to cook lean fish, but fat fish do well with it, too. Fish of any size may be poached. Poaching cooks a fish gently at low temperatures, yet because it is surrounded by hot liquid it cooks quickly, thus retaining maximum flavor and moisture.

Many cooks and connoisseurs consider poaching the best way of cooking fish. It certainly offers many avenues that other cooking methods don't. For example, poached fish can be served either hot or cold. Another option is the use of the cooking liquid as a vehicle for adding flavor to the fish. Sometimes, a sauce can be made from the cooking liquid, as you will see shortly.

Fish is often poached in a liquid known as **court bouillon** (Recipe 12.7). This is a liquid simmered with vegetables (such as onions, carrots, and celery), seasonings (such as herbs), and an acidic product (such as wine or vinegar). It is typically used to poach large whole fish such as salmon or turbot or smaller pieces such as steaks. It may be used to cook fish to be served either hot or cold, but it is not generally used in making sauce.

Usually, you cook the court bouillon before you add the fish. With a little thought, you can see the logic of precooking the bouillon. If you intend to extract any flavor from its flavor builders, you must simmer it long enough to allow the flavors to blend. Small fish and portion-sized pieces should be started in hot precooked bouillon, as in Recipe 12.8. Whole fish should be started in cold liquid for even cooking.

Place the fish on a rack to keep its shape and to simplify handling. If a rack is not available, you may wrap the fish in cheesecloth.

Cooking a large fish may take anywhere from 20 minutes to an hour and a half, depending on its size. You can tell when a whole large fish is done by squeezing it gently at its thickest part. It should feel firm but not hard. Or you can use a meat thermometer, placing the bulb in the thickest part. Fish is edible at an internal temperature of 145°F (63°C) and begins to break down and lose flavor and juices at 150°F (70°C).

Recipe 12-7 COURT BOUILLON

YIELD: ***Approximately 2 quarts (2 L)***

1 1/2 qt	**water**	**1.5 L**
1 pt	**vinegar (or equal parts vinegar and white wine)**	**500 mL**
Mirepoix:		
4 oz	**onions, small dice**	**125 g**
2 oz	**celery, small dice**	**60 g**
2 oz	**carrots, small dice**	**60 g**
5–6	**parsley stems**	
5–6	**peppercorns, crushed**	
1/2	**bay leaf**	
	pinch thyme	
2	**lemons, thinly sliced**	
1/2 tsp	**salt**	**2 mL**

Combine all ingredients and simmer 15–20 minutes.

Note: For salmon or tuna, red wine may be used in place of white wine.

Per quart:		Carbohydrates:	0 g
Calories:	0	Cholesterol:	0 mg
Fat:	0 g	Fiber:	0 g
Protein:	0 g	Sodium:	581 mg

Recipe 12-8 POACHED SALMON STEAKS

YIELD: ***10 6-oz (175 g) portions***

10 6-oz	**salmon steaks or fillets**	**175 g**
	butter as needed	
1 qt	**court bouillon, hot**	**1 L**

1. Place fish in lightly buttered baking dish. Add hot court bouillon to cover.
2. Cover with buttered paper.
3. Poach slowly on range or in 350°F (180°C) oven until done.
4. Remove from liquid and drain well.

Per serving:		Carbohydrates:	0 g
Calories:	160	Cholesterol:	40 mg
Fat:	4 g	Fiber:	0 g
Protein:	32 g	Sodium:	112 mg

When the fish is done, remove it immediately from the bouillon if it is to be served hot. If it is to be served cold, stop the cooking at once by adding ice to the court bouillon. Then cool the fish quickly in the liquid to keep its moisture and flavor from evaporating.

Fish poached in court bouillon go well with rich sauces such as hollandaise for fish served hot. For fish served cold, the traditional sauce is one using mayonnaise. If fat is a concern, a vegetable coulis works well.

Small fish portions such as small fillets, cuts of larger fillets, or steaks are frequently poached in a flavorful fish stock with spices and often white wine added. This liquid then becomes the body of a sauce to be served with the fish. The classical term for this liquid is **fumet** (fue-may). Recipe 12.9 describes these procedures: They combine flesh cookery and sauce cookery in a single dish. Let us examine the recipe in some detail.

First of all, the amount of poaching liquid (stock plus wine) that you will need is whatever will almost cover the fish. It will not necessarily be the exact amount given here but may vary with the size and shape of your pan. If you use either more or less, you should increase or decrease the remaining ingredients accordingly to keep the same proportions.

Recipe 12-9 SOLE IN A WHITE WINE SAUCE

YIELD: ***12 4-oz (125 g) fish with 2 fl oz (60 mL) sauce***

	butter or margarine as needed	
1 Tb	**minced shallots**	**15 mL**
3 lb	**sole fillets**	**1.5 kg**
	salt, cayenne, and lemon juice as needed	
$^1/_2$	**bay leaf**	
	juice from 1 lemon	
1 qt	**fish stock**	**1 L**
1 C	**dry white wine**	**250 mL**
1 qt	**fish velouté**	**1 L**
$^1/_2$ C	**heavy cream**	**125 mL**
	salt and white pepper to season	

1. Coat the bottom of a pan with butter or margarine. Sprinkle with shallots.
2. Season fillets lightly with salt, cayenne, and lemon juice. Place in pan with shallots.
3. Add bay leaf and juice from 1 lemon to the pan. Next, add stock and wine to almost cover. Cover the fish with buttered parchment paper or a lid.
4. Bring liquid to a boil; then reduce to a low simmer and poach until done.
5. Remove fillets from liquid. Keep warm.
6. Reduce the poaching liquid to about one-quarter its volume.
7. Add fish velouté and heavy cream. Bring to a boil.
8. Strain sauce and season to taste.
9. Coat fillets with hot sauce and serve at once.

Per serving:		Carbohydrates:	5 g
Calories:	224	Cholesterol:	71 mg
Fat:	12 g	Fiber:	0 g
Protein:	20 g	Sodium:	353 mg

Now, let us look at the steps involved in making this dish. Step 1 is a method right out of the French kitchen. The shallots add flavor to both fish and sauce. The butter keeps them from burning or sticking to the bottom as the liquid is heated. Of course, it keeps the fish from sticking, too.

The fish is seasoned only lightly in Step 2 because the seasonings dissolve in the liquid. Since the liquid will be reduced in making the sauce, you want only enough seasoning to bring out the fish flavor without spoiling the sauce.

The other ingredients in Step 3 will function in several ways. The liquid will cook the fish. The wine and stock and flavor builders will also give it extra flavor. At the same time, they will build the flavor and body of the sauce to be served with the fish. This fish is covered with buttered parchment paper or a lid to cook the top and simply cook the fish more evenly.

Step 4 describes the basic poaching process. You bring the liquid to the point of general agitation, then reduce the heat immediately. The temperature you want will cause bubbles on the pan bottom and slight action in the liquid, but the surface will be calm. The fillets will poach to doneness very, very quickly. They are done when they become firm and opaque and lose their sheen.

While you are cooking the fish, you are also beginning the sauce. Its flavors are being blended and the liquid is becoming somewhat reduced. You will not need to make a separate flavor reduction because all the ingredients are already there.

In Step 5, you end the cooking of the fish and, in Step 6, reduce the fumet to about one-quarter its volume. In Step 7, you add the velouté and heavy cream and bring to a boil.

Straining and seasoning (Step 8) are the final steps of preparation. Strain the sauce for smoothness. Season it to achieve the flavor most suitable to the fish. A slight taste of lemon does a great deal for fish, so use lemon as much for flavoring as for seasoning.

Step 9 combines both fish and sauce into the final dish. To coat the fish evenly with the sauce is to nap or mask it. **Napping** is a special technique: Using a single swift stroke, you move the ladleful of sauce above the food from one end to

Figure 12-7 SAUCING A FISH

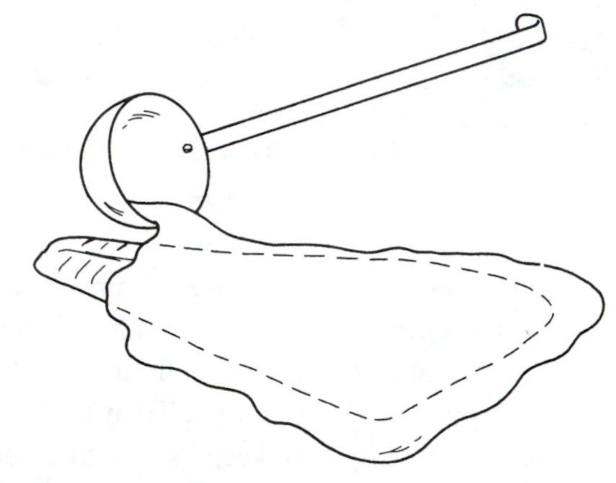

a. Napping or masking.

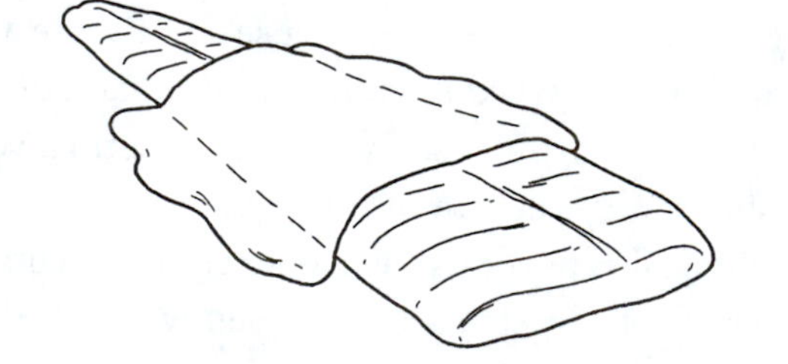

b. Striping.

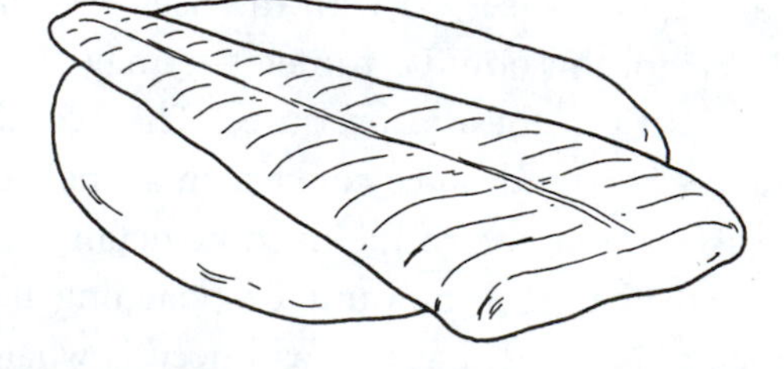

c. Pooling underneath.

the other, emptying it evenly with a smooth rotation of the wrist. For a traditional poached fish dish, the sauce will cover the entire serving. The sauce may be served under the fish or as a broad stripe across it (Figure 12.7).

This dish is a sample of what you can do with a poached fish and a sauce made in the same process. Not only does this method capture every bit of flavor from the fish, it retains the nutrients dissolved in the poaching liquid.

To make this dish even simpler, you can omit the velouté sauce and simply thicken the reduced poaching liquid with heavy cream or raw butter (as in monter au beurre—meaning that a piece of the butter is swirled in the hot sauce at the last minute before serving). You can also simply thicken the reduced poaching liquid with roux or beurre manié and simmer until the starchy taste is cooked out.

You can go in many more directions with this simple beginning. Any number of different dishes can be made by varying flavor builders, combinations of sauces, and garnitures. Recipes 12.9a and 12.9b give you two examples.

STEAMING. Fish are seldom cooked in a cabinet steamer: They tend to overcook in its high heat, and their flavor leaches out. There are, however, delicious ways of steaming them in their own juices. One of these is to cook them in a covered pan with just enough liquid (which usually includes melted butter or oil and wine) to cover the fish halfway, or less, and also to trigger the release of their own flavorful moisture in the form of steam. Some cooks refer to this style of cooking as braising, stewing, or moist baking.

Another way is to enclose each individual portion of fish tightly in parchment paper and bake it in a hot oven. This cooking method is called **en papillote** (on pop-ee-yote). Again, it is the fish's own moisture that steams the flesh to doneness. This method can produce some of the tastiest fish dishes imaginable, as every bit of the fish's own special flavor is captured and blended with the butter, lemon, and other added flavor builders. The paper envelope is opened at the table when served, and the delicious aroma is released to add to the diner's anticipation and pleasure.

An example of this cooking method is given in Recipe 12.10. Pompano en papillote is a fa-

Recipe 12-9a PAUPIETTES OF SOLE BONNE FEMME

To Recipe 12.9, add:

1 lb	**mushrooms, sliced**	**500 g**

1. Add mushrooms to pan with shallots.
2. Form fillets into paupiettes.
3. Proceed as in basic recipe.

Per serving:		Carbohydrates:	6 g
Calories:	234	Cholesterol:	71 mg
Fat:	12 g	Fiber:	0 g
Protein:	22 g	Sodium:	365 mg

Recipe 12-9b SOLE FLORENTINE

To Recipe 12.9, add:

20 oz	**cooked spinach, well drained, buttered, hot**	**600 g**
4–6 oz	**mornay sauce, thick**	**125–175 mL**

Follow Steps 1–6 of Recipe 12.9. Then strain reduced liquid and add enough mornay sauce to produce desired consistency. Season to taste. Place fillets on a bed of hot spinach, 2 oz (60 g) per portion. Coat with sauce and glaze under broiler or salamander until lightly golden.

Per serving:		Carbohydrates:	8 g
Calories:	251	Cholesterol:	74 mg
Fat:	13 g	Fiber:	1 g
Protein:	22 g	Sodium:	505 mg

Recipe 12-10 POMPANO EN PAPILLOTE BELLA VISTA

YIELD: ***10 6–7-oz (175–200 g) portions***

	oil as needed	
10 6–7-oz	pompano fillets	175–200 g
	melted butter, salt, and white pepper as needed	
1 oz	minced shallots	25 g
	chopped parsley as needed	
10	bell pepper slices, 1/4 in. (5 mm)	
10	onion slices, 1/4 in. (5 mm)	
10	tomato slices, 1/4 in. (5 mm)	
10	lemon slices, thin	

1. Cut parchment paper in a heart shape large enough for a fillet to fit on one side with 1/2 in. (1 cm) to spare all around. Oil the paper.
2. Place a fillet on one side of heart. Brush with melted butter, season with salt and white pepper, and sprinkle with shallots and parsley.
3. Overlap 1 slice each of pepper, onion, and tomato across fillet lengthwise. Center lemon slice on top.
4. Fold empty side of heart over fillet and begin making small overlapping folds around edge to enclose fish tightly. Fold point under to hold in place.
5. Place half hearts (papillotes) on lightly oiled sheet pan.
6. Bake in hot oven (400°F/200°C) until paper is puffed and brown (no more than 5–8 minutes).
7. To serve, slide portion onto plate and cut open in front of customer.

Per serving:		Carbohydrates:	6 g
Calories:	217	Cholesterol:	79 mg
Fat:	7 g	Fiber:	2 g
Protein:	32 g	Sodium:	393 mg

mous dish and can be made in many other versions by using such flavor builders as herbs, anchovies, shrimp, or crabmeat. It can also be made with other fish such as mackerel or with less expensive fish such as sole or flounder.

One of the problems in preparing this dish is that you cannot see the fish itself to tell when it is done. This is the reason for the time guideline in Step 6. You would use the lower limit for thin fillets such as sole or flounder and the higher limit for thicker pieces.

You can substitute foil if you do not have parchment paper, folding it carefully in the same way so that no steam escapes. But you will lose the doneness clue of having the paper puffed and brown.

QUALITY STANDARDS AND GUIDELINES FOR FIN FISH

Cooked fish should be moist, sweet, and tender. It is done when it is opaque and gently firm. Fish that is flaky is still edible but has gone beyond perfection. Dry, chewy fish is unacceptable.

Fish should be served as soon as possible, or it will lose the qualities that make it perfect. Presentation is important: A pale, flat fish on a plate needs something to give it height and color—a garnish or garniture, a sauce, a contrasting accompaniment such as a vegetable coulis or salsa. Butter sauces go well with fish. Lemon is a natural for fish, either in cooking or in presentation.

But no matter how elaborate the dish or what you do to dress it up, preserving the fish's own flavor, body, and texture, underlies the quality of the product you serve.

SHELLFISH

Thus far, we have talked mostly about fin fish. Shellfish are different creatures. Figure 12.8 shows the most commonly served shellfish.

Some shellfish live inside a pair of shells, as clams, oysters, mussels, and scallops do, or underneath a single shell, as the abalone does. These are **mollusks.** The whole clam or oyster or mus-

Figure 12-8 COMMONLY USED SHELLFISH

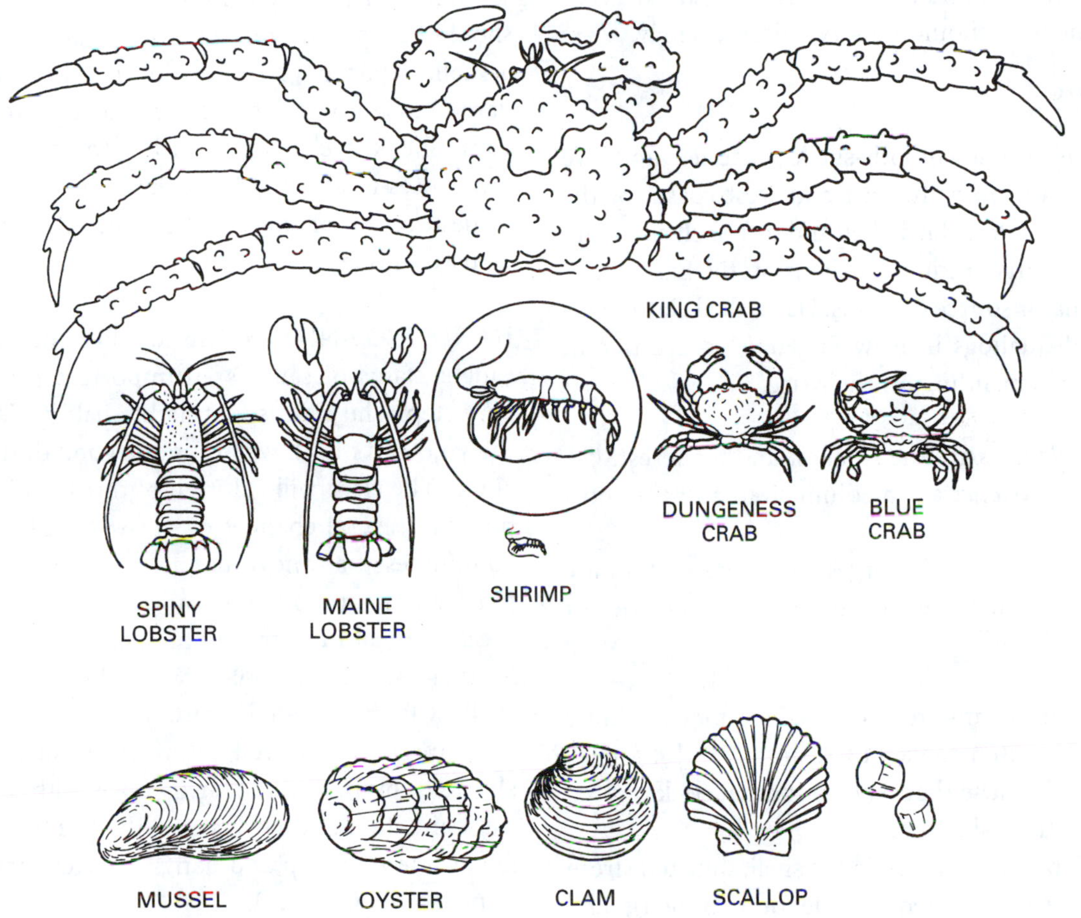

sel is edible, but what we eat as a scallop is only the muscle that opens and closes its shells. The shells themselves are often used as dishes for various sauced fish delicacies, which are then called **en coquille** (on ko-keel). Abalone steaks are also only one muscle, sliced and pounded thin.

Other kinds of shellfish wear jointed suits of armor. These are **crustaceans** (krus-tay-shuns). The ones we eat are crabs, lobsters, shrimp, and crayfish. Shellfish of both types have a prominent place in fish cookery, and they have characteristics all their own.

The flavor of shellfish ranges from mild to full. Scallops, lobster, crayfish, and squid have a mild flavor. Octopus has a moderate flavor, and mussels, oysters, and clams have a full flavor.

There is scarcely any limit to what you do in building mouth-watering shellfish dishes. But underneath everything you do in cooking these delectable creatures are five simple things to remember:

- Shellfish are very lean.
- Moist-heat methods are best.

- Quick cooking is best.
- Lemon should be part of cooking and service.
- Shellfish should be served immediately.

CLAMS

Clams are a smooth-shelled species and are found on both the east and west coasts of the United States. Hard-shell and soft-shell clams are the two major kinds of clams on the East Coast, the major source of clams. Hard-shell clams, also called quahogs in New England, have different names depending on their size.

- *Littlenecks* are the smallest and tenderest.
- *Cherrystones* are medium sized and the most common.
- *Chowders* are the largest and, because they are tough, they are cut up for use in chowder or for frying.

Soft-shell clams are also called steamers, because they are often cooked by steaming, or long-neck clams, because they have necks that stick out between their shells.

Clams are sold live in the shell, shucked (fresh or frozen), canned (whole or chopped), and frozen breaded (raw or cooked). When buying live clams, make sure they have:

- Tightly closed shells (if the shells are opened slightly, tap with a knife, and they should close; discard if they don't close)
- Moist shells that are not cracked, chipped, or broken
- Mild odor

Don't buy live clams that have broken shells or a bad odor. Shucked clams should have plump meat, a mild odor, and a pale- to deep-orange color.

STORING. Live clams carry around their own sea water environment inside their shells. They should be stored at refrigerator temperatures in a shallow pan covered with a wet cloth. Keep damp but not wet. They can be kept up to two days. Shucked clams should be stored in their own juices in a container with a tight lid in the coldest section of your refrigerator. They should be used in one to two days.

HANDLING AND COOKING. Purging freshly caught clams of sand is an important preliminary step. The clam spent its life half buried in the sand and may have brought a good deal of it along. The clam will rid itself of this sand if you put it in several changes of salt water for 15 to 20 minutes at a time; it has a set of siphons that pull water in and out. Or you can sprinkle cornmeal in a pail of clams submerged in brine and let them sit in the cooler overnight. Scrub the shells with fresh water before use.

Clams are removed from their shells, or **shucked,** by prying the shells open with a special knife. It isn't easy, because the live little fellow inside clams up and hangs on. Here are the steps (see Figure 12.9):

1. Place a clam in the palm of your left hand (if you are right-handed, reverse if you are left-handed) with the hinge between the thumb and index finger. Take a clam knife (or dull paring knife) and line it up along the crack between the shells.
2. Curl the fingers of the hand holding the clam around the back of the knife and apply slow steady pressure until the knife slides in. Twist the knife to open the shell wide enough to cut the muscle on top.
3. Break off the top shell and keep the clam level to avoid losing the juice. Cut the clam away

Figure 12-9 HOW TO SHUCK A CLAM

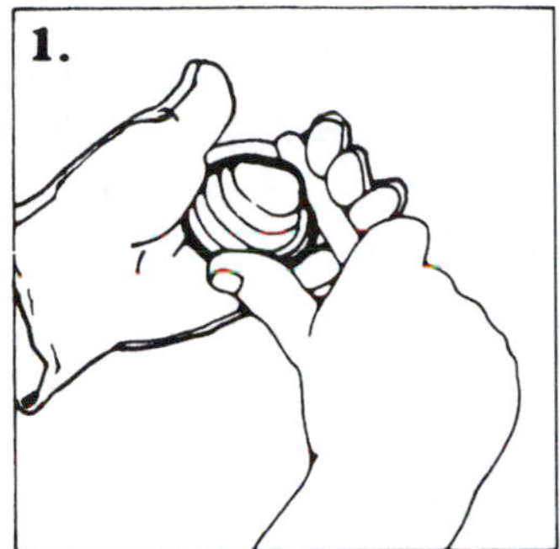

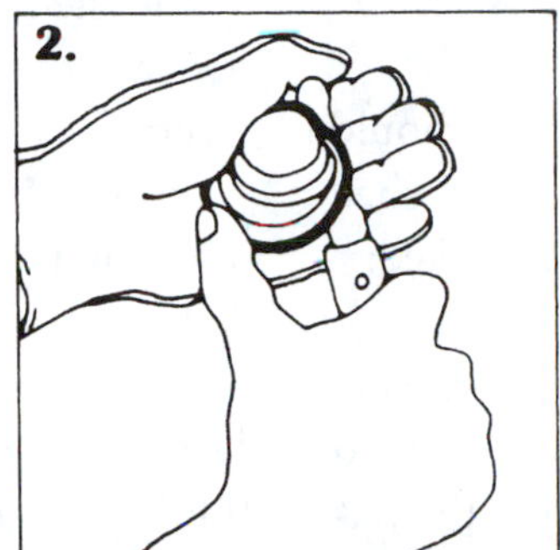

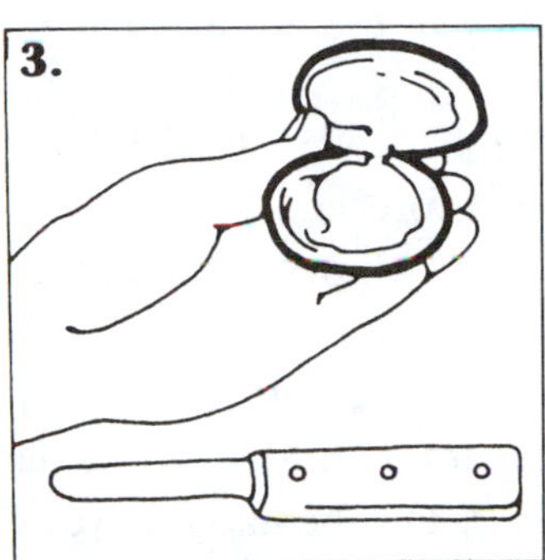

from the bottom shell by scraping with the knife point.

If you find it very difficult to shuck clams, try warming them very briefly in the oven—just until they open wide enough to insert the knife.

Only cook clams that are alive, as evidenced by their closed shell. Clams are often cooked by steaming in their shells, either in a cabinet steamer or in a covered stockpot on the range with a small amount of water on the bottom. The shells open when they are done. Serve them in the shell along with a cup of the rich broth that results from their cooking. Do not season them.

Clams can also be cooked by steaming, baking on the half shell, deep-frying, or simmering in soups and chowders. Remove them one by one as they open and continue cooking until all are done. Shucked clams become plump and opaque when cooked. Do not overcook, as overdone clams are tough.

CRABS

There are various kinds of crabs:

- *Blue crab:* From the East Coast, a small crab ranging from 4 ounces to 1 pound, used often for frozen crabmeat, named for their blue pincers.
- *Soft-shell crab:* Molting blue crabs that have shed their hard shells and are harvested before their new shell hardens. Completely edible after the head, gills, stomach, and intestines are removed.
- *Dungeness crab:* A West Coast favorite, ranges from $1^1/_2$ to $3^1/_2$ pounds in size, meat from the body is white while meat from the claws and legs is red, meat is very sweet.
- *King crab:* Largest of the crabs, ranges in size from 6 to 24 pounds, cooked immediately after harvest, comes from Alaska.
- *Snow crab:* About half the size of the king crab and less expensive, cooked immediately after harvest, also from Alaska.

Few crabs are purchased live, except soft-shell crabs. When bought live, make sure there is some leg movement. Frozen crab (it has already been cooked) is available year-round, and fresh is available during warm months in the areas where the crabs are harvested.

STORING. Live crabs should be kept in the refrigerator for only one to two days in moist packaging (seaweed or damp paper strips). Frozen crabmeat should be kept at or below 0°F (−18°C). Once thawed, use immediately.

HANDLING AND COOKING. Crabs should be alive before cooking. To clean a soft-shell crab, do the following before they are cooked:

1. Place the crab top side up on the work surface. With a knife or shears, cut off the head about $^1/_4$ inch behind the eyes. Be sure the yellowish sand bag (it's the stomach) is removed and discarded. Rinse well under cold running water and pat dry.
2. Turn the crab on its back and cut off the tail flap, or apron, which is triangular in females and T-shaped in males. First, pry the apron up with your fingers and then pull it down and away. Discard the apron and the intestinal tract, which is attached to it.
3. Peel back the pointed shell and scrape or pull out the spongy gills on each side. Rinse the crab with cold water and pat dry.

Don't clean soft-shell crabs until you are ready to cook them. The crab may then be breaded or battered for deep-frying. Soft-shell crabs can also be sautéed or grilled.

Hard-shell crabs do not need to be prepared before cooking. They are usually simmered for 10 to 15 minutes in salted water and then cooled in ice water. They can also be steamed. To pick the meat out of a Dungeness or other hard-shell crab, do the following:

1. Grasp a front claw and twist it, breaking it off where it meets the body. Repeat with the other claw and legs. Crack each piece (a nutcracker comes in handy) and remove the meat.
2. Break off the pointed shell on the underside.
3. Pry off the top shell. Discard the gills, spongy parts, and stomach (behind the eyes) under the shell.
4. Place the knife blade down the center of the crab's body. Tap the knife with a mallet to cut in half. Repeat to cut each half into chunks, placing the knife blade between the leg joints. Pry out the meat.

Frozen crabmeat often is quite watery—squeeze out the moisture before cooking.

LOBSTERS

The most popular lobster is the northern lobster. The meat from its large tail, four pair of legs, and two large frontclaws is eaten. The lobster's shell is dark green, or blue green, but it turns red when cooked. Lobsters are classified by weight: A jumbo lobster is over $2^1/_2$ pounds, a large or select lobster is $1^1/_2$ to $2^1/_2$ pounds, a quarter lobster is about $1^1/_4$ pounds, and a chicken lobster is about 1 pound.

The spiny or rock lobster is not a true lobster, but a type of crayfish. The only usable meat of the spiny lobster is found in the tail, and it is less sweet than lobster.

Lobsters can be purchased live or frozen. When receiving live lobster, make sure there is some leg movement and that the lobster's tail curls under when picked up. Cooked meat, fresh or frozen, is also available.

STORING. Store lobsters in the refrigerator in ventilated containers. Keep moist with seaweed, lettuce leaves, or damp paper towels. Never store in an air-tight container as the lobsters will suffocate and die. Live lobsters should be used within 24 hours; cooked lobster meat within one to two days.

HANDLING AND COOKING. Live lobsters are often cooked by throwing them headfirst into

Recipe 12-11 LOBSTER TAIL

YIELD: ***1 4–5 oz portion (125–150 g)***

1 4–5-oz	**lobster tail**	**125–150 g**
	salt, pepper, melted butter, paprika, and lemon juice as needed	

1. Saddleback the lobster tail.
2. Sprinkle with salt, pepper, melted butter, paprika, and lemon juice.
3. Place in a pan with a small amount of water ($^1/_2$–$^3/_4$ in./1–1.5 cm deep). Cover and steam until done.
4. Serve immediately.

Per serving:		Carbohydrates:	1 g
Calories:	214	Cholesterol:	121 mg
Fat:	12 g	Fiber:	0 g
Protein:	24 g	Sodium:	376 mg

boiling water (this kills them instantly) and simmering for about 6 minutes for each pound. When the lobster is done, remove it immediately from the cooking liquid, cut it in half (lay it back side down and use a heavy knife), and crack the claws. Serve at once with lemon and a dish of melted butter. The guest dips bits of lobster in the butter.

Steaming is a good, quick, moist-heat method to prepare frozen lobster tails. The tails must be thawed shortly before cooking. Recipe 12.11 shows how they are prepared by steaming. Let us look at each step in detail.

Step 1: Figure 12.10 shows how to saddleback the lobster tail.

Step 2: The seasoning is done at this point so that it will penetrate the flesh during cooking. Butter is added for both visual and taste appeal; paprika is largely for looks.

Step 3: The function of the water is to create steam in the covered pan, not to boil the fish. Since the flesh has been placed on top of the shell, it is not immersed in the water. "Done" is when the flesh is firm and opaque. It takes only a few minutes.

Step 4: Serve at once for flavor and eye appeal. Lemon and melted butter (drawn butter,

Figure 12-10 HOW TO SADDLEBACK A LOBSTER TAIL

a.

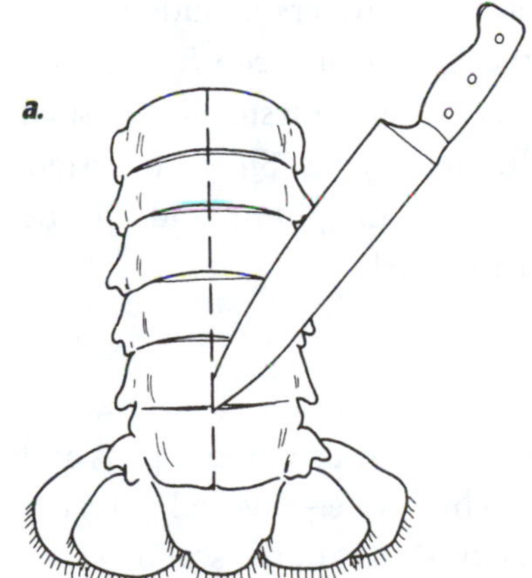

b.

c.

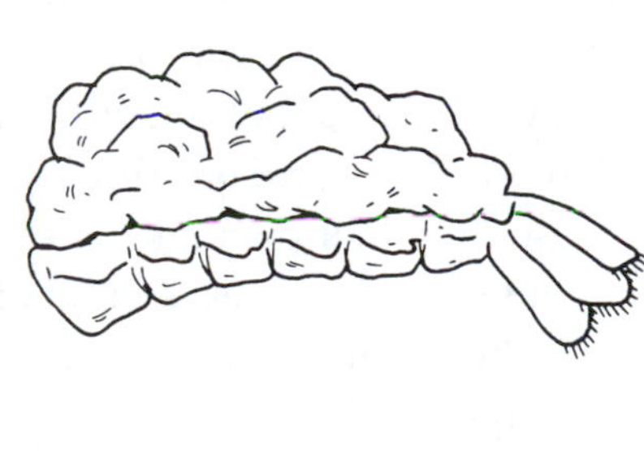

a. Cut through the top shell of the tail (dotted line). ***b.*** Spread the shell open. ***c.*** Pull the flesh out and arrange on top of the shell.

beurre fondu) are indispensable accompaniments to plain hot lobster meat no matter how it is cooked.

Whole or cut-up lobster can also be cooked by broiling, baking, or sautéing.

OYSTERS

Oysters have a rough shell with scalloped edges. They vary in size, texture, and flavor according to where they are harvested. Oysters are found on both the east and west coasts of the United States, and they are often named after the area in which they are harvested. For example, Eastern oysters are taken from the Atlantic Ocean, and Pacific oysters are found along the Oregon and Washington coasts.

Oysters can be purchased live in the shell, shucked (fresh or frozen), breaded (raw or frozen), and canned. When buying live oysters, make sure they have tightly closed shells, a mild odor, and moist shells that are not cracked or broken. Shucked oysters should be plump, with a mild odor, and creamy white in color, but they vary naturally to include green, red, brown, and pink colorations. They should be in a clear liquid.

STORING. Live oysters should be stored in the refrigerator in the cartons they were packed in. Keep them damp, but not wet. They can be kept up to three or four days. Shucked oysters should be stored in their own juices in a container with a tight lid in the coldest section of your refrigerator. They should also be used within three to four days.

HANDLING AND COOKING. At least one hour before shucking, scrub the oysters under cold running water. Discard any oysters that don't have tightly closed shells or shells that close once jiggled.

Figure 12.11 shows one method for shucking an oyster.

1. Shucking an oyster is a question of leverage, not force. To open, place it flat side up, and with a cloth or towel, press it firmly against the work surface. Do not hold it in your hand and try to open it in the air as you would a clam. Place the tip of the oyster knife between the shell near the hinge.
2. Twist the knife up while pushing it in until you hear a snap (that means the hinge is broken).
3. Twist to open the shell wide enough to slide the knife inside the top shell to cut the muscle that closes the shell. Avoid cutting the flesh of the oyster or it will lose its plumpness.
4. Lift the top shell off. Keep the oyster level at all times to save the juice. Cut the lower end of the muscle from the bottom shell to loosen the meat. Remove any pieces of shell that may be in the meat.

Cooking methods for oysters include poaching, baking on the half shell, deep-frying, and simmering in soups or stews. Oysters in the shell are done when the shell opens. Shucked oysters are done when they become plump and opaque and the edges start to curl.

SCALLOPS

The scallop is actually the muscle that opens and closes the shell. This sweet-flavored, creamy white muscle is the only part of the scallop eaten by Americans, but Europeans eat the entire scallop. There are several different kinds of scallops:

Figure 12-11 HOW TO SHUCK AN OYSTER

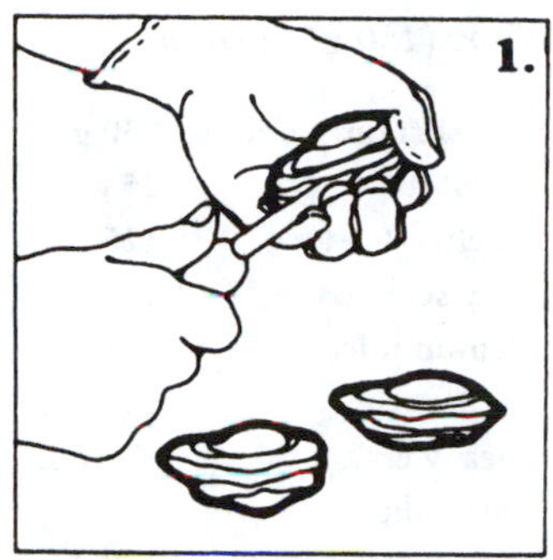

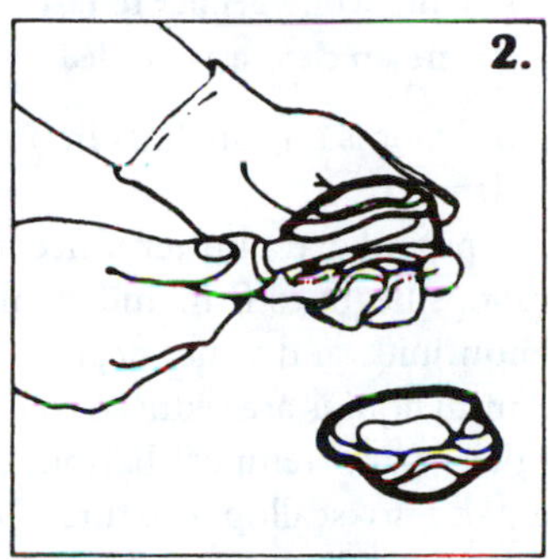

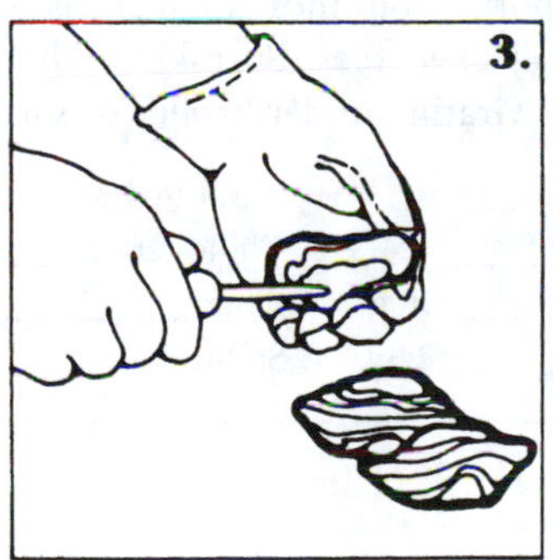

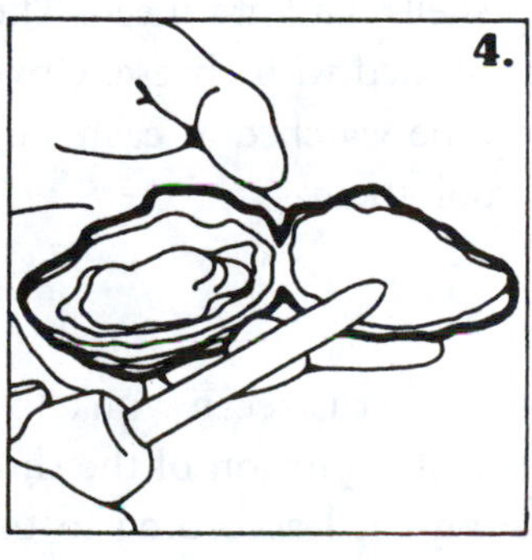

- *Sea scallops* are caught off the coasts of the New England and Middle Atlantic states. They are large and are often cut into smaller pieces.
- *Bay scallops* are caught off the eastern coast of the United States, the Gulf of Mexico, and the North Sea. They are much smaller than sea scallops and are often considered more delicate.
- *Calico scallops* are also small.

Scallops are always sold shucked.

To be fresh, scallops should display the following characteristics:

- Mild, sweet odor.
- Moist looking.
- Varying color. The smaller bay and calico scallops are usually creamy white, with occasional light tan or pink coloration; the larger sea scallops are also creamy white, though they might show light orange or pink color, which is natural

STORING. Scallops can be refrigerated for one to two days covered in their own liquid in a closed container. A sulfur-like smell or brownish color indicates spoilage. The refrigerator temperature should be between 30 and 34°F (−1–1°C). Don't put them on ice—it will ruin their texture.

HANDLING AND COOKING. The only preparation for scallops is to wash them quickly in cold water. Scallops can be cooked using almost any cooking method. Once cooked, scallops turn milky white and become firm. If overdone, they become tough.

Scallops may be broiled in casseroles, similar to a dish called shrimp scampi. They are covered with a layer of bread crumbs before the garlic butter is poured over them, which glazes as they are broiled. The crumbs also protect them from high heat and moisture loss.

Scallops may also be sautéed as shown in Recipe 12.12. The secret here is very quick cooking in butter and oil. Herbs and wine provide a rich and special taste. Scallops are often broiled or poached as well.

A famous scallop dish (Recipe 12.13) blends a number of cooking methods and techniques. The recipe shows you how the dish is built. It begins by adding the scallops to sautéed flavor builders for very brief cooking. The pan is then deglazed with wine and lemon juice and the liquids are reduced, during which the scallops finish cooking by simmering. They are then combined with a liaison-enriched sauce, portioned into scallop shells, and gratinéed. They may be further embellished with cheese. Obviously, the scallops must be watched at each step in order not to overcook them.

Recipe 12-12 SAUTEED HERBED SCALLOPS

YIELD: *10 4-oz (125 g) portions*

$2^1/_2$ lb	**bay or sea scallops**	**1.25 kg**
2 oz	**butter**	**60 g**
2 fl oz	**olive oil**	**60 mL**
$^1/_2$ C	**white wine or sherry**	**125 mL**
4 oz	**chives**	**125 g**
4 oz	**chopped parsley**	**125 g**
	salt to taste	

1. Cut large sea scallops in half. Dry scallops with paper towels.
2. Heat butter and olive oil in a sauté pan.
3. Sauté scallops over moderately high heat until lightly golden on all sides (about 1–2 minutes). Remove scallops from pan and keep warm.
4. Deglaze pan with wine or sherry. Add chives and parsley and pour over scallops.
5. Salt to taste and serve at once.

Per serving:		Carbohydrates:	3 g
Calories:	196	Cholesterol:	50 mg
Fat:	11 g	Fiber:	0 g
Protein:	19 g	Sodium:	230 mg

Recipe 12-13 COQUILLES ST. JACQUES

YIELD: *10 5-oz (150 g) portions*

$^1/_2$ lb	**mushrooms, sliced**	**250 g**
1 oz	**shallots**	**25 g**
$^1/_2$ C	**melted butter**	**125 mL**
$2^1/_2$ lb	**bay scallops**	**1.25 kg**
$^1/_2$ C	**lemon juice**	**125 mL**
1 C	**white wine**	**250 mL**
$^3/_4$ pt	**heavy cream**	**375 mL**
3	**egg yolks**	
$1^1/_4$ qt	**fish velouté, hot**	**1.25 L**
	salt and white pepper to taste	
	Parmesan cheese as needed	

1. Sauté mushrooms and shallots in butter until light golden.
2. Add scallops and extra butter if needed. Cook until scallops begin to firm and change color.
3. Add lemon juice and wine, deglaze pan, and simmer until liquids are reduced by one-third.
4. In another pan, temper liaison into hot velouté. Add to scallop mixture. Season to taste with salt and white pepper.
5. Place portions in individual shells (coquilles) or small casseroles. Sprinkle with Parmesan cheese. Gratiné under broiler or salamander.

Per serving:		Carbohydrates:	11 g
Calories:	424	Cholesterol:	188 mg
Fat:	30 g	Fiber:	0 g
Protein:	24 g	Sodium:	758 mg

SHRIMP

Shrimp is a small crustacean with a long tail and 10 legs. The edible portion of the shrimp is the tail. Tails are graded according to the number per pound in unpeeled form, known as the count. The larger the shrimp, the more expensive they are. The term **prawn** is sometimes used to refer to large shrimp. There are many varieties of shrimp, such as brown, pink, and white, but after cooking, all shrimp are the same color.

Shrimp can be purchased in several forms:

- **Green shrimp**—meaning raw shrimp in the shell
- Peeled and deveined shrimp (P&D)—meaning the shrimp has its shell and vein removed.
- Peeled, deveined, and cooked (PDC)—meaning the shell and vein have been removed and the shrimp is cooked

These three forms are usually sold frozen (unless you are very close to where shrimp are harvested) because shrimp are highly perishable. Shrimp are also available frozen and breaded (raw or cooked), canned, and butterflied (split in the shell).

Raw shrimp should appear moist; the meat should be firm and the shells translucent with a minimum of black spots or edges. Cooked shrimp in the shell should contain firm white meat with pink or reddish shells.

STORING. Fresh shrimp in the shell should be stored on ice in the refrigerator; peeled shrimp can also be stored on ice but only after wrapping them up. Use refrigerated shrimp within one to two days.

HANDLING AND COOKING. Shrimp to be served hot must be peeled and deveined before cooking. If shrimp are to be served cold, they are usually peeled and deveined after cooking to maintain flavor. Figure 12.12 shows how to peel and devein shrimp.

Figure 12-12 HOW TO PEEL AND DEVEIN SHRIMP

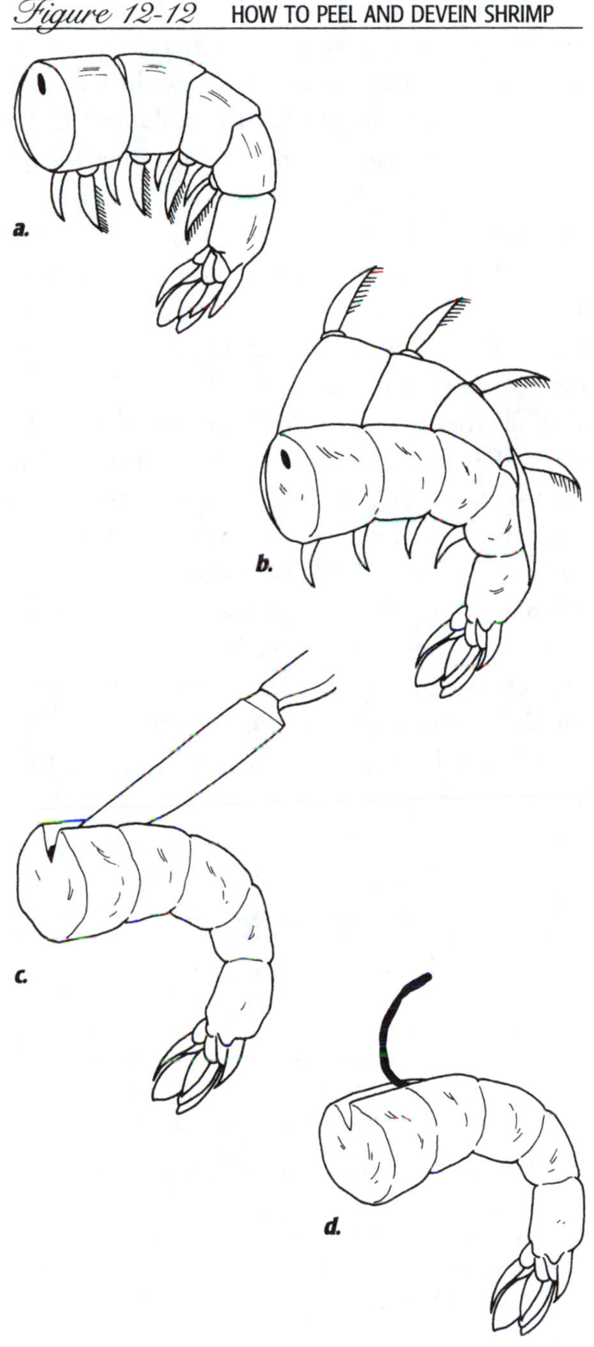

a. Headless shrimp with shell on. ***b.*** Pull off the shell beginning at the leg side. It will come right off. ***c.*** To devein, cut along the curved surface to the black vein, which is the intestine. ***d.*** Pull the vein away or run a knife tip under it.

Like other shellfish, shrimp need to be cooked quickly; otherwise, you risk overcooking them and having a tough product. Cook shrimp just until they curl, the shells turn pink, and their meat turns opaque. Shrimp can be cooked using a variety of methods: simmering, sautéing, broiling, deep-frying, baking, or grilling.

"Boiled" shrimp are really simmered. Recipe 12.14 shows a recipe for simmering shrimp. You will probably notice how similar it is to poaching fish in a court bouillon. The method is essentially the same with a different liquid and different flavor builders and a somewhat higher temperature. You cook the liquid and flavor builders for a few minutes before adding the shrimp, in order to blend and develop flavors. Then you cook the shrimp at a simmer only until they are done. Use this method for either green or peeled shrimp. Cook green shrimp in the shell; the shells have a great deal of flavor.

In broiled shrimp scampi (Recipe 12.15), the shrimp are literally immersed in garlic butter as they cook. The tails stiffen and stand up, providing a handsome and striking presentation for this rich dish.

Recipe 12-14 SIMMERED SHRIMP

Yield: ***3 4-oz (125 g) servings***

2 C	**white stock**	**500 mL**
3 Tb	**red wine vinegar**	**45 mL**
1 Tb	**pickling spice**	**15 mL**
1 lb	**shrimp, peeled and deveined**	**450 g**

1. Bring stock, vinegar, and pickling spice to a boil.
2. Add shrimp and reduce heat to simmer.
3. Simmer 4–8 minutes or until shrimp appear pink and firm.

Per serving:		Carbohydrates:	0 g
Calories:	140	Cholesterol:	276 mg
Fat:	2 g	Fiber:	0 g
Protein:	30 g	Sodium:	317 mg

Recipe 12-15 BROILED SHRIMP SCAMPI

Yield: ***10 portions (5 pieces each)***

50	**shrimp, peeled and deveined (16–20 count), tails left on**	
1/2 oz	**puréed garlic**	**15 g**
4 oz	**butter**	**125 g**
1/2 C	**olive oil**	**125 g**
1 fl oz	**lemon juice**	**30 mL**
1 fl oz	**white wine**	**30 mL**
	salt and pepper to taste	
1/4 C	**chopped parsley**	**60 mL**

1. In small casseroles, place 5 shrimp per portion with tails up.
2. Sauté garlic in butter and olive oil until aroma is evident. Add lemon juice and wine. Season with salt and pepper to taste.
3. Pour butter sauce over shrimp and cook under broiler at medium heat until shrimp are done (pink, firm, and lightly browned tops). Sprinkle with chopped parsley.

Per serving:		Carbohydrates:	0 g
Calories:	240	Cholesterol:	300 mg
Fat:	11 g	Fiber:	0 g
Protein:	30 g	Sodium:	407 mg

SUMMING UP

The flavor, body, and texture of all kinds of fish and seafood are delicate and fragile. Fish is delicate and sweet. It has a high water content that readily evaporates, carrying much flavor with it. In body, fish has little connective tissue, which makes it fall apart easily unless gently handled and gently cooked. It cooks quickly: Its muscle tissue coagulates readily and it is done when opaque and gently firm. In texture, fish is tenderness itself if cooked quickly at low temperatures. If overcooked, its texture becomes tough, dry, and chewy.

The choice of cooking method for a particular kind of fish depends on what will best preserve and enhance its flavor, body, and texture. This depends partly on the fat content of the fish. Fat fish may be cooked with either moist-heat or dry-heat methods. Lean fish do best with moist-heat methods but may be broiled, baked, or fried if protected by butter or oil or a coating of some kind.

All kinds of fish respond especially well to the use of lemon. They are also compatible with many flavor builders, especially wine, butter, mushrooms, herbs, and sauces. As a menu item, fish is versatile: The same fish may be prepared in many different ways, and a given recipe can be varied by substituting different fish.

Like fish, shellfish are very lean. Moist-heat methods work best, along with quick cooking. Lemon should be part of cooking and service, and shellfish should always be served immediately.

The Cook's Vocabulary

court bouillon, fumet

en coquille

en papillote

fin fish

flaking

flatfish

green shrimp

market forms: whole, round, drawn, dressed, steak, fillet, stick, butterflied

napping

paupiette

prawn

round fish

shellfish: mollusks, crustaceans

shuck

Review Questions

Answer each question in complete sentences. Read each question carefully and make sure you answer all parts of the question. Organize your answer into more than one paragraph when appropriate.

1. What are the major considerations in cooking fish? In choosing a cooking method, what difference does it make whether a fish is fat or lean?
2. How does fish compare nutritionally to meat and poultry?
3. Discuss five ways of preparing fish and give an example of a recipe using each method.
4. Suggest ways of preparing and presenting fish to compensate for their flat, colorless appearance.
5. How do shellfish differ from fin fish? What are the best cooking methods for shellfish?
6. What do en papillote, en coquille, and paupiette mean?

Chapter 13

BREAKFAST, BEVERAGES, AND DAIRY PRODUCTS

Breakfast is often defined as the first meal of the day. You probably think of it in terms of 6 A.M. to 9 A.M. But in today's world breakfast may be served at noon, at 9 in the evening, or at 3 A.M. to top off an evening out. It is much more than the day's first meal; it is a group of foods cooked and served in a particular way.

Breakfast is usually eggs with bacon, sausage, or ham, and maybe with hash browns, French fries, or grits, and toast or muffins or cornbread, with fruit or juice to begin with and coffee before, during, and after. The alternative to eggs seems to be pancakes with sausage, or with bacon, or with ham. Or cereal, hot or cold. Or a light continental breakfast of rolls and coffee, or Danish pastry and coffee, or doughnuts and coffee. Or just coffee.

Brunch, another popular meal period, is a combination of breakfast and lunch and is served from late morning until midafternoon, usually on weekends. Here you will find dishes that take off from breakfast eggs and pancakes and bacon and ham and fruit to make light and appetizing luncheon entrées, along with salads, quiche, and other more traditional lunch fare. Sometimes, such a meal is displayed on an eye-catching buffet with ice sculptures and fruit displays—a visual feast.

What will you cook for breakfast and brunch? Many operations use convenience items. They buy readymade Danish pastries, doughnuts, croissants, and rolls. They make cereals, muffins, cornbread, and grits from mixes, flakes, or powders needing only to be baked or boiled as the package directs. They use frozen hash brown potatoes and canned or frozen fruit juices.

So what is left for the cook to do? You will put to work your skills and knowledge to prepare

- Eggs
- Breakfast meats
- Pancakes, waffles, French toast, crêpes
- Beverages
- Brunch dishes

You will learn more about some familiar foods, practice some old techniques, learn some new ones, and get some experience on the griddle.

After completing this chapter, you should be able to:

- Describe the similarities between breakfast and brunch and the differences between them.
- Describe the principal ways of cooking eggs to order.

- Describe how to use the griddle to cook eggs, breakfast meats, pancakes, and French toast.
- Describe how to prepare breakfast ham, bacon, and sausage.
- List the principal breakfast beverages and describe how to use them.
- Name and describe a dozen kinds of cheese.

ABOUT EGGS

An egg is made up of the albumen, or white; the yolk, or yellow; and a porous shell. It is at its best right after it is laid. A cross section of an egg is shown in Figure 13.1. In a fresh egg, the two ropes of chalazae (ka-lay′-zee) hold the yolk firmly in the middle of the egg. There is more thick white than thin white, and the air cell (located at the large end of the egg) is small.

Eggs lose their firmness by the escape of carbon dioxide through the porous shell. As this happens, the air cell enlarges, the chalazae relax, the yolk moves off center, the thick white lessens, and the thin white increases. You can see off-center yolks and large air cell indentations in hard-boiled eggs that have lost quality. Notice the thick white and thin white as you fry and poach eggs, and you'll see why freshness is important.

Figure 13-1 INSIDE THE EGG—A SIMPLIFIED VERSION

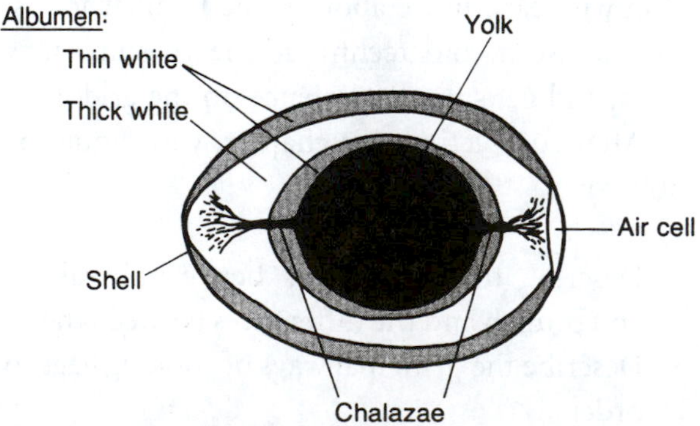

QUALITY AND SIZE

Eggs are graded AA, A, or B under a federal–state program administered by the U.S. Department of Agriculture. You can check for high quality and freshness by noting the egg's appearance when broken. Its yolk should remain whole and stand high, and the white should stand high and close to the yolk. Fresh grade AA eggs are the best for uses in which appearance really counts—such as fried or poached eggs. Grade AA or A eggs work well for boiled eggs (be sure to use eggs that have been in the cooler a few days because very fresh hard-boiled eggs are hard to peel).

The color of the shell has no relation to quality. Shell color is determined by the breed of hen.

Eggs are classified by size as well as by quality. The two classifications have nothing to do with each other. Size classification is actually by weight per dozen, not by the egg, and the eggs in a dozen may not all be the same size. Table 13.1 shows the classification of eggs by size.

MARKET FORMS

In addition to fresh eggs, there are several other market forms. Dried eggs and frozen eggs are available whole or separated into whites and yolks. The biggest demand for processed eggs is in the baking industry, but whole frozen eggs are popular and useful for eggs cooked in quantity and in mass, such as scrambled eggs, omelets, and baked goods.

Egg substitutes are available that are low in cholesterol, but not always low in fat. They are often made from egg whites and vegetable oil.

Table 13-1 EGGS CLASSIFIED BY SIZE

Size	Minimum Weight per Dozen
Jumbo	30 oz (849 g)
Extra large	27 oz (768 g)
Large	24 oz (672 g)
Medium	21 oz (588 g)
Small	18 oz (504 g)
Peewee	15 oz (425 g)

HANDLING AND STORAGE

Proper handling can preserve freshness. Stored in coolers at 36°F (2°C), shell eggs have a shelf life of several weeks with little loss of quality. At room temperature, they deteriorate rapidly. When you hold eggs at the grill for cooking, you are exposing them to rapid quality loss. Store them away from strong-smelling foods. They absorb odors through the shell.

All frozen eggs must be stored at 0°F (−18°C) and thawed in the cooler (allow two days). Dried eggs must be stored in the cooler and reconstituted according to package directions.

All eggs except the frozen pasteurized form are likely to bring salmonella bacteria with them into the kitchen. This is another reason for keeping them refrigerated and handling them with respect at all times. Other rules to follow to prevent salmonella from causing foodborne illness include the following:

- Don't use cracked eggs—throw them out!
- Refrigerate hard-boiled eggs.
- Do not reuse a container after it has had raw-egg mixture in it until it has been washed thoroughly.
- Use an egg separator, instead of the egg shells themselves, to separate the white from the yolk.
- Follow your kitchen's guidelines on using raw eggs in recipes that require no further, or minimal, cooking. Examples include eggnog, Caesar salad dressing, mayonnaise, and hollandaise sauce.

NUTRITIONAL PROFILE

Nutritionally, eggs are good sources of protein, vitamin A, iron, and some B vitamins. The yolk is high in fat and in cholesterol, a fatty substance some people avoid for health reasons. One egg contains 213 milligrams of cholesterol—compare that to the 300 milligrams suggested maximum we eat daily.

COOKING EGGS

The egg is versatile (and also inexpensive). You have already met it as an emulsifier in making butter sauces. You have seen it in the liaison as a binding agent and creator of smooth texture for soups and sauces. You know that it is used to clarify liquids such as consommés. You have used it to hold breading together and make it adhere to the product, and to bind duchesse potatoes.

It has still other uses. Egg thickens custards and puddings. Whipped egg white leavens batters and soufflés and is the essence of meringue. Egg can be brushed on foods to be baked, or added to sauces to be glazed, to produce a shiny golden-brown crust.

Eggs cooked for breakfast are high-grade whole fresh eggs prepared in a number of ways:

- Fried eggs
- Scrambled eggs
- Boiled eggs

- Poached eggs
- Shirred eggs
- Omelets

Recipes for each of these styles are given in Recipes 13.1 to 13.6.

The most important rule for cooking eggs of any kind is to use low to moderate temperatures and short cooking times. Overcooking and high heat cause toughness and loss of flavor. Keep in mind also that egg whites become cooked before the yolk does.

FRIED EGGS

Fried eggs have varying different degrees of firmness of the yolk and white, depending on the guest's specifications. There are also some differences in style in some of the variations. Here are the more common ones:

- *Sunny side up*: fried, not flipped over, the white cooked firm and yolk cooked medium.
- *Basted*: pan-fried, not flipped over, the top cooked by exposing to heat from above in the salamander or by adding a small amount of water to the pan, covering, and steaming. Eggs may also be basted by spooning hot fat from the pan over the yolk while the egg is frying.
- *Over easy*: fried and flipped over, the white barely firm and the yolk just warm.
- *Over medium*: fried and flipped over, the white firm and the yolk partially cooked.
- *Over well (or hard)*: fried and flipped over, both yolk and white cooked firm.

Recipe 13-1 FRIED EGGS

YIELD: ***1 egg***

2 tsp	**butter or margarine**	**10 mL**
1	**egg**	

1. In a sauté pan, melt butter or margarine over medium heat.
2. Break egg into bowl. Pour egg into pan.
3. Reduce heat to low and cook the egg to order.

Per serving:		Carbohydrates:	1 g
Calories:	92	Cholesterol:	211 mg
Fat:	7 g	Fiber:	0 g
Protein:	6 g	Sodium:	162 mg

Cooking fried eggs requires both practice and patience. The cook must learn to achieve a good-looking finished product as well as one that tastes good. An egg to order should be glossy, moist, and tender no matter what its degree of doneness.

Here are some techniques essential to success.

Cook two eggs at a time. Break them into a bowl first. If anything is wrong, such as a broken yolk or a blood spot, you can save them for another use.

Use a well-primed fry pan 6 to 8 inches across at the bottom, just the right size to accommodate the eggs in a nice round shape. Heat the pan over low heat and add $^{1}/_{8}$ inch (3 mm) or so of fat—butter, margarine, or a mixture of butter and oil. When the fat is hot (but not hot enough to sizzle), add the two eggs simultaneously. Cook the first side to the desired degree of doneness.

Flipping eggs is an art that scares and frustrates many novice cooks. The object is to get the eggs turned over without redecorating the floor, range top, or ceiling, and without damaging the eggs. Yolks must remain whole and white unfolded.

To flip eggs successfully, follow the steps below. They are illustrated in Figure 13.2.

1. Cook the eggs on one side, as described, until the white is set.
2. Lift the pan, tilting it away from you so that the eggs start to slide toward the far side of the pan.

Figure 13-2 FLIPPING EGGS IN A PAN

a. Cook the eggs on one side until the white is set.

b. Lift the pan and tilt it away from you so that the eggs begin to climb the far rim of the pan.

c. Flip your wrist around, pulling the pan toward you, and the eggs will turn over. (Photos by Patricia Roberts.)

3. Flip your wrist quickly upward while pulling the pan toward you, and the eggs will turn over. Do not toss them in the air; they should scarcely leave the pan.

Once the eggs are flipped, cook the second side to the desired degree of doneness. Then flip the eggs back again to serve the better-looking side to the guest.

You might practice with a slice of bread rather than eggs until you have the feel for flipping. If you have trouble, you are in good company.

You can also cook eggs to order on a griddle. Figure 13.3 shows you how, from beginning to end. Use a low heat and flip the eggs with a spatula. Sometimes, they are cooked in an egg ring to keep them in a perfectly round shape.

Here are some common pitfalls and ways to avoid them:

- *Eggs brown and crisp:* Too much heat. Use a low heat. Eggs cook at 140 to 158°F (60–70°C).
- *Egg white blistered:* Too much heat or too much fat. Cut down accordingly.
- *Eggs odd shapes:* Eggs not fresh enough. Use only high-grade fresh eggs; they are well shaped and stand tall.
- *Eggs sticking:* Too much heat, too little fat, or a porous cooking surface.

A porous cooking surface is a constant nightmare for the egg cook. A primed surface, whether griddle or pan, is absolutely necessary. A **primed,** or **seasoned, surface** is one that has been polished at a high heat with salt and fat or oil to overcome its porousness.

To prime a pan, follow these steps:

- Heat the pan on a hot fire.
- Remove the pan from the fire and add to it a few drops of oil and a handful of salt.

Figure 13-3 COOKING EGGS ON A GRIDDLE

a. First crack the eggs into a bowl.

b. Holding the bowl close to the griddle surface, tip the eggs all together onto the griddle.

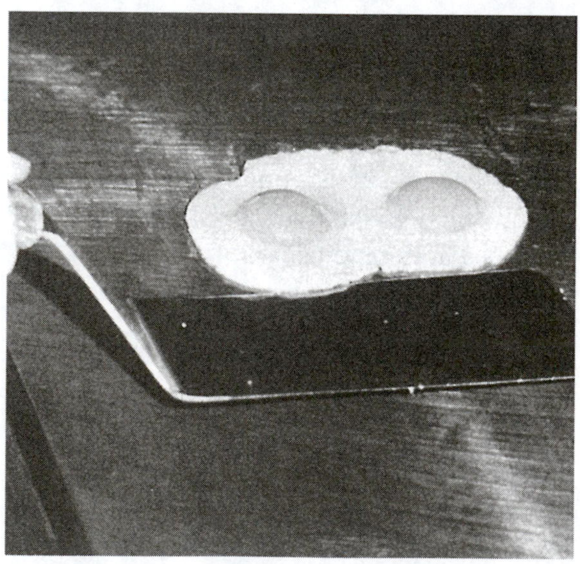

c. When the white is set, place a spatula under one edge of the eggs.

d. Flip them over with a smooth, quick lifting and turning motion so that they scarcely leave the griddle. (Photos by Patricia Roberts.)

- With a soft cloth, rub salt and oil vigorously and with pressure into the surface of the hot pan, as though you were scouring it with cleanser.
- Discard the salt-and-oil mixture and wipe the pan very clean with a soft, dry cloth.
- Repeat until you can cook an egg in the pan without its sticking anywhere.

Water destroys a primed surface. A common cry in the breakfast kitchen is, "Who washed my egg pans??!" Cooking a hamburger or anything else in an egg pan causes the same frustration. Egg pans should be used only for eggs.

Wash your own egg pans when you are through for the day; dry them properly and reprime them. To dry an egg pan, put it on the heat. When it is dry and hot, reprime it before storing and it will work just fine. For extra security, rub it again with oil before you start cooking your next egg.

SCRAMBLED EGGS

To scramble eggs, mix yolks and whites well and add to the preheated pan as for fried eggs. Stir gently with a spoon or spatula from time to time so that the eggs are broken up and cook evenly.

Scrambled eggs held on a steam table can turn an unappetizing green. To avoid this, undercook the eggs and then blend in a small amount of cream or béchamel sauce after they are cooked. This will not only prevent the green but will keep them moist.

BOILED EGGS

Boiled eggs are cooked in a hot liquid. Though they are called boiled, the water should not boil; it should simmer. The rapid action of boiling water will crack the shells as they bump each other.

Recipe 13-2 SCRAMBLED EGGS

YIELD: ***1 serving***

2	**eggs**	
1 Tb	**milk**	**15 mL**
$^1/_4$ tsp	**salt**	**1 mL**
2 tsp	**butter**	**10 mL**

1. Beat eggs in bowl until yolks and whites are mixed. Beat in milk and salt.
2. Melt butter in a pan over a low heat.
3. Add beaten eggs to pan. Stir gently from time to time as eggs become solid.
4. Serve immediately.

Per serving:		Carbohydrates:	3 g
Calories:	238	Cholesterol:	451 mg
Fat:	19 g	Fiber:	0 g
Protein:	14 g	Sodium:	804 mg

Eggs to be simmered should be at room temperature. This will help prevent the shells from cracking when they hit the hot water.

Boiled eggs, like other kinds, are cooked to varying degrees of doneness, usually spelled out in minutes. The times given here refer to eggs at room temperature placed in water that is at a boil when the eggs are put in and then simmered.

- 3 to 5 minutes in simmering water produces a soft egg.
- 6 to 8 minutes produces a medium egg.
- 10 to 15 minutes produces a hard-cooked egg.

The time spans given here are broad. For smaller eggs, use the lower limits; for larger eggs, use the upper limits.

You can also start the eggs in cold water, bring to a boil, and then reduce to a simmer. In this case, the cooking time (once the water simmers) for a soft-cooked egg is about 1 to 2 minutes, 3

Recipe 13-3 HARD-BOILED EGGS

YIELD: *1 egg*

1 egg, at room temperature for 1 hour

1. Place egg into boiling water to cover.
2. Reduce heat to let water simmer. Cover and cook for 15 minutes. (Cook for 4 minutes for soft-cooked eggs or 7 minutes for medium-cooked eggs.)
3. Remove cover, pour off water, and run cold water over egg until cool.
4. Crack shell; then remove shell. Refrigerate immediately.

Per serving:		Carbohydrates:	1 g
Calories:	78	Cholesterol:	212 mg
Fat:	5 g	Fiber:	0 g
Protein:	6 g	Sodium:	62 mg

to 5 minutes for medium cooked, and 10 minutes for hard cooked. For hard-boiled eggs, some cooks remove the pan from the heat once the water boils, cover the pan, and allow 20 minutes cooking time.

The problems with boiled eggs are not with the soft egg but with the hard one. Don't overcook it. An overcooked egg will turn dark around the yolk and have a tough white.

If you are making hard-cooked eggs for something other than breakfast and plan to use them cold, cooling them quickly in ice water will help avoid the dark color around the yolk. Peeling them right away under cold running water is easier than peeling them later.

POACHED EGGS

A poached egg is a shelled egg cooked in hot liquid, usually water. To poach an egg, you drop it gently into hot liquid and let it stand until it reaches the desired doneness.

It is a simple process. But *there are several factors of critical importance* in achieving a good-looking poached egg—one that has a compact, glossy, obviously tender white surrounding an unbroken, somewhat thickened yolk.

The first is the quality of the egg. Only a fresh, high-quality egg will emerge from its hot bath in a state of togetherness. If an older or lower-grade egg is used, add half an ounce (15 mL) of vinegar and a teaspoon (5 mL) of salt to each quart of poaching liquid to help firm up the white and keep it from spreading.

The second consideration is the temperature. It needs to be hot enough to begin cooking the egg as soon as the egg hits the liquid, but not hot enough to produce agitation. Action in the liquid will tend to tear the egg or spoil its shape. What you want is small bubbles rising from the bottom but no agitation. You can use the same criteria you used for poaching poultry or fish.

Recipe 13-4 POACHED EGGS

YIELD: *1 egg*

1 qt	**water**	**1 L**
2 tsp	**white vinegar**	**10 mL**
1	**egg**	

1. Bring water to a simmer. Add vinegar.
2. Crack egg into small bowl or plate.
3. Pour egg off plate gently into simmering water.
4. Simmer about 5 minutes, until whites are solid and yolk is still soft.
5. Remove egg with slotted spoon. Serve immediately.

Per serving:		Carbohydrates:	1 g
Calories:	75	Cholesterol:	212 mg
Fat:	5 g	Fiber:	0 g
Protein:	6 g	Sodium:	62 mg

Recipe 13-4a EGGS BENEDICT

YIELD: ***1 serving***

To Recipe 13.4, add:

1 2-oz	**slice Canadian bacon, grilled**	**60 g**
1	**half English muffin, buttered**	
$1^1/_2$ oz	**hollandaise sauce**	**45 mL**

1. Place Canadian bacon on English muffin. Center a well-drained poached egg on bacon.
2. Nap with hollandaise sauce and serve immediately.

Per serving:		Carbohydrates:	15 g
Calories:	660	Cholesterol:	480 mg
Fat:	58 g	Fiber:	1 g
Protein:	19 g	Sodium:	1260 mg

The third point of concern is the amount of liquid. It should be 3 to 4 inches (7–10 cm) deep in the pan to ensure the egg is completely covered while cooking. It should also be deep enough to cook the egg slightly before it reaches the bottom of the pan, so that it does not stick to the bottom. There should be enough liquid altogether to ensure that adding the egg does not drop the temperature below the 150 to 160°F (66–71°C) necessary for cooking. The amount you need will vary with the number of eggs being poached in one pan.

A fourth factor is the way the egg is put into the pan. Slip it in gently toward the side of the pan. It may be easier to do this from a bowl or saucer than directly from the shell. You'll see the yolk sink quickly to the bottom, with the white flapping upward.

After about 3 to 5 minutes, the whites should be firm and the yolk soft. Take them out carefully with a skimmer or perforated spoon, draining them well.

Eggs for quantity service may be poached in advance. To do so, the eggs are immediately put into ice water after cooking and held in the cooler. At serving time, you can reheat them for 30 to 60 seconds in simmering liquid.

Poached eggs can be served plain on buttered toast or English muffins, or you can combine them with other ingredients as in Recipes 13.4a and 13.4b. A variation on Recipe 13.4b is to make containers of duchesse or baked potatoes or of grilled tomato halves. Or you can substitute other vegetables and sauces to create your own house specialty. The many poached egg dishes you can make as variations of these recipes give you a wealth of entrées for brunch menus.

SHIRRED EGGS

Shirred eggs are eggs cooked and served in the same dish, usually a shallow flat-bottomed earthenware dish. You coat the dish with

Recipe 13-4b EGGS FLORENTINE

YIELD: ***1 serving***

To Recipe 13.4, add:

2 oz	**cooked chopped spinach, seasoned**	**60 g**
3 Tb	**mornay sauce**	**45 mL**
1 tsp	**Parmesan cheese, grated**	**5 mL**

1. Make a nest of hot drained spinach on a serving plate. Place poached egg in center of spinach.
2. Nap with sauce.
3. Sprinkle with Parmesan cheese and gratiné lightly.

Per serving:		Carbohydrates:	6 g
Calories:	186	Cholesterol:	228 mg
Fat:	13 g	Fiber:	2 g
Protein:	12 g	Sodium:	443 mg

Recipe 13-5 SHIRRED EGGS

YIELD: ***1 serving***

butter as needed
2 eggs

1. Butter individual casserole dish.
2. Break eggs into bowl; then place in buttered dish.
3. Set dish directly on the range over a moderate heat until the whites begin to firm.
4. Then place in 350°F (180°C) oven and cook until done.

Per serving:		Carbohydrates:	1 g
Calories:	179	Cholesterol:	430 mg
Fat:	13 g	Fiber:	0 g
Protein:	12 g	Sodium:	146 mg

melted butter and break the eggs into it. For speed, you set it directly on the range until the whites begin to firm. Then you transfer it to a moderate oven (350°F/180°C) for finish cooking or run it under the salamander to cook the top. Be careful not to overcook. Shirred eggs should have the same qualities as eggs sunny side up.

You can make many different brunch dishes with shirred eggs by first placing the raw eggs on hash, bacon, diced tomatoes, or cheese and preparing them the same way. Or you can cook them first and then surround them with mushroom or tomato sauce, grilled meat, hot cream, or asparagus tips.

OMELETS

Of all egg dishes, the omelet is the most difficult to master. Mastery takes patience, practice, and timing. To understand the omelet, study Recipe 13.6 step by step. An omelet pan, by the way, is a primed fry pan slightly larger than a two-egg pan. Figure 13.4 illustrates the last half of the story, from Step 4 to completion.

A perfect **omelet** is fluffy, moist, and tender, soft in the center, yellow in color with no brown at all or just a hint of it, oval in shape, and all in one continuous piece. You can fill it with meat, cheese, jelly, mushrooms, shrimp, or other good things whose flavors complement the eggs. You add the filling before you make the first fold. Or you can make an herb omelet by mixing herbs into the eggs before cooking begins. Some cooks add two or three drops of water per egg before beating them. It makes a somewhat lighter, fluffier omelet.

Recipe 13-6 THREE-EGG OMELET

YIELD: ***1 omelet***

3	**eggs**	
1 Tb	**butter**	**15 mL**

1. Break eggs into a bowl. Beat well with a fork or whip, aerating the eggs slightly.
2. Heat an omelet pan until hot. Add butter to the hot pan and allow time for it to melt and get hot.
3. Add the eggs to the center of the omelet pan.
4. When the edges curl and cook firm, place a plastic spoon or spatula in the center of the pan and vigorously slide the pan back and forth so that the raw eggs on top spill over the cooked edges and cook.
5. When firm on the bottom but still moist on top, remove from heat and fold one edge of the omelet to the center of the pan or a little beyond, using the spatula or spoon.
6. Slide the other edge of the omelet onto a plate and roll the folded part over on top of it to make a second fold—all in one motion.

Per serving:		Carbohydrates:	3 g
Calories:	323	Cholesterol:	687 mg
Fat:	25 g	Fiber:	0 g
Protein:	19 g	Sodium:	352 mg

Figure 13-4 COOKING AND FOLDING AN OMELET

a. When the edges curl and cook firm . . .

b. . . . place a spoon or spatula in the center of the pan and vigorously slide the pan back and forth so that the raw eggs on top spill over the cooked edges and cook.

c. When the bottom is firm but the top is still moist, remove from the heat and fold one edge to the center of the pan or a little beyond.

d. Slide the other edge onto a plate . . .

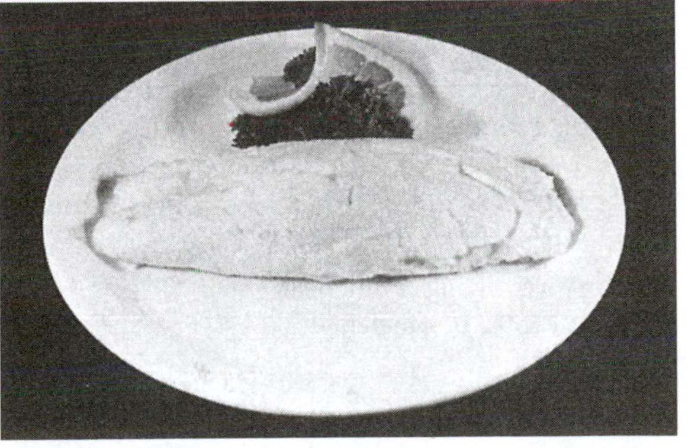

e. . . . roll the folded part over on top of it—all in one motion.

f. "A perfect omelet is fluffy, moist, and tender. . . . " (Photos by Patricia Roberts.)

Recipe 13-6a CHEESE OMELET

YIELD: *1 omelet*

To Recipe 13.6, add:

1 oz	**cheddar or Swiss cheese, grated**	**30 g**

Before removing from heat (Step 5), add cheese across center of omelet. Let it cook for a moment before folding omelet.

Per serving:		Carbohydrates:	4 g
Calories:	437	Cholesterol:	716 mg
Fat:	34 g	Fiber:	0 g
Protein:	26 g	Sodium:	427 mg

Recipe 13-6b WESTERN OMELET

YIELD: *1 omelet*

To Recipe 13.6, add:

2 oz	**western mixture: equal parts small diced ham, onions, and green pepper, sautéed**	**60 g**

Before removing from heat (Step 5), add western mixture across center of omelet.

Per serving:		Carbohydrates:	10 g
Calories:	366	Cholesterol:	687 mg
Fat:	26 g	Fiber:	2 g
Protein:	20 g	Sodium:	371 mg

Recipe 13-6c CURRANT JELLY OMELET

YIELD: *1 omelet*

To Recipe 13.6, add:

1 oz	**red currant jelly**	**30 g**

Before removing from heat (Step 5), add jelly across center of omelet.

Per serving:		Carbohydrates:	23 g
Calories:	351	Cholesterol:	687 mg
Fat:	25 g	Fiber:	0 g
Protein:	19 g	Sodium:	362 mg

Recipes 13.6a to 13.6d give you four more techniques for adding flavorful foods to omelets. In the cheese omelet, you cook the added ingredient as part of making the omelet. In the western omelet, you add a precooked mixture of ingredients during cooking. In the currant jelly omelet, you fill the completed omelet, and in the Spanish omelet you ladle a sauce over it after cooking is done. All make delicious dishes for breakfast, brunch, or lunch.

You can vary the form of the omelet if you wish. Leave it flat and cook it like fried eggs (no stirring); this is called a **frittata** or flat omelet. A frittata is normally started on the stove top and finished under a salamander. Or fold the omelet in half to make it *American style.* However, the form we have pictured here, with the two folds, usually called a French omelet, is the one most people expect an omelet to be.

Like eggs to order, omelets must be made individually. You can, however, preprepare the eggs in quantity, shelling and mixing them as you do for scrambled eggs, then measuring them into individual pans as the omelets are ordered. Where large quantities are required, omelets may be made ahead, chilled, and reheated at service time.

Recipe 13-6d SPANISH OMELET

YIELD: *1 omelet*

To Recipe 13.6, add:

$^{1}/_{4}$ C	**Spanish sauce**	**60 mL**

Nap finished omelet with Spanish sauce.

Per serving:		Carbohydrates:	7 g
Calories:	343	Cholesterol:	687 mg
Fat:	25 g	Fiber:	1 g
Protein:	20 g	Sodium:	582 mg

The omelet is both versatile and challenging. It is well worth the time and practice it takes for mastery.

BREAKFAST MEATS

Any meat can be served for breakfast, but there are some kinds we identify with the breakfast menu. Ham and eggs, bacon and eggs, pancakes and sausage—all are breakfast go-togethers. These products of the pig fall into two groups: ham and bacon, which are smoked or cured, and sausage, which is usually raw fresh pork.

Breakfast ham is typically sliced cooked ham grilled or broiled to order. You need only enough cooking to get it thoroughly hot and to brown the fat around the edges. Use a moderate heat and cook both sides. A typical breakfast portion is 2 to 4 ounces.

The typical portion of *bacon* is two to four slices. The best way to cook bacon is in a moderate oven (300–350°F/150–175°C). Bacon is almost all fat so lower temperatures lessen shrinkage. You can lay the slices out on sheet pans or on racks placed on sheet pans, or you can buy it already laid out on parchment paper that can go right into the oven on a sheet pan. Any of these ways will give you a consistent product, evenly cooked without turning. It looks 400 percent better than pan-fried bacon because it does not curl.

The most difficult part of the cooking is pouring off the grease, which must be done when cooking is complete. Handling a large amount of hot grease in a shallow pan is extremely dangerous and calls for all your caution and skill. Using a rack avoids this problem because you just pick the rack up off the pan, leaving the grease to be dealt with when it is cooler.

Drain the cooked bacon on paper towels or racks. Bacon holds well and can be prepared ahead in considerable quantity.

A second way of cooking bacon is to fry it in a pan or on a griddle. This method is used only for small amounts cooked to order. Preheat the pan, use moderate heat, and turn the slices so as to cook both sides. Bacon may also be broiled to order on the broiler rack of the salamander. It cooks well in the microwave oven, too.

Whatever cooking method you use, cook the bacon to crispness, or a little short of crispness if it is to be held. It should never be allowed to reach the point at which it suddenly turns brown and brittle and changes flavor. It may take a little experience to know how to stop just before the turning point.

One other smoked-pork item used for breakfast and brunch is smoked pork loin that has been boned and rolled. This cut of meat is called *Canadian bacon.* It comes precooked and is handled, stored, sliced, and heated the same way as ham. Look back at Recipe 13.4a for one way to use it.

Sausage used as a breakfast meat comes in two forms: links and patties. Sausage patties can be compared to hamburger patties with one major difference: Sausage is usually fresh pork (it can also be turkey) and must always be cooked well done. This is true for the links, too.

Sausage is cooked like bacon. You pan-fry it or cook it on the griddle for small amounts, and cook it in the oven for larger quantities. Take great pains to cook it done yet not overdone. It is done when it becomes firm and the color is totally changed from gray to brown. Overcooked sausage becomes very dry, crisp, and hard. Crispness may be desirable in bacon but not in sausage.

Other meats, too, can be served for breakfast, and often are—steak, pork chops, chipped beef in white sauce, corned beef hash, chicken livers. Fish are also offered on some menus: mackerel and smoked salt fish such as kippered herring. Meats and fish are prepared for breakfast and brunch exactly as they would be for other meals, except that the portions are smaller—usually 2 to 4 ounces (50–100 g).

PANCAKES, WAFFLES, FRENCH TOAST, CRÊPES

Waffles and pancakes, sometimes called griddle cakes or flapjacks, are typically American breakfast fare. Both are made from batters, but they differ in the way they are cooked.

Pancakes are made from a batter consisting of eggs, flour, water or milk, seasoning, and a leavening agent to make them puff or rise as they cook. The most common leavening agent is baking powder. You can make the batter from Recipe 13.7 or use a prepared mix. In either case, do not overmix it; too much mixing will make it tough. Stop as soon as it is well blended.

To cook pancakes, use a 2-ounce (60 mL) ladle to pour small quantities of batter on a slightly oiled griddle set at low to moderate heat. When they are brown on the bottom and begin to form holes on top, flip them over and brown them on the other side. Serve them immediately—piping hot in a stack with butter and syrup, preserves, or fruit.

Good pancakes are light and slightly spongy in texture. Add nuts or fruit for a special flavor treat.

Waffles are made from a similar but slightly heavier batter with fat or oil added. They are cooked with a waffle iron, a piece of small equipment that has only one use: making waffles. It cooks the batter on the top and bottom simultaneously and makes the waffles look like large plaid pancakes.

You can make waffles from a mix or use one of the recipes from Chapter 16. Cook them in a preheated waffle iron.

A good waffle is light to medium brown, with a crisp, light texture. It should have the exact shape of the waffle iron, with no ragged edges. Serve it like a pancake with butter and syrup, preserves, or fresh fruit.

To clean the waffle iron, simply brush out any crumbs. The iron has a preprimed surface that will be spoiled by water. An occasional light oiling may be necessary.

French toast is a complete breakfast in itself. You may wonder how "French" French toast is, but there is no doubt how American it is. In

Recipe 13-7 PANCAKES

YIELD: ***16 3-in. (7 cm) pancakes***

8 oz	**flour**	**250 g**
1 oz	**sugar**	**30 g**
1/2 tsp	**salt**	**2 mL**
1 Tb	**baking powder**	**15 mL**
2	**eggs**	
1 pt	**milk**	**500 mL**
1/4 C	**oil**	**60 mL**

1. Sift flour, sugar, salt, and baking powder.
2. Mix eggs, milk, and oil, stirring until blended.
3. Add liquid to dry ingredients and mix until barely combined.
4. Using a 2-oz (60 mL) ladle, pour onto griddle set at low to moderate heat, turning when holes begin to appear on top.
5. Cook until bottom is browned. Serve immediately.

Per pancake:			
Calories:	96	Carbohydrates:	11 g
Fat:	5 g	Cholesterol:	22 mg
Protein:	2 g	Fiber:	0 g
		Sodium:	167 mg

Recipe 13-8 FRENCH TOAST

YIELD: ***12 portions (2 slices each)***

10	**eggs**	
3/4 qt	**milk**	**750 mL**
2 tsp	**nutmeg or cinnamon**	**10 mL**
2 tsp	**vanilla**	**10 mL**
1 tsp	**salt**	**5 mL**
24	**slices day-old bread**	

1. Mix eggs, milk, nutmeg or cinnamon, vanilla, and salt until thoroughly combined.
2. Soak bread slices in egg mixture until moistened throughout.
3. Cook on lightly oiled griddle over moderate heat, turning once, until lightly golden on both sides.

Per serving:		Carbohydrates:	33 g
Calories:	297	Cholesterol:	151 mg
Fat:	14 g	Fiber:	4 g
Protein:	10 g	Sodium:	623 mg

France, it is called *pain perdu*, meaning lost bread, because you can use up day-old, slightly stale bread and turn a loss into a profit. Day-old bread absorbs more egg mixture than fresh bread and produces the best French toast.

French toast (Recipe 13.8) is made by soaking bread in seasoned beaten eggs often flavored with vanilla or nutmeg or cinnamon, and then griddling or pan-frying it to a golden brown. Include cream for an extra-rich flavor. French toast is served dusted with powdered sugar with syrup on the side.

Toppings for pancakes, waffles, or French toast do not have to be limited to the traditional butter, syrup, or preserves. Some healthier choices include the following:

- Fruit sauces
- Puréed fruit
- Sliced fresh fruit and powdered sugar
- Yogurt or ricotta cheese with sliced fruit
- Reduced-fat sour cream and berries

We turn now from French toast to a type of pancake from France—**crêpes.** These are quite different from American pancakes: They are very thin, and since they contain no leavening they are flat. They do not make a dish by themselves but are usually rolled around fillings and napped with sauce. Savory fillings produce dishes for brunch, lunch, dinner, or appetizers. A few of the possibilities are creamed chicken, seafood Newburg, or creamed spinach, often topped with a sauce such as mornay and gratinéed lightly.

By adding sugar to the batter, you can make sweet crêpes for desserts. Fill them with fruit, ice cream, preserves, or pudding, then roll them and top with a dessert sauce or confectioners' sugar.

Before you let your imagination run wild, let us examine the crêpe-making procedure. It is nowhere near as simple as our American pancake. Recipe 13.9 spells it all out.

In Step 1, sift the dry ingredients to distribute them thoroughly, just as you did for American-style pancakes. The sugar is included for dessert crêpes, though some cooks use up to a tablespoon (15 mL) in the basic mix to aid in browning.

At this point, the method begins to differ. With a wire whip, either by hand or in the mixer, stir in the eggs (Step 2) and add 2 to 4 oz (60–120 g) of the milk (Step 3). Make sure this mixture is very smooth and lumpfree before adding the rest of the liquids (Step 4). Strain through a fine-mesh china cap (Step 5). You need a smooth texture to make the very thin pancake desired.

But all this mixing causes a substance in the flour called gluten to develop. If you used the batter immediately, this gluten would give you a thin but tough crêpe. This is why you refrigerate the batter (Step 6). By letting it rest, you give the

Recipe 13-9 CRÊPES

YIELD: ***25 6-in. (15 cm) crêpes***

8 oz	**flour**	**250 g**
1 tsp	**salt**	**5 mL**
6	**eggs**	
2 C	**milk**	**500 mL**
3 Tb	**melted butter**	**45 mL**
	oil as needed	

1. Sift dry ingredients into a bowl.
2. Stir eggs into dry ingredients.
3. Add enough milk to make a paste and stir until smooth.
4. Gradually blend in remaining milk and butter.
5. Strain through a china cap. If necessary, adjust texture with water. Batter should be the consistency of heavy cream.
6. Cover bowl with plastic wrap and leave at room temperature for 30–60 minutes.
7. Coat a seasoned crêpe pan very lightly with butter or oil.
8. Heat over moderately high heat until very hot. Remove from pan.
9. Using a small ladle, pour about 3 Tb (45 mL) batter into pan. Immediately swirl pan so that batter coats bottom with a thin, even layer. Pour off excess.
10. Return to heat and cook until bottom is light brown.
11. Turn crêpe and brown second side. Slide onto wire rack to cool.
12. Continue in this way, stacking cooled crêpes with parchment or waxed paper between. Oil pan lightly as needed.
13. Wrap in plastic wrap and refrigerate or freeze until needed.

Per crêpe:		Carbohydrates:	8 g
Calories:	76	Cholesterol:	58 mg
Fat:	3 g	Fiber:	0 g
Protein:	3 g	Sodium:	133 mg

gluten time to relax. Then you are ready to try your hand at cooking the crêpes.

Frying crêpes, like making omelets, takes practice to produce a perfect one. Even experienced French chefs say that the first of any batch is "for the cat" because it is seldom right. After some practice, many cooks can produce crêpes assembly-line style with five or more pans on the fire simultaneously. The first pancake is ready to flip as the batter is poured into the last pan.

The first step is to choose a well-seasoned pan and oil it lightly (Step 7). The crêpe may tear if it sticks, but it will be greasy if you use too much fat. Heat the pan (Step 8). As you ladle the batter in, tilt the pan and swirl the batter gently as it reaches the hot pan (Figure 13.5a) so that a thin, round, even coat will "set" on the bottom of the pan (Step 9). Pour off the excess. All this is accomplished almost in one motion taking only a few seconds.

Return the pan to the heat for a minute or so until the crêpe is a light golden brown (Step 10). Use your fingertips to pull one edge gently up from the side of the pan (Figure 13.5b) to flip the pancake over (Step 11). Cook until it has browned lightly and then use the pan to slide it onto the stack (Figure 13.5c). The first side browns more evenly than the second one. It is used as the presentation side—the outside of the rolled crêpe—so that it looks more attractive to the diner.

Crêpes can be made ahead of time because they store well in the refrigerator or freezer when tightly wrapped and protected from air (Steps 12 and 13). When you have become a confident crêpe maker, you can use some fillings and sauces from previous chapters to create dishes for brunch, lunch, and appetizers—for example, crêpes seafood Newburg in Recipe 13.9a. And keep crêpes in mind for delicious sweet combinations when you reach the dessert chapter (Chapter 17).

Figure 13-5 FRYING CRÊPES

a. Ladle the butter into the pan while tilting and swirling to make a thin, even coating.

b. When the first side is a *light* golden brown, peel it away from the pan to turn it over.

c. When the second side is light golden brown, slide it onto the stack. (Photos by Patricia Roberts.)

Recipe 13-9a CRÊPES SEAFOOD NEWBURG

YIELD: ***1 portion***

2	**crêpes**	
3 oz	**seafood Newburg, hot**	**90 g**
$^1/_4$ C	**mornay sauce, hot**	**60 mL**

1. Place equal amounts of Newburg mixture on each crêpe. Roll up.
2. On serving plate, place rolled crêpes side by side with seam on bottom.
3. Nap with mornay sauce. Gratiné under salamander until light golden.

Per serving:		Carbohydrates:	13 g
Calories:	240	Cholesterol:	130 mg
Fat:	12 g	Fiber:	0 g
Protein:	16 g	Sodium:	383 m

You will find other batter-based products for breakfast and brunch discussed in Chapter 16—muffins, cornbread, sweet rolls, coffee cake, biscuits, brioche. In most kitchens, such products are bought or made from mixes. Certain other prebaked products are standards on most breakfast menus—buttered toast, English muffins, doughnuts, Danish pastries. You simply toast and butter the bread or the muffin, heat the doughnut or danish, and serve it forth.

CEREALS

Cold cereal is the most popular breakfast food. It's easy to understand why—it's fast, doesn't require any cooking or preparation beyond putting it in a bowl and adding milk, and it comes in a wide variety of flavors and forms. Ready-to-eat cereals come as whole grain, refined grain, sweetened, unsweetened, with fruits and nuts, flaked, puffed, and so on.

Cereals vary in the amount of sugar, sodium, and fiber they contain. When made with whole grains such as whole wheat or oatmeal, the cereal contains more fiber than products made with wheat flour or refined rice. In general, cereals are also:

- Low in calories
- High in starch
- Low in fat (except for many granolas)
- A moderate source of protein
- Fortified with iron and a number of vitamins

Hot cereals are nutritious as well.

Though not as popular as cold cereals, hot cereals—such as oatmeal and grits—enjoy much respect on a breakfast menu. Cereals are always cooked in a liquid, usually water but milk and other liquids may often be substituted. Cooking cereals gelatinizes the starch and improves its flavor. Most cereals can be added gradually to boiling water. Simply stir well until it starts to thicken. Then, turn the heat down to simmer, cover the pan, and cook until done (check the package for cooking times). Some finely granulated cereals, such as farina or cornmeal, need to be mixed first with cold water before being adding to the boiling water. This is done to prevent lumpy cereal.

BEVERAGES

To many people, a cup of coffee is the essence of breakfast. Others may feel the same way about tea, but coffee is the great American beverage.

COFFEE

The one thing most likely to leave a lasting impression of the place where it is served is coffee.

There's a good chance it will be both the first and the last thing a customer tastes, especially at breakfast. To ensure a good afterimage, good coffee is a must.

Coffee is made with two ingredients, ground coffee and hot water. It is brewed by passing the water over the coffee in a machine that does most of the work. Simple? It isn't simple at all.

Coffee begins as berries of a tropical tree. Beans come from a variety of coffee trees found in areas such as Colombia, Brazil, and Venezuela. Coffee producers use several varieties of coffee beans to produce their own distinctive blends.

After being cleaned, skinned, and dried, coffee beans are roasted to different degrees—dark, medium, light—to develop their flavor. The amount of roasting affects the color and flavor of the coffee brewed from the beans—the more the bean is roasted, the darker it is and more strongly flavored. Most of the commercial blends of coffee are made from a **city roast,** also called **American** or **medium roast.** It is not nearly as dark as French-roast beans (also called dark roast) or espresso-roast beans, which are roasted until nearly burned.

Coffee beans are then ground so that their flavor can be more easily extracted by water. The **grind** of a coffee refers to the size of the grounds produced from the coffee beans. The finer the grind, the more flavorings will be extracted by the water during the coffee-making process. Therefore, the size of the grind is related to the method of making the coffee. For example, if grounds are subject to hot water for a short time, a fine grind is recommended. Table 13.2 shows types of coffee makers and appropriate grinds to use for each.

A good cup of coffee is a clear, rich-brown, steaming-hot brew with an inviting fragrance. To make good coffee, you must give careful attention to absolutely everything that has to do with making it—equipment, time, temperature, water, as well as the ground coffee and the method of making the brew. Let's look at the basic rules.

Table 13-2 TYPES OF COFFEE MAKERS

Coffee Maker	*Description*	*Coffee Maker*	*Description*
Percolator	Heated water is forced up a tube in the middle of the percolator and sprayed over the coffee grounds held in a basket at the top of the pot. Make sure water level is below the bottom of the basket. *Uses regular (coarse) grind.*	Automatic Drip-Filter Coffee Makers	Enough cold water is poured into the reservoir to make the desired amount of coffee. Water in the reservoir is heated instantly as it flows past the heating element and is sprayed over the finely ground coffee in a basket lined with filter paper. *Uses drip grind or grind made for automatic drip coffee makers.*
Drip	Almost boiling water poured into a filter cone above the coffee pot drips slowly through the grounds held in a basket in the center and drips into the coffee pot. *Uses drip (medium) grind.*		

Use clean equipment. Coffee leaves a barely visible oily residue that will spoil the next potful if it is not cleaned away. One spot can do it. All coffee pots must be cleaned after each brewing, and coffee makers must be cleaned thoroughly once a day.

Use fresh coffee. Only fresh coffee will give you fresh taste. Ground coffee loses flavor quickly. Store in a cool, dry place and use within one week.

Use the right grind. The right grind is whatever is recommended by the manufacturer of your equipment. Too coarse a grind will give you weak, flavorless coffee. Too fine a grind will give you bitter flavor plus the chance of fine grounds in the bottom of the cup.

Use the right proportions. A good ratio of coffee to water is 1 pound to 2 to $2^1/_2$ gallons (450 g to 8–10.5 L). Establish exact amounts for your coffee maker and your clientele by taste and experience. The proportion of brewed coffee to the size of the coffee maker is also important. It is best to use the equipment at its full capacity, or at three-quarters capacity at the very least.

Use fresh water. Draw fresh water for each batch of coffee. Boiled water that stands becomes stale. Use water from the cold tap. Hot tap water may contain residues from the hot-water tank.

Use the right water temperature. The water temperature for brewing should be between 195 and 200°F (90–93°C). Water that is not hot enough will not extract the flavors you want. Water that is too hot can extract some flavors you don't want.

Use a pourover or drip method of brewing. Hot water should pass over the ground coffee one time and one time only. Percolator-style coffee makers boil the water while it is being brewed, so the water passes through the grounds any number of times. Two types of acceptable brewing equipment are shown in Figure 13.6. For small amounts of coffee, the 10-cup automatic drip machine is popular. Many models have as many as six burners for keeping fresh-brewed coffee hot. For larger volume, an urn such as the one pictured brews by spraying hot water over the ground coffee. Urns vary in size from 2 to 100 gallons, but the basics of brewing are the same.

Do not overbrew. Brewing time must be long enough to extract the flavorful soluble solids but not long enough to extract the less soluble and unpleasant-tasting solids. Total brewing time should not exceed 8 minutes. Most coffee is brewed in 4 to 6 minutes. Less than 4 minutes will underextract; more than 8 will certainly overextract.

Remove the grounds as soon as brewing is complete. This prevents further unintentional brewing. Hot brewed coffee will send steam up through the grounds, which condenses and drains back again, leaching undesirable flavors from the grounds.

Do not hold coffee more than an hour. Coffee that stands loses both flavor and aroma and actually undergoes chemical changes that alter its taste. The holding temperature should be between 185 and 190°F (85–88°C).

Cost is often the reason given for not throwing out stale coffee and making a fresh pot. Consider which cost is greater, a few cups of coffee or a customer. Improved planning and timing will solve the waste problem better than pretending stale coffee is good to the last drop.

In addition to regular coffee, most foodservice establishments serve decaffeinated coffee, which is coffee from which the caffeine has been removed. **Caffeine** is a stimulant that is rapidly absorbed into the bloodstream. For most people, it increases heart rate and blood pressure, increases

Figure 13-6 TYPICAL COFFEE MAKERS

a. A 10-cup automatic-drip coffee maker. You place premeasured coffee in the basket and flip a switch. The machine draws the right amount of water, heats it to the right temperature, and makes the coffee. A warming plate on the top keeps one pot hot while the second pot is making.

b. A double spray-over urn. You place premeasured coffee in the basket at the top of the urn, position the spray over it, and flip a switch. Water is heated to the proper temperature in the middle section. (Photos courtesy Bunn-O-Matic Corporation.)

attentiveness and performance, and gives relief from fatigue. In high doses, it can produce insomnia, nervousness, a racing heart, and other troublesome symptoms. Many people build a tolerance to caffeine's effects. When caffeine is withdrawn from the diet, symptoms are felt, including headache, fatigue, and irritability.

Caffeine is present in over 60 plant species in various parts of the world, including coffee beans, tea leaves, kola nuts, and cocoa beans. Coffee, tea, cola, and cocoa are the most common sources of caffeine in the American diet (see Table 13.3).

Espresso, and other coffees made from it, have become very popular in the United States. Table 13.4 describes many of these coffees. In addition, flavored coffees are quite popular—they range from flavors (such as vanilla) added to roasted coffee beans or added after brewing the coffee. Postbrew flavorings include chocolate, hazelnut, almond, caramel, and fruit flavors.

TEA

As legend has it, one day in 2737 B.C. the Chinese emperor Shen Nung was boiling drinking water over an open fire, believing that those who drank boiled water were healthier. Some leaves from a nearby *Camellia sinensis* plant floated into the pot. The emperor drank the mixture and de-

Table 13-3 CAFFEINE IN BEVERAGES

Item	Milligrams Caffeine	
	Average	*Range*
Coffee (5-ounce cup)		
Brewed, drip method	115	60–180
Brewed, percolator	80	40–170
Instant	65	30–120
Decaffeinated, brewed	3	2–5
Decaffeinated, instant	2	1–5
Tea (5-ounce cup)		
Brewed, major U.S. brands	40	20–90
Brewed, imported brands	60	25–110
Instant	30	25–50
Iced (12-ounce glass)	70	67–76
Soft drinks (12-ounce can)		
Cola		30–46
Decaffeinated cola		0–2
Cherry cola		36–46
Lemon–lime		0
Other citrus		0–64
Root beer		0
Ginger ale		0
Tonic water		0
Other regular soda		0–44
Juice added		0
Diet cola		36–50
Decaffeinated diet cola		0–0.2
Diet cherry cola		0–46
Diet lemon–lime, diet root beer		0
Other diets		0–70
Club soda, seltzer, sparkling water		0
Chocolate		
Cocoa beverage (5-ounce cup)		4
Chocolate milk beverage (8 ounces)		5

SOURCE: The Food and Drug Administration.

clared it gave one "vigor of body, contentment of mind, and determination of purpose."

Perhaps as testament to the emperor's assessment, tea—the drink he unwittingly brewed that day—today is second only to water in worldwide consumption. The U.S. population is drinking its fair share of the brew.

Tea comes in black, green, and oolong varieties, all produced from the leaves of *Camellia sinensis,* a white-flowered evergreen (herbal teas come from leaves of other plants). The method of processing the leaf distinguishes the three types.

- **Black tea** is the most popular form of tea in the United States. It is made by fermenting the freshly harvested tea leaves so they turn black. Black tea has a very deep flavor and dark color.
- **Green tea** is made by steaming or otherwise heating the leaves immediately after plucking to prevent the fermentation that makes black tea. Then the leaves are rolled and dried.
- **Oolong tea** is fermented only partially—to a point between black and green.

Flavored and spiced teas are made from black tea. Teas can be flavored with just about anything—peach, vanilla, cherry. The spiced teas, on the other hand, usually contain pieces of spices—cinnamon or nutmeg or orange peel.

However, *orange pekoe tea* does not contain any orange at all. Orange pekoe refers to the size of the tea leaf. The largest leaves are orange pekoe, pekoe, and pekoe souchong. In brewing, flavor and color come out of the larger leaves

Table 13-4 ESPRESSO DRINKS

Name	Description
Espresso	The word espresso refers to the unique process used to brew this coffee. Hot water is forced under high pressure through finely ground coffee that has been compacted. The coffee is made from beans that have been roasted until very dark. Figure 13.7 shows an espresso machine. The serving size is about $1^1/_2$ fluid ounces (45 mL).
Cappuccino	$1^1/_2$ fluid ounces (45 mL) of espresso, topped by frothed milk that is separated into hot milk and foam, in an approximate ratio of one part espresso, one part milk, and one part foam. Usually served in a glass mug.
Latte	A single or double serving of espresso, topped by frothed milk, in a ratio of one part espresso to three parts milk. Usually served in a wide-mouthed glass.
Mocha	A single serving of espresso mixed with about 5 fluid ounces of steamed milk and chocolate syrup to taste. Often topped with whipped cream.

more slowly than they come out of the smaller leaves.

Like coffee, tea is a brew made by exposing the product to hot water over a period of time. However, the tea leaves stand immersed in hot water rather than having the water seep through them and drain off as in coffee making. This process is called **steeping.**

A good cup of tea is a clear, fragrant liquid with a taste often described as brisk—somewhat sweet, somewhat tart, but never bitter. Flavor, aroma, and color vary with the kind and blend

Figure 13-7 AN ESPRESSO MACHINE

(Courtesy Grindmaster Corporation.)

Table 13-5 DESCRIPTIONS OF SPECIALTY TEAS

Name of Tea	Description	Name of Tea	Description
Black dragon	From the Amoy, Foochow, and Canton provinces of China and Taiwan, it has a delicate, fruity taste with a light color. It makes an excellent choice with fruit or fruity dishes.	Earl Grey	An unusual blend of India and China teas flavored with Oil of Bergamot.
		English breakfast	A blend of India and Ceylon teas that is full-bodied and rich.
Ceylon breakfast	A blend of teas grown on the hillsides of Sri Lanka producing a rich golden tea with superb flavor.	Irish breakfast	A blend of teas from Kenya and India traditionally favored by the Irish for its pungent, amber brew.
China black	The traditional blend of Keemun and other fine teas from the Chinese mainland with a mellow character and unusually distinctive smoky taste.	Jasmine	A blend of green and black teas scented with jasmine flowers.
		Lapsang Souchong	A large leaf, black tea with a distinctive smoky flavor.
		Lemon	Lemon-scented tea produced from a Ceylon blend that is particularly enjoyable when made iced.
China oolong	A select blend of large leaf teas from the Orient with excellent flavor and the aroma of fresh peaches.	Orange pekoe	A blend of carefully selected Ceylon teas giving a smooth flavor that is particularly refreshing when served iced.
Darjeeling	A fine blend of teas, from the foothills of the Himalayas, with a subtle flowery bouquet and the delicate muscatel flavor for which the Darjeeling teas are known.	Prince of Wales	A blend of carefully selected finest Keemun black teas considered by connoisseurs to be one of the finest Chinese teas.

of tea, and strength varies with the taste of the diner.

To make good tea, you pour boiling water over the tea bag (you can also buy loose tea) in a preheated pot, let it steep for 3 to 5 minutes, and remove the bag.

As in making coffee, there are some important rules:

- Use the right proportions. A teaspoon (5 mL) of tea, or one portion-sized tea bag, makes one cup of strong tea or two cups of mild tea. An ounce of tea makes a gallon (6–8 grams make 1 L).
- Use boiling-hot water, freshly boiled, for maximum flavor extraction.
- Do not overbrew. Tea steeped more than 5 minutes becomes dark and bitter. Remove the tea bag from the pot at the end of the brewing period.
- Use only pottery, china, glass, or stainless steel for brewing. Metals react with a substance in tea called tannin to produce a metallic taste.

Actually, most operations do not make tea this way. They serve the diner a cup or pot of hot water with a tea bag beside it. They do this for two reasons—because people like their tea in different strengths and because Americans are not great tea drinkers and demand is light. Perhaps dumping a whole shipload of tea into Boston Harbor 200 years ago influenced our drinking habits.

This type of service does not make very good tea because the water is tepid by the time it is served. An individual pot is better than a cup because it keeps the water hotter and allows the diner to pour it over the tea rather than dunk the bag in the tepid water. Preheating the pot helps, too.

Iced tea is made the same way as hot tea, doubling the proportion of tea to water (2 oz or 60 g to 1 gal or 4 L) and using the maximum steeping time. Larger tea bags are made for brewing larger quantities of tea, such as for iced tea. It is made in quantity and held at room temperature. It holds well, up to 4 hours. Pour it over ice just before service. Instant iced tea is often used today to cut preparation time.

Tables 13.5 and 13.6 give additional information on tea.

JUICES

Cold fruit and vegetable juices are a very American way to begin breakfast or brunch. Tangy orange, grapefruit, and pineapple juices as well as ice-cold tomato and vegetable juices are excellent stimulators of the appetite. Chill canned juices thoroughly; reconstitute frozen juices according to package directions and chill. Serve in chilled glasses.

Some restaurants feature freshly made juices using a wide variety of fruits and vegetables. Health-conscious customers have been reaching more and more for this style of beverage. With a high-quality piece of equipment known as a

Table 13-6 MATCHING FOODS TO DIFFERENT TYPES OF TEAS

Food	*Type of Tea*	*Character of Tea*	*Food*	*Type of Tea*	*Character of Tea*
Breakfast	Breakfast teas	Brisk, rich, full-bodied	Dessert	Traditional black tea blends	Bright, balanced
	Traditional black tea blends	Bright, balanced		Flavored teas such as:	
	Early Grey	Fragrant, smooth		Orange	Light
				Lemon	Sweet
				Blackberry	Fragrant
Sandwiches, hamburgers	Traditional black tea blends	Bright, balanced		Peppermint	Refreshing
				Herbal teas such as:	
	Darjeeling	Nutty flavor		Chamomile	Delicate
	Yunnan	Brisk		Hibiscus	Flowery
	Assam	Malty		Almond	Fragrant
	Ceylon	Bright, full of flavor			
Beef, pork, spicy ethnic entrées	Traditional black tea blends	Bright, balanced			
	Spiced blends	Aromatic, pronounced flavor			
	Green tea	Pungent			

juicer, as well as flavorings and dairy products, it is possible to make a wide variety of tasty juices and juice drinks.

DAIRY PRODUCTS

Dairy products, including milk and products made from milk, are among the most versatile foods that are part of many recipes. You cannot overlook the fact that, in addition to the many advantages of nutrition, dairy products are generally inexpensive, and many reduced-fat versions are available.

MILK

Although milk is consumed as a beverage, it is classified as a food. Cold milk not only serves as a delightful beverage, it is also used in cooking and baking. Milk provides substantial amounts of calcium and is a very inexpensive source of protein in the diet. Most milk is also fortified with vitamins A and D.

In its natural state after the cow is milked, milk is an emulsion. When allowed to stand, the fat in the cow's milk floats to the top. This fat is actually cream and the rest of the milk is skim milk—milk without fat. By shaking this milk up, it will form a temporary emulsion and become smooth and blended for a short time. Since milk fat does not combine permanently with the rest of the milk under normal circumstances, today's milk is **homogenized** to create a permanent bond between the milk and cream. Today's milk is also **pasteurized,** meaning it is heated to kill harmful bacteria.

Milk is available in many forms (see Table 13.7). The differences center around the milk's fat content. Milk is also available with some or all of its water content removed.

- Evaporated milk and evaporated skim milk are made by heating milk to stabilize the milk protein and then removing about 60 percent of the water. They are used mostly in cooking and baking.
- Sweetened condensed milk and skimmed milk also have about 60 percent of their water removed. What makes them different is that they are heavily sweetened.
- Nonfat dry milk, also called powdered milk, is made by removing the water from pasteurized skim milk. It is also used in baking and cooking.

Among other milk products are three items made by combining friendly bacteria with a milk product. Buttermilk is skim milk that is cultured with bacteria to produce a tangy beverage. Yogurt is made by fermenting whole, reduced-fat, low-fat or fat-free milk. It is sometimes sweet-

Table 13-7 NUTRIENT COMPOSITION OF 1 CUP[a] OF MILK

Name	*Calories*	*Fat*	*Saturated Fat*	*Calcium*
Whole milk	150	8 g	5 g	300 mg
Reduced-fat milk, also called 2% reduced-fat milk	120	5 g	3 g	300 mg
Lowfat milk, also called 1% lowfat milk	100	2.5 g	1.5 g	300 mg
Fat-free milk, also called skim or nonfat milk	80	0 g	0 g	300 mg

[a]One serving.

Table 13-8 CALORIES AND FAT IN MILK AND CREAM

Product	*Serving Size*	*Calories*	*Fat (grams)*
Skim milk	1 cup	86	0.5
1% milk	1 cup	102	3
2% milk	1 cup	121	5
Whole milk	1 cup	150	8
Half-and-half	1 tablespoon	20	2
Light cream (coffee cream)	1 tablespoon	29	3
Light whipping cream, fluid	1 tablespoon	44	5
Heavy whipping cream, fluid	1 tablespoon	52	6
Sour cream	1 tablespoon	26	3

SOURCE: U.S.D.A.

ened and flavored and served by itself or as part of another dish. Sour cream is 18 percent fat cream, fermented. It has a thick, spoonable consistency and a delicious flavor. It is used in dips and dressings. Table 13.8 compares the calories and fat in milk and other dairy products.

Milk products must always be refrigerated. They are among the foods most likely to encourage bacterial growth. They deteriorate rapidly.

Then there is cheese, an important milk product and an ideal candidate for the brunch menu.

CHEESE

Cheese is a high-protein dairy product made from the milk of domestic animals: cows, sheep, and goats. It is made by curdling milk—that is, separating it into curds and whey—by adding rennet or bacteria or both. The liquid whey is drained off, and the solid mass of curd, or coagulated milk protein, is used to make cheese.

Legend has it that the first cheese was made accidentally from goat's milk that an Arab merchant was carrying in a saddlebag. The jolting of his camel in the hot sun separated the milk into curds and whey. The fact that the saddlebag was made of animal innards may have had something to do with it. Most of the rennet used in cheese making today comes from the lining of a calf's stomach.

KINDS OF CHEESE

There are literally hundreds of different kinds of cheese. They range in taste from mild to sharp and in texture from soft to hard—usually referred to as soft, semisoft, firm, and hard. They are also divided into two groups-**ripened** (fermented with bacteria or molds) and **unripened** (fresh, untreated). Cheeses ripened over a period of time are said to be aged. The longer they age, the sharper their flavor—and the higher their cost. Let's take a look at just the few you are most likely to serve or to use in the kitchen.

Cheddar cheese is a firm ripened type of cheese. It comes in many varieties, ranging in flavor from very mild to very sharp. Cheddar is used in sandwiches and appetizers and as a dessert cheese.

Swiss is another popular type of firm ripened cheese. It is immediately recognizable by its holes, which come from gases that develop during fermentation. The Swiss cheeses have a variety of mild flavors. Two kinds of imported swiss are frequently used in the kitchen: Emmenthaler (em′-un-tahl-er) and Gruyère (groo-yair). They are the cheeses of choice for the cheese–fruit plate and the buffet, as well as for the soufflé, the fondue pot, and the sauce pot. Domestic Swiss is usually used in sandwiches.

A group known collectively as blue cheese are ripened semisoft cheeses with blue–green veins of mold in them. They have a sharp, peppery flavor and crumbly texture that make them look and taste very similar. Among them are some well-known imports—Roquefort from the town of Roquefort, France; Gorgonzola from Italy; and Stilton from England—that could be featured as stars on your buffet, fruit–cheese plate, or dessert menu. The less famous domestic blues are popular in salad dressings, canapé toppings, salads, and sauces, as well as in their own right.

Another well-known flavorer of salad dressings and sauces is Parmesan (par′-ma-zan), a hard, ripe cheese with a sharp and piquant flavor. This is the cheese you shake onto spaghetti. It comes in a soft powdery form, but it is much more delicious if you grate it fresh from the hard piece. Originally an Italian cheese, it is now produced domestically, like nearly all other cheese types. Romano (roh-mahn′-o) is very similar to Parmesan with a slightly sharper, saltier flavor.

Compatriot to Parmesan is mozzarella (motz′-a-rel′-a), the pizza cheese. An unripened cheese of semisoft-to-firm texture, it has a mild but distinctive flavor. No pizza tastes right without it.

Of the other unripened (fresh) cheeses, the most familiar are cottage cheese and cream cheese, both native American products, both versatile mainstays of the cold kitchen. Cottage cheese is an excellent salad cheese; cream cheese is used in sandwiches, canapés, hors d'oeuvres, and dips and is an essential ingredient in cheesecake. They are the only cheeses you could call inexpensive.

At the luxury end of the scale are three soft—almost as soft as a sauce—dessert cheeses: Brie (bree), Camembert (kam′-um-bare), and Limburger (pronounced as spelled). You'll find them in restaurants catering to connoisseurs of food. They taste much better than their aroma and rather unattractive appearance would lead you to believe. But an odor of ammonia tells you when they are past their prime.

Two red-jacketed cheeses from the Netherlands, on the other hand, make bright and attractive buffet items. They are Gouda (goo′da) and Edam (ee′-dum). They have the firm texture and good cheese color of a pale cheddar, and they offer mild but subtly different flavors that are welcome in a dessert cheese or on a cheese board.

There you have a baker's dozen of what are called the **natural cheeses.** Then there is **process cheese.**

Pasteurized process cheese is made by adding an emulsifier and water to grated natural cheese (usually a combination of cheddar and other cheeses) and heating and mixing it all until it becomes homogeneous. One cheese connoisseur has called it "solidified floor wax." But it does have some endearing qualities: It does not spoil easily, it stays moist, it melts well, and it is cheaper than natural cheese. It should never be used as a dessert cheese, but it is found in sandwiches and atop the meat in a cheeseburger. It is what most Americans know as American cheese.

Table 13.9 gives information about these and additional cheeses.

HOLDING, STORAGE, AND SERVICE

Cheeses are both held and stored under refrigeration. They can also stand in bulk at room temperature for several hours, which makes them good buffet items (Figure 13.8). Their most significant limitation is that they dry and harden when exposed to air. This means that as soon as you cut into a cheese you must either use it or wrap it tightly with plastic wrap to exclude the air.

Table 13-9 A GUIDE TO CHEESES

Cheese	*Characteristics*	*Uses*
Unripened		
Cottage	Mild, slightly acid flavor; soft, open texture with tender curds of varying size; white to creamy white	Appetizers, salads, cheesecakes, dips
Cream	Delicate, slightly acid flavor; soft, smooth texture; white	Appetizers, salads, sandwiches, desserts, and snacks
Neufchâtel	Mild, acidic flavor; soft, smooth texture similar to cream cheese but lower in fat; white	Salads, sandwiches, desserts, snacks, dips
Ricotta	Mild, sweet, nutlike flavor; soft, moist texture with loose curds (fresh ricotta) or dry and suitable for grating; white	Salads, main dishes such as lasagne and ravioli, and desserts, mostly in cooked dishes
Soft, Ripened		
Bel Paese	Mild, sweet flavor; light, creamy-yellow interior; slate-gray surface; soft to medium-firm, creamy texture	Appetizers, sandwiches, desserts, and snacks
Brie	Mild to pungent flavor; soft, smooth texture; creamy-yellow interior; edible thin brown and white crust	Appetizers, sandwiches, desserts, snacks, salads
Camembert	Distinctive mild to pungent flavor; soft, smooth texture—almost fluid when fully ripened; creamy-yellow interior; edible thin white or gray–white crust	Appetizers, desserts, and snacks
Limburger	Highly pungent, very strong flavor and aroma; soft, smooth texture that usually contains small irregular openings; creamy-white interior; reddish-yellow surface	Appetizers, desserts, snacks, sandwiches
Semisoft, Ripened		
Blue	Tangy, piquant flavor; semisoft, pasty, sometimes crumbly texture; white interior marbled or streaked with blue veins of mold; resembles Roquefort	Appetizers, salads and salad dressings, desserts, and snacks
Brick	Mild, pungent, sweet flavor; semisoft to medium-firm, elastic texture; creamy white-to-yellow interior; brownish exterior	Appetizers, sandwiches, desserts, and snacks
Gorgonzola	Tangy, rich, spicy flavor; semisoft, pasty, sometimes crumbly texture; creamy-white interior, mottled or streaked with blue–green veins of mold; clay-colored surface	Appetizers, salads, desserts, and snacks
Mozzarella (also called Scamorza)	Delicate, mild flavor; slightly firm, plastic texture; creamy white	Main dishes such as pizza or lasagne, sandwiches, snacks, and salads

(*Continued*)

Table 13-9 (Continued)

Cheese	Characteristics	Uses
Muenster	Mild to mellow flavor; semisoft texture with numerous small openings; creamy-white interior; yellowish-tan or white surface	Appetizers, sandwiches, desserts, and snacks
Port du Salut	Mellow to robust flavor similar to Gouda; semisoft, smooth elastic texture; creamy white or yellow	Appetizers, desserts, and snacks
Roquefort	Sharp, peppery, piquant flavor; semisoft, pasty, sometimes crumbly texture; white interior streaked with blue–green veins of mold	Appetizers, salads and salad dressings, desserts, and snacks
Sapsago	Sharp, pungent, clover-like flavor; very hard texture suitable for grating; light green or sage green	Grated for seasoning
Stilton	Piquant flavor, milder than Gorgonzola or Roquefort; open, flaky texture; creamy-white interior streaked with blue–green veins of mold; wrinkled, melon-like rind	Appetizers, salads, desserts, snacks, in cooked foods
Hard, Ripened		
Cheddar (often called American)	Mild to very sharp flavor; smooth texture, firm to crumbly; light cream to orange	Appetizers, main dishes, sauces, soups, sandwiches, salads, desserts, and snacks
Colby	Mild to mellow flavor, similar to cheddar; softer body and more open texture than cheddar; light cream to orange	Sandwiches, snacks, cooked foods
Edam	Mellow, nutlike, sometimes salty flavor; rather firm, rubbery texture; creamy-yellow or medium yellow–orange interior; surface coated with red wax; usually shaped like a flattened ball	Appetizers, salads, sandwiches, sauces, desserts, and snacks
Gouda	Mellow, nutlike, often slightly acid flavor; semisoft to firm, smooth texture, often containing small holes; creamy-yellow or medium yellow–orange interior; usually has red wax coating; usually shaped like a flattened ball	Appetizers, salads, sandwiches, sauces, desserts, and snacks
Gruyère	Nutlike, salty flavor, similar to Swiss, but sharper; firm, smooth texture with small holes or eyes light yellow	Appetizers, desserts, snacks, fondue and other cooked dishes
Monterey (Jack)	Semisoft; smooth, open texture, mild flavor; cheddar-like; hard when aged	Appetizers, sandwiches, salads
Parmesan	Sharp, distinctive flavor; very hard, granular texture; yellowish white	Grated on cooked (Italian) dishes, salads, as seasoning

Table 13-9 (Continued)

Cheese	Characteristics	Uses
Provolone	Mellow to sharp flavor, smoky and salty; firm, smooth texture; cuts without crumbling; light creamy yellow; light-brown or golden-yellow surface	Appetizers, main dishes, sandwiches, desserts, and snacks
Romano	Very sharp, piquant flavor; very hard, granular texture; yellowish-white interior; greenish-black surface	Seasoning and general table use; when cured a year, it is suitable for grating
Swiss (also called Emmenthaler)	Mild, sweet, nutlike flavor; firm, smooth, elastic body with large round eyes; light yellow	Sandwiches, salads, snacks, fondue and other cooked dishes

Figure 13-8 CHEESE-AND-FRUIT TRAY

This display uses blocks of cheese and fruit pieces like sculptural forms to set the stage for portioned slices. Since slices dry out quickly, only a few are presented. (Photo courtesy Wall's Catering, Dallas, Texas.)

Hard and firm cheeses, properly wrapped, keep from a week to several months in the refrigerator. Even with the best of care, once a whole cheese has been cut it tends to dry out, grow sharper in flavor, and develop inedible molds around the edges. Semisoft and soft cheeses keep one to two weeks refrigerated. Fresh cheeses should be kept no more than a week.

Cheeses should be served at room temperature. Slices and bite-sized pieces of cheese must be cut just before service. Once dried out, they are useless except in sauces and cooked products. This is fine if you serve a lot of cheese sauce. But cheese is too expensive to waste.

COOKING WITH CHEESE

As you may have already discovered, cheese cookery poses no problems as long as you keep the temperature low or the cooking time short or both. The high-protein content of cheese means that it becomes tough and stringy with high temperatures and prolonged cooking. Its fat content may also separate out.

The best way to add cheese to a recipe is to grate it. Grating will break the cheese into small, thin pieces that will melt and blend quickly and evenly into the end product.

Cheese used in a starch-thickened sauce must not be added until after the thickening process is completed. Cheese for gratinéing should be added near the end of the cooking period if it is an oven-cooked product. A glaze administered

Recipe 13-10 QUICHE AU FROMAGE (CHEESE PIE)

YIELD: ***1 pie or 6 servings***

3	**eggs**	
$1^1/_2$ C	**milk**	**375 mL**
$^1/_4$ tsp	**salt**	**1 mL**
	dash nutmeg	
1 C	**shredded Swiss cheese**	**250 mL**
8-in.	**pie shell, unbaked**	

1. Mix together eggs, milk, salt, and nutmeg.
2. Spread cheese along bottom of pie shell.
3. Pour egg mixture into pie shell.
4. Bake in 375°F (190°C) oven for 20–30 minutes, until the filling is set.

Per serving:		Carbohydrates:	21 g
Calories:	291	Cholesterol:	135 mg
Fat:	17 g	Fiber:	0 g
Protein:	13 g	Sodium:	342 mg

Recipe 13-10a QUICHE LORRAINE

YIELD: ***1 pie or 6 servings***

To Recipe 13.10, add:

4 oz	**crumbed bacon, cooked**	**125 g**

Spread bacon with cheese in Step 2.

Per serving:		Carbohydrates:	21 g
Calories:	399	Cholesterol:	151 mg
Fat:	27 g	Fiber:	0 g
Protein:	18 g	Sodium:	644 mg

Recipe 13-10b QUICHE FLORENTINE

YIELD: ***1 pie or 6 servings***

To Recipe 13.10, add:

1 oz	**chopped onion, sautéed**	**30 g**
4 oz	**chopped spinach, sautéed**	**125 g**

Decrease cheese to $^1/_4$ cup (60 mL). Spread onion and spinach with cheese in Step 2.

Per serving:		Carbohydrates:	22 g
Calories:	317	Cholesterol:	135 mg
Fat:	20 g	Fiber:	1 g
Protein:	13 g	Sodium:	356 mg

in the salamander is always a quick trip, whatever the product.

To top off the subject of foods for breakfast and brunch, you can combine cheese and egg cookery in a cheese quiche (Recipe 13.10). A **quiche** (keesh) is a savory pie with a custard base.

Different kinds of quiche can be made by varying the major flavor. Recipes 13.10a and 13.10b give you two ideas. You can use cheese alone as the major flavor, or combine it with other major flavors, or leave it out entirely. Seafood, meat, poultry, and vegetables such as mushrooms, broccoli, or cauliflower can also be used to good advantage.

Bake the pie on the bottom shelf or directly on the floor of a stack oven. This allows the dough to bake fairly quickly and thus avoids a soggy bottom crust. The filling is set when the center no longer jiggles but is firm without being rubbery.

SUMMING UP

Breakfast, first meal of the day, is made up of groups of foods traditionally cooked and served together. Brunch builds on the breakfast menu and moves it to span the middle of the day. Breakfast is likely to be a wake-up, hurry-up affair. Brunch, usually a weekend offering, is a leisurely meal with the accent on pleasure and the chance to explore new dishes.

For both meals, eggs and egg-based dishes are the heart of the menu. Egg cookery is the single most important skill for the breakfast cook to master. Once you are comfortable with the egg, you can combine it with your other cooking knowledge and skills to produce any number of egg dishes—many kinds of omelets, many poached-egg and shirred egg dishes, scrambled eggs, savory quiches.

Another group of breakfast dishes centers around waffles, pancakes, and French toast, with breakfast meats to accompany them. For such dishes, the cook must know how to make a batter that will produce a light and tender product, how to cook on the griddle, and how to prepare the different kinds of breakfast meats. The thin French pancakes known as crêpes offer the cook a real challenge, along with the chance to fill them with delicious mixtures for brunch dishes.

The beverage side of breakfast is making good coffee and good tea and serving the hot beverages hot and the cold ones cold—juices and iced tea and milk. Beverages are routine and unchallenging and are therefore often neglected, but they can make all the difference in the world to the customer—especially the coffee.

Many other foods can be served for breakfast—potatoes, tomatoes, cheese, cornbread, muffins, oysters. Regional preferences often determine the selection of offerings. In some parts of the South, for example, grits are standard breakfast fare; elsewhere, a plate of eggs would be unthinkable without French fries or hash browns.

Many breakfast foods can be featured in other settings. Omelets and shirred eggs are excellent luncheon dishes. Bacon, ham, and sausage are great to use in sandwiches, salads, and entrées. Hard-cooked eggs go anywhere, anytime. Waffles and pancakes suitably sweetened and flavored, double as desserts. Coffee and tea are universal 24-hour pick-me-ups.

Once you can cook them well, use breakfast foods as starters for your own creations, and let your imagination run wild.

The Cook's Vocabulary

brunch
caffeine
cheese: ripened, unripened, natural, process
city roast (also called American or medium roast)
crêpe
espresso
French toast
frittata
grind
homogenized
omelet
primed (seasoned) surface
pancakes
pasteurized
quiche
steeping
tea: black, green, oolong
waffle

Review Questions

Answer each question in complete sentences. Read each question carefully and make sure you answer all parts of the question. Organize your answer into more than one paragraph when appropriate.

1. Describe how each style of egg is prepared.
2. Give four examples of natural cheeses and one example of process cheese.
3. Describe how a French crêpe differs from an American pancake. Why does the crêpe make a more suitable luncheon dish than the pancake?
4. What is the difference between cappuccino, latte, and mocha?
5. Which type of tea is used most often in the United States?
6. In your opinion, which menu items discussed in this chapter make the most suitable brunch dishes? Explain your views.
7. Name several ways in which the tasks of the breakfast cook are different from those of the soup or sauce cook.

Chapter 14

PANTRY PRODUCTION

With this chapter, we enter another realm of the kitchen—the area where cold foods are prepared. It is known variously as the cold kitchen, the pantry, or the garde manger department. What you call it will depend on the kind and size of the operation and on local jargon.

This is not to say that no cooking goes on here. It does. In fact, the cold-food expert must be a master of all the techniques of the kitchen.

Cold foods are important to any foodservice menu. Today's American diner responds to crisp, fresh, and natural foods that have lost nothing in cooking and processing but retain their original color, shape, and flavor. But there is more to cold foods than uncooked fruits and vegetables. To a greater degree than hot foods, cold foods offer opportunities for interesting harmonies and contrasts of textures and tastes as well as of color and shape and pattern. And some popular cold foods are as sophisticated as others are fresh and simple.

The products of the pantry fill many menu roles. Some are used to open a meal—fresh, colorful fruits and vegetables that awaken the appetite, or tangy tidbits that hint of pleasures to come. Some may accompany an entrée or follow it as an accent or a change of pace. Some may be entrées in themselves. Whole meals may be provided from the cold kitchen, from inexpensive salad bars to elaborate party buffets.

We will begin our exploration of cold-food preparation with that most universal of all cold foods, the salad. Then we'll have a look at salad dressings and their close relatives cold sauces, and we'll consider how to put salads and dressings together.

After completing this chapter, you should be able to:

- Identify greens commonly used in salads.
- Describe how to prepare the major salad types.
- Explain and illustrate the principles of salad presentation.
- Describe how to make the major types of salad dressings and cold sauces.

SALADS AND SALAD MAKING

The first salads were simply greens dipped in salt. In fact, the word salad comes from a Latin word meaning "salted." Roman dinners often had a separate salad course of raw greens with a dressing.

Salads vanished from the European diet for a thousand years or more but reappeared in the seventeenth century. At one time, it was not unusual to include flowers such as nasturtiums, marigolds, rose petals, and violets in salads. But though it become common in Europe, salad was seldom the focus of interest for either the cook or the diner.

It was not until the salad crossed the ocean to America that it came into its own. One true claim to fame of the American cook is ingenuity in the preparation of salads. We have gone far beyond the simple salted greens of the past to vegetables of every species, shape, and flavor, and to meats, fish, fruits, cheeses, and eggs. We have moved the salad all over the menu, from appetizer to accompaniment to entrée to dessert to meal-in-itself. And we have taken it from obscurity to stardom. Many a salad is a work of art.

How do we define this versatile food? A salad is a dish that is almost always served cold, usually accompanied by a cold dressing made of oil, vinegar, special flavorings, and often eggs. It usually takes off from a leafy green base and is likely to be piquant in flavor. There are four parts to the structure of the typical salad:

- The *base,* or *underliner:* usually a leafy green such as a lettuce cup or a fine layer of shredded lettuce
- The *body:* the major ingredient or mixture of ingredients
- The *dressing:* sometimes part of the salad, more often not, but always planned to be compatible with it
- The *garnish:* a colorful accent providing eye appeal (often omitted if the salad itself is colorful)

Salads are held in high regard by the health-conscious American customer, and rightly so. Leafy greens and other salad vegetables and fruits are good sources of many essential vitamins and minerals, as well as fiber. But salads are not always the low-calorie foods many people think they are when they include less than moderate amounts of cheese, meats, nuts, and most regular salad dressings.

Let us explore the essentials of salad making by examining some different kinds of salads. We'll group them according to their ingredients and the way they go together.

- Leafy green
- Vegetable
- Cooked
- Fruit
- Combination
- Gelatin or congealed

LEAFY GREEN SALADS

Leafy green salads are made of raw leafy green vegetables, usually of the lettuce or endive families. The most common of these salad greens are listed below, grouped according to type. They are pictured in Figure 14.1.

Crisphead Lettuces

Iceberg: a crisp, green–white lettuce, very mild in flavor

Romaine or cos: a crisp, coarse lettuce with long, flat, bright-green leaves, full of flavor

Butterhead Lettuces

Bibb or limestone: a small, loose-leaved head lettuce having soft, smooth, buttery leaves, yellow white to dark green in color

Boston: similar to Bibb but less sweet, and having a slightly larger head with more yellow tones

Figure 14-1 LEAFY GREENS FOR SALAD

a. Iceberg lettuce. (Photo courtesy Burpee Seeds.)

b. Romaine lettuce. (Photo by Patricia Roberts.)

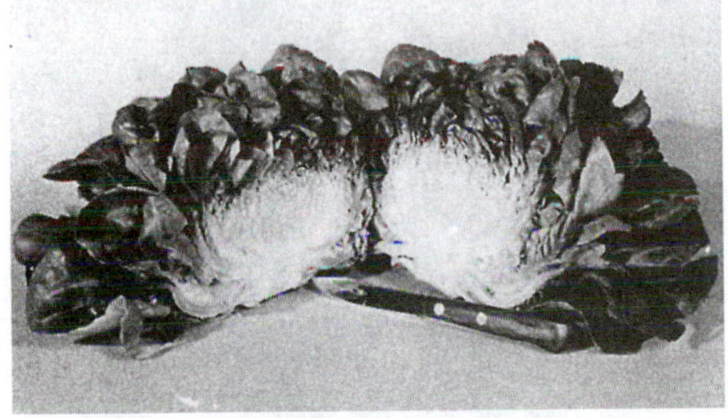

c. Bibb lettuce. (Photo courtesy Burpee Seeds.)

d. Boston lettuce. (Photo courtesy Burpee Seeds.)

e. Green leaf lettuce. (Photo by Patricia Roberts.)

f. Red leaf lettuce. (Photo by Patricia Roberts.)

(*Continued*)

Figure 14-1 (*continued*)

g. Chicory. (Photo by Patricia Roberts.)

h. Belgian endive. (Photo by Patricia Roberts.)

i. Spinach. (Photo courtesy Burpee Seeds)

j. Watercress (Photo courtesy USDA.)

Leaf Lettuces

Green leaf: tender, curly edged, crisp, but softer than the crisphead lettuces; many varieties of many shades of green

Red leaf: curly green leaves with fragile red tips

Endive

Chicory (curly endive): a bunched head having crisp, narrow, curled, feathery dark-green leaves and a slightly bitter taste

Escarole: flat-headed, similar in appearance to chicory but with larger, coarser, firmer, and darker-green leaves; distinctively bitter in taste.

Belgian endive: a pointed cluster of crisp, fleshy, waxy white leaves looking like a short spear; actually the specially cultivated shoot of the curly endive

Variety Greens

Spinach: flat or crinkled dark-green leaves, crisp and flavorful

Watercress: small dark-green leaves on a crisp stem, strong and zesty in flavor; used occasionally in salads, more often as a garnish

These greens can be served separately or in combinations offering texture and color variety. Usually, they are served in bite-sited pieces (except, sometimes, Belgian endive and some of the soft lettuces) with a dressing that is added at the moment of service.

The primary areas of concern to the salad maker are in the handling and serving of a green salad. It goes without saying that the greens should be fresh, high-quality produce. They should be thoroughly washed as described in Chapter 3.

All green salads should be served well chilled. Green salads should be crisp, unless they are made entirely of soft lettuces such as Boston, Bibb, and leaf. These soft lettuces should be fresh and unwilted. Naturally crisp salad greens such as iceberg and romaine should be very crisp when served. If the greens lack crispness, both they and the salad lack quality.

To maintain crispness in cut greens, cut them as close to serving as possible. You can also put them in ice water to crisp them, draining them well before dishing them out.

For true quality in a salad, greens must be cleanly and evenly cut with a sharp stainless steel cutting edge. The size of the cut pieces is very important. Nothing is more frustrating to the diner than to be served a salad of crisp greens with pieces too large to be maneuvered gracefully from plate to mouth.

Controversy has raged for years over whether to cut or to tear lettuce for salads. But try tearing lettuce for a thousand salads—it would take you all day. You can cut it in one-tenth the time.

Consider another factor: Crisp vegetables depend for their crispness on their high water content. When this diminishes, they wilt. Greens that are torn lose their water faster than greens that are cut. It is almost impossible to tear them without bruising the leaves.

A common problem in holding salad greens is the appearance of rust color on the edges. To prevent discoloration, you can rinse them in a mild antioxidant. But proceed with caution: Too strong a solution can produce a bad taste. To prevent browning, also be sure to use a stainless steel knife for cutting.

Precut, prewashed lettuce is available in plastic bags in many areas. It keeps two to three days, and the labor it saves is worth its price for many operations. Once you open a bag, however, the lettuce loses quality quickly.

Leafy green salads are served in various ways. They may be tossed together in a large container until they are evenly mixed, then served on individual plates or perhaps in a large serve-yourself bowl. Or they may be arranged carefully on individual plates for artistic effect. Sometimes greens and dressing are tossed together at tableside. But no dressing is ever added to a tossed salad until the very last minute; it will wilt the lettuce in no time.

Let us look at a basic green salad—mainstay of the typical American menu. The combination of greens in Recipe 14.1 provides variety in color and flavor. The paleness of the iceberg contrasts with the strong green colors of the romaine and watercress, and the iceberg's bland taste is a foil for their assertive flavors. There is textural contrast, too, in the fragile leaves of the watercress among the crisp lettuce pieces. (You will discard the tough watercress stems, using the thinner branches and leaves.)

Notice the care taken to keep the greens fresh and crisp. If holding time is short, you may skip Step 4 and portion the greens directly after toss-

Recipe 14-1 BASIC GREEN SALAD

YIELD: *12 portions*

- **1 head iceberg lettuce, cored**
- **1 head romaine**
- **1/2 bunch watercress**
- **12 tomato wedges**
- **12 black olives**

1. Wash and drain all greens, discarding unusable portions.
2. Cut into bite-sized pieces.
3. Toss gently to distribute all greens evenly.
4. Cover with damp towels and refrigerate.
5. Shortly before service, portion onto chilled plates and refrigerate.
6. Add tomato wedges and black olives at time of service.

Per serving:			
Calories:	20	Cholesterol:	0 mg
Fat:	1 g	Fiber:	2 g
Protein:	1 g	Sodium:	47 mg
		Carbohydrates:	3 g

ing, holding the plated portions in the refrigerator. You will add the garnishes as the salad is served so that their moisture will not wilt the lettuces.

There are countless variations for this recipe. For the watercress, you might substitute a pound of spinach or half a head of curly endive; either of these will give color and flavor contrasts to the lettuces. You might use different garnishes—cucumber or radish slices, a bell pepper ring, a cherry tomato. Try developing your own basic green salad recipe; the possibilities are practically endless.

VEGETABLE SALADS

A **vegetable salad** has one or more nonleafy vegetables as its main ingredients. It does not contain leafy vegetables at all. It may have leafy greens as a base, or underliner, but not as part of the body.

Many vegetable salads are made of raw vegetables cut into various shapes. When two or more vegetables are combined, they should be chosen for their complementary flavors and colors. The following raw vegetables are commonly used in vegetable salads:

Bean sprouts	Broccoli
Cabbage	Mushrooms
Carrots	Onions
Celery	Radishes
Cucumbers	Tomatoes
Green peppers	Zucchini

Cut raw vegetables, like leafy greens, do not hold well. Cut them as close as possible to serving time and place them in ice water so that they do not dry out or shrivel. Wilting and rusting are not the major problems they are with the leafy vegetables, but certain kinds do not hold their color well. White vegetables, such as celery and especially mushrooms, can turn dark or rust. You can prevent this by the same means used for leafy greens—cutting with stainless steel, using (with caution) an antioxidant solution, and storing correctly.

Many cooked vegetables are also used as main ingredients in vegetable salads. Such vegetables are cooked because they are not suitable for salad in their raw state. They, too, may be used singly or in combination. Again, the choice is based on compatible flavors and colors. Choices include:

Artichoke hearts	Carrots
Asparagus	Cauliflower
Beans (all kinds)	Hearts of palm
Olives	Peas
Peppers, roasted	Water chestnuts

Both raw and cooked vegetables for salads can be marinated to give them special flavor. If this is done, the problem of discoloration in raw vegetables is solved by the marinade, which protects the cut surfaces from the air.

Recipe 14-2 VEGETABLES À LA GRECQUE

YIELD: *12 portions*

1 lb	mushrooms, small whole or large quartered	450 g
$^1/_2$ lb	carrots, $^1/_8$-in. (2 mm) slices	250 g
$^1/_2$ lb	green beans, 2-in. (5 cm) pieces	250 g

Marinade:

2 C	water or chicken stock	500 mL
1 C	olive oil	250 mL
3 fl oz	lemon juice	100 mL
1 4-in.	celery rib	10 cm
1 tsp	salt	5 mL

Sachet:

1 tsp	minced garlic or shallots	5 mL
1 tsp	crushed peppercorns	5 mL
1 tsp	coriander seeds	5 mL
$^1/_2$	bay leaf	
$^1/_2$ tsp	thyme	2 mL

1. Wash and dry mushrooms and trim ends.
2. Parboil carrots and green beans separately until 50–75 percent done. Remove from heat and add ice to chill. Drain.
3. Place all marinade ingredients, including sachet, in stainless steel pan and bring to a boil. Simmer 15 minutes.
4. Add mushrooms, carrots, and green beans to marinade and simmer 5 minutes. Remove from heat.
5. When cool, remove sachet and celery. Marinate vegetables overnight in refrigerator.

Per serving:		Carbohydrates:	5 g
Calories:	48	Cholesterol:	0 mg
Fat:	3 g	Fiber:	1 g
Protein:	1 g	Sodium:	42 mg

Vegetable salads, both raw and cooked, are generally arranged on a leafy-green liner, with or without a dressing added at the time of service. One very common vegetable salad—coleslaw, made from shredded cabbage—has a dressing mixed in as an integral part of the salad. If vegetables have been marinated, the marinade replaces a dressing.

Recipe 14.2 is a marinated vegetable salad. You will remember the principles of marinating from Chapter 3 and the partial-cook/quick-chill method of cooking vegetables from Chapter 9. Assembling the chilled ingredients on lettuce cups is the final move that turns it all into a salad. In serving marinated salads, remove the vegetables carefully from the marinade with a slotted spoon to keep the plate free of excess liquid. To assemble, place a $2^1/_2$-ounce (75 g) portion on a lettuce cup on a chilled plate and sprinkle with chopped parsley.

COOKED SALADS

Cooked salads are those that use a single cooked food as the major ingredient. Macaroni salad, tuna salad, and potato salad are everyday examples. Some of the foods commonly cooked to become salads are:

Potatoes	Ham
Rice	Poultry (chicken, turkey)
Pastas	Fish (tuna, salmon)
Eggs	Shellfish (shrimp, lobster, crab)

Cooked vegetable salads may be classified as either cooked or vegetable, since they have characteristics of both.

Cooked salads usually have another feature that sets them apart: They include a dressing as an integral part of their makeup. This dressing provides another characteristic of the cooked salad—its cohesiveness. This quality of sticking together allows it to be portioned with a scoop. It can also be spread as a sandwich filling if the major ingredient is suitable. Egg, ham, chicken, and tuna salad sandwiches are familiar examples.

You can create many variations of the basic cooked salads by using different dressings and different flavor additions. A common addition is something to give crunch, providing texture contrast to the soft cooked food. It might be raw celery, for example. Or it could be crisp pickle or minced onion if the flavor is right for the salad.

Recipe 14.3 shows the structure of a typical cooked salad. Its major ingredient, chicken, is enhanced by the addition of celery for texture contrast and Worcestershire sauce for extra flavor.

The main ingredient in a cooked salad can be marinated to give it special flavor. This is often done with shellfish. A similar trick for flavoring potato salad is to add an oil-and-vinegar dressing to the cooked potatoes while they are hot, so that they soak up the dressing.

Cooked salads are among the hearty salads that can be served as entrées. They are also a pleasing and acceptable way of using suitable leftover cooked foods of high quality.

Recipe 14.4 shows a popular way to dress up a cooked salad entrée. Though the tomato traditionally gets top billing on the menu, it is the cooked salad that provides the character of the dish. The tomato functions as a combination of base, body, and garnish that enlarges the salad to entrée size, both colorfully and economically. It could provide a convenient frame or format for almost any cooked salad. Consider the variations shown in Recipes 14.4a and 14.4b.

Other cup-shaped foods may play the same role—avocado halves stuffed with shrimp or crab

Recipe 14-3 CHICKEN SALAD

YIELD: ***12 4-oz (150 g) portions***

$2\frac{1}{4}$ lb	**cooked chicken, medium dice**	**1 kg**
$\frac{3}{4}$ lb	**celery, small dice**	**375 g**
$\frac{1}{2}$ tsp	**Worcestershire sauce**	**2 mL**
1 tsp	**salt**	**5 mL**
$\frac{1}{4}$ tsp	**white pepper**	**1 mL**
$1\frac{1}{2}$ C	**mayonnaise**	**375 mL**

1. Mix all ingredients.
2. Cover and refrigerate 4–6 hours to blend flavors.

Per serving:		Carbohydrates:	2 g
Calories:	376	Cholesterol:	16 mg
Fat:	33 g	Fiber:	0 g
Protein:	19 g	Sodium:	436 mg

Recipe 14-4 STUFFED TOMATO SALAD

YIELD: ***12 portions***

3 lb	**chicken salad**	**1.4 kg**
12	**tomatoes, cored**	
12	**lettuce leaves**	

Garnish:

12	**black olives**
12	**cucumber slices**
12	**parsley sprigs**

1. Prepare chicken salad as directed in Recipe 14.3.
2. Cut tomatoes into quarters, leaving sections attached at bottom. Spread apart.
3. To serve, place tomatoes on lettuce leaves. Use a No. 8 scoop to center chicken salad in each tomato. Arrange garnish.

Per serving:		Carbohydrates:	8 g
Calories:	409	Cholesterol:	16 mg
Fat:	33 g	Fiber:	2 g
Protein:	20 g	Sodium:	487 mg

Recipe 14-4a TUNA SALAD STUFFING

YIELD: ***12 portions***

Replace body of Recipe 14.4 with:

2 1/4 lb	**tuna**	**1 kg**
3/4 lb	**celery, diced**	**375 g**
2 oz	**onions, diced**	**50 g**
2 fl oz	**lemon juice**	**60 mL**
1 tsp	**tarragon**	**5 mL**
1 1/2 C	**mayonnaise**	**375 mL**

Mix ingredients. Serve as in Recipe 14.4.

Per serving:		Carbohydrates:	8 g
Calories:	344	Cholesterol:	52 mg
Fat:	25 g	Fiber:	2 g
Protein:	22 g	Sodium:	748 mg

salad; pineapple halves filled with fruit salad. The main consideration is the appropriateness of the container to the salad it contains.

FRUIT SALADS

Fruit on the table is certainly not new. Beginning with Eve and the apple, fruit was a popular food in ancient civilizations. Today's table offers fruit in great variety from all parts of the world. Demand has burgeoned as the popularity of fresh natural foods has increased and fresh fruits have become available year-round. Today, fruit salads have become standard menu items—as appetizers, as accompaniments to the main course, as entrées in their own right, and as desserts.

A **fruit salad** is any salad in which fruit predominates. It is generally composed of cut or sectioned fruits served separately or combined. Berries of many varieties are sometimes added to create good flavor and color. Some of the fresh fruits commonly used in salads are:

Apples	Honeydew melon
Apricots	Kiwi
Bananas	Mango
Berries	Oranges
Cantaloupe	Papaya
Coconut	Plums
Grapefruit	Pomegranates
Grapes	Raisins

Handling fruits for salads requires some special product knowledge and techniques. Certain fresh fruits—apples, pears, peaches, bananas, avocados—discolor when exposed to air. Like the lettuces, they must be cut with stainless steel cutting edges. If you combine such fruits with citrus fruits, the high acid content of the latter prevents the rapid discoloration of the fruits that are vulnerable to air. Or you can rinse vulnerable fruits in lemon juice and water or an ascorbic acid solution, though this does compromise their flavor.

Fruits that are not peeled should be washed as close to use time as possible. Berries, in particular, especially strawberries and raspberries, do not hold well. Wash them just before use, drain them well, and add them just before service.

Recipe 14-4b BEEF SALAD STUFFING

YIELD: ***12 portions***

Replace body of Recipe 14.4 with:

2 1/4 lb	**cooked beef, julienne**	**1 kg**
3/4 lb	**onions, chopped**	**375 g**
2 C	**oil-and-vinegar dressing**	**500 mL**

Marinate for 24 hours. Serve as in Recipe 14.4.

Per serving:		Carbohydrates:	9 g
Calories:	222	Cholesterol:	59 mg
Fat:	9 g	Fiber:	2 g
Protein:	26 g	Sodium:	104 mg

Recipe 14-5 FRESH FRUIT PLATTER

YIELD: ***1 serving***

2	**leaves of red-tipped leaf lettuce**	
2	**cantaloupe wedges**	
2	**pineapple rings**	
2	**watermelon cubes**	
2	**orange slices**	
2	**apple or pear slices**	
2	**grapefruit segments**	
	small bunch grapes	
1	**mint sprig**	
$^{1}/_{4}$ C	**yogurt dressing**	**60 mL**

1. Lay lettuce on chilled platter.
2. Arrange fruit attractively on lettuce.
3. Serve with dressing. Add strawberry garnish if desired.

Per serving:		Carbohydrates:	47 g
Calories:	204	Cholesterol:	3 mg
Fat:	2 g	Fiber:	4 g
Protein:	5 g	Sodium:	47 mg

Many canned fruits are good salad material—mandarin oranges, peaches, pears, apricots, grapefruit, pineapple, sweet cherries. Drain them carefully or they will make for a watery plate. Dried fruits—dates and raisins—are also used.

Almost any fruits may be combined. Flavor, color, variety, and availability will determine your choices. The fresh fruit platter in Recipe 14.5 is a colorful arrangement designed as a luncheon entrée. Fruit may vary with seasonal prices. A yogurt dressing complements the fruit.

Other foods may be added to a fruit salad to spark flavor or texture. For example, the famous Waldorf salad combines apples with celery and walnuts. The diced apples, celery, and chopped nuts are mixed with a mayonnaise or Chantilly dressing to hold the salad together.

Fruit salads are usually served on lettuce, but not always. They are usually accompanied by a dressing (sometimes a sweet one), but by no means always.

COMBINATION SALADS

A **combination salad** is just what the name implies—a combining of two or more kinds of ingredients or two or more kinds of salads. A combination salad might combine leafy greens and vegetables, and sometimes foods from this list:

Fruit, fresh, canned, or cooked
Meats, poultry, fish
Cheese, eggs
Bread

This is by no means an exhaustive list. Added to leafy greens and vegetables, these foods multiply the number of potential salad combinations, since each item can combine with many others.

Certain salad combinations have become so popular they are considered standards. For instance:

- *Tossed garden salad:* a combination of leafy greens and garden vegetables in season
- *Chef's salad:* leafy greens, ham, turkey, and cheese, often with a vegetable or egg garnish

Depending on its nature, a combination salad may be combined in a careful arrangement on a serving plate or it may be mixed together in random fashion by tossing. The chef's salad in Recipe 14.6 is an example of an arranged salad. It contains the standard combination of ingredients plus a variety of garnishes chosen for compatibility of flavor as well as eye appeal. A chef's salad is an entrée salad, traditionally served in a

Recipe 14-6 CHEF'S SALAD

YIELD: ***1 portion***

4 oz	**basic green salad**	**150 g**
$^3/_4$ oz	**chicken or turkey white meat, julienne**	**25 g**
$^3/_4$ oz	**ham, julienne**	**25 g**
$^3/_4$ oz	**roast beef, julienne**	**25 g**
$^3/_4$ oz	**Swiss cheese, julienne**	**25 g**
2	**tomato wedges**	
2	**hard-cooked egg quarters**	
4	**cucumber slices**	
1	**olive**	

1. Place basic green salad mixture in chilled bowl.
2. Arrange julienne of meats and cheeses on greens as shown.
3. Arrange garnishes on salad.

Per serving:		Carbohydrates:	7 g
Calories:	256	Cholesterol:	171 mg
Fat:	12 g	Fiber:	1 g
Protein:	29 g	Sodium:	467 mg

bowl with the greens on the bottom. The other major ingredients and garnishes are carefully arranged to form a pleasing pattern. A dressing of the customer's choice is added at the time of service or served separately.

Salads are usually tossed only to mix leafy greens or to mix other foods with leafy greens. But many foods that combine well with greens in flavor and texture do not toss well. Heavy or bulky items sink to the bottom. Juicy foods wilt the greens. Tomato, for instance, has too much juice for tossing in a garden salad. It is best to add the tomato as a garnish after the other ingredients are tossed together. And cucumber used with soft lettuce will deflate the lettuce very quickly.

Occasionally, a salad is tossed at tableside not only to mingle its ingredients but also to blend a dressing with the salad. The Caesar salad described later is often served this way.

The possibilities for combination salads are limited only by the imagination. Let taste and color again be your guides when combining different kinds of foods. Don't put fish with meat or pimientos with blueberries.

GELATIN SALADS

A **gelatin, or congealed, salad** is any salad that has gelatin in its makeup to hold it together. Gelatin comes in three primary forms: clear or unflavored, fruit flavored, and aspic.

Clear or unflavored gelatin comes in two principal forms, powder and leaves. The leaves look like heavy plastic film. Good-quality powdered gelatin has a softness and sheen referred to as bloom.

Fruit-flavored gelatin comes in powdered form in assorted flavors under many familiar brand names. It contains sugar as well as color and flavor.

Aspic is a powdered meat-flavored gelatin. It is usually beef flavored, but it also comes in fish and poultry flavors.

There are two methods of handling gelatin, one for clear gelatin and the other for fruit-flavored gelatin and aspic. For clear gelatin, the first step is to mix it with cold water. Then you stir the mixture into boiling-hot water, dissolve it completely, and cool. Dispersing the gelatin in cold water first will keep it from lumping. Then dissolving it in boiling-hot water, as many product labels advise, will give you the best end results. Technically, gelatin will dissolve at 100°F (38°C), but it may take forever and you may not have that much time.

For aspic and fruit-flavored gelatin, only one step is necessary: Dissolve the powder in very hot water and cool.

The end product for all gelatins is a jellied substance that forms when the mixture is cold. It is important to get the right proportion of liquid to gelatin. Too much liquid will make the gel wobbly; too little will make it rubbery. You can substitute fruit juice or another suitable liquid for part or all of the water.

The tomato aspic in Recipe 14.7 is an example of a salad made with clear gelatin. As you can see, tomato juice provides most of the liquid, as well as the flavor and body of the salad.

Many different fruits, vegetables, and other foods can be added to gelatin as it begins to jell. Drain them well, so that the proportion of liquid to gelatin does not change and spoil the consistency. You can add almost any fruit or vegetable. The few exceptions are raw pineapple, figs, and papaya. These fruits contain certain enzymes that keep the gelatin from congealing. The same fruits cooked or canned cause no trouble.

If you add things before the gelatin has begun to set, some kinds of foods will float to the top. For a good mix, wait until setting begins before adding anything.

After you have added everything and the product is beginning to jell, pour it into individual molds or, for volume production, into large pans. Cut the panful of salad into serving portions after it is firmly jelled—6 to 8 hours at least. It is best to make congealed salads a day ahead.

To unmold individual salads, dip each mold into hot water for a second or two, then flip over onto the salad plate. If you have trouble getting the hang of this, you can invert the plate over the upright mold and then turn everything over together. Refrigerate unmolded salads to restore any firmness they may have lost.

Congealed salads, except dessert salads, are usually served on greens. Sometimes congealed salads are served without a dressing. If a dressing is used, it is generally a mayonnaise or another dressing with considerable body.

Congealed salads must be kept refrigerated until the moment of service or they may lose their firmness. Covered and kept in the cooler in their pans or molds, they will hold well for several days.

Recipe 14-7 TOMATO ASPIC

YIELD: ***About 3 quarts (3 L)***

2 oz	**unflavored gelatin**	**60 g**
1 pt	**cold water**	**500 mL**
2 qt	**tomato juice**	**2 L**
4 oz	**chopped onions**	**125 g**
2 oz	**chopped celery**	**60 g**
1	**bay leaf**	
4	**cloves**	
1 tsp	**dry mustard**	**5 mL**
7 oz	**sugar**	**200 g**
1/2 pt	**lemon juice**	**250 mL**

1. Sprinkle gelatin on cold water and let stand 10 minutes.
2. Simmer tomato juice with remaining ingredients except lemon juice for 5 minutes.
3. Strain mixture and add to gelatin, stirring until gelatin is dissolved.
4. Stir in lemon juice.
5. Pour into two half-size hotel pans or decorative molds and refrigerate until firm.

Per cup:		Carbohydrates:	26 g
Calories:	117	Cholesterol:	0 mg
Fat:	0 g	Fiber:	0 g
Protein:	6 g	Sodium:	601 mg

SALAD ON THE MENU

In discussing various salads, we have noted that many of them can play several menu roles. To adapt them to different roles, you would make several kinds of adjustments. You would use smaller portions for an appetizer or accompaniment and larger portions for an entree. You might extend an entrée salad by adding extra ingredients (such as tomato to the chicken salad in recipe 14.4) or by using hearty garnishes such as hard-cooked egg quarters or a small bunch of grapes. You might use a different dressing for each different menu role—a tangy one for an appetizer salad, a hearty dressing for an entrée, perhaps no dressing at all for a leafy green served between courses to cleanse the palate.

Another menu use of salads is to make them part of a buffet or salad bar. In this case, you will not worry about the underliner and the plate garnish; you will prepare only the body of the salad, though you may use greens and garnish for the serving piece. (You may have noticed that our recipes have usually omitted the base, dressing, and garnish where these do not really affect the nature of the salad. These salad elements will vary from one operation to another and will be included on the standardized recipe card.)

A luncheon plate is another popular menu use of salad: Combine several salads or use them with other cold foods. A typical cold luncheon plate might contain a small sandwich and three salads, such as mixed-fruit salad, potato salad, and vegetable salad. Another might have a salad of avocado stuffed with shrimp accompanied by fruit and relishes.

Still another luncheon plate might be made up entirely of fresh fruits, such as the fruit platter in Recipe 14.5. A fruit salad platter may include yogurt or cheese to provide the protein usually associated with an entrée. Or it may have a scoop of sherbet as a flavor-texture complement.

When you plan a cold luncheon plate, the most important considerations are a good balance of flavors and attractive visual presentation. The same two things hold for all salad making. You already know a good deal about flavor; let's focus on the very important subject of presentation.

SALAD PRESENTATION

Eye appeal is the purpose of every presentation, whether the food is hot or cold. It is especially important for cold foods because they lack the come-on of an appetizing aroma. On the other hand, the fresh colors and textures of many cold foods offer more visual potential than most hot dishes.

There are three essentials to consider in presentation: height, color, and unity.

HEIGHT

Height gives a salad interest and importance. A raised surface or high point calls attention to itself. A flat and level surface is monotonous and self-effacing.

Height in a salad can be in one of two forms: actual or implied. Actual height in a leafy salad, for example, may be achieved by loosely arranging the greens on the plate so that they are higher in the center than toward the edges of the plate. Figure 14.2 shows the difference this makes.

Another way of achieving height is by adding a garnish that has some height. For instance, a plate of sliced cucumbers may be given actual height by adding a bouquet of parsley.

Where actual height is difficult to attain, implied height, or an illusion of height, can often be achieved by causing the eye to focus on a particular point. This can be done in several ways. One is by arranging ingredients in a pattern that

Figure 14-2 ACTUAL HEIGHT IN A SALAD ARRANGEMENT

The romaine leaves on the right, arranged for maximum height, make a far more interesting salad than the flat arrangement on the left. Both quantities are the same. (Photo by Patricia Roberts.)

guides the eye to that point, as in Figure 14.3. Another is to use an eye-catching ingredient or garnish to establish a focal point. If the point is near the center the salad will appear tall.

COLOR

Color is very, very important in cold foods. Take a plain, ungarnished coleslaw and see how dull it looks. Add a wedge of tomato, serve it on bright romaine lettuce, and see how color transforms it.

Figure 14-3 IMPLIED HEIGHT

A pinwheel arrangement gives the effect of height on the plate by focusing the eye on a central point.

Many people feel the more color in a salad the better, but this philosophy doesn't work out well in practice. Too many colors tend to confuse the eye and dissipate the attention. Three colors are really all that are needed. They can even be various shades of the same color, such as the three greens of a cucumber salad served on lettuce and garnished with parsley.

A limit of three colors is not a hard-and-fast rule. There will be salads whose flavor combinations override the color rule, as in a mixed-fruit salad that might have a whole rainbow of color. But as long as a salad has at least three colors, there is no need to add ingredients or garnishes just to add more color.

There are no precise formulas for choosing and arranging colors in a salad. Colors are like flavors: Some go well together and some don't. Bell pepper and tomato colors complement each other; carrot and tomato together create color confusion. The way to learn to handle color in a salad is to experiment with it and follow good examples of other people's work.

UNITY

Creating unity in a food presentation can be compared to putting round pegs in round holes. Unity refers to the relationship of the whole salad to the serving piece on which it is presented. The layout of the salad must fit the shape of the salad plate.

Salads are usually presented on round plates. This means that the lines, forms, and shapes of the salad ingredients must be arranged in a pattern that fits harmoniously into a circle. The pattern may repeat the curve of the plate's edge, or echo its roundness on a smaller scale, or complement it with balance and symmetry.

The pattern begins with the rim of the plate. Never place anything on the rim; it is the frame of your design. If you use a lettuce liner you can arrange it in a circle within the rim to repeat the shape.

The examples given here illustrate how various patterns can be used to complement the circular shape of the plate. Figure 14.4 is a salad of sliced tomato served with egg wedges. Not all these items are round, but they are placed in a circular pattern. This not only unifies the salad but also adds implied height by focusing the eye on the center of the plate.

Figure 14.5 is an arrangement of cucumber slices. They themselves are little circles, and when placed in a circular arrangement, they echo and re-echo the roundness of the plate, creating a unified presentation. Parsley sparks the pattern with contrast.

The cold luncheon plate follows the same rules of presentation. Figure 14.6 shows a harmonious arrangement of the salad–sandwich luncheon plate described earlier.

Figure 14-5 CIRCLES IN CIRCLES ON A CIRCLE

Figure 14-4 ODD SHAPES CAN FORM A CIRCULAR PATTERN

Figure 14-6 SYMMETRICAL ARRANGEMENT FOR A SALAD–SANDWICH PLATE

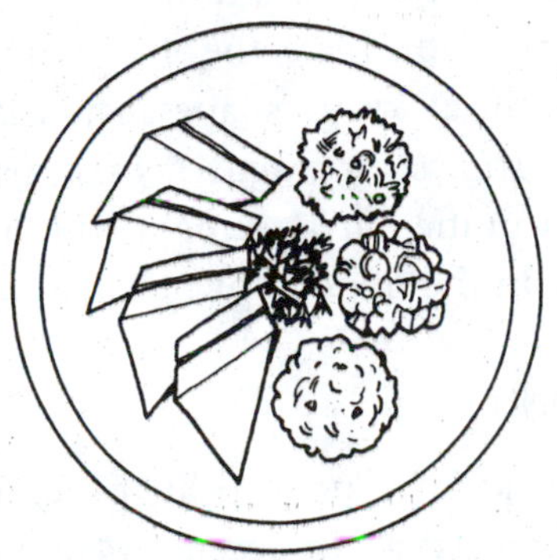

Figure 14-7 PLACING THE GARNISH

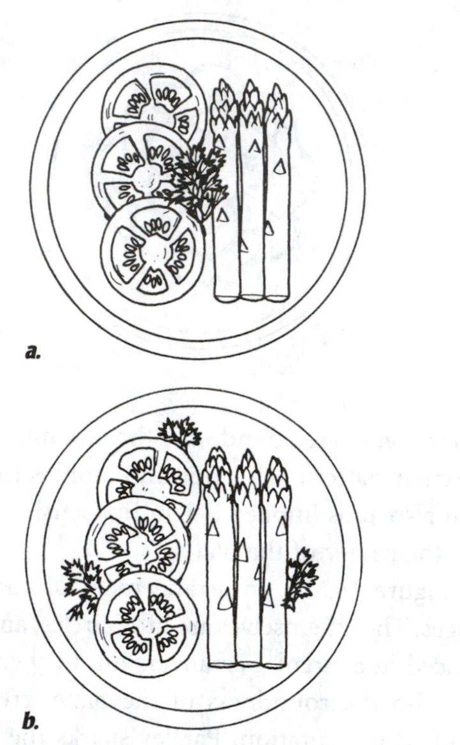

a. Grouping the parsley sprigs in the center pulls the salad together. ***b.*** Placing them symmetrically around the edge scatters the attention and creates a helter-skelter effect even though the arrangement fills out the round form of the plate.

A round lettuce liner can often help to unify a salad composed of stiff linear shapes or a diversity of shapes. Or, if the ingredients are grouped symmetrically and there is a focal point in the center of the plate, the effect is one of unity in spite of the awkward shapes. The salad in Figure 14.7a shows asparagus spears and tomato slices in a unified arrangement with a bouquet of parsley in the middle for height and focus.

GARNISHING

Many a salad is brought to life by an appropriate garnish used as an accent, a color contrast, or a focal point. On the other hand, there is no need to garnish a salad that is already colorful and well designed. An ingredient of the salad itself can often take over the function of a garnish by its position, shape, and color, and there is then no point to adding a further garnish.

The most effective garnish is something bright, eye-catching, contrasting in color, and pleasing in shape. The foods you can use are unlimited. Here are some of the most popular:

Watercress	Pimiento strips
Mint	Lemon slice or wedge
Parsley	Orange slice or twist
Olives, green or black	Hard-boiled egg slice, half, or quarter
Radishes	Berries
Pickles	Cherries
Cherry tomatoes	Grapes
Tomato wedges	Fruit wedge
Pepper rings	Nuts, chopped or whole
Sliced mushrooms	Crumbled cheese

But don't limit your imagination to these. Look at the raw materials available to you in terms of bits of shape and color and be creative. Do limit your choice to things compatible in taste and spirit with the salad itself.

Use your garnishes in odd numbers—one, three, five. Stick to one garnish or a group of such go-togethers as a black olive, a green olive, and a cherry tomato. Place the garnish or group of garnishes in one spot only. To make this point clear, look at the bad example in Figure 14.7b and the good example in Figure 14.7a. The one on the bottom scatters the attention; the one on the top concentrates the attention and thus helps to unify the presentation. The garnish must always be planned as part of the total presentation.

Keep in mind that a garnish should play the

role of an accent and should not steal the show. Garnishes cut into fancy shapes may draw attention to themselves and diminish the salad, as an overdressed woman is outdone by her jewels and furs. In addition, the labor cost of creating such garnishes cannot be justified for the individual salad plate.

GUIDELINES FOR MAKING GOOD SALADS

The job of making salads can be a challenging, enjoyable, and creative endeavor. Here is a summary of the essentials for producing eye-catching, appetizing, and tasty products:

- Use fresh, high-quality ingredients.
- Choose ingredients for compatibility of flavors, textures, and colors.
- Plan your presentation carefully in terms of height, color, and unity. Keep it simple. Do not overcolor. Do not overgarnish. Do not cover the edge of the plate.
- Serve salads well chilled on chilled plates.

SALAD DRESSINGS

Most salads include a dressing. Sometimes, it is an integral part of the salad, as in coleslaw or tuna salad or marinated vegetables. More often, the dressing is a separate companion to the body of the salad. We can define a **salad dressing** as a liquid or semiliquid served with or on a salad to give it specific flavor.

Most salad dressings fall into two categories, those having an oil-and-vinegar base and those based on an egg-and-oil emulsion. Most unthickened dressings have a base of vinegar and oil, while most thickened dressings are emulsion-based using mayonnaise. Let us examine each type in turn.

OIL-AND-VINEGAR DRESSINGS

The simplest group of salad dressings consists of those having an oil-and-vinegar base—the unthickened dressings. These date back to ancient times. Olive oil with lemon was used in the ancient Persian empire. The Greeks and Romans ate salads dressed with olive oil and vinegar. They dipped their bread in the same mixture.

The primary ingredients of this group of dressings are oil, vinegar, and water. Each ingredient has its variations. There are, for example, many oils. Some common ones are:

- Olive oil
- Peanut oil
- Canola oil
- Corn oil
- Soybean oil
- Peanut oil

Descriptions of these oils, as well as others, are found in Table 14.1.

Popular vinegars include *wine vinegars* (made from white wine, red wine, rosé wine, rice wine, champagne, or sherry), *cider vinegar* (made from apples), *white vinegar* (distilled to have a neutral flavor), and *balsamic vinegar.* Balsamic vinegar, a dark-brown vinegar with a rich sweet-and-sour flavor, is made from the juice of a very sweet white grape and is aged for at least 10 years. Vinegars can also be infused, or flavored, with all sorts of ingredients, such as chili peppers, roasted garlic, or any herbs, vegetables, and fruits. These types of vinegars are called *flavored vinegars.* For example, lemon vinegar works well in salad dressings and cold sauces.

In this text, the term vinegar means distilled white vinegar unless another vinegar is specified.

The difficult part of making an oil-and-vinegar dressing is achieving the proper balance of

Table 14-1 VEGETABLE OILS

Oil	Characteristics/Uses	Oil	Characteristics/Use
Canola oil	Light yellow color Bland flavor Good for frying, sautéing, and in baked goods Good for salad dressings	Peanut oil	Pale yellow color Mild nutty flavor Good for frying and sautéing Good for salad dressings
Corn oil	Golden color Mild flavor Good for frying, sautéing, and in baked goods Too heavy for salad dressings	Safflower oil	Golden color Bland flavor Has a higher concentration of polyunsaturated fatty acids than any other oil Good for frying, sautéing, and in baked goods Good for salad dressings
Cottonseed oil	Pale yellow color Bland flavor Good for frying, sautéing, and in baked goods Good for salad dressings	Sesame oil	Light golden color Distinctive, strong flavor Good for sautéing Good for flavoring dishes and in salad dressings Use in small amounts Expensive
Hazelnut oil	Dark amber color Nutty, smoky flavor Not for frying or sautéing as it burns easily Good for flavoring finished dishes and salad dressings Use in small amounts Expensive	Soybean oil	More soybean oil is produced than any other type, used in most blended vegetable oils and margarines Light color Bland flavor Good for frying, sautéing, and in baked goods Good for salad dressings
Olive oil	Varies from pale yellow with sweet flavor to greenish color and fuller flavor to full, fruity taste (color and flavor depend on olive variety, level of ripeness, and how they were processed) Extra virgin or virgin olive oil—don't cook with because it burns, good for flavoring finished dishes and in salad dressings, strong olive taste Pure olive oil—can be used for sautéing and in salad oils, not as strong as olive taste as extra virgin or virgin	Sunflower oil	Pale golden color Bland flavor Good for frying, sautéing, and in baked goods Good for salad dressings
		Walnut oil	Medium yellow to brown color Rich, nutty flavor For flavoring finished dishes and in salad dressings Use in small amounts Expensive

Recipe 14-8 OIL-AND-VINEGAR DRESSING (VINAIGRETTE)

YIELD: ***1 quart (1 L)***

3 C	**salad oil**	**750 mL**
1 C	**wine vinegar**	**250 mL**
1 Tb	**salt**	**15 mL**
1 tsp	**white pepper**	**5 mL**

1. Blend ingredients together vigorously until a temporary emulsion forms.
2. Repeat just before use.

Per ounce:		Carbohydrates:	0 g
Calories:	180	Cholesterol:	0 mg
Fat:	20 g	Fiber:	0 g
Protein:	0 g	Sodium:	218 mg

the primary ingredients. If the oil predominates, it gives the dressing an oily taste. If there is too much vinegar, it drowns out everything else.

Recipe 14.8 gives you a good basic ratio. This simple dressing is called a **vinaigrette.** The standard ratio of oil/vinegar in a French dressing, also called vinaigrette, is 3 parts oil to 1 part vinegar. The ratio given here should be used only as a guideline. Depending on the ingredients being used, as well as the cook preparing it, the ratio may have to go up or down. Also, if using a very strong vinegar, the vinegar may have to be diluted a little with water.

To make an oil-and-vinegar dressing, blend everything together vigorously at room temperature until an emulsion forms. The emulsion will be very temporary and must be re-formed at the moment the dressing is served. There is an old saying that you need a miser to pour in the vinegar, a spendthrift to add the oil, a counselor for the salt, and a madman to shake it all up.

Basic oil-and-vinegar dressing can be used to create many different dressings by adding ingredients to alter the flavor. Here are a few common additives:

Chopped onion	Sugar
Chopped egg	Hot sauce
Chopped pickles	Roquefort cheese
Chopped capers	Parmesan cheese
Chopped parsley	Lemon
Chopped herbs	Lime
Chopped chives	Bacon bits
Crushed peppercorns	Honey
Crushed garlic	Worcestershire sauce
Paprika	Dill
Prepared mustard	

Recipes 14.8a and 14.8b show variations of vinaigrette dressings using some of these ingredients.

Oil-and-vinegar dressings are not as perishable as the emulsified dressings because they contain no eggs and have a high acid content. However, they deteriorate in flavor rapidly. For this reason, it is advisable for optimum flavor to

Recipe 14-8a VINAIGRETTE II

YIELD: ***1+ quart (1+ L)***

$1^1/_2$ pt	**oil**	**750 mL**
$^1/_2$ pt	**vinegar**	**250 mL**
2	**eggs, hard-cooked, chopped**	
1 oz	**onions, chopped fine**	**30 g**
2 Tb	**minced parsley**	**30 mL**
2 tsp	**minced chives**	**10 mL**
	salt and pepper to taste.	

Blend ingredients together vigorously. Salt and pepper to taste.

Per ounce:		Carbohydrates:	0 g
Calories:	186	Cholesterol:	13 mg
Fat:	21 g	Fiber:	0 g
Protein:	0 g	Sodium:	4 mg

Recipe 14-8b ITALIAN DRESSING

YIELD: ***1 quart (1 L)***

$1^1/_2$ pt	**olive oil**	**750 mL**
$^1/_2$ pt	**wine vinegar**	**250 mL**
$1^1/_2$ tsp	**puréed garlic**	**7 mL**
1 Tb	**oregano**	**15 mL**
	salt and pepper to taste.	

Blend ingredients together vigorously. Salt and pepper to taste.

Per ounce:		Carbohydrates:	0 g
Calories:	179	Cholesterol:	0 mg
Fat:	20 g	Fiber:	0 g
Protein:	0 g	Sodium:	0 mg

make no more than a day's supply at a time, although many operations do. If kept overnight, such dressings should be refrigerated. They must be brought to room temperature before service so that the temporary emulsion with its blend of flavors can be re-created.

EMULSIFIED DRESSINGS

The model of all the emulsified dressings is **mayonnaise,** a flavored, seasoned emulsion of egg yolks and oil. If you can make mayonnaise, you can make all the others.

MAYONNAISE. Mayonnaise is a base, or mother sauce, for many salad dressings as well as some important cold sauces. It is also a dressing in its own right.

The origins of mayonnaise go back to a sauce the Romans made by adding egg yolks to an oil-and-garlic sauce that they had borrowed from the Egyptians. Somewhere along the way, the garlic was dropped but the emulsion was kept, thus creating mayonnaise.

It later became a custom in many European towns to have an annual mayonnaise parade. Every chef in town would enter the parade with his bowl of mayonnaise, each one a little bit different, a little bit special. Today's garde manger, too, is likely to have a specially flavored version.

Recipe 14.9 provides a formula for a basic mayonnaise. Before studying it, you may want to review the principles of emulsion in Chapter 8.

Let us review the recipe a step at a time. You begin with the egg yolks (make sure they are very fresh), using six per quart of oil. You whip them with the flavorings you've added until the mixture is smooth and well blended.

Add the oil very slowly (Step 2), especially in the beginning, to keep the emulsion from break-

Recipe 14-9 MAYONNAISE

YIELD: ***1+ quart (1+ L)***

2 Tb	**vinegar**	**30 mL**
2 Tb	**lemon juice**	**30 mL**
1 tsp	**dry mustard**	**5 mL**
6	**egg yolks**	
1 qt	**salad oil**	**1 L**

1. Add half the vinegar and lemon juice and all the mustard to the egg yolks and whip until blended and light in color.
2. Very slowly add oil, whipping rapidly to make an emulsion.
3. When you have added half to three-fourths of the oil, whip in the balance of the vinegar and lemon juice; then slowly whip in remaining oil.
4. Season to taste.

Per ounce:		Carbohydrates:	0 g
Calories:	252	Cholesterol:	40 mg
Fat:	28 g	Fiber:	0 g
Protein:	1 g	Sodium:	1 mg

ing. Add it in a slow, steady stream, whipping all the time, as you did when adding butter in butter sauces (Figure 8.7). If you are making the dressing by hand, place a folded wet towel under the bowl to steady it.

Adding the remaining vinegar and lemon juice midway (Step 3) will tend to stabilize the emulsion. You can add them earlier if your dressing becomes too thick to whip.

The finishing step (Step 4) is to season to taste (subdued taste for a basic dressing) when your emulsion is complete.

If these procedures and precautions look familiar, it is because they should. The making of mayonnaise is very similar to making a butter sauce. But there are some major differences. The eggs are not cooked, the flavor base is not a reduction, and the proportions are different. Egg yolks will hold far more than warm butter—about twice as much.

One more precaution: The ingredients for the mayonnaise should be at room temperature before you start. The reason for this is that cold oil does not readily separate into the tiny fat droplets that are necessary for a stable emulsion. The other ingredients should be the same temperature as the oil in order for emulsion to take place.

You can thin mayonnaise if it is too thick by beating in a few drops of water. If it is too thin, you can thicken it by starting over with new egg yolks and whipping the thin dressing into them. As with butter sauces, this can also be a way of dealing with a broken emulsion.

Mayonnaise is a basic dressing and should be treated as such. Be very careful not to overflavor it with specific ingredients. Keep it uncommitted—bland—so it can go in any direction. For the same reasons, use a mild-tasting vegetable oil rather than olive oil. The latter has a distinctive flavor that is not usually appropriate in a basic dressing.

Seasoning a basic mayonnaise is simpler than seasoning a hot sauce because there is no cooking. The sauce will not be reduced, so there will be no change in the proportion of seasoning to volume of sauce. Therefore, seasoning can be done either before or after the basic mayonnaise is used to make finished dressings. The one potential problem might come in adding a flavoring having a high salt content, such as anchovies, to an already salted mayonnaise.

Finished dressings are made from basic mayonnaise in the same way that finished sauces are made from mother sauces—by seasoning or by adding specific flavors and ingredients to a basic dressing. When we look at finished dressings as a group, however, we find that there are few standard recipes. Each person or establishment may take great pride in a particular recipe for a dressing. Such a dressing is often referred to as a house dressing, and its individuality may well contribute to the success of the house.

Although specific recipes are often well-guarded secrets, there are some general characteristics for certain popular dressings. One or two ingredients may vary, but the general concept is the same. Recipes 14.9a and 14.9b give you two examples made from basic mayonnaise. In addition, you can make:

- *Russian:* mayonnaise, pickle relish, chopped egg, chopped pimiento, seasonings
- *Creamy Roquefort:* mayonnaise; sour cream; Roquefort cheese, crumbled; seasonings
- *Chantilly:* mayonnaise, whipped cream, lemon juice, nutmeg
- Green goddess: mayonnaise, sour cream, anchovy, garlic, tarragon, parsley, chives, seasonings
- *Dill:* mayonnaise, chopped fresh dill

Recipe 14-9a THOUSAND ISLAND DRESSING

YIELD: ***1+ quart (1+ L)***

1½ pt	**mayonnaise**	**750 mL**
½ C	**chili sauce**	**125 mL**
½ C	**catsup**	**125 mL**
6	**eggs, hard-cooked, chopped**	
2 oz	**onion, chopped**	**50 g**
2 oz	**dill pickles, chopped**	**50 g**
	salt and pepper	

Blend mayonnaise, chili sauce, and catsup. Fold in remaining ingredients. Season with salt and pepper to taste.

Per ounce:		Carbohydrates:	3 g
Calories:	172	Cholesterol:	52 mg
Fat:	17 g	Fiber:	0 g
Protein:	2 g	Sodium:	235 mg

Recipe 14-9b BLUE CHEESE DRESSING

YIELD: ***1+ quart (1+ L)***

1 C	**mayonnaise**	**250 mL**
1 C	**blue cheese**	**250 mL**
2 C	**sour cream**	**500 mL**
	juice from 1–2 lemons	
1 Tb	**crushed black pepper**	**15 mL**
2 tsp	**puréed onion**	**10 mL**
1	**garlic clove, puréed**	
	salt and pepper to taste	

Blend mayonnaise, cheese, and sour cream. Fold in remaining ingredients. Season to taste with salt and pepper.

Per ounce:		Carbohydrates:	1 g
Calories:	90	Cholesterol:	13 mg
Fat:	9 g	Fiber:	0 g
Protein:	1 g	Sodium:	105 mg

EMULSIFIED FRENCH DRESSING. Another base used for thickened dressings is called **emulsified French dressing.** A typical formula is given in Recipe 14.10. To make it, you apply techniques similar to those used in making mayonnaise to ingredients similar to those in oil-and-vinegar dressings. The result is that the oil and acids and flavorers are held in suspension in the correct proportions, emulsified by the eggs. This makes a dressing that doesn't have to be blended every time it is served, as an oil-and-vinegar dressing must be, with the chance of too much oil or vinegar being served on a salad. Yet the dressing is thin enough to coat leafy greens.

Paprika, garlic, shallots, herbs, and flavored vinegars and oils offer many ways to vary this basic recipe. The dressing that Americans term French (and the French call American) is a tomato-flavored, sweetened version of this basic dressing. Try using the flavorings from Recipes 14.8a and 14.8b in the emulsified French dress-

Recipe 14-10 BASIC EMULSIFIED FRENCH DRESSING

YIELD: ***1 quart (1 L)***

4 oz	**vinegar**	**125 mL**
2 oz	**lemon juice**	**60 mL**
2	**egg yolks or 1 whole egg**	
1½ pt	**oil**	**375 mL**
	salt and white pepper to taste	

1. Add half the vinegar and lemon juice to eggs and whip until blended and light colored.
2. Add oil slowly to make an emulsion.
3. When half the oil has been added, blend in remaining vinegar and lemon juice.
4. Whip in remaining oil. Adjust texture by whipping in water or additional lemon juice or vinegar a few drops at a time until thin enough to pour.
5. For a finished dressing, season to taste with salt and white pepper.

Per ounce:		Carbohydrates:	0 g
Calories:	185	Cholesterol:	13 mg
Fat:	21 g	Fiber:	0 g
Protein:	0 g	Sodium:	1 mg

ing recipe and compare the texture and flavor differences in the two types of dressings.

Here are some of the flavorful finished dressings made from basic emulsified French dressing:

- *Russian:* French dressing, red caviar, seasonings.
- *Herb:* French dressing, parsley, chervil, oregano, chives, thyme, seasonings.

Herbs should be fresh if possible.

Literally hundreds of other finished dressings can be created by adding one or more of the following items to either basic emulsified French or basic mayonnaise—and this list is by no means exhaustive:

Blue cheese	Caviar
Roquefort cheese	Sweet relish
Parmesan cheese	Dill relish
Other cheeses, shredded	Sweet pickles
Sour cream	Dill pickles
Whipped cream	Brandy
Hard-cooked eggs	Vinegars of different flavors
Worcestershire sauce	Mustard
Tabasco sauce	Fruit juices
Catsup	Fruit rind
Chili sauce	Grapes
Anchovies	Avocado
Capers	Diced vegetables
Ham	Curry powder
Garlic	Chili powder
Fine herbs	Currant jelly

Mayonnaise and emulsified French dressing have a limited shelf life. They must be refrigerated because of their raw-egg content. The vinegar and lemon juice they contain retard bacterial growth. However, they really should be used within three or four days because they lose flavor.

Emulsified dressings actually improve in the first 24 hours as their flavors blend. Then they begin to suffer flavor loss or change. This is particularly true of finished dressings containing onions, garlic, fresh herbs, parsley, and anchovies, all of which turn bitter after a short time. Emulsified dressings should be stored tightly covered in glass or plastic containers, away from foods having odors.

COOKED SALAD DRESSINGS

Cooked salad dressings (Recipe 14.11) are made by thickening a body of milk with a starch thickener and sometimes eggs, with appropriate flavorings and seasonings added. The cooked starch or egg or both form a thickening

Recipe 14.11 COOKED SALAD DRESSING

YIELD: ***10 ounces***

1	**egg**	
3/4 C	**hot milk**	**185 mL**
2 Tb	**flour**	**30 mL**
1 Tb	**sugar**	**15 mL**
1/4 tsp	**salt**	**1 mL**
	cayenne as needed	
2 Tb	**butter**	**30 mL**
1/4 C	**white vinegar**	**60 mL**

1. Beat the egg slightly with a wire whip and add the milk gradually.
2. Combine flour, sugar, salt, and cayenne and mix in the top of a double boiler. Heat and let cool.
3. Add the milk mixture slowly and cook over hot water, stirring until the mixture thickens.
4. Add the butter and vinegar.
5. Refrigerate.

Per ounce:		Carbohydrates:	3 g
Calories:	50	Cholesterol:	30 mg
Fat:	4 g	Fiber:	0 g
Protein:	1 g	Sodium:	99 mg

agent that prevents the oil from separating out upon standing, although only a small amount, or no, oil is used. It is similar in appearance to mayonnaise, but its flavor is more pronounced and tart.

PREPARED DRESSINGS

In many kitchens, salad dressings are purchased already prepared. Prepared dressings are frequently used as bases to which specific ingredients are added to make special finished dressings. It is common, for example, to stock mayonnaise in quantity and make it into Thousand Island, blue cheese, and other dressings as needed. Some prepared salad dressings must be kept refrigerated at all times. Many other dressings must be refrigerated only after opening.

Various finishing ingredients are also available as dried dressing mixes, and they are becoming very popular. You simply add X number of packages to Y amount of basic dressing according to package instructions, and the job is complete. Some of these may be added to buttermilk or cottage cheese as a base to produce tasty low-calorie dressings.

The motivations for using prepared products are certainly valid. Labor is a prime cost in the food industry, and there is a lot of labor in the making of salad dressings. As a result, unless a particular establishment uses enough of the product to warrant the labor, it is likely to choose packaged products.

In terms of quality, the dressings made from scratch are often better than commercially prepared dressings, though the commercial product tends to be more consistent. Dressings made from scratch allow for the expression of individual skill and the creation of that certain flavor people will come back to savor again.

Recipe 14-12 YOGURT DRESSING

YIELD: ***21/2 cups (600 mL)***

1 C	**plain nonfat yogurt**	**250 mL**
1 C	**sour cream**	**250 mL**
$^1/_2$ C	**honey**	**125 mL**
	nutmeg and lemon juice to taste	

1. Blend all ingredients thoroughly.
2. Flavor with nutmeg and lemon juice to taste.

Per ounce:		Carbohydrates:	8 g
Calories:	53	Cholesterol:	4 mg
Fat:	2 g	Fiber:	0 g
Protein:	1 g	Sodium:	15 mg

The imaginative cook can also use other commercial products as bases for dressings. Sour cream and yogurt as well as cottage cheese and buttermilk may be used alone as bases or mixed with other dressings. In fact, you can try almost anything that has a promising texture and a suitable flavor.

Recipe 14.12 is an example of a dressing using sour cream and yogurt as a base. Honey is added to tame the tart yogurt flavor to go with a fruit salad such as the fruit platter in Recipe 14.5.

PUTTING DRESSING AND SALAD TOGETHER

Some people think a salad is not a salad until it has a dressing on it. Others prefer their salad with no dressing at all. Still others will eat only one kind of dressing, no matter what the salad. Because of this variety of tastes, it is customary in American restaurants to offer the guest a salad with a choice of dressings. And, since most salads require the dressing to be added at the last minute, it is often the customer who adds it.

In planning a dressing or a choice of dressings for a salad, keep in mind the purpose of any dressing: It is meant to dress a salad. The dressing should not mask or overwhelm the body of the salad but should blend, contrast, complement, or otherwise enhance it. For example, salads made from mild, tender lettuces such as Boston and Bibb should not be subjected to dressings whose strong taste or heavy texture disguises or drowns the very qualities for which the lettuces are chosen.

There are few rules to curb your imagination in putting dressings and salads together, but some things do go together better than others.

- Vegetables, both raw and cooked, go well with dressings having an acid taste such as vinegar or lemon.
- Meats, fish, shellfish, and poultry typically have dressings with subtler flavorings—herbs, curry, condiments such as mustard or horseradish, tomato (for fish or shellfish), brandy.
- Fruits go well with such sweet–tart dressings as poppy seed or honey and lime.
- Emulsified dressings are usually used when the salad is intended to stay together, as most cooked salads are. They are also typical choices for gelatin salads.
- Oil-and-vinegar dressings or very thin emulsified dressings are usually used when a salad is tossed at tableside.

But, in most instances, the cook does not choose a specific dressing for a salad. Instead, the diner is offered a choice of three or four. For example:

- An oil-and-vinegar dressing, probably a basic dressing or an Italian
- An emulsified dressing, such as French, Thousand Island, or Russian
- The most popular dressing in town
- A house dressing—the cook's specialty

There are very few salads for which there is one specific dressing and no other. Of the few whose body and dressing are inseparable, the most familiar is the Caesar salad. It was invented, so the story goes, by a restaurateur named Caesar in Tijuana, Mexico, who was faced with unexpected numbers of guests and ran out of everything but eggs, romaine, and some stale bread. His solution was to toast cubes of the bread with oil and garlic, coddle the eggs (he simmered them 1 minute), toss it all together with a flourish, along with some zesty flavorings—crushed peppercorns, lemon juice, Parmesan cheese—and serve it as the specialty of the house. The tableside ceremony of putting it all together with a flourish is traditionally as much a part of this salad as the romaine and the dressing.

COLD SAUCES

Cold sauces are thickened, seasoned liquids that are used like hot sauces to enhance dishes of meats, poultry, fish, and vegetables. The reason you find them in this chapter is that most of them are like emulsified dressings in every way but use. In fact, most of them are made from basic mayonnaise as the mother sauce. Like salad dressings, cold sauces are a product of the garde manger or pantry department.

The cold sauces that derive from mayonnaise are just like the emulsified salad dressings from the standpoint of production, handling, and storage. The difference is in their use and in the requirements imposed by use.

The key factors to consider when preparing a cold sauce are:

- The base consistency
- The kind of meat or other product it is to enhance
- A logical balance of flavors

The consistency must meet the description of an ideal sauce, one that seems to be in motion. Because the sauce is cold, it will not run as freely as a hot sauce, but it should be pourable.

The kind of dish with which the sauce is to be served will determine the kinds of products used to flavor it. For example, lemon and dill will complement fish. Fruit flavors will complement game. The options are wide open, but logic must be used in making choices.

Here are a few well-known cold sauces that have mayonnaise as the mother sauce. The mini-recipes show you their structure and proportions.

- *Tartar sauce* (Recipe 14.13). Generally served with fried fish.

Recipe 14-13 TARTAR SAUCE

YIELD: ***Approximately 1 quart (1 L)***

1 qt	**mayonnaise**	**1 L**
1 oz	**dill pickles, chopped**	**30 g**
1 oz	**capers, chopped**	**30 g**
1 tsp	**dry mustard**	**5 mL**
	salt, white pepper, and lemon to taste	

Blend all ingredients.

Per ounce:		Carbohydrates:	1 g
Calories:	198	Cholesterol:	16 mg
Fat:	22 g	Fiber:	0 g
Protein:	0 g	Sodium:	187 mg

Recipe 14-14 RÉMOULADE SAUCE

YIELD: ***5 cups (1250 mL)***

1 qt	**mayonnaise**	**1 L**
4 oz	**Dijon-style mustard**	**120 g**
2 oz	**green onions, finely chopped**	**60 g**
1 oz	**capers, finely chopped**	**30 g**
1 oz	**celery, finely chopped**	**30 g**
1/2 oz	**garlic, puréed**	**15 g**
2 Tb	**lemon juice**	**30 mL**
	salt and white pepper to taste	

1. Blend all ingredients.
2. Add salt and white pepper to taste.

Per ounce:		Carbohydrates:	1 g
Calories:	163	Cholesterol:	13 mg
Fat:	18 g	Fiber:	0 g
Protein:	0 g	Sodium:	157 mg

- *Rémoulade* (ray-ma-lahd) (Recipe 14.14). Served with shellfish; often offered as a "choice of" cocktail sauce along with red sauce.
- *Sauce verte* (vairt) (Recipe 14.15). Served with fish, cold meats and poultry, and cold vegetables.

Another widely used cold sauce is the cocktail sauce for cold shrimp and crab, often called red sauce. It is not based on mayonnaise but uses a blend of tomato products such as catsup, chili sauce, and tomato paste or purée, flavored with horseradish and fresh lemon juice and seasoned. Like many of the hot tomato sauces, it does not derive from a mother sauce. It is made from scratch or bought in prepared form.

Cold sauces are handled and stored following the same rules that apply to salad dressings. Anything having a mayonnaise base must be kept under refrigeration. Cocktail sauce, with its many

Recipe 14-15 SAUCE VERTE

YIELD: ***5 cups (1250 mL)***

5 oz	**parsley**	**150 g**
10	**spinach leaves**	
1 qt	**mayonnaise**	**1 L**
1 tsp	**lemon juice**	**5 mL**
	salt and white pepper to taste	

1. Purée greens in food chopper or blender and squeeze juice through cheesecloth into mayonnaise along with lemon juice.
2. Add salt and white pepper to taste.

Per ounce:		Carbohydrates:	1 g
Calories:	160	Cholesterol:	13 mg
Fat:	18 g	Fiber:	0 g
Protein:	0 g	Sodium:	128 mg

acid ingredients, is much less susceptible to spoilage and health hazards. But it, too, should be refrigerated, not only for health reasons but because it is served with chilled foods.

SUMMING UP

The pantry area of the kitchen produces some of the most interesting and attractive foods on the menu. Here the cook works not only with flavor and texture but with color and shape and visual harmony as well. The products of this kitchen area fill many menu roles—openers, entrées, accompaniments, whole meals, party fare. The principal categories are salads, salad dressings, and cold sauces.

Salads fall naturally into six categories—leafy green, vegetable, cooked, fruit, combination (more than one ingredient type), and gelatin. Within each category, the possibilities of tasty and attractive ingredient combinations are almost limitless.

Most salads are served with a dressing, usually added at serving time. Dressings are of two types—oil and vinegar and emulsified. Oil-and-vinegar dressings require only the right proportions and vigorous blending. Making an emulsified dressing, such as mayonnaise, is more complicated, rather like making a butter sauce. A wide variety of flavorful ingredients can produce hundreds of different dressings, including house specialties.

Most cold sauces are made by adding distinctive ingredients to a basic mayonnaise. A few are made with tomato products as the base. Cold sauces typically accompany fish, seafood, cold meats and poultry, or cold vegetables.

In all cold foods, presentation shares top honors with flavor in creating customer-pleasing products. A well-presented salad or buffet tray will have color, height, and unity to please the eye and stimulate the appetite.

To the uninitiated, the amounts of time, labor, and tender loving care that go into foods that never get near the fire can be eye-opening. Cold food production is a facet of food preparation that can challenge both the innovative culinary artist and the lover of tradition. The payoff for such efforts is obvious as salads and other cold foods increase in popularity almost before our eyes.

The Cook's Vocabulary

aspic
clear or unflavored gelatin
combination salad
cold sauce
cooked salad dressing

cooked salad
dressing
emulsified French dressing
fruit-flavored gelatin
fruit salad
gelatin or congealed salad
leafy green salad
mayonnaise
salad dressing
vegetable salad
vinaigrette

Review Questions

Answer each question in complete sentences. Read each question carefully and make sure you answer all parts of the question. Organize your answer into more than one paragraph when appropriate.

1. What are the six types of salads and how is each one different?
2. List the components of vinaigrette, mayonnaise, emulsified French dressing, and cooked salad dressings. Compare and contrast.
3. In your opinion, what makes a salad bar appeal to customers? Consider actual items that might be offered as well as presentation and freedom of choice.
4. How do the principles of height, color, and unity apply to salads? Do they apply to foods other than salads? If so, which ones and why? If not, why not?
5. If you were asked to use fruits in a cocktail, a salad entrée, and an accompaniment to a poultry entrée, what fruits would you choose for each, how would you present each one, and how would the portions compare?
6. What cold sauces, if any, would you serve with a hot dish?
7. What is it about cold food preparation that challenges creativity?

Chapter 15

HORS D'OEUVRES AND FOOD PRESENTATION

Hors d'oeuvres are another type of food created in the pantry or garde manger department. They are bite-sized pieces or small portions of foods served to stimulate the appetite. Usually, they are very sharp or spicy in taste to wake up the taste buds and make the diner hungry—or thirsty, as the case may be. The ancient Greeks called them "provocatives to drinking" and served them at their version of the cocktail party—a bring-your-own-goatskin-of-wine affair. Included were such items as roasted grasshopper, marinated octopus, and spiced meats wrapped in grape leaves.

Hors d'oeuvres comes from a French expression that literally means "outside the meal" foods. Indeed, the term hors d'oeuvres is sometimes used interchangeably with the term appetizer. **Appetizer** refers to the first course of a meal and features small portions of food meant to stimulate the appetite. Although appetizers share some similarities with hors d'oeuvres, hors d'oeuvres are normally finger foods that are served at receptions and cocktail parties.

It would be impossible to list the many different kinds of hors d'oeuvres. They range all the way from a simple glass of tomato juice to medallions of goose liver pâté in aspic.

The best planned hors d'oeuvres, or any part of the menu, may falter and fail at any moment unless the presentation is well done. A haphazard arrangement of food on a plate can turn off the appetite. An aesthetically pleasing plate can sharpen it. The look of the plate—the diner's first impression of the food on it—is a matter well worth the most careful thought and study.

After completing this chapter, you should be able to:

- Describe the characteristics of canapés, crudités, dips, cocktails, and hot hors d'oeuvres.
- Explain how to prepare hors d'oeuvres in quantity.
- Design plate and platter presentations.
- Plan buffet setups.

HORS D'OEUVRES

The variety of hors d'oeuvres is astonishing. Fortunately, we can break them down into two broad categories: hot or cold. Cold hors d'oeuvres include canapés, crudités, dips, and cocktails. Let's start by looking at these.

CANAPÉS

A **canapé** (can-a-pay) is a bite-sized or two bite-sized finger food consisting of three parts: a base, a spread or topping, and a garnish or garniture. Designed for eye as well as taste appeal, canapés are made in assorted shapes, arranged attractively on trays, and served from the cocktail buffet or passed to the guests.

Canapé bases can be made from a number of foods:

- Breads—white, rye, French, pumpernickel
- Croutons
- Pastry shells
- Cream puff shells
- Melba toast
- Crackers of many varieties

Melba toast and crackers make the simplest bases. They come in assorted standard sizes, shapes, and textures and are all ready for topping and garnish. Breads are more trouble; they must be sliced and cut into shapes—squares, rectangles, circles, triangles, diamonds, and so on. Pastry shells are usually purchased readymade. They come in various shapes ready to hold spicy or cheesy fillings or meat pastes. Croutons are usually made from scratch and commonly take the most preparation time of all the bases.

The **crouton** (kroo-tahn) is a buttered bread shape baked in the oven until crisp and brown. Like other types of canapé bases, croutons are made in a great variety of shapes. (Small cubes of bread fried with herbs and spices and used as garnitures for soups and salads are also called croutons.)

The best way to make croutons for canapé bases is to start by cutting pullman bread lengthwise, as Figure 15.1 shows. You can freeze the bread lightly and use a slicing machine for even thickness. Then you cut your circles, squares, or other shapes from these large slices. Figure 15.2 shows some pleasing shapes.

Figure 15-1 SLICING A PULLMAN LOAF FOR CANAPÉS—LENGTHWISE

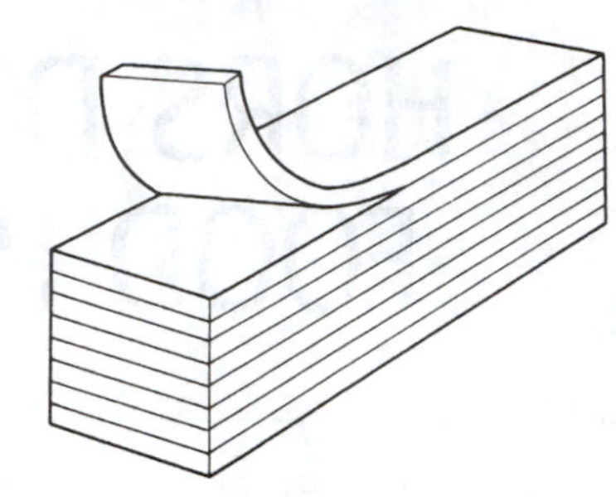

Once you have cut the crouton shapes, use Recipe 15.1 to finish them. Croutons made this way can be stored dry for several days and remain crisp.

But once you have made a crouton into a canapé, you can run into a major problem—keeping it crisp when it is in contact with a moist

Figure 15-2 POPULAR SHAPES FOR CANAPÉ BASES

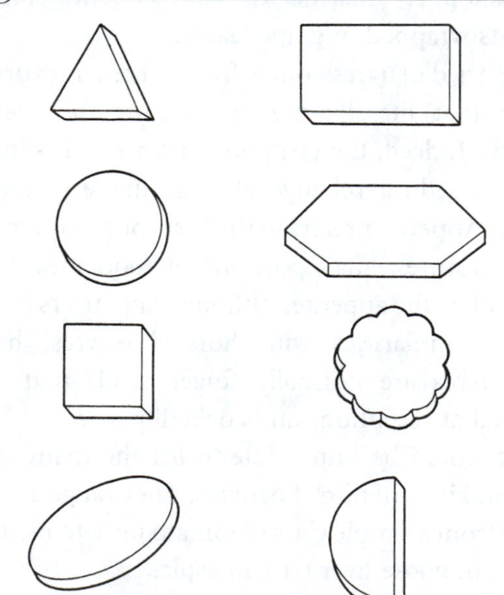

Recipe 15-1 CROUTONS

day-old bread
melted butter as needed

1. Cut bread up into desired shapes for croutons.
2. Coat a sheet pan with butter.
3. Lay bread shapes on buttered pan and brush with melted butter.
4. Bake at 450°F (230°C) until crisp and brown—about 5–8 minutes. Watch carefully.

Per 1/2 ounce:		Carbohydrates:	9 g
Calories:	65	Cholesterol:	1 mg
Fat:	3 g	Fiber:	0 g
Protein:	2 g	Sodium:	174 mg

spread or topping. One way to avoid this problem is to brush the croutons with egg white before they are baked. The baked egg white provides a coating that prevents the croutons from absorbing moisture.

Now, let's consider the second part of the canapé—the topping or spread. It should be something that clings nicely to the base and holds the garnish, so that the canapé does not fall apart in the guest's fingers. Choose it together with the garnish with two things in mind—eye appeal and taste. "Eye-appealing" and "appetizing" go together; we eat with our eyes as well as our taste buds.

Canapés should be sharp in flavor. Sharp contrasting flavors are often used together on the same piece. In creating contrast, you may use sweet/sour, salty/bland, strong/mild, but avoid flavors that do not blend well. A good match would be a mustard butter spread with a ham garnish.

Here are some examples of spreads:

Caviar
Chicken salad
Cheese spread
Egg salad
Flavored butters—such as lemon butter or mustard butter
Flavored cream cheese
Ham salad
Liver pâté
Salmon salad
Shrimp salad
Tuna salad

Many types of butters, meat or fish spreads (Recipe 15.2), and cheeses can be used for toppings.

Garnishes might be capers; olives; slices of eggs, pimientos, bell peppers, or carrots; chopped parsley; or onion. The sole requirement for matching toppings and garnishes is harmony of taste and appearance.

Make each small creation neat, trim, fresh, bright, precisely garnished, and exactly like its brothers of the same kind. They are then ready for arrangement on a tray.

Recipe 15-2 SHRIMP SPREAD

Yield: *Approximately 1 quart (1 L)*

1 lb	**cooked shrimp**	**500 g**
1 C	**mayonnaise**	**250 mL**
2 oz	**minced onion**	**60 g**
1/2 oz	**chopped capers**	**15 g**
	salt, white pepper, and lemon juice to taste	

1. Purée shrimp.
2. Blend mayonnaise, onion, and capers with shrimp.
3. Season to taste with salt, white pepper, and lemon juice.

Per ounce:		Carbohydrates:	0 g
Calories:	67	Cholesterol:	29 mg
Fat:	6 g	Fiber:	0 g
Protein:	3 g	Sodium:	63 mg

Canapés can be made with inexpensive ingredients and efficient use of labor and equipment. At the other end of the scale are the expensive shellfish, caviar, smoked salmon, and puréed meat creations, garnished with precision and flair by the skilled garde manger. Enormous amounts of time and labor can be spent in creating mouth-watering, eye-appealing canapés, and the price per bite can be high indeed.

To the cook or garde manger, they are a versatile and challenging species. Let your taste and imagination run wild. Then work with precision and care to make a fresh, attractive, professional-looking product even from such everyday ingredients as cream cheese, eggs, and olives.

CRUDITÉS

Crudités, also known as relishes, are raw, crisp vegetables such as julienne carrots or celery sticks. Popular vegetables for crudités also include radishes, broccoli and cauliflower florets, sweet peppers, cherry tomatoes, cucumbers, and scallions.

Recipe 15-3 ROQUEFORT OR BLUE CHEESE DIP

YIELD: ***1 pint (500 mL)***

8 oz	**cream cheese**	**250 g**
6 oz	**Roquefort or blue cheese, crumbled**	**175 g**
$^1/_2$ C	**light cream**	**125 mL**
2 tsp	**lemon juice**	**10 mL**
2 Tb	**onion, finely chopped**	**25 mL**

1. Beat cream cheese until soft and fluffy.
2. Blend in remaining ingredients.

Per ounce:		Carbohydrates:	1 g
Calories:	102	Cholesterol:	28 mg
Fat:	9 g	Fiber:	0 g
Protein:	4 g	Sodium:	193 mg

Recipe 15-4 BEAN DIP

YIELD: ***8 1 cup servings (250 mL)***

1 tsp	**vinegar**	**5 mL**
$^1/_4$–1 tsp	**chili powder**	**1–5 mL**
2 oz	**onion, chopped**	**60 g**
2 Tb	**mayonnaise**	**30 mL**
$^3/_4$ C	**pinto or kidney beans, cooked, drained, mashed**	**185 mL**
3 Tb	**celery, chopped**	**45 mL**
4 oz	**tortilla chips**	
$^1/_2$ C	**salsa**	

1. Mix vinegar, chili powder, and onion with mayonnaise in a bowl. Add beans and celery; mix well.
2. Serve with tortilla chips and salsa.

Per serving:		Carbohydrates:	15 g
Calories:	134	Cholesterol:	3 mg
Fat:	8 g	Fiber:	2 g
Protein:	3 g	Sodium:	149 mg

To be used as cold hors d'oeuvres, crudités must be of the highest quality. In other words, they must be fresh and unblemished. Crudités are normally served with dips, our next topic.

DIPS

Dips are informal hors d'oeuvres made with softened cheese, sour cream, mashed avocado, bean purée, or foods of similar consistency flavored to complement crisp, bite-sized foods that are dipped into the product. Recipes 15.3 and 15.4 are examples. The dippers can be chips, crackers, or crudités as just discussed.

Dips are inexpensive, easy to make in volume, and simple to serve—a bowl of dip, a dish of dippers. They hold well and make good buffet items.

COCKTAILS

Most people are familiar with the **cocktail** via the ever-popular shrimp and crab cocktails. The typical cocktail consists of several bite-sized pieces of fish, shellfish, or fruit served with a highly flavored sauce. In the fruit cocktail, the "sauce" would probably be fruit juice flavored with a liqueur or perhaps a bite-sized topping of tangy sherbet. Oysters and clams on the half shell belong to this group of appetizers. The familiar crab cocktail is presented in Recipe 15.5.

OTHER COLD HORS D'OEUVRES

There are many other cold hors d'oeuvres that do not fit into the categories of canapés, crudités, dips, or cocktails. Here are some examples:

- *Cheese:* bite-sized cubes. Cut them shortly before serving because they dry out quickly when exposed to air.

Recipe 15-5 CRAB COCKTAIL

YIELD: ***1 portion***

$1^1/_2$ oz	**crabmeat**	**45 g**
1	**lettuce leaf**	
1 oz	**shredded lettuce**	**25 g**
1 fl oz	**red or rémoulade sauce**	**25 mL**
1	**lemon wedge**	

1. Pick over crabmeat to remove shells.
2. Line plate with lettuce leaf. Top with mound of shredded lettuce.
3. Arrange crabmeat attractively on shredded lettuce. Top with sauce; garnish with lemon.

Per serving:		Carbohydrates:	3 g
Calories:	57	Cholesterol:	43 mg
Fat:	1 g	Fiber:	0 g
Protein:	9 g	Sodium:	344 mg

Recipe 15-6 DEVILED EGGS

YIELD: ***12 portions***

12	**eggs, hard-cooked**	
1 fl oz	**milk**	**30 mL**
6 Tb	**mayonnaise**	**175 mL**
$^1/_2$ tsp	**dry mustard**	**2 mL**
1 fl oz	**vinegar**	**30 mL**
	salt to taste	

1. Peel eggs and cut in half lengthwise.
2. In mixing bowl, mash yolks. Blend in milk, then mayonnaise, mustard, and vinegar.
3. Season to taste with salt.
4. Using pastry bag with plain or star tube, pipe about $1^1/_2$ Tb (20 mL) of yolk mixture into each half egg white.
5. Refrigerate.

Per 2 egg halves:		Carbohydrates:	1 g
Calories:	129	Cholesterol:	216 mg
Fat:	11 g	Fiber:	0 g
Protein:	6 g	Sodium:	102 mg

- *Cheese balls:* bite-sized balls made of cheese blends such as crumbled Roquefort, cream, and grated cheddar. Chill them; roll them in finely chopped nuts or parsley just before service.
- *Deviled eggs:* hard-cooked eggs—the whites stuffed with a spread made from the yolks (Recipe 15.6) or with a spicy meat or fish spread.
- *Ham rolls:* thin slices of cold ham rolled around pickles or asparagus spears or filled with a spread or mousse.
- **Antipasto** (ann-tee-pahs′-toe or ann-teep-ahs′-toe; Italian for "before the food"): a small plate or tray of flavorful bite-sized cold foods—smoked oysters, olives, marinated vegetables, spicy cold meats, fish, shellfish, cheese, and such. The origin of this elegant hors d'oeuvre

was an Italian chef's ingenuity in using far-from-elegant leftovers.

- *Liver pâté* (pah-tay): specially seasoned chicken liver or goose liver paste glazed or baked in a crust, sliced, and served cold.

HOT HORS D'OEUVRES

There is no end to the variety of hot hors d'oeuvres. By mixing and matching a countless number of ingredients, you can create traditional, as well as signature, hors d'oeuvres.

Let's take a look at some of the possibilities:

- Mini-meatballs with sauce, such as Swedish meatballs
- **Brochettes**—small skewers containing meat, poultry, fish, shellfish, or vegetables
- Pastry shells with hot fillings
- Phyllo dough or wonton skins filled with meat, poultry, fish, shellfish, or vegetables, such as a miniature egg roll
- **Rumaki**—bacon wrapped around a food, such as chicken livers or olives, and then cooked
- Breaded and fried meat, poultry, vegetables, and cheese

Figure 15.3 and Recipes 15.7 to 15.9 give even more possibilities.

PREPARING AND HOLDING HORS D'OEUVRES

One person at a party may be expected to eat a total of five or six different hors d'oeuvres and canapés. As you can see, serving a party of 500 could mean making and arranging 3000 or more. The cold-food expert must work with patience and staying power as well as skill and care.

Production must be planned carefully because most canapés and hors d'oeuvres do not hold well. Crisp canapé bases will absorb moisture from their toppings or from the moist air of the cooler. Soft bread canapé bases will dry out quickly if exposed to air. Toppings and garnishes will soon lose their fresh look, and even their contrasts of flavor can blur in time. Cheese cubes will harden and develop ugly, brittle edges. The peaks and ridges of deviled-egg fillings will become crusty.

The solution is to prepare the various parts of these mini-foods separately ahead of time and assemble them as close to serving time as possible. Dry canapé bases, stored dry, keep well for

Figure 15-3 HOT HORS D'OEUVRES

Beef and mushroom turnover
Broccoli cheese puff
Broccoli and cheddar quiche
Buffalo wings
Burrito
Calzone
Chicken cordon bleu
Chicken fingers
Chicken kebab on a skewer
Clam casino
Coconut shrimp
Figs stuffed with turkey wrapped in bacon
Frank in blanket
Mushroom and onion phyllo
Pizza bagel
Potato and onion pierogi
Sausage pizza puff
Shrimp toast
Spinach phyllo
Stuffed cabbage
Vegetable tempura
Zucchini sticks

Recipe 15-7 STUFFED MUSHROOMS

YIELD: ***24 stuffed mushrooms***

24	**medium mushrooms**	
	melted butter as needed	
1/4 lb	**sausage meat**	**125 g**
1/2 C	**shredded mozzarella cheese**	**125 mL**
1/4 C	**bread crumbs**	**60 mL**

1. Wash and pat dry mushrooms.
2. Remove stems from mushrooms. Chop stems. Set aside.
3. Brush mushroom caps with melted butter and set aside.
4. Cook sausage over medium heat until well browned. Drain sausage on absorbent towel.
5. Cook mushroom stems in sausage drippings until tender, about 10 minutes. Remove from heat.
6. Add sausage, cheese, and bread crumbs to pan and stir well.
7. Fill mushroom caps with sausage mixture. Bake at 400°F (200°C) for 10–15 minutes until mushrooms are tender and tops are lightly browned.

Per mushroom:		Carbohydrates:	1 g
Calories:	44	Cholesterol:	10 mg
Fat:	4 g	Fiber:	0 g
Protein:	2 g	Sodium:	78 mg

several days. Bread bases may be cut ahead, but must be kept moist or frozen. Some bread-based canapés can be made ahead and frozen, if their toppings are foods that freeze well. Butters and spreads hold well in the cooler (cover them); some even improve in flavor. But bring them to room temperature before attempting to apply them. Garnishes may be cut ahead, meats sliced, sauces prepared.

Many canapé and hors d'oeuvre ingredients are good bacteria growers—fish, poultry, meats, eggs, egg products—and must not stay long at kitchen temperatures. Keep both raw ingredients and assembled products out of danger zone temperatures while you are working. Chill finished platters before service: Once served, they may have to stay at room temperature for an hour or more before being eaten.

Summing up, here are some general rules for holding:

- Keep holding times for finished products as short as possible.
- Keep moist ingredients moist and dry ingredients dry, and assemble the two kinds as close to use time as possible.
- Keep cold foods cold and hot foods hot, not only for taste and eye appeal but for safety's sake.
- Plan production carefully, with all these other rules in mind.

Recipe 15-8 PUFF PASTRY CHEESE TWISTS

YIELD: ***10 servings***

1	**sheet puff pastry dough (10 × 15 in.) (250 cm × 375 cm)**
2	**beaten eggs**
	Parmesan cheese, grated as needed

1. Roll out sheet of puff pastry dough.
2. Brush with beaten egg; then sprinkle with Parmesan cheese.
3. Use a pastry wheel to cut narrow strips.
4. Pick up each strip and twist it.
5. Arrange twists on sheet pan, pushing ends down.
6. Bake at 375°F (185°C) until puffed and lightly browned.

Per serving:		Carbohydrates:	9 g
Calories:	138	Cholesterol:	51 mg
Fat:	10 g	Fiber:	0 g
Protein:	3 g	Sodium:	153 mg

Recipe 15-9 PUMPERNICKEL–MUENSTER CANAPES

Yield: ***16 appetizers***

8 oz	**Muenster cheese**	**250 g**
1	**onion, sliced thin and separated into rings**	
4	**pumpernickel bread slices**	

1. Place cheese slices and onion slices evenly on top of bread.
2. Place on a sheet pan and broil for 3–5 minutes until cheese is bubbly and light brown.
3. Cut bread slices into triangles and serve immediately.

Per serving:		Carbohydrates:	6 g
Calories:	83	Cholesterol:	13 mg
Fat:	4 g	Fiber:	1 g
Protein:	4 g	Sodium:	144 mg

Appetizers of all kinds provide an avenue for using leftovers and odds and ends, if these are fresh and attractive. This adds profitability to the virtues of these delightful foods. Wide variety and attractive presentation contribute to the success of any party and any operation.

PLATE PRESENTATION

But not all menu planners design plate layouts, and not every menu is planned with plate presentation in mind. Some à la carte menus, in fact, do not offer groups of foods together, and a plate's contents may not be known until the order is turned in to the kitchen. The look of the plate becomes the cook's responsibility.

Though the cook has less flexibility than the menu planner, many a cook has devised many an attractive plate presentation using only foods the menu dictates plus an occasional garnish. With a good knowledge of foods, some rules, and some practice, the cook is well equipped to do a good job.

It is also up to production personnel to see that planned plate layouts are carried out with precision at dish-out time. Some of the remarks in the following discussion apply as much to carrying out a plate design as they do to planning it.

You have learned a good deal about presentation in making salads. Many of the same rules apply to main-dish presentation. In addition, there are a few special ones. Let's talk about the following:

- Don't cover the plate edges.
- Keep garnishes simple and use only when necessary.
- Consider color and unity.
- Position all foods on the plate for the diner's convenience.
- Preserve the identity of individual foods.
- Plan portion sizes in relation to one another.
- Use hot plates for hot food and cold plates for cold.

The border of the plate should never have food on it. Not only should the layout be planned within the borders, but the drips of sauce or juices that might be spilled during dish-out should be carefully removed. Clean plate edges are mandatory.

Garnishes used properly can be profitable. Unnecessary garnishes are costly. To add a garnish simply because you feel you need to garnish everything is a useless and wasteful practice. Many plates do not need garnishes. If they are full and the foods themselves possess all the color necessary, a garnish simply adds confusion. Where a garnish is needed, it should be planned into the layout and its cost should be included in the menu price.

Providing color for a plate of hot foods presents more of a challenge than working with color in cold foods. Many cooked foods have brown and gold tones. Brilliance of natural color is often lost through cooking.

The careful menu writer plans the vegetable accompaniments for main dishes specifically to give color. Two yellow vegetables, for example, do not provide color contrast. When a yellow or red vegetable is served, a green vegetable will give the necessary color contrast.

When the menu writer has not considered color, it becomes the responsibility of the cook to add imaginative garnishes to give the color needed.

Unity is provided by the arrangement of food on the plate. As with cold foods, you want a pattern harmonious with the shape of the plate. The trick is to use food shapes and relationships to create this harmony. Keep the center of the plate in mind and work around it. At the same time, you should balance the colors in the arrangement. Sometimes, an awkward combination of shapes can be avoided by cutting the vegetable differently. Sometimes, it is better to change the vegetable or to add a second vegetable or a garnish. This is a good reason for planning plate layouts before the menu is frozen on a printed card. Sometimes, an oval plate substituted for a round one will solve the problem.

Look carefully at the plate layout patterns in Figure 15.4 to see how food combinations can be laid out to maintain unity and color balance. Notice how color and color contrast have been supplied either by the menu or by the addition of garnishes. The ingredients tend to rotate around the center of the plate, creating unity.

There are rules of service that may complicate the plate layout. The main dish is presented directly in front of the guest, as the illustrations

Figure 15-4 PLATE PRESENTATION

a. New York steak, baked potato, asparagus, broiled tomato.

b. New York steak, baked potato, broiled tomato, parsley. Notice that color contrast is supplied by adding a garnish.

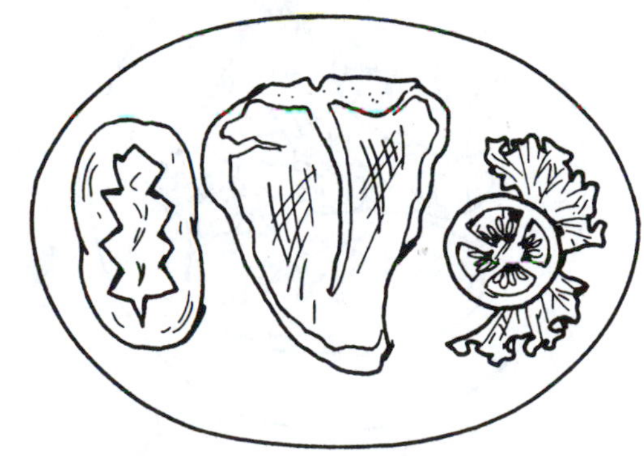

c. T-bone steak, baked potato, garnish of sliced tomato and curly endive.

(*Continued*)

Figure 15-4 (continued)

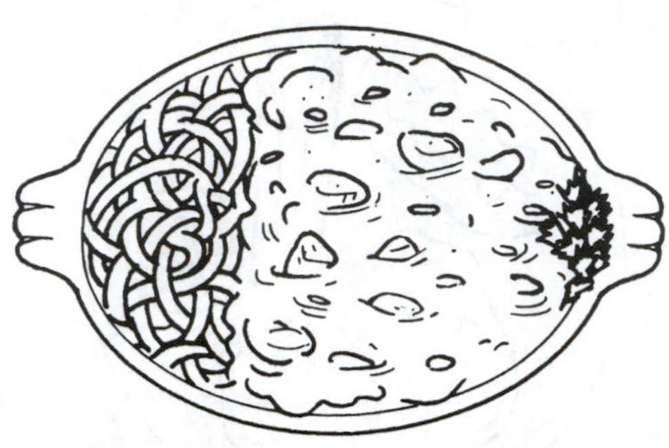

d. Chicken stew in tureen, noodles, parsley.

e. Potato salad, sandwich.

f. Chicken Kiev, rice, Belgian carrots, asparagus.

g. Mexican platter: enchiladas topped with shredded lettuce, cheese, diced tomato with taco, rice, beans.

h. Sliced calf's liver with onions, noodles, sauteed pineapple rings, parsley.

i. Lobster tail, cup of butter, parsley, half lemon.

show. When meat having a fat or bone side is presented, that side should be turned away from the guest. If there is no fat or bone, there is no problem.

These rules force you to work with the meat in a more or less fixed position. It becomes your focal point, which is what you want it to be anyway.

Notice that the individual items in the drawings maintain their separate identities because they are neatly arranged. You can further maintain identity by straining excess liquids from vegetables and using no more than the proper amount of a sauce that is part of a dish.

When determining portion sizes, the menu writer should think of them in relation to one another on the plate, and the production crew should carry out the specifications to the letter. Otherwise, it is possible for the wrong item to become the main object on the plate. Too large a baked potato could make a steak look like a garnish.

Last but not least, always present hot foods on hot plates and cold foods on cold plates. You can blow the whole thing—the days of planning, the hours and hours of production—by allowing a hot meal to be served cold.

BUFFET PRESENTATION

A good buffet sells itself by its visual presentation—the appeal to the senses that whets the appetite. It must be designed as a whole for continuous visual impact. Within the overall design, individual dishes should be designed according to their position on the buffet. Here are the main considerations that underlie the visual art of buffet presentation:

- Height, color, and unity
- Simplicity
- Lasting appeal
- An effect of plenty

HEIGHT, COLOR, AND UNITY

The concepts that govern the design of individual salads apply equally to the design of the whole buffet. Height gives the buffet stature and focus; color sparks interest; unity provides harmony and order.

Height is achieved in many ways. Built-up shelves or empty soft-drink boxes, suitably covered, are often used to add actual height. Tall floral arrangements, candelabra, and even ice carvings are used to lift the line of sight.

Color is essential to a good buffet, but it should be kept simple. Because of the great variety of foods on a buffet, the salad rule of no more than three colors is impractical; nevertheless, food colors should not reach the stage of riot and confusion. There should be a sense of plan and order. This means careful menu design with color in mind and careful layout so that colors next to one another harmonize rather than clash, complement rather than cancel one another out.

Unity on the buffet as a whole means unity in the style of service and in the dishes and utensils. If elegance is the keynote, food will be served on silver, mirrors, and crystal, with silver serving utensils. A buffet for a German Oktoberfest party might use homespun tablecloths and wooden serving dishes and utensils. Platters and bowls should be similar in shape—all curves or all rectangles, not a hodgepodge of shapes and sizes. As with color, the goal is order and harmony. The appointments should complement the food, not detract from it.

SIMPLICITY

Simplicity in everything is the rule of thumb in setting up the buffet. Each individual dish must

Figure 15-5 SIMPLICITY

The garnish for the salad bowl on the left will still be there when the bowl is three-quarters empty. The one on the right will be a jumble after the first serving or two.

be developed in relation to the whole buffet. Garnishes must be kept simple on such items as salad bowls, relish trays, meat trays, and hot foods. If every dish is overgarnished, the combining of overgarnished dishes multiplies confusion and clutters the buffet.

You can see this in the salad bowls in Figure 15.5. The one on the left is garnished with tomato wedges around the edge, nothing more. This presentation is simple. The bowl on the right is elaborately garnished with cherry tomatoes, black olives, parsley, and whatever else the cook could find.

Although the second bowl may be attractive by itself, when displayed on a buffet it is bad for two reasons.

- It is so outstanding it does not complement the buffet as a whole.
- As soon as the first person is served, it loses all its beauty.

Simplicity can have interesting effects on the guests' attitudes. It is much easier to make choices from foods that are simply presented and easily identifiable than from presentations where design and color have taken over and the food is secondary. Timid guests may skip their favorite foods rather than spoil your platter designs, and then they'll feel frustrated with themselves and you.

LASTING APPEAL

It may seem impossible to expect lasting appeal in something that is being constantly diminished by hungry guests. Yet each person viewing the buffet and eating from it has as much right to have the total visual experience as the first person to pass. Remember, too, the guests at a buffet who wait in line gazing at the food while others are making their selections. You want their appetites to be heightened as they survey the display and plan their own selections. Poor layout and platters that lose their looks with the first few servings can easily take the appetite away.

A well-designed buffet will have elements and patterns that hold throughout service—its focal point, its height, its color, its unity, its overall harmonious arrangement of dishes and trays of food. Simplicity is important here. A simple layout will hold its pattern. It is easy to replenish. Platter arrangements of good, simple design will retain rhythm and color and focus when portions are gone. Even an empty tray will still function as part of the overall design.

AN EFFECT OF PLENTY

A good buffet is always full. This will do more than anything else to achieve lasting appeal. Nothing is more discouraging to the appetite than three series of almost empty serving dishes. Good planners in cafeterias, restaurants, and all kinds of buffet establishments make backup platters, bowls, and chafing dishes and hold them in readiness to replace a dish that runs out.

Some tricks of the trade can create the effect of plenty without risking large amounts of leftovers. A plate inverted in the bottom of a salad bowl will make a modest supply look inexhaustible. Platters placed fairly close together give a look of abundance, whereas too much bare tablecloth between dishes makes the total offering look skimpy. Whole foods such as a ham, a whole fish, or a large salad mold may share a platter with serving portions of the same food; these pieces help to fill the plate visually even when the serving portions are almost exhausted. Displays of whole fruits and blocks of cheese from which the guests cut their own portions give a continuing appearance of plenty.

PRESENTATION OF INDIVIDUAL DISHES

Each individual platter, bowl, or tray should take its starting point from its position in the overall buffet layout. The part the dish plays in the overall design can affect the size of the dish itself, the placement of its focal point, the type and size and color of its garnish, and the arrangement of portions on the dish. When you arrange a serving dish for buffet presentation, you must always think of how it will be viewed by the guest and how it will look in relation to its neighbors and to the buffet as a whole.

Salads form a major part of most buffets. They are usually presented in large bowls. These, in turn, are set on a bed of ice, as in the typical cafeteria, or with each salad bowl set in a larger bowl containing ice, as on a typical buffet. Congealed salads are often made in large molds of decorative shapes and presented on well-chilled platters laid on ice. Ring molds are popular, with a bowl of dressing or a contrasting garnish in the center.

Each salad bowl should have its simple garnish to complement the food or accent it. The most successful is a row of a suitable garnish arranged around the edge of the bowl (Figure 15.5). Helpings of the salad will be taken mostly from the middle of the bowl, especially if it is mounded to begin with, so chances are good that the ring of garnish will remain relatively unspoiled. For a coleslaw, for example, you might stand a row of overlapping pineapple slices along the rim. You might ring a bowl of potato salad with halves of hard-cooked eggs, a bowl of mixed-fruit salad with a single row of whole strawberries.

Salad dressings should be placed near the salads they are to dress. If this detail is left to someone who does not understand foods, you may have guests eating apricot glaze on a green salad and vinaigrette on a Bavarian cream.

Cold meats and vegetables, canapés, and many baked desserts are typically arranged in serving portions on flat serving dishes such as platters, trays, and mirrors. Some basic rules of presentation apply to all.

The basic design of a platter is a matter of using lines or rows of foods to create a simple, rather formal pattern. The rim of the platter is the frame of your design. Keep the food patterns within the rim. Not only does this look better, but it makes for easier service and fewer spills.

Once again in platter design, you meet the basics of height, unity, and simplicity. On a platter, height may be something that is physically higher than the rest of the platter or it may be implied height. The function of height is to give focus. You can supply height in several ways. You can use an unportioned piece of a food as a background to arranged portions of the same food, such as a piece of a whole ham on a platter of sliced ham. Or you can use a bowl of cold sauce, or a simple garnish such as parsley, or a cluster of small garnishes of a strong contrasting color—black olives, for example. Whatever it is, it should provide the focal point of your design.

You may have encountered the problem in Figure 15.6 before. The answer is that they are the same length. Line A looks longer because the angles at each end carry the eye outward. The angles on line B hold the eye to a smaller dimension.

Thus, the eye can be made to flow in the direction desired. By using patterns consisting of curves or lines that carry the eye flow in the direction you want it to go, you can make platters both interesting and effective.

Examine the patterns in Figure 15.7. Notice how, in all the figures but *a*, the tendency is for the eye to flow toward the circle. In *a*, the eye flows away. The effect is to sharpen the design in *b, c, d,* and *e* and to dissipate or flatten it in *a*.

In designing a platter, then, establish a focal point and lay out lines that cause the eye to flow to and from that point to create balance and

Figure 15-6 WHICH LINE IS LONGER, A OR B?

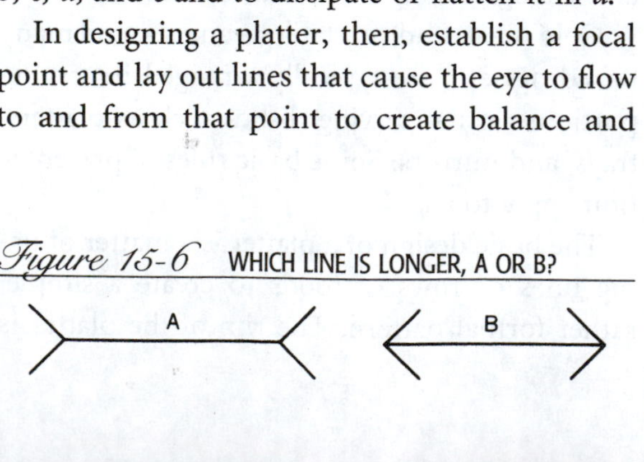

Figure 15-7 EYE FLOW

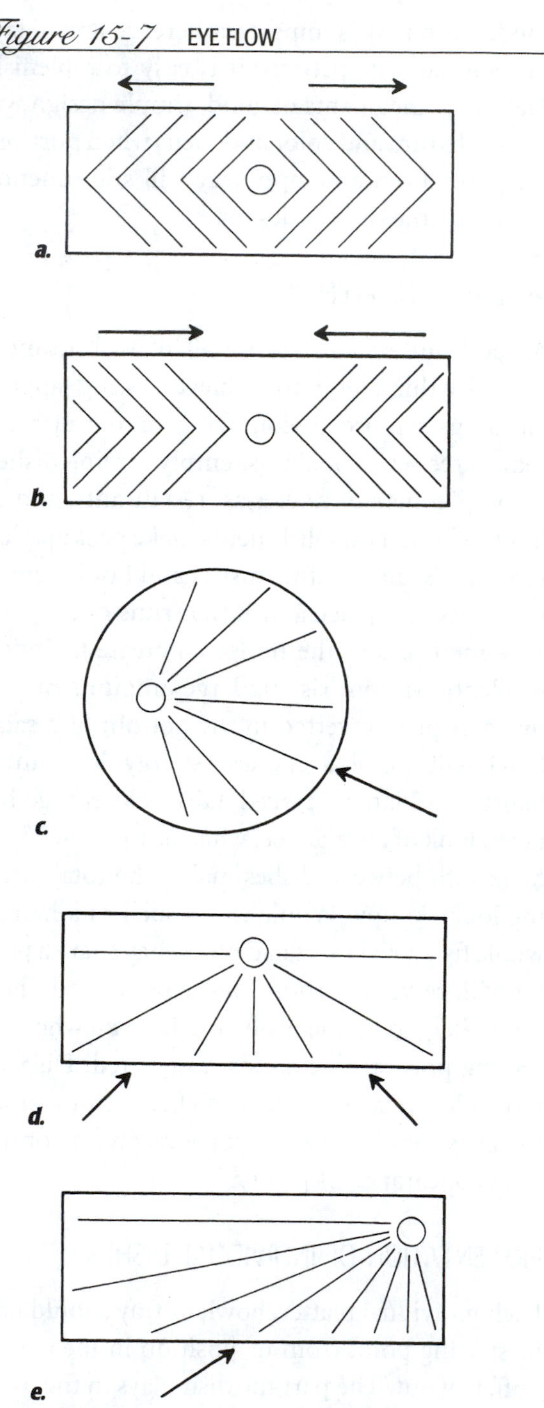

The eye follows the lines. Eye flow gives a flat design the illusion of height when the eye follows lines to a single point as in *b, c, d,* and *e.* Eye flow does nothing for *a,* because the eye does not focus on the center point but is led away.

Figure 15-8 UNITY

Simple line patterns that accentuate platter shape give unity to each.

height. Even if your focal point is physically as flat as the rest of the platter, eye flow will create the illusion of height.

Unity means the same thing in platter arrangement as it does in salads. The lines of your design—that is, your rows of food—should relate to the shape of the platter (Figure 15.8). On a round plate, they may be curves of a circle, or radiating spokes of a pinwheel, or S curves, or straight lines whose length and arrangement are fitted into the roundness. On a rectangular platter, straight or angled lines are harmonious with the shape. So are repeating curves that fit the shape neatly and fill it visually. The portions of food should be uniform in shape and size for a crisp, clean, linear look in your design.

Simplicity of design is important. The pattern should be straightforward and repetitive. This not only gives a pleasing rhythmic look but maintains the basic design while the food is disappearing from the platter.

The position of the platter on the table, plus the direction of traffic flow, will determine where you place your platter's focal point. Plan your presentation from the point of view of the guests as they first see it. Then you can plan your eye flow accordingly. In Figure 15.9, for example, the traffic is approaching from the left and the platter is angled toward the guest. The focal point is placed at the back of the platter, and the rows of food are arranged to face toward the guest and draw the eye toward the focal point.

Another factor to consider is the shape of the food items. You want to angle their best features toward the guest. For example, you would usually arrange wedge-shaped pieces so that the high back of the wedge is away from the guest and the triangular shape slopes forward. Likewise, you would layer rows of sliced foods, such as cold meats, so that the layers face the guests.

Sometimes a platter is positioned so that it is seen from all sides. You would then place your focal point in the center and work outward instead of from the corners or back line of the platter and buffet table.

No matter how you plan your design, the platter must be easy to serve. If getting a portion off the platter disrupts either the whole arrangement or the guest's composure, you have defeated the entire purpose of your display.

The professionally designed platter in Figure 15.8 was a prize winner in a culinary competition. Notice how the skilled specialist follows the simple basic principles of any buffet or platter presentation. Of course, the person who can do show work has added the mastery of advanced techniques and long experience, plus hours and sometimes days of labor for a single piece. But the techniques, experience, and labor are of little value without the basic principles. And these you can apply right now with simple foods using techniques you have already mastered.

PRESENTATION OF HOT FOODS

Most hot foods on the buffet are served from chafing dishes. Whenever possible, hot foods are arranged in portions. This not only looks attractive and makes service easy, it also provides some degree of portion control for these more expensive items. Hot foods are often served by staff, even when the rest of the buffet is self-service. This also helps in controlling portion size.

The fact is that hot foods are difficult to present visually. For appetite appeal, they depend more on their aroma and their reputation than they do on their natural beauty. They are not easily garnished for buffet service: Parsley wilts, and most of the other colorful garnishes used on cold foods do not go well with hot foods or, like parsley, lose their freshness with continued heat. Occasionally, chopped parsley is successful, or slices of parsleyed lemon with fish, or glazed fruits with ham or pork, or pimiento with vegetables or rice, or a bright cheese topping or buttery brown crumbs on a casserole. But, in general, garnishes on chafing dishes begin to look tired very quickly.

However, most hot foods do not need a great deal of attention to visual presentation. If they look as they should—fresh, hot, the fried chicken crisp, the asparagus plump and green, the rice

Figure 15-9 HORS D'OEUVRE PARISIENNE—A SIMPLE, STRAIGHTFORWARD DESIGN

Rows of beef medallions are interspersed with rows of complementary food portions—stuffed artichoke bottoms, tomato cases filled with asparagus, stuffed eggs. The fat sculpture provides focus and height. Its classic look blends with the simplicity of the tray design, yet softens the tray's repetitive regularity. Presentation on a mirror heightens the effect of simple elegance. (Photo by James C. Goering.)

light and fluffy, the baked potatoes mealy white—they sell themselves.

SUMMING UP

Hors d'oeuvres comes from a French expression that literally means "outside the meal" foods. Indeed, the term hors d'oeuvres is sometimes used interchangeably with the term appetizer. Appetizer refers to the first course of a meal and features small portions of food meant to stimulate the appetite. Although appetizers share some similarities with hors d'oeuvres, hors d'oeuvres are normally finger foods that are served at receptions and cocktail parties.

The variety of hors d'oeuvres is astonishing. Fortunately, we can break them down into two broad categories: hot or cold. Cold hors d'oeuvres include canapés, crudités, dips, and cocktails. Hot hors d'oeuvres might include fried vegetables, mini-meatballs, rumaki, or filled pastry shells.

When considering plate presentation, follow these golden rules. Don't cover the plate edges. Keep garnishes simple and use only when necessary. Consider color and unity. Position all foods on the plate for the diner's convenience. Preserve the identity of individual foods. Plan portion sizes in relation to one another. Use hot plates for hot food and cold plates for cold.

Here are the main considerations that underlie the visual art of buffet presentation: height, color, and unity; simplicity; lasting appeal; and an effect of plenty. Each individual platter, bowl, or tray should take its starting point from its position in the overall buffet layout. The part the dish plays in the overall design can affect the size of the dish itself, the placement of its focal point, the type and size and color of its garnish, and the arrangement of portions on the dish. When you arrange a serving dish for buffet presentation, you must always think of how it will be viewed by the guest and how it will look in relation to its neighbors and to the buffet as a whole.

The Cook's Vocabulary

antipasto
appetizer
brochette
canapé
cocktail
crouton
crudité
hors d'oeuvre
rumaki

Review Questions

Answer each question in complete sentences. Read each question carefully and make sure you answer all parts of the question. Organize your answer into more than one paragraph when appropriate.

1. Name the categories of hot and cold hors d'oeuvres. Give two examples from each category.
2. How are appetizers and hors d'oeuvres the same? How are they different?
3. What are the components of canapés?
4. Why is presentation important?
5. What are the essentials in a successful plate layout?
6. What are the essentials in a successful buffet presentation?

Chapter 16

THE BAKESHOP

In this chapter and the next, we look at still another specialized area of cooking—the production of breads, rolls, pies, cakes, and other dessert items. Baked goods and desserts are often neglected menu items that require only a little knowledge and creative flair to become people-pleasing stars. Even small operations can produce freshly baked breads or rolls and specialty desserts to increase profits and keep customers coming back.

Bread has a long history as a staple food, beginning with grain-and-water pastes baked on a hot flat stone—the ancestor of griddle cakes. Some form of pancake is found in every culture of the world.

Early Egyptians were probably the first to produce leavened bread by using wild yeasts and saving a bit of the fermented dough from one batch to start the next—the original sourdough "starter." The Egyptians also invented the oven. Rich Egyptians enjoyed some 30 different kinds of breads and cakes and even measured their wealth in loaves of bread.

Desserts and sweets originated with combinations of nuts and nut pastes, honey, milk, spices, fruits, and meal. Cheesecake was popular in both Greece and Rome. Baked custards were made in Greece and Rome but were considered suitable only for women and children. The art of puff pastry comes to us from Persia by way of ancient Greece.

Until the nineteenth century, methods of baking changed very little. The baker's oven, a dome-shaped brick structure, was still heated with hot coals, and the bread or pastry was set on the oven floor or hearth after the coals were scraped out. There was no way to control the temperature. During the nineteenth century, a stove with a coal-burning fireplace below the oven was invented. Gas and electric ovens soon followed. During the same period, chemical leaveners and commercial yeasts were developed, easing the baker's task.

Today's large commercial bakeries have specialized equipment for almost everything you can think of. But you can make most breads and pastries and sweets with the ovens and mixing equipment you find in the typical quantity kitchen, even without a separate bakeshop area. What you need is to know your ingredients well, to understand how they act and react in the heat of the oven, and to learn a few special techniques.

After completing this chapter, you should be able to:

- Understand and explain what happens in a dough or batter as it is baked.
- Describe the principal baking ingredients and explain the roles they play in baking.

- Scale ingredients accurately.
- Describe the differences in the major types of batters and doughs and explain mixing methods used for each type.
- Explain what is meant by makeup and how this process can turn out different products from the same batter or dough.

THE BAKING PROCESS

You are already familiar with baking as a cooking method—a dry-heat method in which heat is applied to a product by surrounding it with the hot air of an oven. You have learned how to bake vegetables, meats, poultry, fish, and casserole combinations of precooked foods to bring them to the desired degree of doneness.

But, in baking the products that we refer to as baked goods, the transfer of heat brings about far more complicated changes than the simple cooking to doneness that happens in baking a potato or a ham. Baked goods start out as doughs and batters, which are primarily flour-and-water mixtures with other ingredients added. When the heat of the oven travels through these mixtures, it brings about complex physical and chemical changes. The nature of the end product depends on many interactions between ingredients and on the way they are put together, and even small differences in ratios and proportions or in methods of mixing will produce very different results.

Doughs and **batters** are varied from the basic flour–water mix by using another liquid in place of water or by adding other ingredients—eggs, salt, sweetening, fats, leavening, flavoring—any or all of these. Yet all doughs and batters undergo the same basic changes as heat is conducted to and through the product and its temperature rises. In order to control these changes and produce consistently well-made baked goods, it is important to understand what takes place during the **baking process.**

As heat is applied and the temperature of the product rises, gases, such as carbon dioxide, steam, and bubbles of air, form and expand. These gases create the **leavening**, or increase in volume, that occurs during baking. They also increase digestibility and palatability by making the product tender and light.

As these gases expand, they are held within the dough or batter by certain protein substances in the flour known as **gluten.** Gluten has an elastic structure that stretches with the expanding gases yet is strong enough to contain them, forming a network of cells within the dough or batter. If all the gases escaped, the product would be heavy and tough.

As the temperature rises, starches in the flour absorb moisture, and at 150°F (65°C) they begin to firm, or gelatinize. When the product reaches 165°F (74°C), the proteins in the flour, and in eggs if they are present, begin to coagulate, and the elastic gluten stops expanding and becomes rigid. Gelatinization and coagulation contribute to the structure and chewiness of the finished product.

In this development of leavening and structure, correct baking temperatures are crucial. If the oven temperature is too high, coagulation will occur too quickly, the gases won't be able to expand enough, and the baked product will have insufficient volume. If the temperature is too low, coagulation may not occur soon enough and the product may collapse.

Along with these developments in leavening and structure, fats in the batter or dough melt and coat cell walls, which aids in tenderizing. Some fats, as they melt, release air bubbles that help to leaven batters, puff pastry, pie dough, and sponge cakes. Since different fats have different melting points, it is important to choose the correct fat for each use.

As the baking proceeds, some of the surface moisture evaporates and a crust forms on the outside of the product. The crust browns as certain ingredients react to the increase in the temperature of the product, caramelizing or undergoing other chemical changes that produce *browning*. Sugar is often responsible for this turn of events, but milk solids, gluten, and egg proteins also contribute to browning.

When all these processes have been completed, the dough or batter has become a loaf of bread, a cake, a batch of muffins, or whatever, and the product is done.

It is not surprising that bakers and pastry chefs call their recipes **formulas**, referring to the chemical reactions that must take place. There is no leeway in baking: The specific ingredients, the amounts, and their proportions must be followed exactly or the proper reactions will not happen and the product will not turn out as it should. Baking is a precise form of art.

INGREDIENTS AND THEIR FUNCTIONS

Let us look more closely at the most used baking ingredients and the roles they play in the character of the finished product.

FLOUR

Flour of one kind or another is the basic ingredient in baked goods. It performs many functions. As we have seen, it provides the structure and backbone of the finished product: It acts as a body builder as well as a binding agent. It also provides texture, flavor, absorbency, and keeping qualities. Nutritionally, flour contributes starch and protein, as well as small amounts of minerals, vitamins, sugar, and fat. Some flours are enriched with additional vitamins and iron.

Flour is a cereal product made by milling (grinding) the kernel of the grain (Figure 16.1). The flours most used in the bakeshop are made from wheat, because wheat contains the highest proportion of the proteins gliadin and glutenin, which combine to form gluten once the flour is moistened.

White flours are made from the starchy interior of the wheat kernel, which contains the gluten-forming proteins. There are two types of wheat, hard and soft, which make the flours used in every bakeshop—bread flour, cake flour, and pastry flour. Each provides the different qualities needed for different types of doughs and batters.

Bread flour is a strong flour made from hard wheat. It is capable of forming the long, strong gluten strands needed for such crusty, chewy products as French bread and hard rolls.

Figure 16-1 WHEAT KERNEL

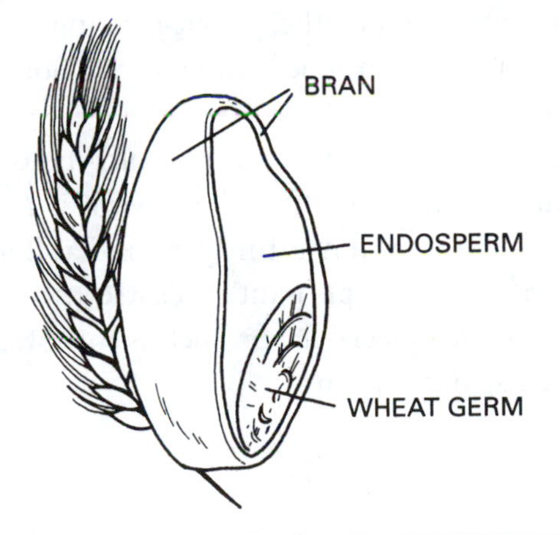

White flours are made from the starchy endosperm. Whole wheat flours are made from the entire kernel.

Cake flour, on the other hand, is known as a weak flour because it is made from soft wheat, which has a good deal less protein. This flour is useful in making soft, tender products such as high-quality cakes and doughnuts.

Pastry flour, another weak flour, has a slightly higher protein content. It is used in pie doughs, quick breads, muffins, biscuits, pastries, and some cookies—products that need a somewhat firmer structure than cakes.

A fourth familiar type of flour, *all-purpose flour*, contains slightly less gluten than bread flour. Because it is all purpose, it does not serve any one purpose as well as a specific flour type. Bakers tend to use the flours made for specific purposes.

Whole wheat flours are milled from the entire kernel. This makes them more nutritionally complete than white flours, but they make a heavier, denser product because their gluten is less elastic. For this reason, they are usually combined with a white flour in making muffins, breads, rolls, and even pie doughs.

Flours made from rye, soybeans, oats, and barley are sometimes chosen for specialty items or to provide menu variety. All these flours have protein, but it is not the gluten-forming kind. They are usually combined with a strong flour to provide gluten.

Meal, especially cornmeal, may also be used in combination with wheat flour. Meal is a cereal product that is not as finely ground as flour. Cornmeal makes pleasantly coarse-textured products with a special flavor, such as cornbread, corn sticks, and muffins.

LIQUIDS

Moisture is necessary to gluten development. Moisture means water specifically, not just any liquid. Oils, for example, are liquids, but they contain no moisture.

Most dough and batter formulas specify water or a milk product, which is mostly water. Other ingredients—eggs, butter, honey, molasses—may also contribute water. You will remember from Chapter 4 that water is the major ingredient in most foods.

Many milk products are used to add flavor, food value, and keeping qualities. They also improve texture: Here are the milk products most commonly used in baking.

Whole milk contributes both water and fat to the batter or dough. Skim milk has had virtually all of the butterfat removed. Buttermilk, since it is slightly acidic, is often used when the leavening agent in a formula is baking soda, which requires an acid to work with. Buttermilk also adds a special flavor and contributes to the tenderness of the finished product.

Dry milk powder, usually made from nonfat (skim) milk, has had all but a fraction of its water removed. It can be added with the dry ingredients in a formula that uses water as the liquid, or it can be reconstituted and added as liquid skim milk.

Cream is seldom an ingredient in batters and doughs but is used in the bakeshop in such dessert items as custards, puddings, fillings, and toppings. Its fat content is important. Half-and-half is 10 to 12 percent fat. It can replace heavy cream in some recipes for lower cost and fewer calories but will not whip up. Heavy cream and whipping cream have a range of 30 to 40 percent butterfat.

Eggs, being 75 percent water, contribute liquid in formulas. Other liquids are occasionally used in baking, such as beer in a coating batter or orange juice, molasses, or burnt sugar syrup for a special flavor.

LEAVENERS

Leavening is the process by which doughs or batters increase in volume through the addition of bubbles of gas. A **leavener** or **leavening agent** initiates the increase in volume by producing the bubbles. As you know, leavening is not complete until the bubbles have been trapped by the structure and the product can hold its shape. Without leavening, baked goods would be heavy, dense, and unpalatable.

Leavening can be achieved in four ways: with yeast, with chemical leaveners, mechanically—that is, by the mixing method—and by turning moisture into steam. The amounts of leaveners are small in comparison with the major ingredients, but the ratios are just as important as any other. Be very careful in measuring these critical ingredients!

YEAST. **Yeast** is a living plant that multiplies under favorable conditions, produces the gas carbon dioxide, and thereby creates light and appetizing rolls, breads, and sweet rolls from heavy doughs. Yeast also has other virtues. It increases digestibility and adds flavor.

The process by which yeast works is called **fermentation.** Three factors are necessary to this process: the right food, the right amount of moisture, and the right temperature. The right food is provided by sugars in wheat flour and by sugar itself. Moisture comes from liquids in the formula. The right dough temperature is 80°F (27°C). During fermentation, the yeast breaks down the sugars into carbon dioxide, alcohol, and water. Rising dough indicates the progress of this leavening action, which takes from 1 to 3 hours.

Fermentation continues until the dough is baked. At 140°F (60°C), the yeasts are killed, but by this time the bubbles they have made are trapped safely in a strong gluten framework. The alcohol evaporates during the baking.

There are two forms of yeast, compressed and active dry. Compressed yeast comes in a springy, yet firm grayish cake. To add it to the dough, you dissolve it in warm liquid from the formula—twice its weight or more. A temperature of 80 to 90°F (26–32°C) makes a good start. Active dry yeast is compressed yeast with the water removed. It is granulated and is either mixed with warm liquid from the formula or added to the dough with the dry ingredients. Since there are many different types of dry yeasts, you must follow the manufacturer's instructions carefully. Compressed yeast should be stored in the refrigerator. Active dry yeast should be stored in a cool, dry place.

CHEMICAL LEAVENERS. The principal chemical leaveners are baking soda and baking powder. **Baking soda**, like yeast, releases carbon dioxide to create its leavening action. To do this, it needs moisture and an acid ingredient to work with. Any of several things could provide the acid—cocoa or chocolate, honey, molasses, buttermilk, or fruit.

Unlike yeast, baking soda produces carbon dioxide without depending on heat. This means that batters made with soda must be baked very soon after mixing or the gases will escape. Baking soda is often used in cookies, muffins, and quick breads.

Baking powder is a combination of 1 part baking soda and 2 parts acid, usually cream of tartar. It is more stable than baking soda and it requires heat for maximum gas production. A baking powder batter can be held for a time without loss of its leavening power. Baking powder is used in biscuits and cakes whose formulas do not have the acid needed by baking soda.

MECHANICAL LEAVENING. Air bubbles may be incorporated mechanically into batters by two different mixing methods—creaming and foaming. In the heat of the oven, these air bubbles expand and act as leaveners.

The **creaming method** consists of whipping air into a fat–sugar combination until the mixture is light and fluffy. Pound cakes and some cookies rely on this method. The **foaming method** incorporates air by beating it into eggs. Whole eggs provide the foam that leavens sponge cakes, and foams from egg whites raise angel food cakes, soufflés, and meringues.

STEAM. Steam may be used as a leavener by vaporizing the moisture in the batter or dough during baking. Water converted to steam can expand up to 1600 times its original volume. This takes a high initial baking temperature: The water must reach 212°F (100°C) to vaporize. Products leavened by steam include pie doughs, cream puffs, popovers, and puff pastry.

EGGS

Eggs are versatile additions to batters and doughs, playing many roles in support of the major ingredients. Egg proteins assist gluten in providing structure. Eggs contribute moisture, since they are three-fourths water. The fat in the yolks can play the role of a shortening in some formulas. And, as noted, eggs become important leavening agents when whipped to incorporate air. Whole eggs when whipped can increase to four times their original volume, whites can reach eight times theirs, and yolks can achieve two and a half times their original volume.

In addition to these major functions, eggs add color, flavor, and texture to baked goods. They can turn a plain white batter golden or produce a shiny golden-brown crust on a pie or puff pastry. Eggs in a batter or dough enrich the flavor of the finished product.

Eggs have the remarkable quality of producing different textures. Whipped egg whites folded into batters make lighter, fluffier products. The yolks are natural emulsifiers: When whipped together with other ingredients, they help to hold batters together.

Besides whole fresh eggs, the bakeshop uses frozen eggs, both whole and separated. They save time and labor, provide consistent quality, and avoid waste since whites or yolks can be bought separately when whole eggs are not needed. But whole fresh eggs are essential when fresh flavor is important to the product.

In baking, you measure eggs by weight rather than by numbers of eggs because not all individual eggs or parts of eggs are the same size. Egg quantities in formulas are given by shelled weight. Chapter 13 contains more information on eggs.

FATS

Bakers use several types of fats, some vegetable and some animal. Their most important function is to shorten gluten strands. This enables a batter or dough to rise higher before the gluten becomes rigid, thus adding bulk as well as softening texture and tenderizing the product. Fat also enhances the keeping qualities of baked goods by retaining moisture.

Fats assist in leavening when they are used as creaming agents. Butter used in pie and puff pastry doughs also leavens by releasing steam, but fats that contain no water do not have this capability. Butter also adds flavor, and even fats with no flavor of their own subtly enhance the flavor of the finished product.

As you can see, the various kinds of fats do not perform alike in baking and are not interchangeable. Let us look at them individually.

Butter is a natural fat with a melt-in-the-mouth quality and flavor that is very desirable in certain desserts and pastries. It is about 80 percent fat, 5 percent milk solids, and 15 percent water, which gives it its leavening ability. Its low melting point has its drawbacks: It makes doughs based on butter more difficult to handle. Butter is also expensive. It is often mixed with shortening or margarine to lower the cost while retaining some of butter's best qualities.

Margarine is a butter substitute made from vegetable oils. Like butter, it contains some water (about 14 percent). It can sometimes replace butter or be mixed with it, but it lacks the distinctive butter flavor.

Shortenings are fats made especially for baking by hydrogenating animal or vegetable fats. They are practically 100 percent fat and contain no water. They have higher melting points than butter or margarine. There are several kinds, falling into two groups.

Regular shortening has a strong, waxy texture, a bland flavor or no flavor, and a high melting point. Shortenings of this class form the small particles that produce the flaky texture of pie doughs and biscuits. They are also good at absorbing and retaining air when creamed, making them good leavening agents. This type of shortening is the one most widely used in baking.

Emulsified shortening, also called **high-ratio shortening**, is softer than regular shortening. It emulsifies easily with other ingredients and can incorporate more air than other shortenings when used in creaming. It is used in formulas having more sugar than flour and in cakes and icings high in sugar and liquid because it can hold everything together without breaking or curdling.

Oils are liquids at room temperature. They are almost 100 percent fat and contain no water. They are seldom used in doughs and batters but are useful in oiling pans, in deep-frying, and sometimes as a wash.

SUGARS

Sugars are included in baked goods primarily for flavor and tenderness. They also add color either through caramelization or by contributing their own color, as brown sugar and molasses do. Sugar will absorb and retain moisture, which influences texture and keeping qualities. Sugars also provide food for yeasts. Sometimes sugar assists in leavening by acting as a mixing agent with butter or as a foaming and stabilizing agent with eggs to incorporate air into batters.

Sugars have different textures and different levels of sweetness, and some have very individual flavors. Here is a rundown on the most used sweetening agents.

Granulated sugars are white sugars made from sugar cane or sugar beets. There are various degrees of refinement. *Granulated, or table, sugar*, is most commonly used. *Confectioners' sugars* are white sugars ground to fine powder. The degree of fineness is identified by the number of X's on the package. Number 10X is the finest and is used in icings, toppings, and fillings.

Brown sugar comes from the same sources as white sugar but is less highly refined and contains caramel and molasses. It is chosen for its flavor, color, and moisture-retaining ability. *Molasses* is a liquid by-product of sugar refining. Its color and flavor are important in gingerbread, cookies, and rye breads. It also has high moisture-retaining ability. It is an acid and is often paired with baking soda.

Honey is a natural liquid sugar made by bees. It is used in special cakes and cookies for its flavor. It is also acidic.

Corn syrup, used in candies and icings, is made from cornstarch. Because of its chemical makeup it inhibits crystallization and produces a smoother texture than other sugars.

SALT

Salt acts as a seasoning, bringing out the flavor of baked goods just as it does in other areas of cooking. In the bakeshop, it also has other important functions, especially in yeast products. Salt inhibits the action of yeast, controlling its rate of growth. It also strengthens gluten, which helps it to trap carbon dioxide more effectively, thus improving texture. It is important to weigh the salt in a formula accurately to ensure the right fermentation rate and the desired texture of the final product.

FLAVORINGS

Most flavorings do not affect the chemistry of baking. Their role is simply to provide interesting flavors and to contribute variety to the baker's output.

Ground spices, especially cinnamon, allspice, ginger, cloves, and nutmeg, are used in a number of products. Use the best quality possible and weigh spices whenever you can rather than measuring them by the spoonful.

Two kinds of liquid flavorings, extracts and emulsions, are used in baked goods and desserts. **Extracts** are oils dissolved in alcohol. Familiar examples are vanilla, lemon, and almond. **Emulsions** are oils emulsified with water. Lemon, orange, and mint emulsions are those most commonly used.

Table 16.1 reviews the functions and forms of many baking ingredients. Additional ingredients not limited to the bakeshop are used for flavor and textural variety. They include fresh and dried fruits, nuts, coconut, chocolate, cocoa, cheeses, herbs, vegetables, and even meats. Most do not affect the baking chemistry, but they do contribute bulk and increase yield to some extent.

Table 16-1 BAKING INGREDIENTS

1. Flour

Function

- Provide the structure of baked goods (needed more in breads than in more tender products such as cakes)

Forms:

- All-purpose—can be used in any recipe that does not specify a particular type of flour
- Bread—a high-protein flour used to make breads and pizza dough
- Cake—a low-protein flour used to make cakes and other delicate baked goods
- Pastry—its gluten content is between cake flour and bread flour, best suited to make pie dough, quick breads, biscuits, and some cookies and pastries

2. Sugars

Functions:

- Add flavor
- Make a fine-textured, tender product
- Prevent staling by holding onto water
- Provide leavening when creamed
- Help crust brown

Table 16-1 (Continued)

Forms

- Fine granulated (table sugar)
- Confectioners' (powdered)—white sugar ground to a fine powder; "10X" is the finest and is used in icings, toppings, and cream fillings
- Brown sugar—table sugar that is not as highly refined, contains some molasses and caramel, used for its flavor and color

3. Milk and cream

Functions:

- Add flavor
- Develop gluten
- Provide nutritional value
- Help crust brown

Forms:

- Whole, low-fat, skim milk
- Buttermilk—is mildly acid; when mixed with baking soda, it produces leavening and also imparts a special flavor
- Dry milk—usually treated as a dry ingredient which is reconstituted when water is added

4. Water

Function:

- Combines with flour to make gluten

5. Eggs

Functions:

- Provide structure
- Provide moisture (water)
- Provide flavor and color
- Provide leavening when whipped (egg white)
- Make batter smooth (egg yolk)

Forms:

- Fresh, frozen, dried

6. Fats

Functions:

- Make product tender
- Add richness
- Prevent staling of baked product
- Provide leavening when creamed

Forms:

- Regular shortening—has waxy texture and no taste, creams well, and is used in pie crusts, biscuits, many pastries and cookies, and breads
- Emulsified or high-ratio shortening—softer and creams better than regular shortening, used in some cakes and icings
- Butter—makes dough hard to handle because it melts at room temperature, tastes better than shortening because it melts in the mouth (shortening leaves a film in the mouth)
- Margarine—can replace butter but lacks the flavor
- Oils—rarely used in baking

7. Leavening agents

Functions:

- Makes baked goods rise by producing bubbles of gas

Forms:

- Baking powder
- Baking soda and acid ingredient such as buttermilk
- Yeast—a live microscopic plant that eats sugar and then produces carbon dioxide gas in bread doughs

8. Seasonings and flavorings

Function:

- Flavoring

Forms:

- Includes salt, chocolate, spices, extracts, etc.

SPECIAL BAKING CONCEPTS AND PROCEDURES

SCALING

Now that we have reviewed ingredient roles, you can appreciate even better the concept of recipes as chemical formulas and the necessity for maintaining accurate ratios and proportions. The most accurate method of controlling amounts and proportions is to weigh all ingredients. This is called **scaling.** Accurate weighing is even more important in baking than in other types of cooking. Dry ingredients must always be weighed. Certain liquid ingredients—water, milk, and eggs—can be measured either by weight or by volume. For these ingredients and these only, "a pint's a pound the world around" is a handy rule to remember.

Scaling is done on a special **baker's balance beam scale** such as the one shown in Figure 16.2. It contains two platforms, a balance beam with a sliding weight for measuring ounces or grams, and several counterweights for measuring pounds or kilograms. A scoop for scaling dry ingredients, shown on the left-hand platform, comes with the scale, along with a counterweight for the right-hand side to balance it exactly.

The principle of using this scale is to set up the right-hand side to the weight desired by using counterweights and the weight beam and then to add the ingredient on the left-hand side until the scale balances. The illustrations show a step-by-step procedure for scaling.

The term scaling applies to the entire process of measuring ingredients. This includes measurement of the completed batter or dough when it is **panned**—that is, put into pans for baking. Measuring the dough or batter for each muffin or roll or loaf of bread is essential to a uniform product—each muffin like every other muffin in size and appearance, each one baking at the same rate. Scaling each one also guarantees that you will produce the number intended.

In scaling the finished dough or batter, you do not always use a scale. You may use a measure such as a scoop or ladle that is equal to the weight of the batter desired per muffin, or a biscuit cutter that produces the size biscuit you want. In making bread or rolls, you will use a dough cutter (Figure 16.3) as well as a scale to divide the dough into equal parts of the required weight.

BAKER'S PERCENTAGES

A system known as **baker's percentages** is another concept that is unique to baking. It is a way of expressing ratios or proportions of ingredients in a given formula. In each case, 100 percent represents, not the total of all ingredients in the formula, but the amount of flour alone. Other ingredients are then expressed as percentages of this amount. For example, if a formula calls for 10 lb flour and 4 lb shortening, the flour is 100 percent and the shortening is 40 percent. If a formula specifies 130 percent sugar for 10 lb flour, you will need 13 lb sugar.

You may find all this confusing at first. Just remember that it expresses ratios, not total percentages. An experienced baker or pastry chef uses baker's percentages when creating new formulas or making major adjustments to old ones.

In this book, we will not be using baker's percentages. But it is a concept you will meet if you pursue a baking career.

POUR BATTERS

Batters and doughs are typically grouped according to the texture of the mixture, which derives mainly from the proportion of flour to liquid.

Figure 16-2 HOW TO USE THE BALANCE BEAM SCALE

a. A balance beam scale with scoop and counterweights. The scale is balanced and ready for weighing (Step 1). If you use a different container, place it on the left-hand platform and move the beam weight along the bar until the scale balances.

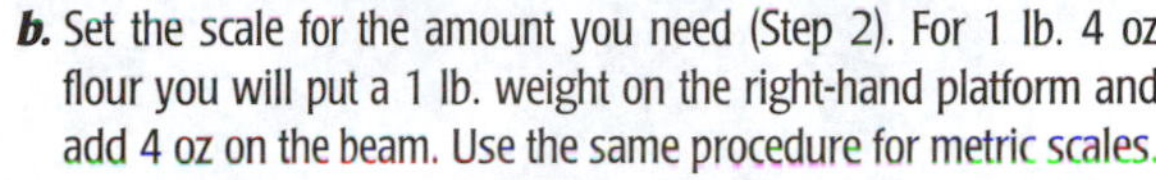

b. Set the scale for the amount you need (Step 2). For 1 lb. 4 oz flour you will put a 1 lb. weight on the right-hand platform and add 4 oz on the beam. Use the same procedure for metric scales.

c. Add the ingredient until the scale balances (Step 3).

d. To weigh additional ingredients increase the amount needed with counterweights and beam. Then add the new ingredient carefully to the container until the scale balances. If you reach 16 oz on the beam, put a 1-lb weight on the right-hand platform and reset the beam to zero so you can use it again. (Photos by Patricia Roberts.)

Pour batters have the lowest ratio of flour to liquid. They can be poured easily in a steady stream.

You have already produced pour batters if you made the pancakes and crêpes in Chapter 13. Another pour batter is given in the formula for waffles (Recipe 16.1). Comparing it with the pancake formula, you will see that it is very similar except that it contains more fat and less liquid.

In pour batters, the dry ingredients are sifted together to mix them well, as in Step 1 of the

Figure 16-3 DOUGH CUTTER

(Photo by Patricia Roberts.)

Recipe 16-1 WAFFLES I

YIELD: ***1 quart (1 L) batter***

8 oz	**flour**	**250 g**
$^1/_2$ oz	**baking powder**	**15 g**
$^1/_2$ tsp	**salt**	**2 mL**
1 oz	**sugar**	**30 g**
3	**eggs**	
12 fl oz	**milk**	**375 mL**
4 fl oz	**melted butter or oil**	**125 mL**

1. Sift flour, baking powder, salt, and sugar together.
2. Combine eggs with milk and butter/oil and fold into dry ingredients.
3. Oil waffle iron (if necessary) and pour in enough batter to cover two-thirds of the surface. Batter will spread to fill.
4. Close iron and cook until steaming stops and waffles are light brown and crisp.

Per 2 oz pancake:		Carbohydrates:	14 g
Calories:	139	Cholesterol:	58 mg
Fat:	8 g	Fiber:	0 g
Protein:	3 g	Sodium:	251 mg

waffle formula. They are then mixed with the liquids just until they are moistened, as in Step 2. Overmixing would develop the gluten, which would make these products tough and chewy. This two-step mixing method is often called the **muffin method** because this is how muffins are made, as we shall see shortly.

You may remember that crêpes are an exception to this method: They must be mixed until they are smooth in order to produce a thin product. Because this develops the gluten, a crêpe batter must rest before baking so that the gluten can relax and yield a tender crêpe as well as a thin one.

To make waffles, preheat the iron and pour enough batter on the middle of the bottom to cover about two-thirds of the surface (Step 3). Close the top and cook (Step 4). Waffle irons signal when done and turn off automatically. If yours doesn't, wait until things stop steaming; then lift the top. It should come up easily. If it resists, cook another 30 seconds and try again. Lift the waffle out carefully, working from one edge. It should emerge all in one piece.

Both pancakes and waffles can be made lighter and fluffier when whipped egg whites are folded into them, as in Recipe 16.la. This is the foam-

Recipe 16-1a WAFFLES II

YIELD: ***1 quart (1 L) batter***

In procedures for Recipe 16.1, make these changes:

Omit sugar in Step 1.

In Step 2, separate eggs. Combine yolks with other liquids and fold into dry ingredients.

Whip egg whites to a soft peak. Add sugar and whip again just until combined. Fold gently into moistened mixture.

Continue with Steps 3 and 4.

ing method of leavening discussed earlier. Make sure that no yolk is present in the whites and that utensils and mixing bowl are grease free. Even the tiniest bit of yolk or fat keeps the egg whites from attaining volume.

To determine a soft peak, lift a small amount of beaten white above the surface. If it stands up but the top or peak falls over, you have reached this consistency.

Making waffles with whipped egg whites takes extra preparation time, and the batter does not hold quite as well, a consideration when you are cooking to order. There are other ways of dressing them up, such as adding extra flavor and texture ingredients. Recipe 16.1b is one suggestion.

Crisp and tender waffles, a delicious addition to the breakfast menu, can also function as a dessert with ice cream and fruit sauce.

Popovers (Recipe 16.2) are made from a pour batter mixed by a completely different method. They are leavened entirely by steam. Because of this, bread flour must be used for its stronger gluten content, and the dough must be well mixed until very smooth so that the gluten is well developed and will form a strong structure to trap the rapidly expanding gases. The popovers are baked at a high temperature to promote quick formation of the steam and coagulation of the proteins in the flour and eggs. The result is a light and airy puff, a dramatic illustration of the leavening power of steam.

Popovers may be used as an accompaniment to a meal or as an interesting container for meat or vegetable salads. For a delicious luncheon entrée, try filling them with such things as chicken à la king or seafood Newburg. When popover batter is made with beef drippings and served with a roast, it is called Yorkshire pudding.

Recipe 16-1b WAFFLES III

YIELD: *6 cups (1.5 L) batter*

To ingredients in Recipe 16.1, add:

1 tsp	**cinnamon**	**5 mL**
4 oz	**nuts, chopped**	**125 g**
6 oz	**fruit, small pieces, drained**	**175 g**

Follow instructions in Recipe 16.1 or 16.1a, adding cinnamon in Step 1 and folding in nuts and fruit at end of Step 2.

Per 2 oz waffle:		Carbohydrates:	13 g
Calories:	145	Cholesterol:	45 mg
Fat:	9 g	Fiber:	1 g
Protein:	3 g	Sodium:	193 mg

Recipe 16-2 POPOVERS

YIELD: *6 popovers*

2	**eggs**	
1 C	**flour**	**250 mL**
$^1/_2$ tsp	**salt**	**2 mL**
1 C	**milk**	**250 mL**

1. Beat eggs slightly. Beat in flour, salt, and milk until very smooth.
2. Fill greased muffin cups about three-quarters full.
3. Bake at 425°F (220°C) until firm with a dry, medium-brown crust—about 30–40 minutes.

Per serving:		Carbohydrates:	17 g
Calories:	120	Cholesterol:	76 mg
Fat:	3 g	Fiber:	1 g
Protein:	5 g	Sodium:	235 mg

DROP BATTERS

A great variety of products are made from the somewhat rough-textured, often lumpy semiliquids known as **drop batters.** The differences in

Recipe 16-3 PLAIN MUFFINS

YIELD: *12 muffins*

2 C	**flour**	**500 mL**
1/3 C	**sugar**	**80 mL**
1 Tb	**baking powder**	**15 mL**
1 tsp	**salt**	**5 mL**
1	**egg**	
3/4 C	**milk**	**180 mL**
1/2 C	**oil**	**125 mL**

1. Sift dry ingredients into a bowl.
2. In another bowl, beat eggs and then add milk and oil.
3. Fold liquids into dry ingredients until barely blended.
4. Fill greased muffin cups about three-quarters full.
5. Bake at 400°F (200°C) until firm but springy—about 20 minutes.
6. Remove from pan onto wire rack to cool.

Per serving:		Carbohydrates:	21 g
Calories:	189	Cholesterol:	20 mg
Fat:	11 g	Fiber:	1 g
Protein:	3 g	Sodium:	306 mg

product may come from the diversity of ingredients or simply from the mixing, panning, or baking method. Ranging from muffins and tea breads to gingerbread, scones, dumplings, and coating batters, they have in common a similar batter texture and most of them use the muffin method of mixing.

Many of these products belong to a group known as **quick breads** because they are quickly and easily put together and they are breadlike in texture and in menu use. The chief reason they are quick and easy is that they are leavened with a chemical leavener; this is simply added to the dry ingredients, and there is no need for the time and activity required by other leavening methods.

In the muffin formulas (Recipe 16.3 and its variations), you see the muffin mixing method in action again. Figure 16.4 illustrates the essential steps. First, the dry ingredients are sifted together to ensure even distribution in the batter. The liquids are blended together and then folded in, mixing only enough to barely combine the ingredients. Don't worry if a few small lumps remain; they will disappear during baking. To produce a tender product, you want to avoid overmixing: Once the gluten has access to moisture, it will begin to develop if manipulated, thus diminishing tenderness.

In mixing the whole wheat muffins (Recipe 16.3a), you do not sift the dry ingredients because this would sift out the wheat germ, which is an integral part of the flavor and texture. Baking soda is used to take advantage of the acidity of the molasses or honey and to bring out its special flavor.

Recipe 16-3a WHOLE WHEAT MUFFINS

YIELD: *12 muffins*

Replace 1 C flour with 1 C whole-wheat flour.

Per serving:		Carbohydrates:	20 g
Calories:	188	Cholesterol:	20 mg
Fat:	11 g	Fiber:	1 g
Protein:	3 g	Sodium:	306 mg

Recipe 16-3b BLUEBERRY NUT MUFFINS

YIELD: *12 muffins*

After Step 3, fold in 1 C (250 mL) fresh blueberries and 4 Tb (60 mL) nuts.

Per serving:		Carbohydrates:	23 g
Calories:	211	Cholesterol:	20 mg
Fat:	12 g	Fiber:	2 g
Protein:	4 g	Sodium:	307 mg

Figure 16-4 MUFFIN MIXING METHOD

a. Sift the dry ingredients.

b. Fold liquids into dry ingredients to barely combine. Batter should be lumpy.

c. To make up, portion into prepare pans. (Photos by Patricia Roberts.)

Because of the type of leavener used, all three of these batters must be baked very soon after mixing, especially the whole wheat muffins, so that no volume is lost.

Formulas for muffins can be baked as loaf breads or sheet cakes and vice versa. They can be varied by replacing part of the liquid with fruit juice or buttermilk and by adding nuts, bran, fruit, and spices, or even cheese, herbs, and vegetables, to produce breads to be served at lunch, tea, and dinner as well as breakfast. The added ingredients will not change the basic chemistry

Recipe 16-4 COATING BATTER

YIELD: ***Approximately 1 quart (1 L)***

12 oz	**flour**	**375 g**
$^{3}/_{4}$ oz	**baking powder**	**22 g**
$^{3}/_{4}$ tsp	**salt**	**3 g**
$^{3}/_{4}$ oz	**sugar**	**22 g**
8 oz	**beaten eggs**	**240 g**
12 fl oz	**milk**	**375 mL**
	flour for dredging	

1. Sift together dry ingredients.
2. Mix beaten eggs and milk. Fold into dry ingredients.
3. Refrigerate, covered, 4–8 hours before using.
4. Dredge product in flour and dip in batter to cover completely.
5. Deep-fry at 350°F (180°C) until golden. Drain well and serve immediately.

Per ounce:		Carbohydrates:	10 g
Calories:	61	Cholesterol:	35 mg
Fat:	1 g	Fiber:	0 g
Protein:	2 g	Sodium:	143 mg

of the formula but may increase the yield slightly. Recipe 16.3b is one of dozens of possible variations.

The last drop batter we will examine (Recipe 16.4) has many uses in the hot-food kitchen. You can use it as a coating for all sorts of deep-fried foods, such as onion rings, mushrooms, or rounds or batonnets of zucchini or eggplant; or you can add things to the batter to make fritters. Fruit fritters (Recipe 16.4a) can be dusted with powdered sugar and served at breakfast with syrup or preserves, or at lunch or dinner to accompany entrées. Vegetable fritters (Recipe 16.4b) or batter-fried vegetables are popular snacks or side dishes.

This batter is made with the by-now-familiar muffin method. Refrigerating it for several hours relaxes the gluten, increasing tenderness. Like pancake or waffle batter, it can be made lighter by separating the eggs and folding in stiffly beaten whites separately. You can make a beer batter from this formula by omitting the baking powder and replacing the milk with beer. The carbonation in the beer acts as the leavener and

Recipe 16-4a FRUIT FRITTERS

YIELD: ***About 24 fritters***

To Recipe 16.4, add:

$^{3}/_{4}$ oz	**sugar**	**22 g**
1 lb	**diced fruit (apples, berries, pineapple, etc.) well drained**	**450 g**

Dredge fruit in flour and fold into batter at end of Step 2.

In Step 5, using a No. 24 scoop, drop batter directly into deep fryer.

Per fritter:		Carbohydrates:	17 g
Calories:	98	Cholesterol:	46 mg
Fat:	2 g	Fiber:	1 g
Protein:	3 g	Sodium:	192 mg

Recipe 16-4b VEGETABLE FRITTERS

YIELD: ***About 24 fritters***

To Recipe 16.4, add:

1 lb	**diced cooked vegetables (corn, carrots, zucchini, eggplant)**	**450 g**

Dredge vegetables in flour and fold into batter at end of Step 2.

In Step 5, using a No. 24 scoop, drop batter directly into deep fryer.

Per serving:		Carbohydrates:	16 g
Calories:	96	Cholesterol:	46 mg
Fat:	2 g	Fiber:	1 g
Protein:	4 g	Sodium:	197 mg

the beer adds its distinctive flavor. Both these variations increase the crisp texture so desirable in fried foods. Some cooks add a small amount of paprika to coating batters to aid in coloring.

Avoid frying these products at too high a temperature or making the fritters too large because the outside will darken too quickly before the interior is cooked. Like other fried foods, these products are at their peak when served immediately but can be held successfully for a short time in a warm place, uncovered.

PASTES

Pastes have a texture that is stiffer than batters and softer than doughs. They are usually piped from a pastry bag and are firm enough to maintain their shape. The best known paste, **éclair paste**, is a flour–liquid mixture like the other doughs and batters. Cookie pastes, which require different ingredients and a different mixing method, are discussed later.

Éclair paste is also called choux paste, from the French *pâté à choux* meaning cabbage paste, so called because the mounds of paste look like little cabbages. Familiar choux paste products include cream puffs and éclairs—tender puffed-up crusts with hollow centers like popovers—and crullers or French doughnuts.

Choux paste makes a great variety of menu items. Small cream puffs, called **profiteroles**, are served with soup. Bite-sized cream puff shells can be flavored by stirring grated cheese, herbs, minced meat, seafood, or poultry or combinations of these into the mixture before cooking, or the shells can be filled after baking with savory mixtures for delightful hors d'oeuvres. And, of course, there are éclairs and cream puffs for dessert, filled with delicate cream fillings. You have also met choux paste in an entirely different role—providing structure and texture in duchesse potatoes (Chapter 9).

Recipe 16.5 details the ingredients and procedures for choux paste. You will notice that this formula is not unlike the other baking mixtures you have dealt with, except for the large amount of butter and eggs. Like popovers, it uses bread flour because, like popovers, choux paste is leavened by steam and needs the extra gluten to con-

Recipe 16-5 PÂTE À CHOUX (CHOUX PASTE, ECLAIR PASTE)

YIELD: ***12 éclair or cream puff shells***

1 C	**water**	**250 mL**
4 oz	**butter**	**125 g**
$^1/_8$ tsp	**salt**	**0.5 mL**
1 C	**flour**	**250 mL**
4	**eggs**	

1. In a heavy pan, bring water, butter, and salt to a full boil.
2. Remove from heat and add flour all at once, stirring rapidly with a wooden spoon.
3. Over moderate heat, continue to cook and stir until mixture is smooth, pulls away from pan, and forms a ball-like mass.
4. Remove from heat. Continue stirring, until mixture cools to 140°F (60°C).
5. Beat in eggs a little at a time, incorporating them completely each time until batter is smooth and glossy. When all eggs are absorbed, mixture should be thick and able to stand alone.
6. Pipe or pan out into desired shape and size.
7. Bake at 400°F (200°C) until crisp, brown, and dry.

Per serving:		Carbohydrates:	8 g
Calories:	128	Cholesterol:	92 mg
Fat:	9 g	Fiber:	0 g
Protein:	3 g	Sodium:	123 mg

tain the tremendous expansion. The butter and eggs are for tenderness, flavor, and texture. The eggs also emulsify the butter–flour–liquid mixture and hold it together. Milk is used for flavor, too, especially for dessert items, but water also makes an excellent product. Sugar is used for a sweet product and omitted for a nonsweet or savory item.

The procedures, on the other hand, are something new. Let us go through them step by step.

Make sure the liquid is at a rolling boil in Step 1. The fat must be completely melted and mixed with the liquid before the flour is added, so that the ingredients are evenly distributed. In Step 2, removing the mixture from the heat, adding the flour all at once, and stirring like crazy is the easiest way to produce the smooth, lumpfree mixture.

In Step 3, rapid stirring continues over moderate heat (to avoid scorching) to begin gluten development and to allow the flour to absorb moisture and gelatinize. (Does this remind you of making roux?) When the mixture forms a ball, you know the process is complete. At this point (Step 4), remove the mixture from the heat and let it cool slightly so that the eggs won't cook when you add them. You can transfer the mixture to a mixer with the paddle or continue stirring by hand.

Perhaps you can guess why you add the eggs little by little in Step 5—to avoid lumping. They must be evenly distributed to form a uniform emulsion. When all the eggs have been beaten in, you should have a thick, smooth, glossy paste, able to stand alone, ready to be piped out. With a little practice, pâté à choux takes only a few minutes to prepare and should be piped out (Step 6) and baked as soon as possible.

To form cream puffs, use a plain tip to pipe out quarter- to half-dollar-sized rounds, depending on the final size desired. A mound about $1^1/_2$ inches (4 cm) in diameter is usual; a well-made paste will increase three to five times when baked. Space on pans to allow for expansion. Use paper-lined sheet pans; oiled pans will cause the paste to flatten out. For éclairs, pipe out 1 × 4-in. (2.5 × 10 cm) oblong shapes, using the same procedure.

In baking (Step 7), the oven temperature is high in order to create the steam that expands and puffs the paste. The continued heat coagulates the gluten and the egg protein to firm and set the structure. Some chefs bake at 425°F (220°C) for 10 minutes and reduce the temperature to 375°F (190°C) for the remaining time. Baking time varies according to product size. Cream puffs and other choux paste products must be thoroughly baked—well browned and crisp—and cooled slowly or they will collapse.

Cream puffs and éclairs may be filled with whipped cream, pastry cream, ice cream, or a fruit filling. They are then dusted with confectioners' sugar or topped with a dessert sauce or chocolate fondant (more on these good things later). Hold them in the refrigerator or, for an ice cream filling, in the freezer.

Unfilled pâté à choux products that have been thoroughly cooled may be placed in plastic bags and stored in the refrigerator for up to a week, or frozen and stored longer. They keep very well and can be freshened by heating in a moderate oven for a few minutes.

SOFT DOUGHS

Soft doughs include biscuits and yeast breads and rolls. A soft dough has a higher flour-to-liquid ratio than a drop batter—enough to make a firm but elastic dough that is soft to the touch.

These doughs can be rolled, cut, or formed into various shapes and sizes to make a variety of products. They are also varied by the use of different ingredients and mixing methods.

BISCUITS

Biscuits (Recipe 16.6) are usually considered quick breads because they are fast and simple to make, whereas yeast breads take 2 to 3 hours and require more preparation. The mixing method used for biscuits is called the **pastry method** because it is also used for pie doughs, as you will see in the next chapter. It requires that the fat be rubbed or cut into the dry ingredients before liquids are added. You can cut in the fat with a fork, pastry cutter, or mixer, or by rubbing the fat and flour together between the palms of your hands.

Let us look at the formula in detail. The mixture of flours is used for two different but complementary purposes. Bread flour contributes the stronger gluten structure needed during leavening. Cake flour moderates this effect, allowing the biscuit to be tender and flaky. The other ingredients perform their usual functions: baking powder for leavening, salt for flavor, fat for tenderness, milk to provide liquid for the gluten and for starch gelatinization, as well as to add flavor. Butter will add flavor, too.

Now, let us examine the mixing method step by step. In Step 1, you sift the dry ingredients to distribute them evenly, as in the muffin method. It is equally important to distribute the fat throughout (Step 2) until the mixture resembles a coarse meal or, for a flakier biscuit, until the fat is pea sized.

When adding the liquid ingredients (Step 3), mix as little as possible because this is when the gluten begins developing and you want to control this development. At this point, the dough will resemble a drop batter and can be treated like one. You can drop 2-oz biscuits onto paper-lined pans, skipping Steps 4 to 7, and bake them in this form. They will be very tender but irregular in appearance.

Beginning in Step 4, traditional biscuits differ from most quick breads. A moderate amount of gluten development is desirable to support the structure during leavening. You accomplish this by **kneading.** Kneading manipulates the dough to stretch the gluten strands and develop their elastic qualities. For biscuits, the kneading is gentle. Place the dough in one lump on a lightly floured surface and use the heels of your hands

Recipe 16-6 BISCUITS

YIELD: ***12 biscuits***

1 C	**bread flour**	**250 mL**
1 C	**cake flour**	**250 mL**
$1\frac{1}{2}$ tsp	**baking powder**	**8 mL**
$\frac{1}{2}$ tsp	**baking soda**	**2 mL**
$\frac{1}{2}$ tsp	**salt**	**2 mL**
4 Tb	**butter or shortening**	**60 mL**
$\frac{3}{4}$ C	**buttermilk**	**185 mL**

1. Sift together dry ingredients.
2. Cut fat into dry ingredients.
3. Fold in buttermilk until barely combined.
4. Turn out onto lightly floured surface and knead lightly, making four quarter turns of the dough.
5. Roll out to $\frac{1}{2}$-in. (1 cm) thickness.
6. Cut into desired shape and place on paper-lined or lightly oiled baking sheets.
7. Brush tops with milk or egg wash.
8. Bake at 425°F (220°C) until doubled in height and golden brown—about 15–20 minutes.

Per serving:		Carbohydrates:	16 g
Calories:	122	Cholesterol:	14 mg
Fat:	5 g	Fiber:	1 g
Protein:	3 g	Sodium:	267 mg

to push the bulk of the dough away from you. Fold it in half back on top of itself and turn the dough in a quarter circle. Repeat three times until the circle is completed.

This is the entire kneading procedure for biscuits. We will see in the next section that yeast products require more gluten development, and the kneading takes place in the mixer.

After kneading, the dough is ready to be rolled out to a uniform thickness (Step 5). This is done with a small broomstick pin (Figure 16.5) and is known as **pinning out.**

Cut the biscuits into the desired shape (Step 6) using a lightly floured cutter. If you use a round cutter, cut the biscuits as close together as possible. The scraps between the biscuits have to be reworked and won't be as tender. You can avoid this problem by cutting the biscuits in squares or triangles with a floured knife or dough cutter. Whatever their shape, space the biscuits 1/2 inch (1 cm) apart on a lightly oiled or paper-lined sheet pan. For softer, less crusty biscuits, place them almost touching each other.

Figure 16-5 ROLLING PINS

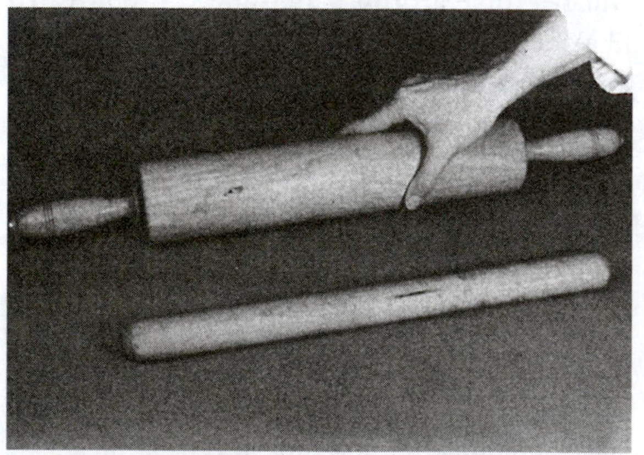

Top, ball bearing pin. Bottom, broomstick pin. (Photo by Patricia Roberts.)

Recipe 16-6a SWEET BISCUITS

YIELD: ***12 biscuits***

Add 1/2 C (125 mL) raisins just before Step 3.

Per serving:		Carbohydrates:	20 g
Calories:	140	Cholesterol:	14 mg
Fat:	5 g	Fiber:	1 g
Protein:	3 g	Sodium:	267 mg

A milk or egg wash (Step 7) helps to produce an attractive, shiny brown crust. Milk wash makes a softer top crust, and egg wash produces a crisper, browner crust. The baking temperature is high (Step 8) to make the biscuits rise quickly and to create a firm structure.

Biscuits are traditionally served at breakfast in certain areas of the country. You might want to try some variations to produce a sweet shortcake for fruit (Recipe 16.6a) or bite-sized savory biscuits to serve as an hors d'oeuvre (Recipe 16.6b). Any of these biscuits can be a welcome addition to the bread basket at any time of day.

YEAST DOUGHS

Most soft doughs are yeast doughs. The products they make range from French and Italian loaves to sweet rolls and Danish pastry. As in other

Recipe 16-6b SAVORY BISCUITS

YIELD: ***12 biscuits***

Add 1/2 C (125 mL) grated cheese and/or 2 Tb (30 mL) dill just before Step 3.

Per serving:		Carbohydrates:	16 g
Calories:	144	Cholesterol:	20 mg
Fat:	7 g	Fiber:	1 g
Protein:	4 g	Sodium:	301 mg

types of baked products, the differences come from ingredients and makeup.

Differences in ingredients produce two types of yeast doughs—lean and rich. **Lean doughs** are low in fat and sugar. They include crusty breads and rolls and pizza dough as well as whole wheat and rye bread and rolls. **Rich dough** formulas contain more fat and sugar and often include eggs. Brioche, challah breads, sweet rolls, and coffee cakes are examples.

All yeast doughs, lean or rich, go through the same series of production steps—12 of them. It is a long process, but the baker is actively involved only a small part of the time. It is an in-and-out process in which the baker is very busy for short periods. In between, the baker puts the dough to work by itself. It goes like this:

Baker	*Dough Alone*
1. Scaling ingredients	
2. Mixing	
	3. Fermenting (1–2$^{1}/_{2}$ hours)
4. Punching	
5. Scaling the dough	
6. Rounding	
	7. Bench proofing (10–20 minutes)
8. Makeup and panning	
	9. Proofing (1–2 hours)
	10. Baking (20–90 minutes)
	11. Cooling (3–45 minutes)
	12. Storage

The baker is responsible for beginning and ending the "dough alone" steps properly but is not actively involved.

Let us look at these steps briefly to gain an overview of the process. Then we will examine some formulas to gain a better understanding of what goes on and why.

Scaling ingredients (Step 1) is already familiar to you. In yeast doughs as elsewhere, careful weighing is essential, especially for salt, which affects both fermentation and gluten development.

Mixing (Step 2) is the most complex and possibly the single most important step. It must accomplish two things of key importance to the finished product. First, it must distribute all ingredients evenly throughout the batter, for correct leavening action and a uniform product. Second, it must develop the gluten properly.

Two major mixing methods are used. The **straight dough method** has one step: You place all the ingredients in the mixer bowl and combine them, using the dough arm. Some rich doughs require a **modified straight dough method** in which the ingredients are combined in installments to ensure that such ingredients as fat and sugar are completely integrated into the dough.

The second major method—the **sponge dough method**—has two steps. In the first step, the liquid, part of the flour, and the yeast are mixed to a smooth, thick batter, or sponge, which is fermented until doubled in volume. The sponge is then mixed with the remaining flour and other ingredients to form the dough.

Fermenting (Step 3) follows mixing in the straight dough method. Fermentation begins during mixing and continues until the yeast is killed when the dough temperature reaches 140°F (60°C) in the oven. Between these two events, it needs time to work its chemical magic. So you place the dough in a **proof box**—a special cabinet with controlled temperature and high humidity. If you do not have a proof box, you place the dough in an oiled container, oil the dough surface, and cover the container to prevent a crust from forming. You let it ferment until it has doubled in volume and does not spring

Figure 16-6 TESTING THE RISING

back but remains indented when you press it lightly with your fingertips (Figure 16.6). The best temperature for fermenting is to keep the dough at about 80°F (27°C).

In the sponge method, the sponge alone is fermented. After the remaining ingredients are added, another brief fermentation period usually follows.

Punching (Step 4) is the next step in the straight dough method. This is done by pulling up the sides of the dough mass and pushing them down into the center until the dough has deflated. This equalizes the temperature, allows the gluten to relax, and redistributes the yeast so the dough will rise again.

You do not punch the sponge after it ferments. Mixing in the remaining ingredients accomplishes the same things.

Scaling the dough (Step 5) comes next—weighing it into portions of the desired size. The dough is divided on the bench, the baker's wood-surfaced worktable. You dust the surface lightly with flour, cut the dough with a dough cutter or sharp knife to avoid stretching it, and weigh it on the balance scale. After you weigh out the first portion correctly, you can use it as a counterweight and weigh the remaining portions against it.

Rounding (Step 6) is a preliminary makeup technique. Your aim is to form each portion into a round ball with a smooth skin that will contain the gases effectively. You use the cupped palm of your hand to roll the dough around on the bench while pressing it against the bench surface with the outside edge of your hand.

Bench proofing (Step 7) means fermenting at the bench. The balls of dough are covered and allowed to rest at the bench for 10 to 20 minutes as fermentation continues. This relaxes the gluten and makes makeup easier.

Makeup and panning (Step 8) bring you closer to the final product. Makeup means forming the dough into its final shape. The goal of this step is familiar: uniformity of size and appearance to produce attractive, evenly baked portions. An immense variety of shapes and sizes is possible. After makeup, bread and rolls are placed in pans or molds or properly spaced on sheet pans. Those baked on sheet pans are called hearth breads, from the days when they were placed directly on the oven floor or hearth for baking.

Proofing (Step 9) is another fermentation period. Bakers use the term proofing to distinguish this leavening period from the first fermentation. The best conditions for proofing are a humidity of 85 percent and a temperature of 90 to 100°F (32–38°C) to keep the dough at 80°F (27°C). If a proof box is not available, duplicate these conditions as closely as possible and cover the dough to retain moisture and prevent a skin from forming. Proofing is "done" when the dough has doubled and remains indented when pressed. Handle with care: It is very fragile and is easily deflated.

Baking (Step 10) comes next. Before going into the oven, loaves and some rolls are cut or **docked** by slashing the top with a sharp knife. This allows even expansion in the oven. Most products are brushed with a wash to provide shine, crispness, browning, or all three. Pans are then placed carefully in the oven. Lean doughs and small rolls bake quickly at high temperatures, but rich doughs and large loaves bake at lower temperatures for a longer time.

Yeast products rise rapidly in the oven at first as gases expand. Fermentation ends as the temperature rises, and the product firms as the starches gelatinize and the proteins coagulate. The crust forms and browns. Doneness is signaled when the crust is golden brown and the loaves sound hollow when tapped lightly.

You may think of baking as the final step, but two more steps are the baker's responsibility in order to preserve that fresh-baked quality.

Cooling (Step 11) allows excess moisture to escape. Products baked in molds should be removed and placed on screens or racks so that air can circulate around them. Bread and rolls baked on sheet pans can be left on the pans to cool. Keep drafts away from hot breads or the crusts may split.

Storage (Step 12) is the final step for all baked goods. Its goal is to inhibit staling—deterioration of texture and aroma caused by loss of moisture and changes in the structure of the starches.

Staling begins very soon after baking, but bread, rolls, biscuits, and quick breads to be served within 8 hours can be stored at room temperature. If they must be kept longer, wrap them in plastic wrap or place in plastic bags after they are thoroughly cool. If they are not cool, moisture will collect and make the product soggy—particularly undesirable in hard-crusted goods. Always store them in the freezer. Refrigeration actually increases staling, so don't follow this common practice. Freshen frozen baked goods in the oven at a low temperature for a short time, or simply let them thaw.

Now, let us examine some formulas for different types of breads and rolls. You will see that they all have the basic steps in common; the only differences are in mixing method and makeup techniques.

HARD ROLL DOUGH. Hard roll dough (Recipe 16.7) is a lean dough that makes chewy, hard-crusted rolls or French- or Italian-style bread. True French bread has only flour, yeast, water, and salt. The small amounts of fat and sugar in this formula contribute to keeping qualities. Bread flour is used for its strong gluten content.

Recipe 16-7 HARD ROLL DOUGH

YIELD: ***4 lb 7½ oz (2.1 kg)***

1½ oz	**compressed yeast**	**45 g**
1 lb 8 oz	**water**	**720 g**
2 lb 10 oz	**bread flour**	**1.3 kg**
1 oz	**salt**	**30 g**
1 oz	**sugar**	**30 g**
1 oz	**shortening**	**30 g**
1 oz	**egg whites**	**30 g**
	lean egg wash or water as needed	
	cornmeal for pans as needed	

1. Dissolve yeast in 3 oz (100 mL) water, warmed to 90°F (32°C).
2. Using straight dough method, mix all ingredients at medium speed for about 12 minutes.
3. Ferment at 80°F (27°C) until doubled (about 1 hour).
4. Punch down, scale, round, and bench-proof 10–20 minutes.
5. Make up as desired and pan.
6. Proof at 90°F (32°C) until doubled. Test with fingertips.
7. Slash top, brush with wash, and bake at 400°F (200°C) with steam for 10 minutes. Continue without steam until crust is firm and golden brown.

This formula is an example of the straight dough method. After dissolving the yeast in part of the water (Step 1), you place all the ingredients in the bowl of the mixer. Don't let the yeast come into direct contact with the salt; this would inhibit fermentation.

During mixing (Step 2), the ingredients are distributed evenly in the first few minutes, and the dough forms a mass around the dough hook. The slapping of the dough against the sides of the bowl kneads and stretches the gluten strands, making them stronger and more elastic. If the dough has not lost its sticky look and feel when two-thirds of the mixing time is up, you should add a little more flour.

Twelve minutes for mixing is only a guideline. Watch for clues: Lean doughs when properly mixed look and feel smooth and resilient. The dough clears the bowl in a smooth mass. Both undermixing and overmixing can produce poor volume and texture in the final product.

During fermentation (Step 3), the yeast multiplies and produces carbon dioxide, causing the dough to rise. Punching in Step 4 deflates it. Punching, along with scaling, rounding, and bench proofing, prepares the dough for makeup. If you take special care during rounding to form smooth balls, makeup will be much easier and will produce more attractive finished products. (You could even choose to bake these balls as buns or round loaves without further handling.)

For Step 5, the makeup technique for club rolls is illustrated in Figure 16.7. The technique of rolling and sealing (Steps 5a, b, and c) is the same for French- and Italian-style (hearth) loaves and pan bread (bread baked in loaf pans). This technique produces a uniform roll or loaf with a smooth, even surface—one that will keep its shape.

Use the same steps for hearth and pan breads. These breads are scaled at anywhere from 12 to 16 ounces (360–500 g) or more depending on the size loaf desired. For pan breads, the width of your rectangle in Step 5a is the length of the loaf pan. The made-up loaf should touch the ends of the pan.

Rolls and loaves from this dough are traditionally baked with a thin layer of cornmeal on sheet pans. This practice stems from the days when cornmeal was sprinkled on the hearth to keep the bread from sticking. The cornmeal on the pan still performs this function as well as adding texture and flavor. If you use loaf pans or molds, oil them lightly instead. Placing the rolls or loaves seam side down makes the dough rise evenly and keeps the crust from cracking during baking. Spacing on the pan must allow for expansion.

Now, going back again to the dough formula in Recipe 16.7, you proof the made-up dough (Step 6). If you don't have a proof box, put the pans in a warm place and cover the dough with plastic wrap or lightly dampened towels. If a crust forms before baking, the dough cannot expand properly.

Figure 16-7 MAKING CLUB ROLLS

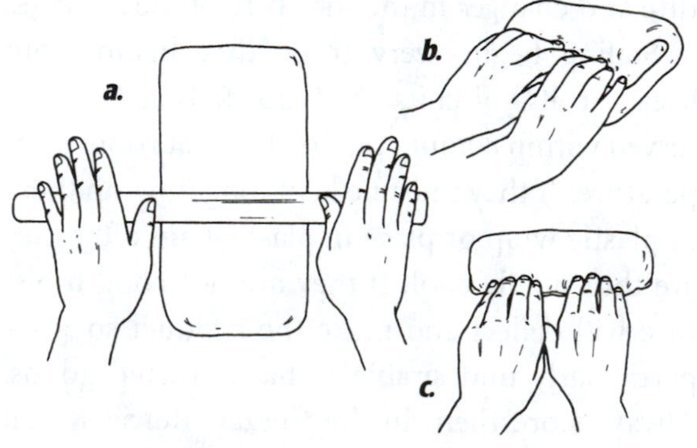

a. Roll each round into a rectangle twice as long as wide and the thickness of a finger. ***b.*** Tightly roll up the strip of dough, sealing it to itself with your fingertips as you roll. ***c.*** Stretch end of strip to width of roll and seal.

Recipe 16-7a CLUB ROLLS

Yield: *About 4 dozen rolls*

Using hard roll dough in Recipe 16.7:

In Step 4, scale at $1^1/_2$ oz (45 g) per roll. In Step 5, make up and pan as follows:

a. Roll each round into a rectangle twice as long as wide and the thickness of a finger.
b. Tightly roll up the strip of dough, sealing it to itself with your fingertips as you roll.
c. Stretch end of strip to width of roll and seal.
d. Sprinkle cornmeal on sheet pans. Place rolls 2 in. (5 cm) apart with seam on bottom.

Total baking time: About 15–20 minutes.

Per roll:		Carbohydrates:	19 g
Calories:	97	Cholesterol:	0 mg
Fat:	1 g	Fiber:	1 g
Protein:	3 g	Sodium:	231 mg

In Step 7, cut a lengthwise slash on top for club rolls, or two or three diagonal parallel cuts in loaves. Without any cut, a crack appears on the side of a loaf as it rises and forms its crust. Rolls are cut mainly for appearance. Brushing with wash helps create a thin, crispy crust during baking. Use your pastry brush with a light touch to avoid collapsing the dough. Place your pans gently in the oven. If the dough is banged or knocked around, the fragile structure will collapse, ruining all your hard work.

Lean doughs are the only kind that use steam in baking. Some stack ovens have a generator that can inject steam into the oven. This helps these doughs develop a thin, crispy crust. If steam is not available, you can still produce an excellent product, but it will have a slightly thicker crust. Total baking times will be 15 to 20 minutes for rolls and 40 to 75 minutes at 375°F (190°C) for loaves and pan breads, depending on size.

SOFT ROLL DOUGH. Soft roll dough (Recipe 16.8) creates a softer, less chewy texture than hard roll dough because of the higher sugar and fat content. The milk solids also give it a slightly different flavor and texture. Use the straight dough method, observing the same guidelines as in mixing the hard roll dough. You can either dissolve the milk powder in the water or simply add it directly to the mixing bowl.

As with other yeast doughs, you have your choice of many sizes and shapes of finished products. Among these are single-knot rolls (Recipe 16.8a) and butterflake rolls (Recipe 16.8b). Figures 16.8 and 16.9 illustrate how to make these rolls. Other possibilities are buns, figure 8's, and

Recipe 16-8 SOFT ROLL DOUGH

Yield: *4 lb 13 oz (2.3 kg) dough*

2 oz	**compressed yeast**	**60 g**
1 lb 8 oz	**water**	**720 g**
2 lb 8 oz	**bread flour**	**1.2 kg**
1 oz	**salt**	**30 g**
4 oz	**sugar**	**125 g**
4 oz	**shortening or margarine**	**120 g**
2 oz	**dry milk solids**	**60 g**
	water, milk, or lean egg wash as needed	

1. Dissolve yeast. Using straight dough method, mix all ingredients at medium speed for about 12 minutes.
2. Ferment at 80°F (27°C) until doubled (about 1 hour). Test with fingertips.
3. Punch down, scale, and round. Bench-proof 10–20 minutes.
4. Make up as desired. Place on paper-lined sheet pans or in greased molds.
5. Proof at 90°F (32°C) until doubled. Test with fingertips.
6. Brush with wash. Bake at 400°F (200°C) until golden.

Recipe 16-8a SINGLE-KNOT ROLLS

YIELD: *About 6 dozen rolls*

Using soft roll dough made in Recipe 16.8:

In Step 3, scale at 1 oz (30 g).

In Step 4, make up and pan as shown in Figure 16.8.

Place on paper-lined pans 2 in. (5 cm) apart.

Baking time: About 15–20 minutes.

Per roll:		Carbohydrates:	14 g
Calories:	81	Cholesterol:	0 mg
Fat:	2 g	Fiber:	0 g
Protein:	2 g	Sodium:	157 mg

braided rolls. Most rolls from soft dough are spaced about $2^1/_4$ inches (5 cm) apart. Rolls baked closer together or in molds have less crust.

Brush rolls with a wash for a shiny glazed look when baked. A lean egg wash is made with water and has more whites than yolks. Baking time for rolls is usually 15 to 20 minutes.

You can also make white pan bread—the familiar American-style loaf—with this formula. Makeup and panning are the same as for hard roll dough. Baking time for loaves is 45 to 75 minutes at 375°F (190°C).

You can make whole wheat bread and rolls from this formula by adding $1^1/_2$ lb (720 g) whole wheat flour and reducing the bread flour to 1 lb (480 g). These items, too, can be made up in all these different ways.

Using Recipe 16.9, you can make the crust for the all-American favorite: pizza. Add sauce, cheese, and toppings and bake in the oven until the crust is lightly browned and cheese is melted.

SWEET ROLL DOUGH. Doughs used for sweet rolls and coffee cakes need the modified straight dough method in order to incorporate the fat, sugar, and eggs evenly. Recipe 16.10 is a typical **sweet roll dough** illustrating this method. You add the ingredients step by step for thorough mixing, and you mix the first three groups of ingredients with the paddle, which does a better mixing job than the dough arm.

You switch to the dough arm when you add the flour in Step 2d because the paddle would

Recipe 16-8b BUTTERFLAKE ROLLS

YIELD: *About 6 dozen rolls*

Using soft roll dough made in Recipe 16.8:

In Step 3, scale three 24-oz (720 g) pieces of dough.

In Step 4, make up and pan as shown in Figure 16.9.

Place pieces on end in greased muffin tins.

Baking time: About 15–20 minutes.

Per serving:		Carbohydrates:	14 g
Calories:	81	Cholesterol:	0 mg
Fat:	2 g	Fiber:	0 g
Protein:	2 g	Sodium:	157 mg

Figure 16-8 MAKING SINGLE-KNOT ROLLS

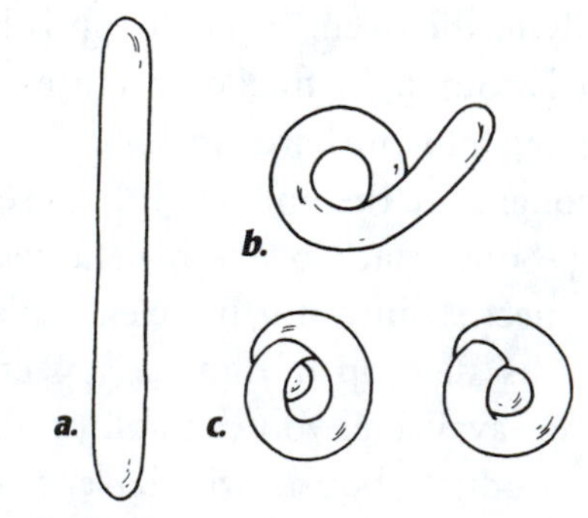

a. With your palms, roll each piece of dough into a rope 5″ (12 cm) long and $^1/_2$ inch (1 cm) thick. ***b.*** Form one half into a doughnut shape. ***c.*** Roll the other half over and then under the doughnut and push end up through center to form a button.

Figure 16-9 MAKING BUTTERFLAKE ROLLS

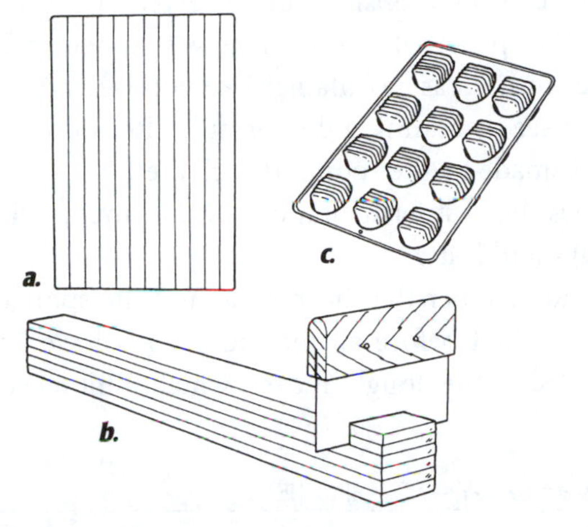

a. Roll out dough into a very thin rectangle 12 × 18 inches (30 × 45 cm). Brush with melted butter and cut into lengthwise strips 1 × 18 inches (2.5 × 45 cm). **b.** Make stacks of 6 strips each. Cut each stack into $1^1/_2$-inch (3.5 cm) pieces. **c.** Place pieces on end in greased muffin tins.

Recipe 16-9 PIZZA DOUGH

YIELD: ***1 crust***

1	**package active dry yeast**	
1 C	**warm water (105–115°F)**	**250 mL**
1 tsp	**sugar**	**5 mL**
1 tsp	**salt**	**5 mL**
2 Tb	**oil**	**30 mL**

1. Dissolve yeast in warm water.
2. Stir in remaining ingredients. Beat vigorously.
3. Knead for 2–3 minutes.
4. Let dough rest about 5 minutes.

(To make pizza, press dough into greased pan and top with sauce, cheese, and toppings. Bake at 425°F/220°C for 20–24 minutes.)

Per crust:		Carbohydrates:	7 g
Calories:	281	Cholesterol:	0 mg
Fat:	28 g	Fiber:	2 g
Protein:	3 g	Sodium:	232 mg

Recipe 16-10 SWEET ROLL DOUGH

YIELD: ***5 lb 11/2 oz (2.5 kg) dough***

1 lb	**milk**	**500 g**
3 oz	**compressed yeast**	**90 g**
8 oz	**butter/margarine/shortening**	**250 g**
8 oz	**sugar**	**250 g**
$^1/_2$ oz	**salt**	**15 g**
6 oz	**eggs**	**185 g**
1 lb 12 oz	**bread flour**	**875 g**
12 oz	**pastry flour**	**375 g**
	egg wash as needed	

1. Heat milk to 100°F (38°C) and dissolve yeast in it.
2. Mix using modified straight dough method.
   a. In mixer, using paddle, combine fat, sugar, and salt at low speed.
   b. When smooth, add eggs; mix thoroughly.
   c. Mix in liquid and yeast.
   d. Add flour and mix with dough arm 4–5 minutes at medium speed.
3. Ferment at 80°F (27°C) until doubled (about $1^1/_2$ hours). Test with fingertips.
4. Punch down, scale, and round. Bench-proof 10–20 minutes.
5. Make up as desired and pan.
6. Proof at 90°F (32°C) until doubled. Test with fingertips.
7. Brush with egg wash and bake at 375°F (190°C) until golden brown.

cut the gluten strands. You can see why when you compare it with the dough arm. A short mix with the dough arm develops the gluten to the proper degree for this dough.

Notice that the fermentation period is longer than that for the other two doughs. It is harder for the yeast to expand this sweet, rich dough.

Rich doughs generally use the familiar egg wash of 2 parts egg to 1 part water. For an extra-rich wash, use milk in place of water, or add extra yolks, or do both. Egg wash provides ex-

Recipe 16-10a CINNAMON ROLLS

YIELD: ***48–50 rolls***

Using sweet roll dough from Recipe 16.10:

In Step 4, scale four $1^1/_4$ lb (635 g) pieces.
In Step 5, make up as follows:

a. Roll out each round into a rectangle 12 × 8 × $^1/_2$ in. (30 × 20 × 1 cm). Brush with melted butter and sprinkle with cinnamon sugar.
b. Roll lengthwise tightly; seal seam.
c. Slice into $1^1/_4$-in. (2.5 cm) pieces.
d. Place in oiled muffin tins or on sheet pans 1 in. (2.5 cm) apart.

Bake for 20–25 minutes.

Per roll:		Carbohydrates:	30 g
Calories:	226	Cholesterol:	27 mg
Fat:	10 g	Fiber:	1 g
Protein:	4 g	Sodium:	163 mg

tra browning of the crust as well as a very shiny look.

For special flavors, you can add spices such as nutmeg and cinnamon along with the fat and sugar in Step 2a. Or you can use special fillings such as cinnamon sugar when you make up the dough. To make cinnamon sugar, mix $^1/_2$ ounce (15 g) of cinnamon with 1 pound (480 g) of sugar.

Recipe 16.10a makes this dough into cinnamon rolls. Roll up the dough tightly and evenly, but seal only the seam. This makes an attractive swirl when the dough is cut. You can add raisins, chopped dates, or nuts with the cinnamon sugar.

You can produce a variety of pastries for breakfast and coffee break by adding fillings of caramel, nuts, cheese, dried fruit, or preserves. You can make up the dough like cinnamon rolls, or flatten $1^1/_2$-ounce (45 g) rounds of dough and put the filling in an indentation in the center. You can make it into a coffee cake.

BRIOCHE. The rich, delicate roll known as **brioche** (bree-ohsh) is often served at breakfast in Europe, but it can be served with lunch or dinner or used as a container like popovers. As you can see by scanning the formula (Recipe 16.11), it is made by the sponge dough method. This allows the best fermentation for a formula rich in eggs and butter.

Remember that in this method the sponge is fermented before all the ingredients have been added to the dough. Butter, which inhibits yeast

Recipe 16-11 BRIOCHE

YIELD: ***3 lb $2^1/_2$ oz to 3 lb $6^1/_2$ oz (1685–1810 g) dough***

Sponge:

8 oz	**milk**	**250 g**
1 oz	**compressed yeast**	**30 g**
8 oz	**bread flour**	**250 g**
8 oz	**eggs**	**310 g**
1 lb	**bread flour**	**500 g**
1 oz	**sugar**	**30 g**
$^1/_2$ oz	**salt**	**15 g**
10–14 oz	**butter, softened**	**300–425 g**
	egg wash as needed	

1. Heat milk to 100°F (38°C). Stir in yeast and flour to form the sponge.
2. Cover and let ferment until doubled—about $1^1/_2$ to 2 hours.
3. In mixer, with paddle at medium speed, gradually add eggs to sponge. Beat in dry ingredients. Add butter little by little until absorbed.
4. Ferment covered in refrigerator overnight or at 90°F (32°C) for 20 minutes.
5. Punch down, scale, and round. Bench-proof 10–20 minutes.
6. Make up and pan as desired.
7. Proof at 90°F (32°C) until doubled. Test with fingertips.
8. Brush with egg wash. Bake at 400°F (200°C) until golden and firm.

growth, is not included in the sponge. The mixing time for the sponge is short to avoid gluten development (enough gluten will develop during fermentation). Even with all these conditions favorable to yeast growth, the fermentation time is long.

When the rest of the ingredients are added, the mixing time is short. The paddle mixes better than the dough arm, and since strong gluten development is not wanted in a tender roll, cutting the gluten strands is not a concern. Mixing ends when the butter is absorbed. The dough will be very soft and sticky.

Because of this soft, sticky consistency many bakers cover the dough at this point and put it in the refrigerator, where it will ferment very slowly. The cold dough will be easier to handle during the remaining steps. If not refrigerated, doughs made by the sponge method will follow mixing with the usual fermentation step, but the dough will double in half the usual time.

Recipe 16-11a TRADITIONAL BRIOCHE

YIELD: *3 dozen rolls*

Using brioche dough from Recipe 16.11:

In Step 5, scale at $1^1/_2$ oz (50 g).
In Step 6, make up and pan as follows.

1. Using the edge of your hand, roll one-fourth of the rounded dough away from the rest without separating. Continue rolling until both pieces are smooth and round.
b. Place large-end-first into oiled fluted tin and lightly press the small ball into the larger ball.

Baking time: About 20–25 minutes.

Per serving:		Carbohydrates:	15 g
Calories:	140	Cholesterol:	44 mg
Fat:	7 g	Fiber:	1 g
Protein:	3 g	Sodium:	380 mg

Figure 16-10 MAKING BRIOCHE

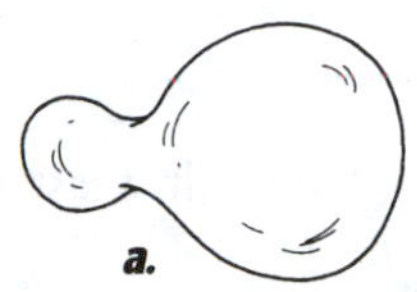

a. Using the edge of your hand, roll one-fourth of the rounded dough away from the rest without separating. Continue rolling until both pieces are smooth and round. ***b.*** Place large-end-first into oiled fluted tin and lightly press the small ball into the larger ball.

The traditional brioche shown in Figure 16.10 is made up in a fluted tin, with a small round piece on top of a large ball as shown in the drawing. Pressing down the small ball keeps it from separating too much during proofing and baking. Egg wash helps provide the shiny golden-brown color of the finished roll. Brioche can also be baked in loaf pans, as muffins, or in many other shapes.

ROLLED-IN YEAST DOUGHS. Croissants and Danish pastry are made with rich yeast doughs into which butter is rolled in the makeup process. After a short mixing and chilling period the dough is rolled out, the butter is applied, and dough and butter are folded into layers and refrigerated for 3 to 4 hours. The rolling, chilling, and folding are repeated twice, trapping 300 layers of butter between thin layers of dough and creating a tender, flaky roll.

These delectable rolls are seldom made in the ordinary kitchen; they require a great deal of time and a certain amount of skill. It is more practical to buy the frozen dough or the fresh-baked product.

Now, you have read about a wide variety of yeast doughs. By scaling accurately and following procedures carefully, you can avoid most problems in your finished breads and rolls. But

Figure 16-11 SOME COMMON PROBLEMS WITH YEAST PRODUCTS AND THEIR CAUSES

PROBLEM: Incorrect volume.
CAUSES: Too much or too little salt, yeast, or dough scaled. Improper mixing or fermentation. Weak flour.
PROBLEM: Poor shape, split or blistered crust.
CAUSES: Careless molding and shaping. Underproofed or overproofed. Too much liquid. Weak flour.
PROBLEM: Texture too dense.
CAUSES: Not enough yeast. Underproofed.
PROBLEM: Crumbly texture, gray color.
CAUSES: Incorrect mixing. Too much dusting flour. Overproofed. Fermentation temperature too high. Fermentation time too long. Baking temperature too low.
PROBLEM: Crust too dark.
CAUSES: Baking time too long. Baking temperature too high. Too much milk or sugar.
PROBLEM: Crust too pale.
CAUSES: Baking time too short. Baking temperature too low. Overfermented. Too little sugar or milk.
PROBLEM: Poor flavor.
CAUSES: Poor-quality ingredients. Too little salt. Improper fermentation. Poor sanitation. Improper storage.

sometimes things don't come out well and you wonder what went wrong. Common problems and their causes are outlined in Figure 16.11.

STIFF DOUGHS

Stiff doughs, when made up, have the firmest texture and the highest flour-to-liquid ratios of all the baking mixtures. The major types are pie doughs, short doughs, and puff pastry. They are all composed mainly of flour, fat, and liquid. The wide variety of products you can make from them comes mainly from mixing and makeup techniques as well as final assembly with other preparations.

Pie doughs and short doughs are used mostly for desserts, and are treated in detail in the next chapter. **Puff pastry dough**, on the other hand, is used almost as much in the hot-food kitchen as for desserts. For puff pastry, fat—usually butter—is rolled into the dough as for croissants and Danish pastry, but puff pastry depends solely on steam from the butter for its leavening. When properly made and baked it can rise up to eight times its thickness!

The dough consists of flour, liquid, salt, and a small amount of butter, mixed until combined. After a period of relaxing, a large amount of additional butter is rolled into the dough in the manner of rolled-in yeast doughs. The amount can range from 50 to 100 percent of the weight of the flour. Since it is the steam from the water in the butter that provides the leavening during baking, 100% butter yields the largest increase in volume.

The dough is rolled and folded from four to six times, depending on whether it is folded in quarters (called 4-folds) or in thirds (3-folds). Since this makes 1280 layers, it is easy to see why the French give the name *mille-feuilles*—a thousand loaves—to desserts made with this pastry.

Napoleons, tart shells, cheese straws, turnovers, and cream horns are a very few of the desserts made with this amazing dough. In the hot-food kitchen, you can make patty shells and vol-au-vents (vo-lo-von) as containers for sauced foods, or bake chicken breasts, fish fillets, or beef tenderloin wrapped in puff pastry for elegant en croute (on kroot, meaning "in crust") entrées. Figure 16.12 illustrates a few of these possibilities.

Puff pastry dough demands not only time but skill. The rolling-out must be uniform and the corners must be kept square and the edges even or the layers will not build up evenly and the dough won't rise uniformly in baking. You must avoid pulling and stretching. The temperature must be just right so the butter is neither too firm nor too soft. All in all, this is a dough for the experienced pastry chef.

Most kitchens without pastry chefs take advantage of the frozen puff pastry dough products available. These include 15-pound blocks of dough that can be rolled, shaped, or cut. Even easier are prerolled sheets and squares.

Figure 16-12 PUFF PASTRY DOUGH PRODUCTS

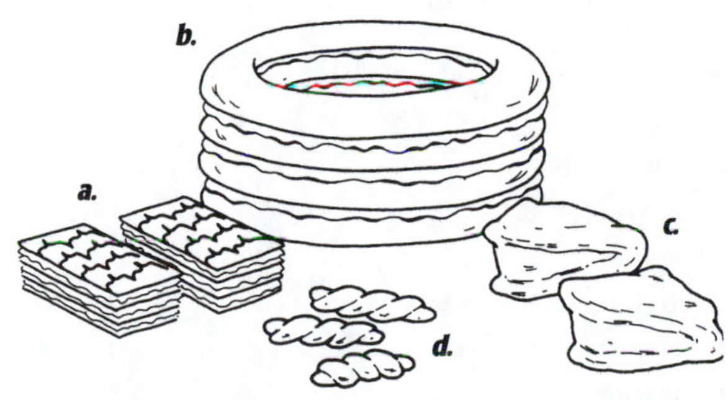

a. Napoleons. ***b.*** Patty shells (vol-au-vent). ***c.*** Turnovers, sweet and savory. ***d.*** Cheese straws.

Here are some guidelines for working with puff pastry:

- Avoid pulling or stretching the dough when rolling or shaping it; it will cause shrinking and toughening.
- For proper rising during baking, keep the dough cool while you are working with it. Don't let egg wash or your fingers touch the edges, or the layers may stick together. Make straight, even cuts with a sharp knife.
- Refrigerate items before baking. Bake at 400°F (200°C) until thoroughly done. Products should be very crisp and brown or they will be too chewy.

SUMMING UP

Baking is very different from making a soup or a sauce or cooking a steak to doneness, even though many of the same physical and chemical reactions take place in the cooking. In baking, it is essential to use exact ingredients and amounts to achieve a successful product. You can add salt to a soup at the end of cooking. But if you forget to put salt in the bread dough, the baked bread is a failure.

There is a definite pattern to the baking process. As heat is applied, the rising temperature within the dough or batter causes bubbles of gas provided by leaveners to form and expand. The elastic gluten in the flour expands to contain the bubbles and form a network of cells around them. As the internal temperature continues to rise, starches absorb moisture and gelatinize, proteins coagulate, the gluten becomes rigid, the inner structure of the finished product firms, and the outer crust browns. When all these processes are completed, the product is done.

Batters and doughs are primarily flour–liquid mixtures with one or more added ingredients—leavening, eggs, fat, sugar, salt, flavorings. Each ingredient contributes certain qualities, and in each product the proportions of ingredients are critical to the final product. If you understand your ingredients and what they are supposed to do, you will know how to use them properly and can avoid faults in the finished product.

The basic flour–liquid mixtures vary in texture from the thin pour batters that make pancakes and popovers to the stiff doughs that make pie crusts, tarts, and puff pastry. Different mixing methods are called for, appropriate to the batter type. The goal is to distribute the ingredients evenly and at the same time achieve just the right gluten development—a neat trick.

When the dough or batter is properly mixed, it is prepared for baking by makeup into rolls, loaves, muffins, or whatever the product is to be. This is done by scaling the mixture into equal pieces, forming these pieces into the proper shapes, and panning them for baking. Some, especially yeast doughs and stiff doughs, can be turned into many different products simply by making them up differently.

After baking, the product must be cooled and stored properly to keep staling to a minimum. Products like waffles, pancakes, and fritters are cooked to order and served at once (have you ever tasted a cold pancake?). Products to be stored any length of time must be frozen.

Some of the products we have explored in this chapter are complete in themselves. Others, such as choux paste products and puff pastry, are only the starting point for delectable desserts and pastries. We will have more to say about these in the next chapter.

The Cook's Vocabulary

baker's percentages
baking powder
baking process
baking soda
batters: pour, drop
bench proofing
brioche
creaming method
dock
doughs: soft, stiff
éclair paste (choux paste)
emulsified or high-ratio shortening
emulsion
extract
fermentation
foaming method
formula
gluten
kneading
leavener or leavening agent
leavening
makeup
modified straight dough method
muffin method
panned
pastry method
pinning out
popover
profiterole
proofing
proof box
puff pastry dough
punching
quick bread

rounding
scaling
shortening
sponge dough method
straight dough method
yeast
yeast doughs: lean, rich, hard roll, soft roll, sweet roll, rolled-in

Review Questions

Answer each question in complete sentences. Read each question carefully and make sure you answer all parts of the question. Organize your answer into more than one paragraph when appropriate.

1. What do you think is the greatest difference between baking and other kinds of cooking? Explain your answer.
2. Describe the changes that heat brings about during baking and explain why bakers call their recipes formulas.
3. Explain the role of gluten in baking. Mention several ways to develop gluten and several ways to relax it or avoid its development.
4. How do leaveners increase volume?
5. What are the biggest differences between yeast doughs and other doughs and batters? How do these differences affect the product?
6. Name two products made from pour batters, drop batters, pastes, hard roll dough, soft roll dough, sweet roll dough, rolled-in yeast dough, and stiff doughs. State 2 characteristics of each batter or dough.

Chapter 17

DESSERTS

For centuries, people have been putting together delicious combinations of fruits, sugars, eggs, milk, butter, and grain products to satisfy their sweet tooth. An array of such dishes appears today on the typical menu card for a delightful finish to a dinner, lunch, or brunch. These dishes are mostly products of the bakeshop, whether they are bought from a bakery or come out of a special corner of the kitchen.

This chapter completes the story of basic bakeshop production, building on the knowledge of ingredients, mixing methods, and techniques you gained in Chapter 16. You will find it useful to dip back into that chapter now and then to reinforce your understanding of the baking process and of baking ingredients, mixing methods, and such techniques as whipping eggs, scaling, makeup, and panning.

Even though you may never become a baker, you can use your knowledge, understanding, and baking skills in the hot-food kitchen. They will enable you to make great quiche, pancakes, popovers, patty shells, biscuits, fritters, savory soufflés, en croûte entrées, and many other products featured on other parts of the menu. And when you see in this chapter how hundreds of products are made by putting together a few basic components in different ways, you can apply this idea not only to creating your own dessert specialties but also to making all kinds of menu dishes.

After completing this chapter, you should be able to:

- Describe three cookie mixing methods and seven cookie makeup styles and apply them in making cookies.
- Describe three mixing methods for cakes, explain when and why they are used, and apply them in making cakes.
- Explain how to make icings, fillings, toppings, and glazes and how to use them in finishing cakes and cookies.
- Explain the roles of eggs in making custards, meringues, and soufflés, and deal with eggs correctly in making these products.
- Describe or demonstrate how to make pie doughs, fillings, and finished pies.

COOKIES

Fresh cookies can provide a special accompaniment to ice cream or sherbet, variety on a dessert buffet, or even treats "to go." Cookies are made in more sizes, shapes, flavors, and textures than any other type of baked item. Several factors account for this great variety. One is differences in ingredients and proportions. Another is three different mixing methods. Still another is seven different makeup styles. When you add to all this the many different flavorers you can use and the many ways you can decorate cookies, you have infinite variety at your fingertips.

ABOUT COOKIES IN GENERAL

Cookies draw on the same groups of ingredients as the baked goods in Chapter 16, but as desserts they are higher in fat and sugar, and they avoid high-gluten flours in favor of melt-in-the-mouth tenderness. They have their own special mixing methods—three of them—since certain combinations of ingredients must be put together in a certain way or they won't form a smooth, uniform dough. So we have:

- The **creaming method,** used for doughs that are high in fat. In this method, you cream fat, sugar, and flavorings together with the paddle, add eggs and liquid, and mix in flour and leavener last.
- The **one-stage method**—the simplest and quickest—used for doughs that are low in moisture, high in fat and sugar, and can stand some gluten development. In this method, you mix everything together at once.
- The **foam method** (sometimes termed **sponge method**), used for doughs that are high in eggs and low or lacking in fat. In this method, you whip the whole eggs, yolks, or whites with sugar and carefully fold in the remaining ingredients by hand.

The texture of cookie doughs varies from soft but firm to very stiff according to the proportions of flour, sugar, fat, and liquid. The creaming and one-stage methods are used for firm and stiff doughs. Doughs made by the foam method resemble the pastes in Chapter 16 and can be piped out like pâte à choux. The texture of the doughs does not necessarily correspond to the texture of the finished cookie, which may be crisp, soft, or chewy depending on such factors as the characteristics of the ingredients; the amounts of sugar, fat, and liquid; the makeup style; the size of the cookie; and the baking time.

We will examine each of the three mixing methods in detail by following a formula through all the procedures. We will also examine the seven makeup styles: drop, bar, bagged, rolled, icebox, molded, sheet. In the meantime, let us look at some guidelines that apply to all kinds of cookies made in all kinds of ways:

- In all three methods, ingredients must be at room temperature before mixing. Otherwise, they will not mix properly, and if they are not properly mixed, they will not turn into the excellent product you want to serve your guests.
- All ingredients must be scaled accurately and all instructions must be followed carefully. Cookies are no different from other baked product: They are chemical formulas and must be followed exactly.
- Scale all cookies in a batch to a uniform size. This makes an attractive appearance and ensures even baking.
- Before baking, you may decorate cookies with nuts, candied fruit, sugar, coconut, or chocolate sprinkles. After baking, you can ice them with frosting or melted chocolate or dust them with powdered sugar.
- Many cookie doughs made by the one-stage or creaming method can be refrigerated or frozen before baking. This allows you to bake them as needed. Foam-method cookies must be baked immediately.

- Choose clean pans that are not warped. Line them with parchment paper (for most cookies). It eliminates the need to grease or flour and saves time, money, and labor.
- Doughs that are very rich in fat may burn on the bottom. To prevent this, double-pan them: Place a second pan of the same size under the pan with the cookies.
- Baking times are short with relatively high temperatures. Most cookies have reached doneness when the edges and bottoms take on a light golden color. Watch them very carefully because they can overbake in as little as one minute.
- Cookies continue to bake after you take them out of the oven because of heat stored in the pan. Allow for this in judging doneness.
- Cool cookies slowly away from drafts or they may crack. Soft cookies should cool and firm up before you remove them from the pan. Others can be removed while still warm. Like bread, cookies should be completely cool before being stored so that moisture won't accumulate and make them soggy.
- All cookies should be wrapped with plastic film when cool. Exposure to air increases staling.
- When carefully wrapped, cookies can be held or stored at room temperature for two days to a week, depending on the type of cookie. All cookies can be frozen after baking to maintain freshness. Simply let them thaw or reheat them very briefly at a low temperature.

Recipe 17-1 CHOCOLATE CHIP COOKIES

YIELD: *50 cookies*

$2^1/_4$ C	**flour**	**550 mL**
1 tsp	**baking soda**	**5 mL**
1 tsp	**salt**	**5 mL**
1 C	**softened butter, margarine, or shortening**	**250 mL**
$^3/_4$ C	**white sugar**	**185 mL**
$^3/_4$ C	**brown sugar, firmly packed**	**185 mL**
2 eggs		
$^1/_2$ tsp	**water**	**2 mL**
1 tsp	**vanilla**	**5 mL**
2 C	**chocolate chips**	**500 mL**
$^3/_4$ C	**nuts**	**185 mL**

1. Combine butter, margarine, or shortening, and sugars in mixer. Beat until creamy with paddle.
2. Stop the mixer and scrape down the bowl.
3. Slowly beat in eggs, water, and vanilla. Mix until light and fluffy.
4. Sift together flour, baking soda, and salt.
5. Add flour mixture all at once and blend on low speed just until combined.
6. Blend chocolate chips and nuts on low speed.
7. Drop by teaspoonfuls onto greased sheet pans.
8. Bake at 375°F (190°C) for 8–12 minutes until edges are lightly colored.

Per cookie:		Carbohydrates:	13 g
Calories:	118	Cholesterol:	19 mg
Fat:	7 g	Fiber:	1 g
Protein:	1 g	Sodium:	116 mg

CREAMING METHOD

Now, let's take a step-by-step look at cookies mixed by the creaming method. Recipe 17.1 gives us the ever-popular chocolate chip cookie as an example. You start with all ingredients at room temperature and you scale them accurately, of course.

In Step 1, the fat and sugar are beaten with the paddle at medium speed to form an emulsion that will hold the liquids when they are added. At the same time, the paddle beats in bubbles of air, which are held in the emulsion and will provide leavening during baking to lighten texture. You use the paddle rather than the whip because this mixture is too stiff for the whip and may break it. Do not use high speed for creaming, thinking you will save time. Not as many air cells will form.

Notice the instruction to **scrape down** at the end of Step 2. For this, you stop the motor and use a plastic dough scraper (Figure 17.1a) or rubber spatula to scrape the bottom and sides of the bowl and the paddle completely. If you skip this step, some ingredients will cling to the bowl and paddle and will not be incorporated completely into the dough. You will use this important technique in many kinds of dessert formulas. *Always turn the motor off before scraping down to avoid accidents.*

In most cookies made by the creaming method, the butter and sugar are mixed until the volume has increased considerably and the texture is light and fluffy. The exceptions are dense, chewy cookies, such as oatmeal cookies, that need to keep their shape during baking; they are mixed only until a paste is formed. The paste will not spread as much during baking. Salt, flavoring, and spices are often added at this stage to distribute them evenly.

In Step 3, you add the eggs and other liquids little by little to give them time to be absorbed completely. Continue mixing until light and fluffy—as much as 5 minutes—to increase the eggs' ability to emulsify and hold the other ingredients without curdling. Don't forget to scrape down.

Sifting the flour and soda in Step 4 distributes the soda evenly. Add the sifted mixture all at once, mixing on low speed to avoid flour dust flying everywhere! To avoid toughness in the finished cookies, mix only until combined so that gluten will not build up. Add the chocolate chips and nuts last, and again mix only until they are distributed evenly.

The **drop method** of makeup (Step 7) is one of the fastest and easiest. Use a portion scoop for uniformity. A No. 30 scoop makes 1 ounce (30 g) of dough that will spread into a fairly large chocolate chip cookie. Space evenly about 2 inches (5 cm) apart for a cookie this size. For smaller cookies, use a higher numbered scoop.

The drop method can be used for almost every kind of cookie. Likewise, cookies made by the creaming method can be made up by any other method.

Bake these chocolate chip cookies only until the edges have colored and firmed slightly (Step 8). Remember that they will continue to bake somewhat after you take them out of the oven. Cool them on the pan.

Figure 17-1 DESSERT EQUIPMENT

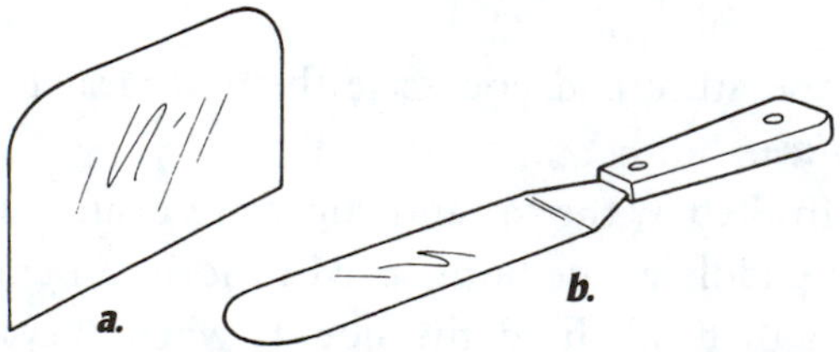

a. Dough scraper, a flexible piece of plastic 4 × 6 inches (8 × 12 cm) used for scrape down and folding. ***b.*** A cake spatula, used to smooth cake batters and to apply icing and fillings.

ONE-STAGE METHOD

The next recipe (Recipe 17.2) illustrates the one-stage mixing method. You may recognize this method as a counterpart of the straight dough yeast method (Chapter 16). Before you begin the mixing, there are two preliminary steps: preparing the raisins and sifting the dry ingredients. Then you just mix everything together thoroughly on low speed (Step 3), scraping down

Recipe 17-2 RAISIN SPICE BARS

YIELD: *6 dozen bars 1 × 3 in. (2.5 3 8 cm)*

1 lb 8 oz	**pastry flour**	**750 g**
1/4 oz	**baking soda**	**7 g**
1/4 oz	**salt**	**7 g**
1/4 oz	**cinnamon**	**7 g**
8 oz	**butter, margarine, or shortening**	**250 g**
1 lb	**granulated sugar**	**500 g**
8 oz	**brown sugar**	**250 g**
8 oz	**eggs**	**250 g**
1 lb 8 oz	**raisins**	**750 g**
	egg wash as needed	
	confectioners' sugar as needed	

1. If raisins are hard, soak in hot water until soft. Drain and dry thoroughly.
2. Sift together flour, baking soda, salt, and cinnamon.
3. One-stage mixing method:
   a. Place all ingredients in a mixer bowl and mix with paddle on low speed.
   b. When partially combined, scrape down bowl.
   c. Continue mixing until blended.
4. Bar makeup method:
   a. Scale dough into four equal units. Chill thoroughly.
   b. Form chilled dough into rolls as long as the width of a sheet pan. Space rolls evenly on a paper-lined pan.
   c. Flatten each roll until about 3 in. (8 cm) wide.
5. Brush tops with egg wash.
6. Bake at 350°F (180°C) until firm and lightly golden (about 12–15 minutes).
7. When cool, cut into 1 in. (2.5 cm) bars. Ice or dust with confectioners' sugar.

Per bar:		Carbohydrates:	24 g
Calories:	126	Cholesterol:	20 mg
Fat:	3 g	Fiber:	1 g
Protein:	2 g	Sodium:	98 mg

midway in the process. Finished dough will be blended but not ultrasmooth. Don't overmix or the gluten will develop too much.

You may notice that there is no milk or water in this formula. Liquid is provided by the eggs and butter. This is a very stiff dough.

The **bar method** of makeup is used in Step 4. You could also make up these cookies with the drop, sheet, icebox, rolled, or molded method, but this dough is too stiff to bag.

The bar method requires chilled dough for easy handling. Form it into rolls on a dusted bench. Space the rolls across the sheet pan, and flatten them with your fingers or a pin.

Brush the tops with egg wash for a shiny look, but don't let the wash drip down the sides or the bars will stick to the paper. Bake these strips until firm but still springy and lightly colored on the edges. Let them cool completely in the pan, then cut crosswise into uniform bars, using a sharp or serrated knife. Dust with powdered sugar or use an icing to frost them.

FOAM (SPONGE) METHOD

Recipe 17.3, ladyfingers, demonstrates the foam, or sponge, method. Notice that the formula contains no butter, no milk or water, and no leavening other than the air you will beat into the batter. It is all eggs, sugar, and flour. The foam method whips and folds them step by step into a soft, delicate batter. The method is not limited to fat-free batters, however; brownies, which are heavy in butter and chocolate, are often made by the foam method. The key to foams is the role of the eggs, which emulsify the other ingredients and add leavening at the same time.

You begin by whipping yolks and sugar at high speed, maximizing the emulsifying power of the yolks and incorporating the most air possible.

Recipe 17-3 LADYFINGERS

YIELD: ***8 dozen ladyfingers***

8 oz	**egg yolks**	**240 g**
8 oz	**granulated sugar**	**240 g**
8 oz	**pastry flour, sifted**	**240 g**
10 oz	**egg whites**	**300 g**
2 oz	**granulated sugar**	**60 g**
	powdered sugar as needed	

1. Foam mixing method:
   a. In a mixer bowl, using whip, whip egg yolks with 8 oz (240 g) sugar on high speed until very thick and light—about 10–12 minutes.
   b. Remove bowl from machine. With scraper or spatula, fold in sifted flour.
   c. In another mixer bowl, whip egg whites on high speed to a soft peak. Add 2 oz (60 g) sugar and whip to stiff peak.
   d. By hand, carefully fold whites into yolk mixture.
2. Bagged makeup method:
   a. Place mixture in pastry bag fitted with a large plain tube.
   b. Pipe out 3 × $^3/_4$ in. (8 × 2 cm) strips onto parchment-lined sheet pans.
   c. Dust lightly with powdered sugar.
3. Bake at 375°F (190°C) until edges are very light brown (about 10 minutes).

Per serving:		Carbohydrates:	5 g
Calories:	30	Cholesterol:	30 mg
Fat:	1 g	Fiber:	0 g
Protein:	1 g	Sodium:	6 mg

The mixture will be very thick and pale yellow and should double or triple its original volume.

Before adding the flour in Step 1b, you sift it to eliminate lumps and to lighten it. Carefully fold it in by hand (Figure 17.2), maintaining as much volume as possible. This is the folding technique described in Chapter 3.

To fold in flour, use a plastic scraper or rubber spatula. Sift the flour onto the top of the batter. Start folding by moving the scraper down the side and across the bottom of the bowl. Then bring it up the opposite side, bringing batter with it, and turn it to spread the batter over the flour on top. Continue this motion, moving around the bowl, until the flour is blended with the foam. Avoid cutting through the batter. The goal is to avoid deflating it as much as possible.

Whipping the egg whites (Step 1c) also deserves special attention. Soft peak and stiff peak can be considered "degrees of doneness" for egg whites. You will remember from making waffles in Chapter 16 that egg whites beaten to a soft peak will stand up but the top will curl over. In many formulas for cakes and cookies, after the soft-peak stage is reached, part or all of the sugar

Figure 17-2 FOLDING

To fold ingredients into a mixture, use a spatula to go down the side, across the bottom and up the opposite side as you rotate the bowl.

from the formula is added and the mixture is then whipped to a stiff peak, meaning that the top or peak will stand up without curling over. It is very important to stop beating as soon as a stiff peak will form. If you are not careful, you can very quickly overbeat the whites. They should look moist and shiny. If they look dry and form large lumps or curds, they are overbeaten and much of their leavening ability is lost.

After you have whipped the egg whites with the sugar to a stiff but moist peak, fold them in until no streaks remain. Use the same folding technique, and once again keep as much volume as possible.

In Step 2, you make up the ladyfingers using the **bagged method.** This method can be used for almost any kind of dough that is soft enough to bag out, but it is used most often for doughs made by the foam method.

Follow the steps in the formula. You may want to glue the corners of the parchment to the pan with a dab of the mixture. This keeps the paper from pulling up when you pull up with the bag at the end of each strip of dough. Dust lightly with confectioners' sugar, and bake at once.

Foam cookies must be baked immediately because the air incorporated in beating, which will turn to steam in the oven, is often the only leavening agent. A high temperature is needed to create the steam. Cooking time is short: These cookies will be done when they are a very pale golden brown. Cool completely before removing them from pans for storing.

MAKEUP METHODS

The mixing method for any given formula depends on ingredients and ratios. The makeup method, on the other hand, usually depends an how the cookie should look. Most cookie doughs can be made up by nearly all seven methods, with a different look for each. The method chosen will often depend on what the cookies will be used for and the demands of production as much as on the traditional look of the particular cookie.

Here is a quick summary of the seven makeup styles, including those you have already examined closely:

- Drop. Use a portion scoop to place uniform amounts of dough onto sheet pans.
- Bar. Form equal pieces of chilled dough into cylinders. Space three or four logs crosswise on a sheet pan. Flatten with fingers or roll to make strips. Cut strips into 1-inch (2.5 cm) pieces after baking.
- Bagged (sometimes called spritz or pressed). Use a pastry bag to press out onto sheet pans uniform amounts of dough in the size and shape desired. To use this method, the dough must be soft enough to pipe. Foam cookies are most often bagged.
- **Rolled.** Chill a stiff dough. On a lightly dusted bench with a lightly dusted pin, roll dough to a uniform thickness of $^1/_8$ to $^1/_4$ inch (3–6 mm). Press cookie cutters dipped in flour into the dough as close together as you can. Slide a straight cake spatula (Figure 17.1b) under the cut-out cookies to lift them and place on paper-lined pans.

  Rolled cookies are often decorated before baking with nuts, sugar, and so on. After baking, they can be iced and decorated, or you can put two together with frosting or melted chocolate for a delicious sweet sandwich.
- **Icebox or refrigerator.** Scale a stiff dough into equal units and form them into cylinders of uniform dimensions—usually 1 to 2 inches (2–5 cm). Wrap in parchment or waxed paper and chill at least 4 to 6 hours. Slice into

uniform slices and place on paper-lined sheet pans.

These cookies can also be decorated. Or you can color part of a batch and form it into logs. Pin out remaining dough 1/4 inch (5 mm) thick and the same length as the logs. Brush lightly with egg wash to act as glue, and wrap around the logs (Figure 17.3a). Wrap, chill, slice, and bake.

To make pinwheels, pin out equal-sized sheets of colored and white dough. Egg-wash the colored sheet, place the white sheet on top, and roll up to form a log (Figure 17.3b). Wrap, chill, slice, and bake.

- **Molded.** Shape uniform portions of dough by hand or place in special molds to bake.

  Madeleines, for example, which are made from a sponge dough, are baked in special molds. The familiar peanut butter cookie, made from a stiff dough, is also molded. To mold it, place balls of 1/2 to 1 ounce (15–30 g) on paper-lined pans 1 to 2 inches (2–5 cm) apart. Dip a fork in sugar to prevent sticking and press down on each ball to flatten and make the traditional crisscross marks. Other molded cookies may use a weight or the bottom of a glass to flatten.

- **Sheet.** Spread or roll dough evenly into sheet pans lined with parchment or greased and floured, making sure the dough fills the corners completely. After baking, cool and cut into squares or rectangles.

Figure 17-3 REFRIGERATOR COOKIES

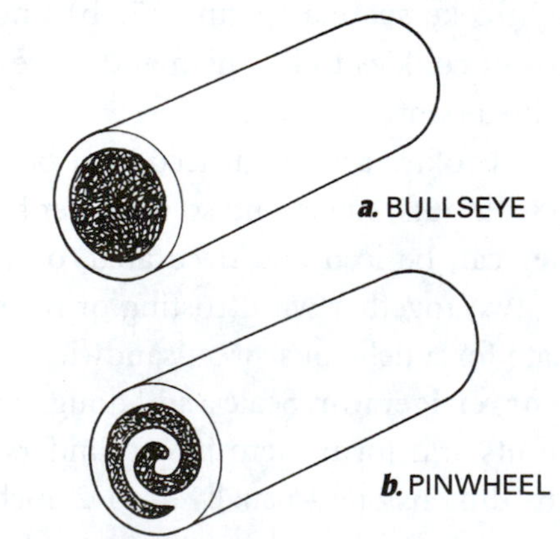

a. Bullseye. ***b.*** Pinwheel.

The word cookie means "little cake." We will see in the next section that the two have more similarities than differences.

CAKES

Cakes are another baked product made in incredible variety using a few basic methods and the same kinds of ingredients used for all baked goods.

ABOUT CAKES IN GENERAL

Cakes, like cookies, are high in sugar and usually in fat and low in gluten, since tenderness is the goal. Most are made with cake flour, which has the least gluten of the white flours.

The biggest difference between cake and cookie batters is in the amount of liquid used. Most cake batters are thin and pour readily. They typically have high ratios of liquid to flour, sugar, and fat. Incorporating all this liquid without making the mixture curdle requires special care in mixing.

Like cookies, cakes are mixed by three basic methods. They correspond fairly closely to the three cookie-mixing methods, but you will see some definite differences. The creaming method is essentially the same as the creaming method for cookies. The **two-stage method** is similar to the one-stage cookie method, but it incorporates the liquid in two distinct stages—hence, its name. The foam method corresponds to the foam method for cookies.

We will look at the three methods in detail, using a formula as an example for each. But, first, here are some guidelines for making cakes by any method:

- Have all ingredients at room temperature and scale them accurately.
- Follow instructions carefully. Do not try to take shortcuts or combine steps. Cake emulsions must be built little by little.
- Scale batter uniformly into pans lined with parchment or greased and floured (except for foam cakes, which require ungreased pans). Smooth batter in pan.
- Rap pans sharply on the bench (again, except for foam cakes) to release large air bubbles that may be trapped in the batter. They will make tunnels in the finished cake.
- Bake promptly.
- Don't let pans touch each other in the oven; the heat cannot circulate and the cakes will not bake evenly.
- The correct temperature is very important: Too high and the crust will form too early; too low and the dough will not expand properly.
- There are three tests of doneness. The sides begin to pull away from the edges of the pan. The center is firm and springy. A wooden toothpick inserted in the center comes out clean.
- When the cake is done, remove it from the oven and let it cool in the pan away from drafts. Cakes are tender and fragile and will break or crack if removed from the pan when more than barely warm. After the initial cooling, turn cakes out of pans bottoms up onto racks to cool completely. This allows air to circulate around them, preventing a soggy bottom.
- When completely cool, wrap cakes in plastic wrap and hold in a cool place or in the freezer.

CREAMING METHOD

Pound cake (Recipe 17.4) is an example of the many butter cakes made by the creaming method. It is one of the oldest and simplest cakes. This method of mixing was the only one avail-

Recipe 17-4 POUND CAKE

YIELD: ***1 cake or 10 servings***

1 1/2 C	**flour**	**375 mL**
1/4 tsp	**baking powder**	**1 mL**
1/2 C	**butter, room temperature**	**125 mL**
1 C	**sugar**	**250 mL**
1/2 tsp	**vanilla**	**2 mL**
3	**eggs, room temperature**	
1/2 C	**sour cream, room temperature**	**125 mL**

1. Mix together flour and baking powder.
2. In a mixing bowl, beat butter on medium speed for 30 seconds. Gradually add sugar, beating about 10 minutes or until very light and fluffy. Beat in vanilla.
3. Blend in a little of the flour mixture; then add eggs 1 at a time and blend until incorporated.
4. Scrape down bowl. Beat until light and fluffy—about 5 minutes.
5. Mix in remaining flour mixture on low speed until just blended.
6. Pour batter into greased baking pan.
7. Bake at 350° (180°C) until done—about 1 hour.

Per serving:		Carbohydrates:	33 g
Calories:	268	Cholesterol:	94 mg
Fat:	13 g	Fiber:	0 g
Protein:	4 g	Sodium:	134 mg

able for high-fat cakes until the development of emulsified shortening. It produces a coarser, slightly less tender cake than the other two methods.

Compare the instructions for pound cake with those for chocolate chip cookies. You will find them similar except where you add just a little of the flour. This prevents the mixture from curdling when the rest of the eggs are added.

This cake can be flavored with nutmeg or finely grated orange or lemon zest. Raisins, nuts, and candied fruit are other possibilities. To make into a chocolate cake, cocoa is used.

TWO-STAGE METHOD

The two-stage method of mixing cakes was developed when emulsified shortenings became available. You will remember from Chapter 16 that this type of fat can carry a higher percentage of sugar to flour and larger amounts of liquid without curdling. This mixing method corresponds to the one-stage cookie method, except that the liquids are added in two stages. The method and the shortening type produce a smooth, liquid batter that bakes into a moist and tender cake with a texture like velvet.

The general pattern of the two-stage method is to mix the dry ingredients, the fat, and part of the liquid for 7 to 8 minutes with several scrapedowns. This is Stage 1. Sometimes the mixing is broken into several steps, with the liquid added as a separate step. In Stage 2, additional liquid is mixed with the eggs and added in three parts.

Everybody's favorite, chocolate cake (Recipe 17.5), is an example of the two-stage method. It breaks Stage 1 into three steps, with the chocolate added as a separate step to incorporate it thoroughly before the liquid is added. Low speed is used throughout the mixing.

Recipe 17-5 CHOCOLATE CAKE

YIELD: ***12 8-in. (20 cm) round layers***

2 lb	**cake flour**	**1 kg**
3/4 oz	**salt**	**25 g**
3/4 oz	**baking powder**	**25 g**
1/4 oz	**baking soda**	**7 g**
2 lb 8 oz	**sugar**	**1.2 kg**
1 lb	**emulsified shortening**	**450 g**
8 oz	**baker's chocolate, melted**	**250 g**
1 lb 4 oz	**skim milk**	**625 g**
1 lb 4 oz	**eggs, lightly beaten**	**625 g**
12 oz	**skim milk**	**375 g**

Stage 1

1. Sift flour with salt, baking powder, and baking soda. Place with sugar and fat in mixer bowl and mix with paddle on low speed for 2 minutes. Scrape down.
2. Add melted chocolate and blend on low speed for 2 minutes. Scrape down.
3. Add the first amount of skim milk and blend on low speed for 3–5 minutes, stopping mixer to scrape down several times during this mixing period.

Stage 2

1. Combine eggs with remaining skim milk. Add this mixture in 3 parts with machine running on low. Scrape down after each addition is blended in. Total mixing time for this step should be 5 minutes.
2. Scale at 12 oz (375 g) into 8-in. (20 cm) round pans.
3. Bake immediately at 375°F (190°C) until done—about 25 minutes.

Per cake:		Carbohydrates:	164 g
Calories:	1169	Cholesterol:	202 mg
Fat:	53 g	Fiber:	4 g
Protein:	17 g	Sodium:	1145 mg

A series of thorough scrape-downs is one of the most important features of this method, to keep the ingredients within reach of the paddle. They are especially important in Stage 2 when the batter becomes more liquid with each egg–milk addition. Ingredients left on the sides of the bowl do not emulsify properly and may form lumps that will cause faults in the cake. Continue mixing after the last addition until a smooth liquid batter forms.

Two-stage cakes are usually scaled with a volume measure because the batter is so thin. You balance the scale with an empty volume measure on the left. Place the desired weight on the scale and pour batter into the measure until it balances. Note the volume level that equals the weight desired, then pour the batter into a pan, using a rubber spatula to empty the measure completely. Scale the rest of the batter by using the volume measure at the level noted. For this very liquid batter, this method is much quicker and easier than weighing out.

Both creamed and two-stage batters can easily be turned into cupcakes and sheet cakes. Scale cupcakes at 1 1/2 ounce (45 g) into paper-lined or greased and floured pans. Bake them at 385°F (195°C) until done (about 15–20 minutes). Scale sheet cakes at 6 to 8 pounds (3–3.6 kg) into paper-lined sheet pans. Bake at 360°F (180°C) until springy in the center (about 35 minutes).

FOAM METHOD

Cakes made by the foam method are leavened primarily by air whipped into an egg foam. They contain little or no fat compared to other types of cakes. Sponge, angel food, and chiffon cakes are the kinds made by this method. Recipe 17.6 shows the techniques this method requires.

Sponge cake, called *génoise* (zhunwahz) by the French, uses whole eggs for the foam. The eggs must be at room temperature or warmed slightly to aid in increasing the volume. To warm them (Step 1), place the mixer bowl in water just below a simmer either in a pan on the stove or in a bain-marie. Keep stirring and do not overheat or you will make sweetened scrambled eggs. The egg mixture should reach 110°F (43°C)—slightly warmer than body temperature. You can sense a change when it is ready: It will feel looser and less viscous.

This step can be omitted, but mixing times will be longer and volume and texture will suffer. With warmed eggs, an increase in volume of three times or more is possible in Step 2. (You

Recipe 17-6 BUTTER SPONGE CAKE

YIELD: ***5 1/2 lb (2.8 kg) batter***

2 lb	**eggs**	**1 kg**
1 lb 8 oz	**sugar**	**750 g**
1/2 oz	**vanilla or other flavoring**	**15 g**
1 lb 8 oz	**cake flour**	**750 g**
8 oz	**butter, melted**	**250 g**

1. Place eggs, sugar, and flavoring in a mixer bowl. Place bowl in a bain-marie. Heat to 110°F (43°C) , stirring constantly.
2. Using whip attachment, whip on highest speed of mixer until increased in volume, thick, and light in color (about 15–30 minutes).
3. Sift flour onto top of foam and carefully fold in with rubber spatula until no streaks remain.
4. By hand, fold in melted butter just until combined.
5. Scale batter into pans prepared on the bottom only. Spread smooth.
6. Bake at 375°F (190°C) until done (about 20–25 minutes).

Figure 17-4 A ROLLED CAKE

a. Sprinkle top lightly with granulated sugar.

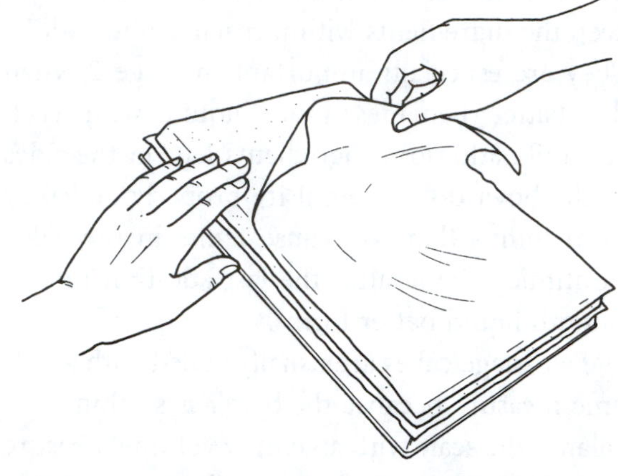

b. Place clean parchment paper on top of cake and place an inverted sheet pan over it. Turn cake out of pan onto inverted sheet pan.

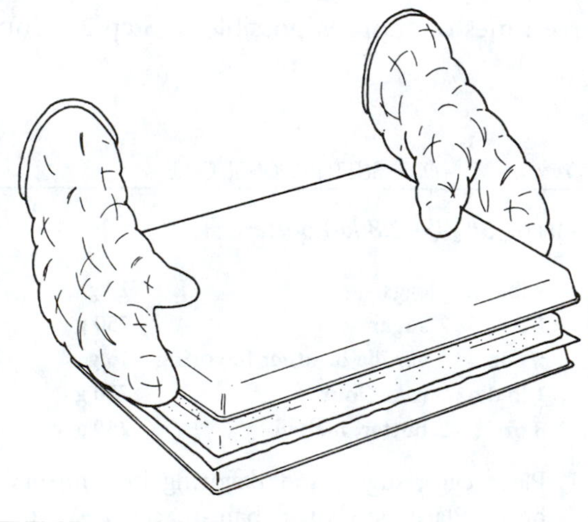

c. Carefully peel paper off cake.

d. Roll up cake in the clean parchment paper and cool.

e. To assemble, unroll and spread an even layer of jelly, preserves, buttercream, or ice cream.

f. Reroll. Ice and decorate as desired.

can also use this technique in making ladyfingers.)

Steps 3 and 4 use the folding technique described for mixing ladyfingers. In formulas having other dry ingredients, such as cocoa, cornstarch, or chemical leaveners, these would be sifted with the flour in Step 3.

In order to handle the batter as little as possible during scaling (Step 5), use a volume measure as in the two-stage scaling method. Weights for round layers are 10 to 16 ounces (280–450 g), sheet cakes scale at $2^1/_2$ pounds (1.2 kg), and cupcakes at 10 ounces (280 g) per dozen. Only the bottoms of the pans are greased or lined with paper because this batter needs to cling to the sides slightly during baking in order to rise properly.

Bake immediately. Foam batters require a higher temperature than most cakes to create the steam needed for leavening and setting. Cakes are done when the center is springy and a toothpick in the center comes out clean. This type of cake does not pull away from the sides as much as the other two types. Run a cake spatula around the sides to loosen if necessary. Cool slightly, then turn out onto racks to complete cooling.

You can make a chocolate sponge cake from Recipe 17.6 by substituting 4 ounces (125 g) of cocoa for 4 ounces of the flour. Sift the cocoa together with the remaining flour in Step 3.

You can also make a rolled cake from a sponge cake—a product of great versatility. In order to roll it, you must omit the butter from the formula to keep the cake from cracking. You scale $2^1/_2$ to 3 pounds (1–1.5 kg) of dough into a paper-lined sheet pan and bake as usual. Immediately after baking follow the steps in Figure 17.4.

Angel food cakes are made from egg white foams that require some variations in technique. You whip warmed egg whites on high speed, adding salt, cream of tartar, and flavoring when they are foamy. Continuing to whip, you add the sugar gradually, and whip until a stiff peak is reached. Mix the remaining sugar with the flour for even distribution, and fold in, using the same technique as for a sponge cake. Bake in un-

Recipe 17-6a ANGEL FOOD CAKE

YIELD: ***1 cake (12 slices)***

1 C	**cake flour**	**250 mL**
1 $^5/_8$ C	**sugar**	**400 mL**
12	**egg whites, room temperature**	
$1^1/_2$ tsp	**cream of tartar**	**8 mL**
$^1/_4$ tsp	**salt**	**1 mL**
$1^1/_2$ tsp	**vanilla**	**8 mL**
$^1/_2$ tsp	**almond flavoring**	**2 mL**

1. Sift flour and $^3/_4$ C (185 mL) sugar together.
2. Using electric mixer and whip, beat egg whites until foamy. Add cream of tartar and salt.
3. On medium speed, beat in remaining sugar a little at a time, beating for 10 seconds after each addition.
4. Continue beating, now at high speed on mixer, until whites are firm and hold stiff peaks when whip is pulled out.
5. Fold in flavorings with rubber spatula.
6. Fold in flour mixture a little at a time until it disappears.
7. Use rubber scraper and push batter from mixing bowl into tube pan (ungreased). Spread and level batter against tube and sides of pan. Cut through batter gently with a knife.
8. Bake at 350°F (175°C) for 30–45 minutes or until no imprint remains when finger lightly touches top of cake.
9. Invert cake immediately on rack. Remove cake from pan when cooled.

Per serving:		Carbohydrates:	33 g
Calories:	149	Cholesterol:	0 mg
Fat:	0 g	Fiber:	0 g
Protein:	4 g	Sodium:	104 mg

Recipe 17-6b CHIFFON CAKE

YIELD: ***1 cake, 12 servings***

$2^1/_4$ C	**cake flour**	**560 mL**
$1^1/_2$ C	**sugar**	**375 mL**
1 Tb	**baking powder**	**15 mL**
$^1/_4$ tsp	**salt**	**1 mL**
$^1/_2$ C	**cooking oil**	**125 mL**
7	**egg yolks**	
2 tsp	**lemon peel, shredded**	**10 mL**
1 tsp	**vanilla**	**5 mL**
7	**egg whites**	
$^1/_2$ tsp	**cream of tartar**	**2 mL**

1. Sift together flour, sugar, baking powder, and salt into a mixing bowl.
2. In a separate bowl, beat lightly oil, egg yolks, lemon peel, vanilla, and $^3/_4$ C (185 mL) cold water.
3. Make a well in the dry ingredients and pour in the wet ingredients. Beat on low speed until combined; then beat on high speed for 5 minutes or until very smooth.
4. Thoroughly wash beaters.
5. In a separate bowl, beat egg whites and cream of tartar on medium speed until egg whites hold stiff peaks.
6. Fold batter with rubber spatula gently into whipped egg whites.
7. Pour into a tube pan (ungreased).
8. Bake at 350°F (175°C) for 60–70 minutes or until no imprint remains when finger lightly touches top of cake.
9. Invert cake immediately on rack. Remove cake from pan when cooled.

Per serving:		Carbohydrates:	41 g
Calories:	294	Cholesterol:	124 mg
Fat:	12 g	Fiber:	0 g
Protein:	5 g	Sodium:	184 mg

greased tube pans, at a lower temperature, 350°F (180°C), to avoid early crust formation. Cool cakes completely upside down on racks to maintain their volume. Loosen with a spatula to remove from the pan.

For **chiffon cakes,** whipped egg whites are folded into a batter of flour, liquid, eggs, and oil. They are baked and cooled the same way as angel food cakes.

CONVENIENCE MIXES

Many convenience mixes are available for all types of cakes. They save a great deal of time and labor. Follow their instructions carefully and apply your knowledge of mixing methods, baking, and cooling to produce a consistently reliable result.

The cake is baked. Now let's look at some icings and see how to assemble everything for a popular finishing touch to any meal.

ICINGS AND TOPPINGS

Icings, also called **frostings,** are used to top or coat a cake and are sometimes spread between layers as a **filling.** They are made primarily of sugar, with fat, eggs, and flavorings often added. Icings serve three functions:

- They make cakes more attractive and decorative.
- They add flavor and richness.
- They improve keeping qualities by forming a protective coating around the cake.

The six basic types are fondant, flat, buttercream, royal or decorator's, boiled or foam, and fudge.

Fondant is a smooth, shiny white icing made of very fine crystallized sugar. It is difficult to make, and most bakeshops buy it as a moist paste or a dry powder to which water is added. Store both types covered at room temperature.

Fondant is sometimes thinned with **simple syrup.** This syrup is made with equal parts sugar and water heated and stirred until the sugar has dissolved and combined with the water. It is a basic preparation of many uses that should be a part of every baker's mise en place. Cover and store it at room temperature.

Here are the procedures for using fondant:

- Heat and stir the desired amount over hot water. Do not heat over 100°F (38°C) or fondant will lose its shine.
- If necessary, thin with water or simple syrup until icing is easily pourable.
- Stir in flavoring and coloring as desired.
- Pour fondant over a cake set on a rack over a sheet pan. Smooth with a cake spatula dipped in hot water (Figure 17.5a). You can scrape up the excess and strain for another use.

To make chocolate fondant, stir in 3 ounces of melted bitter chocolate per pound of fondant (90 g per 500 g) and thin to the right consistency. Many other colors and flavors can be used. For all icings, use a light hand with color and the best quality flavors possible. Pastel colors and delicate flavors are preferred.

Flat icing (Recipe 17.7) is almost a simple fondant and can be substituted for it in an emergency. Simply combine all ingredients until smooth, juggling the amounts of sugar and water to achieve a fairly stiff consistency. It will become more liquid when it is warmed for use. You can replace part of the water with milk, cream, or fruit juice, and color or flavor it as desired.

This icing is often used on coffee cakes and sweet rolls. It can also provide a simple coating for pound cakes, angel food cakes, cupcakes, and cookies.

Buttercreams are the most familiar frostings. Recipe 17.8 gives a basic recipe. Butter provides the most desirable flavor, but you can mix it with margarine or with emulsified shortening for a more stable emulsion, especially in hot weather. Salt functions as it does in other kitchen areas—as a seasoning.

Figure 17-5 ASSEMBLING CAKES AND ICINGS

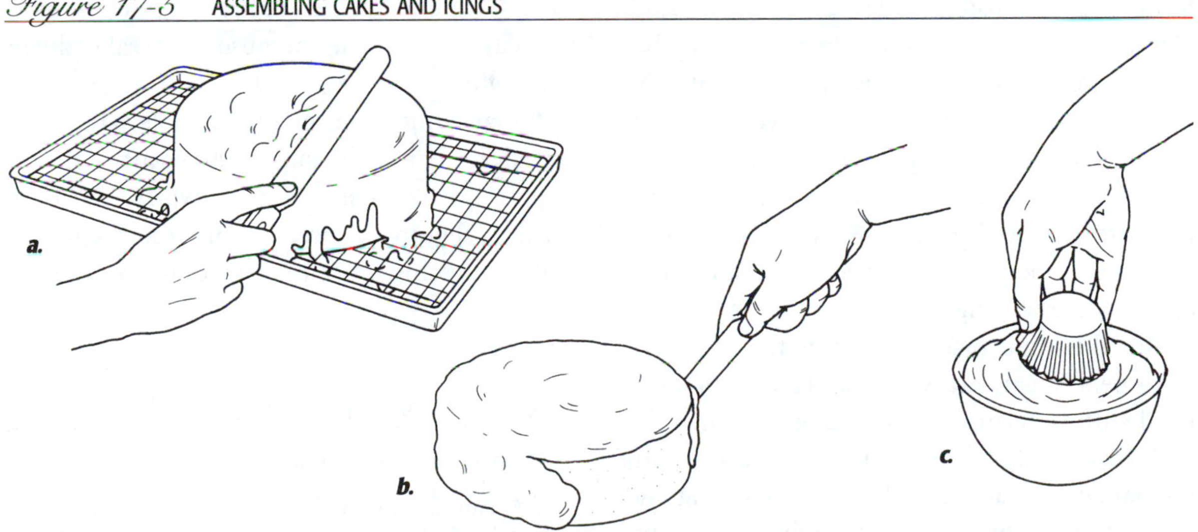

a. Pour icing in center of cake and spread to edge and around sides. **b.** Push icing ahead of spatula to keep it free of crumbs. **c.** Dip tops of cupcakes into softened icing, twist a quarter turn, and remove with a quick smooth motion.

Recipe 17-7 FLAT ICING

YIELD: ***5–6 lb 4 oz (2.6–3.1 kg) icing***

4–5 lb	**confectioners' sugar**	**2–2.5 kg**
12 fl oz	**hot water**	**375 mL**
4 oz	**corn syrup**	**125 g**
1 Tb	**vanilla or other flavoring**	**15 mL**

1. With paddle, on low speed, mix all ingredients until smooth.
2. To use, heat over low heat or in bain-marie and apply as for fondant.

Per ounce:		Carbohydrates:	24 g
Calories:	90	Cholesterol:	0 mg
Fat:	0 g	Fiber:	0 g
Protein:	0 g	Sodium:	0 mg

If you have fondant on hand, use Recipe 17.8a for the easiest basic buttercream. Recipe 17.8b calls for cream cheese for a specialty flavor popular on carrot cakes and others.

Buttercream is made in many flavors: In place of vanilla, use lemon, orange, almond, peppermint, and so on. For chocolate buttercream, add unsweetened chocolate (Recipe 17.8c). For coffee, make with instant coffee as in Recipe 17.8d. Combine the two and you have mocha. Any basic buttercream can be made up in quantity and used to make many different flavors, as you would make a large supply of a basic sauce for many small sauces. Cover and store in the refrigerator, where it will keep several days. Bring to room temperature, add the desired flavor, and apply to the waiting cake.

Royal icing is made by beating together confectioners' sugar, egg whites, and cream of tartar until stiff. It becomes hard and brittle when dry and is used only on cakes that will be served immediately. It is also called decorator's icing and is often used for flowers and other decorative work.

Recipe 17-8 BUTTERCREAM FROSTING

YIELD: ***Approximately $2^1/_2$ cups (625 mL)***

$^1/_2$ C	**butter or margarine, softened to room temperature**	**125 mL**
1 lb	**confectioners' sugar**	**450 g**
$^1/_4$ tsp	**salt**	**1 mL**
5–6 Tb	**light cream**	**75–90 mL**
2 tsp	**vanilla**	**10 mL**

1. Cream butter or margarine until fluffy. Beat in sugar and salt a little at a time, until combined thoroughly, texture is light, and volume is increased.
2. Add remaining ingredients and beat on high speed until very fluffy.

Per ounce:		Carbohydrates:	23 g
Calories:	140	Cholesterol:	16 mg
Fat:	6 g	Fiber:	0 g
Protein:	0 g	Sodium:	80 mg

Boiled icing is a foamy, airy icing used on angel food and chiffon cakes. To make it, you mix hot simple syrup into whipped egg whites and then flavor and color as desired. It must be used the day it is made because it breaks down overnight.

Fudge icing also uses a hot simple syrup. It is mixed slowly into fat, sugar, and cocoa. A dense, rich, candylike icing results, which must be warmed slightly to spread. Store it in the refrigerator, covering it to prevent a crust from forming.

Recipe 17-8a BUTTERCREAM II

equal parts fat and fondant

1. Cream fat until light and fluffy.
2. Add fondant by handfuls and beat until fluffy.

Recipe 17-8b CREAM CHEESE ICING

Yield: ***Approximately $2^1/_2$ cups (625 mL)***

Replace butter or margarine with cream cheese.

Per ounce:		Carbohydrates:	23 g
Calories:	117	Cholesterol:	9 mg
Fat:	3 g	Fiber:	0 g
Protein:	1 g	Sodium:	48 mg

Recipe 17-8d COFFEE BUTTERCREAM

Yield: ***Approximately $2^1/_2$ cups (625 mL)***

Beat 2 tsp (10 mL) instant coffee powder into creamed butter before adding sugar.

Per ounce:		Carbohydrates:	23 g
Calories:	140	Cholesterol:	16 mg
Fat:	6 g	Fiber:	0 g
Protein:	0 g	Sodium:	80 mg

Some other coatings and toppings are often used to enrich and enhance cakes and other pastries. Among these are **glazes**—transparent coatings that take the place of icings and display the product instead of covering it up. They are brushed on rich cakes and fruit tarts for a simple yet elegant topping and a dazzling shine.

Apricot glaze is among the most popular. It is usually bought readymade, and you simply melt it over low heat or in a water bath, thin with water or simple syrup, and apply with a pastry brush. You can make this glaze by melting and thinning apricot preserves and straining or puréeing them. Red currant jelly and some other jellies are also used in this manner.

Sweet sauces made with butterscotch, fruit, chocolate, caramelized sugar, and custards are another category of coatings and toppings. They can be napped across or pooled under slices of pound cake and cheesecake, for example. They are often purchased readymade, but you will have a chance to make at least one kind of sweet sauce later in this chapter.

Simple syrup also has its own roles in finishing desserts for service. European-style cakes often use simple syrup flavored with liqueur or wine to saturate cake layers before assembling. This has the added advantage of maintaining a moist, fresh taste and appearance longer on the pastry cart or display case. Flavored simple syrups are also used to poach fruits. These may be served as simple fruit compotes or combined with cake or a frozen product for a more elaborate dessert.

Recipe 17-8c CHOCOLATE BUTTERCREAM

Yield: ***Approximately $2^1/_2$ cups (625 mL)***

Blend 1 oz (30 g) melted unsweetened chocolate into creamed butter before adding sugar.

Per ounce:		Carbohydrates:	23 g
Calories:	148	Cholesterol:	16 mg
Fat:	6 g	Fiber:	0 g
Protein:	0 g	Sodium:	81 mg

ASSEMBLING AND DECORATING CAKES

Putting cake and icing together to make a handsome product has secrets of its own. Here are the major procedures and techniques for combining icings with sheet, layer, or cupcakes.

Choose icings and fillings that complement the cake in color, flavor, and texture. Sponge cakes are iced and filled with fruit, buttercream, fondant, pastry cream, or whipped cream. Angel food and

Figure 17-6 SPLITTING A CAKE INTO LAYERS

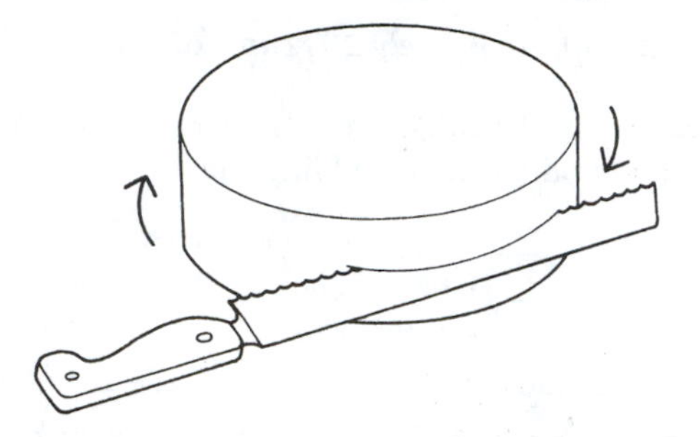

Rotating the cake, use a serrated blade to cut in 1 inch (2 cm) all around edge. Without removing the knife, continue to rotate and cut until cake is cut through in even layers.

chiffon cakes need only flat, fondant, or fluffy boiled icings. Heavier cakes made by the creaming or two-stage methods can carry a denser buttercream or fudge icing or any of the other icing types.

Cool cakes completely before finishing. Icings will not maintain their texture if applied when the cake is even slightly warm. Cakes can be wrapped when completely cool, frozen for a short time, and assembled and finished as needed with good results.

Remove crumbs from cakes by brushing or tapping gently. Loose crumbs give a messy look when they become mixed with the icing.

Trim ragged or crusty edges evenly from layer and sheet cakes, if necessary. This helps make a uniform, attractive appearance in the finished cake.

Split round cakes into layers if you are going to use a filling. Figure 17.6 shows you how to do this.

Place the bottom layer cut side down on a cardboard cake circle on a turntable or serving plate. Spread a thin, even layer of filling to within $^1/_8$ to $^1/_4$ inch (0.25–0.5 cm) of the edge. Place the top layer cut side down on the filling.

To apply fondants and flat icings, pour onto the center of the cake. Use a cake spatula dipped in hot water to spread to the edges and down and around the sides (Figure 17.5a). For the other icing types, place some of the icing in the center and spread to the edges. Dip out more with the spatula as needed to cover the entire cake with an even coat.

To avoid getting crumbs mixed with the icing, always push it ahead of the spatula (Figure 17.5b). Do not let the spatula touch the surface of the cake.

Cupcakes can be iced by either of the methods described, or you can use the faster, more efficient technique shown in Figure 17.5c. For volume service, use sheet cakes iced on the top only.

For all kinds of cakes, you can either swirl the icing into peaks or smooth it and practice your pastry bag techniques of pressure, motion, and

Figure 17-7 SIMPLE DECORATIONS AND BORDERS

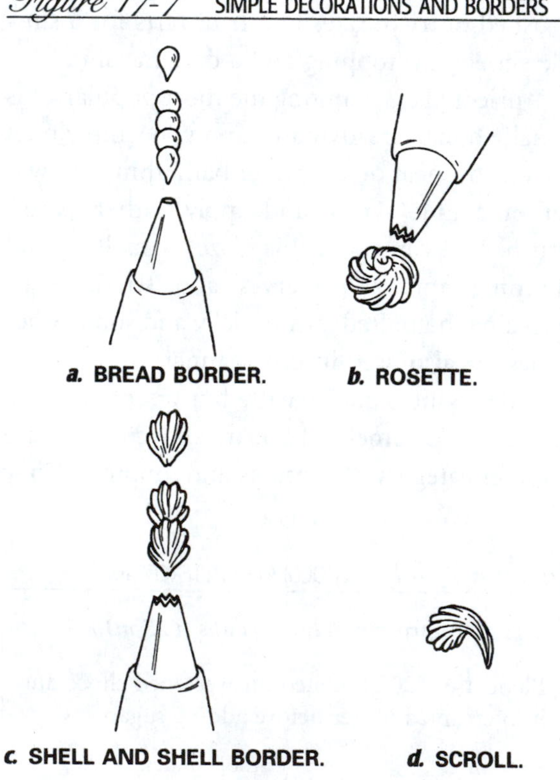

***a.* BREAD BORDER.** ***b.* ROSETTE.**

***c.* SHELL AND SHELL BORDER.** ***d.* SCROLL.**

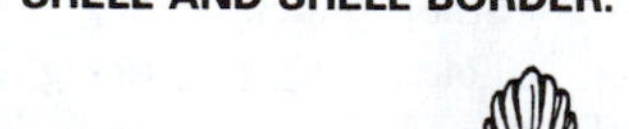

***e.* FLEUR DE LIS.**

Figure 17-8 PAPER CONES

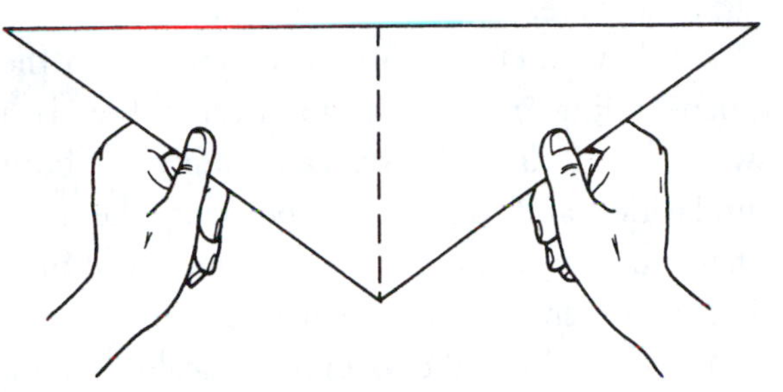

a. Cut a triangle from parchment paper.

b. Roll into a cone beginning at a point slightly left of center.

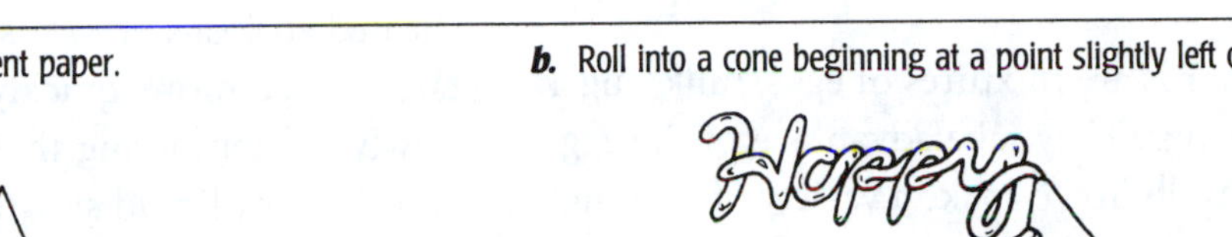

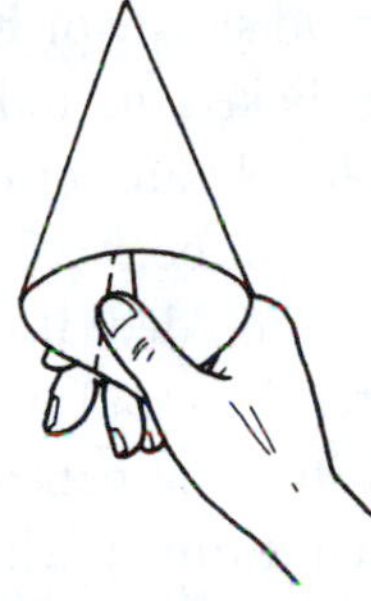

c. Finish rolling the cone, pulling it to close tip completely. Fold in flap at open end to prevent unrolling.

d. Fill two-thirds full and fold over corners and top to close. Snip off point for desired-size hole. Use gentle pressure to apply inscriptions and line designs.

release to perfect the simple decorations and borders illustrated in Figure 17.7.

For inscriptions and finer designs, make a paper cone as shown in Figure 17.8. Fill it two-thirds full and fold the corners and top to close. Using the right hand to exert pressure and the left hand to guide (as you do with the pastry bag), write Happy Birthday or make designs. The paper cone can also be used with pastry tips.

Whatever decorations you choose, keep them simple in kind, amount, and color, just as you do for salads, buffets, and garnishing. This not only saves time and labor but results in a more attractive and professional-looking cake.

Divide cakes into uniform portions, marking them into halves, then quarters, with the dull edge of a long knife. Mark each quarter into the number of portions desired.

Cut the cake as close to service time as possible to prevent drying. Dip the knife into hot water after each cut.

CUSTARDS, MERINGUES, AND SOUFFLÉS

In this section, we encounter once again the versatility of the egg and its key role in dishes for every part of the menu. Three types of dessert preparations are built almost entirely on its ability to incorporate air, to emulsify, to coagulate, to thicken, and to develop a product with a delightfully smooth and tender consistency.

Reviewing the nature and behavior of the egg and the techniques of egg cookery will help you tackle these formulas. Follow sanitation rules carefully in handling eggs to avoid the hazards of bacteria they are likely to carry.

CUSTARDS

Sweet custards are mixtures of eggs, milk, sugar, and flavorings. They take advantage of the egg's emulsifying ability to make a variety of toppings, fillings, puddings, and sauces. Two preparation techniques produce two types of custards. **Baked custards** (Recipe 17.9) are baked in an oven until they are set. **Stirred custards** (Recipes 17.10 and 17.11) are stirred over gentle heat until the eggs coagulate.

You have met a savory baked custard in the quiche filling in Chapter 13. Recipe 17.9 is a sweet baked custard. You can readily see both similarities and differences between the two. These custards are easy to make; they need only thorough blending of ingredients.

A whisk does the blending. Scalded milk (heated to just below a simmer) helps the custard to set more quickly in the oven. Add it slowly, remembering that an egg mixture must absorb a hot liquid slowly or it will curdle.

Custards are baked in individual metal or porcelain cups, hotel pans, or other baking pans and molds. They can be served in the mold but are more often unmolded. If custards are to be unmolded, butter the molds lightly. After pouring the custard into the pan or molds, remove any bubbles that formed when pouring. The bubbles will scorch and spoil the texture. Place the pan or molds in a larger pan, put in the oven, and add hot water to reach halfway up the sides of the custard pan or molds. Baking in hot water moderates the heat and keeps the egg protein from toughening. The water should stay just below a simmer during baking.

The test for doneness is a knife inserted an inch or two (2–5 cm) from the edge. If it comes out clean, the custard is done. The center won't be as firm as the edges but will finish cooking after you take it out of the oven.

Remove the custard pans from the hot water, cover, and store in the refrigerator. Serve cold, unmolding at service time if desired. To unmold, gently loosen the edges with a cake spatula, place the serving plate over the mold, and reverse with a sharp, jerking motion to release the custard in one piece.

Recipe 17-9 BASIC BAKED CUSTARD

YIELD: *6 custards*

3	**eggs**	
3 Tb	**sugar**	**45 mL**
	pinch salt	
1/2 tsp	**vanilla**	**2 mL**
2 C	**milk**	**500 mL**

1. Beat eggs in a bowl with a whisk. Add sugar, salt, and vanilla.
2. Scald the milk and pour slowly into the egg mixture, stirring constantly with a whisk.
3. Pour into ramekins and place in shallow roasting pan.
4. Pour boiling water into the baking pan to the level of the custard.
5. Bake at 325°F (160°C) until mixture is firm—about 45 minutes.

Per serving:		Carbohydrates:	10 g
Calories:	112	Cholesterol:	117 mg
Fat:	5 g	Fiber:	0 g
Protein:	6 g	Sodium:	130 mg

Recipe 17-9a CREME CARAMEL

YIELD: *6 custards*

Heat $^1/_2$ C (120 mL) sugar and $^1/_4$ C (60 mL) water in a saucepan over medium heat until the mixture is light brown. Use this caramel sugar to coat the bottom of each custard cup with 1 tsp (5 mL) by swishing it around. Make custard according to Recipe 17.9 and pour into custard cups lined with caramel sugar.

Per serving:		Carbohydrates:	26 g
Calories:	174	Cholesterol:	117 mg
Fat:	5 g	Fiber:	0 g
Protein:	6 g	Sodium:	130 mg

Crème caramel (Recipe 17.9a) turns a plain baked custard into a dish with great style. To make the caramelized sugar syrup, you heat 2 to 3 parts sugar to 1 part water in a heavy saucepan, stirring until the sugar is dissolved, and then cook at a low boil. As the temperature increases, the water evaporates and the sugar begins to brown. The syrup reaches the amber-colored caramel stage at the high temperature of 320 to 340°F (160–170°C), so handle it very carefully. It must be poured into the pans while hot because when cool it is unpourable, hard, and brittle. Don't cook it past the amber color or it will be bitter. Créme caramel is always served unmolded so that the caramel syrup forms the topping.

This caramel syrup is usually made up in quantity and forms a standard part of a bakeshop mise en place. You can make it into a dessert sauce of many uses. Heat until liquefied and carefully thin the hot mixture with regular simple syrup, water, or cream until it reaches the desired consistency.

A heartier version of baked custard is bread pudding (Recipe 17.9b)—a delicious and profitable way to use up day-old bread. It is usually portioned and served with a dessert sauce. You can add raisins or nuts for extra flavor.

Now, let us look at a stirred custard. The *custard sauce* in Recipe 17.10 is a basic preparation served with cakes, puddings, ice creams, and pastries. Making a custard sauce takes advantage of the emulsifying and thickening ability of eggs and uses techniques similar to those used in butter sauces.

Whipping the egg yolks and sugar in Step 1 starts emulsification. When the mixture has lightened and thickened enough to show traces of the whip, add the milk slowly (Step 2) to avoid scrambled eggs. This is the same technique you used in Chapter 6 in adding a liaison to a hot liquid.

In Step 3, heat makes the eggs coagulate, thickening and binding the mixture. The heat must be gentle and you must stir constantly to prevent scorching and overheating. If the sauce gets too hot, it will curdle. When the sauce will

Recipe 17-9b BREAD PUDDING

YIELD: *6 servings*

To Recipe 17.9, add:

2	**slices bread**	
1 oz	**melted butter**	**30 g**
pinch cinnamon and nutmeg		

1. Brush melted butter on both sides of bread. Overlap slices in small baking dish.
2. Prepare custard and pour over bread. Dust with spices.
3. Bake as in Step 5.

Per serving:		Carbohydrates:	30 g
Calories:	230	Cholesterol:	128 mg
Fat:	9 g	Fiber:	0 g
Protein:	7 g	Sodium:	214 mg

Recipe 17-10 VANILLA CUSTARD SAUCE (CRÈME ANGLAISE)

YIELD: ***$2^1/_2$ pints (1.25 L)***

6 oz	**egg yolks**	**175 g**
8 oz	**sugar**	**250 g**
1 qt	**milk, scalded**	**1 L**
1 Tb	**vanilla**	**15 mL**

1. Whip yolks and sugar by hand or in mixer until pale yellow and thickened.
2. Temper in hot milk.
3. Place in trunnion kettle or place bowl in hot water on stove. Using low heat (185°F/85°C), stir constantly until thickened.
4. Remove from heat. Stir in vanilla.
5. Cool by placing bowl in cold water, stirring occasionally.

Per $^1/_2$ cup serving:		Carbohydrates:	31 g
Calories:	237	Cholesterol:	257 mg
Fat:	9 g	Fiber:	0 g
Protein:	7 g	Sodium:	62 mg

lightly coat a spoon, it has reached the right consistency. If the sauce does begin to curdle, you have a chance to bring it back by taking it off the heat and whipping it little by little into a tablespoon (15 mL) of cold milk, either by hand or in a blender.

Recipe 17-10a CHOCOLATE CUSTARD SAUCE

YIELD: ***2-$^3/_4$ pints (1.3 L)***

To Recipe 17.10, add:

6 oz	**sweet chocolate**	**180 g**

Melt chocolate and stir into warm sauce in Step 4.

Per serving:		Carbohydrates:	38 g
Calories:	294	Cholesterol:	231 mg
Fat:	14 g	Fiber:	0 g
Protein:	7 g	Sodium:	57 mg

Recipe 17-11 BASIC PASTRY CREAM (CRÈME PÂTISSIÈRE)

YIELD: ***Approximately $2^1/_2$ quarts (2.5 L)***

2 qt	**milk**	**2 L**
4 oz	**sugar**	**125 g**
1 lb	**eggs**	**500 g**
5 oz	**cornstarch**	**150 g**
5 oz	**cake flour**	**150 g**
12 oz	**sugar**	**375 g**
4 oz	**butter, softened**	**125 g**
$^1/_2$ oz	**lemon juce**	**15 mL**
$^1/_2$ oz	**vanilla**	**15 mL**
	melted butter and sugar as needed	

1. In a trunnion kettle or heavy saucepan, heat milk and 4 oz (125 g) sugar to a low boil.
2. In a mixing bowl, stir eggs with a whip until blended fairly smooth.
3. Sift cornstarch, cake flour, and sugar together over eggs. With whip, blend until very smooth and thoroughly combined.
4. Temper in hot milk.
5. Return to pan or kettle and heat slowly, stirring constantly, until mixture thickens and reaches a full boil. Remove from heat.
6. Stir in butter, lemon juice, and vanilla until combined.
7. Pour into shallow pan. Brush lightly with melted butter or sprinkle with granulated sugar to prevent crust. Cover with paper and refrigerate immediately.

Per $^1/_2$ cup serving:		Carbohydrates:	40 g
Calories:	277	Cholesterol:	122 mg
Fat:	10 g	Fiber:	0 g
Protein:	7 g	Sodium:	124 mg

Cool quickly, stirring so that a crust doesn't form, and refrigerate, covered, as soon as possible, remembering the health risks of keeping egg products at room temperature. Store this sauce a few days at most, and never mix new with old for sanitation safety.

Custard sauces can be flavored in the same ways as buttercreams. Recipe 17.10a is one example.

Pastry cream is another stirred custard used as is or flavored to produce cake and pie fillings, puddings, fillings for éclairs, or, when thinned with milk, a light custard sauce. As you see in Recipe 17.11, it is made by the same basic technique as custard sauce but contains starch and flour and must be heated to a higher temperature to reach its firmer consistency.

A trunnion kettle is easiest to use, but a heavy saucepan produces good results with careful heating and constant stirring. In Step 1, some sugar heated with the milk helps prevent scorching. While the milk is heating, mix the eggs in another bowl and blend in the dry ingredients (Steps 2 and 3). In Step 4, stir in the hot milk slowly to raise the temperature gradually, and then put everything back into the kettle or pan. Slowly cook and stir the mixture until it reaches a *full boil*—but no longer. The custard will be firm and thick and the starchy taste will be gone. (Don't go on cooking it as you would a soup or sauce. The cornstarch and the slow cooking make the difference.)

After blending in the butter and flavorings, pour into shallow pans. The melted butter or sugar in Step 7, along with the paper, prevent a filmy crust from forming. Refrigerate for a quick exit from the danger zone.

Recipes 17.11a and 17.11b show two popular ways to vary the basic pastry cream. You can substitute other flavorings for the vanilla, such as almond, orange, or lemon.

Before we leave custards, let's look at a popular dessert that is normally thought of as a cake—cheesecake (Recipe 17.12). Despite its name, it is a form of baked custard since its structure is provided by coagulation of the eggs during baking. The cheese provides the major body, and the cornstarch and flour act as thickeners and binders. All this gives the cheesecake a very different texture from other baked custards.

The mixing method is more like making a cake than a custard: It is similar to the creaming method. As in cakes, scrape-downs are important in producing a smooth, homogeneous, lumpfree mixture.

Cheesecakes are often baked in springform pans, which make it easy to remove the baked cheesecake. If you use this type of pan, place the panned cakes on a rack in the oven with a pan of hot water underneath. If you use solid pans, put them right in the pan of water. The steam from the water will keep the custards from cracking during baking.

Recipe 17-11a CHOCOLATE PASTRY CREAM

YIELD: ***Approximately 2$^{3}/_{4}$ quarts (2.5 L)***

To Recipe 17.11, add:

8 oz semisweet chocolate, melted 250 g

Stir chocolate into hot pastry cream in Step 6.

Per serving:			
Calories:	301	Carbohydrates:	43 g
Fat:	12 g	Cholesterol:	111 mg
Protein:	7 g	Fiber:	1 g
		Sodium:	114 mg

Recipe 17-11b CHANTILLY PASTRY CREAM

YIELD: ***Approximately 3 quarts (3 L)***

To Recipe 17.11, add:

$^{1}/_{2}$–1 pt heavy cream 250–500 mL

Whip cream and fold into chilled pastry cream.

Per serving:			
Calories:	265	Carbohydrates:	33 g
Fat:	12 g	Cholesterol:	115 mg
Protein:	6 g	Fiber:	0 g
		Sodium:	107 mg

Recipe 17-12 CHEESECAKE NEW YORK STYLE

YIELD: ***1 cake (16 slices)***

1 lb	**cream cheese, softened**	**450 g**
3 C	**sour cream**	**750 mL**
1 C	**sugar**	**250 mL**
2 Tb	**flour**	**30 mL**
3 Tb	**cornstarch**	**45 mL**
1 tsp	**vanilla**	**5 mL**
3	**eggs**	
2 Tb	**lemon juice**	**30 mL**

1. In mixer, using paddle, beat cream cheese on medium speed until soft, light, and fluffy.
2. Stir in sour cream until combined. Scrape down.
3. Sift dry ingredients together. Stir in on low speed until combined. Scrape down.
4. Add eggs little by little, waiting until each addition is absorbed. Scrape down.
5. Stir in lemon juice; then cream until combined.
6. Bake at 375°F (190°C) until set—about 1 hour. Cool completely in pan.

Per serving:		Carbohydrates:	17 g
Calories:	247	Cholesterol:	87 mg
Fat:	18 g	Fiber:	0 g
Protein:	5 g	Sodium:	115 mg

Bake until the center is set and the sides have pulled away slightly from the pan. Cool the cakes completely in the pans. When cool, invert onto cardboard cake circles, wrap, and refrigerate until needed—up to several days.

Use a long-blade knife dipped in hot water to cut each piece cleanly and neatly. Serve with a choice of fruit sauces for an added treat.

Some other familiar desserts use custards as a base. **Bavarian creams** are flavored, light custard sauces with gelatin and whipped cream. **Chiffons** are a stirred custard base with gelatin and beaten egg whites. Many types of dishes are called mousses, but the sweet ones are often stirred custards with whipped cream or stiff egg whites or both.

MERINGUES

Meringues are egg whites whipped with sugar, which produces still another multiuse preparation. They come in two types—soft and hard—and are made by three procedures.

Soft meringues (Recipe 17.13a) are made with equal parts of sugar and egg whites. Pie toppings are their most common use. They are also folded into cakes, soufflés, and icings.

Hard meringues (Recipe 17.13b) contain up to twice as much sugar as egg whites. They are usually formed into shells, nests, cookies, or layers (Figure 17.9) and are baked in a low-heat oven (200°F/100°C) for 1 to 2 hours until dry and crisp without browning. They are combined with ice cream, fruit sauces, and other preparations for finished desserts.

Recipe 17-13a SOFT MERINGUE

YIELD: ***Approximately 4 small meringue shells***

2	**egg whites**	
5 Tb	**granulated sugar**	**75 mL**

1. Beat egg whites in a stainless steel bowl with a whisk until a coarse foam appears.
2. Add $^{1}/_{2}$ Tb (8 mL) sugar at a time and continue beating.
3. After addition of all sugar, continue beating until peaks are formed.
4. Shape into desired forms.
5. Bake at 350°F (180°C) until light and dry.

Per serving:		Carbohydrates:	15 g
Calories:	66	Cholesterol:	0 mg
Fat:	0 g	Fiber:	0 g
Protein:	2 g	Sodium:	28 mg

Recipe 17-13b HARD MERINGUE

Yield: ***Approximately 6 small meringue shells***

2	**egg whites**	
1 C	**granulated sugar**	**250 mL**

1. Beat egg whites in a stainless steel bowl with a whisk until a coarse foam appears.
2. Add 1 Tb (15 mL) sugar at a time and continue beating until all sugar is added.
3. Mixture should be stiff and glossy.
4. Shape into desired forms and place on greased baking sheet dusted with cornstarch.
5. Bake at 350°F (180°C) until light and dry.

Per serving:		Carbohydrates:	48 g
Calories:	194	Cholesterol:	0 mg
Fat:	0 g	Fiber:	0 g
Protein:	2 g	Sodium:	28 mg

SOUFFLÉS

Soufflés have a formidable reputation among beginners. But examine Recipe 17.14. In it, you can see that a soufflé has a base of white sauce, flavored. A meringue is folded in and the mixture is baked. What could be easier since you are combining familiar products and basic techniques?

The basic procedures are indeed familiar and uncomplicated, and if you carry out the techniques correctly, your soufflé will not fall. Here are some points to watch:

- Don't overbeat the egg whites and sugar.
- Fold them in carefully to maintain volume.
- Bake at the correct temperature to create the steam for leavening.

Figure 17-9 MERINGUES

a. Meringue shells. ***b.*** Meringue cookies. ***c.*** Meringue layers. ***d.*** Meringue nests.

Recipe 17-14 VANILLA SOUFFLÉ

Yield: ***10 $4^1/_2$-oz (125 g) portions***

3 oz	**flour**	**100 g**
3 oz	**butter, softened**	**100 g**
1 C	**milk, scalded**	**250 mL**
6 oz	**egg yolks**	**200 g**
8–10 oz	**egg whites**	**250–300 g**
6 oz	**sugar**	**175 g**
2 tsp	**vanilla**	**10 mL**
$^1/_2$ tsp	**salt**	**2 mL**
	butter and sugar as needed	

1. Make a paste of flour and butter (beurre manié).
2. In a heavy saucepan, add beurre manié to hot milk, whipping until smooth. Simmer, stirring, until no starch taste remains.
3. Cool to warm. Stir in egg yolks until blended.
4. Whip egg whites to stiff peaks with sugar, vanilla, and salt. Fold into base mixture.
5. Place in buttered and sugared baking dishes, smoothing tops carefully.
6. Bake at 375°F (190°C) until puffed and golden (about 15–20 minutes for individual portions).

Per serving:		Carbohydrates:	25 g
Calories:	248	Cholesterol:	240 mg
Fat:	13 g	Fiber:	0 g
Protein:	7 g	Sodium:	243 mg

- Handle carefully when putting a soufflé into the oven and removing it. Don't bang the oven door.
- Don't open the oven door until the guideline time is nearly up.

Soufflés can hold without collapsing in a turned-off warm oven for a short time, but careful coordination of timing with service personnel gets the soufflé to the guest with all its impressive height.

Recipes 17.14a and 17.14b are easy variations. In savory soufflés such as Recipe 17.14b, you merely omit all the sugar and use cheese in place of sugar to coat the pans. You can also use a thick béchamel sauce as a base and stir in cooked, drained chopped vegetables or other flavor ingredients.

Recipe 17-14a CHOCOLATE SOUFFLÉ

Yield: ***10 portions***

To Recipe 17.14, add:

5 oz bittersweet chocolate, melted 150 g

Add chocolate at end of Step 3.

Per serving:		Carbohydrates:	33 g
Calories:	317	Cholesterol:	240 mg
Fat:	18 g	Fiber:	0 g
Protein:	8 g	Sodium:	244 mg

PIES AND TARTS

PIE DOUGHS

Pies, tarts, tartlettes, and quiche (as in Chapter 13) are only a few of the good things to eat that

Recipe 17-14b CHEESE SOUFFLÉ

Yield: ***10 portions***

In Recipe 17.14, make these changes:

Omit sugar.
Add 8–10 oz (250–300 g) grated cheese.
Add seasonings (salt to taste).

Stir in cheese at end of Step 2, off heat, and season as for a béchamel.

In Step 5, replace sugar with finely grated cheese.

Per serving:		Carbohydrates:	17 g
Calories:	343	Cholesterol:	264 mg
Fat:	25 g	Fiber:	1 g
Protein:	14 g	Sodium:	385 mg

come from pie or pastry dough. Two types of this stiff dough—**flaky** and **mealy**—are needed to make good pies. Both are mixed by the pastry method used in making biscuits. The difference between them comes in mixing the fat and flour and in the amount of liquid used. In flaky dough, you leave the fat in larger pieces. This forms layers of fat and flour that produce flakiness when rolled and baked. Flaky dough is used for top crusts and unfilled or prebaked shells. In mealy dough, you mix the fat into the flour more completely. This dough is more tender and less likely to absorb moisture and is therefore used for bottom crusts. Recipe 17.15 includes both types.

As you examine the formula, look first at the ingredients. Pastry flour is used for its moderate gluten content. You have a choice of fats. Regular shortening is most often the choice for cost and consistency. Emulsified shortening should not be used. Butter combined with shortening gives a pleasing flavor and an easily handled dough. If you use all butter, you have a very tender, rich dough that is more difficult to handle. It will require less liquid because of the moisture in the butter.

The water must be cold—40°F (4°C) or less—to help keep the dough cool. The dough should stay at or below 60°F (15°C) to keep the fat soft but not too soft and to prevent gluten from developing too quickly. Salt, and sugar if used, is dissolved in the liquid for even distribution. (Sugar may be added for flavor; it also increases browning.) Notice that the formula has no leavener: This is a dough that is leavened by steam.

Now, for the action. Beginning with Step 1, you can mix a large amount (at least three times this formula) as quickly and easily by hand as in the machine with the dough hook. It is also easier to judge the readiness of the dough. Place a dampened towel under the bowl to keep it steady. Rub the flour and fat together with the palms of your hands (Step 2), until you achieve the consistency you want (flaky or mealy) and the fat and flour are evenly distributed.

Proceed with Steps 3 and 4. Make a hole in the middle of the mixture and pour in most of the liquid. Use your fingertips to go down the sides of the bowl to the bottom and then up. As the water is absorbed, begin to try to shape the dough into a solid mass. Add the rest of the water as necessary to form a ball. If you use too lit-

Recipe 17-15 PIE DOUGH

YIELD: ***2 9-in. (23 cm) crusts***

$2^1/_4$ C	**pastry flour**	**560 mL**
9 Tb	**shortening butter chilled**	**135 mL**
1 tsp	**salt**	**5 mL**
4–5 Tb	**water, ice cold**	**60–75 mL**

1. Place flour and fat in a bowl.
2. For flaky crust, rub fat and flour until $^1/_4$-in. (5 mm) particles of fat are evenly distributed. For mealy crust, rub fat and flour until mixture has a coarse, crumbly texture.
3. Dissolve salt in 3 Tb of the cold water and add to flour mixture.
4. Toss mixture, adding more liquid as necessary, until it forms a mass of dough.
5. Cover and refrigerate 4 hours or more.
6. Dust bench, rolling pin, and dough lightly with flour.
7. Divide dough in half. Roll each crust into a circle $^1/_8$ in. (3 mm) thick, working from the center outward. Turn, lift, and dust dough if necessary to prevent sticking.
8. Place in pan. Trim or flute as desired. Refrigerate again.

Per crust:		Carbohydrates:	96 g
Calories:	953	Cholesterol:	0 mg
Fat:	59 g	Fiber:	2 g
Protein:	10 g	Sodium:	1165 mg

tle liquid, the baked crust will crack and fall apart. If you use too much, the crust will be tough. Mealy dough requires less liquid than flaky. Do not overwork the dough. If you overmix it after adding the liquid, you end up with a tough piece of shoe leather instead of a tender container for the filling.

Some gluten development is unavoidable, so the dough is allowed to relax in the refrigerator (Step 5). Cover it well with plastic film so that a crust doesn't form.

Steps 6 to 8 carry the dough through makeup and panning. Use as little flour as possible to dust the bench, dough, and pin. Scale the dough. Shape the crust into a flattened ball, and roll out. Steady, even pressure from the center outward in all directions makes it easiest to roll a perfect circle of uniform thickness (Figure 17.10a). Lift the dough once or twice to make sure it isn't sticking, and dust if necessary. Avoid pulling or stretching the dough here or gluten will develop. Roll it as close as possible to the size you need. Allow an extra 2 inches (5 cm) for a bottom crust.

In Step 8, roll up the circle of dough around the rolling pin and unroll it into the pan (Figure 17.10b). Use gentle pressure to eliminate air pockets and shape the dough into the pan. Again, avoid stretching or pulling or the crust will shrink during baking.

A single-crust pie can now be fluted or crimped and trimmed. To make a fluted edge, place a thumb or finger inside the edge of the crust. Use the forefinger and thumb of the other hand to pinch up the dough (Figure 17.10c). Continue this process around the crust, spacing evenly. You can make a simpler edge by **crimping**—pressing the tines of a fork around the rim (Figure 17.10d).

To pinch off excess dough, press your palms against the rim while rotating the pie plate. Another technique is to use a knife to cut against the rim while rotating the pie above the bench with the other hand. Either way, make a neat and even edge with no jagged pieces.

Tarts, cream pies, and chiffon pies, among others, require a prebaked shell for filling. With a fork, dock the bottom of the unbaked crust by piercing rows of evenly spaced holes (Figure 17.10e). This will prevent air pockets and blisters in the finished crust. Place another pie pan of the same size inside the dough. Put pans and dough upside down on a sheet pan and bake until done. This procedure keeps the crust from shrinking.

A double-crust pie begins by placing the rolled-out mealy dough in the pan and shaping it. Fill the pie carefully. Don't let any filling get on the edges or the steam from the pie as it bakes will break through the sealed edge and leave more filling on the outside than the inside. Brush the rim with egg wash; it will act as glue to seal the top to the bottom and keep the bubbling liquid from escaping during baking. Roll out flaky pie dough, dock the crust or cut decorative steam vents (Figure 17.10f), and place on the pie. Use the techniques for finishing and trimming single crusts, making sure the edges are well sealed.

Colorful fruit pies (cherry, blueberry) may have a lattice crust of crisscross strips of pie dough to show off their beauty. Either type of crust can be brushed with milk or egg wash and sugar to aid in browning and produce a shiny crust.

SHORT DOUGH

Short dough is another type of stiff pastry dough, used mainly for tartlettes and tarts. These are European style pastries finished with a custard-type filling, fruit, or both. This dough is actually con-

Figure 17-10 MAKEUP FOR PIE CRUSTS

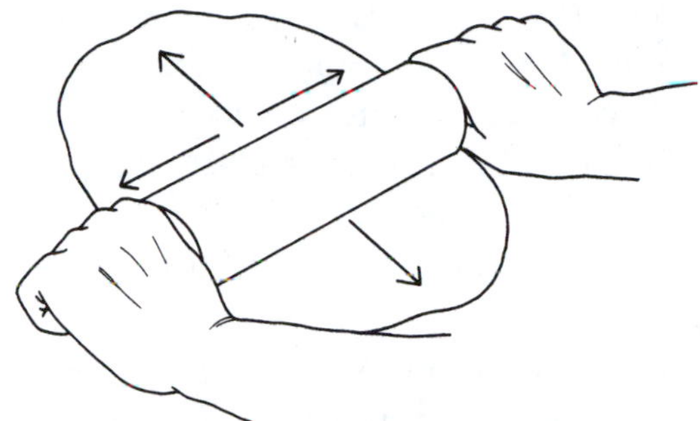

a. Rolling the dough.

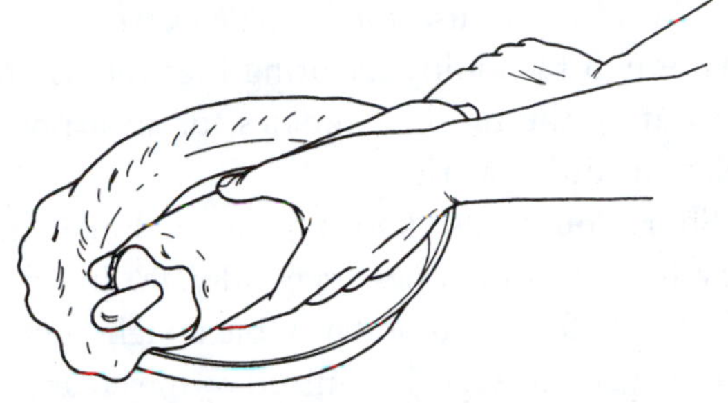

b. Placing dough in pan.

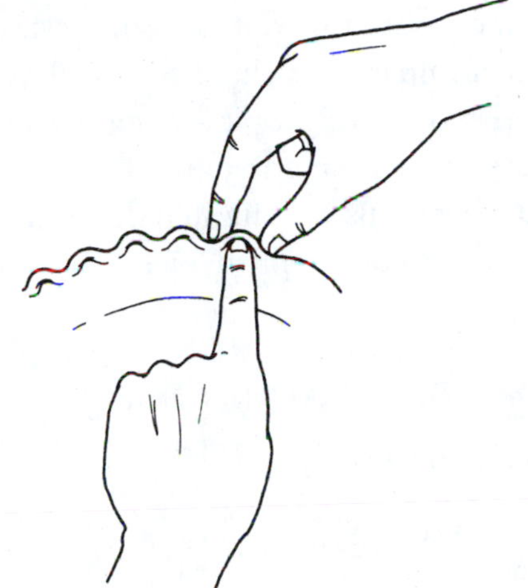

c. Fluting the edge.

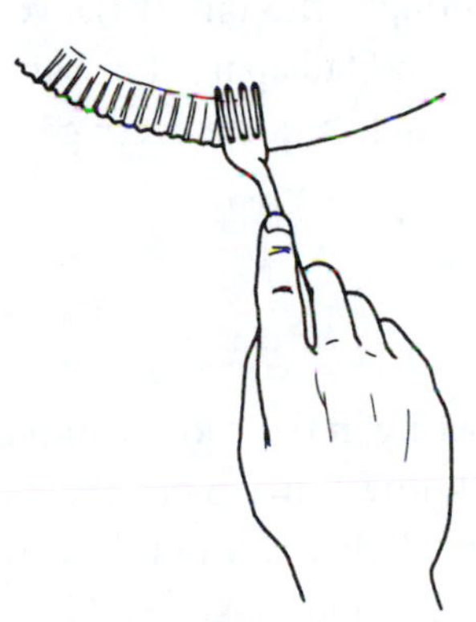

d. Crimping the edge.

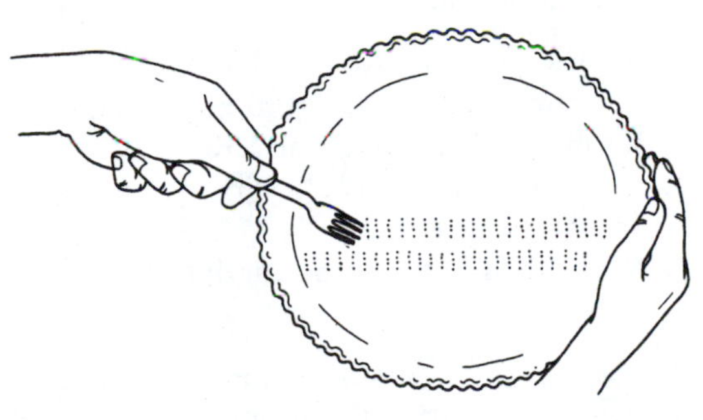

e. Docking the bottom.

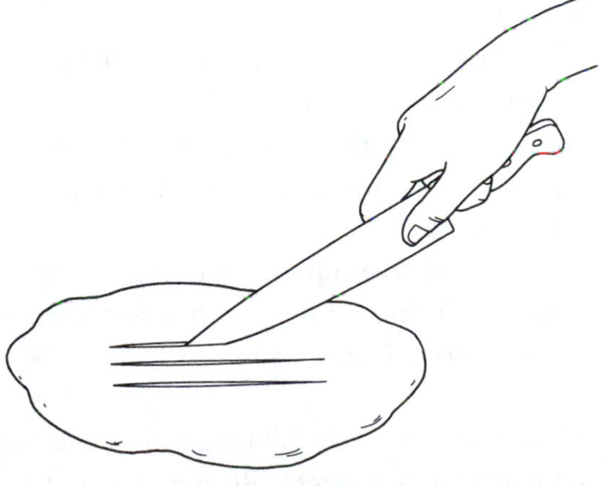

f. Cutting steam vents.

sidered a rich cookie dough and can be used for sugar cookies and other types of rolled or molded cookies. You can use your cookie expertise with this dough by adding flavoring ingredients and decorating the finished cookies for an array of delicious little pastries.

Short dough, also known as sweet dough, is a very tender, sometimes fragile dough. In addition to the flour and butter of pie dough, it contains sugar and eggs. It is mixed by the creaming method and chilled. If it warms as you work with it, the dough becomes very sticky and hard to handle. For tarts, the dough is rolled out thicker than pie dough—about $^1/_4$ inch (5 mm) thick. If it is not thick enough, the tart shells you make with it may crack and fall apart after baking. The fragility of this dough requires very gentle handling.

PIE FILLINGS

The dough is relaxing in the cooler, but you can't relax until you know how to fill the pies. But don't panic. You will discover in this section that assembling a baked or unbaked pie is simply a matter of putting together several different preparations you have already learned how to make.

Unbaked pies are baked, cooled shells that are filled with a finished filling. The filling is often topped with meringue, sweetened whipped cream, or other ingredients such as fruit, coconut, or nuts.

A variety of **cream pies,** for example, are easily made by using a filling with a pastry cream base. Here are a few:

- *Chocolate cream pie.* Fill baked pie shells with chocolate pastry cream (Recipe 17.11a). Chill.
- *Banana cream pie.* In baked pie shells, layer one sliced banana per pie with vanilla pastry cream (Recipe 17.11).
- *Coconut cream pie.* Stir 8 ounces (250 g) of toasted coconut into vanilla pastry cream (Recipe 17.11). Fill baked pie shells.

Lemon pie filling (Recipe 17.16) is a stirred, thickened custard just like pastry cream. Water replaces milk, and, of course, lemon provides the major flavor. You can make an orange or lime pie filling by substituting orange or lime zest and juice. To intensify the flavor of a citrus filling, increase the amount of zest. It is the zest, not the juice, that imparts the characteristic flavor.

For a lemon meringue pie—or for any **meringue pie**—use a soft meringue (Recipe 17.13a). Spread a generous coating in a decorative manner over the cooled filled pie. Make sure the

Recipe 17-16 LEMON PIE FILLING

YIELD: ***1 quart (1 L)***

8 oz	**sugar**	**250 g**
1 qt	**water**	**1 L**
4	**egg yolks**	
2	**eggs**	
3 oz	**cornstarch**	**90 g**
2 Tb	**grated lemon zest**	**30 mL**
$^1/_2$ C	**lemon juice**	**125 mL**

1. Bring sugar and water to a low boil.
2. Mix remaining ingredients together and temper in hot sugar–water mixture.
3. Return to heat and cook, stirring constantly, until thickened.
4. Cool slightly before pouring into baked pie shells.

Per quart:		Carbohydrates:	317 g
Calories:	1618	Cholesterol:	1276 mg
Fat:	31 g	Fiber:	1 g
Protein:	24 g	Sodium:	166 mg

meringue is spread all the way to the edges of the shell with no gaps, to keep it from slipping. Place in a hot oven (400°F/200°C) for a few minutes until light golden.

Chiffon pies are made by adding gelatin to a stirred, thickened custard base and folding in whipped cream, meringue, or both before the gelatin sets. This combination produces a filling that is both firm and fluffy.

Baked pies start with unbaked single mealy-dough shells. These are filled with an uncooked mixture and then baked. They include pourable fillings that set during baking when the eggs coagulate—in other words, custards. Here are three examples of **custard pie:**

- *Custard pie.* Fill unbaked pie shells with the mixture for baked custard (Recipe 17.9). Dust with nutmeg. Bake for 10 minutes at 400°F (200°C). Reduce to 325°F (160°C). Bake until filling is set at edges.
- *Pecan pie.* Mix sugar, butter, and salt. Mix in eggs, corn syrup, and vanilla, and pour this translucent custard over pecan pieces spread in shell. Bake as for custard pie, dropping the temperature to 350°F (180°C) after 10 minutes.
- *Pumpkin pie.* Mix canned puréed pumpkin with brown sugar, spices, and a little bit of flour. Mix in eggs, milk, and corn syrup for a custard-like batter. Bake as for custard pie, dropping the temperature to 350°F (180°C) after 10 minutes.

You will notice that at first a high temperature is used to bake these pies. This is to set and seal the mealy dough and avoid a soggy, unappetizing crust. Use the baked custard test for doneness to prevent overbaking and curdling.

Fruit pies use an unbaked shell of mealy dough that is filled with fruit and usually topped with a flaky top crust or lattice. Recipe 17.17 gives a basic method for making a fruit filling. The method can be used with fresh, canned, or frozen fruit. In effect, you are making a dessert sauce to which you add fruit. Since the fruit is not cooked before baking, it retains a firm texture instead of becoming mushy.

The variable amounts of sugar and starch depend on the natural sweetness and thickening

Recipe 17-17 FRUIT PIES

YIELD: ***4 9-in. (23 cm) pies***

1	**No. 10 can fruit, water packed**	
	water as needed	
3 oz	**cornstarch**	**90 g**
1 lb 8 oz	**sugar**	**750 g**
1 tsp	**salt**	**5 mL**
	flavorings to taste	
4	**bottom crusts and 4 top crusts**	

1. Drain liquid from No. 10 can. Add water to juice to equal 1 qt (1 L).
2. In a heavy saucepan, bring $1^1/_2$ pt (0.75 L) juice/water to boil.
3. Mix remaining juice/water with cornstarch and stir into hot liquid.
4. Simmer until thickened to desired consistency.
5. Stir in sugar, salt, and flavorings to taste. Bring back to a simmer and then remove from heat.
6. Gently combine with drained fruit. Cool slightly.
7. Fill and top pies. Bake at 400°F (200°C) for 10 minutes. Reduce heat to 350°F (180°C) and bake until crust is golden.

Note: 5 lb (2.5 kg) fresh or frozen fruit may be substituted for canned fruit. Appropriate fruit are apples, cherries, peaches, berries, etc.

Per serving (1/8 of pie):		Carbohydrates:	51 g
Calories:	273	Cholesterol:	0 mg
Fat:	8 g	Fiber:	2 g
Protein:	1 g	Sodium:	22 mg

ability of the fruit chosen (for example, apples and peaches are high in **pectin,** a natural jelling ingredient, so they require less starch). If you use fresh fruit, you can sprinkle it with some of the sugar to draw out the juices. Drain and combine with water in Step 1.

Choose flavorings—cinnamon, nutmeg, cloves, extracts, lemon zest—compatible with each fruit. Salt and lemon juice bring out the natural flavor.

COMBINING DESSERTS AND BAKED PRODUCTS

All the techniques, ingredients, methods, and finished products may be a jumble in your mind by now. But when you analyze the roles of ingredients and the methods of mixing and assembling, you can see there are only a few. Even a small bakeshop area can produce a few basic items in a multitude of ways to add sparkle and variety to a dessert menu.

Here are a few suggestions to get you started—but don't limit yourself to these!

- *Black Forest cake.* Soak split chocolate cake layers with kirsch-flavored simple syrup. Fill with dark sweet cherry filling. Ice with sweetened whipped cream. Decorate with shaved chocolate and additional cherries.
- *Pear belle-Hélène.* Place a poached pear on a slice of pound cake. Top with chocolate sauce.
- *Napoleons.* Sandwich pastry cream between three layers of thin baked puff pastry. Ice with fondant.
- *Boston cream pie.* Fill split layers of white or yellow cake with pastry cream. Frost with fudge icing.
- *Vacherin.* Sandwich layers of ice cream between baked meringue layers. Ice and decorate with whipped cream.
- *Charlottes.* Line a mold with ladyfingers. Pour in bavarian cream. Chill and unmold for service.
- *Éclairs or cream puffs.* Fill baked pâte à choux shapes with pastry cream. Ice with chocolate fondant.
- Crêpes. Fill with mousse, ice cream, or fruit and top with appropriate sauce.

SUMMING UP

Desserts—sweet selections on the menu to finish the meal—complete the story of bakeshop production. This side of baking is referred to as the pastry shop, though the kinds of products described in this chapter can be made in any kitchen. In addition to such baked goods as cookies, cakes, and pies, dessert production includes icings, custards, pastry creams, pie fillings, and meringues—everything you need to make dozens of different desserts.

Cookies are easily made. They are mixed by the creaming method, the one-stage method, or the foam method, depending on ingredient combinations. There are seven methods of makeup—drop, bar, bagged, rolled, refrigerator, molded, and sheet.

Cake batters are high in sugar, fat, and liquid and need special care in mixing. Three cake-mixing methods—creaming, two-stage, and foam—are appropriate to different ingredient combinations. For icing on the cake, there are six choices—fondant, flat, buttercream, royal, boiled, and fudge. Coatings and toppings such as glazes and sweet sauces are also used. Assembling cake and icing is a skill in itself and must be done with care and precision.

Custards can be complete desserts in themselves, or they can be used as pie fillings, toppings, and sauces, or even baked as cheesecake.

Meringues—hard and soft—are egg whites mixed with sugar. They combine with many other pastry shop products to create finished desserts.

Soufflés are made by folding meringue into a thick béchamel and baking—good for luncheon items as well as desserts.

Pie and short doughs are stiff doughs used to make shells for tarts, cream pies, custard pies, chiffon pies, fruit fillings, and countless other variations. You can use them for quiche at lunch as well as for dessert.

All the products of the bakeshop and pastry shop require the utmost care and concentration at every step to prepare them correctly. Baking is, as we have said, a precise form of art. But most of the products we have examined here are within reach of the professional cook in the typical kitchen. The career of pastry chef has a much broader repertoire and requires considerable additional training and experience, but the rewards and satisfactions are great.

The Cook's Vocabulary

angel food cake
Bavarian cream
chiffon
chiffon cake
creaming method
crimping
custards: baked, stirred
filling
foam (sponge) method
fondant
frosting (icing)
glaze
makeup methods: bagged, bar, drop, icebox or refrigerator, molded, rolled, sheet
meringue: hard, soft, common, Swiss, Italian
one-stage method
pastry cream
pectin
pies: cream, meringue, chiffon, custard, fruit, baked, unbaked
pie dough: flaky, mealy, short
scrape down
simple syrup
soufflé
sponge cake
types of icings: flat, buttercream, royal, boiled, fudge
two-stage method

Review Questions

Answer each question in complete sentences. Read each question carefully and make sure you answer all parts of the question. Organize your answer into more than one paragraph when appropriate.

1. What are the differences and similarities in mixing and makeup for cookies and cakes?
2. What other makeup methods could be used for ladyfingers? Raisin spice bars? Chocolate chip cookies?
3. Why are two methods necessary in producing pie doughs? Name pies that use each method.
4. What are the tests of doneness for cookies? Cakes? Custards? Soufflés? Describe the differences in the textures of these products.
5. What other flavors of cream pie filling could you make? How does a fruit pie differ from a custard pie?

Glossary

À la carte cookery (ah la kart) When each menu is cooked to the diner's order just before being served.

À la carte menu A menu on which each item is offered separately, priced separately, and selected separately by the diner.

Administrative dietitian A person, often a **registered dietitian,** who works in a foodservice, usually a healthcare-related foodservice.

Aging Holding of meats over a period of time long enough for enzymatic action to tenderize them.

Al dente (ahl den-tay) Firm to the bite, crisp-tender.

American Dietetic Association A national association that represents most **registered dietitians (RDs)** and registered dietetic technicians in the United States.

Angel food cakes A type of cake made from egg white foams that does not contain any fat.

Anthocyanins Pigments in red vegetables; red in an acid medium, changing to blue or purple in an alkaline medium.

Antipasto A small plate or tray of flavorful, bite-sized cold foods.

Appetizer The first course of a meal.

Apprentice An individual who is receiving formal training for a career.

Aspic A powdered meat-flavored gelatin.

As purchased (AP) Referring to a product as it comes from the purveyor before it undergoes any processing.

Au gratin (oh grat-un) Having a glazed or crusty top surface, especially a sauced food topped with bread crumbs of cheese and baked in a hot oven or glazed under the broiler.

Au jus (oh zhue) Served with its natural juices, which are usually mixed with stock and enriched by simmering with a mirepoix.

Authority The right and power to make the necessary decisions and take the necessary actions to get the job done.

Bacteria Tiny, single-cell organisms seen only with a microscope that cause more foodborne illness than any other hazard.

Bacterial infection A type of foodborne illness caused by eating food that contains harmful bacteria.

Bagged method A makeup method in which a dough is bagged out using a pastry bag and tip.

Bake To cook by heated air in an enclosed area, usually an oven.

Baker's percentages A system for expressing ratios of ingredients in baking formulas; the weight of the flour is always 100%, and the weight of each other ingredient is expressed as a percentage of the weight of the flour.

Bain-marie A vat of hot water kept at 180°F (82°C), or thereabouts, for holding hot liquids such as soups or sauces in readiness for service.

Baked custard Custards baked in an oven until they are set.

Baked pie Pies with unbaked single crusts that are filled with an uncooked mixture and then baked.

Baking process What occurs when heat is applied to doughs and batters while they are baked.

Baking powder A chemical leavener composed of baking soda and an acid; it releases carbon dioxide gas in the presence of moisture and heat.

Baking soda (sodium bicarbonate) An alkaline chemical leavener; it releases carbon dioxide gas in the presence of moisture and heat.

Bar method A makeup method for making cookies in which the cookies are cut into bars after baking.

Barbecue A special dry-heat method in which heat is created by a wood fire at the bottom of an oven or barbecue pit.

Basic sauces (mother or leading sauces) Sauces from which other sauces are made.

Batonnet A precision cut $^1/_4" \times {}^1/_4" \times 3"$ (6 mm × 6 mm × 8 cm).

Batter A semiliquid mixture of flour, liquid, and eggs used to make cakes, cookies, and quick breads or as a coating for foods to be fried. *To batter* is to coat with batter for frying. A *drop batter* is a semiliquid batter, often rough-textured or lumpy. A *pour batter* is one having a low ratio of flour to liquid that can be poured easily in a steady stream.

Bavarian cream Flavored, light custard sauces with gelatin and whipped cream.

Béarnaise (bare-naze or bay-er-nez) A butter sauce made with an emulsion of egg yolks, clarified butter, and a reduction containing tarragon and other finely minced herbs, unstrained.

Beat To move an implement back and forth to blend foods together or to achieve a smooth texture.

Béchamel (bay-sha-mel or besh-a-mel) A white sauce made by thickening milk with white roux. Basic béchamel is one of the mother sauces.

Bench proofing In yeast dough production, fermenting at the bench.

Beurre manié (burr man-yay) A thickening agent of butter and flour in a 1-to-1 ratio by weight, made by kneading ingredients together to form a paste.

Bind To cause a mixture of two or more ingredients to cohere as a homogeneous product, usually by adding a binding agent such as starch or gelatin.

Biological hazards Bacteria, viruses, and parasites that can be carried by food, or multiply in food, and cause foodborne illness.

Bisque A thickened shellfish soup.

Black butter Butter cooked until it is dark brown.

Blanching Plunging a food into boiling water briefly (generally less than a minute) and then plunging it into cold water to stop the cooking. Raw vegetables are often blanched to kill the enzymes in them that make them discolor and deteriorate quicker.

Blend To mix two or more ingredients so completely that they lose their separate identities.

Body The substance and volume of a dish.

Boil To cook food submerged in a boiling liquid or to cook the liquid itself at a boil.

Boiled icing A foamy, airy icing used on angel food and chiffon cakes. It is made from hot simple syrup, whipped egg whites, and flavorings.

Boning knife A knife used to remove bones from raw meat, poultry, and fish.

Borscht A Russian or Polish soup made with beets and other ingredients.

Botulism A foodborne illness caused by a family of bacteria that produce deadly toxins in nonacid foods in the absence of air.

Bouillabaisse (boo-yah-bess) A fish soup or stew from France.

Bouillon Seasoned stock.

Bouquet garni (boo-kay gar-nee) Classically, sprigs of parsley, bay leaf, and thyme, tied together in a bundle with string, often with a celery rib used to flavor stocks, soups, and sauces; more commonly, bouquet garni includes parsley stems, thyme sprigs, bay leaf, leeks, celery, and sometimes carrots.

Braise To cook food until tender with a small amount of liquid in a covered container, usually after browning.

Bran The outer covering of a cereal grain.

Brigade system (brigade de cuisine—bree-gahd de kwee-zeen) A crew or team of chefs, station heads, cooks, and helpers in a classically organized kitchen.

Brioche (bree-ohsh) A cakelike bread with a light texture made of rich yeast dough.

Brochettes Small skewers containing meat, poultry, fish, shellfish, or vegetables.

Broil To cook with radiant heat from above.

Broth The liquid in which a food, usually meat, poultry, or vegetable has been cooked.

Brown butter Butter cooked to a golden brown.

Brown sauce A sauce made by thickening a dark stock with brown roux or cornstarch.

Brown stock A type of stock made from the browned bones of beef or veal and browned mirepoix.

Brunch A late morning or early afternoon meal with breakfast and lunch foods.

Buffalo chopper The same as the food chopper, a piece of foodservice equipment which cuts, chops, and grates.

Buttercream A familiar frosting made with butter or other fat.

Butterflied fish Fillets from both sides of a fish connected by a strip of flesh.

Butter sauce A sauce that uses butter.

Campylobacteriosis A foodborne illness caused by *Campylobacter jejuni,* a bacteria.

Canapé A bite-sized (or two bite-sized) finger food consisting of a base, spread, or topping, and a **garnish** or **garniture.**

Caramelization The process by which sugar, when heated, turns brown.

Carbohydrates A group of nutrients that includes starches, sugars, and fibers.

Carotenes Pigments in yellow vegetables.

Carryover cooking The increase in internal temperature of a food (usually a roast) after removal from the heat source.

Chemical hazards Poisonous substances unintentionally added to foods, such as pesticides or cleaning chemicals.

Chiffon A stirred custard base with gelatin and beaten egg whites.

Chiffon pie A pie made by adding gelatin to a stirred, thickened custard base and folding in whipped cream, meringue, or both before the gelatin sets.

Chlorophyll Pigment that makes vegetables green, with changes to olive green in an acid medium.

Cholesterol A fatlike substance found only in animal foods that the human body needs, but too much of it is not desirable.

Choice grade The second-highest USDA quality grade for meat, indicating high quality, generally tender and juicy.

Chop To cut into pieces of no specified shape.

Chowder Chunky, hearty soups of fish or vegetables, with a large proportion of solid ingredients served in the liquid.

City roast (American or medium roast) A style of roasted coffee beans that is popular in the United States.

Clarification The process of clearing a liquid of all solid particles.

Clarified butter Butter without any milk solids or water.

Clean Free of visible dirt or soiling.

Clearmeat A mixture of lean ground meat, mirepoix, water, and egg whites, used to make consommé.

Clear soup An unthickened soup, usually translucent.

Clinical dietitian A person, often a **registered dietitian,** who provides nutrition services such as nutrition counseling.

Coating Covering a food with a layer of crumbs, meal, flour, or other fine substance before cooking it.

Cocktail An appetizer typically consisting of several bite-sized pieces of meat, fish, shellfish, or fruit with a highly flavored sauce, usually served at a table as the opener to a meal.

Cold sauce A cold, usually thickened, seasoned liquid used to enhance a meat, poultry, fish, or vegetable dish or a sweet.

Collagen White connective tissue in meats, capable of tenderization by moist-heat cooking.

Combination salad A salad that combines two or more ingredients, or two or more kinds of salads.

Compound butter A blend of softened butter and puréed or finely chopped ingredients.

Concasser To cut rough-shaped but even-sized pieces.

Condiments Highly flavored bottled sauces that are added to a dish as flavorings after the cooking is complete, usually by the diner.

Conduction The transfer of heat from something hot to something touching it that is cooler.

Consommé (kon-sum-may) An enriched, clarified stock served as a soup.

Convection The spread of heat by a flow of hot air or steam or liquid.

Converting the recipe Increasing or decreasing the amounts of ingredients in the correct proportions to produce a larger or smaller quantity of the same product.

Cook Any person responsible for the preparation of food.

Cooked salad dressing A salad dressing made by thickening milk with a starch thickener and sometimes eggs, with appropriate flavorings and seasonings added.

Cooked salads Salads that use a single cooked food as the major ingredient.

Court bouillon An acid and highly flavored poaching liquid used to cook fish.

Cream pies An unbaked pie filled with a pastry cream base.

Creaming method A method used for making dough that is high in fat. In this method, you cream fat, sugar, and flavorings together with the paddle, add eggs and liquid, and mix in flour and leavener last.

Cream soups A soup thickened with a thickening agent.

Crêpe A thin pancake used for both desserts and entrées.

Critical control point Any point, step, or procedure in which a food safety hazard can be prevented, eliminated, or reduced.

Critical limits The criteria that must be met for each control procedure in a HACCP program.

Cross-contamination The spread of bacteria from one food to another via a dirty knife, towel, counter, sink, dish, hands, or other means.

Crouton A buttered bread shape baked in the oven until crisp and brown that is often used on top of salads and soups.

Crudités Raw, crisp vegetables.

Crustaceans Shellfish whose shells are like jointed suits of armor, such as shrimp or lobster.

Cured meats Meats preserved in salt or by drying.

Custard An egg-and-milk mixture that is either stirred over heat or baked until the egg coagulates.

Custard pie A baked pie containing custard.

Cut To divide into pieces or to shape using a knife.

Cycle menu A menu planned for a set period of time, such as 4 weeks. At the end of the 4-week cycle, the menu repeats itself.

Dark meat Meat in poultry that is fattier and cooks longer than light meat.

Deep-fry To cook food submerged in hot fat.

Deglaze To dissolve the glaze of drippings in the bottom of a pan by adding cold liquid to the hot pan and stirring.

Demiglace (dem-ee-glass or dem-ee-glaze) A sauce made from equal parts espagnole and brown stock, reduced by half; often used as a base for other sauces.

Dice To cut into small uniform cubes.

Dietetic technician A professional who works as a member of a foodservice or health team under the supervision of a dietitian in a healthcare setting. Most have completed a two-year college program approved by the **American Dietetic Association** and have passed a credentialing exam.

Director of food and nutrition services A job title found in healthcare for the person who oversees the department, providing foods to patients and/or employees/visitors, as well as nutrition services.

Dock To cut a bread dough with a knife or to perforate a pie dough with a fork to allow steam to escape.

Doneness The exact point to which meat has progressed from a raw to a cooked state. *Rare:* cool and red in the center. *Medium rare:* slightly warm in the center with deep-pink or pale-red center color. *Medium:* warm and pink in the center. *Medium well:* slightly hot and slightly pink in the center. *Well done:* fully cooked, hot in the center with no pink, but still moist.

Dough A flour–liquid mixture, thicker than a batter, used to make biscuits, breads, rolls, pies, and pastries. *Lean yeast doughs* are low in fat and sugar. *Rich yeast doughs* contain more fat and sugar and often include eggs.

Drawn butter Melted butter.

Drawn fish Fish that are eviscerated.

Dredging A three-step process of coating a food with crumbs or meal.

Dressed fish Fish that are eviscerated and scaled or skinned.

Dressing (1) For salads, a flavorful liquid or semi-liquid used to enhance a salad. (2) For poultry, an accompaniment or stuffing consisting of a bread product or rice mixed with flavorful foods such as onions, herbs, sausage, usually moistened with fat or stock.

Drop method A makeup method for cookies in which a scoop is used to spread the dough on the pan.

Dry aging The aging of meat by hanging the carcass for three to six weeks in a refrigerator with carefully controlled temperature, air flow, and humidity.

Dry sauté To cook food quickly with little or no added fat in a pan over high heat.

Dry storage area A cool, dry place used for storing canned goods and other foods that do not require refrigeration or freezing.

Duchesse potatoes Potato purée mixed with egg yolks and butter.

Du jour menu A menu that changes daily.

Éclair paste (choux paste) A paste of flour, butter, egg, and water or milk, used for cream puffs and certain potato dishes.

Edible portion (EP) The weight or quantity of food remaining after trimming and processing.

Egg wash A mixture of eggs and liquid used in breading a product for cooking; also used in baking for coating doughs to produce good color and gloss.

Elastin Tough yellow connective tissue in meat, which cannot be tenderized by cooking.

Émincer To mince or to cut into thin uniform strips.

Emulsified French dressing A thin emulsified salad dressing made by whipping oil and vinegar slowly into whipped egg yolks or whole eggs and thinning to a pourable consistency.

Emulsify To form an emulsion.

Emulsified (high-ratio) shortening A special type of shortening used in the bake shop because it emulsifies easily with other ingredients and can incorporate more air than other shortenings when used in creaming.

Emulsion A mixture of two liquids in which one, evenly dispersed in the other, is held in suspension. Oils emulsified with water (lemon emulsion) are an example.

Endosperm The large center area in a grain that is rich in starch.

En papillote (on pap-eeyote) Steaming a food wrapped in foil or parchment paper.

Entremetier (on-tra-met-yay) Station chef responsible for vegetables and soups.

Espagnole (ess-pan-yole) A brown sauce made from an enriched beef stock thickened with roux. Espagnole is a mother sauce for many small sauces.

Executive chef (chef de cuisine) Manager responsible for all kitchen operations, for the quality of the menu and the products served, for hiring and managing the kitchen staff, for controlling costs and meeting budgets, and for coordinating with other departments.

Expediter The title of the person in a kitchen responsible for getting à la carte entrées from the cooks to the servers.

Espresso A style of coffee made using the espresso process of forcing hot water through finely ground coffee (roasted very dark) that has been compacted.

Extracts Oils dissolved in alcohol.

Fat A nutrient found in such foods as meat, poultry, milk, and nuts.

Fermentation In yeast doughs, the action by which yeast breaks down the sugars in flour, releasing carbon dioxide, which leavens the dough.

Fiber A carbohydrate found abundantly in plant foods that cannot be digested.

Fillet A side of a fish that has been removed from the bones.

Fin fish Fish that have fins and a skeleton.

Finish cooking To complete the cooking of a food, usually just before service.

Fires: Class A (burning wood, paper, or cloth), Class B (a grease or oil fire), and Class C (an electrical fire).

Fish station chef (poissonnier—pwa-sawn-yay) Station chef responsible for all fish dishes.

Fish stick A crosscut of a fish fillet.

Fish stock A type of stock made like a white stock but that uses fish bones and/or crustacean shells.

Flaking In fish, when the muscle starts to naturally separate due to cooking. Fish is considerated done just before it flakes.

Flaky Description of a pie dough that forms layers of fat and flour (flakiness). Flaky pie dough is used for top crusts and unfilled or prebaked shells.

Flavones Pigments in white vegetables: white in an acid medium, yellow in an alkaline medium.

Flavor (1) The way a food tastes, through a combination of sweet, sour, bitter, and salt tastes, perceived by the tongue and the aromas perceived by the nose. (2) To flavor is to add an ingredient whose distinctive taste complements the predominant flavor of a dish without masking that flavor or losing its own identity.

Flavor builder An ingredient added in cooking to enrich the flavor of the main ingredient.

Flavor building Producing a blend of flavors to reinforce the flavor and body of a liquid.

Flavoring The addition of a product for the purpose of adding its own distinctive flavor to the final dish.

Foam method In baking, a method of mixing ingredients used for dough that are high in eggs and low in fat. In this method, you whip the eggs, yolk, or whites with sugar and carefully fold in the remaining ingredients by hand.

Fold To mix a whipped ingredient lightly with another ingredient or mixture by gently turning one over and under the other with a flat implement.

Fondant A smooth, shiny white icing made of very fine crystallized sugar.

Fond lié (fawn lee-ay) A brown sauce made by thickening a dark stock with cornstarch.

Food additives Substances added to food, intentionally or unintentionally.

Food and beverage director A job title found in hotels for the person who has responsibility for foods, beverages, and service. In a hotel, the executive chef reports to the food and beverage director.

Foodborne hazards Biological, chemical, or physical hazards that can be carried by food, or can multiply in food, and cause foodborne illness.

Foodborne illness The sickness that results from eating foods contaminated with harmful bacteria and other microorganisms.

Food cost percentage Percentage of food cost in relation to dollar sales in a given operation.

Food Guide Pyramid A food guidance system developed by the U. S. Department of Agriculture (USDA).

Food production manager The job title of the person who is responsible for all levels of food handling, production, and often service of food.

Food spoilage Any change in food that causes undesirable flavors, textures, or appearance. It is caused by the action of bacteria, yeast, and molds on food.

Formula A recipe, especially one used in the bakeshop.

Freezer burn On foods, white spots having off flavors and pulpy texture, caused by dehydration through exposure to air at below-freezing temperatures.

French knife A fairly thick, rigid, wide-bladed knife with a distinctive triangular profile.

French toast Fried bread that has been soaked in an egg-and-milk mixture.

Fritter Breaded or battered vegetables that are deep-fried.

Fruit pie An unbaked shell of mealy dough that is filled with fruit and usually topped with a flaky top crust or lattice.

Fruit salad Any salad in which fruit predominates.

Fudge icing An icing made from hot, simple syrup, fat, sugar, and cocoa.

Fumet (fue-may) A flavorful stock, usually fish, used for poaching and frequently used as the body of an accompanying sauce.

Function sheet An order form for one-time special events, such as banquets.

Fusion cooking Blending of ingredients, flavors, and techniques from various ethnic cuisines to develop new dishes.

Fry station chef (friturier—free-tour-yay) Station chef responsible for all fried foods.

Game The flesh of wild animals such as rabbits or squirrels.

Garnish To add a colorful edible accent to a finished dish entirely for eye appeal. A garnish may be eaten, but that is not its purpose.

Garniture Something edible added to a finished dish for eye appeal, flavor, and often textural contrast. It becomes part of the dish and is eaten with it.

Gazpacho A Spanish soup that is an uncooked vegetable purée thickened with bread crumbs and served cold.

Gelatin (1) A semisolid jellylike substance, or gel, used as a binding agent in salads, desserts, and cold entrées, (2) *Clear or unflavored gelatin* comes in dry powder or leaves that are dissolved to produce the gel. Powdered *fruit-flavored gelatin* has sugar added.

Gelatin (congealed) salad Any salad that has gelatin in its makeup to hold it together.

Gelatinization The reaction of starch to heat and moisture in which dry starch granules absorb liquid, swell, and become jellylike, thickening and binding a product with which they are mixed.

Germ The area of the grain kernel that sprouts when allowed to germinate.

Glaze (1) To add a shine or gloss to the surface of a product for taste or eye appeal by basting during cooking, by coating with a sauce. Baked products are glazed with egg wash, coating, and icing. (2) A stock reduced to a gelatinous consistency.

Gluten The protein substance that provides structure in baked goods. Moisture is necessary for gluten to develop.

Grade A measure of the quality of a food product.

Gratiné (gra-tee-nay) Glazed in the salamander or broiler.

Green meat Meat that has not had time to be softened by enzymatic action following the onset of rigor mortis.

Green shrimp Raw shrimp in the shell.

Griddling Cooking on a griddle.

Grill To cook on an open grill with heat from below; also a radiant-heat process.

Grill station chef (grillardin—gree-yar-dan) Station chef responsible for grilled and broiled meats, seafood, and poultry.

Grind coffee The size of the grounds produced from coffee beans. The size of the grind is related to the method of making the coffee.

Guiding hand When using a knife, the hand that holds the food lightly.

Gumbo A soup thickened with brown roux and crowded with meat or fish and vegetables, usually served with rice.

Hard roll dough A lean dough that makes chewy, hard-crusted rolls or French- or Italian-style bread.

Hazard Analysis Critical Control Point (HACCP) A prevention-based food safety system designed to prevent the occurrence of foodborne illness.

Helper A person in training or one lacking the skills necessary to merit the title of cook.

Herbs The leafy parts of certain plants that grow in temperate climates.

Holding The keeping of a food product for a short period before its intended use at a specific time.

Hollandaise (hol-lun-daze) Butter sauce made with an emulsion of egg yolks, clarified butter, and a flavor reduction. One of the five mother sauces.

Homogenized A process in which milk is treated so the fat does not separate from the liquid.

Hors d'oeuvres Bite-sized pieces or small portions of foods served to stimulate the appetite.

Hot tops Ranges with large, flat metal heating surfaces.

Icing (frosting) A sweet mixture, made mostly of sugar, used for coating and filling pastries, cakes, cookies, and breads.

Induction cooking Cooking with equipment that uses induction heating. Cooking equipment remains cool while pots and pans heat up.

Inspection A process in which certain foods, such as meats and eggs, must be examined by the federal government to make sure they are wholesome.

Intoxication A type of foodborne illness caused by eating foods containing toxins that bacteria made while in the food.

Julienne A precision cut $^1/_8$" × $^1/_8$" × $1^1/_2$ to 2" (6 mm × 6 mm × 4–5 cm).

Knead To manipulate dough in order to develop gluten.

Leafy green salads Salads made of raw leafy green vegetables.

Leaven, leavener Any agent that introduces air or gas into a batter or dough, causing it to rise.

Leavening Increase in volume that occurs during baking.

Legumes Dried beans and peas.

Liaison (lee-ay-zon) A combination of egg yolks and cream (in a ratio of 1 to 2 by volume) used to give a velvety texture to soups and sauces.

Light meat Meat in poultry that is more tender and cooks faster than dark meat.

Macaroni Pastas made from flour and water.

Maître d'hôtel butter A compound butter made with lemon juice and chopped parsley or other fresh herbs.

Major flavor The predominant flavor of a dish.

Makeup To form a dough or batter into uniform shapes and sizes prior to baking.

Marbling Fat distributed throughout meat.

Marinade A seasoned liquid used for **marinating** foods. Marinades are usually based on an acidic food, such as vinegar.

Marinating Soaking a food in a seasoned liquid (called a **marinade**) or applying a dry marinade (called a **rub**) to add flavor or to tenderize, or both.

Market menus Menus based on product availability.

Mayonnaise A flavored, seasoned emulsion of egg yolks and oil. Mayonnaise can be a finished salad dressing, a basic dressing for other salad dressings, or a mother sauce for other cold sauces.

Mealy pie dough A type of pie crust in which you mix the fat into the flour more completely, resulting in a crust that is less likely to absorb moisture. Mealy pie dough is used for bottom crusts.

Mealy or starchy potatoes Potatoes that are high in starch and low in sugar. Best for French-fried, mashed, and baked potatoes.

Meat The flesh of domestic animals.

Medical nutrition therapy The process of assessing a patient's nutritional status and then treating the patient as needed with a modified diet and/or nutrition counseling.

Menu (1) List of the dishes offered for service at a meal. (2) The card on which the dishes offered for service are listed for the guest, usually with their prices.

Meringue Egg whites whipped until stiff with sugar, used in making desserts. *Hard meringues* use 2 parts sugar to 1 part white. *Soft meringues* are made with equal parts sugar and whites.

Meringue pie A pie topped with meringue.

Midscale (midpriced) restaurant A restaurant that offers food at moderate prices and that usually has table service.

Mince To chop very fine.

Minerals Minute components in food that are essential for growth and good health.

Minestrone An unthickened soup full of vegetables and pasta that can easily be a meal in itself.

Mirepoix (mee-ra-pwah) A standard flavor builder for stocks, soups, and sauces made up of onions, carrots, celery, and sometimes leeks.

Mise en place (meez on plass) Everything in its proper place; a good production setup with everything ready to go.

Mix To combine ingredients in such a way that the parts of each ingredient are evenly dispersed in the total product.

Mollusks Shellfish that live inside a pair of shells, such as clams, or underneath a single shell, such as abalone.

Monounsaturated fat Fats found in plant oils, such as olive oil, that help keep blood cholesterol levels down.

Monter au beurre (mawn-tay oh burr) To swirl butter into a hot sauce just before serving.

Mother sauces (leading sauces) Basic sauces from which other sauces are made.

Muffin method In baking, a two-step mixing method in which the dry ingredients are sifted together and then mixed with the liquids just until they are moistened.

Mulligatawny A curry-flavored chicken soup from India.

Mycotoxins A type of toxin produced by molds growing on food.

Napping To coat evenly with a sauce, usually with one stroke of the ladle.

Natural cheese Cheese made by curdling milk and ripening the curds.

Naturally thickened soups (purée soups) Soups that are naturally thickened by a purée of its major ingredients.

Nonselective menu A menu that offers virtually no food choices.

Noodles Pastas made from flour, water, and eggs.

Nutrient-dense foods Foods that provide many nutrients for the calories they contain.

Nutrients The nourishing substances in food that provide energy.

Nutrition A science that studies nutrients in foods and in the body, and how these nutrients are related to health and disease. Nutrition also examines the processes by which you choose what to eat and the balance of foods in nutrients in your diet.

One-stage cookie method The simplest and quickest method of mixing ingredients used for dough that are low in moisture and high in fat and sugar. In this method, you mix everything together at once.

Onion piqué (pee-kay) A flavor builder for soups and sauces made by affixing a bay leaf to a small peeled onion with a clove.

Organic foods Food grown without nearly any synthetic insecticides, fungicides, herbicides, and fertilizers.

Organization chart A diagram of a company's organization showing levels of management and lines by which authority and responsibility are transmitted.

Oven-frying To brown in a fry pan and finish-cook in an oven; a common way of producing fried chicken in volume.

Pan-broil To cook uncovered in a sauté pan or skillet without adding any fat or liquid. Fat is drained off as it accumulates.

Pancake A fried cake made from a batter of flour, water or milk, eggs, seasonings, and a leavening agent.

Pan-fry To cook food in a small to moderate amount of fat in a pan over moderate heat.

Pan gravy A sauce made in a pan from the juices or drippings of the items cooked in the pan.

Panned The process of putting the completed batter or dough into pans for baking.

Pantry chef (garde manger—gardmon-shay) Station chef responsible for the preparation of all cold foods.

Parasites Small organisms that must live on or inside another organism to survive.

Parboiling To partially cook a food by boiling.

Paring knife A small knife used for preparing fruits and vegetables.

Partial cooking Any cooking process that is stopped before the product reaches doneness.

Pasteurized A process in which milk is heated to kill harmful bacteria.

Pastry chef (pâtissier—pa-tees-yay) Station chef responsible for the preparation of all baked items, including desserts, breads, and pastries.

Pastry cream Stirred custard used as is or flavored to produce cake and pie fillings, puddings, fillings for éclairs, or when thinned with milk, a light custard sauce.

Pastry method A mixing method in baking that requires fat to be cut into dry ingredients before liquids are added.

Paupiette (pope-yet) A fish fillet or a thin slice of meat rolled into a cylinder shape around another bit of food and poached or braised.

Paysanne A triangular or quarter slice of uniform thickness.

Pectin A natural jelling ingredient found in fruit.

Peeler A piece of small equipment used to peel fruits and vegetables.

Personal hygiene The actions we take to promote our health and cleanliness.

Physical hazards Foreign objects, such as glass fragments, that can get into food and cause harm.

Phytochemicals Disease-fighting chemicals found in plant foods.

Pigments Colors in vegetables.

Pilaf method A method of cooking rice, covered, with sautéed onion and just enough stock to be completely absorbed.

Pinning out Rolling out a dough to a uniform thickness, usually done with a small broomstick pin.

Poach To cook food submerged in liquid at a temperature of roughly 160–180°F (71–82°C).

Polyunsaturated fat Fats such as corn oil that may help reduce blood cholesterol.

Popovers A muffin made from a poured flour-egg-milk batter.

Pot roasts A large cut of meat braised whole in a pot and sliced for service.

Poultry Edible birds domestically raised for human consumption.

Prawn Large shrimp.

Prepreparation All the cleaning, cutting, processing, setting up, and production that is done before final preparation of food for service.

Primal cuts Large divisions or wholesale cuts of meats.

Primed (seasoned) surface A cooking surface treated at high heat with salt and fat or oil to overcome its porousness.

Prime grade The highest USDA quality grade for meat, indicating thick, white, brittle fat cover, fine-textured flesh, and abundant marbling.

Process cheese Cheese made by grinding one or more natural cheeses, heating and blending them with emulsifiers and other ingredients, and pouring the mixture into molds to become solid.

Processing An inclusive term referring to all the things done to foods in getting them ready to cook or serve, such as cleaning, cutting, mixing, breading, puréeing.

Production The part of a foodservice operation in which foods from the market are transformed into finished dishes for service.

Production schedule An overall plan for a specific production period stating who is responsible for what products and when each product must be ready.

Production worksheet A written work schedule for a person or department for a given product period stating all information necessary for production, such as food to be prepared, quantity needed, time needed, and so on.

Profiteroles Small cream puffs.

Proof To ferment a yeast dough a second time.

Protein A nutrient found in meats, poultry, fish, milk, legumes, nuts, and seeds that is a major structural part of animal tissue.

Puff pastry A rolled-in stiff dough leavened by steam from butter, which produces a light, flaky pastry when baked.

Punch, punch down To deflate a yeast dough after fermentation, to expel gas, redistribute the yeast, and equalize the temperature.

Purée To mash a cooked product to a fine pulp, usually by forcing it through a sieve or putting it into a blender.

Quiche (keesh) A savory pie with a custard base.

Quick bread An easily and quickly made bread leavened chemically or by steam; biscuits, muffins, and pancakes are examples.

Quickservice restaurant A restaurant with a limited menu requiring a minimum of cooking equipment and cooking skills.

Radiation The transfer of heat through energy waves radiating directly from a heat source to the food. In foodservice, microwave radiation and infrared radiation are used in some cooking/reheating processes.

Raft Clearmeat after it has coagulated in clarifying a consommé.

Recipe An abbreviated set of directions for making a product, including a list of ingredients and instructions for combining them.

Reduce To boil or simmer a liquid down to a smaller volume.

Registered dietitians (RDs) Credentialed professionals in the nutrition field who have specialized education in human anatomy and physiology, medical nutrition therapy, foods and food science, the behaviors sciences, and foodservice management, RDs must complete at least a bachelor's degree, an internship or equivalent experience, and a qualifying exam.

Relief cook (tournant—toor-non) A station chef who relieves other station chefs, also called swing cook or rounds cook.

Relishes Chunky mixtures of vegetables and/or fruits and flavor ingredients served cold as sauces for meat, poultry, and seafood.

Responsibility The obligation an individual has to carry out certain duties and activities.

Ripened cheese Cheese that has been fermented with bacteria or molds.

Roast To cook by heated air, usually in an enclosed space such as an oven or barbecue pit. The food is not covered.

Roast station chef (rôtisseur—ro-tee-sur) Station chef responsible for roasted and braised meats and meat dishes.

Rolled-in dough A soft or stiff dough with fat rolled in layers with the flour-liquid mixture.

Rotating stock To put new products either behind or under existing supplies of the same product, to ensure that the oldest will be used first.

Rough prep (prepping) Kitchen slang meaning to clean fresh produce.

Rounding A step in making yeast dough in which you try to make each piece of dough round by rolling the dough around on the bench while pressing it against the bench surface with the outside edge of your hand.

Round fish (1) A whole fish. (2) A fish having a rounded bony structure, such as trout or salmon, as opposed to a flatfish such as flounder.

Roux (roo) A thickening agent of fat and flour in a 1-to-1 ratio by weight, made by blending and cooking over moderate heat. A *white roux* is cooked until the mixture is foamy and begins to have a chalky look. A *blond roux* is cooked somewhat longer, until the roux is slightly darker than white roux. *Brown roux* is cooked until the color is brown. *Dark brown or black roux* is cooked until the roux is deep brown in color.

Royal icing An icing made by beating together confectioners' sugar, egg whites, and cream of tartar until stiff.

Rub A dry marinade made of herbs and spices (and other seasonings), sometimes moistened with a little oil, and rubbed (or patted) on the surface of meat, poultry, or fish (which is then refrigerated and cooked at a later time).

Rumaki Bacon wrapped around a food, such as chicken liver, and then cooked. A popular hot hors d'oeuvres.

Sachet Any mixture of herbs and spices tied in a square of cheesecloth and added to the cooking pot or pan for flavor.

Salamander Small overhead broiler used for quick glazing and browning of foods already cooked.

Salsa A chunky mixture of vegetables and/or fruits and flavor ingredients served cold as sauces for meat, poultry, and seafood.

Sanitary Free of harmful numbers of disease-causing microorganisms.

Sanitation Taking measures to keep food free of anything that might cause disease.

Saturated fat A type of fat found mostly in animal foods that leads to high blood cholesterol levels.

Sauce A seasoned liquid, usually thickened, that enhances a dish.

Sauté To cook food quickly in a small amount of hot fat in a pan over high heat.

Sauté station chef (saucier—so-see-ay) A station chef responsible for all sautéed items and for sauces.

Scaling Using a scale to weigh ingredients or doughs and batters to be evenly divided for baking.

Sear To expose the surfaces of a piece of meat to extreme heat before cooking at a lower temperature.

Seasoning The addition of substances that heighten the taste of a food without altering that taste or adding their own flavors.

Selective menu A menu that allows the customer to choose what to eat.

Select quality A USDA meat grade for meat that is lean but not as fine or as tender as higher grades, such as Choice.

Semi à la carte menu A menu with some separately priced items along with a set price for an entrée and its accompaniments.

Semiselective menu Menus that allow the customer to make some, but not all, choices of what to eat.

Semolina The roughly milled endosperm of a type of what called durum wheat; used almost exclusively for making pasta.

Shelf life Safe keeping time of a food.

Shellfish Fish that wear their skeleton on the outside.

Short dough Another type of stiff pastry dough used mainly for tartlettes and tarts.

Shortening Fat made especially for baking by hydrogenating animal or vegetable fats.

Shuck To remove the outer covering, such as shells from oysters or husks from corn.

Simmer To cook food submerged in liquid just below a boil or to cook the liquid itself at temperatures of 180°F (85°C) to just short of the boiling point.

Simple butter A sauce that contains nothing but butter.

Simple syrup A solution of sugar in water, used to thin fondant or flavored to become a dessert syrup.

Skim To remove foam, scum, or fat from the surface of a stock, soup, or sauce.

Slack time Time allowed during preparation for a product to undergo a change—a frozen product to thaw, juices in cooked meats to settle, gluten in dough to relax before baking.

Slice To cut into uniform slices, usually across the grain.

Slicer A knife used to slice cooked meats or, if serrated, breads, cakes, and other items you don't want to crush during the slicing process.

Slurries A thickener made of starch and water.

Small sauce (finished sauce) A sauce made by adding one or more ingredients to a basic or leading sauce.

Smoked meats Meat preserved by exposing them to the drying effect of a wood chip fire—the choice of wood affects the flavor of the smoked product.

Soft doughs A type of dough used to make biscuits, yeast breads, and rolls.

Soft roll dough A dough used to make a softer, less chewy product than hard roll dough.

Soufflés (soo-flay) A light and fluffy sweet or savory dish, made with heavy béchamel, egg yolks, and a major flavor ingredient, folded with whipped egg whites, baked, and served immediately.

Soup station chef (potager—poh-ta-zhay) A station chef responsible for preparation of soups and stocks.

Sous-chef (soo-shef) A production supervisor reporting to an executive chef. A sous-chef fills in for the executive chef and directly supervises food production.

Spices The roots, bark, seeds, flowers, buds, and fruits of certain tropical plants.

Spit-roasting A method for cooking poultry in which birds are trussed, oiled, and placed on spits that revolve before a hot fire or in an oven.

Sponge cake A light butterless cake made rich with beaten eggs.

Sponge dough method In baking, a method for preparing yeast doughs.

Standardized recipe A recipe developed for use in a particular operation to record the way the operation makes a given dish.

Starch A form of carbohydrate present in flour, cereals, pastas, potatoes, vegetables, and legumes.

Static menu A menu that is the same every day.

Station (1) A functional area of a kitchen layout, such as a salad station or a vegetable station. (2) Any area set up with supplies and equipment in order to complete a production task; a work station.

Station cook or line cook Cook responsible for preparing certain menu items.

Station head or chef (chefs de partie—shef de partee) A person in charge of all production for a given station or department. A station head may be both supervisor and working cook.

Steak (1) Fish: A crosscut section of the body of a large pan-dressed fish. (2) Meat: A tender cut from the rib, loin, sirloin, tenderloin, round, or chuck.

Steam To cook foods by exposing them to steam, either with or without pressure.

Steel A piece of equipment used to remove burrs from the knife edge and maintain the knife's edge.

Steeping In tea, exposing the tea leaves to hot water over a period of time.

Stiff doughs A dough with the highest flour-to-liquid ratios used to make pie doughs, short doughs, and puff pastry.

Stir-fry To cook bite-sized ingredients over high heat in a small amount of oil, usually in a bowl-shaped pot called a wok.

Stirred custards Custard stirred over gentle heat until the eggs coagulate.

Stock A flavored liquid used in making soups, sauces, and sauce-based entrées.

Stone (whetstone) A piece of equipment used to sharpen knives, usually along with a **steel.**

Storage The keeping of a food product for future use for an unspecified period of time.

Straight dough method In baking, placing all the ingredients in the mixer bowl and combining them with the dough arm. In the *modified straight dough method,* the ingredients are combined in installments to ensure that the fat and sugar are completely integrated into the dough.

Stuffing A flavorful product stuffed into a cavity in a bird, fish, meat, or vegetable.

Sugars Simple carbohydrates that occur naturally in fruits and milk, and in refined forms such as table sugar.

Suprême (1) A dish of cold food served embedded in ice. (2) A boneless poultry breast.

Sweat To cook slowly in fat over low or moderate heat without browning, sometimes with a cover on the pan.

Sweet butter Unsalted butter.

Sweet roll dough A dough used for sweet rolls and coffee cakes.

Table d'hôte menu A menu on which a price is given for a whole dinner, as opposed to à la carte pricing of each item.

Tang The extension of a knife's blade into the handle.

Tea A drink made by brewing tea leaves. *Black tea* is made by fermenting the tea leaves so they turn black. *Green tea* is made by steaming or otherwise heating the leaves to prevent the fermentation that makes black tea. *Oolong tea* is fermented only partially—to a point between black and green.

Temperature danger zone The temperatures (from 40°–140°F or 4°–60°C) in which bacteria grow.

Tempering The process of adding a hot liquid little by little to a cold liquid to raise its temperature slowly.

Texture The quality of a product or dish perceivable by the sense of feel: its consistency and its thick-thin, smooth-coarse, tender-tough, crisp-soft qualities.

Thickening agents An ingredient whose primary function is to thicken.

Tomato sauce Any red sauce made from stock thickened with tomatoes and sometimes a thickening agent.

Toxin-mediated infection A type of foodborne illness in which the bacteria produce toxins once they have entered the body (specifically, the intestines).

Trueing the edge To use a **steel** to remove burrs from the edge of a knife in order to keep it sharp.

Trussing To tie meat or poultry into a compact shape, such as tying the legs and wings of a bird close to the body for even cooking.

Two-stage cake method A method for making cakes in which the liquid is incorporated in two distinct stages.

Unbaked pies Baked, cooled shells that are filled with a finished filling.

Unripened cheese Cheese that is freshly made, such as cream cheese

Utility knife A narrow, pointed knife used mostly in fruit and vegetable preparation and also for carving chicken.

Vegetable salad A salad with one or more nonleafy vegetables as its main ingredients.

Vegetable station chef (légumier—lay-gu-myay) Station chef responsible for preparation of vegetables and starches.

Vegetable stock A type of stock made without any animal products. Vegetables, herbs, and spices are simmered in water and wine may be added.

Velouté (ve-loo-tay) A sauce made from a light stock and thickened with roux.

Vinaigrette (vin-a-gret) A salad dressing of oil and vinegar.

Viruses Very small living organisms that can cause diseases, such as foodborne illness.

Vitamins Minute components in food that are essential for growth and good health.

Waffle A crisp, cake egg batter baked in a greased waffle iron. Its batter is slightly heavier (more fat) than pancake batter.

Water A nutrient that is the major ingredient in most foods.

Waxy or new potatoes Potatoes high in sugar and low in starch.

Wet aging A process in which meat is vacuum-packed in moisture-vapor-proof plastic bags and aged under refrigeration. Also called Cryovac-aged.

Whip To beat with a rapid lifting motion to incorporate air into a food.

White sauces A sauce made by thickening milk with a white roux.

White stock Those stocks made by simmering chicken, beef, or veal bones in water with flavor builders.

Whitewash A thickening agent made of flour and water.

Whole (round) fish Fish as they are caught.

Yeast A living plant used to make a bread rise as it produces carbon dioxide gas.

Zest Colored outer portion of a citrus fruit, containing flavorful oils.

Bibliography

Amendola, Joseph. 1993. *The Baker's Manual.* New York: John Wiley & Sons.

Amendola, Joseph, and Lungdberg, Donald. 1992. *Understanding Baking.* New York: John Wiley & Sons.

Bailey, Adrian, and Dowell, Philip. 1980. *Cooks' Ingredients.* New York: William Morrow.

Corriher, Shirley O. 1997. *CookWise: The Hows and Whys of Successful Cooking.* New York: William Morrow.

———. 1996. *The New Professional Chef.* New York: John Wiley & Sons.

Culinary Institute of America. 1993. *Techniques of Healthy Cooking.* New York: John Wiley & Sons.

Drummond, Karen Eich. 1997. *Nutrition for the Foodservice Professional.* New York: John Wiley & Sons.

Educational Foundation of the National Restaurant Association. 1992. *Applied Foodservice Sanitation.* New York: John Wiley & Sons.

Escoffier, A. 1969. *The Escoffier Cook Book.* New York: Crown Publishers.

Gisslen, Wayne. 1998. *Professional Cooking* (4th ed.). New York: John Wiley & Sons.

Holden, Chet. 1993. *Cooking for Fifty.* New York: John Wiley & Sons.

Kapoor, Sandy. 1995. *Professional Healthy Cooking.* New York: John Wiley & Sons.

Katsigris, Costas. 1999. *Design and Equipment for Restaurants and Foodservice.* New York: John Wiley & Sons.

Kimbrough, Mary, and Gielisse, Victor. 1998. *In Good Taste: A Contemporary Approach to Cooking.* Englewood Cliffs, NJ: Prentice Hall.

Labensky, Sarah, and Hause, Alan. 1995. *On Cooking.* Englewood Cliffs, NJ: Prentice Hall.

Loken, Joan K. 1995. *The HACCP Food Safety Manual.* New York: John Wiley & Sons.

McGee, Harold. 1984. *On Food and Cooking.* New York: Scribners.

Miller, Jack E., and Hayes, David K. 1993. *Basic Food and Beverage Cost Control.* New York: John Wiley & Sons.

Pennington, Jean A. T. 1998. *Bowes & Church's Food Values of Portions Commonly Used.* Philadelphia: Lippincott.

Peterson, James. 1997. *Sauces.* New York: John Wiley & Sons.

Powers, Jo Marie. 1979. *Basics of Quantity Food Production.* New York: John Wiley & Sons.

Stefanelli, John M. 1997. *Purchasing: Selection and Procurement for the Hospitality Industry.* New York: John Wiley & Sons.

Time-Life Books. *The Good Cook: Techniques and Recipes* series.

WEB SITES

Books for Cooks
http://www.vdsys.com/bfc

Cordon Bleu Cooking School
http://www.cordonbleu.org/

Epicurious Food
http://www.epicurious.com

Food Net
http://www.foodnet.com/

Food Network
http://www.foodtv.com/index.htm

Food & Nutrition Information Center
http://www.nal.usda.gov/fnic/

Great Chefs Online
http://www.multicom.com/greatchefs

Grains Nutrition Information Center
http://www.wheatfoods.org

Internet Chef
http://www.ichef.com

National Dairy Council
http://www.dairyinfo.com

Yahoo Cooking
http://www.yahoo.com/entertainment/cooking

Subject Index

Index of Recipes